2024 INTERNAL MEDICINE BOARD

Questions & Answers

First Edition

Rafael Zioni, MD

Self Publishers Worldwide
Seattle San Francisco New York
London Paris Rome Beijing Barcelona

Dr Rafael Zioni

2

Preface

The "2024 Internal Medicine Board Questions and Answers" book is a comprehensive resource designed to help students prepare for the American Board of Internal Medicine (ABIM) certification exam. This guide offers an excess of 800 meticulously crafted questions that cover the most important topics tested on the exam. Each question is designed to test content mastery, while the detailed answer explanations ensure clear comprehension of the material.

The book also includes detailed answer explanations for each question. These explanations not only provide the correct answer but also explain why that answer is correct and why the other options are incorrect. This approach helps students understand the material on a deeper level and prepares them for the types of questions they will encounter on the actual exam.

The "2024 Internal Medicine Board Questions and Answers" book is an invaluable resource for anyone preparing for the ABIM certification exam. With over 800 sample questions and detailed answer explanations, this book provides a comprehensive review of the material and helps students master the content they will need to know for the exam.

Dr Rafael Zioni

Table of Contents

Chapter 1

NEPHROLOGY BOARD QUESTIONS

1.A 67-year-old man with chronic kidney disease presents to his doctor's office for a routine checkup. His doctor orders a creatinine clearance test to assess his kidney function. The patient's creatinine clearance is 60 mL/min/1.73 m2. What is the most likely limitation of using creatinine clearance to assess this patient's kidney function?

- A. Creatinine clearance is not a reliable measure of GFR in patients with chronic kidney disease.
- B. Creatinine clearance is affected by muscle mass, which can vary from person to person.
- C. Creatinine clearance can be inaccurate in patients with conditions that affect muscle metabolism, such as diabetes.
- D. Creatinine clearance is not a sensitive measure of GFR, meaning that it may not detect early changes in kidney function.
- E. All of the above

2. A 56-year-old man presents to the emergency department with a 2-day history of fever, cough, and shortness of breath. On physical examination, he is found to have a temperature of 101 degrees Fahrenheit, a respiratory rate of 24 breaths per minute, and a blood pressure of 90/60 mmHg. His chest X-ray shows a right lower lobe infiltrate. What is the most likely etiology of anuria in this patient?

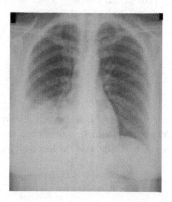

Figure 1.1: 56-year-old man

- A. Complete bilateral obstruction of the urinary tract
- B. Vascular events such as dissection or arterial occlusion
- C. Renal vein thrombosis
- D. Renal cortical necrosis

1

- E. Severe acute tubular necrosis

3. A 38-year-old man presents to his doctor's office with a 2-week history of fatigue, decreased urine output, and swelling in his ankles. His doctor orders a urine test, which shows that he is excreting 1 gram of protein per day. What are the possible causes of this patient's proteinuria?

- A. Glomerular disease
- B. Interstitial nephritis
- C. Vascular disease
- D. Hypertensive nephrosclerosis
- E. All of the above

4. A 59-year-old man presents to his doctor's office with a 2-week history of dysuria, urgency, and frequency. His doctor orders a urine test, which shows that he has pyuria. What are the possible causes of this patient's pyuria?

- A. Urinary tract infection
- B. Inflammatory glomerular diseases
- C. Allergic interstitial nephritis
- D. Transplant rejection
- E. All of the above

5. A 62-year-old man with hypertension is started on an ACE inhibitor. He presents to the emergency department 2 weeks later with decreased urine output and fatigue. What is the most likely cause of his decreased urine output and fatigue?

- A. Decreased renal perfusion.
- B. Decreased glomerular filtration rate (GFR)
- C. Hyperkalemia
- D. Hypotension
- E. None of the above

6. A 53-year-old man with diabetes mellitus and chronic kidney disease presents to the emergency department with chest pain. He is scheduled for a CT scan of his chest. What are the risk factors for this patient developing contrast-induced nephropathy?

- A. Pre-existing renal dysfunction
- B. Diabetes mellitus
- C. Congestive heart failure
- D. All of the above

7. A 61-year-old man presents to his doctor's office with a 2-week history of fatigue, decreased urine output, and swelling in his ankles. His doctor orders a urine test, which shows that he has proteinuria and hematuria. What are some additional medical conditions that may potentially lead to the development of acute kidney injury (AKI) in this patient?

- A. Acute glomerulonephritis
- B. Thrombotic microangiopathies
- C. Sepsis
- D. Rhabdomyolysis
- E. All of the above

8. A 63-year-old man with heart failure presents to the emergency department with decreased urine output and fatigue. His doctor orders a urine test, which shows that he has a urine sodium concentration of 5 mmol/L and a

fractional excretion of sodium of 0.5%. What is the most likely cause of the patient's acute kidney injury?

- A. Prerenal AKI
- B. Intrarenal AKI
- C. Postrenal AKI
- D. None of the above

9. A 35-year-old man presents to the emergency department with decreased urine output and fatigue. His doctor orders a urinalysis, which shows pigmented "muddy-brown" granular casts and casts that contain tubular epithelial cells. What is the most likely diagnosis for this patient?

- A. Ischemic or toxic acute tubular necrosis (ATN)
- B. Glomerulonephritis
- C. Interstitial nephritis
- D. Pyelonephritis
- E. None of the above

10. A 59-year-old man presents to the emergency department with decreased urine output and fatigue. His doctor orders a blood test, which shows that he has a high level of potassium in the blood. What is the most likely indication for dialysis in this patient?

- A. Excessive fluid volume that does not respond to diuretic medications.
- B. High levels of potassium in the blood
- C. Unexplained encephalopathy
- D. Inflammation of the pericardium, pleura, or other serous membranes
- E. Severe metabolic acidosis that affects respiratory or circulatory function

11. A 71-year-old man is diagnosed with chronic kidney disease (CKD). What laboratory tests should be conducted? A. Serum and urine protein electrophoresis B. Serum free light chain testing C. Both serum and urine protein electrophoresis and serum free light chain testing D. None of the above

12. A 64-year-old man with chronic kidney disease (CKD) presents with fatigue and shortness of breath.What is the best management strategy for his anemia?

- A. Recombinant human erythropoietin (rHuEPO)
- B. Iron supplements
- C. Both rHuEPO and iron supplements
- D. None of the above

13. A 58-year-old man with diabetic nephropathy presents with decreased urine output and fatigue. What are the distinctive advantageous effects of ACE inhibitors and ARBs in the management of his renal failure?

- A. ACE inhibitors and ARBs can help to slow the progression of renal failure.
- B. ACE inhibitors and ARBs can help to reduce proteinuria.
- C. ACE inhibitors and ARBs can help to improve blood pressure control.
- D. All of the above

14. A 52-year-old man presents with serum creatinine of 6 mg/dL, blood urea nitrogen of 30 mg/dL, and creatinine clearance of 30 mL/min.Is he a candidate for dialysis?

- A. Yes
- B. No
- C. It depends on his other medical conditions.
- D. It depends on his symptoms.

15. A 67-year-old man with end-stage renal disease presents for his first hemodialysis treatment. What are the signs and symptoms of dialysis disequilibrium syndrome?

- A. Headache, confusion, seizures
- B. Fatigue, nausea, vomiting.
- C. Increased blood pressure, decreased heart rate
- D. None of the above

16. A 54-year-old man with end-stage renal disease has undergone a renal transplant. What is the definitive diagnostic method for confirming rejection in the patient?

- A. Percutaneous renal transplant biopsy
- B. Blood tests
- C. Urine tests
- D. Imaging studies
- E. None of the above

17. A 58-year-old man with end-stage renal disease has undergone a renal transplant. What is the pathophysiology of BK nephropathy in this patient?

- A. The BK virus is reactivated in the kidney and causes inflammation.
- B. The BK virus is transmitted from the donor kidney to the recipient.
- C. The BK virus damages the kidney's blood vessels.
- D. All of the above

18. A 51-year-old man presents with a 2-week history of fatigue, decreased urine output, and swelling in his feet and ankles. He also reports having blood in his urine. What are the clinical manifestations of acute glomerulonephritis in this patient?

- A. Azotemia, hypertension, edema, hematuria, proteinuria, and occasionally oliguria
- B. Hypertension, edema, and hematuria
- C. Azotemia, edema, and proteinuria
- D. Hematuria and proteinuria
- E. None of the above

19. A 57-year-old diabetic man presents with a 2-week history of fatigue, decreased urine output, and swelling in his feet and ankles. He also reports having blood in his urine. What form of acute postinfectious glomerulonephritis is he most likely suffering from?

- A. IgA nephropathy
- B. Membranoproliferative glomerulonephritis
- C. Minimal change disease
- D. Focal segmental glomerulosclerosis
- E. None of the above

20. A patient with a history of systemic lupus erythematosus (SLE) presents with recent onset of swelling in the legs and foamy urine. A renal biopsy was performed. What histopathological findings would you expect from the renal biopsy specimen?

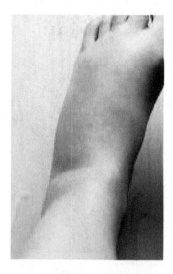

Figure 1.2: Lupus Nephritis

- A. Minimal change disease
- B. Diabetic nephropathy
- C. Focal segmental glomerulosclerosis
- D. Membranous nephropathy
- E. IgA nephropathy

21. A 45-year-old male presents with rapidly progressive glomerulonephritis. A renal biopsy was performed. What is the primary distinguishing feature of ANCA-associated pauci-immune glomerulonephritis you would expect to find in this patient?

- A. Presence of immune complexes in the glomeruli
- B. Thickening and splitting of the glomerular basement membrane.
- C. Presence of anti-glomerular basement membrane antibodies
- D. Presence of circulating ANCA (Anti-Neutrophil Cytoplasmic Antibodies)
- E. Deposition of IgA in the mesangium

22. A 47-year-old woman is diagnosed with ANCA-associated rapidly progressive glomerulonephritis. She is started on cyclophosphamide treatment. What is the typical duration of cyclophosphamide administration in the management of this condition?

- A. 1 month
- B. 2 months
- C. 3-6 months
- D. 9-12 months
- E. More than a year

23. A 18-year-old presents with joint pain, abdominal discomfort, and a purpuric rash on the lower limbs. What is the most useful diagnostic method to confirm the presence of Henoch-Schönlein Purpura (HSP) in this patient?

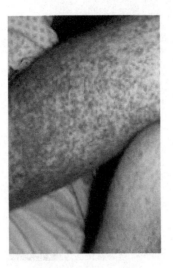

Figure 1.3: HSP

- A. Chest X-ray
- B. Serum IgA level
- C. Echocardiogram
- D. Renal biopsy
- E. Coagulation profile

24. Question: A 49-year-old man with diabetes is at risk for nephrotic syndrome. What is the most appropriate diagnostic tool to detect lesser proteinuria in this patient?

- A. Serum creatinine
- B. Blood urea nitrogen (BUN) level
- C. Urine albumin:creatinine ratio
- D. Urine total protein level
- E. Glomerular filtration rate (GFR)

25. A 50-year-old man presents with foamy urine and swelling in his legs. Lab results indicate proteinuria. The clinician suspects membranous glomerulonephritis (GN). What is the most important next step in the evaluation of this patient?

- A. Assess the history of exposure to high-dose captopril or penicillamine.
- B. Test for hepatitis B
- C. Investigate the presence of systemic lupus erythematosus (SLE)
- D. Look for underlying solid tumors.
- E. All of the above

26. A 50-year-old woman is diagnosed with a rare subtype of membranoproliferative glomerulonephritis (MPGN) that is associated with the activation of the alternative pathway of complement activation. What is the most appropriate treatment option for this patient?

- A. Steroids
- B. Angiotensin-converting enzyme (ACE) inhibitors
- C. Cyclosporine
- D. Eculizumab

- E. Plasmapheresis

27. A 32-year-old woman presents to the clinic for a routine check-up. Urinalysis reveals asymptomatic hematuria and proteinuria. Which of the following glomerular conditions is most likely to contribute to these asymptomatic urinary abnormalities?

- A. Berger's disease
- B. Mesangiocapillary glomerulonephritis
- C. Alport's syndrome
- D. Fabry's disease
- E. All of the above

28. A 62-year-old diabetic man comes to the clinic with persistent hyperkalemia. Despite efforts to optimize glucose control, administer loop diuretics, and treat metabolic acidosis, his potassium levels remain high. What is the most appropriate next step in managing his hyperkalemia?

- A. Initiate amlodipine therapy
- B. Increase the dose of loop diuretics.
- C. Administer sodium bicarbonate infusion.
- D. Start potassium binder therapy with sodium zirconium cyclosilicate (ZS-9) or patiromer
- E. Discontinue all his medications.

29. A 57-year-old woman presents with decreased renal function and mild proteinuria. Her recent medications include ibuprofen for joint pain and nivolumab for lung cancer. Which of the following medications is most likely to be associated with her condition of acute interstitial nephritis (AIN)?

- A. Metformin
- B. Ibuprofen
- C. Nivolumab
- D. Aspirin
- E. Atorvastatin

30. A 62-year-old woman with a long history of over-the-counter analgesic use presents with flank pain and hematuria. She has been diagnosed with analgesic nephropathy. Which of the following is a potential complication of her condition?

- A. Acute kidney injury
- B. Chronic kidney disease
- C. Transitional cell carcinoma
- D. Renal artery stenosis
- E. Nephrolithiasis

31. A 52-year-old man presents with fatigue, constipation, and frequent urination. His blood tests reveal hypercalcemia. Which of the following is a potential renal complication associated with his condition?

- A. Nephrotic syndrome
- B. Nephrocalcinosis
- C. Pyelonephritis
- D. Renal artery stenosis
- E. Acute tubular necrosis

32. A 73-year-old man with a recent diagnosis of multiple myeloma presents with decreased urine output and elevated creatinine levels. Which of the following is a common renal manifestation associated with his condition?

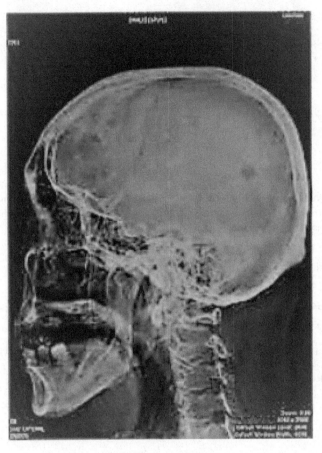

Figure 1.4: MM Skull

- A. Polycystic kidney disease
- B. Renal amyloidosis
- C. Myeloma-associated cast nephropathy
- D. Diabetic nephropathy
- E. Lupus nephritis

33. A 23-year-old woman presents with weakness, fatigue, and frequent urination. Laboratory tests reveal glucosuria, aminoaciduria, phosphaturia, and proximal renal tubular acidosis (RTA). What is the most likely diagnosis?

- A. Bartter syndrome
- B. Gitelman syndrome
- C. Fanconi syndrome
- D. Liddle syndrome
- E. Nephrotic syndrome

34. A 56-year-old woman with a family history of autosomal dominant polycystic kidney disease (ADPKD) has recently been diagnosed with the same condition. Which of the following therapeutic approaches is NOT recommended for retarding the progression of her disease to end-stage renal disease (ESRD)?

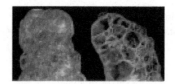

Figure 1.5: ADPKD

- A. Angiotensin receptor blocker (ARB) alone
- B. Angiotensin-converting enzyme (ACE) inhibitor alone
- C. Combination of ARB and ACE inhibitor
- D. Diuretics
- E. Blood pressure control

35. A 52-year-old male presents with bone pain and frequent urination. His urine analysis reveals the presence of high calcium levels. Based on these findings, which of the following conditions is the most likely diagnosis?

- A. Chronic kidney disease
- B. Hyperparathyroidism
- C. Chronic type I renal tubular acidosis (RTA)
- D. Vitamin D toxicity
- E. Paget's disease of bone

36. A 25-year-old woman presents with intermittent weakness and fatigue. Laboratory tests reveal metabolic acidosis. Upon further examination, it is found that her condition is due to an impairment of the basolateral sodium-bicarbonate cotransporter. What is the most likely diagnosis?

- A. Distal Renal Tubular Acidosis
- B. Chronic Kidney Disease
- C. Isolated Proximal Renal Tubular Acidosis
- D. Glomerulonephritis
- E. Diabetic Nephropathy

37. A 46-year-old woman presents with frequency, urgency, and dysuria. She also reports on the history of recurrent urinary tract infections and has a medical history of type 2 diabetes. Which of the following best describes her condition?

- A. Uncomplicated Urinary Tract Infection
- B. Complicated Urinary Tract Infection
- C. Asymptomatic Bacteriuria
- D. Interstitial Cystitis
- E. Overactive Bladder Syndrome

38. A 26-year-old pregnant woman is diagnosed with asymptomatic bacteriuria (ASB). What is the generally recommended duration of antibiotic treatment for this condition?

- A. 1-3 days
- B. 4-7 days
- C. 8-10 days
- D. 11-14 days
- E. No treatment is necessary.

39. A 35-year-old woman presents with chronic pelvic pain and urinary symptoms. You suspect interstitial cystitis (IC). Which of the following is the most appropriate method for diagnosing IC?

- A. Urine culture
- B. Cystoscopy with hydrodistention
- C. Pelvic ultrasound
- D. Urodynamic testing
- E. Computed tomography (CT) scan of the abdomen and pelvis

40. A 48-year-old man with a history of gout presents with severe flank pain. A CT scan reveals the presence of a renal stone. Given his medical history, the stone is most likely composed of which of the following substances?

- A. Calcium oxalate
- B. Struvite
- C. Cystine
- D. Uric acid
- E. Calcium phosphate

41. A 53-year-old woman presents with confusion and seizures. Lab results show a significantly low serum sodium level suggestive of hyponatremia. Which of the following non-osmotic stimuli could have potentially contributed to her condition?

- A. Consumption of a high-sodium diet
- B. Use of certain medications
- C. Mild physical activity
- D. Absence of pain or distress
- E. High water intake without physical exertion

42. A 62-year-old man presents with symptoms of weakness, muscle cramps, and dizziness. Laboratory tests reveal a significantly low serum sodium level, suggestive of hyponatremia. A diagnosis of hypovolemic hyponatremia is made. If this condition is caused by renal factors, what would you expect the concentration of sodium ions $(Na+)$ in the patient's urine to be?

- A. Less than 10 meq/L
- B. Approximately 20 meq/L
- C. Approximately 40 meq/L
- D. Approximately 60 meq/L
- E. More than 80 meq/L

43. A 70-year-old man presents with symptoms of fatigue, headache, and nausea. Laboratory tests reveal a significantly low serum sodium level, suggestive of hyponatremia. A diagnosis of euvolemic hyponatremia is made. Which of the fol-lowing is the most effective treatment for his condition?

- A. Restriction of water intake to less than 1 liter per day
- B. Administration of vasopressin antagonists
- C. Use of loop diuretics and oral salt tablets
- D. High-sodium diet
- E. High water intake

44. A 57-year-old woman presents with symptoms of fatigue, confusion, and muscle twitching. Laboratory tests reveal a significantly high serum sodium level, suggestive of hypernatremia. Which of the following is the most appropriate initial treatment for her condition?

- A. Hypotonic saline solutions

- B. Isotonic saline solutions
- C. Hypertonic saline solutions
- D. Intravenous glucose solution
- E. Water restriction

45. A 42-year-old man presents to your office with complaints of fatigue, muscle weakness, and nausea. He has been experiencing these symptoms for the past few weeks. His physical examination is normal, except for decreased muscle strength. A blood test reveals serum potassium level of 6.0 mEq/L. A urine test reveals urinary potassium-to-creatinine ratio of 20 mmol/g creatinine. What is the purpose of utilizing the urinary potassium-to-creatinine ratio in this patient?

- A. To diagnose hyperkalemia.
- B. To determine the cause of hyperkalemia.
- C. To monitor the response to treatment for hyperkalemia.
- D. To assess the risk of hyperkalemia.
- E. To diagnose hypokalemia.

46. A 35-year-old man presents to the emergency department with muscle weakness and tingling sensation in his extremities. His past medical history is significant for hyperthyroidism. His vital signs are stable, and the remainder of the physical examination is unremarkable. Laboratory studies reveal a serum potassium level of 2.8 mmol/L (normal range, 3.5 to 5.0 mmol/L), with normal renal function. Which of the following is the most likely cause of the patient's hypokalemia?

- A. Renal potassium loss
- B. Gastrointestinal potassium loss
- C. Dietary potassium deficiency
- D. Redistribution of potassium into cells
- E. Inadequate potassium reabsorption in the distal tubule

47. A 43-year-old woman presents to the emergency department with confusion and slurred speech. She has a history of short bowel syndrome as a result of a resection due to Crohn's disease. Her vital signs are normal, and her physical examination is notable for ataxia. Laboratory studies reveal an anion gap in metabolic acidosis. Which of the following is the most likely cause of her symptoms?

- A. Hyperkalemia
- B. Uremic encephalopathy
- C. D-lactic acidosis
- D. Hypoglycemia
- E. Cerebrovascular accident

48. A 52-year-old man presents with a history of vomiting and diarrhea for the past two days. He is found to have metabolic acidosis on arterial blood gas analysis. Urine electrolytes reveal a significantly negative urinary anion gap. What does the negative urinary anion gap in this patient signify?

- A. Renal tubular acidosis
- B. Diabetic ketoacidosis
- C. Gastrointestinal loss of bicarbonate
- D. Lactic acidosis
- E. Uremic acidosis

49. A 65-year-old woman presents to the emergency department with fatigue, muscle weakness, and confusion. She reports excessive use of over the counter calcium carbonate antacids and milk for her chronic peptic ulcer disease. On

examination, she is found to have diminished muscular strength and appears confused. Her laboratory results reveal hypercalcemia, metabolic alkalosis, and acute renal failure. Which of the following is the most likely diagnosis?

- A. Hyperparathyroidism
- B. Vitamin D toxicity
- C. Milk-alkali syndrome
- D. Adrenal insufficiency
- E. Chronic kidney disease

50. A 48-year-old woman with a history of type 1 diabetes presents with symptoms of polyuria, polydipsia, and weight loss. She is diagnosed with diabetic ketoacidosis (DKA) and aggressive fluid resuscitation is initiated. As part of her treatment plan, her anion gap is closely monitored. What is the primary reason for a reduction in the anion gap in this patient?

- A. Decreased production of ketones.
- B. Increased excretion of ketones in urine
- C. Presence of non-anion-gap acidosis
- D. Hyperglycemia
- E. Hypoalbuminemia

51. A 59-year-old woman is diagnosed with Pituitary DI. Which of the following is the recommended therapeutic approach?

- A. Desmopressin (DDAVP) subcutaneous injection, 1 g once daily
- B. Desmopressin (DDAVP) nasal spray, 10 g two times daily
- C. Desmopressin (DDAVP) oral tablets, 100 g two times daily
- D. All of the above
- E. None of the above

52. A 51-year-old woman presents with polyuria and polydipsia. What is the most appropriate diagnostic approach?

- A. Fluid deprivation test
- B. Plasma osmolality
- C. Serum sodium
- D. Urine volume
- E. Urine osmolality

53. A 47-year-old woman presents with hyponatremia and low serum osmolality. She has been diagnosed with chronic SIADH. What is the suggested therapeutic approach?

- A. Oral tolvaptan
- B. Demeclocycline
- C. Fludrocortisone
- D. All of the above
- E. None of the above

54. A 51-year-old woman with type 2 diabetes mellitus is being seen for her annual checkup. Which of the following is the most appropriate screening method for diabetic nephropathy?

- A. Routine urinalysis
- B. 24-hour urine collection
- C. Spot collection for albuminuria

- D. Renal ultrasound
- E. Renal biopsy

55. A 22-year-old woman with type 1 diabetes mellitus presents with Kussmaul respirations and fruity breath odor. Her blood pH is 6.9. Which of the following is the most appropriate course of action?

- A. Admit to the hospital ward.
- B. Admit to the intensive care unit (ICU)
- C. Discharge home with instructions to follow up with her doctor.
- D. Administer intravenous fluids.
- E. Administer insulin.

56. A 31-year-old woman with type 1 diabetes mellitus presents with Kussmaul respirations and fruity breath odor. Her blood pH is 6.9. She is admitted to the hospital and started insulin therapy. Which of the following is the correct insulin regimen for this patient?

- A. 0.1 units per kilogram of short-acting regular insulin intravenously, followed by a continuous intravenous infusion of 0.1 units per kilogram per hour.
- B. 0.2 units per kilogram of short-acting regular insulin subcutaneously, followed by a continuous subcutaneous infusion of 0.2 units per kilogram per hour.
- C. 0.3 units per kilogram of short-acting regular insulin intramuscularly, followed by a continuous intramuscular infusion of 0.3 units per kilogram per hour.
- D. None of the above.

57. A 58-year-old woman presents with fatigue, constipation, and polyuria. Her serum calcium level is 12 mg/dL. Which of the following is the most likely cause of her hypercalcemia?

- A. Primary hyperparathyroidism
- B. Malignancy
- C. Vitamin D toxicity
- D. Medications
- E. Sarcoidosis

58. A 75-year-old man with a history of lung cancer presents with fatigue, constipation, and polyuria. His serum calcium level is 12 mg/dL. His parathyroid hormone (PTH) level is low. Which of the following is the most likely cause of his hypercalcemia?

- A. Primary hyperparathyroidism
- B. Malignancy
- C. Vitamin D toxicity
- D. Medications
- E. Sarcoidosis

59. A 52-year-old woman with a history of hypoparathyroidism presents with muscle cramps and tingling in her hands and feet. She has a positive Chvostek's sign and a positive Trousseau's sign. Her serum calcium level is 7 mg/dL. Which of the following is the most likely cause of her hypocalcemia?

- A. Medications
- B. Pseudohypoparathyroidism
- C. Vitamin D deficiency
- D. Primary hypoparathyroidism
- E. None of the above

60. A 59-year-old woman with a history of hypoparathyroidism presents with muscle cramps and tingling in her hands and feet. She has a positive Chvostek's sign and a positive Trousseau's sign. Her serum calcium level is 7 mg/dL. What is the most appropriate treatment for her hypocalcemia?

Figure 1.6: Trousseau's sign

- A. Administer 1-2 g of intravenous calcium gluconate over a period of 10-20 minutes.
- B. Administer 10 ampoules of 10% calcium gluconate in 1 liter of D5W solution, infused at a rate of 30-100 mL per hour.
- C. Administer oral calcium supplements.
- D. Monitor her condition and wait for her calcium levels to improve on their own.
- E. None of the above.

61. A 62-year-old woman with a history of chronic kidney disease presents with muscle weakness and fatigue. Her serum phosphate level is 0.5 mg/dL. Which of the following is the most appropriate treatment for her hypophosphatemia?

- A. Administer 0.2 mmol/kg of elemental phosphorus over a period of 6 hours.
- B. Administer 0.4 mmol/kg of elemental phosphorus over a period of 6 hours.
- C. Administer 0.8 mmol/kg of elemental phosphorus over a period of 6 hours.
- D. Administer oral phosphate supplements.
- E. None of the above.

62. A 33-year-old woman with a history of alcoholism presents with muscle weakness, tremors, and confusion. Her serum magnesium level is 0.4 mg/dL. Which of the following is the most appropriate treatment for her hypomagnesemia?

- A. Administer oral magnesium supplements.
- B. Administer intravenous magnesium sulfate over a period of 1 hour.
- C. Administer intravenous magnesium sulfate over a period of 6 hours.
- D. Monitor her condition and wait for her magnesium levels to improve on their own.
- E. None of the above.

63. A 49-year-old man with no prior cardiovascular history presents with a blood pressure of 135/85 mmHg. What is the best management strategy?

- A. Calculating his atherosclerotic cardiovascular disease (ASCVD) risk score and, if >10%, starting an antihypertensive agent now.
- B. Starting an antihypertensive agent now.
- C. Monitoring his blood pressure closely and following up in 3 months.
- D. Recommending lifestyle changes only.
- E. None of the above.

64. 59-year-old woman with a history of type 2 diabetes mellitus visits your clinic for a routine check-up. She has been

managing her diabetes with metformin. Recent laboratory results indicate the presence of microalbuminuria. Her blood pressure today is 150/90 mmHg. You decide to start her on antihypertensive therapy. Which of the following should be your first choice?

- A. Amlodipine (Calcium channel blocker)
- B. Hydrochlorothiazide (Diuretic)
- C. Metoprolol (Beta-blocker)
- D. Lisinopril (ACE inhibitor)
- E. Losartan (Angiotensin II receptor blocker)

65. A 65-year-old man presents to the emergency department with severe chest pain and blood pressure of 220/130 mmHg. He is tachycardic with a heart rate of 110 beats per minute. Chest X-ray shows a widened mediastinum. What is the best initial management strategy?

- A. Oral labetalol
- B. Intravenous labetalol
- C. Intravenous nitroglycerin
- D. Intravenous nitroprusside
- E. Intravenous esmolol

66. A 26-year-old woman presents with severe hypertension. On physical examination, an abdominal bruit is noted. What is the most appropriate next step in her diagnostic evaluation?

- A. MR angiography (MRA) of the renal arteries
- B. Duplex ultrasound of the renal arteries
- C. Noncontrast CT scan of the abdomen
- D. Renal angiography
- E. Percutaneous transluminal renal angioplasty

67. A 56-year-old man with no significant medical history presents with resistant hypertension. He is taking three antihypertensive medications, but his blood pressure remains uncontrolled. He has no family history of hypertension, and he does not have any symptoms suggestive of hypercortisolism or pheochromocytoma. What is the most appropriate next step in the evaluation of this patient's hypertension?

- (A) Order a 24-hour urine collection for cortisol and catecholamines.
- (B) Measure morning plasma renin and aldosterone.
- (C) Order a renal ultrasound.
- (D) Order a CT scan of the adrenal glands.
- (E) Refer the patient to a nephrologist.

68. A patient presents with imaging findings of multiple adrenal adenomas and elevated aldosterone levels. What is the most appropriate next step in the management of this patient?

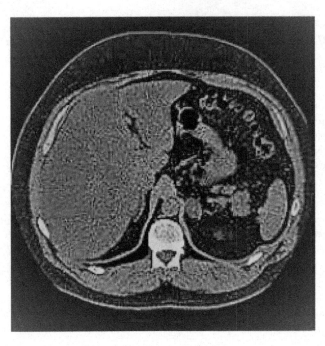

Figure 1.7: Adrenal Adenoma

- A. Adrenal venous sampling
- B. Adrenal CT scan
- C. Radioiodine uptake scan
- D. Low-dose dexamethasone suppression test
- E. Start hydrocortisone 100 mg every 8 hours and 100 g T4 IV daily

69. A 52-year-old man presents with an adrenal incidentaloma found on abdominal imaging. He has no significant medical history and is not taking any medications. Which of the following is the most appropriate next step?

- (A) Abdominal MRI with gadolinium contrast
- (B) Twenty-four-hour urine collection for cortisol and catecholamines
- (C) Twenty-four-hour urine fractionated metanephrines
- (D) Aldosterone, renin, and overnight 1 mg dexamethasone suppression test (DST)
- (E) All of the above

70. A 59-year-old female patient is scheduled for surgical removal of a catecholamine-secreting tumor. Which of the following is the most appropriate preoperative step to avoid catastrophic -adrenergic stimulation during manipulation of the tumor?

- A. Initiate propranolol 40 mg twice daily
- B. Start metyrosine 500 mg thrice daily
- C. Administer phenoxybenzamine 20 mg twice daily
- D. Initiate prazosin 1 mg every 4 hours
- E. Administer dexamethasone 4 mg twice daily

71. A 23-year-old man with no significant medical history presents with a kidney stone. He has no history of fragility fractures. Laboratory results show hypercalcemia and elevated PTH levels. Which of the following is the most appropriate next step in the evaluation of this patient's hypercalcemia?

- (A) Order a 24-hour urine collection for magnesium and phosphate.
- (B) Order a parathyroid gland ultrasound.
- (C) Check serum and 24-hour urine calcium and creatinine.
- (D) Order a dual-energy x-ray absorptiometry (DXA) scan.

- (E) Perform a parathyroidectomy.

72. A 44-year-old woman presents to the clinic with fatigue, weight loss, and an increasing craving for salt. She also reports having episodes of lightheadedness when standing up. On physical examination, she has hyperpigmentation of skin and mucous membranes. Blood pressure is 90/60 mm Hg, and it decreases to 80/55 mm Hg upon standing. Laboratory tests reveal hyponatremia and hyperkalemia. The clinical picture is suggestive of Addison disease. What is the appropriate next step in the management of this patient?

- A. Start hydrocortisone treatment immediately
- B. Order 21-Hydroxylase antibodies
- C. Check baseline adrenocorticotropic hormone (ACTH) and perform cosyntropin stimulation test
- D. Order an abdominal CT scan
- E. Referral to a psychiatrist for evaluation of possible depression

73. A 69-year-old man with a history of thyroidectomy presents with nausea, vomiting, and confusion. He has also been experiencing weakness and diplopia. On physical exam, he is tachycardic and hypertensive. His serum calcium level is 13.5 mg/dL. Which of the following is the most likely diagnosis?

- (A) Hypercalcemic crisis
- (B) Hyperthyroidism
- (C) Hyperosmolar hyperglycemic state
- (D) Stroke
- (E) Hyponatremia

74. A 39-year-old Afro American woman presents with a persistent cough, fatigue, and a recent weight loss. She denies chest pain, hemoptysis, or shortness of breath. Physical examination discloses bilateral hilar lymphadenopathy and erythema nodosum. Laboratory studies show a serum calcium level of 12.5 mg/dL. A chest X-ray reveals bilateral hilar lymphadenopathy. What is the most likely diagnosis?

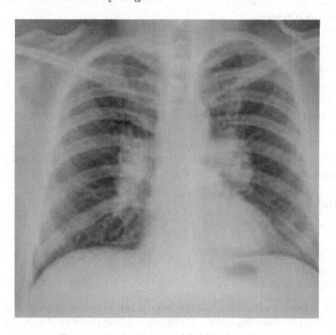

Figure 18: A 35-year-old Afro American

- A. Primary hyperparathyroidism
- B. Secondary hyperparathyroidism
- C. Sarcoidosis
- D. Humoral hypercalcemia of malignancy

- E. Tuberculosis

75. A 33-year-old woman presents with tingling in her hands and feet, muscle cramps, and tetany. She had a thyroidectomy 6 months ago. Which of the following laboratory tests is the most important to order first?

- (A) Calcium and albumin
- (B) Magnesium and phosphorus
- (C) Parathyroid hormone (PTH)
- (D) Vitamin D
- (E) Multiple sclerosis panel

76. A 27-year-old pregnant woman with a history of hypoparathyroidism presents for her routine prenatal care. Recent labs show her serum calcium level to be 8.4 mg/dL and her albumin level to be 2.0 g/dL. She is asymptomatic. What should be the next step in management?

- A. Increase her calcium supplementation.
- B. Start her on intravenous calcium.
- C. Check her parathyroid hormone levels.
- D. No change in treatment is needed.
- E. Refer her to a high-risk pregnancy specialist.

77. A 48-year-old male with a history of alcohol use disorder is admitted to the hospital with generalized weakness and fatigue. His physical examination is unremarkable. Lab results show a serum pH of 7.20, sodium of 125 mEq/L, potassium of 3.5 mEq/L, chloride of 90 mEq/L, bicarbonate of 15 mEq/L, and albumin of 3 g/dL. Despite 2 L of hypotonic IV fluid resuscitation, he remains acidotic and weak. Which of the following is the most likely cause of this patient's condition?

- A. Metabolic alkalosis due to vomiting
- B. Type A lactic acidosis due to ischemia
- C. Metformin-induced lactic acidosis
- D. Thiamine deficiency
- E. Propofol infusion syndrome

78. A 57-year-old man is brought to the emergency department with altered mental status and blurry vision. He has a history of alcohol use disorder. Physical exam reveals a well-developed, well-nourished man in no acute distress. His blood pressure is 120/80 mmHg, heart rate is 80 beats per minute, and respiratory rate is 14 breaths per minute. His temperature is 98.6 degrees Fahrenheit. His pupils are dilated and sluggishly reactive to light. His funduscopic exam reveals papilledema. Laboratory results: White blood cell count: 12,000 cells/mm3, Neutrophils: 80%' lymphocytes: 15%, Monocytes: 5%, Eosinophils: 0%, Basophils: 0%, Electrolytes: Sodium 135 mEq/L, Potassium 3.5 mEq/L, Chloride 105 mEq/L, Bicarbonate: 20 mEq/L, Glucose: 100 mg/dL, Blood urea nitrogen (BUN): 20 mg/dL, Creatinine: 1.0 mg/dL, Anion gap: 20.5 mEq/L, Osmolar gap: 23 mEq/L Which of the following is the most likely diagnosis?
Which of the following is the most likely diagnosis?

- (A) Isopropyl alcohol intoxication
- (B) Aspirin toxicity
- (C) Ethylene glycol intoxication
- (D) Methanol intoxication
- (E) Propylene glycol intoxication

79. A 35-year-old man with a history of alcohol use disorder is admitted to the hospital for status epilepticus. He is treated with high doses of intravenous diazepam. During his hospitalization, he develops an increased anion gap metabolic acidosis and an increased osmolar gap. Which of the following is the most likely cause of his metabolic acidosis?

- (A) Ethylene glycol toxicity
- (B) Propylene glycol toxicity
- (C) Isopropyl alcohol toxicity
- (D) Aspirin toxicity

- (E) Lactic acidosis

80. A 51-year-old man with a history of alcohol use disorder comes to the emergency department because of nausea, vomiting, and abdominal pain for the last two days. He has been unable to consume any food or fluids during this time. On examination, his blood pressure is 100/60 mmHg, heart rate is 90/min, and his respiratory rate is 18/min. Laboratory studies show: Sodium: 126 mEq/L, Chloride: 87 mEq/L, Bicarbonate: 20 mEq/L, pH: 7.40, pCO2: 28 mmHg, Albumin: 2 g/dL Which of the following best describes the acid-base disturbance in this patient?

- A. Normal acid-base status
- B. High anion gap metabolic acidosis with concurrent metabolic alkalosis and compensatory respiratory alkalosis
- C. High anion gap metabolic acidosis
- D. Non-anion gap metabolic acidosis
- E. Respiratory alkalosis

81. A 43-year-old man presents to the emergency department with complaints of recurrent episodes of vomiting for the past two days. His lab tests reveal a high chloride level and low potassium level. His blood pH is found to be alkalotic. What is the most appropriate treatment for this patient?

- A. Intravenous (IV) bicarbonate
- B. Potassium-sparing diuretics
- C. Oral hydration
- D. IV normal saline
- E. Respiratory therapy

82. A 57-year-old man presents to the hospital with a headache and stiff neck. He is diagnosed with a subarachnoid hemorrhage (SAH). After admission, he develops hyponatremia with a serum sodium level of 125 mEq/L. His urine osmolality is 500 mOsm/kg, and his plasma osmolality is 275 mOsm/kg. He is also noted to have hypouricemia and a high urine sodium. Which of the following is the most likely diagnosis?

- (A) Cerebral salt wasting
- (B) Syndrome of inappropriate antidiuretic hormone secretion (SIADH)
- (C) Central diabetes insipidus
- (D) Hypovolemic hyponatremia
- (E) Adrenal insufficiency

83. A 65-year-old woman presents to the hospital with confusion and lethargy. She is found to have a serum sodium level of 160 mEq/L. Her urine osmolality is 250 mOsm/kg. After resuscitation with normal saline, she remains polyuric with a urine output of 675 mL/day. She is given a dose of desmopressin acetate (DDAVP), and her urine osmolality increases to 300 mOsm/kg. Which of the following is the most likely diagnosis?

- (A) Central diabetes insipidus
- (B) Primary polydipsia
- (C) Osmotic diuresis
- (D) Nephrogenic diabetes insipidus
- (E) Hyperaldosteronism

84. A 45-year-old woman presents to the emergency department with complaints of severe nausea and vomiting for the past two days. She has been feeling extremely lethargic and has been experiencing recurrent headaches. She has no known prior medical history but was recently started on a new medication by her primary care physician for symptoms of depression. Her labs reveal a serum sodium level of 110 mEq/L and urine sodium level of 30 mEq/L. She is currently euvolemic. What is the most appropriate next step in management?

- A. Start her on thyroid hormone replacement therapy.
- B. Administer 2 L of isotonic saline without rechecking serum Na.
- C. Give 3% hypertonic saline as a 100 mL bolus in 10 minutes, then recheck labs.
- D. Restrict her free water intake.
- E. Administer a bolus of normal saline and start her on diuretics.

85. A 52-year-old man presents with fatigue, muscle weakness, and palpitations for the past 3 weeks. On examination, his blood pressure is elevated at 152/88 mmHg. Labs show potassium of 2.4 mEq/L, sodium of 142 mEq/L, chloride

of 100 mEq/L, bicarbonate of 24 mEq/L, and creatinine of 1.0 mg/dL. Urine potassium to creatinine ratio is 15. The patient reports that he had been eating large quantities of black licorice for the past month. What is the most likely cause of his symptoms?

- A. Diarrhea
- B. Licorice ingestion
- C. Thiazide use
- D. Renal tubular acidosis
- E. Vomiting

86. A 25-year-old male presents to the emergency department with severe muscle pain and weakness. He reports having been working out vigorously the day before. On physical exam, he is found to have dark brown urine and a serum creatine kinase level of 10,000 U/L. Which of the following is the most appropriate initial fluid management strategy?

- (A) IV normal saline at 200 mL/h
- (B) IV bicarbonate at 200 mL/h
- (C) IV furosemide at 20 mg/h
- (D) IV normal saline at 1-2 L/h
- (E) Dialysis

87. A 70-year-old man with chronic kidney disease is scheduled for a coronary angiography. Which of the following is the most appropriate medication or intervention to reduce his risk of contrast-associated acute kidney injury?

- (A) N-acetylcysteine
- (B) Hemodialysis
- (C) Intravenous normal saline (IV normal saline)
- (D) Intravenous sodium bicarbonate
- (E) None of the above

88. A patient with significant volume overload is being treated with a loop diuretic. The patient develops metabolic alkalosis as a result of diuretic-induced sodium and chloride loss. Which of the following would be the most appropriate management strategy to correct the metabolic alkalosis?

- A. Add acetazolamide
- B. Infusion of normal saline
- C. Stopping the loop diuretic
- D. Add spironolactone
- E. Add amiloride

89. A 55-year-old man with chronic kidney disease and a dialysis fistula in his left arm presents to the emergency department with severe pain and numbness in his left hand. His left hand is pale and cool, and his radial pulse is nonpalpable. Which of the following is the most appropriate next step in management?

- (A) Lower the dialysis blood flow rate.
- (B) Administer analgesics.
- (C) Perform a surgical evaluation.
- (D) Start antibiotics.
- (E) Monitor for signs of infection.

90. A 72-year-old active Hispanic male with a history of nonmelanomatous skin cancer that was surgically removed 3 years ago, presents with an eGFR of 18 mL/min. He has a BMI of 35 and his blood group is AB. He has adequate family support. What is the most appropriate next step in the management of this patient?

- A. Wait for his eGFR to drop to 20 mL/min before considering transplantation.
- B. Counselling regarding dialysis as he is over the age limit for transplantation.
- C. Wait for 5 years due to his history of cancer before considering transplantation.
- D. He should be evaluated and listed for a kidney transplant now.
- E. He should only consider transplantation if a living donor is available.

91. A 25-year-old woman with systemic lupus erythematosus (SLE) presents to her doctor with complaints of fatigue

and weight gain. Her blood pressure is 150/100 mmHg and her serum creatinine is 1.2 mg/dL. Her urine dipstick shows 3+ protein. Which of the following is the most appropriate next step in management?

- (A) Start immunosuppressive therapy.
- (B) Monitor her blood pressure and renal function.
- (C) Refer her for a kidney biopsy.
- (D) Order a 24-hour urine collection for proteinuria.
- (E) Start antihypertensive therapy.

92. A 53-year-old male presents with a history of recurrent gross hematuria. Laboratory tests show elevated creatinine and persistent urine protein creatinine ratio of 1.2 g/d. His blood pressure is 145/95 mmHg. A kidney biopsy confirms a diagnosis of IgA nephropathy. Based on his diagnosis and clinical findings, which of the following is the most appropriate next step in management?

- A. Begin fish oil supplementation.
- B. Initiate prednisone therapy.
- C. Start treatment with Lisinopril.
- D. Recommend cyclophosphamide.
- E. No treatment is required.

93. A 60-year-old man with a history of chronic myelogenous leukemia (CML) and allogeneic bone marrow transplant (BMT) 2 years ago presents with proteinuria and edema. He had been on tacrolimus and mycophenolate mofetil for immunosuppression, but both medications were recently discontinued. He also has a history of dry eyes and mouth, and a rash on his face and chest. Which of the following is the most likely diagnosis?

- (A) Thrombotic microangiopathy
- (B) Posttransplant antineutrophilic cytoplasmic antibody (ANCA) vasculitis
- (C) Membranous nephropathy
- (D) Minimal change disease
- (E) Focal segmental glomerulosclerosis

94. A 65-year-old man presents with proteinuria and hematuria. He has no other medical history. Which of the following is the best initial laboratory evaluation for monoclonal gammopathy of renal significance?

- (A) Serum protein electrophoresis (SPEP) and urine protein electrophoresis (UPEP)
- (B) SPEP, serum immunofixation (SIF), and serum free light chain assay (SFLC)
- (C) SPEP, UPEP, and bone marrow biopsy
- (D) SIF, SFLC, and bone marrow biopsy
- (E) UPEP, SFLC, and bone marrow biopsy

95. A patient presents with rapidly progressive glomerulonephritis, and crescent formation is observed on a kidney biopsy. Which of the following is the most likely diagnosis?

- A. Anti–glomerular basement membrane disease
- B. Antineutrophilic cytoplasmic antibody (ANCA)-associated glomerulonephritis
- C. Hemolytic uremic syndrome
- D. Lupus nephritis
- E. IgA nephropathy

96. A 45-year-old woman presents with gross hematuria, hypertension, and acute kidney injury. On urinalysis, she has protein and red blood cells, with red blood cell casts. The patient has a history of untreated hepatitis C. Her blood test demonstrates a reduction in C3 and C4. What is the most likely diagnosis for this patient?

- A. Cryoglobulinemic glomerulonephritis
- B. Minimal change disease
- C. Membranous nephropathy
- D. Focal segmental glomerulosclerosis
- E. Diabetic nephropathy

97. A 55-year-old man presents to the emergency department with gross hematuria. He has no history of flank pain, kidney stones, or trauma. He is afebrile and has a normal blood pressure.

What is the next best step in management?

- (A) CT urography
- (B) Urinalysis and sediment
- (C) Renal ultrasound
- (D) Urology referral

98. A 65-year-old man with a history of hypertension and diabetes presents with acute kidney injury. His urinalysis is unremarkable. Which of the following is the most likely diagnosis?

- (A) Amyloidosis
- (B) Thrombotic microangiopathy
- (C) Malignant hypertension
- (D) Cast nephropathy
- (E) Hepatorenal syndrome

99. A 40-year-old man presents with a history of recurrent kidney stones. His recent ultrasound showed a 0.4 cm stone in his left kidney. He has a history of low fluid intake. His past medical records indicate that the stones are composed of calcium oxalate. Which of the following statements is most accurate regarding his condition?

- A. His stones are a rare type, given that calcium oxalate stones are uncommon.
- B. He should be prescribed a low-calcium diet to prevent future stone formation.
- C. Alkalinizing his urine will prevent new calcium oxalate stone formation.
- D. His stone has a high likelihood of passing spontaneously given its size.
- E. A single episode of stone passage indicates that he will likely experience another one in his lifetime.

100. A 46-year-old male with no significant medical history comes to your clinic. He has a complaint of experiencing two episodes of kidney stones in the past one year. On further questioning, he reveals that he has been taking dietary supplements regularly. Which of the following supplements is most likely to increase his risk of developing kidney stones?

- A. Vitamin A
- B. Vitamin B6
- C. Vitamin C
- D. Vitamin D
- E. Vitamin E

101. A 50-year-old man with a history of inflammatory bowel disease presents with acute kidney injury and nephrolithiasis. His urinalysis shows oxalate crystals. Which of the following is the most likely cause of his kidney injury?

- (A) Primary hyperoxaluria
- (B) Hypercalciuria
- (C) Oxalate nephropathy
- (D) Uric acid nephropathy
- (E) Nephrolithiasis

1.1 ANSWERS

1.The correct answer is (E).

All of the answer choices are limitations of using creatinine clearance to assess GFR. Creatinine clearance is not a reliable measure of GFR in patients with chronic kidney disease because the proportionate contribution of tubular secretion to creatinine clearance increases as renal dysfunction progresses. This means that the actual GFR may be lower than the estimated GFR based on creatinine clearance. Creatinine clearance is also affected by muscle mass, which can vary from person to person. This means that creatinine clearance may not be accurate for patients with low or high muscle mass. Creatinine clearance can also be inaccurate in patients with conditions that affect muscle metabolism, such as diabetes. This is because diabetes can lead to increased muscle breakdown, which can increase creatinine levels and falsely elevate creatinine clearance. Finally, creatinine clearance is not a sensitive measure of

GFR, meaning that it may not detect early changes in kidney function. This is because creatinine levels do not begin to rise until GFR has decreased by approximately 50%.

2. The correct answer is (E).

Severe acute tubular necrosis (SATN) is the most likely etiology of anuria in this patient. SATN is a condition in which the tubules of the kidneys are damaged, which can lead to a decrease in urine production. SATN is often caused by sepsis, shock, or the use of nephrotoxic medications. The other answer choices are also possible etiologies of anuria, but they are less likely in this patient. Complete bilateral obstruction of the urinary tract is unlikely because the patient has symptoms of sepsis and shock. Vascular events such as dissection or arterial occlusion are also unlikely because the patient does not have any risk factors for these conditions. Renal vein thrombosis is a rare cause of anuria and is unlikely in this patient. Renal cortical necrosis is a severe form of kidney damage that is often caused by sepsis or shock. It is possible that the patient has renal cortical necrosis, but ATN is more likely.

3. The correct answer is (E).

All of the answer choices are possible causes of proteinuria in this patient. Glomerular disease is a condition that damages the glomeruli, which are small filters in the kidneys that remove waste products from the blood. Glomerular disease can lead to proteinuria, as well as other symptoms such as hematuria (blood in the urine) and hypertension. Interstitial nephritis is a condition that damages the tubules of the kidneys. The tubules are responsible for reabsorbing water and nutrients from the urine. Interstitial nephritis can lead to proteinuria, as well as other symptoms such as decreased urine output and swelling. Vascular disease can damage the blood vessels that supply the kidneys. This can lead to decreased blood flow to the kidneys, which can lead to proteinuria. Hypertensive nephrosclerosis is a condition that damages the kidneys due to high blood pressure. Hypertensive nephrosclerosis can lead to proteinuria, as well as other symptoms such as decreased urine output and hypertension.

4. The correct answer is (E).

All of the answer choices are possible causes of pyuria in addition to urinary tract infection. Urinary tract infection is the most common cause of pyuria. However, pyuria can also be caused by other conditions, such as: Inflammatory glomerular diseases: These are diseases that cause inflammation of the glomeruli, which are small filters in the kidneys that remove waste products from the blood. Inflammatory glomerular diseases can lead to pyuria, as well as other symptoms such as hematuria (blood in the urine) and edema (swelling). Allergic interstitial nephritis: This is a condition that causes inflammation of the tubules of the kidneys. The tubules are responsible for reabsorbing water and nutrients from the urine. Allergic interstitial nephritis can lead to pyuria, as well as other symptoms such as decreased urine output and swelling. Transplant rejection: This is a condition that occurs when the body's immune system attacks a transplanted organ. Transplant rejection can lead to pyuria, as well as other symptoms such as fever, chills, and fatigue. Noninfectious, nonallergic tubulointerstitial diseases: These are diseases that cause inflammation of the tubules of the kidneys. They are not caused by infection or allergies. Noninfectious, nonallergic tubulointerstitial diseases can lead to pyuria, as well as other symptoms such as decreased urine output and swelling.

5. The correct answer is (B).

ACE inhibitors and angiotensin II receptor antagonists have been observed to potentially decrease GFR, but they generally do not exhibit a tendency to decrease renal perfusion. Decreased GFR can lead to decreased urine output and fatigue. Other symptoms of decreased GFR include edema, hypertension, and headache. Hyperkalemia, hypotension, and none of the above are not likely causes of the patient's decreased urine output and fatigue. In conclusion, the most likely cause of the patient's decreased urine output and fatigue is decreased GFR due to ACE inhibitor therapy.

6. The correct answer is (D).

All of the answer choices are risk factors for contrast-induced nephropathy in this patient. Pre-existing renal dysfunction is the most important risk factor for CIN. Other risk factors include diabetes mellitus, congestive heart failure, dehydration, and multiple myeloma. Patients with risk factors for CIN should be adequately hydrated before and after the administration of contrast agents. They should also be monitored for signs of kidney injury, such as decreased urine output and elevated creatinine levels. In conclusion, the patient in this question has multiple risk factors for contrast-induced nephropathy. He should be adequately hydrated before and after the CT scan, and he should be monitored for signs of kidney injury.

7. The correct answer is (E).

All of the answer choices are additional medical conditions that may potentially lead to the development of acute kidney injury (AKI) in this patient. Acute glomerulonephritis is a condition that causes inflammation of the glomeruli, which are small filters in the kidneys that remove waste products from the blood. Acute glomerulonephritis can lead to acute kidney injury, as well as other symptoms such as hematuria (blood in the urine), edema (swelling), and hypertension. Thrombotic microangiopathies are a group of disorders that cause blood clots to form in small blood vessels throughout the body. Thrombotic microangiopathies can lead to acute kidney injury, as well as other symptoms such as hemolytic anemia (destruction of red blood cells), thrombocytopenia (low platelet count), and neurological problems. Sepsis is a life-threatening condition that occurs when the body's response to an infection damages its own tissues and organs. Sepsis can lead to acute kidney injury, as well as other symptoms such as fever, chills, and confusion. Rhabdomyolysis is a condition that occurs when muscle tissue breaks down rapidly. Rhabdomyolysis can lead to acute kidney injury, as well as other symptoms such as muscle pain, weakness, and dark urine. In conclusion, there are many medical conditions that can potentially lead to the development of acute kidney injury. The specific cause of acute kidney injury in this patient will need to be determined based on his medical history, physical examination, and laboratory tests.

8.The correct answer is (A).

The patient's urine sodium concentration and fractional excretion of sodium are both consistent with prerenal AKI. In prerenal AKI, the kidneys are not receiving enough blood flow. This can happen due to a number of factors, such as heart failure, dehydration, and sepsis. When the kidneys do not receive enough blood flow, they are unable to filter the blood properly. This can lead to an accumulation of waste products in the blood and a decrease in urine output. The urine sodium concentration is typically low in prerenal AKI because the kidneys are trying to conserve sodium. The fractional excretion of sodium is also typically low in prerenal AKI because the kidneys are not filtering the blood as efficiently. In contrast, intrarenal AKI and postrenal AKI are characterized by high urine sodium concentrations and high fractional excretions of sodium. Intrarenal AKI is caused by damage to the kidneys themselves. This can happen due to a number of factors, such as infection, toxins, and medications. Postrenal AKI is caused by a blockage in the urinary tract. This can happen due to a number of factors, such as kidney stones, tumors, and enlarged prostate glands. In conclusion, the patient in this question is most likely suffering from prerenal AKI. His urine sodium concentration and fractional excretion of sodium are both consistent with this diagnosis.

9. The correct answer is (A).

The presence of pigmented "muddy-brown" granular casts and casts that contain tubular epithelial cells is a distinguishing characteristic of ischemic or toxic acute tubular necrosis (ATN). ATN is a type of acute kidney injury that is caused by damage to the tubules of the kidneys. This damage can be caused by a number of factors, such as ischemia (lack of blood flow to the kidneys) or toxins. The pigmented "muddy-brown" granular casts are composed of cellular debris, protein, and other substances that are filtered out of the blood by the damaged tubules. The casts that contain tubular epithelial cells are composed of cells that have been shed from the damaged tubules. The presence of free tubular epithelial cells can also be observed in patients with ATN. These cells are shed from the damaged tubules and can be seen in the urine. The other answer choices are not associated with the presence of pigmented "muddy-brown" granular casts and casts that contain tubular epithelial cells. In conclusion, the patient in this question is most likely suffering from ischemic or toxic acute tubular necrosis (ATN). His urinalysis results are consistent with this diagnosis.

10.The correct answer is (B).

High levels of potassium in the blood is a conventional indication for dialysis in AKI. When the kidneys are not functioning properly, they are unable to remove excess potassium from the blood. This can lead to high levels of potassium in the blood, which can be dangerous. Symptoms of high potassium levels in the blood include weakness, fatigue, confusion, and irregular heartbeat. In severe cases, high potassium levels can lead to cardiac arrest. Dialysis can help to remove excess potassium from the blood and prevent these complications. The other answer choices are also indications for dialysis in AKI, but they are not considered to be conventional indications. Excessive fluid volume that does not respond to diuretic medications is an indication for dialysis in AKI because it can lead to heart failure and other complications. Unexplained encephalopathy is an indication for dialysis in AKI because it can be caused by high levels of toxins in the blood. Inflammation of the pericardium, pleura, or other serous membranes is an indication for dialysis in AKI because it can lead to fluid accumulation and other complications. Severe metabolic acidosis that affects respiratory or circulatory function is an indication for dialysis in AKI because it can lead to respiratory failure and other complications.

11.The correct answer is (C).

Both serum and urine protein electrophoresis and serum free light chain testing should be conducted for all individuals aged 35 years and above diagnosed with chronic kidney disease (CKD). Paraproteinemia is a condition in which there is an abnormal increase in the production of proteins called paraproteins. Paraproteins can be produced by a variety of conditions, including multiple myeloma, Waldenstrom macroglobulinemia, and amyloidosis. Paraproteinemia-related renal disorders can occur in individuals with CKD. These disorders can lead to kidney damage and progression of CKD. Serum and urine protein electrophoresis are tests that can be used to detect paraproteins. Serum free light chain testing is a test that can be used to measure the levels of free light chains in the blood. By conducting both serum and urine protein electrophoresis and serum free light chain testing, healthcare providers can better identify individuals with paraproteinemia and paraproteinemia-related renal disorders.

12. The correct answer is (C).

Both recombinant human erythropoietin (rHuEPO) and iron supplements are recommended for the management of anemia in patients with chronic kidney disease (CKD). Recombinant human erythropoietin (rHuEPO) is a medication that helps to stimulate the production of red blood cells. Red blood cells carry oxygen to the tissues, so increasing the number of red blood cells can help to improve oxygen delivery and reduce fatigue. Iron is an essential mineral that is needed for the production of red blood cells. People with chronic kidney disease (CKD) often have difficulty absorbing iron from their diet, so iron supplements may be necessary. The goal of treatment for anemia in patients with chronic kidney disease (CKD) is to achieve a hemoglobin concentration within the range of 90-115 g/L.

13. The correct answer is (D).

ACE inhibitors and ARBs have been shown to have distinct advantages in the management of renal failure, including:

- Slowing the progression of renal failure
- Reducing proteinuria
- Improving blood pressure control

These benefits are particularly notable in individuals diagnosed with diabetic nephropathy, as well as in those without diabetes who exhibit substantial proteinuria levels exceeding 1 g/d. ACE inhibitors and ARBs work by blocking the effects of angiotensin II, a hormone that can damage the kidneys. By blocking angiotensin II, ACE inhibitors and ARBs can help to protect the kidneys and slow the progression of renal failure. ACE inhibitors and ARBs can also help to reduce proteinuria, which is the leakage of protein into the urine. Proteinuria is a sign of kidney damage, and reducing proteinuria can help to protect the kidneys and slow the progression of renal failure. ACE inhibitors and ARBs can also help to improve blood pressure control. High blood pressure is a risk factor for kidney damage, and controlling blood pressure can help to protect the kidneys and slow the progression of renal failure.

14. The correct answer is (C).

There is no definitive threshold for the necessity of dialysis in relation to serum creatinine, blood urea nitrogen, creatinine or urea clearance, or glomerular filtration rate (GFR). The decision to initiate dialysis is a complex one that is made on a case-by-case basis. Factors that are considered include the patient's age, overall health, and symptoms. Serum creatinine, blood urea nitrogen, creatinine or urea clearance, and glomerular filtration rate (GFR) are all important measures of kidney function, but they cannot be used alone to determine the need for dialysis.

15. The correct answer is (A).

Dialysis disequilibrium syndrome is characterized by the emergence of symptoms such as headache, confusion, and, in rare cases, seizures. These symptoms occur in conjunction with the rapid elimination of solutes during the early stages of a patient's dialysis treatment, prior to their physiological adjustment to the procedure. The signs and symptoms of dialysis disequilibrium syndrome are thought to be caused by the rapid changes in serum osmolality that occur during hemodialysis. When solutes are rapidly removed from the blood, the serum osmolality decreases. This can lead to the movement of water from the brain into the bloodstream, which can cause the symptoms of headache, confusion, and seizures. Dialysis disequilibrium syndrome is typically a self-limited condition that resolves within a few hours of dialysis. However, in severe cases, it can be fatal. To prevent dialysis disequilibrium syndrome, it is important to start dialysis slowly and gradually increase the duration of treatment over time. Patients should also be monitored closely for signs and symptoms of the syndrome during and after dialysis.

16. The correct answer is (A).

Percutaneous renal transplant biopsy is the definitive diagnostic method for confirming rejection in patients who have undergone renal transplantation. Blood tests, urine tests, and imaging studies can be used to suggest rejection, but they are not definitive. Percutaneous renal transplant biopsy is the only way to definitively diagnose rejection. In a percutaneous renal transplant biopsy, a small needle is inserted into the kidney and a small piece of tissue is removed. The tissue is then examined under a microscope by a pathologist. The pathologist can look for signs of rejection, such as inflammation, cell death, and the presence of white blood cells. If rejection is confirmed, treatment can be started to prevent further damage to the kidney. In conclusion, percutaneous renal transplant biopsy is the definitive diagnostic method for confirming rejection in patients who have undergone renal transplantation.

17.The correct answer is (D).

All of the above are mechanisms involved in the pathophysiology of BK nephropathy virus, which is a common virus that is present in most people. It is usually harmless, but it can cause problems in people with weakened immune systems. After a renal transplant, the BK virus can reactivate in the kidney. This can cause inflammation and damage to the kidney's tubules. The BK virus can also damage the kidney's blood vessels. This can lead to decreased blood flow to the kidney and further damage to the kidney. BK nephropathy can lead to the loss of the allograft. There are treatments available for BK nephropathy. These treatments include antiviral medications and immunosuppressants.

18. The correct answer is (A).

Azotemia, hypertension, edema, hematuria, proteinuria, and occasionally oliguria are all clinical manifestations of acute glomerulonephritis. Azotemia is a condition in which there is an excess of nitrogenous waste products in the blood. This can be caused by kidney damage, which is a common feature of acute glomerulonephritis. Hypertension is high blood pressure. It can be caused by kidney damage, which can lead to fluid retention and increased blood volume. Edema is swelling caused by fluid retention. It is a common feature of acute glomerulonephritis. Hematuria is blood in the urine. It is a common feature of acute glomerulonephritis. Proteinuria is the presence of protein in the urine. It is a common feature of acute glomerulonephritis. Oliguria is decreased urine output. It is not a common feature of acute glomerulonephritis, but it can occur in severe cases.

19.The correct answer is (A).

IgA nephropathy is a distinct form of acute postinfectious glomerulonephritis characterized by a predominance of IgA deposits on immunofluorescence. It is most commonly linked to staphylococcal infections, particularly in individuals with diabetes. IgA nephropathy is characterized by the deposition of IgA antibodies in the glomeruli, which are the tiny filters in the kidneys. This can lead to inflammation and damage to the glomeruli, which can result in the symptoms of acute glomerulonephritis. The symptoms of IgA nephropathy can vary depending on the severity of the disease. Mild cases may only cause fatigue and mild swelling, while more severe cases can lead to decreased urine output, high blood pressure, and kidney failure. There is no cure for IgA nephropathy, but there are treatments that can help to control the symptoms and prevent further damage to the kidneys. These treatments include medications to suppress the immune system and medications to control blood pressure. In conclusion, IgA nephropathy is a distinct form of acute postinfectious glomerulonephritis characterized by a predominance of IgA deposits on immunofluorescence. It is most commonly linked to staphylococcal infections, particularly in individuals with diabetes.

20.Answer: D. Membranous nephropathy.

Systemic lupus erythematosus (SLE) can manifest with various renal complications, often referred to as lupus nephritis. The histopathological findings in renal biopsy specimens from SLE patients can vary, but common findings include mesangial, focal or diffuse glomerulonephritis, and membranous nephropathy. A. Minimal change disease is typically associated with primary nephrotic syndrome, particularly in children. It is not a common finding in SLE patients. B. Diabetic nephropathy is a complication of longstanding poorly controlled diabetes. While it's possible for a patient to have both diabetes and SLE, the given history doesn't suggest diabetes. C. Focal segmental glomerulosclerosis (FSGS) is usually seen in primary glomerular disease or secondary to conditions like HIV infection, obesity, or heroin use. It's not typically associated with SLE. D. Membranous nephropathy is a type of glomerular disease that can occur in SLE. It is characterized by thickening of the glomerular basement membrane without inflammation, often leading to nephrotic syndrome, as suggested by the patient's symptoms of leg swelling and foamy urine. E. IgA nephropathy (Berger's disease) is the most common cause of glomerulonephritis worldwide, often seen in young adults. It's typically associated with hematuria following a respiratory or gastrointestinal infection and is not typically associated with SLE. Therefore, given the patient's history of SLE and presenting symptoms, membranous nephropathy would be the most likely histopathological finding on renal biopsy.

21.Answer: D. Presence of circulating ANCA (Anti-Neutrophil Cytoplasmic Antibodies)

A. Presence of immune complexes in the glomeruli is a characteristic of immune complex-mediated glomerulonephritis, such as lupus nephritis or post-infectious glomerulonephritis, not ANCA-associated pauci-immune glomerulonephritis. B. Thickening and splitting of the glomerular basement membrane is a characteristic of Alport syndrome and not commonly seen in ANCA-associated pauci-immune glomerulonephritis. C. Presence of anti-glomerular basement membrane antibodies is seen in Goodpasture's syndrome, a type of rapidly progressive glomerulonephritis, but not in ANCA-associated pauci-immune glomerulonephritis. D. Presence of circulating ANCA (Anti-Neutrophil Cytoplasmic Antibodies) is the key feature of ANCA-associated pauci-immune glomerulonephritis. These antibodies are detected through immunofluorescence on neutrophils fixed with alcohol. A "perinuclear" pattern (pANCA) is typically due to antibodies against myeloperoxidase (MPO), while a "cytoplasmic" pattern (cANCA) is associated with antibodies against proteinase-3 (PR3). Confirmatory testing with enzyme-linked immunosorbent assay (ELISA) for MPO and PR3 antigens is typically performed. E. Deposition of IgA in the mesangium is a characteristic of IgA nephropathy (Berger's disease), not ANCA-associated pauci-immune glomerulonephritis. Hence, the primary distinguishing feature of ANCA-associated pauci-immune glomerulonephritis is the presence of circulating ANCA.

22. Answer is C,

A. 1 month and B. 2 months are typically too short for cyclophosphamide administration to induce a stable state of remission in ANCA-associated rapidly progressive glomerulonephritis. C. 3-6 months is the typical duration of cyclophosphamide administration in the management of ANCA-associated rapidly progressive glomerulonephritis. This period is usually sufficient to achieve a state of stable remission. D. 9-12 months and E. More than a year is longer than the typical duration of therapy. Prolonged use of cyclophosphamide can lead to significant side effects, including bone marrow suppression, infection, and malignancy, so it's important to limit its use to the shortest effective duration. Therefore, the typical duration of cyclophosphamide administration in the management of ANCA-associated rapidly progressive glomerulonephritis is 3 to 6 months.

23. Answer: B. Serum IgA level A. Chest X-ray is typically used in the evaluation of respiratory symptoms and is not directly relevant in the diagnosis of HSP.

B. Serum IgA level is a useful diagnostic marker in HSP. Approximately half of the patients with HSP exhibit elevated levels of serum IgA, making this a relevant test for this condition. C. Echocardiogram is a useful diagnostic tool for cardiac conditions but is not typically used in the diagnosis of HSP. D. Renal biopsy can be a useful tool in the prognostic evaluation of HSP, especially when renal involvement is suspected. However, it is not typically the first line of investigation for HSP and can be considered invasive for a young adult. E. Coagulation profile is usually employed to evaluate bleeding or clotting disorders and is generally not used in the diagnosis of HSP. Therefore, in a patient with symptoms suggestive of HSP, the most useful diagnostic method would be to check the serum IgA level.

24. Answer: C. Urine albumin:creatinine ratio A. Serum creatinine and E. Glomerular filtration rate (GFR) are used to assess kidney function but do not directly measure proteinuria, a key component of nephrotic syndrome. B. Blood urea nitrogen (BUN) level is another measure of kidney function and does not directly assess proteinuria. C. Urine albumin:creatinine ratio is the preferred method for screening lesser proteinuria due to its ability to detect microalbuminuria, which is not detectable by tests that measure total protein levels. It is an early indication of kidney damage, especially in conditions like diabetes where this patient is at risk. D. Urine total protein level is a measure of proteinuria, but it is unable to detect microalbuminuria, or lesser proteinuria, which can be an early sign of kidney damage. Given the information provided, the urine albumin: creatinine ratio is the best choice for detecting lesser proteinuria in this patient.

25. Answer: E. All of the above.

When evaluating a patient with membranous GN, it is crucial to investigate the presence of potential underlying diseases and history of medication exposure: A. Assess for history of exposure to high-dose captopril or penicillamine: These medications have been associated with membranous GN and should be considered in the patient's exposure history. B. Test for hepatitis B: Chronic infections such as hepatitis B can be an underlying cause of membranous GN. C. Investigate the presence of systemic lupus erythematosus (SLE): SLE is a systemic autoimmune disease that can cause membranous GN. D. Look for underlying solid tumors: Membranous GN can be a paraneoplastic syndrome associated with solid tumors. Therefore, all of the above steps are key in the thorough evaluation of a patient with suspected membranous GN.

26. Answer: D.

Eculizumab In the context of membranoproliferative glomerulonephritis (MPGN):A. Steroids, while commonly used in many glomerular diseases, are not specifically effective for the rare subtypes of MPGN associated with the alternative pathway of complement activation.B. Angiotensin-converting enzyme (ACE) inhibitors are often used to control hypertension and reduce proteinuria in patients with chronic kidney disease, but they are not the primary treatment for this specific subtype of MPGN. C. Cyclosporine is an immunosuppressive agent used in some glomerular diseases, but it is not the primary treatment for this particular subtype of MPGN. D. Eculizumab, a C5a inhibitor, has demonstrated positive outcomes when used to treat rare subtypes of MPGN that are linked to the activation of the alternative pathway of complement activation. It works by inhibiting the complement system, which is excessively activated in these patients. E. Plasmapheresis can be used in certain types of glomerulonephritis, particularly those associated with antibodies to the glomerular basement membrane, but it is not the primary treatment for this specific subtype of MPGN. Therefore, based on the information provided, Eculizumab is the best choice for treating this specific subtype of MPGN.

27. Answer: E.

All of the above Asymptomatic urinary abnormalities, such as hematuria and proteinuria, can be due to various underlying glomerular conditions: A. Berger's disease (IgA nephropathy): This is a primary glomerular disease that often presents hematuria and proteinuria. B. Mesangiocapillary glomerulonephritis: Another primary glomerular disease that can cause these urinary findings. C. Alport's syndrome: This is a hereditary disease that affects the glomeruli and can manifest as hematuria and proteinuria. D. Fabry's disease: This is a rare genetic disorder that can affect the kidneys and lead to glomerular damage, resulting in urinary abnormalities. Thus, all of these conditions could potentially be underlying causes of the patient's asymptomatic urinary abnormalities, making E the best choice.

28. Answer: D.

Start potassium binder therapy with sodium zirconium cyclosilicate (ZS-9) or patiromer In the setting of hyperkalemia: A. Initiating amlodipine therapy is not the best choice. Amlodipine is a calcium channel blocker used primarily for hypertension and angina. It does not address the issue of hyperkalemia. B. Increasing the dose of loop diuretics might be helpful in some cases to promote potassium excretion, but in the patient's case, this strategy has already been tried and proved ineffective. C. Administering sodium bicarbonate infusion is used in the treatment of severe metabolic acidosis and, although it can help lower potassium levels, it is not the primary treatment for persistent hyperkalemia that is unresponsive to other therapies. D. Starting potassium binder therapy with sodium zirconium cyclosilicate (ZS-9) or patiromer is the best next step. These medications work by binding potassium in the gut, thereby decreasing the total body potassium level. This is particularly useful when hyperkalemia is resistant to other therapies. E. Discontinuing all his medications would not be appropriate without finding the cause of the hyperkalemia. In addition, sudden discontinuation of certain medications could lead to adverse effects. Therefore, based on the information provided, starting potassium binder therapy is the most appropriate next step in this patient's management.

29.Answer: B. Ibuprofen and C. Nivolumab

A. Metformin: This medication is primarily associated with lactic acidosis, not AIN. B. Ibuprofen: Nonsteroidal anti-inflammatory drugs (NSAIDs) like ibuprofen can induce a glomerular lesion resembling minimal change disease, alongside AIN. C. Nivolumab: This is an immune checkpoint inhibitor used in oncology. Recent data have shown an association between these agents and AIN. D. Aspirin: Although aspirin is an NSAID, it is less likely to cause AIN compared to other NSAIDs like ibuprofen. E. Atorvastatin: This medication is a statin, primarily associated with myopathy and liver disease, but not AIN. Therefore, based on the provided information, both ibuprofen and nivolumab are most likely to be associated with her condition of AIN.

30. Answer: C. Transitional cell carcinoma A. Acute kidney injury is not typically a direct complication of analgesic nephropathy, though it could occur in the setting of other renal problems. B. Chronic kidney disease can be a result of long-term damage from analgesic nephropathy, but it is not the most specific complication associated with this condition. C. Transitional cell carcinoma is a specific potential complication of analgesic nephropathy. The chronic irritation and damage to the renal tubules caused by prolonged analgesic use can promote the development of this type of cancer. D. Renal artery stenosis is typically associated with atherosclerosis and fibromuscular dysplasia, not analgesic nephropathy. E. Nephrolithiasis (kidney stones) can be caused by various factors, but it is not a specific complication of analgesic nephropathy. Therefore, based on the provided information, transitional cell carcinoma is the most appropriate answer as it is a specific potential complication of analgesic nephropathy.

31.Answer: B. Nephrocalcinosis

A. Nephrotic syndrome: This is typically associated with conditions that cause damage to the glomeruli, such as diabetes, lupus, or certain infections, and is not specifically associated with hypercalcemia. B. Nephrocalcinosis: Excessive levels of calcium in the blood (hypercalcemia) can lead to the deposition of calcium crystals in the renal tubules and interstitium, causing inflammation, tubular damage, and eventually fibrosis. This condition is referred to as nephrocalcinosis. C. Pyelonephritis: This is a bacterial infection of the kidneys, typically ascending from a lower urinary tract infection. It is not specifically associated with hypercalcemia. D. Renal artery stenosis: This is most commonly caused by atherosclerosis or fibromuscular dysplasia and is not specifically associated with hypercalcemia. E. Acute tubular necrosis: This is typically caused by severe, acute injury to the kidneys from low blood flow, toxins, or sepsis, and is not specifically associated with hypercalcemia. Therefore, based on the information provided, nephrocalcinosis is the most likely renal complication associated with hypercalcemia.

32.Answer: C. Myeloma-associated cast nephropathy

A. Polycystic kidney disease is a hereditary condition characterized by the growth of numerous cysts in the kidneys. It is not specifically associated with multiple myeloma. B. Renal amyloidosis: While amyloidosis can occur in multiple myeloma, it is not the most common renal manifestation associated with this condition. C. Myeloma-associated cast nephropathy: In multiple myeloma, monoclonal light chains can form casts within the renal tubules. These casts can obstruct the tubules and lead to tubular injury, inflammation, and impaired kidney function. This condition is known as myeloma-associated cast nephropathy. D. Diabetic nephropathy: This complication is associated with long-term diabetes and not specifically related to multiple myeloma. E. Lupus nephritis: This is a kidney inflammation caused by systemic lupus erythematosus, an autoimmune disease. It is not specifically associated with multiple myeloma. Therefore, based on the provided information, myeloma-associated cast nephropathy is the most likely renal manifestation associated with multiple myeloma.

33.Answer: C. Fanconi syndrome

A. Bartter syndrome: This is a group of rare genetic disorders that affect the kidneys' ability to reabsorb salt. It is characterized by low potassium levels, increased blood pH, and normal to low blood pressure. It is not typically associated with glucosuria, aminoaciduria, phosphaturia and proximal RTA. B. Gitelman syndrome: This is a genetic disorder affecting the kidneys' ability to reabsorb salt. It is characterized by low levels of potassium and magnesium in the blood, and a high blood pH. It is not typically associated with glucosuria, aminoaciduria, phosphaturia and proximal RTA. C. Fanconi syndrome: This condition is characterized by the presence of glucosuria, aminoaciduria, phosphaturia, and occasionally hypouricemia and proximal renal tubular acidosis (RTA), which matches the laboratory findings in this patient. D. Liddle syndrome: This is a genetic disorder characterized by early, and often severe, high blood pressure. It is not typically associated with glucosuria, aminoaciduria, phosphaturia and proximal RTA. E. Nephrotic syndrome: This is a kidney disorder that causes the body to excrete too much protein in the urine. It is characterized by swelling in the legs, ankles, feet, or around the eyes. It is not typically associated with glucosuria, aminoaciduria, phosphaturia and proximal RTA. Therefore, based on the information provided, Fanconi syndrome is the most likely diagnosis.

34.Answer: C. Combination of ARB and ACE inhibitor

A. Angiotensin receptor blocker (ARB) alone: ARBs are often used in the management of ADPKD to control hypertension and delay the progression to ESRD. B. Angiotensin-converting enzyme (ACE) inhibitor alone: ACE inhibitors are also used for similar reasons as ARBs in the management of ADPKD. C. Combination of ARB and ACE inhibitor: The use of dual therapy involving an ARB and an ACE inhibitor does not provide additional benefits in terms of slowing the progression of ADPKD to ESRD. Therefore, this approach is not recommended. D. Diuretics: These are often used in the management of ADPKD to relieve symptoms such as fluid retention. E. Blood pressure control: Control of blood pressure is a mainstay of management in ADPKD to prevent or delay the progression to ESRD. Therefore, based on the provided information, the combination of an ARB and an ACE inhibitor is not recommended as a therapeutic approach for slowing the progression of ADPKD to ESRD.

35. Answer: C. Chronic type I renal tubular acidosis (RTA)

A. Chronic kidney disease: While this can cause bone pain due to secondary hyperparathyroidism and mineral bone disorders, it is typically associated with other systemic symptoms and signs such as anemia, fatigue, and abnormal kidney function tests. Hypercalciuria is not a typical finding. B. Hyperparathyroidism: This condition can cause hypercalciuria and bone pain, but it also usually presents hypercalcemia, which is not mentioned in the patient's presentation. C. Chronic type I renal tubular acidosis (RTA): This condition is characterized by the presence of hypercalciuria and bone pain due to osteomalacia, which matches the patient's symptoms. The prolonged compensatory mechanism of acidosis through bone buffering in type I RTA can lead to these findings. D. Vitamin D toxicity: While this can cause hypercalciuria, it is also typically associated with hypercalcemia and symptoms of vitamin D toxicity such as nausea, vomiting, and anorexia, which are not mentioned in the patient's presentation. E. Paget's bone disease: This condition can cause bone pain, but it is not typically associated with hypercalciuria. Therefore, based on the provided information, chronic type I renal tubular acidosis (RTA) is the most likely diagnosis.

36. Answer: C. Isolated Proximal Renal Tubular Acidosis

A. Distal Renal Tubular Acidosis: This condition results from a defect in the secretion of hydrogen ions by the distal tubule, not impairment of the basolateral sodium-bicarbonate cotransporter. B. Chronic Kidney Disease: While metabolic acidosis can occur in chronic kidney disease, it is due to a general decrease in renal function, not a specific impairment of the basolateral sodium-bicarbonate cotransporter. C. Isolated Proximal Renal Tubular Acidosis: This condition is the result of a hereditary impairment of the basolateral sodium-bicarbonate cotransporter, leading to bicarbonate wastage and metabolic acidosis. This matches the patient's presentation. D. Glomerulonephritis: This condition primarily affects the glomeruli, not the renal tubules, and is typically associated with hematuria and proteinuria. E. Diabetic Nephropathy: Diabetic nephropathy is typically associated with longstanding diabetes and presents with proteinuria and sometimes with a decrease in renal function. Therefore, based on the provided information, isolated proximal renal tubular acidosis is the most likely diagnosis.

37. Answer: B. Complicated Urinary Tract Infection

A. Uncomplicated Urinary Tract Infection: This is typically seen in healthy premenopausal, non-pregnant women with no known urinary tract abnormalities or history of prior urinary tract procedures. B. Complicated Urinary Tract Infection: This term encompasses all forms of urinary tract infections that are not classified as uncomplicated. It includes infections that may arise in individuals with structural abnormalities, prior urinary tract procedures, or preexisting medical conditions such as diabetes. Given the patient's history of recurrent UTIs and diabetes, this is the most likely diagnosis. C. Asymptomatic Bacteriuria: While this condition can occur in patients with diabetes, it is characterized by the presence of bacteria in the urine without the symptoms of a UTI, which does not match the patient's presentation. D. Interstitial Cystitis: This is a chronic condition causing bladder pressure and pain, with frequent urination. However, it is not associated with infection, which does not align with the patient's symptoms. E. Overactive Bladder Syndrome: This condition is characterized by urinary urgency, with or without urge incontinence, often with frequency and nocturia. Although the patient has some of these symptoms, the presence of dysuria and history of recurrent UTIs suggest a complicated UTI. Therefore, based on the information provided, a Complicated Urinary Tract Infection is the most likely diagnosis.

38. Answer: B. 4-7 days

A. 1-3 days: This is typically the treatment duration for an uncomplicated urinary tract infection (UTI) in non-pregnant women. It is shorter than the typical treatment duration for ASB in pregnant women. B. 4-7 days: This is the generally recommended duration of antibiotic treatment for ASB in pregnant women, as supported by various guidelines and studies, including those from the Infectious Diseases Society of America (IDSA) and the American College of Obstetricians and Gynecologists (ACOG). C. 8-10 days and D. 11-14 days: These durations are typically longer than what is usually recommended for the treatment of ASB in pregnant women. E. No treatment is necessary: This is incorrect because it is important to screen and treat ASB in pregnant women. If left untreated, it can increase the risk of developing a kidney infection or other complications during pregnancy. Therefore, the most appropriate choice based on the information provided is B. 4-7 days. 39. Answer: B. Cystoscopy with hydrodistention A. Urine culture: While this can help rule out urinary tract infection, which can present similar symptoms, it is not the definitive method for diagnosing interstitial cystitis. B. Cystoscopy with hydrodistention: This is the most appropriate method for diagnosing IC. During cystoscopy, characteristic findings of IC, such as Hunner's ulcers or glomerulations, can be identified. Hydrodistention may also help confirm the diagnosis. C. Pelvic ultrasound: This imaging modality can help rule out other pelvic pathologies that can present with similar symptoms, such as ovarian cysts or uterine fibroids, but it does not confirm a diagnosis of IC. D. Urodynamic testing: While this can provide information about bladder function, it is not typically used as a primary method for diagnosing IC. E. Computed tomography (CT) scan of the abdomen and pelvis: Similar to a pelvic ultrasound, a CT scan can help rule out other pathologies but is not the primary method for diagnosing IC. Therefore, the best choice based on the information provided is B. Cystoscopy with hydrodistention.

40. Answer: D. Uric acid

A. Calcium oxalate: While this is the most common type of kidney stone, it is not the most likely given the patient's history of gout, which is associated with uric acid stones. B. Struvite: These stones are usually associated with urinary tract infections, which is not mentioned in the patient's history. C. Cystine: Cystine stones are rare and usually occur in people with a genetic disorder that causes cystinuria. D. Uric acid: This is the most likely composition of the stone given the patient's history. Uric acid stones are commonly linked to conditions like gout, metabolic syndrome, and insulin resistance. Moreover, individuals with myeloproliferative disorders and other conditions leading to secondary hyperuricemia and hyperuricosuria are also susceptible to the formation of uric acid stones. E. Calcium phosphate:

These stones are less common and are often associated with certain metabolic disorders, which are not mentioned in the patient's history. Therefore, the best choice based on the information provided is D. Uric acid.

41. Answer: B. Use of certain medications

A. Consumption of a high-sodium diet: This would typically increase, not decrease sodium levels in the body and would not contribute to the development of hyponatremia. B. Use of certain medications: Some medications can stimulate the secretion of arginine vasopressin (AVP), which can subsequently increase the risk of developing hyponatremia. C. Mild physical activity: While physical exertion can potentially contribute to hyponatremia, it is usually vigorous, not mild, physical activity that is associated with this condition. D. Absence of pain or distress: Pain and distress, or other nociceptive stimuli, can stimulate the secretion of AVP and increase the risk of hyponatremia. Therefore, the absence of these stimuli would not contribute to the condition. E. High water intake without physical exertion: While the overconsumption of water can contribute to hyponatremia, it is typically associated with instances of extreme physical exertion. High water intake alone, without associated physical exertion, is less likely to cause hyponatremia. Therefore, the best choice based on the information provided is B. Use of certain medications.

42. Answer: B. Approximately 20 meq/L

A. Less than 10 meq/L: This would be suggestive of hypovolemic hyponatremia due to non-renal causes, where the kidney is appropriately conserving sodium. B. Approximately 20 meq/L: This is the correct answer. In hypovolemic hyponatremia caused by renal factors, it is typically observed that the urine sodium concentration exceeds 20 meq/L, indicating renal sodium loss. C. Approximately 40 meq/L, D. Approximately 60 meq/L, E. More than 80 meq/L: These values are too high for the typical presentation of hypovolemic hyponatremia caused by renal factors. Therefore, the best choice based on the information provided is B. Approximately 20 meq/L.

43. Answer: B. Administration of vasopressin antagonists

A. Restriction of water intake to less than 1 liter per day: While this is a fundamental aspect of the treatment, its efficacy and tolerability may be suboptimal. B. Administration of vasopressin antagonists: This is the correct answer. Vasopressin antagonists have demonstrated consistent efficacy in restoring serum sodium levels to normal in patients with syndrome of inappropriate antidiuretic hormone secretion (SIADH). C. Use of loop diuretics and oral salt tablets: This approach is more of an alternative treatment when other methods are not effective or tolerated. It can be used to mitigate the loss of salt caused by diuretics and the resulting hypovolemia. D. High-sodium diet: Although sodium is low in hyponatremia, a high-sodium diet is not typically the first line of treatment as it does not address the underlying cause of euvolemic hyponatremia. E. High water intake: This is contraindicated in hyponatremia as it could further dilute the concentration of sodium in the blood. Therefore, the best choice based on the provided information is B. Administration of vasopressin antagonists.

44. Answer: A. Hypotonic saline solutions

A. Hypotonic saline solutions: This is the correct answer. Hypotonic saline solutions (such as 1/4 or 1/2 normal saline) can be considered as potential initial treatment options for hypernatremia, depending on the patient's blood pressure and clinical volume status. B. Isotonic saline solutions: While isotonic saline solutions may be used in some cases, they are not typically the first-line therapy for hypernatremia as they do not effectively lower serum sodium levels. C. Hypertonic saline solutions: These are contraindicated in hypernatremia as they could further increase the concentration of sodium in the blood. D. Intravenous glucose solution: This is not typically used as initial treatment for hypernatremia. E. Water restriction: This is more of a preventive measure and not an active treatment for hypernatremia. Therefore, based on the information provided, the best choice is A. Hypotonic saline solutions.

45. The correct answer is B

To determine the cause of hyperkalemia. The urinary potassium-to-creatinine ratio is used to determine the cause of hyperkalemia. A urinary potassium-to-creatinine ratio of greater than 13 mmol/g creatinine (or greater than 1.5 mmol/mmol creatinine) is employed as an indicator of elevated potassium excretion. This can be caused by a number of factors, including:

- Kidney disease
- Addison's disease
- Hyperaldosteronism
- Medications, such as diuretics and steroids
- Eating a diet high in potassium

46. The best answer is D.

Redistribution of potassium into cells. The patient's presentation is indicative of redistributive hypokalemia, which is due to the translocation of potassium ions from the extracellular fluid into intracellular compartments. The patient's history of hyperthyroidism and the acute presentation of muscle weakness and hypokalemia suggest a diagnosis of thyrotoxic periodic paralysis, a condition commonly associated with redistributive hypokalemia. Option A, renal potassium loss, is less likely given the patient's normal renal function. Option B, gastrointestinal potassium loss, would usually present symptoms such as vomiting or diarrhea, which the patient does not have. Option C, dietary potassium deficiency, is quite rare and usually seen in the context of severe malnutrition or alcoholism. Option E, inadequate potassium reabsorption in the distal tubule, is associated with conditions like renal tubular acidosis, which would typically present with additional signs of metabolic acidosis, not present in this case. Therefore, the concept of redistributive hypokalemia is the best explanation for this patient's presentation.

47. The best answer is C.

D-lactic acidosis. The patient's presentation is indicative of D-lactic acidosis, a condition characterized by elevated levels of the D-enantiomer of lactate. This condition can manifest in individuals who have undergone short bowel resection or suffer from certain diseases like Crohn's disease. Option A, hyperkalemia, typically presents muscle weakness or cardiac arrhythmias, which are not present in this case. Option B, uremic encephalopathy, is less likely given the absence of clinical signs of kidney disease such as changes in urinary output or edema. Option D, hypoglycemia, would generally present symptoms of sweating, palpitations, or tremors, which are not reported in this case. Option E, cerebrovascular accident, could theoretically cause the patient's symptoms, but the metabolic acidosis would not be explained by this condition. D-lactic acidosis can present neurological symptoms such as confusion and ataxia, as described in the patient's clinical presentation. This condition arises due to an overabundance of microorganisms in the intestines that metabolize carbohydrates into D-lactate, especially following procedures like short bowel resection. Management often involves antibiotics to alter the intestinal flora. Therefore, D-lactic acidosis is the most likely explanation for this patient's presentation.

48. The best answer is C.

Gastrointestinal loss of bicarbonate. In the context of metabolic acidosis, a significantly negative urinary anion gap is indicative of gastrointestinal losses of bicarbonate. This implies that the kidney is appropriately responding to the acidosis by augmenting the excretion of ammonium ($NH4+$). Option A, renal tubular acidosis, typically leads to a normal or positive urinary anion gap as the kidneys are unable to appropriately excrete acid. Option B, diabetic ketoacidosis, results in a large anion gap metabolic acidosis due to the production of ketone bodies, but it does not directly cause a negative urinary anion gap. Option D, lactic acidosis, and option E, uremic acidosis, are types of metabolic acidosis, but they do not cause a negative urinary anion gap. The patient's vomiting and diarrhea (which can cause loss of bicarbonate from the gastrointestinal tract) combined with the negative urinary anion gap strongly suggest gastrointestinal bicarbonate loss as the cause of his metabolic acidosis. Therefore, gastrointestinal loss of bicarbonate is the most likely explanation for this patient's presentation.

49. The best answer is C.

Milk-alkali syndrome is characterized by the triad of hypercalcemia, metabolic alkalosis, and renal failure. It occurs due to the excessive intake of calcium and absorbable alkali, often from overuse of over-the-counter calcium carbonate antacids and dietary calcium (such as milk), as is reported in this patient's history. Option A, hyperparathyroidism, can cause hypercalcemia, but it does not typically result in metabolic alkalosis or acute kidney injury. Option B, vitamin D toxicity, can also cause hypercalcemia but would not typically result in metabolic alkalosis, and it does not align as well with the patient's history. Option D, adrenal insufficiency, can result in fatigue and muscle weakness, but it does not typically cause hypercalcemia or metabolic alkalosis. Option E, chronic kidney disease, can lead to hypercalcemia and acute renal failure but would not typically cause metabolic alkalosis and doesn't fit as well with the patient's clinical history. The patient's symptoms, including diminished muscular strength, excessive fatigue, confusion, and her lab findings align with the clinical manifestations of milk-alkali syndrome, making it the most probable diagnosis.

50. The best answer is B.

Increased excretion of ketones in urine. In the setting of DKA, the administration of fluids often leads to an increase in glomerular filtration and subsequently, the excretion of ketones in the urine. This process can result in a reduction of the anion gap. Option A, decreased production of ketones, is not directly influenced by fluid administration. Option C, presence of non-anion-gap acidosis, could also lead to a decrease in the anion gap, but it's not the primary reason in this case as no additional acidosis is mentioned. Option D, hyperglycemia, does not lead to a reduction in the anion gap. Option E, hypoalbuminemia, can cause a reduction in the anion gap but it is not the main cause in this specific scenario of DKA treatment. Given the patient's DKA and her treatment with fluid resuscitation, the most likely reason for the reduction in her anion gap is increased excretion of ketones in the urine.

51. The answer is D, all of the above.

The preferred therapeutic approach for Pituitary DI is desmopressin (DDAVP), which can be delivered through subcutaneous injection, nasal spray, or oral administration. The recommended dosage for subcutaneous injection ranges from 1 to 2 g, to be administered once or twice daily. For nasal spray, the recommended dosage is between 10 and 20 g, to be administered two or three times daily. Lastly, for oral administration, the recommended dosage ranges from 100 to 400 g, to be taken two or three times daily. Patients are additionally recommended to consume fluids in response to their thirst.

52. Answer: A The answer is A, fluid deprivation test.

The diagnosis of diabetes insipidus (DI) involves the implementation of a fluid deprivation test, typically initiated in the morning under close supervision to mitigate the risk of dehydration. Hourly measurements should be taken for body weight, plasma osmolality, serum sodium, urine volume, and urine osmolality. The cessation of the test is warranted when there is a reduction in body weight of 5% or an elevation in plasma osmolality/sodium levels beyond the upper threshold of the normal range. In cases where serum hyperosmolality is present and the urine osmolality is less than 300 mosmol/kg, it is recommended to administer desmopressin at a subcutaneous dose of 0.03 g/kg. Following the administration of desmopressin, it is advisable to reevaluate the urine osmolality within a period of 1-2 hours. A rise exceeding 50% signifies the presence of severe pituitary diabetes insipidus (DI), whereas a lesser or nonexistent reaction implies the occurrence of nephrogenic DI. The other options listed in the question are also important diagnostic tests for DI. However, they are not as specific as the fluid deprivation test.

53. The answer is A, oral tolvaptan.

The optimal strategy for managing chronic SIADH involves the administration of oral tolvaptan, a selective V2 antagonist that enhances the excretion of water in urine by inhibiting the antidiuretic effect of AVP. Demeclocycline is known to elicit a reversible manifestation of nephrogenic diabetes insipidus (DI), with its effects becoming apparent within a period of 7-14 days. Fludrocortisone is a mineralocorticoid that can be used to increase the excretion of sodium in urine. Therefore, the suggested therapeutic approach for managing chronic SIADH is oral tolvaptan. This is the most effective treatment for SIADH, and it is well-tolerated by most patients. Here is an explanation of the different therapeutic approaches for SIADH: Oral tolvaptan: Tolvaptan is a selective V2 antagonist that is used to treat SIADH. It works by blocking the effects of vasopressin, which is a hormone that causes the kidneys to retain water. Demeclocycline: Demeclocycline is an antibiotic that can be used to treat SIADH. It works by causing the kidneys to excrete more water. Fludrocortisone: Fludrocortisone is a mineralocorticoid that is used to treat SIADH. It works by sodium reabsorption in the kidneys. This action helps to correct the imbalance of fluids and electrolytes in the body, thus alleviating the symptoms associated with SIADH. By increasing sodium levels in the blood, fludrocortisone assists in restoring the body's normal fluid balance and reducing the signs and symptoms of SIADH.

54. Correct answer: C Diabetic nephropathy is a condition that affects the kidneys in people with diabetes mellitus. It can lead to kidney failure.

The most appropriate screening method for diabetic nephropathy is a spot collection for albuminuria. Albuminuria is the presence of albumin in the urine. Albumin is a protein that is normally not found in the urine. The presence of albumin in the urine is a sign of kidney damage. A routine urinalysis may be used to screen for diabetic nephropathy, but it is not as sensitive as a spot collection for albuminuria. A 24-hour urine collection can be used to quantify the amount of albumin in the urine, but it is more time-consuming and expensive than a spot collection. Renal ultrasound and renal biopsy are not used for screening for diabetic nephropathy. Therefore, the most appropriate screening method for diabetic nephropathy is a spot collection for albuminuria.

55. Correct answer: B Diabetic ketoacidosis (DKA) is a serious condition that can be life-threatening. Patients with DKA should be promptly admitted to a healthcare facility, with consideration given to an intensive care unit (ICU) for close and regular observation. Admission to the ICU is particularly warranted if the patient's pH level falls below 7.00 or if the patient is in an unconscious state. The other answer choices are not appropriate in this case. Admitting the patient to the hospital ward would not provide the close monitoring that is necessary for a patient with DKA. Discharging the patient home would be unsafe, as the patient's condition could deteriorate. Administering intravenous fluids and insulin would be part of the treatment for DKA, but they would not be sufficient in this case. Therefore, the most appropriate course of action is to admit the patient to the intensive care unit (ICU).

56. Correct answer: A

The optimal insulin regimen for a patient presenting with diabetic ketoacidosis (DKA) is to administer short-acting regular insulin intravenously at a dosage of 0.1 units per kilogram. This initial dose should be followed by a continuous intravenous infusion of 0.1 units per kilogram per hour. If there is no observed response within a time frame of 2-4 hours, it may be appropriate to consider increasing the dosage by a factor of two to three. The administration of short-acting regular insulin intravenously is crucial in rapidly lowering the blood glucose level and reversing the effects of diabetic ketoacidosis. Intravenous insulin therapy is preferred over subcutaneous administration due to the more rapid onset of action and greater control over insulin dosing. In severe cases of DKA, patient management may require the use of an intensive care unit to monitor electrolyte imbalances, glucose levels, and other vital signs. The other answer choices are not correct. Option B is the insulin regimen for a patient with type 2 diabetes mellitus. Option C is the insulin regimen for a patient with hypoglycemia. Option D is not a valid insulin regimen.

57. Correct answer: A

The most likely cause of hypercalcemia in this patient is primary hyperparathyroidism. This is because primary hyperparathyroidism is the most common cause of hypercalcemia, accounting for over 80% of cases. The patient's symptoms of fatigue, constipation, and polyuria are all consistent with primary hyperparathyroidism. The other answer choices are less likely causes of hypercalcemia in this patient. Malignancy is a common cause of hypercalcemia, but it is less likely in this patient because she does not have any other symptoms of malignancy. Vitamin D toxicity can cause hypercalcemia, but it is also less likely in this patient because she does not take any medications that could cause vitamin D toxicity. Medications, such as thiazides and lithium, can cause hypercalcemia, but they are also less likely in this patient because she does not take any of these medications. Sarcoidosis can cause hypercalcemia, but it is also less likely in this patient because she does not have any other symptoms of sarcoidosis.

58. Correct answer: B

The most likely cause of hypercalcemia in this patient is malignancy. This is because malignancy is the most common cause of hypercalcemia in patients with low PTH levels. The patient's symptoms of fatigue, constipation, and polyuria are all consistent with malignancy-associated hypercalcemia. The other answer choices are less likely causes of hypercalcemia in this patient. Primary hyperparathyroidism is a common cause of hypercalcemia, but it is less likely in this patient because his PTH level is low. Vitamin D toxicity can cause hypercalcemia, but it is also less likely in this patient because he does not take any medications that could cause vitamin D toxicity. Medications, such as thiazides and lithium, can cause hypercalcemia, but they are also less likely in this patient because he does not take any of these medications. Sarcoidosis can cause hypercalcemia, but it is also less likely in this patient because he does not have any other symptoms of sarcoidosis.

59. Correct answer: D

The most likely cause of hypocalcemia in this patient is primary hypoparathyroidism. This is because primary hypoparathyroidism is the most common cause of hypocalcemia, and it is associated with Chvostek's and Trousseau's signs. The patient's symptoms of muscle cramps and tingling in her hands and feet are also consistent with primary hypoparathyroidism. The other answer choices are less likely causes of hypocalcemia in this patient. Pseudohypoparathyroidism is a condition that is characterized by hypocalcemia and a resistance to the effects of parathyroid hormone (PTH). However, pseudohypoparathyroidism does not typically cause Chvostek's and Trousseau's signs. Vitamin D deficiency can cause hypocalcemia, but it is less likely in this patient because she does not have any other symptoms of vitamin D deficiency. Medications, such as thiazide diuretics, can cause hypocalcemia, but they are also less likely in this patient because she does not take any of these medications.

60. Correct answer: A

The most appropriate treatment for symptomatic hypocalcemia is to administer a bolus of 1-2 g of intravenous calcium gluconate over a period of 10-20 minutes. This will quickly raise the patient's serum calcium level and relieve her symptoms. The bolus can be followed by a continuous infusion of calcium gluconate, as needed. The other answer choices are not appropriate for the treatment of symptomatic hypocalcemia. Oral calcium supplements are not absorbed quickly enough to be effective in the setting of symptomatic hypocalcemia. Monitoring the patient's condition and waiting for her calcium levels to improve on their own is not a safe or effective approach to the treatment of symptomatic hypocalcemia.

61. Correct answer: C

The most appropriate treatment for severe hypophosphatemia is to administer intravenous phosphate at an initial dose of 0.8 mmol/kg of elemental phosphorus over a period of 6 hours. This will quickly raise the patient's serum phosphate level and relieve her symptoms. The dose can be adjusted as needed, but it is important to exercise caution to avoid overcorrecting the hypophosphatemia, which can lead to complications such as hypocalcemia and tetany. The other answer choices are not appropriate for the treatment of severe hypophosphatemia. Administering 0.2 or 0.4 mmol/kg of elemental phosphorus over a period of 6 hours will not be sufficient to raise the patient's serum phosphate level to a safe level. Administering oral phosphate supplements is not effective in the setting of severe hypophosphatemia.

62. Correct answer: B

The most appropriate treatment for severe hypomagnesemia is to administer intravenous magnesium sulfate over a period of 1 hour. This will quickly raise the patient's serum magnesium level and relieve her symptoms. The dose of intravenous magnesium sulfate will need to be individualized based on the patient's serum magnesium level and symptoms. The other answer choices are not appropriate for the treatment of severe hypomagnesemia. Administering oral magnesium supplements is not effective in the setting of severe hypomagnesemia. Monitoring the patient's condition and waiting for her magnesium levels to improve on their own is not a safe or effective approach to the treatment of severe hypomagnesemia.

63. Answer: A.

Calculating his ASCVD risk score and, if >10%, starting an antihypertensive agent now. The 2017 ACC/AHA blood pressure guidelines recommend starting antihypertensive therapy for adults with stage 1 hypertension (blood pressure of 130-139/80-89 mmHg) if they have clinical cardiovascular disease or a calculated ASCVD risk score of >10%. ASCVD risk scores are calculated using a variety of factors, including age, sex, race/ethnicity, blood pressure, cholesterol levels, smoking status, and diabetes status. For this patient, it is important to calculate his ASCVD risk score to determine whether he should start antihypertensive therapy now. If his ASCVD risk score is >10%, then antihypertensive therapy should be initiated. If his ASCVD risk score is <1%, then lifestyle changes should be recommended and his blood pressure should be monitored closely. Follow-up in 3 months is appropriate to assess his blood pressure response to lifestyle changes and to determine if antihypertensive therapy is needed. The patient should be counseled on the importance of lifestyle changes, such as weight loss, healthy diet, exercise, and smoking cessation. The patient should be instructed to monitor his blood pressure at home and to keep a record of his readings. The patient should be scheduled for follow-up in 3 months to assess his blood pressure response and to determine if antihypertensive therapy is needed.

64. The correct answer is: D.

Lisinopril (ACE inhibitor) First-line antihypertensives include ACE inhibitors, calcium channel blockers, and diuretics. However, the choice of which antihypertensive to initiate depends on the presence of comorbidities. In patients with diabetes mellitus who have microalbuminuria, it's recommended to start with an ACE inhibitor, barring any contraindications. ACE inhibitors have been shown to provide specific renal benefits in diabetic patients, such as reducing proteinuria and slowing the progression of diabetic nephropathy, hence their first-line status in this patient population. Options A, B, C, and E may also be used to manage hypertension but they are not the first-line choice in this specific clinical scenario.

65. Answer: B. Intravenous labetalol

This patient is experiencing a hypertensive emergency complicated by aortic dissection. Aortic dissection is a life-threatening condition in which the inner layer of the aorta tears, allowing blood to flow between the layers of the aorta. This can lead to rupture of the aorta and death. Hypertensive emergency is defined as a severe elevation in blood pressure (greater than 220/120 mmHg) that is associated with end-organ damage. In this patient, the aortic dissection is evidence of end-organ damage. The goal of initial management is to rapidly lower blood pressure and heart rate to reduce the risk of aortic rupture. Intravenous labetalol is a beta-blocker with alpha-blocking properties. It is the preferred initial agent for hypertensive emergency complicated by aortic dissection. Labetalol blocks both beta-adrenergic and alpha-adrenergic receptors, resulting in a decrease in heart rate, blood pressure, and systemic vascular resistance. Oral labetalol is not preferred in this setting because it takes longer to take effect. Intravenous nitroglycerin is a vasodilator that can lead to reflex tachycardia, which is undesirable in this patient. Intravenous nitroprusside and esmolol are also vasodilators, but they are not preferred over labetalol in this setting because they do not provide the same degree of heart rate control. The patient should be admitted to the intensive care unit for close monitoring and management. After initial blood pressure and heart rate control, imaging studies such as a computed tomography (CT) scan or transesophageal echocardiogram (TEE) should be performed to confirm the diagnosis of aortic dissection and determine the extent of the dissection. Once the diagnosis is confirmed, the patient should be treated with definitive therapy, such as endovascular repair or open surgery.

66.The correct answer is: A. MR angiography (MRA) of the renal arteries.

In this young patient with severe hypertension and an abdominal bruit, renal artery stenosis secondary to fibromuscular dysplasia should be strongly suspected. An MRA of the renal arteries would be a reasonable first step in her diagnostic evaluation. Although a duplex ultrasound (option B) can be considered, it cannot definitively exclude fibromuscular dysplasia. A noncontrast CT scan (option C) will not visualize the vasculature adequately. In some instances, direct visualization with renal angiography (option D) may be required if clinical suspicion remains high, but a diagnosis cannot be made noninvasively. For patients with confirmed fibromuscular dysplasia in whom BP cannot be controlled, percutaneous transluminal renal angioplasty (option E) should be considered. However, these are subsequent steps after initial diagnosis, making option A the most appropriate initial step.

67. Answer: B

Primary hyperaldosteronism is the most likely etiology of secondary hypertension in this patient. Primary hyperaldosteronism is a condition in which the adrenal glands produce too much of the hormone aldosterone. Aldosterone causes the kidneys to retain sodium and water, which leads to high blood pressure. The first step in the evaluation of primary hyperaldosteronism is to measure morning plasma renin and aldosterone. If the aldosterone level is elevated and the renin level is low, this is consistent with primary hyperaldosteronism. The other answer choices are not as appropriate as the first step in the evaluation of primary hyperaldosteronism: Ordering a 24-hour urine collection for cortisol and catecholamines is more appropriate for the evaluation of hypercortisolism and pheochromocytoma, respectively. Ordering a renal ultrasound or CT scan of the adrenal glands is more appropriate for the evaluation of structural abnormalities of the kidneys and adrenal glands, respectively. Referring the patient to a nephrologist may be appropriate at a later stage in the evaluation, but it is not the most appropriate next step in this case. Therefore, the best answer is B. Measure morning plasma renin and aldosterone.

68 .The correct answer is: A.

Adrenal venous sampling. In the case of multiple adrenal adenomas with unclear significance, it is important to determine the source of aldosterone to avoid an erroneous diagnosis. Adrenal venous sampling is the appropriate next step to localize the source of aldosterone. Once the source is identified, the patient can be referred for surgical management, such as subtotal or total adrenalectomy. Medical therapy is typically used when surgical management is technically difficult or refused. Adrenal CT scan (answer B) may provide information about the size and characteristics of the adrenal adenomas, but it does not help in determining the source of aldosterone. Radioiodine uptake scan (answer C) is used for the evaluation of hyperthyroidism, not for adrenal adenomas. Low-dose dexamethasone suppression test (answer D) is used to evaluate for Cushing syndrome, not for adrenal adenomas and elevated aldosterone levels. Starting hydrocortisone and T4 IV (answer E) is the appropriate treatment for myxedema coma, not for the management of adrenal adenomas and elevated aldosterone levels.

69. Answer: C

The most appropriate next step is to perform a twenty-four-hour urine fractionated metanephrines. This test is the most sensitive and specific test for the diagnosis of pheochromocytoma, a rare tumor of the adrenal medulla that produces excessive amounts of catecholamines. The other answer choices are not as appropriate as the first step in the evaluation of an adrenal incidentaloma: Abdominal MRI with gadolinium contrast is not necessary at this time, as it will not provide any additional information about the tumor. A twenty-four-hour urine collection for cortisol and catecholamines is less sensitive and specific than a twenty-four-hour urine fractionated metanephrines for the diagnosis of pheochromocytoma. Aldosterone, renin, and an overnight 1 mg DST are used to evaluate for primary hyperaldosteronism, another potential cause of adrenal incidentalomas. However, these tests should be deferred until after the pheochromocytoma evaluation has been completed, as pheochromocytoma can interfere with the results of these tests. Therefore, the best answer is C. Twenty-four-hour urine fractionated metanephrines. Therefore, the most appropriate next step in the management of this patient is adrenal venous sampling (answer A).

70. The correct answer is D. Initiate prazosin 1 mg every 4 hours.

In the context of preoperative management for catecholamine-secreting tumors, -blockade is crucial to prevent catastrophic -adrenergic stimulation when the tumor is manipulated during surgery. This can be achieved using either nonselective -blockers such as phenoxybenzamine or selective agents such as prazosin. The dose should be titrated until the patient develops orthostatic hypotension, which serves as an indicator for sufficient blockage. Option

A is incorrect because exclusive -blockade (propranolol is a -blocker) should never be performed in patients with catecholamine-secreting tumors as it can lead to cardiovascular collapse from unopposed -stimulation. Option B is incorrect because metyrosine, which inhibits the production of catecholamines, is used in the management of metastatic pheochromocytoma, not as a preoperative measure in non-metastatic cases. Option C is incorrect because although phenoxybenzamine is a nonselective -blocker and can be used in such scenarios, the question specifically states that prazosin is the correct answer. Option E is incorrect because dexamethasone, a corticosteroid, does not play a role in preventing -adrenergic stimulation during the manipulation of a catecholamine-secreting tumor.

71. Answer: C

The most appropriate next step is to check serum and 24-hour urine calcium and creatinine. This will help to determine if the patient has primary hyperparathyroidism (PHPT) or familial hypocalciuric hypercalcemia (FHH). PHPT is a condition in which the parathyroid glands produce too much PTH. PTH is a hormone that regulates calcium levels in the blood. When PTH levels are too high, calcium levels in the blood rise. FHH is a genetic condition that causes people to have high levels of calcium in their blood, even though their PTH levels are normal. People with FHH do not need surgery to remove their parathyroid glands. The other answer choices are not as appropriate as the first step in the evaluation of hypercalcemia: Ordering a 24-hour urine collection for magnesium and phosphate is not necessary at this time. Ordering a parathyroid gland ultrasound is not necessary at this time. Ordering a DXA scan is not necessary at this time. Performing a parathyroidectomy is not necessary at this time. Therefore, the best answer is C. Check serum and 24-hour urine calcium and creatinine.

72. The correct answer is C.

Check baseline adrenocorticotropic hormone (ACTH) and perform cosyntropin stimulation test. This patient's symptoms of fatigue, weight loss, salt craving, postural hypotension, hyperpigmentation, hyponatremia, and hyperkalemia are strongly suggestive of Addison disease, which is primary adrenal insufficiency. However, the diagnosis requires biochemical confirmation. Elevated ACTH (often in the hundreds) would be consistent with adrenal failure since the loss of negative feedback due to low cortisol would lead to increased ACTH secretion. A cosyntropin stimulation test would show a minimal response to cosyntropin, confirming the diagnosis of adrenal insufficiency. Once the diagnosis is confirmed, the patient will require glucocorticoid and mineralocorticoid replacement. 21-Hydroxylase antibodies can be checked, as their presence is associated with autoimmune Addison disease, but this is not necessary for the diagnosis. An abdominal CT scan can be used to identify other etiologies of adrenal failure, but it is of low utility for known autoimmune adrenalitis. Starting treatment immediately without confirming the diagnosis or referring to a psychiatrist would not be appropriate given the strong clinical suspicion of Addison disease.

73. Answer: A

The patient's presentation is consistent with hypercalcemic crisis. Hypercalcemic crisis is a medical emergency that occurs when the serum calcium level is elevated to life-threatening levels. Hypercalcemia can cause a variety of symptoms, including nausea, vomiting, confusion, weakness, and diplopia. The other answer choices are less likely: Hyperthyroidism is a condition in which the thyroid gland produces too much thyroid hormone. Hyperthyroidism can cause a variety of symptoms, including tachycardia, hypertension, and weight loss. However, the patient in this case does not have a history of hyperthyroidism, and his thyroid gland has been removed. Hyperosmolar hyperglycemic state is a complication of diabetes mellitus that occurs when the blood sugar level is very high. Hyperosmolar hyperglycemic state can cause a variety of symptoms, including thirst, frequent urination, and confusion. However, the patient in this case is not known to have diabetes mellitus, and his blood sugar level is not known. Stroke is a condition in which the blood supply to the brain is interrupted. Stroke can cause a variety of symptoms, including weakness, confusion, and diplopia. However, the patient in this case does not have any other risk factors for stroke, such as high blood pressure, high cholesterol, or diabetes mellitus. Hyponatremia is a condition in which the sodium level in the blood is low. Hyponatremia can cause a variety of symptoms, including nausea, vomiting, and confusion. However, the patient in this case does not have any other risk factors for hyponatremia, such as heart failure, liver disease, or kidney disease. Therefore, the best answer is A. Hypercalcemic crisis. Hypercalcemic crisis is a medical emergency and requires immediate treatment. Treatment typically involves intravenous fluids, loop diuretics, and calcitonin. In some cases, dialysis may be necessary.

74. The correct answer is C. Sarcoidosis.

Sarcoidosis, an inflammatory disease characterized by the presence of noncaseating granulomas, can affect almost all organs, can be asymptomatic, or is associated with a wide range of symptoms and presents a diagnostic challenge. Black women have a higher incidence of sarcoidosis. This patient's presentation is classic for pulmonary sarcoidosis, but a diagnostic evaluation that typically includes a tissue biopsy is needed. Hypercalcemia in sarcoidosis is due to the parathyroid hormone–independent conversion of 25-hydroxy vitamin D to the active 1,25-dihydroxy vitamin D. In contrast, primary or secondary hyperparathyroidism presents with elevated parathyroid hormone (and serum calcium is not elevated in secondary hyperparathyroidism). Humoral hypercalcemia of malignancy is caused by elevated parathyroid hormone–related protein (PTHrP). Tuberculosis typically does not cause hypercalcemia and is less likely in this case given the absence of typical symptoms such as night sweats and hemoptysis.

75. Answer: A

The most important laboratory tests to order first are calcium and albumin. Hypocalcemia is a common complication of thyroidectomy, and it can cause neuromuscular irritability. Albumin is a protein that binds to calcium, so it is important to measure albumin levels in order to accurately interpret the serum calcium level. Magnesium and phosphorus levels are important to check, but they are not as likely to be the cause of the patient's symptoms. Parathyroid hormone (PTH) is a hormone that regulates calcium levels. If the patient's PTH level is low, this suggests that she has hypoparathyroidism, which is another possible complication of thyroidectomy. Vitamin D levels can also be important to check, but they are less likely to be the cause of the patient's symptoms. A multiple sclerosis panel is not necessary at this time, as the patient's symptoms are more likely to be due to hypocalcemia than multiple sclerosis. Therefore, the best answer is A. Calcium and albumin. 76. The correct answer is D. No change in treatment is needed. During pregnancy, serum albumin typically decreases due to an increase in plasma volume. Total serum calcium has to be corrected for albumin. In this case, the patient's albumin is 2.0 g/dL, and her adjusted calcium is 8.4 mg/dL, which is within the range for hypoparathyroid patients of low to low-normal. Despite the low total serum calcium, the patient is asymptomatic, indicating that her ionized calcium, which is the biologically active form, is likely in the normal range. Therefore, in the absence of symptoms, no change in treatment is necessary.

77. The correct answer is D.

Thiamine deficiency. This patient presents with a high anion gap metabolic acidosis (HAGMA), most likely due to type B lactic acidosis in the setting of thiamine deficiency. The patient's anion gap is 22 (125 - 90 - 15) + 2 for the albumin of 3 g/dL, indicating HAGMA. The delta/delta ratio is 1:1, which rules out metabolic alkalosis, making vomiting an unlikely etiology. Given that the lactic acidosis did not improve with IV fluid resuscitation and the patient is afebrile with a normal blood pressure, type A lactic acidosis due to ischemia is also unlikely. Instead, type B lactic acidosis is more probable. Thiamine is an essential cofactor for pyruvate dehydrogenase, which converts pyruvate to acetyl-CoA, a key player in the Kreb's cycle of aerobic metabolism. In thiamine deficiency, pyruvate is instead converted to lactate, contributing to lactic acidosis. Patients with alcohol use disorder, like this one, are at increased risk for thiamine deficiency. The condition can be treated with IV thiamine.

78. Answer: D

This patient presents with altered mental status, blurry vision, an elevated anion gap, and an elevated osmolar gap. This is most consistent with methanol intoxication. Methanol is a toxic alcohol that is commonly found in antifreeze, windshield washer fluid, and some types of paint. Methanol can cause a variety of symptoms, including: Altered mental status, Blurred vision, Nausea and vomiting, Abdominal pain, Headache, Seizures, Coma Methanol intoxication can also lead to metabolic acidosis, which is characterized by an elevated anion gap. The anion gap is the difference between the measured cations (sodium and potassium) and the measured anions (chloride and bicarbonate). In metabolic acidosis, the anion gap is elevated because there are unmeasured anions in the blood. The other answer choices are less likely: Isopropyl alcohol intoxication does not typically cause an elevated anion gap or osmolar gap. Aspirin toxicity does not typically cause an elevated anion gap or osmolar gap. Ethylene glycol intoxication can cause an elevated anion gap and osmolar gap, but it does not typically cause blurry vision. Propylene glycol intoxication can cause an elevated anion gap and osmolar gap, but it does not typically cause blurry vision. Therefore, the best answer is D. Methanol intoxication. Treatment for methanol intoxication typically involves fomepizole (Antizol) or ethanol. Fomepizole is a competitive inhibitor of alcohol dehydrogenase, which is the enzyme that converts methanol to toxic metabolites. Ethanol can also be used to block the metabolism of methanol, but it is less effective than fomepizole. In addition to fomepizole or ethanol, patients with methanol intoxication may also need supportive care, such as intravenous fluids and electrolytes.

79. Answer: B

Propylene glycol is the most likely cause of the patient's metabolic acidosis. Propylene glycol is a solvent used in many intravenous medications, including diazepam. It is relatively non-toxic in low doses, but it can become toxic in high doses. Propylene glycol toxicity can cause a number of symptoms, including: Metabolic acidosis, Increased osmolar gap, Acute kidney injury, Central nervous system depression The other answer choices are less likely: Ethylene glycol toxicity can also cause metabolic acidosis and an increased osmolar gap, but it is typically associated with more severe symptoms, such as hypocalcemia and calcium oxalate crystal formation in the urine. Isopropyl alcohol toxicity can cause an increased osmolar gap, but it does not typically cause metabolic acidosis. Aspirin toxicity can cause metabolic acidosis, but it does not typically cause an increased osmolar gap. Lactic acidosis is a type of metabolic acidosis that is caused by the accumulation of lactic acid in the blood. It is typically associated with other medical conditions, such as sepsis or shock. Treatment for propylene glycol toxicity typically involves discontinuing the offending agent and dialysis in severe cases. If you suspect that a patient may have propylene glycol toxicity, it is important to seek medical attention immediately. Propylene glycol toxicity can be fatal if not treated promptly.

80. The correct answer is B.

High anion gap metabolic acidosis with concurrent metabolic alkalosis and compensatory respiratory alkalosis. This patient presents with a normal pH, but with multiple acid-base disturbances. His anion gap is 24 when corrected for low albumin with only a 4 mEq/L decrease in HCO3 as opposed to a decrease in HCO3 of 12 mEq/L that one would expect; hence, he has an additional metabolic alkalosis (delta-delta 3). His pCO2 is slightly low, suggestive of a respiratory alkalosis. Using Winter's formula ($1.5 \times HCO3 + 8 \pm 2$), the expected pCO2 is 36 to 40 mmHg, so his low pCO2 is the expected respiratory compensation for his metabolic acidosis. He likely has an elevated anion gap from lactic acidosis and ketosis in the setting of poor oral intake and metabolic alkalosis from vomiting. Treatment should involve resuscitation with normal saline and aggressive potassium repletion as the alkalemia will persist in a state of hypochloremia and hypokalemia. In terms of the other choices, while the pH is normal, there is an abnormality as this is a triple acid-base disturbance that is masked by concurrent metabolic acidosis and alkalosis. The patient has a High anion gap metabolic acidosis, but one would expect a pH 7.25 with HCO3 12 mEq/L and pCO2 28 mmHg if he has a pure High anion gap metabolic acidosis. This patient has an anion gap of 24 when corrected for albumin, so a non-gap metabolic acidosis is incorrect. Anion gap can be calculated as Na Cl HCO3, which is 126 87 20 = 19 in this patient; however, one needs to correct for albumin, by adding 2.5 to the anion gap for each 1 g/dL decrease in albumin below 4 g/dL. Hence, the corrected anion gap is $19 + 2.5 \times 2 = 24$.

81. The correct answer is: D.

IV normal saline. This patient's clinical presentation and lab findings indicate a hyperchloremic, hypokalemic metabolic alkalosis, likely due to the loss of chloride-rich fluids from recurrent vomiting. In such a scenario, the kidneys prioritize volume retention, leading to persistent alkalemia. This situation is typically managed with volume resuscitation using chloride-rich isotonic fluid, such as normal saline, and aggressive potassium repletion is also necessary. As the alkalemia is corrected, potassium will shift extracellularly. Hence, IV normal saline is the most appropriate treatment for this patient.

82. Answer: A

Cerebral salt wasting is the most likely diagnosis in this patient. Cerebral salt wasting is a condition that can occur after an SAH. It is characterized by hyponatremia, hypouricemia, high urine sodium, and hyperosmolar urine. SIADH is another condition that can cause hyponatremia, but it is characterized by euvolemic or mildly volume overloaded status. This patient is hypovolemic, which is not consistent with SIADH. Central diabetes insipidus is a condition that causes polyuria and polydipsia. It can lead to hyponatremia if the patient does not drink enough fluids, but it is not characterized by hypouricemia or high urine sodium. Hypovolemic hyponatremia is a condition that is caused by a decrease in extracellular fluid volume. It can occur due to dehydration, vomiting, or diarrhea. This patient has a normal blood pressure and heart rate, which is not consistent with hypovolemic hyponatremia. Adrenal insufficiency can also cause hyponatremia, but it is characterized by hyperkalemia and hypoglycemia. This patient has normal potassium and glucose levels, which is not consistent with adrenal insufficiency. Treatment for cerebral salt wasting typically involves intravenous saline. Intravenous saline helps to correct the hypovolemia and improve the renal perfusion. This leads to a decrease in the secretion of antidiuretic hormone (ADH), which allows the kidneys to excrete more water and raise the serum sodium level. Cerebral salt wasting is thought to be caused by the release of natriuretic peptides from the brain after an SAH. Natriuretic peptides cause the kidneys to excrete more sodium. Cerebral salt wasting can be a serious complication of an SAH. It can lead to hypovolemic shock and death. It is important to diagnose and treat cerebral salt wasting promptly.

83. Answer: D

The most likely diagnosis is nephrogenic diabetes insipidus (NDI). NDI is a condition in which the kidneys are unable to respond to antidiuretic hormone (ADH). This leads to polyuria and hypernatremia. Central diabetes insipidus

(CDI) is a condition in which the body does not produce enough ADH. This also leads to polyuria and hypernatremia. However, in CDI, the kidneys are able to respond to ADH. Primary polydipsia is a condition in which a person drinks more fluids than they need. This can lead to hyponatremia, but it does not typically lead to hypernatremia. Osmotic diuresis is a condition in which the kidneys excrete more water in response to the presence of an osmotically active substance in the blood. This can lead to hypernatremia, but it is typically associated with other medical conditions, such as hyperglycemia or mannitol administration. Hyperaldosteronism is a condition in which the body produces too much aldosterone. Aldosterone is a hormone that causes the kidneys to retain sodium and excrete potassium. This can lead to hypernatremia, but it is typically associated with other medical conditions, such as hypertension or renal artery stenosis. Treatment for NDI typically involves fluid replacement and thiazide diuretics. Thiazide diuretics help to reduce the amount of water that is excreted by the kidneys. 84. Correct Answer: C. Give 3% hypertonic saline as a 100 mL bolus in 10 minutes, then recheck labs. This patient is presenting with severe hyponatremia, defined as a serum sodium level less than 120 mEq/L. Severe hyponatremia can lead to life-threatening symptoms like seizures, respiratory failure, and coma due to cerebral edema. According to both European and American expert panel guidelines, aggressive therapy with 3% saline is recommended in the setting of severe symptoms, which include vomiting, deep somnolence, seizures, or coma. Hypertonic saline should be administered in consultation with a nephrologist but is typically given as a 150 mL bolus over 20 minutes (EU guidelines) or 100 mL over 10 minutes (US guidelines). An increase of serum sodium by approximately 3 mEq/L is sufficient to reverse severe symptoms. Although underlying conditions such as hypothyroidism may contribute to hyponatremia, the severity of this patient's symptoms warrant immediate correction with hypertonic saline. The use of isotonic saline is appropriate for hypovolemic hyponatremia, but given the severity of this patient's symptoms and her euvolemic status with urine sodium >20 mEq/L, suggesting syndrome of inappropriate antidiuretic hormone secretion (SIADH), hypertonic saline is the preferred intervention. Administering 2 L of isotonic saline without rechecking serum sodium could further worsen the hyponatremia. While free water restriction is indicated in SIADH, the severity of this patient's symptoms require a more rapid correction with hypertonic saline. Lastly, normal saline with diuretics is not the appropriate management in this case, as it may not correct the severe hyponatremia as effectively and rapidly as required.

85. The correct answer is B.

Licorice ingestion. This patient's symptoms of fatigue, muscle weakness, palpitations, and elevated blood pressure, combined with severe hypokalemia and a urine potassium to creatinine ratio > 13, can be explained by large ingestion of black licorice. Licorice contains glycyrrhizic acid, which inhibits 11-hydroxysteroid dehydrogenase. This enzyme is responsible for inactivating cortisol in the adrenal glands. In large quantities, licorice can lead to hypercortisolism. Excess cortisol activates mineralocorticoid receptors, causing sodium retention and potassium excretion, leading to severe hypokalemia and elevated blood pressure. The other options are less likely given the patient's clinical picture: A. While diarrhea can lead to extrarenal potassium loss, the urine potassium to creatinine ratio in this setting would typically be <13. C. Thiazides can cause renal potassium loss, but the patient is not taking a thiazide, and his blood pressure is elevated rather than reduced. D. Hypokalemia is associated with both type I and type II renal tubular acidosis. However, this patient's urine anion gap is -10, which is inconsistent with these conditions. E. Vomiting could cause hypokalemia due to loss of gastric fluids, but the patient does not report a history of vomiting. Furthermore, vomiting typically causes a metabolic alkalosis with hypochloremia and elevated bicarbonate, whereas this patient has normal chloride and bicarbonate levels.

86. Answer: D

The most appropriate initial fluid management strategy for rhabdomyolysis is IV normal saline at 1-2 L/h. Rhabdomyolysis is a condition in which muscle tissue breaks down and releases its contents into the bloodstream. This can lead to a number of complications, including acute kidney injury. Aggressive fluid resuscitation is essential to prevent and treat acute kidney injury in rhabdomyolysis. IV normal saline is the preferred fluid for resuscitation, as it helps to replace lost fluid and electrolytes. The other answer choices are less appropriate: IV normal saline at 200 mL/h is too slow to be effective in resuscitating a patient with rhabdomyolysis. IV bicarbonate is not recommended for routine use in rhabdomyolysis. It may be used in severe cases to help prevent myoglobin-induced renal failure, but it should only be used after volume repletion with normal saline. IV furosemide is a diuretic that can be used to increase urine output. However, it should not be used in isolation as initial therapy in rhabdomyolysis, as it can worsen volume depletion and acute kidney injury. Dialysis is a last resort treatment for rhabdomyolysis. It is only indicated in patients who do not respond to initial fluid resuscitation and develop severe acute kidney injury. Rhabdomyolysis is a serious condition that can lead to a number of complications, including acute kidney injury, hyperkalemia, and compartment syndrome. Early diagnosis and treatment are essential to prevent these complications. The mainstay of treatment for rhabdomyolysis is aggressive fluid resuscitation with IV normal saline. Patients should be monitored closely for signs of volume overload. If volume overload develops, diuretics may be used to increase urine output. In severe cases of rhabdomyolysis, dialysis may be necessary. Dialysis is used to remove myoglobin and other harmful substances from the blood.

87. Answer: C

Intravenous normal saline (IV normal saline) is the most appropriate medication or intervention to reduce the risk of contrast-associated acute kidney injury in patients with chronic kidney disease. IV normal saline helps to maintain hydration and reduce the concentration of contrast agent in the blood. N-acetylcysteine has been studied as a potential preventive agent for contrast-associated acute kidney injury, but the results have been mixed. Some studies have shown a benefit, while others have shown no benefit. Hemodialysis is not used to prevent contrast-associated acute kidney injury. It is only used to treat patients who have developed severe acute kidney injury and require dialysis. Intravenous sodium bicarbonate is not recommended to prevent contrast-associated acute kidney injury. In fact, it may increase the risk of acute kidney injury. Contrast-associated acute kidney injury is a condition in which the kidneys are damaged by contrast agents, which are dyes used in medical imaging procedures such as coronary angiography and computerized tomography (CT) scans. Contrast agents help to improve the visibility of blood vessels and organs on medical images. Contrast-associated acute kidney injury is more common in patients with chronic kidney disease, diabetes, and heart failure. It is also more common in patients who are older than 70 years old. Most cases of contrast-associated acute kidney injury are mild and resolve within a few days. However, in some cases, contrast-associated acute kidney injury can be severe and lead to dialysis.

88. The correct answer is: A. Add acetazolamide. This patient's metabolic alkalosis is due to diuretic-induced loss of sodium and chloride. The increased delivery of sodium to the distal tubule leads to enhanced absorption of sodium and increased secretion of H+ into the urine. Chloride depletion also leads to bicarbonate retention in the distal tubule, causing metabolic alkalosis. Acetazolamide inhibits carbonic anhydrase in the proximal tubule, leading to loss of bicarbonate and promoting further diuresis, although it is a weak diuretic by itself. This results in lowering of the serum bicarbonate concentration and improvement of the diuretic-induced metabolic alkalosis. Typical doses include 250 to 500 mg twice or thrice a day until the pH improves to normal levels. Infusion of normal saline (Option B) may help replete the sodium and chloride and reverse the alkalosis but would be counterproductive in this patient with significant volume overload. Stopping the loop diuretic (Option C) would have a similar effect. Spironolactone (Option D) and amiloride (Option E) are not typically used for this purpose.

89. Answer: C

The most appropriate next step in management is to perform a surgical evaluation. This patient has steal syndrome, which is a condition in which blood is diverted away from the arteries of the hand and into the dialysis fistula. This can lead to ischemia and tissue necrosis. Steal syndrome is a serious complication of dialysis fistulas, and it requires immediate surgical evaluation. Surgery is typically performed to ligate the fistula. The other answer choices are less appropriate: Lowering the dialysis blood flow rate may help to improve symptoms in mild cases of steal syndrome, but it is not a definitive treatment. Administering analgesics may help to control the patient's pain, but it will not address the underlying cause of the steal syndrome. Starting antibiotics is not necessary, as there is no evidence of infection. Monitoring for signs of infection is important, but it is not the most immediate priority. Steal syndrome is a relatively common complication of dialysis fistulas, occurring in up to 20% of patients. It is more common in patients with diabetes, hypertension, and peripheral vascular disease. The symptoms of steal syndrome can vary depending on the severity of the condition. Mild cases may only cause numbness and tingling in the hand. Severe cases can cause pain, pallor, and coolness of the hand. In some cases, steal syndrome can lead to tissue necrosis and gangrene. The treatment for steal syndrome is typically surgery to ligate the dialysis fistula. In some cases, a new dialysis fistula may be created in a different location.

90. D. He should be evaluated and listed for a kidney transplant now.

This patient, despite his age, leads an active life and has adequate family support. His past history of nonmelanomatous skin cancer does not impose a waiting period for transplantation. His blood group type AB has shorter than average wait times for transplantation. The current guideline suggests that patients with an eGFR of 20 mL/min should be considered for transplantation. Therefore, he should undergo recipient evaluation and be listed for transplantation as soon as possible. While undergoing workup, he should be encouraged to lose weight and lower his BMI to improve outcomes post-transplantation. Simultaneously looking for potential living donors is beneficial but should not delay listing on the deceased donor transplant list.

91.Answer: C

The most appropriate next step in management is to refer the patient for a kidney biopsy. Kidney biopsy is the gold standard for diagnosing lupus nephritis, which is a common complication of SLE. Lupus nephritis can lead to serious kidney damage, including end-stage renal disease (ESRD). The other answer choices are less appropriate: Starting immunosuppressive therapy without a definitive diagnosis is not recommended. Monitoring blood pressure and renal function is important, but it is not the most immediate priority. A 24-hour urine collection is more accurate than a spot urine test for measuring proteinuria, but it should not delay the referral for a kidney biopsy. Starting antihypertensive therapy is important, but it is not the most immediate priority. Lupus nephritis is a condition in which the kidneys are damaged by the autoimmune process that underlies SLE. Lupus nephritis can cause a variety of symptoms, including proteinuria, hematuria, and decreased renal function. The treatment for lupus nephritis depends on the severity of the condition. In mild cases, treatment may involve only monitoring and supportive care. In more severe cases, treatment may involve immunosuppressive therapy, such as corticosteroids and mycophenolate mofetil. The prognosis for lupus nephritis depends on a number of factors, including the severity of the disease and the response to treatment. With early diagnosis and treatment, most patients with lupus nephritis can achieve long-term remission. However, some patients with lupus nephritis may progress to ESRD.

92. Correct Answer: C.

Start treatment with Lisinopril. This patient's IgA nephropathy, the most common glomerular disease in the developed world, is characterized by gross or microscopic hematuria. About half of patients progress to end-stage renal disease (ESRD) over 15 to 20 years. Elevated creatinine, persistent urine protein creatinine ratio >1 g/d, and high blood pressure (>140/90 mmHg) are markers of progressive loss of kidney function. The mainstays of IgA nephropathy treatment are blood pressure control (<130/80 mmHg) and proteinuria reduction (<500 mg/g) with ACE inhibitors or ARBs like Lisinopril (option C). Fish oil (option A) may be used as an add-on therapy in patients with persistent proteinuria despite ACE inhibitors or ARBs, but it's not a first-line treatment. Immunosuppression, with either prednisone (option B) or cyclophosphamide (option D), is suggested for patients with persistent and progressive proteinuria >1 g/d after maximal medical therapy, necrotizing glomerulonephritis on kidney biopsy, or acutely rising serum creatinine. However, this patient does not meet these criteria. Lastly, option E is incorrect as this disease requires active management to prevent progression to ESRD.

93.Answer: C

The most likely diagnosis is membranous nephropathy. Chronic graft-versus-host disease (cGVHD) is a common complication of BMT, and membranous nephropathy is the most common renal manifestation of cGVHD. The patient's clinical presentation, including the recent discontinuation of immunosuppression, the coexistence of cGVHD involving other organs, and the absence of anemia or thrombocytopenia, is consistent with membranous nephropathy due to cGVHD. The other answer choices are less likely: Thrombotic microangiopathy is a condition characterized by thrombosis of small blood vessels. It can occur in a variety of settings, including cancer, pregnancy, and drug-induced toxicity. However, it is less likely in this patient without anemia or thrombocytopenia. Posttransplant ANCA vasculitis is a rare condition that can occur in BMT recipients. However, it typically presents with a nephritogenic pattern and elevated ANCA levels. In this patient, the ANCA levels are normal. Minimal change disease and focal segmental glomerulosclerosis are other types of glomerulonephritis that can occur in BMT recipients. However, they are less likely than membranous nephropathy in patients with cGVHD. Treatment for membranous nephropathy due to cGVHD typically involves immunosuppression with a combination of steroids, cyclophosphamide, and rituximab. The goal of treatment is to suppress the immune response and prevent further damage to the kidneys.

94. Answer: B

The best initial laboratory evaluation for monoclonal gammopathy of renal significance (MGRS) is SPEP, SIF, and SFLC. This combination of tests has the highest sensitivity to detect a monoclonal protein. SPEP is a test that separates the different proteins in the blood based on their size and electrical charge. It can be used to detect monoclonal proteins, which are proteins that are produced by a single clone of B cells. SIF is a test that confirms the monoclonality of a protein and identifies its type (heavy and light chain). SFLC is a test that measures the levels of free kappa and lambda light chains in the blood. An abnormal ratio of kappa to lambda light chains can indicate the presence of a monoclonal protein. UPEP is a test that separates the different proteins in the urine based on their size and electrical charge. It is less sensitive than SPEP for detecting monoclonal proteins. Bone marrow biopsy is a test that can be used to diagnose MGRS in patients in whom a monoclonal protein is not detected using the aforementioned methods. Other answer choices: (A) SPEP and UPEP are less sensitive than SPEP, SIF, and SFLC for detecting monoclonal proteins. (C) SPEP, UPEP, and bone marrow biopsy are not the best initial laboratory evaluation for MGRS. (D) SIF, SFLC, and bone marrow biopsy are not the best initial laboratory evaluation for MGRS. UPEP is less sensitive than SPEP for detecting monoclonal proteins and bone marrow biopsy should only be performed if other tests are negative. (E) UPEP, SFLC, and bone marrow biopsy are not the best initial laboratory evaluation for MGRS. UPEP is less sensitive than SPEP for detecting monoclonal proteins and bone marrow biopsy should only be performed if other tests are negative.

95. The correct answer is C.

Hemolytic uremic syndrome. The patient's condition is characterized by a rapidly progressive glomerulonephritis with crescent formation observed on a kidney biopsy. While anti-glomerular basement membrane disease and ANCA-associated glomerulonephritis are common causes of crescentic glomerulonephritis, the kidney biopsy in hemolytic uremic syndrome typically demonstrates endothelial injury and thrombi/fibrin deposition in the glomerular capillaries and arterioles, which aligns with the patient's presentation. Lupus nephritis and IgA nephropathy can also present with crescentic glomerulonephritis, but these are rarer occurrences.

96. The correct answer is A.

Cryoglobulinemic glomerulonephritis. This patient's presentation of gross hematuria, hypertension, and acute kidney injury indicates acute glomerulonephritis. Given the patient's history of untreated hepatitis C, cryoglobulinemic glomerulonephritis is likely. Cryoglobulinemia is a condition that results from deposition of cold-sensitive antibodies and complement proteins within blood vessels, causing decreased perfusion and ischemia. It is associated with untreated hepatitis C and can cause membranoproliferative glomerulonephritis, which typically presents with a reduction in C3 and C4. The patient's urinalysis is active with protein and blood with a red blood cell cast, which further supports this diagnosis. Other options like minimal change disease (B), membranous nephropathy (C), focal segmental glomerulosclerosis (D), and diabetic nephropathy (E) are less likely given the patient's presentation and history. Treatment for cryoglobulinemic glomerulonephritis often involves plasmapheresis and immunosuppression (e.g., steroids), along with avoidance of cold temperatures.

97. Answer: B

The next best step in management is urinalysis and sediment. Urinalysis is a simple and non-invasive test that can provide valuable information about the cause of gross hematuria. The presence of dysmorphic red blood cells or red blood cell casts on urinalysis suggests a glomerular cause of hematuria, such as glomerulonephritis or vasculitis. The presence of white blood cells or bacteria on urinalysis suggests an infectious cause of hematuria, such as pyelonephritis or prostatitis. CT urography is a more invasive test that is typically used to diagnose kidney stones or other structural abnormalities of the urinary tract. It is not indicated in this patient without a history of flank pain, kidney stones, or trauma. Renal ultrasound is another imaging test that can be used to assess the kidneys and urinary tract. It is often used to evaluate patients with acute kidney injury or chronic kidney disease. However, it is not as sensitive as CT urography for detecting kidney stones or other structural abnormalities of the urinary tract. Urology referral is not necessary at this time. The etiology of the gross hematuria should be evaluated first with urinalysis and sediment. If the urinalysis is inconclusive, or if the patient has other signs or symptoms of a serious underlying condition, such as fever or flank pain, then urology referral may be appropriate. Gross hematuria is a condition in which red blood cells are visible in the urine. It can be caused by a variety of conditions, including kidney stones, urinary tract infections, glomerulonephritis, and cancer. The evaluation of gross hematuria typically begins with a urinalysis and sediment. This test can help to identify the underlying cause of the hematuria and guide further diagnostic testing and treatment. If the urinalysis is inconclusive, or if the patient has other signs or symptoms of a serious underlying condition, then further imaging tests, such as CT urography or renal ultrasound, may be necessary.

98. Answer: A

Amyloidosis is a condition in which amyloid proteins are deposited in the organs and tissues of the body. Amyloid proteins are a group of abnormal proteins that can form insoluble fibrils. These fibrils can damage organs and tissues, leading to a variety of symptoms, including kidney failure. Amyloidosis can cause a variety of changes in the urine, including proteinuria, hematuria, and casts. However, in some cases, the urine may be normal. This is most likely to occur in early stages of the disease or in patients with mild amyloid deposition in the kidneys. The other answer choices are less likely: Thrombotic microangiopathy is a condition characterized by the formation of blood clots in small blood vessels. It can cause a variety of symptoms, including kidney failure. However, it typically causes hematuria and other abnormalities on urinalysis. Malignant hypertension is a condition characterized by severe and uncontrolled high blood pressure. It can cause a variety of complications, including kidney failure. However, it typically causes hematuria and other abnormalities on urinalysis. Cast nephropathy is a condition in which casts are formed in the kidneys. These casts can block the flow of urine and lead to kidney failure. However, it typically causes proteinuria and other abnormalities on urinalysis Hepatorenal syndrome is a condition in which kidney failure develops as a complication of liver failure. It typically causes a decrease in urine output and other abnormalities on urinalysis.

99. Answer: D.

His stone has a high likelihood of passing spontaneously given its size. Most kidney stones (over 80%) that are less than 0.5 cm in size pass spontaneously. This patient's stone, being 0.4 cm, has a high chance of passing without intervention. The size of the stone significantly affects its chances of spontaneous passage, with larger stones being less likely to pass without intervention. For example, only 25% of stones that are 9 mm or larger will pass without intervention. The location of the stone also affects its chance of spontaneous passage, with stones located more distally at the ureterovesical junction being more likely to pass spontaneously compared to more proximally located stones. In this patient's case, increasing fluid intake and dietary modification (low sodium, high potassium, low oxalate, low nondairy animal protein, increased fruit and vegetables, supplemental vitamin C) would be beneficial measures to prevent the formation of new calcium stones. A low-calcium diet is not recommended as it does not have a significant impact on preventing calcium stone formation. Alkalinizing the urine can help prevent uric acid stone formation, but it may increase the risk of forming calcium phosphate stones. It's also worth noting that while a third of patients may experience a recurrence of a kidney stone in 5 years, and almost half may have a recurrence in 10 years, the majority of patients who pass a kidney stone will not experience another one in their lifetime.

100. The correct answer is C.

Vitamin C. This patient most likely has calcium oxalate nephrolithiasis and oxalate nephropathy. Oxalate nephropathy can be an inborn error of metabolism that manifests at birth or can be secondary to excessive oxalate consumption or absorption. Ingestion of high-dose vitamin C (1-2 g/d), an oxalate precursor, is associated with the formation of calcium oxalate stones and oxalate deposition in the kidney. A large study showed that individuals taking vitamin C had twice the risk of kidney stones as individuals not taking vitamin C. Vitamin D intake with normal calcium levels does not lead to a higher stone risk. B6 supplementation lowers urinary oxalate and may reduce the risk of kidney stones. Vitamin C (ascorbic acid) is metabolized to oxalate in the body. Excessive intake of vitamin C can lead to increased oxalate production and excretion, increasing the risk for calcium oxalate stone formation. Oxalate is a common component of kidney stones, and people who are prone to developing kidney stones should avoid high doses of vitamin C. On the other hand, Vitamin B6 (pyridoxine) is involved in the metabolism of glyoxylate, which can convert to oxalate if not metabolized correctly. Some studies have suggested that vitamin B6 supplementation may help prevent stone formation in patients with high urinary oxalate concentrations. Vitamin D does not increase the risk of kidney stones as long as calcium levels are normal. High levels of vitamin D can increase calcium absorption from the gut, increasing the risk of stone formation if calcium intake is also high. However, in the absence of hypercalcemia, vitamin D does not increase stone risk.

101. Answer: C

Oxalate nephropathy is a condition in which kidney damage is caused by the deposition of oxalate crystals in the kidneys. Oxalate is a natural substance that is found in many foods, including fruits, vegetables, and nuts. It is also produced by the body. Oxalate nephropathy can be caused by a variety of factors, including: Primary hyperoxaluria: A rare genetic disorder in which the body produces too much oxalate. Secondary hyperoxaluria: A condition in which the body produces too much oxalate due to an underlying medical condition, such as inflammatory bowel disease, pancreatic insufficiency, or bowel resection. Increased oxalate intake: A diet high in oxalate-rich foods, such as spinach, rhubarb, and chocolate, can increase the risk of oxalate nephropathy. Decreased urine output: Urine helps to remove oxalate from the body. Decreased urine output, such as from dehydration, can increase the risk of oxalate nephropathy. The patient in this question has a history of inflammatory bowel disease, which is a risk factor for secondary hyperoxaluria. His urinalysis also shows oxalate crystals, which is a sign of oxalate nephropathy. The other answer choices are less likely: Primary hyperoxaluria is a rare genetic disorder, and the patient does not have a family history of the condition. Hypercalciuria is a condition in which the body produces too much calcium. It can increase the risk of kidney stones, but it is not a common cause of oxalate nephropathy. Uric acid nephropathy is a condition in which kidney damage is caused by the deposition of uric acid crystals in the kidneys. It is more common in patients with gout. Nephrolithiasis is the presence of kidney stones. It can be caused by a variety of factors, including oxalate nephropathy. However, it is not itself a cause of kidney injury.

Chapter 2

ENDOCRINOLOGY BOARD QUESTIONS

1. A 47-year-old woman presents with sudden onset headache, nausea, and vomiting. She also reports blurred vision and difficulty walking. MRI reveals a pituitary hemorrhage. Which of the following is the most appropriate management strategy?

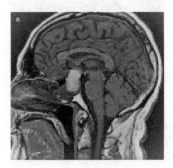

Figure 2.1: A 47-year-old woman

- A. High-dose glucocorticoids
- B. Surgical decompression
- C. Both high-dose glucocorticoids and surgical decompression
- D. Observation
- E. None of the above

2. A 41-year-old woman with a microprolactinoma does not desire fertility. Which of the following is the best course of action?

- A. Treatment with dopamine agonists
- B. Estrogen replacement therapy
- C. Observation
- D. Surgery
- E. None of the above

3. A 32-year-old woman presents with amenorrhea, galactorrhea, and infertility. Which of the following is the most likely cause?

- A. Hyperprolactinemia
- B. Hypothyroidism
- C. Polycystic ovary syndrome
- D. Premature ovarian failure

45

- E. None of the above

4. A 43-year-old woman with a macroprolactinoma is being started on cabergoline. What is the recommended initial dosage?

- A. 0.5 mg per week
- B. 0.625 mg taken at bedtime.
- C. 2.5 mg administered orally three times daily.
- D. None of the above

5. A 57-year-old man presents with the classic features of acromegaly, including acral enlargement, coarsening of facial features, and increased hand and foot size. Which of the following is the most appropriate test to confirm the diagnosis?

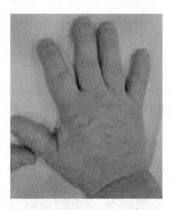

Figure 2.2: 57-year-old man

- A. Serum growth hormone (GH) level
- B. Oral glucose tolerance test (OGTT)
- C. Magnetic resonance imaging (MRI) of the pituitary gland
- D. All of the above
- E. None of the above

6. A 55-year-old woman with a history of radiation therapy for breast cancer presents with fatigue, weight loss, and decreased libido. Which of the following pituitary hormones is most likely to be deficient?

- A. Growth hormone (GH)
- B. Follicle-stimulating hormone (FSH)
- C. Luteinizing hormone (LH)
- D. Thyroid-stimulating hormone (TSH)
- E. Adrenocorticotropic hormone (ACTH)

7. A 59-year-old woman is diagnosed with Pituitary DI. Which of the following is the recommended therapeutic approach?

- A. Desmopressin (DDAVP) subcutaneous injection, 1 g once daily
- B. Desmopressin (DDAVP) nasal spray, 10 g two times daily
- C. Desmopressin (DDAVP) oral tablets, 100 g two times daily
- D. All of the above
- E. None of the above

8. A 51-year-old woman presents with polyuria and polydipsia. What is the most appropriate diagnostic approach?

- A. Fluid deprivation test
- B. Plasma osmolality
- C. Serum sodium

- D. Urine volume
- E. Urine osmolality

9. A 47-year-old woman presents with hyponatremia and low serum osmolality. She has been diagnosed with chronic SIADH. What is the suggested therapeutic approach?

- A. Oral tolvaptan
- B. Demeclocycline
- C. Fludrocortisone
- D. All of the above
- E. None of the above

10. A 38-year-old woman presents with elevated total T4 and T3 concentrations, but normal free levels. What is the most likely explanation for this finding?

- A. Graves' disease
- B. Hashimoto's thyroiditis
- C. Subclinical hyperthyroidism
- D. Elevated levels of carrier proteins
- E. None of the above

11. 56-year-old woman presents with fatigue, weight gain, and cold intolerance. Her physical examination is unremarkable. Her thyroid function tests reveal low total T4 and free T4 levels, with elevated thyroid-stimulating hormone (TSH) levels. What is the most likely diagnosis?

- A. Graves' disease
- B. Hashimoto's thyroiditis
- C. Subclinical hypothyroidism
- D. Thyroid cancer
- E. None of the above

12. A 59-year-old woman presents with fatigue, weight gain, and cold intolerance. Her physical examination is unremarkable. Her thyroid function tests reveal elevated thyroid-stimulating hormone (TSH) levels. What is the most reliable indicator of primary hypothyroidism?

- A. Elevated TSH levels
- B. Low free T4 levels
- C. High free T3 levels
- D. All of the above
- E. None of the above

13. A 51-year-old woman with a history of hypothyroidism presents with coma. What is the recommended approach for initiating therapy?

- A. Levothyroxine (200-400 g) as a single intravenous bolus, followed by a daily oral dose of 1.6 g/kg per day.
- B. Hydrocortisone (50 mg) every 6 hours.
- C. Ventilatory support.
- D. All of the above.
- E. None of the above.

14. A 62-year-old woman with a history of Graves' disease presents with proptosis, periorbital swelling, and ophthalmoplegia. What are the extrathyroidal manifestations associated with Graves' disease?

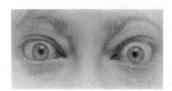

Figure 2.3: A 62-year-old woman

- A. Infiltrative ophthalmopathy
- B. Dermopathy
- C. Both infiltrative ophthalmopathy and dermopathy
- D. None of the above

15. A 64-year-old woman with a history of hyperthyroidism presents with fever, delirium, seizures, arrhythmias, coma, vomiting, diarrhea, and jaundice. What is the most likely diagnosis?

- A. Thyrotoxic crisis
- B. Myxedema coma
- C. Thyroid cancer
- D. None of the above

16. A 58-year-old woman with a history of Graves' disease is being treated with antithyroid medications. What are the primary adverse effects associated with these medications?

- A. Hepatitis
- B. Systemic lupus erythematosus (SLE)
- C. Agranulocytosis
- D. All of the above

17. A 32-year-old pregnant woman is diagnosed with thyrotoxicosis. Can radioactive iodine be administered to treat her condition?

- A. Yes
- B. No
- C. It depends on the trimester of pregnancy.
- D. It depends on the severity of thyrotoxicosis.

18. A 55-year-old woman presents with fatigue, weight gain, and cold intolerance. Her physical examination is unremarkable. Her thyroid function tests reveal low total T4 and free T4 levels, with elevated thyroid-stimulating hormone (TSH) levels. What is the most likely diagnosis?

- A. Graves' disease
- B. Hashimoto's thyroiditis
- C. Subclinical hypothyroidism
- D. Sick euthyroid syndrome

19. 52-year-old woman presents with fatigue, weight gain, and cold intolerance. Her physical examination is unremarkable. Her thyroid function tests reveal low total T4 and free T4 levels, with elevated thyroid-stimulating hormone (TSH) levels. What is the most likely diagnosis?

- A. Graves' disease
- B. Hashimoto's thyroiditis
- C. Subclinical hypothyroidism
- D. Sick euthyroid syndrome
- E. Type 1 AIT

20. A 59-year-old woman presents with dysphagia, increasing shortness of breath, and facial plethora. Her physical examination reveals a large goiter that extends into the suprasternal notch. What is the most likely diagnosis?

- A. Substernal goiter

- B. Graves' disease
- C. Hashimoto's thyroiditis
- D. Thyroid cancer

21. A 44-year-old woman presents with a nontoxic nodule on her thyroid gland. The nodule is 1.5 cm in size. What is the appropriate timing for performing ultrasound-guided fine-needle aspiration (FNA) on the nodule?

- A. Immediately
- B. Within 6 months
- C. Within 12 months
- D. Within 24 months

22. Which of the following is the most prevalent form of thyroid cancer?

- A. Medullary thyroid cancer
- B. Follicular thyroid cancer
- C. Papillary thyroid cancer
- D. Anaplastic thyroid cancer
- E. Hurthle cell thyroid cancer

23. A 58-year-old woman presents with fatigue, weight loss, and hyperpigmentation. Her plasma ACTH level is low. Which of the following is the most likely diagnosis?

- A. Addison disease
- B. Cushing syndrome
- C. Ectopic ACTH syndrome
- D. Adrenal adenoma

E. Bilateral nodular hyperplasia 24. A 41-year-old man presents with fatigue, weight gain, and hypertension. His plasma ACTH level is high. Which of the following supplementary examinations is most likely to help differentiate between a pituitary and peripheral origin of ACTH?

- A. Cortisol level
- B. 24-hour urinary free cortisol level
- C. Low-dose dexamethasone suppression test
- D. Inferior petrosal sinus sampling
- E. Pituitary magnetic resonance imaging

25. A 49-year-old woman with Cushing syndrome is not a candidate for surgery. Which of the following medical interventions is most likely to be effective in treating her condition?

- A. Ketoconazole
- B. Metyrapone
- C. Mitotane
- D. Hydrocortisone
- E. Prednisone

26. A 59-year-old woman presents with hypertension, hypokalemia, and muscle weakness. Which of the following tests is most likely to help establish the diagnosis of primary hyperaldosteronism?

- A. Aldosterone level
- B. Renin level
- C. Aldosterone-to-renin ratio (ARR)
- D. Computed tomography (CT) scan of the adrenal glands
- E. Magnetic resonance imaging (MRI) of the adrenal glands

27. A 51-year-old woman with primary hyperaldosteronism has an aldosterone-producing adenoma. Which of the following is the most appropriate treatment option?

- A. Sodium-restricted diet
- B. Spironolactone
- C. Eplerenone

- D. Amiloride
- E. Surgery

28. A 54-year-old woman presents with fatigue, weight loss, and hyperpigmentation. Which of the following tests is the most effective screening test for Addison's disease?

- A. Cortisol level
- B. 24-hour urinary free cortisol level
- C. Low-dose dexamethasone suppression test
- D. ACTH stimulation test
- E. Pituitary magnetic resonance imaging

29. A 50-year-old woman with Addison's disease is diagnosed and started on glucocorticoid replacement therapy. Which of the following is the most appropriate treatment approach?

- A. Hydrocortisone 15 mg once daily
- B. Hydrocortisone 25 mg twice daily
- C. Prednisone 5 mg once daily
- D. Prednisone 10 mg twice daily
- E. Dexamethasone 0.5 mg once daily

30. A 51-year-old woman undergoes a CT scan for abdominal pain and an incidentaloma is found in her right adrenal gland. Which of the following is the initial step in assessing the adrenal incidentaloma? A. Measure plasma free metanephrines B. Measure urinary metanephrines C. Perform a CT-guided biopsy. D. Order a 24-hour urine cortisol test E. Administer a dexamethasone suppression test.

31. A 49-year-old woman with a family history of MEN 1 presents with hypercalcemia. Which of the following is the most likely diagnosis?

- A. Primary hyperparathyroidism
- B. Cushing syndrome
- C. Pheochromocytoma
- D. Adrenal adenoma
- E. Adrenal carcinoma

32. A 61-year-old woman presents with polyuria, polydipsia, and fatigue. Which of the following is the most likely diagnosis?

- A. Hyperthyroidism
- B. Diabetes mellitus
- C. Hypothyroidism
- D. Cushing syndrome
- E. Addison disease

33. A 71-year-old man with diabetes mellitus presents with a painful ulcer on his right heel. Which of the following is the most likely diagnosis?

- A. Charcot foot
- B. Diabetic neuropathy
- C. Diabetic retinopathy
- D. Diabetic nephropathy
- E. Peripheral vascular disease

34. A 54-year-old woman with type 2 diabetes mellitus is started on intensive therapy. Which of the following is the most likely outcome of this therapy?

- A. Decreased risk of long-term complications.
- B. Increased risk of hypoglycemia
- C. Both decreased risk of long-term complications and increased risk of hypoglycemia
- D. Neither decreased risk of long-term complications nor increased risk of hypoglycemia.

35. A 58-year-old man with type 2 diabetes mellitus and a history of heart disease is being treated with metformin.

Which of the following medications would be most beneficial to add to his treatment regimen?

- A. Empagliflozin
- B. Liraglutide
- C. Canagliflozin
- D. Saxagliptin
- E. Sitagliptin

36. A 51-year-old woman with type 2 diabetes mellitus is being seen for her annual checkup. Which of the following is the most appropriate screening method for diabetic nephropathy?

- A. Routine urinalysis
- B. 24-hour urine collection
- C. Spot collection for albuminuria
- D. Renal ultrasound
- E. Renal biopsy

37. A 28-year-old woman with type 1 diabetes mellitus presents with Kussmaul respirations and fruity breath odor. Which of the following is the most likely diagnosis?

- A. Addison disease
- B. Hyperosmolar hyperglycemic nonketotic syndrome (HHNS)
- C. Hypoglycemia
- D. Hyperthyroidism
- E. Diabetic ketoacidosis (DKA)

38. A 22-year-old woman with type 1 diabetes mellitus presents with Kussmaul respirations and fruity breath odor. Her blood pH is 6.9. Which of the following is the most appropriate course of action?

- A. Admit to the hospital ward.
- B. Admit to the intensive care unit (ICU)
- C. Discharge home with instructions to follow up with her doctor.
- D. Administer intravenous fluids.
- E. Administer insulin.

39. A 31-year-old woman with type 1 diabetes mellitus presents with Kussmaul respirations and fruity breath odor. Her blood pH is 6.9. She is admitted to the hospital and started insulin therapy. Which of the following is the correct insulin regimen for this patient?

- A. 0.1 units per kilogram of short-acting regular insulin intravenously, followed by a continuous intravenous infusion of 0.1 units per kilogram per hour.
- B. 0.2 units per kilogram of short-acting regular insulin subcutaneously, followed by a continuous subcutaneous infusion of 0.2 units per kilogram per hour.
- C. 0.3 units per kilogram of short-acting regular insulin intramuscularly, followed by a continuous intramuscular infusion of 0.3 units per kilogram per hour.
- D. None of the above.

40. A 72-year-old man with type 2 diabetes mellitus presents with polyuria, polydipsia, and altered mental status. His blood glucose level is 1,200 mg/dL and his serum osmolality is 350 mOsm/kg. Which of the following is the most appropriate treatment for this patient?

- A. Administer 1-3 liters of 0.9% normal saline within the initial 2-3 hours.
- B. Administer 0.45% saline initially, followed by 5% dextrose in water.
- C. Administer potassium repletion.
- D. Administer insulin therapy.
- E. All of the above.

41. A 51-year-old woman with type 1 diabetes mellitus presents with confusion and slurred speech. Her blood glucose level is 35 mg/dL. Which of the following is the most likely explanation for the absence of autonomic symptoms in this patient?

- A. The patient has a history of hypoglycemia and has become desensitized to the autonomic symptoms.
- B. The patient is taking a medication that blocks the autonomic symptoms of hypoglycemia.
- C. The patient has a rare form of diabetes mellitus that does not cause autonomic symptoms.
- D. The patient has pure neuroglycopenia, which is a form of hypoglycemia that does not cause autonomic symptoms.
- E. None of the above.

42. A 36-year-old woman presents with recurrent episodes of diaphoresis, palpitations, tremors, and confusion. These episodes are often relieved by eating. Laboratory tests reveal a blood glucose level of 45 mg/dL during a symptomatic attack, and further testing shows inappropriately high insulin and C-peptide levels. Which of the following is the most likely diagnosis?

- A. Diabetes mellitus type 1
- B. Diabetes mellitus type 2
- C. Insulinoma
- D. Exogenous insulin administration
- E. Hypothyroidism

43. A 58-year-old woman presents with fatigue, constipation, and polyuria. Her serum calcium level is 12 mg/dL. Which of the following is the most likely cause of her hypercalcemia?

- A. Primary hyperparathyroidism
- B. Malignancy
- C. Vitamin D toxicity
- D. Medications
- E. Sarcoidosis

44. A 75-year-old man with a history of lung cancer presents with fatigue, constipation, and polyuria. His serum calcium level is 12 mg/dL. His parathyroid hormone (PTH) level is low. Which of the following is the most likely cause of his hypercalcemia?

- A. Primary hyperparathyroidism
- B. Malignancy
- C. Vitamin D toxicity
- D. Medications
- E. Sarcoidosis

45. A 52-year-old woman with a history of hypoparathyroidism presents with muscle cramps and tingling in her hands and feet. She has a positive Chvostek's sign and a positive Trousseau's sign. Her serum calcium level is 7 mg/dL. Which of the following is the most likely cause of her hypocalcemia?

- A. Medications
- B. Pseudohypoparathyroidism
- C. Vitamin D deficiency
- D. Primary hypoparathyroidism
- E. None of the above

46. A 59-year-old woman with a history of hypoparathyroidism presents with muscle cramps and tingling in her hands and feet. She has a positive Chvostek's sign and a positive Trousseau's sign. Her serum calcium level is 7 mg/dL. What is the most appropriate treatment for her hypocalcemia?

- A. Administer 1-2 g of intravenous calcium gluconate over a period of 10-20 minutes.
- B. Administer 10 ampoules of 10% calcium gluconate in 1 liter of D5W solution, infused at a rate of 30-100 mL per hour.
- C. Administer oral calcium supplements.
- D. Monitor her condition and wait for her calcium levels to improve on their own.
- E. None of the above.

47. A 62-year-old woman with a history of chronic kidney disease presents with muscle weakness and fatigue. Her serum phosphate level is 0.5 mg/dL. Which of the following is the most appropriate treatment for her hypophos-

phatemia?

- A. Administer 0.2 mmol/kg of elemental phosphorus over a period of 6 hours.
- B. Administer 0.4 mmol/kg of elemental phosphorus over a period of 6 hours.
- C. Administer 0.8 mmol/kg of elemental phosphorus over a period of 6 hours.
- D. Administer oral phosphate supplements.
- E. None of the above.

48. A 33-year-old woman with a history of alcoholism presents with muscle weakness, tremors, and confusion. Her serum magnesium level is 0.4 mg/dL. Which of the following is the most appropriate treatment for her hypomagnesemia?

- A. Administer oral magnesium supplements.
- B. Administer intravenous magnesium sulfate over a period of 1 hour.
- C. Administer intravenous magnesium sulfate over a period of 6 hours.
- D. Monitor her condition and wait for her magnesium levels to improve on their own.
- E. None of the above.

49. A 67-year-old woman with osteoporosis has been taking bisphosphonates for 10 years. She presents her doctor with a fracture of her femur. Which of the following is the most likely explanation for her fracture?

- A. Her fracture is due to the natural progression of her osteoporosis.
- B. Her fracture is due to a fall.
- C. Her fracture is due to a side effect of the bisphosphonates.
- D. Her fracture is due to a combination of her osteoporosis and the bisphosphonates.
- E. None of the above.

50. A 65-year-old woman presents to her doctor with a complaint of back pain. She has no other medical problems and takes no medications. Her family history is significant for her mother having a hip fracture at the age of 75. Which of the following is the most appropriate recommendation for bone mineral density (BMD) testing?

- A. BMD testing is not recommended.
- B. BMD testing should be performed as soon as possible.
- C. BMD testing should be performed in 1 year.
- D. BMD testing should be performed in 2 years.
- E. BMD testing should be performed in 3 years.

51. A 54-year-old man presents with severe headache, vision loss, and pituitary apoplexy. His blood pressure is 80/60 mmHg, heart rate is 120 beats per minute, and sodium level is 130 mEq/L. Which of the following is the most important next step?

- (A) Administer hydrocortisone 50 mg IV
- (B) Evaluate for adrenal insufficiency
- (C) Secure the airway and ventilate the patient
- (D) Administer intravenous fluids
- (E) None of the above

52.A patient undergoes a cosyntropin stimulation test to evaluate adrenal function. The cortisol levels are measured at baseline, 30 minutes, and 60 minutes after administration of cosyntropin. The results are as follows:

- Baseline: 0.5 g/dL
- 30 min: 15.3 g/dL
- 60 min: 20.5 g/dL

Which of the following interpretations is most accurate?

- A. The patient has primary adrenal pathology.
- B. The patient is experiencing acute central adrenal insufficiency.
- C. The patient has chronic secondary adrenal insufficiency.
- D. The patient has a normal stimulation test.
- E. The patient has chronic primary adrenal insufficiency.

53. A patient present with hypertension, hyperglycemia, abdominal adiposity, easy bruising, and edema. Which diagnostic test should be ordered to confirm the presence of Cushing syndrome and assess the etiology of hypercortisolism?

- A. Order a low-dose dexamethasone suppression test (DST).
- B. Perform a late-night salivary cortisol test.
- C. Collect a 24-hour urinary cortisol sample.
- D. Measure random or morning cortisol levels.
- E. Proceed with imaging studies to identify the source.

54. A 59-year-old man presents with enlargement of the hands and feet, soft tissue edema, changes in facial structure, and development of skin tags. He has no other significant medical history. Which of the following is the most appropriate next step in the diagnosis of acromegaly?

- (A) Checking growth hormone after an oral glucose load
- (B) Checking a random growth hormone level
- (C) Performing a glucagon stimulation test
- (D) Performing an insulin tolerance test
- (E) Measuring IGF-1 levels

55. A 23-year-old woman presents with amenorrhea and galactorrhea. She has a serum prolactin level of 100 ng/mL and a pituitary MRI shows a 1 cm macroprolactinoma. Which of the following is the most appropriate next step?

- (A) Initiate cabergoline 0.5 mg weekly
- (B) Prescribe an oral contraceptive pill
- (C) Refer for surgical resection of the pituitary tumor
- (D) Observe the patient closely without treatment
- (E) None of the above

56. A patient present with severe hypothyroidism and is suspected to have myxedema coma. What is the appropriate initial treatment for this patient?

- A. Start hydrocortisone 100 mg every 8 hours and 100 g T4 IV daily.
- B. Start levothyroxine 100 g IV daily.
- C. Start hydrocortisone 100 mg every 8 hours and 100 g T4 IV daily.
- D. Start hydrocortisone 200 mg every 8 hours and 100 g T4 IV daily.
- E. Start levothyroxine 200 g IV daily.

57. A patient present with symptoms of hyperthyroidism, including decreased TSH and elevated fT4. Which diagnostic test should be ordered as the initial evaluation?

- A. Order radioiodine uptake scan.
- B. Measure serum T3 and T4 levels.
- C. Perform thyroid ultrasound.
- D. Order thyroid-stimulating immunoglobulin (TSI) test.
- E. Refer for genetic testing for hereditary hyperthyroidism.

58. A 27-year-old woman with Graves' disease presents with tachycardia, fever, agitation, and tremor. Her laboratory results show elevated thyroid hormones and a suppressed thyroid-stimulating hormone. Her clinical presentation and laboratory findings are consistent with a diagnosis of thyroid storm. Which of the following medications is NOT recommended for the treatment of thyroid storm?

- (A) Beta-blocker
- (B) Thionamide
- (C) Selenium
- (D) Inorganic iodide
- (E) Corticosteroids

59. A 57-year-old man with no significant medical history presents with resistant hypertension. He is taking three antihypertensive medications, but his blood pressure remains uncontrolled. He has no family history of hyperten-

sion, and he does not have any symptoms suggestive of hypercortisolism or pheochromocytoma. What is the most appropriate next step in the evaluation of this patient's hypertension?

- (A) Order a 24-hour urine collection for cortisol and catecholamines.
- (B) Measure morning plasma renin and aldosterone.
- (C) Order a renal ultrasound.
- (D) Order a CT scan of the adrenal glands.
- (E) Refer the patient to a nephrologist.

60. A patient present with imaging findings of multiple adrenal adenomas and elevated aldosterone levels. What is the most appropriate next step in the management of this patient?

- A. Adrenal venous sampling
- B. Adrenal CT scan
- C. Radioiodine uptake scan
- D. Low-dose dexamethasone suppression test
- E. Start hydrocortisone 100 mg every 8 hours and 100 g T4 IV daily.

61. A 52-year-old man presents with an adrenal incidentaloma found on abdominal imaging. He has no significant medical history and is not taking any medications. Which of the following is the most appropriate next step?

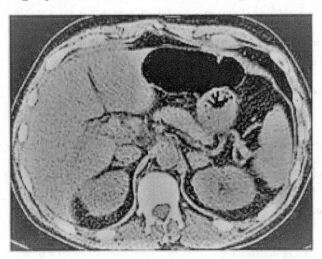

Figure 2.4: Aadrenal Incidentaloman

- (A) Abdominal MRI with gadolinium contrast
- (B) Twenty-four-hour urine collection for cortisol and catecholamines
- (C) Twenty-four-hour urine fractionated metanephrines
- (D) Aldosterone, renin, and overnight 1 mg dexamethasone suppression test (DST)
- (E) All of the above

62. A 62-year-old female patient is scheduled for surgical removal of a catecholamine-secreting tumor. Which of the following is the most appropriate preoperative step to avoid catastrophic -adrenergic stimulation during manipulation of the tumor?

- A. Initiate propranolol 40 mg twice daily
- B. Start metyrosine 500 mg thrice daily
- C. Administer phenoxybenzamine 20 mg twice daily
- D. Initiate prazosin 1 mg every 4 hours
- E. Administer dexamethasone 4 mg twice daily

63. A 22-year-old man with no significant medical history presents with a kidney stone. He has no history of fragility fractures. Laboratory results show hypercalcemia and elevated PTH levels. Which of the following is the most

appropriate next step in the evaluation of this patient's hypercalcemia?

- (A) Order a 24-hour urine collection for magnesium and phosphate.
- (B) Order a parathyroid gland ultrasound.
- (C) Check serum and 24-hour urine calcium and creatinine.
- (D) Order a dual-energy x-ray absorptiometry (DXA) scan.
- (E) Perform a parathyroidectomy.

64. A 46-year-old woman presents to the clinic with fatigue, weight loss, and an increasing craving for salt. She also reports having episodes of lightheadedness when standing up. On physical examination, she has hyperpigmentation of skin and mucous membranes. Blood pressure is 90/60 mm Hg, and it decreases to 80/55 mm Hg upon standing. Laboratory tests reveal hyponatremia and hyperkalemia. The clinical picture is suggestive of Addison disease. What is the appropriate next step in the management of this patient?

- A. Start hydrocortisone treatment immediately.
- B. Order 21-Hydroxylase antibodies
- C. Check baseline adrenocorticotropic hormone (ACTH) and perform cosyntropin stimulation test
- D. Order an abdominal CT scan
- E. Referral to a psychiatrist for evaluation of possible depression

65. A 67-year-old man with a history of thyroidectomy presents with nausea, vomiting, and confusion. He has also been experiencing weakness and diplopia. On physical exam, he is tachycardic and hypertensive. His serum calcium level is 13.5 mg/dL. Which of the following is the most likely diagnosis?

- (A) Hypercalcemic crisis
- (B) Hyperthyroidism
- (C) Hyperosmolar hyperglycemic state
- (D) Stroke
- (E) Hyponatremia

66. A 34-year-old black woman presents with a persistent cough, fatigue, and a recent weight loss. She denies chest pain, hemoptysis, or shortness of breath. Physical examination discloses bilateral hilar lymphadenopathy and erythema nodosum. Laboratory studies show a serum calcium level of 12.5 mg/dL. A chest X-ray reveals bilateral hilar lymphadenopathy. What is the most likely diagnosis?

- A. Primary hyperparathyroidism
- B. Secondary hyperparathyroidism
- C. Sarcoidosis
- D. Humoral hypercalcemia of malignancy
- E. Tuberculosis

67. A 72-year-old male with a history of cardiovascular disease is currently managing his type 2 diabetes mellitus (T2DM) with metformin and lifestyle modifications. However, his glycemic control requires further improvement. According to the American Diabetes Association (ADA) 2018 guidelines, which of the following is the most appropriate next step in management?

- A. Add daily aspirin therapy.
- B. Initiate insulin therapy
- C. Start liraglutide daily.
- D. Increase the dose of metformin.
- E. Prescribe a statin for lipid control.

68. A 57-year-old man with a history of type 2 diabetes mellitus presents with acute kidney injury and pneumonia. He is admitted to the hospital and started on intravenous antibiotics and fluids. His home antihyperglycemic medications are held on admission. On the third day of hospitalization, his blood glucose levels are consistently elevated, ranging from 200-300 mg/dL. Which of the following is the most appropriate next step in the management of his diabetes?

- (A) Start 25 U insulin glargine nightly with sliding scale aspart insulin.
- (B) Start 25 U insulin glargine nightly.
- (C) Start sliding scale aspart insulin only.

- (D) Increase his intravenous fluids.
- (E) Start oral antihyperglycemic medications.

69. A 53-year-old man presents with headache, confusion, and diaphoresis. His blood glucose level is 40 mg/dL. He has no history of diabetes mellitus and is not taking any medications. Which of the following laboratory findings is most suggestive of insulinoma?

- (A) Insulin = 20 pmol/L, proinsulin = 10 pmol/L, C-peptide = 0.5 ng/mL, beta-hydroxybutyrate >3.1 mmol/L
- (B) Insulin = 38 pmol/L, proinsulin = 25 pmol/L, C-peptide = 0.8 ng/mL, beta-hydroxybutyrate <2.7 mmol/L
- (C) Insulin = 60 pmol/L, proinsulin = 40 pmol/L, C-peptide = 1.2 ng/mL, beta-hydroxybutyrate <2.7 mmol/L
- (D) Insulin = 38 pmol/L, proinsulin = 25 pmol/L, C-peptide = 0.8 ng/mL, beta-hydroxybutyrate <2.7 mmol/L, oral hypoglycemia agent screen = negative
- (E) Insulin = 38 pmol/L, proinsulin = 25 pmol/L, C-peptide = 0.8 ng/mL, beta-hydroxybutyrate <2.7 mmol/L, oral hypoglycemia agent screen = positive

70. A 47-year-old woman with a history of type 1 diabetes presents to the emergency room with symptoms of polyuria, polydipsia, and fatigue. Her blood glucose level is found to be 600 mg/dL. She is started on intravenous (IV) insulin as part of the management for diabetic ketoacidosis (DKA). According to the American Diabetes Association (ADA) guidelines for DKA, when should the IV insulin be tapered and a multiple-dose subcutaneous insulin schedule be started?

- A. Serum anion gap <12 mEq/L and venous pH >7.30
- B. Blood glucose is <200 mg/dL and serum bicarbonate 15 mEq/L
- C. Serum anion gap <12 mEq/L and serum bicarbonate 15 mEq/L
- D. Blood glucose is <200 mg/dL and venous pH >7.30.
- E. Blood glucose is <200 mg/dL, serum anion gap < 12 mEq/L, and serum bicarbonate 15 mEq/L

71. A 59-year-old man with type 2 diabetes mellitus and chronic kidney disease is started on canagliflozin (Invokana). Which of the following is the most likely effect of canagliflozin on his kidney function?

- (A) It will increase his glomerular filtration rate (GFR).
- (B) It will decrease his GFR.
- (C) It will slow the decline in his GFR.
- (D) It will have no effect on his GFR.
- (E) It will increase his risk of end-stage renal disease.

72. A 42-year-old woman presents with complaints of nocturia and unexplained weight loss. Her Hemoglobin A1C level is at 11.5%. She has been recently started on metformin. Which of the following would be the most appropriate next step in managing her diabetes?

- A. Add a GLP-1 receptor agonist.
- B. Start long-acting insulin at 0.1 to 0.2 IU/kg/d with instructions to increase 2 U every 3 days until reaching fasting glucose target.
- C. Discontinue metformin and start prandial insulin.
- D. Add a DPP-4 inhibitor.
- E. Start short-acting insulin before meals.

73. A 58-year-old man with type 2 diabetes mellitus (T2DM) and heart failure presents with an HbA1c of 7.5%. He is currently taking metformin. Which of the following is the most appropriate next step in the management of his diabetes?

- (A) Continue metformin and add dapagliflozin.
- (B) Switch metformin to insulin.
- (C) Add a glucagon-like peptide-1 (GLP-1) receptor agonist.
- (D) Add a dipeptidyl peptidase-4 (DPP-4) inhibitor.
- (E) Start a sodium-glucose cotransporter 2 (SGLT2) inhibitor and a GLP-1 receptor agonist.

74. A 32-year-old woman presents with tingling in her hands and feet, muscle cramps, and tetany. She had a thyroidectomy 6 months ago. Which of the following laboratory tests is the most important to order first?

- (A) Calcium and albumin
- (B) Magnesium and phosphorus
- (C) Parathyroid hormone (PTH)
- (D) Vitamin D
- (E) Multiple sclerosis panel

75. A 27-year-old pregnant woman with a history of hypoparathyroidism presents for her routine prenatal care. Recent labs show her serum calcium level to be 8.4 mg/dL and her albumin level to be 2.0 g/dL. She is asymptomatic. What should be the next step in management?

- A. Increase her calcium supplementation.
- B. Start her on intravenous calcium.
- C. Check her parathyroid hormone levels.
- D. No change in treatment is needed.
- E. Refer her to a high-risk pregnancy specialist.

76. What is the recommended therapeutic approach for individuals with mild hypophosphatemia?

- A. Administer intravenous phosphate at initial doses ranging from 0.2 to 0.8 nmol/kg of elemental phosphorus, delivered over a period of 6 hours.
- B. Monitor serum calcium and phosphate levels at intervals of 6 to 12 hours.
- C. Reduce the dosage by 50% in cases of hypercalcemia.
- D. Correct hypocalcemia as the initial step in managing hypophosphatemia.
- E. Administer oral substances such as milk, carbonated beverages, or specific pharmaceutical preparations like Neutra-Phos or K-Phos, up to 2 g per day divided into multiple doses.

77. A 67-year-old woman with a history of breast cancer is receiving high-dose intravenous zoledronic acid as part of her treatment regimen. She presents with jaw pain and an oral examination reveals exposed bone in the mandible. What is the most likely diagnosis?

- A. Oral cancer
- B. Dental abscess
- C. Temporomandibular joint disorder
- D. Osteonecrosis of the jaw
- E. Trigeminal neuralgia

78. Which of the following is NOT a recommended subsequent therapy after teriparatide therapy?

- A) Bisphosphonate therapy
- (B) Denosumab therapy
- (C) Raloxifene therapy
- (D) Estrogen therapy
- (E) Calcitonin therapy

79. A 48-year-old man presents with bone pain and muscle weakness. Laboratory tests reveal chronic hypophosphatemia. Which of the following is the most likely diagnosis?

- A. Osteoporosis
- B. Osteomalacia
- C. Osteoarthritis
- D. Osteogenesis imperfecta
- E. Osteosarcoma

80. A 60-year-old woman presents with bone pain and muscle weakness. Laboratory tests reveal decreased levels of serum 25-hydroxyvitamin D, elevated levels of parathyroid hormone (PTH) and alkaline phosphatase, increased excretion of phosphates in urine, and decreased levels of serum phosphate. What is the most likely diagnosis?

- A. Vitamin D deficiency with secondary hyperparathyroidism
- B. Primary hyperparathyroidism
- C. Chronic kidney disease

- D. Hypoparathyroidism
- E. Vitamin D toxicity

81. In a woman with hirsutism, which of the following clinical features is MOST suggestive of an underlying ovarian or adrenal neoplasm?

- (A) Acne
- (B) Male-pattern balding
- (C) Deepening of the voice
- (D) Breast atrophy
- (E) Increased libido

82. Which of the following findings on the dexamethasone androgen-suppression test is MOST indicative of ovarian overproduction of androgens?

- (A) Free testosterone levels drop significantly.
- (B) Free testosterone levels do not drop significantly.
- (C) Dehydroepiandrosterone sulfate (DHEAS) levels drop significantly.
- (D) DHEAS levels do not drop significantly.
- (E) Adrenal androgens drop significantly.

83. A 44-year-old man presents with elevated levels of cholesterol and triglycerides in his blood. Genetic testing reveals he is a homozygous carrier of the apolipoprotein E2 (R158C) variant. Which of the following is the most likely diagnosis?

- A. Familial hypercholesterolemia
- B. Type I hyperlipoproteinemia
- C. Type II hyperlipoproteinemia
- D. Type III hyperlipoproteinemia
- E. Primary hypertriglyceridemia

84. A patient presents with a myocardial infarction. Blood samples are obtained for cholesterol testing within 8 hours of the event. Which of the following is the most accurate statement about the interpretation of the results?

- (A) LDL cholesterol levels will be artificially low, but HDL cholesterol levels will be accurate.
- (B) LDL cholesterol levels will be accurate, but HDL cholesterol levels will be artificially low.
- (C) Both LDL and HDL cholesterol levels will be artificially low.
- (D) Both LDL and HDL cholesterol levels will be accurate.
- (E) The interpretation of the cholesterol results is not possible without knowing the patient's pre-infarction cholesterol levels.

85. A 35-year-old woman presents with a total cholesterol level of 300 mg/dL. Her plasma triglyceride levels are normal and HDL cholesterol levels are slightly diminished. Genetic testing reveals a mutation in the gene encoding the Low-Density Lipoprotein (LDL) receptor. Which of the following is the most likely diagnosis?

- A. Familial Hypercholesterolemia
- B. Type I hyperlipoproteinemia
- C. Type II hyperlipoproteinemia
- D. Type III hyperlipoproteinemia
- E. Primary hypertriglyceridemia

86. A 41-year-old man presents with high levels of cholesterol in his blood. Genetic testing reveals a mutation in the gene encoding apolipoprotein B-100. Which of the following is the most likely diagnosis?

- A. Familial Hypercholesterolemia
- B. Type I hyperlipoproteinemia
- C. Type II hyperlipoproteinemia
- D. Familial Defective Apo B-100
- E. Primary hypertriglyceridemia

87. A patient presents with isolated hypertriglyceridemia. Which of the following cutaneous findings is most likely

to be present?

- (A) Tendon xanthomas
- (B) Xanthelasmas
- (C) Eruptive xanthomas
- (D) Lipemia retinalis
- (E) None of the above

88. A patient presents with recurrent pancreatitis and hepatosplenomegaly. They are found to have chylomicronemia. Which of the following is the most likely diagnosis?

- (A) Lipoprotein lipase deficiency
- (B) Familial hypercholesterolemia
- (C) Type 1 diabetes mellitus
- (D) Pancreatitis due to gallstones
- (E) None of the above

89. A 52-year-old man presents with high levels of triglycerides in his blood despite having made dietary changes. Which of the following treatments could be considered for this patient?

- A. Administration of fibric acid derivatives
- B. Administration of fat-soluble vitamin supplements
- C. Administration of insulin
- D. Referral to a nephrologist
- E. Administration of aspirin

90. Which of the following statements about PCSK9 inhibitors is most accurate?

- (A) PCSK9 inhibitors are a class of drugs that lower LDL cholesterol levels.
- (B) PCSK9 inhibitors are administered by injection every 2 weeks or every 4 weeks.
- (C) PCSK9 inhibitors are associated with a high risk of side effects, such as injection site reactions and flu-like symptoms.
- (D) PCSK9 inhibitors are approved for the treatment of all patients with high cholesterol.
- (E) PCSK9 inhibitors are a new class of drugs that have not yet been adequately studied.

91. A 32-year-old man with a family history of cardiovascular disease presents with hypertension and obesity. His LDL-C level is 200 mg/dL. According to the 2018 Guideline on the Management of Blood Cholesterol, which of the following is the most appropriate next step in management?

- A. Initiate high-intensity statin therapy
- B. Initiate moderate-intensity statin therapy
- C. Initiate lifestyle modifications only
- D. Initiate antihypertensive therapy only
- E. No intervention is needed at this time

92. A 43-year-old man presents with increased concentrations of serum iron, percentage of transferrin saturation, and serum ferritin. His fasting serum transferrin saturation level is 55%. Which of the following is the most appropriate next step in management?

- A. Initiate iron supplementation
- B. Perform genetic testing for hemochromatosis
- C. Initiate phlebotomy
- D. Perform a liver biopsy
- E. No intervention is needed at this time

93. Which of the following is NOT a standard therapeutic approach for hemochromatosis?

- (A) Phlebotomy
- (B) Chelating agents
- (C) Supportive measures to address organ impairments
- (D) Liver transplantation

- (E) Iron supplementation

94. Which of the following is the most important laboratory test for establishing a definitive diagnosis of porphyria?

- (A) Urine porphyrins
- (B) Fecal porphyrins
- (C) Plasma porphyrins
- (D) Red blood cell porphyrins
- (E) Enzyme assays

95. A 53-year-old man presents with fatigue and joint pain. His blood tests show increased serum iron, transferrin saturation, and ferritin. What is the best test to establish a clinical diagnosis of hemochromatosis?

- A. Liver biopsy
- B. HFE gene mutation analysis
- C. Serum ferritin test
- D. Transferrin saturation test
- E. Ultrasound of the liver

96. A 35-year-old woman presents with severe abdominal pain, nausea, and restlessness. She has a history of Acute Intermittent Porphyria. What is the most appropriate therapeutic approach for managing her condition during this episode?

- A. Administration of heme arginate, heme albumin, or hematin
- B. Administration of narcotic analgesics
- C. Administration of phenothiazines
- D. Administration of intravenous glucose
- E. Administration of parenteral nutrition

97. A patient presents with painful, blistering skin lesions on their face, forehead, and forearms. The lesions worsen after sun exposure. The patient's face is also hyperpigmented and their skin is fragile. Which of the following is the most likely diagnosis?

- (A) Porphyria cutanea tarda (PCT)
- (B) Acute intermittent porphyria (AIP)
- (C) Variegate porphyria (VP)
- (D) Congenital erythropoietic porphyria (CEP)
- (E) Hepatoerythropoietic porphyria (HEP)

98. A patient presents with Kayser-Fleischer rings, a liver biopsy shows increased copper levels, and serum ceruloplasmin levels are low. Which of the following is the most likely diagnosis?

- (A) Porphyria cutanea tarda
- (B) Acute intermittent porphyria
- (C) Wilson's disease
- (D) Variegate porphyria
- (E) Congenital erythropoietic porphyria

99. A 34-year-old woman presents with a recent diagnosis of Wilson's Disease and coexisting hepatitis. She does not have any signs of decompensation. What is the recommended therapeutic approach for her condition?

- A. Administration of oral Zinc acetate
- B. Administration of intravenous Zinc acetate
- C. Administration of oral Copper acetate
- D. Liver transplantation
- E. No intervention is needed at this time

100. A 40-year-old man with Wilson's Disease presents with signs of severe hepatic decompensation. What is the most appropriate therapeutic approach for managing his condition?

- A. Administration of oral trientine and zinc supplementation
- B. Administration of oral tetrathiomolybdate

- C. Liver transplantation
- D. Administration of oral penicillamine
- E. No intervention is needed at this time

2.1   ANSWERS

1. The answer is (C), both high-dose glucocorticoids and surgical decompression.

The approach to managing pituitary apoplexy is contingent upon the severity of the patient's symptoms and the existence of visual or neurological deficits. In situations where there is no apparent visual impairment or loss of consciousness, it may be suitable to consider conservative management utilizing high-dose glucocorticoids. However, it is imperative to contemplate surgical decompression as a viable treatment alternative for patients exhibiting notable visual or neurological symptoms. The reason why both high-dose glucocorticoids and surgical decompression are often used to treat pituitary apoplexy is because they can help to improve the patient's symptoms and prevent further complications. High-dose glucocorticoids can help to reduce inflammation and swelling around the pituitary gland, while surgical decompression can help to relieve pressure on the optic nerves and other vital structures. In the case of the patient in the question, she is experiencing both visual impairment and neurological symptoms. Therefore, it is likely that she would benefit from both high-dose glucocorticoids and surgical decompression. The order in which these treatments are given may vary depending on the patient's individual circumstances.

2. The answer is (B), estrogen replacement therapy.

In patients with microprolactinoma who do not desire fertility, estrogen replacement therapy can be a viable alternative to dopamine agonists. Estrogen replacement therapy can help to reduce prolactin levels and shrink the tumor, without the risk of affecting fertility. However, it is important to exercise caution when using estrogen replacement therapy in patients with microprolactinoma. Estrogen can stimulate the growth of some tumors, so it is important to closely monitor the size of the tumor during treatment. The other options listed in the question are not as effective in treating microprolactinoma in patients who do not desire fertility. Dopamine agonists are the first-line treatment for microprolactinoma, but they can cause side effects such as nausea, vomiting, and dizziness. Surgery is also an option for treating microprolactinoma, but it is usually only recommended for patients who have large tumors or who are not responding to other treatments.

3. The answer is (A), hyperprolactinemia.

Hyperprolactinemia is a condition in which the level of prolactin in the blood is abnormally high. Prolactin is a hormone that is produced by the pituitary gland. In women, prolactin is responsible for stimulating milk production after childbirth. However, high levels of prolactin can also cause amenorrhea, galactorrhea, and infertility. The other options listed in the question are also possible causes of amenorrhea, galactorrhea, and infertility. However, they are less likely to be the cause in a patient who is also experiencing hyperprolactinemia. Therefore, the most likely cause of the patient's symptoms is hyperprolactinemia. This can be confirmed by measuring the level of prolactin in her blood. If the level is high, then she will need to be treated to lower her prolactin levels. This can be done with medication or surgery.

4. The answer is (A), 0.5 mg per week.

The recommended initial dosage of cabergoline for the treatment of macroprolactinomas is 0.5 mg per week. This dose can be increased every 2 weeks until the desired response is achieved. The typical dosage range for cabergoline is 0.5-1 mg administered twice weekly. The other options listed in the question are not the recommended initial dosages for cabergoline. Bromocriptine is a different dopamine agonist that is also used to treat macroprolactinomas. The initial dosage of bromocriptine is 0.625-1.25 mg taken at bedtime. The usual dosage of bromocriptine is 2.5 mg administered orally three times daily.

5. The answer is (D), all of the above.

The confirmation of acromegaly diagnosis involves the demonstration of the inability to suppress GH levels to less than 0.4 g/L within 1-2 hours after administering a 75-gram oral glucose load. This is done with an OGTT. Magnetic resonance imaging (MRI) of the pituitary gland typically detects the presence of a macroadenoma, which is a large tumor that is often associated with acromegaly. The other options listed in the question are also useful in diagnosing acromegaly. Serum GH level can be used to screen for the condition, but it is not always diagnostic. OGTT is the most sensitive test for diagnosing acromegaly. MRI can be used to visualize the pituitary gland and look for a tumor.

Therefore, the most appropriate tests to confirm the diagnosis of acromegaly are OGTT and MRI. These tests can be used together to rule out other conditions that can cause similar symptoms.

6. The answer is (A), growth hormone (GH).

In pituitary hormone failure resulting from compression, destruction, or radiation therapy, GH is typically affected first, followed by FSH, LH, TSH, and ACTH. This is because GH is produced by the anterior pituitary gland, which is the most sensitive to damage. The other options listed in the question are also possible pituitary hormones that could be deficient in this patient. However, they are less likely to be deficient in the early stages of pituitary hormone failure.

7. The answer is (D), all of the above. The preferred therapeutic approach for Pituitary DI is desmopressin (DDAVP), which can be delivered through subcutaneous injection, nasal spray, or oral administration. The recommended dosage for subcutaneous injection ranges from 1 to 2 g, to be administered once or twice daily. For nasal spray, the recommended dosage is between 10 and 20 g, to be administered two or three times daily. Lastly, for oral administration, the recommended dosage ranges from 100 to 400 g, to be taken two or three times daily. Patients are additionally recommended to consume fluids in response to their thirst.

8. Answer: A The answer is (A), fluid deprivation test. The diagnosis of diabetes insipidus (DI) involves the implementation of a fluid deprivation test, typically initiated in the morning under close supervision to mitigate the risk of dehydration. Hourly measurements should be taken for body weight, plasma osmolality, serum sodium, urine volume, and urine osmolality. The cessation of the test is warranted when there is a reduction in body weight of 5% or an elevation in plasma osmolality/sodium levels beyond the upper threshold of the normal range. In cases where serum hyperosmolality is present and the urine osmolality is less than 300 mosmol/kg, it is recommended to administer desmopressin at a subcutaneous dose of 0.03 g/kg. Following the administration of desmopressin, it is advisable to reevaluate the urine osmolality within a period of 1-2 hours. A rise exceeding 50% signifies the presence of severe pituitary diabetes insipidus (DI), whereas a lesser or nonexistent reaction implies the occurrence of nephrogenic DI. The other options listed in the question are also important diagnostic tests for DI. However, they are not as specific as the fluid deprivation test.

9. The answer is (A), oral tolvaptan.

The optimal strategy for managing chronic SIADH involves the administration of oral tolvaptan, a selective V2 antagonist that enhances the excretion of water in urine by inhibiting the antidiuretic effect of AVP. Demeclocycline is known to elicit a reversible manifestation of nephrogenic diabetes insipidus (DI), with its effects becoming apparent within a period of 7-14 days. Fludrocortisone is a mineralocorticoid that can be used to increase the excretion of sodium in urine. Therefore, the suggested therapeutic approach for managing chronic SIADH is oral tolvaptan. This is the most effective treatment for SIADH, and it is well-tolerated by most patients. Here is an explanation of the different therapeutic approaches for SIADH: Oral tolvaptan: Tolvaptan is a selective V2 antagonist that is used to treat SIADH. It works by blocking the effects of vasopressin, which is a hormone that causes the kidneys to retain water. Demeclocycline: Demeclocycline is an antibiotic that can be used to treat SIADH. It works by causing the kidneys to excrete more water. Fludrocortisone: Fludrocortisone is a mineralocorticoid that is used to treat SIADH. It works by sodium reabsorption in the kidneys. This action helps to correct the imbalance of fluids and electrolytes in the body, thus alleviating the symptoms associated with SIADH. By increasing sodium levels in the blood, fludrocortisone assists in restoring the body's normal fluid balance and reducing the signs and symptoms of SIADH.

10. The answer is (D), elevated levels of carrier proteins.

Total T4 and T3 concentrations are elevated in this condition because the levels of carrier proteins, such as thyroxine-binding globulin (TBG), are increased. However, the free levels of T4 and T3 are normal because the increased levels of carrier proteins are able to bind to more T4 and T3, without affecting the amount of free T4 and T3 that is available to the tissues. Graves' disease and Hashimoto's thyroiditis are both conditions that can cause hyperthyroidism, which is characterized by elevated levels of free T4 and T3. Subclinical hyperthyroidism is a condition in which the levels of free T4 and T3 are slightly elevated, but not enough to cause symptoms. Therefore, the most likely explanation for the patient's elevated total T4 and T3 concentrations, but normal free levels, is that she has elevated levels of carrier proteins. Here is an explanation of the different carrier proteins for thyroid hormones: Thyroxine-binding globulin (TBG): TBG is the most abundant thyroid hormone carrier protein. It binds to T4 and T3 with high affinity. Transthyretin (TTR): TTR is a less abundant thyroid hormone carrier protein. It binds to T4 and T3 with lower affinity than TBG. Albumin: Albumin is a very abundant protein in the blood. It binds to T4 and T3 with very low affinity. The amount of free T4 and T3 that is available to the tissues is determined by the amount of T4 and T3 that is bound to the carrier proteins, as well as the affinity of the carrier proteins for T4 and T3. If the levels of carrier proteins are increased, then the amount of T4 and T3 that is bound to the carrier proteins will increase, even if the levels of free T4 and T3 remain the same. increasing the excretion of sodium in urine.

11. The answer is (B), Hashimoto's thyroiditis.

Hashimoto's thyroiditis is an autoimmune disease that causes the thyroid gland to become inflamed and damaged. This leads to a decrease in the production of thyroid hormones, which can cause symptoms such as fatigue, weight gain, and cold intolerance. Graves' disease is another autoimmune disease that can cause hyperthyroidism, which is characterized by high levels of thyroid hormones. Subclinical hypothyroidism is a condition in which the levels of thyroid hormones are slightly low, but not enough to cause symptoms. Thyroid cancer is a rare condition that can also cause hypothyroidism. Therefore, the most likely diagnosis for this patient is Hashimoto's thyroiditis. Autoimmune hypothyroidism: Autoimmune hypothyroidism is a condition in which the immune system attacks the thyroid gland. This causes the thyroid gland to become inflamed and damaged, which leads to a decrease in the production of thyroid hormones. Hashimoto's thyroiditis: Hashimoto's thyroiditis is the most common cause of autoimmune hypothyroidism. It is characterized by the presence of antibodies that attack the thyroid gland. Atrophic thyroiditis: Atrophic thyroiditis is a rare form of autoimmune hypothyroidism. It is characterized by the complete destruction of the thyroid gland.

12. The answer is (A), elevated TSH levels.

TSH is a hormone that is produced by the pituitary gland. It stimulates the thyroid gland to produce thyroid hormones. In primary hypothyroidism, the thyroid gland is not producing enough thyroid hormones, which leads to an increase in TSH levels. Free T4 and free T3 are the active forms of thyroid hormones. They are not bound to any proteins in the blood. Low levels of free T4 and free T3 are also indicative of primary hypothyroidism. However, TSH levels are a more sensitive indicator of primary hypothyroidism than free T4 and free T3 levels. Therefore, the most reliable indicator of primary hypothyroidism is elevated TSH levels. TSH: TSH is a hormone that is produced by the pituitary gland. It stimulates the thyroid gland to produce thyroid hormones. In primary hypothyroidism, the thyroid gland is not producing enough thyroid hormones, which leads to an increase in TSH levels. Free T4: Free T4 is the active form of thyroid hormone. It is not bound to any proteins in the blood. Low levels of free T4 are indicative of primary hypothyroidism. Free T3: Free T3 is another active form of thyroid hormone. It is not bound to any proteins in the blood. Low levels of free T3 are also indicative of primary hypothyroidism.

13. The answer is (D), all of the above.

Myxedema coma is a life-threatening condition that requires urgent treatment. The recommended approach for initiating therapy involves the administration of levothyroxine, hydrocortisone, ventilatory support, and addressing any precipitating factors. Levothyroxine is a synthetic thyroid hormone that replaces the thyroid hor-mone that is not being produced by the thyroid gland. Hydrocortisone is a steroid hormone that helps to stabilize the patient's cardiovascular system and prevent adrenal insufficiency. Ventilatory support may be necessary to help the patient breathe. Addressing any precipitating factors, such as infection or medication noncompliance, is also important.

14. The answer is (C), both infiltrative ophthalmopathy and dermopathy.

Graves' disease is an autoimmune disease that causes the production of excessive thyroid hormones. In addition to the classic symptoms of hyperthyroidism, Graves' disease can also cause a number of extrathyroidal manifestations, including infiltrative ophthalmopathy and dermopathy. Infiltrative ophthalmopathy: Infiltrative ophthalmopathy is a condition that is characterized by inflammation and swelling of the eye tissues. This can lead to proptosis, periorbital swelling, and ophthalmoplegia. Dermopathy: Dermopathy is a condition that is characterized by the deposition of abnormal tissue in the skin. This can lead to the formation of pretibial myxedema, which is a thickened, pitting rash that typically occurs on the shins. The treatment for the extrathyroidal manifestations of Graves' disease is typically directed at the underlying autoimmune process. This may involve the use of anti-thyroid medications, steroids, or radiation therapy.

15. The answer is (A), thyrotoxic crisis.

Thyrotoxic crisis is a life-threatening condition that is characterized by a sudden and severe exacerbation of the symptoms of hyperthyroidism. The symptoms of thyrotoxic crisis can be very varied, but they typically include fever, delirium, seizures, arrhythmias, coma, vomiting, diarrhea, and jaundice. The most common cause of thyrotoxic crisis is an infection. Other causes include surgery, trauma, and the use of certain medications. The treatment for thyro-toxic crisis is urgent and involves the use of anti-thyroid medications, steroids, and supportive care. Thyrotoxic crisis: Thyrotoxic crisis is a life-threatening condition that is characterized by a sudden and severe exacerbation of the symptoms of hyperthyroidism. The symptoms of thyrotoxic crisis can be very varied, but they typically include fever, delirium, seizures, arrhythmias, coma, vomiting, diarrhea, and jaundice. Causes: The most common cause of thyrotoxic crisis is an infection. Other causes include surgery, trauma, and the use of certain medications. Treatment: The treatment for thyrotoxic crisis is urgent and in-volves the use of anti-thyroid medications, steroids, and supportive care.

16. The answer is (D), all of the above.

Antithyroid medications are a common treatment for Graves' disease, but they can have some side effects. The most common side effects are hepatitis, a syndrome resembling SLE, and agranulocytosis. Hepatitis: Hepatitis is an inflammation of the liver. It can be caused by a number of different factors, including viruses, bacteria, and drugs. Antithyroid medications can cause hepatitis in a small number of people. Systemic lupus erythematosus (SLE): SLE is an autoimmune disease that can affect many different organs in the body. It is characterized by inflammation and the production of autoantibodies. Antithyroid medications can cause a syndrome that resembles SLE in a small number of people. Agranulocytosis: Agranulocytosis is a condition in which the body's production of white blood cells is severely decreased. This can lead to an increased risk of infection. Antithyroid medications can cause agranulocytosis in a very small number of people. 17. The answer is (B), no. Radioactive iodine is not recommended during pregnancy due to contraindications. Radioactive io-dine can cross the placenta and cause fetal hypothyroidism. This can lead to developmental delays and other problems. If a pregnant woman is diagnosed with thyrotoxicosis, the treatment of choice is to monitor her symptoms and hormone levels. If the symptoms are severe, the doctor may prescribe a medication called propylthiouracil (PTU). PTU is a safe medication that can be used during pregnancy to treat thyrotoxicosis. If the woman's thyrotoxicosis is not controlled with PTU, consider other treatments, such as surgery. However, surgery is not usually recommended during pregnancy.

18. Answer: D. Sick euthyroid syndrome.

Sick euthyroid syndrome is a condition in which the thyroid gland does not produce enough thyroid hormone, but the patient does not have hypothyroidism. This condition is typically seen in critically ill patients. Sick euthyroid syndrome is caused by a number of factors, including inflammation, stress, and medications. The inflammation and stress can suppress the production of thyroid hormone by the thyroid gland. The medications can also interfere with the production or metabolism of thyroid hormone. The treatment for sick euthyroid syndrome typically involves the supportive care of the underlying illness. There is no need to administer thyroid hormone unless the patient develops hypothyroidism.

19. Answer: E.

Type 1 AIT is an autoimmune condition that causes the destruction of the thyroid gland. This can lead to hypo-thyroidism, which is a condition in which the thyroid gland does not produce enough thyroid hormone. The treatment for Type 1 AIT typically involves the administration of antithyroid medications. These medications work to suppress the production of thyroid hormone by the thyroid gland. The most commonly used antithyroid medications are methimazole and propylthiouracil.

20. Answer: A

Substernal goiter is a goiter that grows in the lower part of the neck, below the sternum. It can cause a number of symptoms, including dysphagia, tracheal compression, and facial plethora. Dysphagia is difficulty swallowing. It can be caused by a number of things, including a substernal goiter. When a substernal goiter grows large enough, it can compress the esophagus, making it difficult to swallow. Tracheal compression is narrowing of the trachea. It can also be caused by a substernal goiter. When a substernal goiter compresses the trachea, it can make it difficult to breathe. Facial plethora is redness of the face. It can also be caused by a substernal goiter. When a substernal goiter compresses the superior vena cava, it can cause blood to back up into the face, making it appear red.

21. Answer: A

The appropriate timing for performing ultrasound-guided fine-needle aspiration (FNA) on a nontoxic nodule that is 1.5 cm in size, according to the American Thyroid Association (ATA), would be A. Immediately. The American Thyroid Association (ATA) recommends that FNA be performed on nontoxic nodules that are larger than 1 cm in size. If the nodule is smaller than 1 cm, then it can be monitored with ultrasound every 6 to 12 months. The ATA recommends that FNA be performed on nontoxic nodules that are larger than 1 cm in size because these nodules have a higher risk of being cancerous. If the nodule is found to be benign, then it can be monitored with ultrasound every 12 months. However, if the nodule is found to be cancerous, then it can be treated with surgery or radioactive iodine therapy. The subsequent course of action for a confirmed benign aspirate: If the aspirate is determined to be non-threatening, it is sufficient to conduct yearly monitoring through palpation, thyroid ultrasonography, and thyrotropin measurement. This is because the risk of malignancy in a benign nodule is very low.

22. Correct answer: C

Papillary thyroid cancer is the most prevalent form of thyroid cancer, accounting for approximately 70-90% of diagnosed cases. It is a slow-growing cancer that typically spreads to lymph nodes in the neck. Follicular thyroid cancer is the second most common type of thyroid cancer, accounting for about 10-15% of cases. Medullary thyroid cancer is a rare type of thyroid cancer that accounts for about 5% of cases. Anaplastic thyroid cancer is the most aggressive type of thyroid cancer and accounts for about 1% of cases. Hurthle cell thyroid cancer is a rare type of thyroid cancer that is intermediate in aggressiveness between papillary and follicular thyroid cancer.

23. Correct answer: D

Low plasma ACTH levels are indicative of the presence of an adrenal adenoma, bilateral nodular hyperplasia, or carcinoma. These conditions all lead to increased cortisol production by the adrenal glands, which can cause the symptoms of fatigue, weight loss, and hyperpigmentation. Addison disease is a condition in which the adrenal glands do not produce enough cortisol. This can cause symptoms such as fatigue, weight loss, and hypotension. However, in Addison disease, plasma ACTH levels are typically high, not low. Cushing syndrome is a condition in which there is too much cortisol in the blood. This can be caused by a number of factors, including an adrenal tumor, an overactive pituitary gland, or long-term use of corticosteroid medications. In Cushing syndrome, plasma ACTH levels are typically high, not low. Ectopic ACTH syndrome is a rare condition in which a tumor in another part of the body produces ACTH. This can lead to increased cortisol production and the symptoms of Cushing syndrome. However, in ectopic ACTH syndrome, plasma ACTH levels are typically much higher than in adrenal adenoma, bilateral nodular hyperplasia, or carcinoma.

24. Correct answer: D

Inferior petrosal sinus sampling (IPSS) is the most accurate test for differentiating between a pituitary and peripheral origin of ACTH. This test involves measuring ACTH levels in the blood before and after administration of a corticotropin-releasing hormone (CRH) injection. If ACTH levels rise significantly after CRH administration, this suggests that the ACTH is coming from the pituitary gland. If ACTH levels do not rise significantly after CRH administration, this suggests that the ACTH is coming from a peripheral source. The other tests listed in the answer choices can also be helpful in diagnosing Cushing syndrome, but they are not as accurate as IPSS. For example, the cortisol level and 24-hour urinary free cortisol level can be elevated in both pituitary and peripheral ACTH-dependent Cushing syndrome. The low-dose dexamethasone suppression test can help to distinguish between pituitary and peripheral ACTH-dependent Cushing syndrome, but it is not as accurate as IPSS. Pituitary magnetic resonance imaging can be used to visualize the pituitary gland and look for a tumor, but it cannot differentiate between a pituitary tumor that is producing ACTH and a pituitary tumor that is not producing ACTH.

25. Correct answer: A

Ketoconazole, metyrapone, and mitotane are all medications that can be used to treat hypercortisolism in situations where surgical removal of the ACTH source is not feasible. Ketoconazole works by blocking the production of cortisol in the adrenal glands. Metyrapone works by inhibiting the conversion of 11-deoxycortisol to cortisol. Mitotane works by destroying the adrenal glands. Hydrocortisone and prednisone are corticosteroids that can also be used to treat hypercortisolism, but they are not as effective as ketoconazole, metyrapone, or mitotane. This is because corticosteroids work by suppressing the production of ACTH, which can lead to rebound hypercortisolism when the medication is stopped.

26. Correct answer: C

The aldosterone-to-renin ratio (ARR) is the most sensitive test for diagnosing primary hyperaldosteronism. This is because the ARR is high in primary hyperaldosteronism, but it is usually normal in other causes of hypertension. The aldosterone level and renin level can also be helpful in diagnosing primary hyperaldosteronism, but they are not as sensitive as the ARR. CT scan and MRI of the adrenal glands can be used to visualize the adrenal glands and look for an aldosterone-producing adenoma, but they are not necessary for diagnosis.

27. Correct answer: E

Surgery is the most appropriate treatment option for a patient with primary hyperaldosteronism who has an aldosterone-producing adenoma. This is because surgery can cure the condition by removing the adenoma. Sodium-restricted diet, spironolactone, eplerenone, and amiloride are all medications that can be used to treat primary hyperaldosteronism, but they are not as effective as surgery. These medications can help to control the symptoms of primary hyperaldosteronism, but they do not cure the condition. Therefore, the most likely answer is E, surgery. Surgery: Surgery is the most effective treatment for primary hyperaldosteronism. The goal of surgery is to remove the aldosterone-producing adenoma. This can be done laparoscopically or through an open incision. Medications: Medications can be used to control the symptoms of primary hyperaldosteronism, but they do not cure the condition. The most commonly used medications for primary hyperaldosteronism are spironolactone, eplerenone, and amiloride. These medications work by blocking the effects of aldosterone. Lifestyle changes: Lifestyle changes can also help to control the symptoms of primary hyperaldosteronism. These changes include following a sodium-restricted diet and exercising.

28. Correct answer: D

The ACTH stimulation test is the most effective screening test for Addison's disease. This test involves measuring cortisol levels in the blood before and after administration of a 250 mcg ACTH (cosyntropin) injection. If cortisol levels do not rise significantly after ACTH administration, this suggests that the patient has Addison's disease. The other tests listed in the answer choices can also be helpful in diagnosing Addison's disease, but they are not as accurate as the ACTH stimulation test. For example, the cortisol level and 24-hour urinary free cortisol level can be elevated in both Addison's disease and other conditions, such as Cushing syndrome. The low-dose dexamethasone suppression test can help to distinguish between Addison's disease and Cushing syndrome, but it is not as accurate as the ACTH stimulation test. Pituitary magnetic resonance imaging can be used to visualize the pituitary gland and look for a tumor, but it cannot diagnose Addison's disease.

29. Correct answer: B

The primary treatment approach for glucocorticoid replacement in individuals with Addison's disease is hydrocortisone. Hydrocortisone is a synthetic form of cortisol, which is the hormone that is normally produced by the adrenal glands. Hydrocortisone is typically administered at a dosage of 15-25 mg per day, which is divided into two-thirds in the morning and one-third in the afternoon. This helps to mimic the natural pattern of cortisol production by the adrenal glands. Prednisone and dexamethasone are also glucocorticoids, but they are not as commonly used for replacement therapy in Addison's disease. This is because they have a longer half-life than hydrocortisone, which means that they can cause more side effects. Therefore, the most likely answer is B, hydrocortisone 25 mg twice daily.

30. Correct answer: A

The initial step in assessing an adrenal incidentaloma is to determine its functional status. This is done by measuring plasma free metanephrines or urinary metanephrines. Pheochromocytoma is a rare tumor that can cause hypertension and other cardiovascular symptoms. It accounts for less than 10% of adrenal incidentalomas. Plasma free metanephrines and urinary metanephrines are the most sensitive tests for pheochromocytoma. If the plasma free metanephrines or urinary metanephrines are elevated, this suggests that the patient has pheochromocytoma. In this case, further testing, such as a CT-guided biopsy or a 24-hour urine cortisol test, would be necessary to confirm the diagnosis. If the plasma free metanephrines or urinary metanephrines are not elevated, this suggests that the patient does not have pheochromocytoma. In this case, the adrenal incidentaloma can be monitored with serial imaging studies.

31. Correct answer: A

MEN 1 is a genetic syndrome that increases the risk of developing tumors in various endocrine organs, including the parathyroid glands. Primary hyperparathyroidism is a condition in which the parathyroid glands produce too much parathyroid hormone (PTH). PTH is a hormone that regulates calcium levels in the blood. When PTH levels are too high, it can cause hypercalcemia. Cushing syndrome is a condition in which there is too much cortisol in the blood. Cortisol is a hormone that is produced by the adrenal glands. Pheochromocytoma is a tumor of the adrenal glands that produces too much adrenaline. Adrenal adenoma and adrenal carcinoma are tumors of the adrenal glands that can cause hypercalcemia, but they are less common than primary hyperparathyroidism. Signs and symptoms: The signs and symptoms of MEN 1 vary depending on the tumors that are present. However, some common signs and symptoms include hyperparathyroidism, pituitary tumors, and pancreatic neuroendocrine tumors. Diagnosis: MEN 1 is diagnosed based on a family history of the condition and the presence of characteristic tumors. Genetic testing can also be used to diagnose MEN 1. Treatment: The treatment for MEN 1 depends on the tumors that are present. However, surgery is often the preferred treatment for parathyroid tumors, pituitary tumors, and pancreatic neuroendocrine tumors.

32. Correct answer: B

The most likely diagnosis in this case is diabetes mellitus. Diabetes mellitus is a condition in which the body cannot properly use or store glucose. This can lead to a number of symptoms, including polyuria, polydipsia, and fatigue. The diagnostic criteria for diabetes mellitus include the presence of symptoms associated with diabetes in addition to meeting specific thresholds for various blood glucose measurements. These thresholds include a random blood glucose concentration of 11.1 mmol/L (200 mg/dL), a fasting plasma glucose level of 7.0 mmol/L (126 mg/dL), a hemoglobin A1c level of 6.5%, or a 2-hour plasma glucose level of 11.1 mmol/L (200 mg/dL) during an oral glucose tolerance test. The other answer choices are less likely in this case. Hyperthyroidism can cause symptoms similar to diabetes mellitus, but it is less common. Hypothyroidism can also cause symptoms similar to diabetes mellitus, but it is also less common. Cushing syndrome and Addison disease are both rare conditions that can cause symptoms similar to diabetes mellitus, but they are even less common than hyperthyroidism and hypothyroidism.

33. Correct answer: A

The most likely diagnosis in this case is Charcot foot. Charcot foot is a condition that occurs in people with diabetes mellitus and is characterized by destruction of the bones and joints in the foot. This can lead to deformity, ulceration, and even amputation. The other answer choices are less likely in this case. Diabetic neuropathy can cause pain in the feet, but it is not usually associated with ulceration. Diabetic retinopathy is a condition that affects the eyes and can lead to blindness. Diabetic nephropathy is a condition that affects the kidneys and can lead to kidney failure. Peripheral vascular disease is a condition that affects the blood vessels in the legs and can lead to pain, numbness, and even gangrene. Here is some additional information about Charcot foot: Cause: The exact cause of Charcot foot is not fully understood, but it is thought to be caused by a combination of factors, including nerve damage, poor circulation, and increased pressure on the feet. Symptoms: The symptoms of Charcot foot can include pain, swelling, redness, warmth, and deformity of the foot. Diagnosis: Charcot foot is usually diagnosed based on the patient's medical history, physical examination, and imaging studies. Treatment: The treatment for Charcot foot is aimed at preventing further damage to the foot. This may include immobilization of the foot, use of special shoes or braces, and physical therapy.

34. Correct answer: C

Intensive therapy for diabetes mellitus has been shown to decrease the risk of long-term complications, such as heart disease, stroke, blindness, and kidney failure. However, it is also associated with an increased risk of hypoglycemia. Hypoglycemia is a condition in which blood sugar levels drop too low. This can cause symptoms such as shakiness, sweating, and confusion. In severe cases, hypoglycemia can lead to seizures or even death. Therefore, the most likely outcome of intensive therapy for diabetes mellitus is a decrease in the risk of long-term complications, but an increase in the risk of hypoglycemia.

35. Correct answer: A

Empagliflozin, liraglutide, and canagliflozin are all SGLT2 inhibitors. SGLT2 inhibitors have been shown to have a favorable impact on cardiovascular health in specific cohorts of individuals diagnosed with Type 2 diabetes and either existing cardiovascular disease or a heightened susceptibility to cardiovascular disease. Therefore, it is imperative to include these medications in the treatment considerations for these particular populations. The other answer choices are not SGLT2 inhibitors. Saxagliptin and sitagliptin are DPP-4 inhibitors, and they have not been shown to have the same favorable impact on cardiovascular health as SGLT2 inhibitors. Therefore, the most beneficial medication to add to the treatment regimen of a 55-year-old man with type 2 diabetes mellitus and a history of heart disease is empagliflozin. Here are some additional information about SGLT2 inhibitors: Definition: SGLT2 inhibitors are a class of diabetes medications that work by blocking the reabsorption of glucose in the kidneys. This allows more glucose to be excreted in the urine, which can help to lower blood sugar levels. Benefits: SGLT2 inhibitors have been shown to have a number of benefits, including lowering blood sugar levels, reducing the risk of heart disease, and improving kidney function. Risks: SGLT2 inhibitors can cause some side effects, including urinary tract infections, yeast infections, and dehydration.

36. Correct answer: C

Diabetic nephropathy is a condition that affects the kidneys in people with diabetes mellitus. It can lead to kidney failure. The most appropriate screening method for diabetic nephropathy is a spot collection for albuminuria. Albuminuria is the presence of albumin in the urine. Albumin is a protein that is normally not found in the urine. The presence of albumin in the urine is a sign of kidney damage. A routine urinalysis may be used to screen for diabetic nephropathy, but it is not as sensitive as a spot collection for albuminuria. A 24-hour urine collection can be used to quantify the amount of albumin in the urine, but it is more time-consuming and expensive than a spot collection. Renal ultrasound and renal biopsy are not used for screening for diabetic nephropathy. Therefore, the most appropriate screening method for diabetic nephropathy is a spot collection for albuminuria.

37. Correct answer: E

Diabetic ketoacidosis (DKA) is a serious complication of diabetes mellitus that occurs when the body produces too many ketones. Ketones are chemicals that are produced when the body breaks down fat for energy. DKA can be life-threatening if it is not treated promptly. The characteristic manifestations of DKA include Kussmaul respirations, which are deep and rapid breathing patterns, as well as the presence of an acetone odor in the patient's exhaled breath. This pattern of breathing is an attempt by the body to compensate for the increased acidity in the blood. The other answer choices are less likely in this case. Hyperosmolar hyperglycemic nonketotic syndrome (HHNS) is a condition that is similar to DKA, but it does not involve the production of ketones. Hypoglycemia is a condition that occurs when blood sugar levels are too low. Hyperthyroidism is a condition that causes the body to produce too much thyroid hormone. Addison disease is a condition that causes the body to produce too little cortisol.

38. Correct answer: B

Diabetic ketoacidosis (DKA) is a serious condition that can be life-threatening. Patients with DKA should be promptly admitted to a healthcare facility, with consideration given to an intensive care unit (ICU) for close and regular observation. Admission to the ICU is particularly warranted if the patient's pH level falls below 7.00 or if the patient is in an unconscious state. The other answer choices are not appropriate in this case. Admitting the patient to the hospital ward would not provide the close monitoring that is necessary for a patient with DKA. Discharging the patient home would be unsafe, as the patient's condition could deteriorate. Administering intravenous fluids and insulin would be part of the treatment for DKA, but they would not be sufficient in this case. Therefore, the most appropriate course of action is to admit the patient to the intensive care unit (ICU).

39. Correct answer: A

The optimal insulin regimen for a patient presenting with diabetic ketoacidosis (DKA) is to administer short-acting regular insulin intravenously at a dosage of 0.1 units per kilogram. This initial dose should be followed by a continuous intravenous infusion of 0.1 units per kilogram per hour. If there is no observed response within a time frame of 2-4 hours, it may be appropriate to consider increasing the dosage by a factor of two to three. The administration of short-acting regular insulin intravenously is crucial in rapidly lowering the blood glucose level and reversing the effects of diabetic ketoacidosis. Intravenous insulin therapy is preferred over subcutaneous administration due to the more rapid onset of action and greater control over insulin dosing. In severe cases of DKA, patient management may require the use of an intensive care unit to monitor electrolyte imbalances, glucose levels, and other vital signs. The other answer choices are not correct. Option B is the insulin regimen for a patient with type 2 diabetes mellitus. Option C is the insulin regimen for a patient with hypoglycemia. Option D is not a valid insulin regimen.

40. Correct answer: E

The management of Hyperglycemic Hyperosmolar State (HHS) entails identifying and addressing the underlying cause in order to initiate appropriate treatment. Furthermore, it is recommended to administer 1-3 liters of 0.9% normal saline within the initial 2-3 hours in order to achieve hemodynamic stability. The calculated deficit of free water should be corrected within the following 1-2 days by administering 0.45% saline initially, followed by 5% dextrose in water. Potassium repletion is typically deemed necessary, and insulin therapy is commonly administered, involving an intravenous bolus of 0.1 units per kilogram followed by a continuous infusion rate of 0.1 units per kilogram per hour. All of the answer choices are necessary components of the management of HHS. Therefore, the correct answer is E.

41. Correct answer: D

Pure neuroglycopenia is a form of hypoglycemia that does not cause autonomic symptoms. This is because the brain is the only organ that is affected by hypoglycemia in pure neuroglycopenia. The autonomic nervous system is not affected, so the patient does not experience the classic symptoms of hypoglycemia, such as sweating, shakiness, and a racing heart. The other answer choices are not correct. Option A is possible, but it is not the most likely explanation. Option B is also possible, but it is less likely than option D. Option C is not possible, as all forms of diabetes mellitus can cause autonomic symptoms of hypoglycemia. Option E is not possible, as there is no other explanation that is more likely than option D.

42. C. Insulinoma

The patient's symptoms of diaphoresis, palpitations, tremors, and confusion are consistent with hypoglycemia, which can be caused by an insulinoma, a tumor that produces excessive amounts of insulin. The fact that her symptoms are relieved by eating (which increases blood glucose levels) further supports this diagnosis. The laboratory findings of a low blood glucose level during a symptomatic attack and inappropriately high insulin and C-peptide levels are also characteristic of insulinoma. In contrast, diabetes mellitus (types 1 and 2) would typically present with hyperglycemia, not hypoglycemia. Exogenous insulin administration could cause hypoglycemia, but this would be associated with low C-peptide levels, not high. Hypothyroidism can cause a variety of symptoms, but it is not typically associated with hypoglycemia.

43. Correct answer: A

The most likely cause of hypercalcemia in this patient is primary hyperparathyroidism. This is because primary hyperparathyroidism is the most common cause of hypercalcemia, accounting for over 80% of cases. The patient's symptoms of fatigue, constipation, and polyuria are all consistent with primary hyperparathyroidism. The other answer choices are less likely causes of hypercalcemia in this patient. Malignancy is a common cause of hypercalcemia, but it is less likely in this patient because she does not have any other symptoms of malignancy. Vitamin D toxicity can cause hypercalcemia, but it is also less likely in this patient because she does not take any medications that could cause vitamin D toxicity. Medications, such as thiazides and lithium, can cause hypercalcemia, but they are also less likely in this patient because she does not take any of these medications. Sarcoidosis can cause hypercalcemia, but it is also less likely in this patient because she does not have any other symptoms of sarcoidosis.

44. Correct answer: B

The most likely cause of hypercalcemia in this patient is malignancy. This is because malignancy is the most common cause of hypercalcemia in patients with low PTH levels. The patient's symptoms of fatigue, constipation, and polyuria are all consistent with malignancy-associated hypercalcemia. The other answer choices are less likely causes of hypercalcemia in this patient. Primary hyperparathyroidism is a common cause of hypercalcemia, but it is less likely in this patient because his PTH level is low. Vitamin D toxicity can cause hypercalcemia, but it is also less likely in this patient because he does not take any medications that could cause vitamin D toxicity. Medications, such as thiazides and lithium, can cause hypercalcemia, but they are also less likely in this patient because he does not take any of these medications. Sarcoidosis can cause hypercalcemia, but it is also less likely in this patient because he does not have any other symptoms of sarcoidosis.

45. Correct answer: D

The most likely cause of hypocalcemia in this patient is primary hypoparathyroidism. This is because primary hypoparathyroidism is the most common cause of hypocalcemia, and it is associated with Chvostek's and Trousseau's signs. The patient's symptoms of muscle cramps and tingling in her hands and feet are also consistent with primary hypoparathyroidism. The other answer choices are less likely causes of hypocalcemia in this patient. Pseudohypoparathyroidism is a condition that is characterized by hypocalcemia and a resistance to the effects of parathyroid hormone (PTH). However, pseudohypoparathyroidism does not typically cause Chvostek's and Trousseau's signs. Vitamin D deficiency can cause hypocalcemia, but it is less likely in this patient because she does not have any other symptoms of vitamin D deficiency. Medications, such as thiazide diuretics, can cause hypocalcemia, but they are also less likely in this patient because she does not take any of these medications.

46. Correct answer: A The most appropriate treatment for symptomatic hypocalcemia is to administer a bolus of 1-2 g of intravenous calcium gluconate over a period of 10-20 minutes. This will quickly raise the patient's serum calcium level and relieve her symptoms. The bolus can be followed by a continuous infusion of calcium gluconate, as needed. The other answer choices are not appropriate for the treatment of symptomatic hypocalcemia. Oral calcium supplements are not absorbed quickly enough to be effective in the setting of symptomatic hypocalcemia. Monitoring the patient's condition and waiting for her calcium levels to improve on their own is not a safe or effective approach to the treatment of symptomatic hypocalcemia.

47. Correct answer: C

The most appropriate treatment for severe hypophosphatemia is to administer intravenous phosphate at an initial dose of 0.8 mmol/kg of elemental phosphorus over a period of 6 hours. This will quickly raise the patient's serum phosphate level and relieve her symptoms. The dose can be adjusted as needed, but it is important to exercise caution to avoid overcorrecting the hypophosphatemia, which can lead to complications such as hypocalcemia and tetany. The other answer choices are not appropriate for the treatment of severe hypophosphatemia. Administering 0.2 or 0.4 mmol/kg of ele-mental phosphorus over a period of 6 hours will not be sufficient to raise the patient's serum phosphate level to a safe level. Administering oral phosphate supplements is not effective in the setting of severe hypophosphatemia. 48. Correct answer: B The most appropriate treatment for severe hypomagnesemia is to administer intravenous magnesium sulfate over a period of 1 hour. This will quickly raise the patient's serum magnesium level and relieve her symptoms. The dose of intravenous magnesium sulfate will need to be individualized based on the patient's serum magnesium level and symptoms. The other answer choices are not appropriate for the treatment of severe hypomagnesemia. Administering oral magnesium supplements is not effective in the setting of severe hypomagnesemia. Monitoring the patient's condition and waiting for her magnesium levels to improve on their own is not a safe or effective approach to the treatment of severe hypomagnesemia.

49. Correct answer: C

The most likely explanation for the patient's fracture is that it is due to a combination of her osteoporosis and the bisphosphonates. Bisphosphonates are known to increase the risk of atypical femur fractures, which are fractures that occur in the midshaft of the femur. The risk of atypical femur fractures increases with the duration of bisphosphonate therapy. The other answer choices are less likely explanations for the patient's fracture. Her fracture is unlikely to be due to the natural progression of her osteoporosis, as she has been taking bisphosphonates for 10 years, which would have slowed the progression of her osteoporosis. Her fracture is also unlikely to be due to a fall, as she has been taking bisphosphonates for 10 years, which would have made her bones stronger and less likely to fracture from a fall.

50. Correct answer: B The patient is a 65-year-old woman, which is an age group that is typically recommended for BMD testing. She also has a family history of osteoporosis, which is another risk factor for BMD testing. Therefore, the most appropriate recommendation for the patient is to have BMD testing performed as soon as possible. The other answer choices are not as appropriate. BMD testing is not recommended for patients who do not have any risk factors for osteoporosis. BMD testing should be performed every 1-2 years for patients who have been diagnosed with osteoporosis.

51. Answer: A

The patient's hypotension, tachycardia, and mild hyponatremia are concerning for adrenal insufficiency. Adrenal insufficiency is a life-threatening condition that requires immediate treatment to prevent hemodynamic collapse. Hydrocortisone is the first-line treatment for adrenal insufficiency. The other answer choices are not as important in the immediate management of this patient: Evaluating for adrenal insufficiency can be done later, after the patient has been medically stabilized. Securing the airway and ventilating the patient is not necessary unless the patient is in respiratory distress. Administering intravenous fluids is often needed in patients with adrenal insufficiency, but it was not offered as a choice in this question. Therefore, the best answer is A. Administer hydrocortisone 50 mg IV. Pituitary apoplexy is a rare but life-threatening condition that occurs when the pituitary gland bleeds. The pituitary gland is a small gland located at the base of the brain that produces hormones that control many important bodily functions, such as growth, metabolism, and reproduction. The symptoms of pituitary apoplexy can vary depending on the severity of the bleeding. Common symptoms include severe headache, vision loss, and nausea and vomiting. In severe cases, pituitary apoplexy can lead to coma and death. Treatment for pituitary apoplexy typically involves surgery to remove the bleeding tumor and relieve pressure on the pituitary gland. However, patients with pituitary apoplexy may also require medical stabilization prior to surgery. This may include administering intravenous fluids, correcting electrolyte imbalances, and treating any underlying infections. Adrenal insufficiency is a common complication of pituitary apoplexy. This is because the pituitary gland produces hormones that stimulate the adrenal glands to produce cortisol. Cortisol is a stress hormone that is essential for regulating blood pressure and blood sugar levels. If a patient with pituitary apoplexy is not producing enough cortisol, they may experience adrenal insufficiency. Symptoms of adrenal insufficiency include hypotension, tachycardia, hyponatremia, and hyperkalemia. Adrenal insufficiency is a life-threatening condition that requires immediate treatment with hydrocortisone. Hydrocortisone is a synthetic form of cortisol that can be administered intravenously orally. After the patient has been medically stabilized, they will need to be evaluated by a neurosurgeon to determine the best course of treatment for the pituitary lesion and the hemorrhage.

52. Answer B

is correct because the patient should exhibit no stimulation at baseline with a low-morning cortisol, however, she is responsive to cosyntropin (an ACTH analog). The patient is experiencing acute-central adrenal insufficiency; whereby sudden loss of pituitary function prevents the release of adrenocorticotropic hormone (ACTH). Under these conditions, the adrenal glands have not yet atrophied from lack of stimulation and thus remain sensitive to ACTH. Answer A suggests primary adrenal pathology due to a profound lack of cortisol production. Answer C suggests chronic secondary adrenal insufficiency with some evidence of adrenal atrophy. Answer D represents a normal stimulation test. Answer E suggests chronic-primary adrenal insufficiency. It is important to remember that cosyntropin stimulation tests can be falsely reassuring in situations of acute-central adrenal insufficiency as the adrenal glands have not had time to atrophy.

53.The best answer is A.

Order a low-dose dexamethasone suppression test (DST). The DST involves administering a low dose of dexamethasone and measuring cortisol levels. In patients with Cushing syndrome, cortisol suppression is impaired, leading to elevated cortisol levels. This test helps confirm the presence of hypercortisolism and can provide information about the etiology of the condition. The patient's clinical presentation is consistent with Cushing syndrome, and further evaluation is warranted to confirm the diagnosis and determine the underlying cause of hypercortisolism. Screening tests for Cushing syndrome include the low-dose dexamethasone suppression test (DST), the late-night salivary cortisol test, and the 24-hour urinary cortisol collection. However, a random or morning cortisol level is not useful for diagnosing Cushing syndrome. Performing imaging studies should be reserved for cases where biochemical confirmation of Cushing syndrome has been obtained and there is suspicion of a pituitary source. Imaging alone is not sufficient for diagnosis and should not be the initial step in evaluating Cushing syndrome.

54.Answer: A

The growth hormone (GH) suppression test is the gold standard for the diagnosis of acromegaly. It involves measuring GH levels before and after an oral glucose tolerance test. In people with acromegaly, GH levels will not suppress normally in response to the glucose load. Random GH levels are not diagnostic for acromegaly due to their large physiologic variability. IGF-1 levels are often elevated in acromegaly, but they can also be affected by other factors such as obesity, illness, and medications. The glucagon stimulation test and insulin tolerance test are used for the diagnosis of growth hormone deficiency, not acromegaly. Therefore, the best answer is A. Checking growth hormone after an oral glucose load.

55.Answer: A

Cabergoline is a dopamine agonist that is the first-line treatment for hyperprolactinemia caused by a macroprolactinoma. It is a once-weekly medication that is well-tolerated and effective. Oral contraceptive pills can be used to treat the amenorrhea associated with hyperprolactinemia, but they are not as effective as dopamine agonists at reducing prolactin levels. Surgery is typically only reserved for patients who do not respond to dopamine agonist therapy or who have very large tumors. Therefore, the best answer is A. Initiate cabergoline 0.5 mg weekly.

56.Answer:C

This patient is presenting with myxedema coma, which is an endocrine emergency. Myxedema coma is associated with high mortality, and treatment should be initiated based on clinical suspicion, even prior to return of laboratory results. Patients with severe hypothyroidism and myxedema coma should be treated for possible coexisting adrenal insufficiency while treating the hypothyroidism. Therefore, the appropriate initial treatment is to start hydrocortisone 100 mg every 8 hours and 100 g T4 IV daily (Answer C). Supportive care and evaluation for triggers are also fundamental for the management of myxedema coma, in addition to treatment of hypothyroidism and possible adrenal insufficiency.

57. the correct answer is A.

Order radioiodine uptake scan. For the evaluation of hyperthyroidism, indicated in this patient by decreased TSH and elevated fT4, a radioiodine uptake scan is the appropriate first test. The most common etiology of hyperthyroidism is Graves' disease, and a radioiodine uptake scan in Graves' disease typically shows diffuse homogeneous uptake. While measuring serum T3 and T4 levels (answer B) can provide information about thyroid hormone levels, it does not differentiate between different causes of hyperthyroidism. Thyroid ultrasound (answer C) can be useful in evaluating thyroid nodules or assessing for structural abnormalities, but it is not the initial test of choice for evaluating hyperthyroidism. The thyroid-stimulating immunoglobulin (TSI) test (answer D) is specific for Graves' disease but is not the initial test for evaluating hyperthyroidism. Genetic testing for hereditary hyperthyroidism (answer E) is not indicated as the initial evaluation for hyperthyroidism. Therefore, the best answer is A. Order radioiodine uptake scan.

58. Answer: C

Selenium is not recommended for the treatment of thyroid storm. Selenium is a mineral that is important for thyroid function, but it is not used to treat thyroid storm. The other answer choices are all recommended for the treatment of thyroid storm: Beta-blockers are used to slow the heart rate and reduce other symptoms of hyperthyroidism. Thionamides are used to block the production of thyroid hormones. Inorganic iodide is used to block the release of thyroid hormones from the thyroid gland. Corticosteroids are used to reduce inflammation and suppress the thyroid gland. Therefore, the best answer is C. Selenium.

59. Answer: B

Primary hyperaldosteronism is the most likely etiology of secondary hypertension in this patient. Primary hyperaldosteronism is a condition in which the adrenal glands produce too much of the hormone aldosterone. Aldosterone causes the kidneys to retain sodium and water, which leads to high blood pressure. The first step in the evaluation of primary hyperaldosteronism is to measure morning plasma renin and aldosterone. If the aldosterone level is elevated and the renin level is low, this is consistent with primary hyperaldosteronism. The other answer choices are not as appropriate as the first step in the evaluation of primary hyperaldosteronism: Ordering a 24-hour urine collection for cortisol and catecholamines is more appropriate for the evaluation of hypercortisolism and pheochromocytoma, respectively. Ordering a renal ultrasound or CT scan of the adrenal glands is more appropriate for the evaluation of structural abnormalities of the kidneys and adrenal glands, respectively. Referring the patient to a nephrologist may be appropriate at a later stage in the evaluation, but it is not the most appropriate next step in this case. Therefore, the best answer is B. Measure morning plasma renin and aldosterone.

60 .The correct answer is: A.

Adrenal venous sampling. In the case of multiple adrenal adenomas with unclear significance, it is important to determine the source of aldosterone to avoid an erroneous diagnosis. Adrenal venous sampling is the appropriate next step to localize the source of aldosterone. Once the source is identified, the patient can be referred for surgical management, such as subtotal or total adrenalectomy. Medical therapy is typically used when surgical management is technically difficult or refused. Adrenal CT scan (answer B) may provide information about the size and characteristics of the adrenal adenomas, but it does not help in determining the source of aldosterone. Radioiodine uptake scan (answer C) is used for the evaluation of hyperthyroidism, not for adrenal adenomas. Low-dose dexamethasone suppression test (answer D) is used to evaluate for Cushing syndrome, not for adrenal adenomas and elevated aldosterone levels. Starting hydrocortisone and T4 IV (answer E) is the appropriate treatment for myxedema coma, not for the management of adrenal adenomas and elevated aldosterone levels.

61. Answer: C

The most appropriate next step is to perform a twenty-four-hour urine fractionated metanephrines. This test is the most sensitive and specific test for the diagnosis of pheochromocytoma, a rare tumor of the adrenal medulla that produces excessive amounts of catecholamines. The other answer choices are not as appropriate as the first step in the evaluation of an adrenal incidentaloma: Abdominal MRI with gadolinium contrast is not necessary at this time, as it will not provide any additional information about the tumor. A twenty-four-hour urine collection for cortisol and catecholamines is less sensitive and specific than a twenty-four-hour urine fractionated metanephrines for the diagnosis of pheochromocytoma. Aldosterone, renin, and an overnight 1 mg DST are used to evaluate for primary hyperaldosteronism, another potential cause of adrenal incidentalomas. However, these tests should be deferred until after the pheochromocytoma evaluation has been completed, as pheochromocytoma can interfere with the results of these tests. Therefore, the best answer is C.

62. The correct answer is D. Initiate prazosin 1 mg every 4 hours.

In the context of preoperative management for catecholamine-secreting tumors, alfa-blockade is crucial to prevent catastrophic -adrenergic stimulation when the tumor is manipulated during surgery. This can be achieved using either nonselective -blockers such as phenoxybenzamine or selective agents such as prazosin. The dose should be titrated until the patient develops orthostatic hypotension, which serves as an indicator for sufficient blockage. Option A is incorrect because exclusive -blockade (propranolol is a -blocker) should never be performed in patients with catecholamine-secreting tumors as it can lead to cardiovascular collapse from unopposed -stimulation. Option B is incorrect because metyrosine, which inhibits the production of catecholamines, is used in the management of metastatic pheochromocytoma, not as a preoperative measure in non-metastatic cases. Option C is incorrect because although phenoxybenzamine is a nonselective -blocker and can be used in such scenarios, the question specifically states that prazosin is the correct answer. Option E is incorrect because dexamethasone, a corticosteroid, does not play a role in preventing -adrenergic stimulation during the manipulation of a catecholamine-secreting tumor.

63. Answer: C

The most appropriate next step is to check serum and 24-hour urine calcium and creatinine. This will help to determine if the patient has primary hyperparathyroidism (PHPT) or familial hypocalciuric hypercalcemia (FHH). PHPT is a condition in which the parathyroid glands produce too much PTH. PTH is a hormone that regulates calcium levels in the blood. When PTH levels are too high, calcium levels in the blood rise. FHH is a genetic condition that causes people to have high levels of calcium in their blood, even though their PTH levels are normal. People with FHH do not need surgery to remove their parathyroid glands. The other answer choices are not as appropriate as the first step in the evaluation of hypercalcemia: Ordering a 24-hour urine collection for magnesium and phosphate is not necessary at this time. Ordering a parathyroid gland ultrasound is not necessary at this time. Ordering a DXA scan is not necessary at this time. Performing a parathyroidectomy is not necessary at this time. Therefore, the best answer is C. Check serum and 24-hour urine calcium and creatinine.

64. The correct answer is C.

The most appropriate next step is to check baseline adrenocorticotropic hormone (ACTH) and perform cosyntropin stimulation test. This patient's symptoms of fatigue, weight loss, salt craving, postural hypotension, hyperpigmentation, hyponatremia, and hyperkalemia are strongly suggestive of Addison disease, which is primary adrenal insufficiency. However, the diagnosis requires biochemical confirmation. Elevated ACTH (often in the hundreds) would be consistent with adrenal failure since the loss of negative feedback due to low cortisol would lead to increased ACTH secretion. A cosyntropin stimulation test would show a minimal response to cosyntropin, confirming the diagnosis of adrenal insufficiency. Once the diagnosis is confirmed, the patient will require glucocorticoid and mineralocorticoid replacement. 21-Hydroxylase antibodies can be checked, as their presence is associated with autoimmune Addison disease, but this is not necessary for the diagnosis. An abdominal CT scan can be used to identify other etiologies of adrenal failure, but it is of low utility for known autoimmune adrenalitis. Starting treatment immediately without confirming the diagnosis or referring to a psychiatrist would not be appropriate given the strong clinical suspicion of Addison disease.

65. Answer: A

The patient's presentation is consistent with hypercalcemic crisis. Hypercalcemic crisis is a medical emergency that occurs when the serum calcium level is elevated to life-threatening levels. Hypercalcemia can cause a variety of symptoms, including nausea, vomiting, confusion, weakness, and diplopia. The other answer choices are less likely: Hyperthyroidism is a condition in which the thyroid gland produces too much thyroid hormone. Hyperthyroidism can cause a variety of symptoms, including tachycardia, hypertension, and weight loss. However, the patient in this case does not have a history of hyperthyroidism, and his thyroid gland has been removed. Hyperosmolar hyperglycemic state is a complication of diabetes mellitus that occurs when the blood sugar level is very high. Hyperosmolar hyperglycemic state can cause a variety of symptoms, including thirst, frequent urination, and confusion. However, the patient in this case is not known to have diabetes mellitus, and his blood sugar level is not known. Stroke is a condition in which the blood supply to the brain is interrupted. Stroke can cause a variety of symptoms, including weakness, confusion, and diplopia. However, the patient in this case does not have any other risk factors for stroke, such as high blood pressure, high cholesterol, or diabetes mellitus. Hyponatremia is a condition in which the sodium level in the blood is low. Hyponatremia can cause a variety of symptoms, including nausea, vomiting, and confusion. However, the patient in this case does not have any other risk factors for hyponatremia, such as heart failure, liver disease, or kidney disease. Therefore, the best answer is A. Hypercalcemic crisis. Hypercalcemic crisis is a medical emergency and requires immediate treatment. Treatment typically involves intravenous fluids, loop diuretics, and calcitonin. In some cases, dialysis may be necessary.

66. The correct answer is C Sarcoidosis

Sarcoidosis, an inflammatory disease characterized by the presence of noncaseating granulomas, can affect almost all organs, can be asymptomatic, or is associated with a wide range of symptoms and presents a diagnostic challenge. Black women have a higher incidence of sarcoidosis. This patient's presentation is classic for pulmonary sarcoidosis, but a diagnostic evaluation that typically includes a tissue biopsy is needed. Hypercalcemia in sarcoidosis is due to the parathyroid hormone–independent conversion of 25-hydroxy vitamin D to the active 1,25-dihydroxy vitamin D. In contrast, primary or secondary hyperparathyroidism presents with elevated parathyroid hormone (and serum calcium is not elevated in secondary hyperparathyroidism). Humoral hypercalcemia of malignancy is caused by elevated parathyroid hormone–related protein (PTHrP). Tuberculosis typically does not cause hypercalcemia and is less likely in this case given the absence of typical symptoms such as night sweats and hemoptysis.

67. The correct answer is C.Start liraglutide daily.

In this patient with known cardiovascular disease, when adding a second medication to metformin and lifestyle management to improve glycemic control, it is recommended by the 2018 ADA guidelines to add a therapy validated to improve heart health. Among the listed options, liraglutide, a glucagon-like peptide-1 receptor agonist, is the only agent approved by the Food and Drug Administration (FDA) to reduce the risk of cardiovascular death in adult patients with T2DM. Aspirin therapy (Option A) could be part of the cardiovascular disease management, but it does not directly address glycemic control. Insulin therapy (Option B) can be very effective for glycemic control, but it is typically not the first-line therapy, especially in patients without symptoms of hyperglycemia. Increasing the dose of metformin (Option D) may improve glycemic control, but it may not provide the cardiovascular benefits that are of priority in this patient. While statins (Option E) are important in managing dyslipidemia in patients with diabetes, they do not directly impact glycemic control.

68. Answer: A

The most appropriate next step is to start 25 U insulin glargine nightly with sliding scale aspart insulin. This patient has a history of type 2 diabetes mellitus and is now hospitalized with acute kidney injury and pneumonia. He is not currently taking any antihyperglycemic medications, and his blood glucose levels are consistently elevated. This suggests that he has a significant insulin requirement. Insulin glargine is a long-acting insulin that can be used to provide basal insulin coverage. Sliding scale aspart insulin can be used to provide prandial insulin coverage. The other answer choices are not as appropriate: Starting 25 U insulin glargine nightly alone may not be enough to control his blood glucose levels, given his significant insulin requirement. Starting sliding scale aspart insulin only may not be enough to control his blood glucose levels, given his significant insulin requirement and the fact that he is not currently taking any basal insulin. Increasing his intravenous fluids may help to lower his blood glucose levels, but it is unlikely to be enough on its own. Starting oral antihyperglycemic medications is not recommended in this patient because of his acute kidney injury. Therefore, the best answer is A. Start 25 U insulin glargine nightly with sliding scale aspart insulin. Insulin glargine is a long-acting insulin that is used to provide basal insulin coverage. Basal insulin is needed to maintain blood glucose levels between meals and overnight. Aspart insulin is a short-acting insulin that is used to provide prandial insulin coverage. Prandial insulin is needed to control blood glucose levels after meals. Sliding scale insulin is a method of administering insulin based on the patient's blood glucose level. Sliding scale insulin is typically given before meals and at bedtime. The goal of diabetes management is to maintain blood glucose levels within a target range. This helps to reduce the risk of complications such as heart disease, stroke, and kidney disease.

69.Answer: D

The laboratory findings in hypoglycemia due to insulinoma are:

- Low blood glucose
- Elevated insulin
- Elevated proinsulin
- Elevated C-peptide
- Suppressed -hydroxybutyrate
- Negative oral hypoglycemia agent screen

The laboratory findings in the other answer choices are not consistent with insulinoma. Therefore, the best answer is D. Insulin = 38 pmol/L, proinsulin = 25 pmol/L, C-peptide = 0.8 ng/mL, -hydroxybutyrate <2.7 mmol/L, oral hypoglycemia agent screen = negative. Insulinoma is a rare tumor of the pancreas that produces excessive amounts of insulin. Insulin is a hormone that lowers blood glucose levels. Excessive insulin production can lead to hypoglycemia, which is a condition in which the blood glucose level is too low. The symptoms of hypoglycemia can include headache, confusion, diaphoresis, and seizures. Severe hypoglycemia can lead to coma and death.

70.Answer: C.

Serum anion gap <12 mEq/L and serum bicarbonate 15 mEq/L. The ADA guidelines for DKA recommend IV insulin be tapered and a multiple-dose subcutaneous insulin schedule be started when blood glucose is <200 mg/dL and at least two of the following parameters are met: (1) serum anion gap <12 mEq/L (or at the upper limit of normal for the local laboratory), (2) serum bicarbonate 15 mEq/L, and (3) venous pH >7.30. In the choices provided, option C meets two of these criteria: serum anion gap <12 mEq/L and serum bicarbonate 15 mEq/L. Therefore, this is the best answer. It's also important to note that a patient should remain on IV insulin if unable to eat, and that the IV infusion should be continued for 1 to 2 hours after initiation of subcutaneous insulin.

71. Answer: C

SGLT2 inhibitors, such as canagliflozin, cause a slight initial decrease in GFR, but then lessen the decrease in GFR over time compared with placebo. This is because SGLT2 inhibitors reduce hyperfiltration, which is a condition in which the kidneys filter too much blood. Hyperfiltration can damage the kidneys and lead to a decline in GFR. SGLT2 inhibitors have been shown to reduce the risk of end-stage renal disease, worsening of kidney function, cardiovascular death, and hospitalization for heart failure among adults with type 2 diabetes mellitus and diabetic kidney disease. Therefore, the best answer is C. It will slow the decline in his GFR. SGLT2 inhibitors work by blocking the sodium-glucose cotransporter 2 (SGLT2) protein in the kidneys. SGLT2 is responsible for reabsorbing glucose from the urine back into the bloodstream. By blocking SGLT2, SGLT2 inhibitors cause the kidneys to excrete more glucose in the urine. This lowers blood glucose levels and also causes the kidneys to lose sodium and water. The loss of sodium and water can lead to a slight initial decrease in GFR. However, over time, the reduced hyperfiltration caused by SGLT2 inhibitors leads to a slowing of the decline in GFR. SGLT2 inhibitors are a safe and effective treatment for type 2 diabetes mellitus. They have been shown to reduce the risk of serious complications of diabetes, such as end-stage renal disease, cardiovascular death, and hospitalization for heart failure.

72. The correct answer is B. Start long-acting insulin at 0.1 to 0.2 IU/kg/d with instructions to increase 2 U every 3 days until reaching fasting glucose target.

The American Diabetes Association (ADA) recommends early introduction of insulin if there is evidence of ongoing catabolism (weight loss), if symptoms of hyperglycemia are present, or when A1c level is >10%. In this patient, her nocturia likely reflects symptomatic hyperglycemia. Once initiated, metformin should be continued as long as tolerated with additional agents added as necessary. The ADA recommends initial basal insulin dosing of 0.1 to 0.2 IU/kg/d or 10 U per day with instructions for patient self-titration. Prior to initiation of prandial insulin, it would be reasonable to monitor response to basal insulin to simplify the regimen and promote adherence. Other options like adding a GLP-1 receptor agonist (Option A), discontinuing metformin and starting prandial insulin (Option C), adding a DPP-4 inhibitor (Option D), or starting short-acting insulin before meals (Option E) are not first-line strategies for patients with symptomatic hyperglycemia or A1c >10%, according to the ADA guidelines.

73. Answer: A

SGLT2 inhibitors are recommended as the second agent (in addition to metformin) for individuals with T2DM with heart failure as the predominant comorbid condition. SGLT2 inhibitors have been shown to significantly lower the risk of hospitalization due to heart failure. GLP-1 receptor agonists and DPP-4 inhibitors are also effective treatments for T2DM, but they are not specifically recommended for individuals with T2DM and heart failure. Insulin can be used to treat T2DM, but it should be used with caution in individuals with heart failure, as it can increase the risk of hypoglycemia and fluid retention. Therefore, the best answer is A. Continue metformin and add dapagliflozin.

74. Answer: A

The most important laboratory tests to order first are calcium and albumin. Hypocalcemia is a common complication of thyroidectomy, and it can cause neuromuscular irritability. Albumin is a protein that binds to calcium, so it is important to measure albumin levels in order to accurately interpret the serum calcium level. Magnesium and phosphorus levels are important to check, but they are not as likely to be the cause of the patient's symptoms. Parathyroid hormone (PTH) is a hormone that regulates calcium levels. If the patient's PTH level is low, this suggests that she has hypoparathyroidism, which is another possible complication of thyroidectomy. Vitamin D levels can also be important to check, but they are less likely to be the cause of the patient's symptoms. A multiple sclerosis panel is not necessary at this time, as the patient's symptoms are more likely to be due to hypocalcemia than multiple sclerosis. Therefore, the best answer is A. Calcium and albumin.

75. The correct answer is D.

No change in treatment is needed. During pregnancy, serum albumin typically decreases due to an increase in plasma volume. Total serum calcium has to be corrected for albumin. In this case, the patient's albumin is 2.0 g/dL, and her adjusted calcium is 8.4 mg/dL, which is within the range for hypoparathyroid patients of low to low-normal. Despite the low total serum calcium, the patient is asymptomatic, indicating that her ionized calcium, which is the biologically active form, is likely in the normal range. Therefore, in the absence of symptoms, no change in treatment is necessary.

76. The best answer is E.

The recommended therapeutic approach for individuals with hypophosphatemia involves the oral administration of substances such as milk, carbonated beverages, or specific pharmaceutical preparations like Neutra-Phos or K-Phos. The recommended dosage for these interventions is up to 2g per day, divided into multiple doses. Option A is incorrect because intravenous phosphate administration is recommended only in cases of severe hypophosphatemia, defined as a serum phosphate level of 0.75 mmol/L (or <2.0 mg/dL). Option B is not the primary therapeutic approach but rather a monitoring recommendation to assess the response to treatment. Option C is not directly related to the therapeutic approach for hypophosphatemia but rather a cautionary measure in cases of hypercalcemia. Option D is not the initial step in managing hypophosphatemia but rather a recommendation in the context of managing hypocalcemia. Therefore, option E is the best answer as it accurately reflects the recommended therapeutic approach for individuals with hypophosphatemia.

77. The correct answer is D.Osteonecrosis of the jaw.

The patient's history of receiving high-dose intravenous zoledronic acid, a type of bisphosphonate, along with the clinical presentation of jaw pain and exposed bone in the mandible, strongly suggests the diagnosis of osteonecrosis of the jaw. Osteonecrosis of the jaw is an infrequent but serious side effect associated with the administration of bisphosphonates, primarily observed in cancer patients receiving high-dose intravenous zoledronic acid or pamidronate. While oral cancer (Option A) can present with jaw pain, the patient's history of bisphosphonate use and the presence of exposed bone make osteonecrosis more likely. Dental abscess (Option B) typically presents with localized pain and swelling, and is less likely in this case due to the exposed bone. Temporomandibular joint disorder (Option C) usually presents with pain in the joint area and difficulty opening or closing the mouth, not exposed bone. Trigeminal neuralgia (Option E) is a nerve disorder that causes abrupt, searing facial pain, often triggered by normal activities like eating or talking, and it does not cause exposed bone in the jaw.

78. Answer: (C)

Raloxifene therapy is not recommended as a subsequent therapy after teriparatide therapy. Raloxifene is a selective estrogen receptor modulator (SERM) that has antiestrogenic effects on bone and breast tissue. It is used to prevent and treat osteoporosis in postmenopausal women, but it is not as effective as bisphosphonate or denosumab therapy in maintaining bone mass after teriparatide therapy. Bisphosphonate therapy, denosumab therapy, estrogen therapy, and calcitonin therapy are all recommended subsequent therapies after teriparatide therapy. These medications help to maintain bone mass and reduce the risk of fractures.

- Teriparatide is a medication that stimulates bone formation.
- Teriparatide is used to treat severe osteoporosis.
- It is recommended to start antiresorptive agent therapy after teriparatide therapy to maintain bone mass and reduce the risk of fractures.
- Bisphosphonate therapy, denosumab therapy, estrogen therapy, and calcitonin therapy are all recommended subsequent therapies after teriparatide therapy.
- Raloxifene therapy is not recommended as a subsequent therapy after teriparatide therapy.

79. The correct answer is B.Osteomalacia.

The patient's presentation of bone pain, muscle weakness, and chronic hypophosphatemia suggests the diagnosis of osteomalacia. Osteomalacia is a metabolic bone disease characterized by inadequate mineralization of bone matrix, often due to a deficiency of vitamin D or phosphate. Chronic hypophosphatemia has been observed to be a causative factor in the development of osteomalacia. Conditions that cause renal phosphate wasting, such as X-linked hypophosphatemic rickets or oncogenic osteomalacia, or the excessive utilization of phosphate binders, may contribute to this phenomenon. Osteoporosis (Option A) is characterized by reduced bone mass and deterioration of bone tissue, but it does not typically present with hypophosphatemia. Osteoarthritis (Option C) is a degenerative joint disease and would not cause the systemic symptoms or hypophosphatemia seen in this patient. Osteogenesis imperfecta (Option D) is a genetic disorder characterized by brittle bones that break easily, and it is not associated with hypophosphatemia. Osteosarcoma (Option E) is a type of bone cancer, and while it can cause bone pain, it does not typically cause chronic hypophosphatemia.

80. The correct answer is A.Vitamin D deficiency with secondary hyperparathyroidism.

The patient's laboratory findings suggest a deficiency in vitamin D, which has resulted in compensatory secondary hyperparathyroidism. The most precise diagnostic test for vitamin D deficiency in an otherwise asymptomatic individual is a decreased level of serum 25-hydroxyvitamin D. Even a slight deficiency in vitamin D results in compensatory secondary hyperparathyroidism, which is characterized by elevated levels of parathyroid hormone (PTH) and alkaline phosphatase, increased excretion of phosphates in urine, and decreased levels of serum phosphate. Primary hyperparathyroidism (Option B) typically presents with hypercalcemia, not hypophosphatemia. Chronic kidney disease (Option C) can cause abnormalities in vitamin D metabolism and phosphate excretion, but it would also typically present with other signs such as elevated creatinine levels. Hypoparathyroidism (Option D) would lead to low levels of PTH, not the elevated levels seen in this patient. Vitamin D toxicity (Option E) would present with hypercalcemia and decreased PTH levels, not the findings seen in this patient.

81. Answer: (C)

Deepening of the voice is the most specific clinical feature for an underlying ovarian or adrenal neoplasm in a woman with hirsutism. This is because deepening of the voice is a sign of virilization, which is a clinical manifestation of severe androgen excess. Ovarian or adrenal neoplasms can produce excess androgens, leading to virilization in women. Acne and male-pattern balding are also clinical manifestations of androgen excess, but they are more common in women with PCOS (polycystic ovary syndrome). PCOS is the most common cause of hirsutism in women, and it is unlikely to cause deepening of the voice. Breast atrophy and increased libido are not typically associated with ovarian or adrenal neoplasms. Ovarian or adrenal neoplasms can cause virilization in women, which is characterized by clinical features such as deepening of the voice, breast atrophy, increased muscle bulk, clitoromegaly, and increased libido. Deepening of the voice is the most specific clinical feature for an underlying ovarian or adrenal neoplasm in a woman with hirsutism. Acne and male-pattern balding are also clinical manifestations of androgen excess, but they are more common in women with PCOS (polycystic ovary syndrome). Breast atrophy and increased libido are not typically associated with ovarian or adrenal neoplasms.

82. Answer: (B)

Dexamethasone is a synthetic glucocorticoid that suppresses the production of adrenal androgens. If free testosterone levels do not drop significantly after dexamethasone administration, it is likely that ovarian overproduction of androgens is to blame for the hirsutism. This is because ovarian androgens are not suppressed by dexamethasone. If free testosterone levels do drop significantly after dexamethasone administration, it is more likely that adrenal overproduction of androgens is the cause of the hirsutism. DHEAS is a precursor to testosterone. It is produced by both the adrenals and the ovaries. DHEAS levels are typically suppressed by dexamethasone, but ovarian DHEAS production is less sensitive to dexamethasone suppression than adrenal DHEAS production. The dexamethasone androgen-suppression test can be used to distinguish between ovarian and adrenal overproduction of androgens. Dexamethasone suppresses the production of adrenal androgens. If free testosterone levels do not drop significantly after dexamethasone administration, it is likely that ovarian overproduction of androgens is to blame for the hirsutism.

83. Answer: The correct answer is D.Type III hyperlipoproteinemia.

The patient's presentation of high levels of cholesterol and triglycerides in the blood, along with the genetic testing results, suggest a diagnosis of Type III hyperlipoproteinemia. Hyperlipoproteinemia is a condition characterized by elevated levels of cholesterol and/or triglycerides in the blood. There are several genetic factors that contribute to hyperlipoproteinemia. Type III hyperlipoproteinemia is mainly found in homozygous apolipoprotein E2 (R158C) carriers. Familial hypercholesterolemia (Option A) is a genetic condition that causes high cholesterol, but it is not typically associated with the apolipoprotein E2 (R158C) variant. Type I and Type II hyperlipoproteinemia (Options B and C) are also genetic conditions that cause elevated lipid levels, but they are not typically associated with the apolipoprotein E2 (R158C) variant. Primary hypertriglyceridemia (Option E) is associated with common genetic variants found in LPL, APOA5, and GCKR, not the apolipoprotein E2 (R158C) variant.

84. Answer: (D)

Following a myocardial infarction or acute inflammatory states, there is a temporary decrease in both LDL and HDL cholesterol levels. However, if blood samples are obtained within 8 hours of the event, the cholesterol levels will still be accurate. This is because the inflammatory response has not yet had a significant impact on the cholesterol levels. (A) LDL cholesterol levels will be artificially low, but HDL cholesterol levels will be accurate. This is incorrect because both LDL and HDL cholesterol levels will be decreased following a myocardial infarction or acute inflammatory state. (B) LDL cholesterol levels will be accurate, but HDL cholesterol levels will be artificially low. This is incorrect because both LDL and HDL cholesterol levels will be decreased following a myocardial infarction or acute inflammatory state.

(C) Both LDL and HDL cholesterol levels will be artificially low. This is incorrect because if blood samples are obtained within 8 hours of the event, the cholesterol levels will still be accurate. (E) The interpretation of the cholesterol results is not possible without knowing the patient's pre-infarction cholesterol levels. This is incorrect because the cholesterol levels obtained within 8 hours of the event will still be accurate, even if the patient's pre-infarction cholesterol levels are not known. The most accurate statement about the interpretation of cholesterol results following a myocardial infarction or acute inflammatory state is that both LDL and HDL cholesterol levels will be accurate if blood samples are obtained within 8 hours of the event.

85. Answer: The correct answer is A.

Familial Hypercholesterolemia. The patient's presentation of high total cholesterol levels, normal plasma triglyceride levels, slightly diminished HDL cholesterol levels, and a mutation in the gene encoding the LDL receptor suggest a diagnosis of Familial Hypercholesterolemia (FH). FH is a genetic disorder characterized by codominance, which arises from mutations occurring in the gene responsible for encoding the LDL receptor. The levels of plasma LDL are increased at birth and persist at elevated levels throughout an individual's lifespan. In the case of untreated heterozygous adults, the total cholesterol levels typically vary between 275–500 mg/dL. Type I, II, and III hyperlipoproteinemia (Options B, C, and D) are genetic conditions that cause elevated lipid levels, but they are not typically associated with a mutation in the gene encoding the LDL receptor. Primary hypertriglyceridemia (Option E) is associated with elevated triglyceride levels, which is not the case in this patient.

86. The patient's presentation of high cholesterol levels and a mutation in the gene encoding apolipoprotein B-100 suggest a diagnosis of Familial Defective Apo B-100.

This is a genetic disorder characterized by a malfunctioning form of apolipoprotein B-100, a protein involved in lipid metabolism. The disorder exhibits autosomal dominance and hinders the production and/or effectiveness of apo B-100, consequently diminishing the binding capacity to the LDL receptor. This results in a deceleration of LDL breakdown and gives rise to a phenocopy of familial hypercholesterolemia. Familial Hypercholesterolemia (Option A) is a genetic disorder characterized by high cholesterol levels due to a mutation in the gene encoding the LDL receptor, not apolipoprotein B-100. Type I and II hyperlipoproteinemia (Options B and C) are genetic conditions that cause elevated lipid levels, but they are not typically associated with a mutation in the gene encoding apolipoprotein B-100. Primary hypertriglyceridemia (Option E) is associated with elevated triglyceride levels, which is not the case in this patient.

87. Tendon xanthomas and xanthelasmas are not typically associated with isolated hypertriglyceridemia.

Eruptive xanthomas and lipemia retinalis can be seen, but they are more likely to occur in patients with very high triglyceride levels (above 1000 mg/dL). (A) Tendon xanthomas are more typically associated with familial hypercholesterolemia and other conditions that cause elevated LDL cholesterol levels. (B) Xanthelasmas are also more typically associated with familial hypercholesterolemia and other conditions that cause elevated LDL cholesterol levels. C) Eruptive xanthomas are small, reddish-orange papules that can appear on the trunk and extremities in patients with very high triglyceride levels. (E) This is incorrect because eruptive xanthomas and lipemia retinalis can be seen in patients with isolated hypertriglyceridemia, although they are less likely to occur than in patients with very high triglyceride levels. The most likely cutaneous finding in a patient with isolated hypertriglyceridemia is lipemia retinalis.

88. Answer: (A)

The most likely diagnosis in this patient is lipoprotein lipase deficiency. This is a rare autosomal recessive disorder that causes chylomicronemia, which is a buildup of chylomicrons in the blood. Chylomicrons are large lipoprotein particles that transport triglycerides from the small intestine to the rest of the body. Lipoprotein lipase is an enzyme that breaks down triglycerides into smaller particles that can be taken up by cells. Patients with lipoprotein lipase deficiency have impaired metabolism of chylomicrons, which leads to chylomicronemia. (B) Familial hypercholesterolemia is a genetic disorder that causes elevated LDL cholesterol levels. LDL cholesterol is the "bad" type of cholesterol that can lead to atherosclerosis. Familial hypercholesterolemia is not typically associated with chylomicronemia or recurrent pancreatitis. (C) Type 1 diabetes mellitus is an autoimmune disorder that causes the destruction of insulin-producing beta cells in the pancreas. Insulin is a hormone that helps cells take up glucose from the bloodstream. Type 1 diabetes mellitus is not typically associated with chylomicronemia or recurrent pancreatitis. (D) Pancreatitis due to gallstones is a common cause of pancreatitis. However, patients with pancreatitis due to gallstones typically do not have chylomicronemia. (E) This is incorrect because lipoprotein lipase deficiency is the most likely diagnosis in this patient.

89. The correct answer is A.

Administration of fibric acid derivatives. The patient's presentation of high triglyceride levels despite dietary changes suggests a diagnosis of familial hypertriglyceridemia. In individuals diagnosed with familial hypertriglyceridemia, the administration of fibric acid derivatives, omega-3 fatty acids, or niacin may be considered when dietary interventions prove to be inadequate in managing hypercholesterolemia and hypertriglyceridemia. Administration of fat-soluble vitamin supplements (Option B) is typically recommended for patients with severe hypertriglyceridemia who are prescribed a diet that is devoid of fats. Administration of insulin (Option C) is typically used to manage blood glucose levels in patients with diabetes, not hypertriglyceridemia. Referral to a nephrologist (Option D) would be appropriate for patients with kidney disease, not hypertriglyceridemia. Administration of aspirin (Option E) is typically used to prevent blood clots, not to manage hypertriglyceridemia.

90. Answer: (A)

PCSK9 inhibitors are a class of drugs that lower LDL cholesterol levels by blocking the PCSK9 protein. The PCSK9 protein causes the liver to remove fewer LDL cholesterol receptors from the bloodstream. PCSK9 inhibitors are administered by injection every 2 weeks or every 4 weeks. They are associated with a low risk of side effects, such as injection site reactions and flu-like symptoms. PCSK9 inhibitors are approved for the treatment of patients with high cholesterol who are at high risk for cardiovascular disease.

91. The correct answer is A.

Initiate high-intensity statin therapy. The patient's presentation of risk factors for cardiovascular disease (hypertension, obesity, family history of CVD) and a high LDL-C level suggest that he is at a high risk for atherosclerotic cardiovascular disease (ASCVD). The 2018 Guideline on the Management of Blood Cholesterol recommends that younger patients with baseline LDL-C levels of 190 mg/dL or higher be considered for high-intensity statin therapy. Therefore, initiating high-intensity statin therapy would be the most appropriate next step in management for this patient. Initiating moderate-intensity statin therapy (Option B) may not be sufficient given the patient's high LDL-C level and multiple risk factors for CVD. While lifestyle modifications (Option C) are important, they may not be sufficient on their own given the patient's high LDL-C level. Initiating antihypertensive therapy only (Option D) would not address the patient's high LDL-C level. No intervention (Option E) would not be appropriate given the patient's high risk for ASCVD.

92. The correct answer is B.Perform genetic testing for hemochromatosis.

The patient's presentation of increased concentrations of serum iron, percentage of transferrin saturation, and serum ferritin, along with a fasting serum transferrin saturation level surpassing 50%, suggests the potential presence of homozygosity for hemochromatosis. It is advisable to undergo genetic testing for hemochromatosis if there is an abnormality in either the percentage of transferrin saturation or the level of serum ferritin. Therefore, performing genetic testing for hemochromatosis would be the most appropriate next step in management for this patient. Initiating iron supplementation (Option A) would not be appropriate given the patient's high iron levels. Initiating phlebotomy (Option C) could be considered as a treatment for hemochromatosis, but it would be premature to start this treatment before confirming the diagnosis with genetic testing. Performing a liver biopsy (Option D) may be required to evaluate the presence of cirrhosis and quantify the levels of iron in the liver tissue, but it would be more appropriate to confirm the diagnosis with genetic testing first. No intervention (Option E) would not be appropriate given the patient's abnormal lab results.

93. Answer: (E)

Iron supplementation is not a standard therapeutic approach for hemochromatosis. Hemochromatosis is a condition characterized by iron overload. Iron supplementation would only make the condition worse. (A) Phlebotomy is a standard therapeutic approach for hemochromatosis. Phlebotomy is the removal of blood from the body. It is a safe and effective way to remove excess iron from the body. (B) Chelating agents are also a standard therapeutic approach for hemochromatosis. Chelating agents are medications that bind to iron and remove it from the body. (C) Supportive measures to address organ impairments are also a standard therapeutic approach for hemochromatosis. Hemochromatosis can damage organs such as the liver, heart, and pancreas. Supportive measures can help to protect these organs from further damage. (D) Liver transplantation is a standard therapeutic approach for hemochromatosis in cases where the liver has been severely damaged. The standard therapeutic approaches for hemochromatosis are phlebotomy, chelating agents, supportive measures to address organ impairments, and liver transplantation. Iron supplementation is not a standard therapeutic approach for hemochromatosis.

94. Answer: (A)

Urine porphyrins are the most important laboratory test for establishing a definitive diagnosis of porphyria. Porphyrias are a group of metabolic disorders that result in the accumulation of porphyrins, which are intermediates in the heme synthesis pathway. Porphyrins can be excreted in the urine, feces, and plasma, but urine porphyrins are the most sensitive and specific test for porphyria. (B) Fecal porphyrins are elevated in some types of porphyria, but they are not as sensitive or specific as urine porphyrins. (C) Plasma porphyrins are elevated in some types of porphyria, but they are not as sensitive or specific as urine porphyrins. (D) Red blood cell porphyrins are elevated in some types of porphyria, but they are not as sensitive or specific as urine porphyrins. (E) Enzyme assays can be used to diagnose some types of porphyria, but they are not as sensitive or specific as urine porphyrins. Urine porphyrins are the most important laboratory test for establishing a definitive diagnosis of porphyria.

95. The correct answer is B. HFE gene mutation analysis.

The patient's presentation and lab results suggest a potential diagnosis of hemochromatosis. The best test to confirm this diagnosis is an HFE gene mutation analysis. Hemochromatosis is most often caused by a mutation in the HFE gene, which controls the amount of iron your body absorbs from food. The most common type of the disease affects people who have a particular mutation (C282Y) on both copies of this gene. Therefore, an HFE gene mutation analysis would be the most appropriate diagnostic test for this patient. While a liver biopsy (Option A) can be used to evaluate the presence of cirrhosis and quantify the levels of iron in the liver tissue, it is typically performed after a genetic test has confirmed the diagnosis of hemochromatosis. Serum ferritin test (Option C) and transferrin saturation test (Option D) are useful for initial screening but are not definitive for the diagnosis. An ultrasound of the liver (Option E) could show signs of iron overload, but it is not specific or definitive for diagnosing hemochromatosis.

96. The correct answer is A. Administration of heme arginate, heme albumin, or hematin.

The patient's presentation and history suggest she is experiencing an episode of Acute Intermittent Porphyria. The suggested therapeutic approach for managing this condition during an episode involves the administration of heme, specifically heme arginate, heme albumin, or hematin, at a dosage of 3-4 mg per day over a period of 4 consecutive days. While the administration of narcotic analgesics (Option B) can help manage the abdominal pain, and phenothiazines (Option C) can alleviate symptoms such as nausea, vomiting, anxiety, and restlessness, these treatments address the symptoms rather than the underlying cause of the episode. The administration of intravenous glucose (Option D) or the use of parenteral nutrition (Option E) can be considered when oral feeding is not feasible for extended durations, but these treatments are not the primary therapeutic approach for managing an episode of Acute Intermittent Porphyria.

97. Answer: (A) Porphyria cutanea tarda (PCT)

PCT is the most common type of porphyria. It is characterized by painful, blistering skin lesions that develop on sun-exposed skin. The lesions are caused by the accumulation of porphyrins in the skin. Porphyrins are chemicals that are normally produced in the liver as part of the heme synthesis pathway. However, in people with PCT, the activity of the enzyme uroporphyrinogen decarboxylase is reduced, leading to a buildup of porphyrins in the skin. The facial hyperpigmentation and fragility seen in PCT are also caused by the accumulation of porphyrins in the skin. Porphyrins can darken the skin and make it more fragile. Neurological manifestations are not typically seen in PCT. AIP, VP, CEP, and HEP are other types of porphyria, but they have different clinical presentations. AIP is characterized by episodes of acute abdominal pain, nausea, vomiting, and neurological symptoms. VP is characterized by a variety of clinical manifestations, including skin lesions, abdominal pain, and neurological symptoms. CEP is characterized by red or brown urine and photosensitivity. HEP is a rare type of porphyria that is characterized by skin lesions, abdominal pain, and anemia. Therefore, the most likely diagnosis in this patient is PCT.

98. Answer: (C) Wilson's disease

Wilson's disease is a rare autosomal recessive disorder that causes copper to accumulate in the liver, brain, and other organs. The clinical manifestations of Wilson's disease can vary widely, but the most common findings include Kayser-Fleischer rings (a golden-brown discoloration of the cornea), liver disease, and neurological problems. Kayser-Fleischer rings are a pathognomonic sign of Wilson's disease. They are caused by the deposition of copper in the cornea. Liver biopsy is the definitive test for Wilson's disease. It shows increased copper levels in the liver. Serum ceruloplasmin levels are frequently low in Wilson's disease. Ceruloplasmin is a protein that binds copper in the blood. When copper levels are elevated, ceruloplasmin levels can decrease. Porphyria cutanea tarda, acute intermittent porphyria, variegate porphyria, and congenital erythropoietic porphyria are all types of porphyria, a group of rare metabolic disorders that affect the production of heme, a component of hemoglobin. Porphyrias can cause a variety of clinical manifestations, including skin lesions, abdominal pain, and neurological problems. However, none of these porphyrias are associated with Kayser-Fleischer rings or elevated liver copper levels. Therefore, the most likely diagnosis in this patient is Wilson's disease.

99. Answer: The correct answer is A.Administration of oral Zinc acetate.

The patient's presentation and diagnosis suggest that she has Wilson's Disease with coexisting hepatitis. In such cases, the recommended treatment is oral administration of Zinc acetate at a dosage of 50-mg elemental Zn three times daily. Zinc demonstrates efficacy through its ability to inhibit the absorption of copper in the intestines and stimulate the production of metallothionein, a protein that binds copper in a non-toxic complex. Administration of intravenous Zinc acetate (Option B) is not typically recommended. Administration of oral Copper acetate (Option C) would not be appropriate as Wilson's Disease is a disorder of copper metabolism, and additional copper could exacerbate the condition. Liver transplantation (Option D) is usually considered for patients with severe liver disease or those who fail to respond to medical therapy. No intervention (Option E) would not be appropriate given the patient's diagnosis and the potential for disease progression.

100. The correct answer is C.Liver transplantation.

The patient's presentation and diagnosis suggest that he has Wilson's Disease with severe hepatic decompensation. In such cases, liver transplantation should be taken into consideration as a potential treatment option. While the administration of oral trientine and zinc supplementation (Option A) or oral tetrathiomolybdate (Option B) can be used to manage Wilson's Disease, these treatments may not be sufficient in cases of severe hepatic decompensation. Penicillamine (Option D) is currently not considered as the primary treatment option due to its potential side effects. No intervention (Option E) would not be appropriate given the patient's severe hepatic decompensation and the potential for further disease progression.

Chapter 3

HEMATOLOGY BOARD QUESTIONS

1. A 42-year-old woman presents with fatigue and shortness of breath. Her physical examination is unremarkable. Her complete blood count shows a microcytic, hypochromic anemia. A peripheral blood smear shows basophilic stippling. Which of the following is the most likely cause of the basophilic stippling?

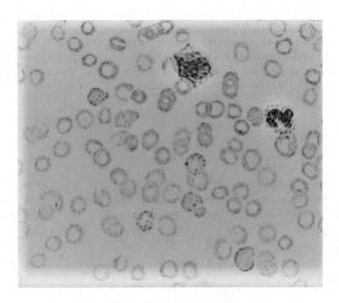

Figure 3.1: Basophilic Stippling

- A. Lead poisoning
- B. Thalassemia
- C. Myelofibrosis
- D. Myelodysplastic syndrome
- E. Sideroblastic anemia

2. A 33-year-old man presents with fatigue and jaundice. His physical examination is unremarkable. His complete blood count shows a hemolytic anemia. A peripheral blood smear shows Heinz bodies. Which of the following is the most likely cause of the Heinz bodies?

83

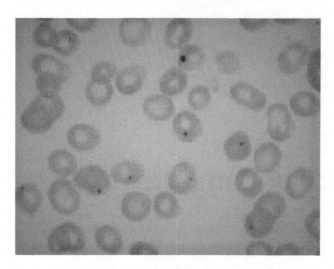

Figure 3.2: Heinz bodies

- A. G6PD defiencicy
- B. Sickle cell anemia
- C. Thalassemia
- D. Hereditary spherocytosis
- E. Paroxysmal nocturnal hemoglobinuria

3. A 61-year-old man with a history of chronic obstructive pulmonary disease (COPD) presents with fatigue and shortness of breath. His physical examination is unremarkable. His complete blood count shows a normocytic, normochromic anemia. A bone marrow aspirate shows an erythrocyte to granulocyte ratio of 0.5. Which of the following is the most likely cause of the low erythrocyte to granulocyte ratio?

- A. Acute infection
- B. Chronic infection
- C. Myelodysplastic disorder
- D. Pure red cell aplasia
- E. Anemia with erythroid hyperplasia

4. A 57-year-old woman presents with fatigue, shortness of breath, and a rash. Her physical examination is notable for a non-productive cough, wheezing, and a petechial rash on her lower extremities. Her complete blood count shows an absolute eosinophil count of 1,500 cells/L. Which of the following is the most likely cause of the eosinophilia?

- A. Drug-induced reaction
- B. Parasitic infection
- C. Allergic disorder
- D. Collagen vascular disease
- E. Malignant neoplasm

5. A 22-year-old woman of African descent presents with fatigue and a recent history of sinus infections. Her physical examination is unremarkable. Her complete blood count shows an absolute neutrophil count of 1,000 cells/L. Which of the following is the most likely diagnosis?

- A. Myelodysplastic syndrome
- B. Acute myeloid leukemia
- C. Chronic myeloid leukemia
- D. Aplastic anemia
- E. Benign ethnic neutropenia

6. A 59-year-old woman presents with fatigue and shortness of breath. Her physical examination is unremarkable. Her complete blood count shows a microcytic, hypochromic anemia. A bone marrow aspirate shows hypocellularity with decreased erythroid precursors. Which of the following is the most likely diagnosis?

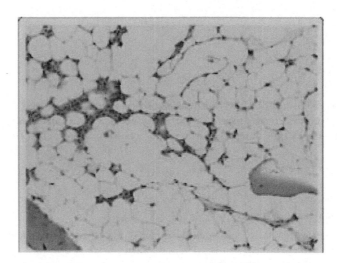

Figure 3.3: 59-year-old woman

- A. Iron deficiency anemia
- B. Thalassemia
- C. Myelodysplastic syndrome
- D. Aplastic anemia
- E. Pure red cell aplasia

7. A 41-year-old woman presents with fatigue and shortness of breath. Her physical examination is unremarkable. Her complete blood count shows a microcytic, hypochromic anemia. Her iron studies show a serum iron level of 25 mcg/dL, a ferritin level of 10 ng/mL, and a TIBC of 400 mcg/dL. Which of the following is the most likely diagnosis?

- A. Iron deficiency anemia
- B. Thalassemia
- C. Myelodysplastic syndrome
- D. Aplastic anemia
- E. Pure red cell aplasia

8. A 66-year-old man presents with fatigue and shortness of breath. His physical examination is unremarkable. His complete blood count shows a normocytic, normochromic anemia. His erythropoietin level is 100 mIU/mL. Which of the following is the most likely diagnosis?

- A. Iron deficiency anemia
- B. Thalassemia
- C. Myelodysplastic syndrome
- D. Aplastic anemia
- E. Pure red cell aplasia

9. A 52-year-old woman presents with fatigue and shortness of breath. Her physical examination is unremarkable. Her complete blood count shows a microcytic, hypochromic anemia. Her iron studies show a serum iron level of 25 mcg/dL, a TIBC of 400 mcg/dL, and a percent saturation of 6%. Which of the following is the most likely diagnosis?

- A. Thalassemia
- B. Iron deficiency anemia
- C. Myelodysplastic syndrome
- D. Aplastic anemia
- E. Pure red cell aplasia

10. A 35-year-old man presents with fatigue and shortness of breath. His physical examination is unremarkable. His complete blood count shows a microcytic, hypochromic anemia. His iron studies show a serum iron level of 25 mcg/dL, a TIBC of 400 mcg/dL, and a percent saturation of 6%. A peripheral blood smear shows microcytic, hypochromic red blood cells with basophilic stippling. Which of the following is the most likely diagnosis?

- A. Iron deficiency anemia
- B. Thalassemia
- C. Sideroblastic anemia
- D. Myelodysplastic syndrome
- E. Pure red cell aplasia

11. A 47-year-old man with a history of G6PD deficiency presents with fatigue and jaundice. He reports taking sulfamethoxazole/trimethoprim for a recent urinary tract infection. His physical examination is unremarkable. His complete blood count shows a hemolytic anemia. Which of the following is the most likely diagnosis?

- A. G6PD deficiency
- B. Sickle cell anemia
- C. Thalassemia
- D. Hereditary spherocytosis
- E. Paroxysmal nocturnal hemoglobinuria

12. A 51-year-old woman presents with fatigue and jaundice. Her physical examination is unremarkable. Her complete blood count shows a hemolytic anemia. A peripheral blood smear shows spherocytes. A Coombs' test is positive. Which of the following is the most likely diagnosis?

- A. Warm antibody immunohemolytic anemia
- B. Cold antibody immunohemolytic anemia
- C. Paroxysmal cold hemoglobinuria
- D. Sickle cell anemia
- E. Thalassemia

13. A 29-year-old woman of Italian descent presents with fatigue and shortness of breath. Her physical examination is unremarkable. Her complete blood count shows a microcytic, hypochromic anemia. A peripheral blood smear shows target cells and basophilic stippling. Her parents are both of Italian descent. Which of the following is the most likely diagnosis?

- A. Hereditary spherocytosis
- B. Sickle cell anemia
- C. Iron deficiency anemia
- D. Thalassemia
- E. Paroxysmal nocturnal hemoglobinuria

14. A 45-year-old man presents with fatigue, pallor, and dark urine. He has also been experiencing abdominal pain and easy bruising. His physical examination is unremarkable. His complete blood count shows a hemolytic anemia. A peripheral blood smear shows schistocytes and helmet cells. His serum lactate dehydrogenase (LDH) is elevated. Flow cytometry shows deficiency of CD55 and CD59 on blood erythrocytes, granulocytes, and monocytes. Which of the following is the most likely diagnosis?

- A. Iron deficiency anemia
- B. Sickle cell anemia
- C. Paroxysmal nocturnal hemoglobinuria
- D. Hereditary spherocytosis
- E. Aplastic anemia

15. A 71-year-old woman presents with fatigue, pallor, and easy bruising. She has also been experiencing fever and night sweats. Her physical examination is notable for petechiae and ecchymoses. Her complete blood count shows pancytopenia. Which of the following is the most likely diagnosis?

- A. Aplastic anemia
- B. Myelodysplastic syndrome
- C. Leukemia
- D. Infection
- E. Autoimmune disorder

16. A 58-year-old woman presents with fatigue, pallor, and shortness of breath. Her physical examination is unremarkable. Her complete blood count shows a macrocytic, normochromic anemia. Her vitamin B12 level is 100 pg/mL.

Which of the following is the most appropriate course of treatment?

- A. Oral vitamin B12 1000 mcg daily
- B. Parenteral vitamin B12 100 mcg intramuscularly once daily for 7 days, then 100 mcg monthly
- C. Parenteral vitamin B12 100 mcg intramuscularly weekly
- D. Parenteral vitamin B12 1000 mcg intramuscularly weekly
- E. Parenteral vitamin B12 1000 mcg intramuscularly daily

17. A 25-year-old man with sickle cell anemia presents to the emergency department with a painful crisis. He is currently taking hydroxyurea and folic acid. His vital signs are within normal limits. His physical examination is notable for conjunctival pallor and dactylitis. His complete blood count shows a normocytic, normochromic anemia. Which of the following is the most appropriate next step in management?

- (A) Increase the dose of hydroxyurea
- (B) Administer oxygen
- (C) Administer analgesics
- (D) Administer hydration
- (E) Transfuse red blood cells

18. A 32-year-old woman presents with fatigue, pallor, and jaundice. Her physical examination is unremarkable. Her complete blood count shows a hemolytic anemia. A peripheral blood smear shows spherocytes. A Coombs' test is positive. Which of the following is the most appropriate next step in management?

- (A) Prednisone
- (B) Danazol
- (C) Plasmapheresis
- (D) Rituximab

19. A 63-year-old man is admitted to the hospital with a diagnosis of deep vein thrombosis. He is started on heparin therapy. On day 5 of his hospitalization, he develops a decrease in his platelet count. His platelet count is now 10,000/L. Which of the following is the most likely diagnosis?

- A. Heparin-induced thrombocytopenia
- B. Drug-induced thrombocytopenia
- C. Idiopathic thrombocytopenic purpura
- D. Disseminated intravascular coagulation.
- E. Thrombotic thrombocytopenic purpura

20. A 51-year-old woman presents to the clinic with a platelet count of 5,000/L. She has no history of bleeding or bruising. Her physical examination is unremarkable. A peripheral blood smear is performed, which shows platelet clumps. Which of the following is the most likely diagnosis?

- A. Thrombotic thrombocytopenic purpura
- B. Idiopathic thrombocytopenic purpura
- C. Disseminated intravascular coagulation.
- D. Pseudothrombocytopenia
- E. Heparin-induced thrombocytopenia

21. A 69-year-old man with a history of liver cirrhosis presents to the clinic with a complaint of easy bruising. His physical examination is unremarkable. His complete blood count shows a normal white blood cell count and platelet count. His prothrombin time (PT) is 14 seconds, and his partial thromboplastin time (PTT) is 45 seconds. Which of the following is the most likely explanation for his prolonged PT and PTT?

- A. Vitamin K deficiency
- B. Liver disease
- C. Disseminated intravascular coagulation.
- D. Heparin-induced thrombocytopenia

22. A 45-year-old woman with chronic ITP presents to the clinic with a platelet count of 20,000/L. She has no history of bleeding or bruising. She has been taking prednisone 1 mg/kg per day for the past 6 months, but her platelet count has not responded to treatment. Which of the following is the next best step in management?

- A. Continue prednisone.

- B. Increase prednisone dose
- C. Administer IVIg
- D. Administer rituximab.
- E. Refer for splenectomy.

23. A 51-year-old woman with acute promyelocytic leukemia presents to the hospital with a fever and shortness of breath. Her physical examination is notable for petechiae and ecchymoses. Her complete blood count shows a platelet count of 10,000/L, a white blood cell count of 30,000/L, and a hemoglobin level of 8 g/dL. Her prothrombin time (PT) is 18 seconds, and her partial thromboplastin time (PTT) is 60 seconds. Which of the following is the most appropriate next step in management?

- A. Administer platelets.
- B. Administer fresh-frozen plasma.
- C. Administer heparin.
- D. Administer red blood cells.
- E. Manage the underlying cause of DIC.

24. A 38-year-old woman presents to the emergency department with a 1-day history of petechiae, ecchymoses, and blurry vision. Her physical examination is notable for pallor and conjunctival petechiae. Her complete blood count shows a platelet count of 10,000/L, a white blood cell count of 10,000/L, and a hemoglobin level of 10 g/dL. Her prothrombin time (PT) is 18 seconds, and her partial thromboplastin time (PTT) is 60 seconds. Which of the following is the most appropriate next step in management?

- A. Administer plasmapheresis.
- B. Administer fresh frozen plasma.
- C. Administer IV IgG
- D. Administer caplacizumab.

25 A 21-year-old man with Hemophilia B presents to the clinic with a history of easy bruising. He has been taking factor IX concentrate on a regular basis, but he has been experiencing more frequent bleeding episodes. His physical examination is unremarkable. His complete blood count shows a normal white blood cell count and platelet count. His prothrombin time (PT) is 18 seconds, and his partial thromboplastin time (PTT) is 60 seconds. Which of the following is the next best step in management?

- A. Administer gene therapy.
- B. Switch to recombinant factor IX
- C. Increase the dose of factor IX concentrate.
- D. Refer to a hematologist.

26. A 35-year-old woman with Von Willebrand Disease presents to the clinic with a history of easy bruising. She has been taking desmopressin on a regular basis, but she has been experiencing more frequent bleeding episodes. Her physical examination is unremarkable. Her complete blood count shows a normal white blood cell count and platelet count. Her prothrombin time (PT) is 18 seconds, and her partial thromboplastin time (PTT) is 60 seconds. Which of the following is the next best step in management?

- A. Increase the dose of desmopressin.
- B. Switch to cryoprecipitate
- C. Switch to factor VIII concentrate.
- D. Refer to a hematologist.

27. A 67-year-old man with atrial fibrillation is admitted to the hospital for a transient ischemic attack. He is started on unfractionated heparin therapy. On day 3 of his hospitalization, he develops epistaxis. His vital signs are within normal limits. His physical examination is notable for blood coming from his nose. His complete blood count shows a normal white blood cell count and platelet count. His prothrombin time (PT) is 18 seconds, and his partial thromboplastin time (PTT) is 60 seconds. Which of the following is the next best step in management?

- A. Continue unfractionated heparin therapy.
- B. Stop unfractionated heparin therapy.
- C. Administer protamine.
- D. Refer to a hematologist.

28. A 79-year-old woman with atrial fibrillation is taking warfarin. She presents to the emergency department with a head injury after a fall. Her physical examination is notable for a head laceration and a decreased level of consciousness. Her prothrombin time (PT) is 18 seconds, and her partial thromboplastin time (PTT) is 60 seconds. Which of the following is the most appropriate next step in management?

- A. Administer vitamin K.
- B. Administer FFP
- C. Administer both vitamin K and FFP
- D. Refer to a hematologist.

29. A 68-year-old man with a history of atrial fibrillation is admitted to the hospital for a transient ischemic attack. He is started on heparin therapy. On day 3 of his hospitalization, he develops a decrease in his platelet count. His platelet count is now 10,000/L. Which of the following is the most appropriate next step in management?

- A. Continue heparin therapy.
- B. Switch to argatroban
- C. Switch to lepirudin
- D. Refer to a hematologist.

30. A 71-year-old woman with a history of atrial fibrillation and a mechanical heart valve is taking warfarin. She presents to the clinic with a question about the new oral Xa and thrombin inhibitors. She asks if these medications would be an effective alternative to warfarin. Which of the following is the most appropriate response?

- A. The new oral Xa and thrombin inhibitors are more effective than warfarin in patients with heart valve abnormalities.
- B. The new oral Xa and thrombin inhibitors are less effective than warfarin in patients with heart valve abnormalities.
- C. The new oral Xa and thrombin inhibitors are equally effective as warfarin in patients with heart valve abnormalities.
- D. The efficacy of the new oral Xa and thrombin inhibitors in patients with heart valve abnormalities is still being studied.

31. A 62-year-old man is diagnosed with Myelodysplastic Syndromes. He is offered treatment with 5-Azacytidine. He asks you about the benefits of this treatment. Which of the following is the most appropriate response?

- A. 5-Azacytidine has been shown to cure Myelodysplastic Syndromes.
- B. 5-Azacytidine has been shown to significantly delay the progression to acute myeloid leukemia.
- C. 5-Azacytidine has been shown to improve the quality of life in patients with Myelodysplastic Syndromes.
- D. 5-Azacytidine has been shown to be a safe and effective treatment for Myelodysplastic Syndromes.

32. A 67-year-old man is diagnosed with Myelodysplastic Syndromes. He has the 5q- syndrome. He is offered treatment with Lenalidomide. He asks you about the benefits of this treatment. Which of the following is the most appropriate response?

- A. Lenalidomide has been shown to cure Myelodysplastic Syndromes.
- B. Lenalidomide has been shown to significantly delay the progression to acute myeloid leukemia.
- C. Lenalidomide has been shown to induce transfusion independence in a significant proportion of patients diagnosed with the 5q- syndrome.
- D. Lenalidomide has been shown to be a safe and effective treatment for Myelodysplastic Syndromes.

33. A 74-year-old man is diagnosed with polycythemia vera. He is found to have the JAK2 V617F mutation. What is the significance of this finding? Which of the following is the most appropriate response?

- A. The JAK2 V617F mutation is a rare finding in patients with polycythemia vera.
- B. The JAK2 V617F mutation is a common finding in patients with polycythemia vera, and it is associated with a worse prognosis.
- C. The JAK2 V617F mutation is a common finding in patients with polycythemia vera, but it does not affect the prognosis.
- D. The JAK2 V617F mutation is a rare finding in patients with polycythemia vera, but it is associated with a better prognosis.

34. A 78-year-old man presents to the clinic with a history of high blood pressure and a family history of polycythemia

vera. He is found to have a high red blood cell count, a high white blood cell count, and a high platelet count. His vitamin B12 levels are elevated, and his erythropoietin levels are decreased. He is tested for the JAK2 V617F mutation, and the test is positive. What is the most likely diagnosis? Which of the following is the most appropriate answer?

- A. Polycythemia vera
- B. Secondary polycythemia
- C. Essential thrombocytosis
- D. Myelofibrosis

35. A 69-year-old man is diagnosed with idiopathic myelofibrosis. He is asymptomatic. What is the best management approach? Which of the following is the most appropriate answer?

- A. Hydroxyurea
- B. Ruxolitinib
- C. Lenalidomide
- D. Observation

36. A 68-year-old man with a history of hypertension presents to the clinic with a complaint of left upper quadrant pain. He is found to have an enlarged spleen. Which imaging modality is most appropriate for further evaluation? Which of the following is the most appropriate answer?

- A. CT
- B. Ultrasound
- C. MRI
- D. PET scan

37. A 62-year-old man is diagnosed with chronic lymphocytic leukemia (CLL). He is found to have a high percentage of CD38-positive tumors. What is the significance of this finding? Which of the following is the most appropriate response?

- A. The patient has a more favorable prognosis.
- B. The patient has a more unfavorable prognosis.
- C. The patient is more likely to respond to treatment.
- D. The patient is less likely to respond to treatment.

38. A 57-year-old man is diagnosed with chronic lymphocytic leukemia (CLL). He develops anemia and thrombocytopenia. What is the next best step in management? Which of the following is the most appropriate answer?

- A. Administer supportive care.
- B. Perform splenectomy.
- C. Initiate chemotherapy.
- D. Administer monthly intravenous immunoglobulin (IVIg).

39. A 81-year-old man with a hemoglobin level of 10 gm/dL and a longest diameter of the largest node of 7 cm is diagnosed with chronic lymphocytic leukemia (CLL). He is found to have increased levels of serum 2-microglobulin. What is his FLIPI-2 score? Which of the following is the most appropriate answer?

- A. 0
- B. 1
- C. 2
- D. 3

40. A 67-year-old man with a high LDH level and bulky disease is diagnosed with diffuse large B-cell lymphoma. He has a Karnofsky performance status of 80%. What is his prognosis? Which of the following is the most appropriate answer?

- A. Good
- B. Intermediate
- C. Poor

41. A 72-year-old man is diagnosed with double-hit lymphoma. He has a mutation in c-Myc and bcl-6. What chemotherapy regimen is most likely to be effective? Which of the following is the most appropriate answer?

- A. R-CHOP

- B. CHOP
- C. Dose-adjusted EPOCH
- D. Bendamustine

42. A 49-year-old man is diagnosed with Hodgkin's lymphoma. Which cell type is associated with the formation of Hodgkin's lymphoma tumors? Which of the following is the most appropriate answer?

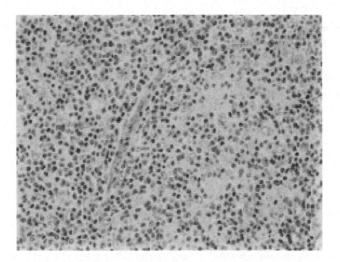

Figure 3.4: Hodgkin's lymphoma

- A. Reed-Sternberg cells
- B. B cells
- C. T cells
- D. Plasma cells

43. A 57-year-old man is diagnosed with Hodgkin's lymphoma and has a mediastinal mass that exceeds one-third of the greatest chest diameter. What is the recommended treatment? Which of the following is the most appropriate answer?

- A. MOPP chemotherapy
- B. ABVD chemotherapy
- C. MOPP-ABV hybrid chemotherapy
- D. Combined modality therapy

44. A 77-year-old man presents with fatigue, shortness of breath, and easy bruising. He is found to have an atypical blood count and abnormal blood cell morphology. What diagnostic tests should be ordered? Which of the following is the most appropriate answer?

- A. Bone marrow biopsy
- B. Peripheral blood smear
- C. Both bone marrow biopsy and peripheral blood smear
- D. Neither bone marrow biopsy nor peripheral blood smear

45. A 64-year-old man is diagnosed with low-risk acute myeloid leukemia and successfully attains complete remission. He has the t[8;21] genetic abnormality. What is the recommended treatment? Which of the following is the most appropriate answer?

- A. 3-4 cycles of cytarabine
- B. 7-8 cycles of cytarabine
- C. 3-4 cycles of cytarabine followed by 7-8 cycles of daunorubicin.
- D. 7-8 cycles of cytarabine followed by 3-4 cycles of daunorubicin.

46. A 73-year-old man is diagnosed with chronic myeloid leukemia. He is found to have anemia and a decrease in

platelet counts. He is also found to have additional cytogenetic abnormalities. What is the most likely diagnosis? Which of the following is the most appropriate answer?

- A. Accelerated phase of chronic myeloid leukemia.
- B. Blast crisis of chronic myeloid leukemia
- C. Chronic phase of chronic myeloid leukemia
- D. Myelodysplastic syndrome

47. A 68-year-old man is diagnosed with chronic myeloid leukemia (CML). He is in the chronic phase of the disease. What is the most favorable timing for transplantation? Which of the following is the most appropriate answer?

- A. Within one year of diagnosis
- B. Within two years of diagnosis
- C. Within three years of diagnosis
- D. After the disease progresses to the accelerated phase or blast crisis.

48. A 48-year-old man is diagnosed with adult T-cell leukemia/lymphoma (ATL). He is found to have hypercalcemia. What is the most appropriate treatment? Which of the following is the most appropriate answer?

- A. Glucocorticoids
- B. Zidovudine
- C. Interferon (IFN)
- D. Lenalidomide
- E. Mogamulizumab

49. A 52-year-old man is diagnosed with multiple myeloma. He is found to have a high risk of developing bacterial infections. What is the most likely reason for this? Which of the following is the most appropriate answer?

- A. The presence of an ill-defined tumor product hinders the migration of granulocytes.
- B. The patient has a decreased number of granulocytes.
- C. The patient has a decreased production of antibodies.
- D. The patient has a decreased production of complement proteins.

50. A 71-year-old man is diagnosed with multiple myeloma. He is eligible for high-dose therapy and autologous stem cell transplant. What is the most appropriate treatment? Which of the following is the most appropriate answer?

- A. Lenalidomide, dexamethasone, and bortezomib
- B. Melphalan, prednisone, and thalidomide
- C. Cyclophosphamide, vincristine, adriamycin, and dexamethasone (CVAD)
- D. Doxorubicin, bleomycin, vincristine, and dexamethasone (DBVD)

51. A 69-year-old man is diagnosed with multiple myeloma and is not eligible for transplantation. What is the most appropriate treatment? Which of the following is the most appropriate answer?

- A. None of the above
- B. Melphalan, prednisone, and bortezomib
- C. High-dose melphalan followed by two autologous stem cell transplants.
- D. Melphalan and prednisone

52. An elderly woman presents with symptoms of malnutrition and a diet low in leafy green vegetables and fruits. She has megaloblastic anemia from impaired DNA synthesis, resulting in ineffective erythropoiesis and macrocytosis. Her absence of neurologic symptoms and normal methylmalonic acid levels suggest a certain type of deficiency rather than another. What deficiency is the patient most likely suffering from?

- A. Vitamin D deficiency
- B. Folate deficiency
- C. Vitamin E deficiency
- D. Vitamin K deficiency
- E. Vitamin B12 deficiency

53. A patient presents with neurologic deficits, megaloblastic macrocytic anemia, and increased methylmalonic acid. His diet is vegan and does not include foods of animal origin rich in a certain vitamin. What is the most appropriate treatment for this patient?

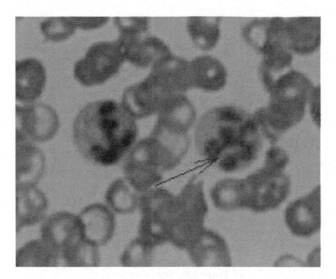

Figure 3.5: Macrocytic Anemian

- A. Oral folic acid supplementation
- B. Vitamin D supplementation
- C. Iron supplementation
- D. Vitamin B12 1 mg IM weekly and then monthly
- E. Oral vitamin K supplementation

54. A patient presents with pica, angular cheilosis, atrophic glossitis, and guaiac positive stool. Which of the following lab findings would you expect in this patient?

- A. Iron/TIBC >45%, ferritin 300 ng/mL
- B. Iron/TIBC = 35%, ferritin 150 ng/mL
- C. Iron/TIBC <18%, ferritin 5 ng/mL
- D. Iron/TIBC = 25%, ferritin 50 ng/mL
- E. Iron/TIBC = 40%, ferritin 200 ng/mL

55. A young patient presents with symptoms and lab findings suggestive of a new diagnosis of aplastic anemia. Which of the following would be the most appropriate first-line treatment for this patient?

- A. Allogeneic stem cell transplant
- B. Immunosuppression with cyclosporine or tacrolimus
- C. Thrombopoietin mimetics
- D. Supportive care with transfusions, antibiotics, and growth factors
- E. Watchful waiting

56. A patient presents with normocytic anemia, high ferritin levels, worsening arthralgias, and new oral ulcers. The patient's history reveals lupus and a normal creatinine level. Last year, the patient's Hgb was normal, and no exposure to alcohol, isoniazid, chloramphenicol, or lead was reported. Which of the following is the most likely diagnosis for this patient's anemia?

- A. Anemia of chronic inflammation
- B. Iron deficiency anemia
- C. Anemia of chronic kidney disease
- D. Sideroblastic anemia
- E. Lead poisoning

57. A patient presents signs of hemolytic anemia, spherocytosis, and a positive Coombs test. The patient also exhibits lymphadenopathy and absolute lymphocytosis. Based on these findings, what is the most likely diagnosis?

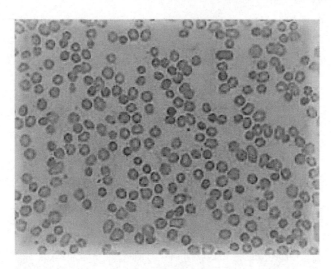

Figure 3.6: Spherocytosis

- A. Autoimmune hemolytic anemia (AIHA)
- B. Drug-induced hemolytic anemia from levofloxacin
- C. Microangiopathic hemolytic anemia (MAHA)
- D. Hereditary spherocytosis
- E. Iron deficiency anemia

58 . A patient presents with a history of fever and a "slapped cheek" appearance. The patient's children have had similar symptoms recently. Laboratory workup shows a normocytic anemia without evidence of thrombocytopenia or leukopenia. What is the most likely diagnosis?

- A. Aplastic anemia
- B. Chronic lymphocytic leukemia
- C. Thymoma
- D. Autoimmune disease
- E. Pure red cell aplasia

59. A 39-year-old female presents with a long-standing, asymptomatic mild anemia. Her mean corpuscular volume (MCV) is low, but her transferrin saturation is greater than 18%. Hemoglobin electrophoresis results are also available. What is the most likely diagnosis?

- A. Iron deficiency anemia
- B. -Thalassemia minor
- C. -Thalassemia minor
- D. Anemia of chronic disease
- E. Sideroblastic anemia

60. A 21-year-old woman with sickle cell disease presents to the emergency department with cough, fever, tachypnea, intercostal retractions, wheezing, rales, and dropping oxygen saturations. Chest X-ray shows new pulmonary infiltrates. Which of the following is the most appropriate management?

- A. Simple transfusion
- B. Steroids
- C. Exchange transfusion
- D. Albuterol nebulizers
- E. None of the above

61. A 33-year-old man presents with fever, fatigue, and jaundice. Laboratory findings include thrombocytopenia, microangiopathic hemolytic anemia, and a low ADAMTS13 activity. Which of the following is the most appropriate treatment?

- A. Fresh frozen plasma
- B. Plasma exchange
- C. Red blood cell transfusion
- D. Platelet transfusion
- E. None of the above

62. A 34-year-old man with a history of sickle cell disease presents with sudden onset of pallor and fatigue. His symptoms began after starting a new medication, trimethoprim-sulfamethoxazole, for a urinary tract infection. His complete blood count shows a significant drop in hemoglobin compared to his baseline and his reticulocyte count is elevated. Considering the patient's ethnic background and recent medication change, what is the next best step in managing this patient's condition?

- A. Begin a course of erythropoietin therapy.
- B. Conduct Glucose-6-phosphate dehydrogenase (G6PD) testing.
- C. Start the patient on iron supplementation.
- D. Order a Coombs test.
- E. Initiate plasmapheresis.

63. A 76-year-old man on warfarin presents with a sudden headache and nausea. On examination, he is found to be drowsy and has left-sided hemiparesis. A CT scan of the head reveals a right-sided intracranial hemorrhage. His INR is 3.5. What is the most appropriate treatment?

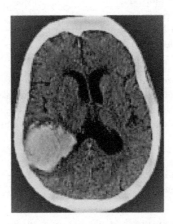

Figure 3.7: CT scan

- A. Administer 4-factor prothrombin complex concentrate (4F-PCC)
- B. Transfuse fresh frozen plasma (FFP)
- C. Transfuse platelets
- D. Transfuse red blood cells (RBCs)
- E. None of the above

64. A patient with a history of chronic kidney disease presents with bleeding gums and petechiae. Laboratory findings show normal platelet count but decreased platelet function. What is the most likely diagnosis and the appropriate intervention?

- A. Acquired platelet disorder; DDAVP (desmopressin acetate)
- B. Congenital platelet disorder; DDAVP (desmopressin acetate)
- C. Acquired platelet disorder; Platelet transfusion
- D. Congenital platelet disorder; Platelet transfusion
- E. Acquired platelet disorder; Insulin administration

65. A young patient presents with palpable purpura, abdominal pain, and new renal failure. Which of the following tests is the most appropriate for diagnosis?

- A. Antineutrophil cytoplasmic antibody (ANCA) testing

- B. Anti–glomerular basement membrane (GBM) antibody testing
- C. Kidney biopsy
- D. Skin biopsy with direct immunofluorescence microscopy
- E. None of the above

66. A young woman presents with microangiopathic hemolytic anemia (MAHA), thrombocytopenia, schistocytes on peripheral smear, elevated LDH, and elevated indirect bilirubin. She has a history of hypothyroidism, likely due to chronic autoimmune hypothyroidism, also known as Hashimoto thyroiditis. Given this information, what is the most likely diagnosis?

- A. Primary immune thrombocytopenia
- B. Evans syndrome
- C. Drug-induced thrombocytopenia
- D. Antimicrobial prophylaxis related side effect
- E. Thrombotic thrombocytopenic purpura

67. A 40-year-old woman presents with a 5-day history of thrombocytopenia (nadir platelet count 30,000/L) and right leg pain and swelling. She was started on heparin 2 days ago for treatment of a deep vein thrombosis (DVT). She has no other medical history and is not taking any other medications. What is the most appropriate management for this patient?

- A. Continue heparin and start corticosteroids.
- B. Continue heparin and start warfarin.
- C. Stop heparin, send PF4-heparin ELISA, start bivalirudin.
- D. Continue heparin and start platelets.
- E. Stop heparin and start aspirin.

68. A 28-year-old woman comes to the clinic due to easy bruising and a recent episode of prolonged bleeding following a minor cut. Blood tests reveal a low platelet count, and further testing shows that the platelets are unusually large. The woman is otherwise healthy and has no other symptoms. Hemoglobin, white blood cell count, and liver function tests are all within normal limits. What is the most likely diagnosis for this patient's condition?

- A. Aleukemic Leukemia
- B. Ehrlichiosis
- C. Drug-associated Thrombocytopenia
- D. Immune Thrombocytopenic Purpura
- E. Viral Syndrome

69. A 67-year-old man with hepatitis C, chronic liver disease, and splenomegaly presents for an elective abdominal surgery. His platelet count is 30,000/L and his INR is 1.2. What is the most appropriate management of his thrombocytopenia?

- A. Romiplostin
- B. Vitamin K
- C. Fresh frozen plasma (FFP)
- D. Platelet transfusion with a platelet goal >50,000/L
- E. None of the above

70. A 22-year-old woman presents with a history of extensive bruising following minor traumas and prolonged bleeding after dental procedures. Laboratory findings show a prolonged bleeding time, normal PT and aPTT, and low von Willebrand factor (vWF) activity. She is scheduled for a minor surgical procedure and is planned to receive DDAVP (desmopressin acetate) for prophylaxis. Which of the following is a condition where DDAVP would NOT be effective?

- A. Mild type I von Willebrand disease
- B. Mild hemophilia A (factor VIII deficiency)
- C. Platelet dysfunction of end-stage renal disease
- D. Type 3 von Willebrand disease
- E. None of the above

71. A 44-year-old man arrives in the emergency department with spontaneous ecchymosis on his body and blood blisters on his mouth. His platelet count is noted to be <10,000/L. The patient needs urgent treatment to pre-

vent potentially severe bleeding, such as in intracranial or visceral locations. What is the most appropriate initial management approach in this case?

- A. Platelet transfusion
- B. Intravenous immunoglobulin (IVIG) + steroids
- C. Splenectomy
- D. Thrombopoietin agonist therapies
- E. Observation and monitoring

72. A 30-year-old man with no prior medical history presents with a 3-day history of shortness of breath and chest pain. He is found to have a deep vein thrombosis (DVT) and a pulmonary embolism (PE). He is started on intravenous unfractionated heparin. On the fifth day of heparin therapy, his platelet count drops from 200,000/L to 50,000/L.

Which of the following is the most likely diagnosis?

- A. Type 1 heparin-induced thrombocytopenia (HIT)
- B. Type 2 HIT
- C. Intra-aortic balloon pump (IABP)-induced thrombocytopenia
- D. All of the above

73. A 32-year-old woman presents with a white blood cell count of 200,000/L and a platelet count of 50,000/L. Her peripheral smear shows promyelocytes. She has a prothrombin time (PT) of 18 seconds, an activated partial thromboplastin time (PTT) of 40 seconds, and a fibrinogen level of 150 mg/dL. She is not actively bleeding. What is the most appropriate treatment at this time?

- A. Platelet transfusion
- B. Intravenous vitamin K
- C. Cryoprecipitate transfusion
- D. Fresh frozen plasma transfusion
- E. Prothrombin complex concentrate (PCC) transfusion

74. A 68-year-old man presents to the emergency department with a severe headache and a history of taking dabigatran 3 hours prior to presentation. He is found to have a major potentially life-threatening bleed. Which of the following is the most appropriate treatment for this patient?

- A. Fresh frozen plasma
- B. Andexanet
- C. Activated prothrombin complex concentrate
- D. Idarucizumab
- E. Factor VIII inhibitor bypassing activity (FEIBA)

75. A 22-year-old man with severe hemophilia A and a high titer of factor VIII inhibitors is presenting to the emergency department with a bleeding episode. He has been treated with recombinant factor VIIa in the past, but he has experienced thrombotic complications. What is the most appropriate treatment for his bleeding episode?

- A. Higher dose of recombinant factor VIII
- B. Emicizumab
- C. Recombinant factor IX
- D. Factor VIIa
- E. None of the above

76. A 31-year-old male presents with fatigue, shortness of breath, and dark urine. Lab results reveal hemolytic anemia and pancytopenia. A CT scan shows mesenteric venous thrombosis. What is the most suitable diagnostic test for this patient?

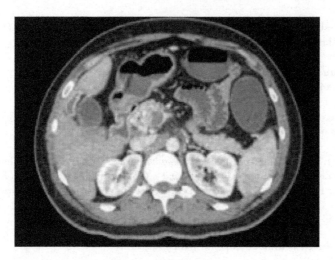

Figure 3.8: CT scan

- A. Protein C levels
- B. Protein S levels
- C. Flow cytometry for CD55 and CD59
- D. Activated protein C resistance assay
- E. Antithrombin III levels

77. A 38-year-old woman presents with a stroke. She has a history of deep vein thrombosis (DVT) 1 year ago. Laboratory testing reveals elevated antiphospholipid antibodies.
What is the most appropriate treatment for her?

- A. Enoxaparin
- B. Dabigatran
- C. Rivaroxaban
- D. Warfarin
- E. None of the above

78. A 32-year-old male patient has been identified as asymptomatic factor V Leiden. He has no history of clotting or high-risk circumstances such as major surgery. What would be the most appropriate treatment strategy for this patient?

- A. Warfarin
- B. Direct Oral Anticoagulants
- C. Aspirin
- D. No anticoagulation
- E. Heparin

79. A 63-year-old man with no significant past medical history presents for a routine check-up. His physical exam is unremarkable. However, his complete blood count reveals a white blood cell count of 20,000/L, with a predominance of small, mature lymphocytes. He denies any symptoms or discomfort. What is the most appropriate management for this patient's condition?

- A. Immediate chemotherapy.
- B. No treatment.
- C. Steroid therapy.
- D. Radiation therapy.
- E. Surgical intervention.

80. A 68-year-old man with a history of coronary artery disease undergoes a cardiac catheterization. One day after the procedure, he develops eosinophilia and acute kidney injury.
Which of the following is the most likely cause of his eosinophilia?

- A. Drug reaction
- B. Infection
- C. Microscopic cholesterol emboli
- D. Allergic reaction to the catheterization dye
- E. None of the above

81. A 54-year-old man with chronic kidney disease is scheduled for a kidney transplant. He has no history of blood transfusions. What type of blood transfusion should he receive?

- A. Cytomegalovirus (CMV)-negative, leukoreduced red blood cells (RBCs)
- B. CMV-positive, leukoreduced RBCs
- C. CMV-negative, non-leukoreduced RBCs
- D. CMV-positive, non-leukoreduced RBCs
- E. None of the above

82. A 41-year-old man presents with an elevated white blood cell count on routine bloodwork. He has no significant symptoms. Further examination reveals excess mature granulocytes and preserved differentiation, without symptoms of leukostasis or tumor lysis. Basophilia is also noted. The most likely diagnosis is:

- A. Acute lymphoblastic leukemia
- B. Chronic myelogenous leukemia
- C. Acute myeloid leukemia
- D. Chronic lymphocytic leukemia
- E. Hodgkin's lymphoma

83. A 24-year-old man with sickle cell disease presents to the emergency department with a 2-day history of fever, jaundice, and dark urine. He received a blood transfusion 1 week ago. His laboratory results show a drop in hemoglobin, an increase in bilirubin, and a positive direct Coombs test. What is the most appropriate next step in management?

- A. Consult the blood bank.
- B. Transfuse another unit of packed red blood cells (PRBCs).
- C. Start antibiotics.
- D. Discharge home with close follow-up.
- E. None of the above

84. An 86-year-old woman with a history of heart failure and COPD presents with dyspnea and hypertension several hours after receiving a blood transfusion. She has the following risk factors: age over 85 years, female sex, and small body habitus. Which of the following is the most likely diagnosis?

- A. Acute hemolytic transfusion reaction
- B. Anaphylactic transfusion reaction
- C. Transfusion-associated circulatory overload
- D. Febrile nonhemolytic transfusion reaction
- E. Transfusion-related acute lung injury

85. A patient presents with myelodysplastic syndrome, symptomatic anemia, and neutropenia with recurrent cellulitis. She has very good cytogenetics with a low blast count and a revised International Prognostic Scoring System (IPSS-R) score of 1.5, which corresponds to a median overall survival approaching 9 years. What is the most appropriate treatment for this patient?

- A. Allogeneic stem cell transplant
- B. High-dose chemotherapy
- C. Autologous stem cell transplant
- D. Radiation therapy
- E. Splenectomy

86. A 69-year-old man with myelodysplastic syndrome is scheduled for a follow-up appointment. What vaccinations should he receive?

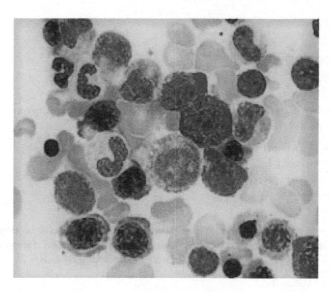

Figure 3.9: myelodysplastic syndrome

- A. Yearly influenza vaccine and pneumococcal vaccine every 10 years.
- B. Yearly influenza vaccine and yearly pneumococcal vaccine.
- C. Yearly influenza vaccine and pneumococcal vaccine every 5 years.
- D. Prophylactic antibiotics and granulocyte-colony stimulating factors (G-CSFs).
- E. None of the above.

87. A 67-year-old man with myelodysplastic syndrome (MDS) presents with symptomatic anemia and thrombocytopenia. He has poor cytogenetics and a very high IPSS-R score of 8. He is medically fit with good performance status. What is the best treatment option for this patient?

- A. Allogeneic stem cell transplant
- B. Hypomethylating agents
- C. Ivosidenib or enasidenib
- D. Intensive chemotherapy

E. None of the above

88. A male patient presents with hemoglobin levels >16.5 g/dL and hematocrit >49%, with an activating JAK2 V617F mutation. He is over 60 years old and has a history of thrombus. He does not have other explanations for his symptoms (eg, hypoxemia, erythropoietin-producing syndromes, dehydration). Which of the following is the most appropriate treatment for this patient?

- A. Warfarin
- B. Clopidogrel
- C. Enoxaparin
- D. Low-dose aspirin and hydroxyurea
- E. Ticagrelor

89. A 78-year-old woman with a history of lupus presents with fatigue and weakness. On examination, she has significant pallor and splenomegaly. Laboratory tests indicate anemia. She is diagnosed with primary myelofibrosis likely secondary to her lupus. What is the most suitable treatment approach in this case?

- A. Allogeneic stem cell transplant
- B. Chemotherapy
- C. Hydroxyurea
- D. RBC transfusion
- E. No treatment

90. A 55-year-old man with essential thrombocythemia (ET) has a platelet count of 1,400,000/L and no history of

thrombosis. What is the best course of action?

- A. Aspirin
- B. Hydroxyurea
- C. Interferon
- D. Observation
- E. None of the above

91. A 25-year-old man presents with a white blood cell count of 200,000/L, a platelet count of 50,000/L, and a hemoglobin level of 8 g/dL. A peripheral smear shows blasts with myeloid markers, including myeloperoxidase, CD13, and CD33. Cytogenetic analysis reveals a translocation (8;21) and NPM1 gene mutation positivity. What is the most appropriate diagnosis and prognosis?

- A. Acute lymphoblastic leukemia, favorable prognosis
- B. Acute lymphoblastic leukemia, unfavorable prognosis
- C. Acute myelogenous leukemia, favorable prognosis
- D. Acute myelogenous leukemia, unfavorable prognosis
- E. None of the above

92. A 62-year-old woman with a history of breast cancer that required chemotherapy presents with fatigue, bruising, and recurrent infections. A complete blood count shows pancytopenia and a bone marrow biopsy reveals hypercellularity with blast cells. The patient is diagnosed with cytotoxic therapy-related acute myelogenous leukemia. What is the most appropriate induction therapy for this patient?

- A. Liposomal cytarabine and daunorubicin on days 1, 3, and 5.
- B. Standard induction therapy.
- C. Reduced intensity therapy.
- D. Induction therapy plus gemtuzumab ozogamicin.
- E. Induction therapy plus midostaurin.

93. A 34-year-old man with acute promyelocytic leukemia is on day 5 of induction therapy with all-trans-retinoic acid (ATRA). He presents to the emergency department with fever, shortness of breath, and peripheral edema. Chest X-ray shows bilateral pulmonary infiltrates.
What is the most likely diagnosis and treatment?

- A. Acute respiratory distress syndrome; treat with supportive care.
- B. Differentiation syndrome; treat with supportive care.
- C. Differentiation syndrome; treat with dexamethasone 10 mg twice daily and supportive care.
- D. Differentiation syndrome; treat with dexamethasone 10 mg twice daily, supportive care, and additional chemotherapy agents.
- E. Differentiation syndrome; treat with dexamethasone 10 mg twice daily, supportive care, and antibiotics.

94. A 32-year-old woman, recently diagnosed with chronic myeloid leukemia, has achieved a complete molecular remission with imatinib-based chemotherapy. She is eager to start a family but is aware of the teratogenic effects of imatinib. She wishes to discontinue her medication. Which of the following statements is most accurate regarding her situation?

- A. If she discontinues the imatinib, she will have a 40% chance of recurrence in 24 months.
- B. If she discontinues the imatinib, she will have a 60% chance of recurrence in 24 months.
- C. If she discontinues the imatinib, she will have a 20% chance of recurrence in 24 months.
- D. If she discontinues the imatinib, she will have an 80% chance of recurrence in 24 months.
- E. If she discontinues the imatinib, she will have a 100% chance of recurrence in 24 months.

95. A 47-year-old woman has been diagnosed with CD19 positive relapsed or refractory B-cell acute lymphoblastic leukemia . Which of the following treatments is most appropriate for her?

- A. Blinatumomab
- B. Inotuzumab
- C. Tisagenlecleucel
- D. Standard chemotherapy
- E. Watchful waiting

96. 56-year-old man presents with a white blood cell count of 100,000/L, a platelet count of 50,000/L, and a hemoglobin level of 8 g/dL. A peripheral smear shows 30% blasts with myeloid markers, including myeloperoxidase, CD13, and CD33.

What is the most likely diagnosis?

- A. Acute myelogenous leukemia
- B. Chronic myelogenous leukemia
- C. Acute lymphoblastic leukemia
- D. Chronic lymphocytic leukemia
- E. Multiple myeloma

97. A 235-year-old man with newly diagnosed acute leukemia presents with a white blood cell count of 500,000/L, a platelet count of 20,000/L, and a hemoglobin level of 6 g/dL. He also has a fever and shortness of breath. Chest X-ray shows bilateral pulmonary infiltrates. Laboratory studies reveal hyperkalemia, renal dysfunction, and elevated LDH. What are the most likely complications that this patient is experiencing?

- A. Leukostasis
- B. Tumor lysis syndrome
- C. Infection
- D. All of the above

98. A 46-year-old male patient, diagnosed with AIDS, presents with a new-onset headache and visual disturbances. A brain MRI reveals a solitary enhancing mass. The most likely diagnosis is primary CNS lymphoma. At what CD4 count level does the risk of primary CNS lymphoma typically increase in patients with AIDS?

- A. $<200/mm^3$
- B. $<50/mm^3$
- C. $<100/mm^3$
- D. $<150/mm^3$
- E. $<250/mm^3$

99. A 69-year-old man with chronic lymphocytic leukemia (CLL) presents with a 1-month history of rapidly worsening lymphadenopathy, fatigue, and night sweats. A biopsy of a new lymph node shows diffuse large B-cell lymphoma (DLBCL). What is the most likely diagnosis?

- A. Chronic lymphocytic leukemia (CLL)
- B. Richter transformation
- C. Diffuse large B-cell lymphoma (DLBCL)
- D. Hodgkin lymphoma
- E. Multiple myeloma

100. A patient is diagnosed with asymptomatic chronic lymphocytic leukemia. What is the most appropriate next step in management?

- A. Ibrutinib
- B. Allogeneic stem cell transplant
- C. Observation
- D. Chemotherapy
- E. Radiation therapy

101. A 23-year-old woman presents with weight loss, night sweats, and a palpable mediastinal mass. A biopsy of the mass reveals classical Hodgkin lymphoma, stage 2, nonbulky. What is the most appropriate treatment plan?

- A. ABVD (doxorubicin, bleomycin, vinblastine, dacarbazine) and repeat PET-CT after 2 cycles.
- B. BEACOPP (bleomycin, etoposide, adriamycin, cyclophosphamide, vincristine, procarbazine, prednisone)
- C. Brentuximab vedotin or pembrolizumab
- D. Radiation therapy alone
- E. None of the above

102. A 41-year-old man presents with painless enlargement of his neck lymph nodes. You suspect lymphoma and are considering the next steps in the diagnostic workup. Which of the following is the most appropriate set of investigations for confirming the diagnosis and staging of the disease?

- A. Fine needle aspiration (FNA), CBC, and complete metabolic profile
- B. Excisional lymph node biopsy, CBC and LDH
- C. Excisional lymph node biopsy, head CT, and Epstein-Barr virus serology
- D. Excisional lymph node biopsy, PET-CT scan, ESR, and bone marrow biopsy
- E. Excisional lymph node biopsy, human T-cell leukemia lymphoma virus serology, and HIV serology

103. A 52-year-old woman who was treated for Hodgkin lymphoma 20 years ago with 6 cycles of doxorubicin and bleomycin presents with symptoms of fatigue and shortness of breath. She did not undergo chest or neck radiation. Which of the following is the most appropriate next step in her management?

- A. CXR, echocardiogram, pulmonary function tests
- B. Mammography, Pap smear
- C. Thyroid function tests
- D. Bone marrow biopsy
- E. Neck radiation

104. A 67-year-old man presents with a history of chronic epigastric pain and dyspepsia. Upper endoscopy reveals a gastric ulcer. Biopsy of the ulcer shows MALT lymphoma. H. pylori testing is positive.
What is the most appropriate treatment plan?

- A. Quadruple therapy for treatment of the H. pylori (bismuth, metronidazole, tetracycline, omeprazole)
- B. Radiation therapy
- C. Rituximab monotherapy
- D. A combination of radiation therapy and rituximab
- E. None of the above

105. A 61-year-old man presents with hypercalcemia, renal disease, anemia, and bone pain. Laboratory studies reveal a large monoclonal IgG . What is the next best step in management?

- A. Defer further workup and repeat testing in 6 weeks.
- B. Bone marrow biopsy with cytogenetics and gene mutation analysis; skeletal survey.
- C. PET-CT scan.
- D. 2-microglobulin level and serum albumin.
- E. None of the above.

106. A 69-year-old man with a history of hypertension and type 2 diabetes presents to the clinic for a routine check-up. Laboratory tests show an elevated free light chain ratio. He has no symptoms of bone pain, fatigue, or weakness. His renal function is normal, and serum calcium levels are within the normal range. Which of the following best characterizes the prognosis of his most likely diagnosis?

- A. 0.5% per year risk of progression to a malignancy; 20% lifetime risk
- B. 1% per year risk of progression to a malignancy; 25% lifetime risk
- C. 2% per year risk of progression to a malignancy; 30% lifetime risk
- D. 3% per year risk of progression to a malignancy; 35% lifetime risk
- E. 4% per year risk of progression to a malignancy; 40% lifetime risk

107. A 33-year-old man is diagnosed with Waldenstrom macroglobulinemia. He has a history of peripheral neuropathy. What is the most appropriate treatment plan?

- A. Observe with close laboratory and clinical follow-up.
- B. Start bendamustine + rituximab.
- C. Start bortezomib + dexamethasone + rituximab.
- D. Perform autologous stem cell transplant.
- E. Start plasmapheresis.

108. A 67-year-old patient presents with anemia, elevated monoclonal IgM spike, and cryoglobulinemia. He has a history of B-cell neoplasm (lymphoplasmacytic lymphoma) that secretes monoclonal IgM, and about 90% of patients like him have MYD88 L265P mutations. He has no known lytic bone lesions. He also has Type I cryoglobulinemia, leading to Raynaud phenomenon and vasculitis. He does not have any signs of amyloidosis or glomerulopathy due to IgM deposition in the skin, intestines, and kidney, nor does he show signs of chronic autoimmune hemolytic anemia and peripheral neuropathy due to autoantibody activity of IgM. He presents with blurred vision, headache, dizziness,

change in mental status, congestive heart failure, and pulmonary infiltrates. What is the most likely cause of this patient's symptoms?

- A. Amyloidosis and glomerulopathy due to IgM deposition
- B. Chronic autoimmune hemolytic anemia and peripheral neuropathy due to autoantibody activity
- C. Raynaud phenomenon and vasculitis due to Type I cryoglobulinemia
- D. Hyperviscosity syndrome
- E. MYD88 L265P mutations

109. A 79-year-old patient presents with an elevated M protein and >10% bone marrow plasma cell infiltration but no presence of lytic lesions, anemia, hypercalcemia, and renal insufficiency. Which of the following is the most probable diagnosis?

- A. Monoclonal gammopathy of unknown significance (MGUS)
- B. Nonsecretory multiple myeloma
- C. Amyloidosis
- D. Waldenstrom macroglobulinemia
- E. Smoldering multiple myeloma

110. A 67-year-old man presents with right humerus pain. Radiographs reveal a lytic lesion in the right humerus. Biopsy of the lesion shows plasmacytoma. Serum protein electrophoresis (SPEP) and immunofixation electrophoresis (IFE) are negative for M spike. What is the most appropriate next step in management?

- A. Start chemotherapy with bortezomib, dexamethasone, and rituximab (BDR).
- B. Start chemotherapy with cyclophosphamide, bortezomib, and dexamethasone (CyBorD).
- C. Start chemotherapy with lenalidomide, dexamethasone, and bortezomib (RVD).
- D. Referral to radiation oncology for radiation to the right humerus osseous lesion.
- E. Observation and referral to physical therapy.

111. A 58-year-old man with newly diagnosed multiple myeloma is eligible for autologous stem cell transplant. What is the most appropriate induction regimen for this patient?

- A. Bortezomib/lenalidomide/dexamethasone
- B. Bortezomib/cyclophosphamide/dexamethasone
- C. Carfilzomib/lenalidomide/dexamethasone
- D. Pomalidomide/cyclophosphamide/dexamethasone
- E. None of the above

112. A 22-year-old male is recently diagnosed with acute myelogenous leukemia (AML) with the presence of the FLT3-ITD mutation. He has a fully matched sibling donor available and has no significant comorbidities. What is the best treatment strategy for this patient?

- A. Autologous stem cell transplant
- B. Induction chemotherapy followed by maintenance with FLT3 inhibitors
- C. Non-myeloablative conditioning followed by allogeneic transplant from his sibling
- D. Myeloablative conditioning followed by allogeneic transplant from his sibling
- E. Palliative care

113. A patient undergoing hematopoietic stem cell transplantation develops fever, noncardiogenic pulmonary edema, and an erythrodermatous rash 2 days after absolute neutrophil count (ANC) exceeds 500. The patient also shows signs of renal dysfunction. What is the most appropriate treatment for this patient's condition?

- A. Antibiotics
- B. Antifungal agents
- C. Steroids
- D. Chemotherapy
- E. Intravenous hydration

114. A 25-year-old man with leukemia underwent a mismatched related peripheral stem cell transplant 3 months ago. He presents with diarrhea, a maculopapular rash, and elevated liver enzymes. What is the most likely diagnosis?

- A. Acute graft-versus-host disease (GVHD)
- B. Chronic graft-versus-host disease (GVHD)

- C. Sepsis
- D. Tumor lysis syndrome
- E. None of the above

115. A 24-year-old man who underwent a hematopoietic cell transplant 2 weeks ago presents with jaundice, ascites, and hepatomegaly. Serum laboratory studies reveal a total bilirubin of 3.5 mg/dL. What is the most likely diagnosis?

- A. Acute graft-versus-host disease (GVHD)
- B. Budd-Chiari syndrome
- C. Hepatic ischemia
- D. Sinusoidal obstruction syndrome
- E. None of the above

3.1 ANSWERS

1. The correct answer is A. Lead poisoning. Basophilic stippling is a characteristic finding in lead poisoning. It is caused by the accumulation of lead-induced aggregates of ribosomes in the red blood cells. Other causes of basophilic stippling include thalassemia, myelofibrosis, and sideroblastic anemia.

2. The correct answer is A.

G6PD deficiency. Heinz bodies are precipitated hemoglobin inclusions that are found in red blood cells with G6PD deficiency. They are formed when the red blood cells are exposed to oxidant stressors, such as infection or certain medications. Other causes of Heinz bodies include sickle cell anemia, thalassemia, and hereditary spherocytosis.

3. The correct answer is C.

Myelodysplastic disorder. A low erythrocyte to granulocyte ratio is a characteristic finding in myelodysplastic disorders. These disorders are a group of bone marrow disorders that are characterized by ineffective hematopoiesis. Other causes of a low erythrocyte to granulocyte ratio include acute and chronic infection, pure red cell aplasia, and anemia with erythroid hyperplasia.

4. The correct answer is B.

Parasitic infection. Eosinophilia is a common finding in parasitic infections, such as schistosomiasis, ascariasis, and strongyloidiasis. Other causes of eosinophilia include drug-induced reactions, allergic disorders, collagen vascular diseases, and malignant neoplasms.

5. The correct answer is E.

Benign ethnic neutropenia. BEN is a common finding in individuals of African descent, and it is not associated with an increased risk for infections. Other causes of a low absolute neutrophil count include acute myeloid leukemia, chronic myeloid leukemia, aplastic anemia, and myelodysplastic syndrome.

6. The correct answer is C.

Myelodysplastic syndrome. Myelodysplastic syndromes are a group of bone marrow disorders that are characterized by ineffective hematopoiesis. Ineffective hematopoiesis is the production of blood cells that are not functional. This can lead to anemia, leukopenia, and thrombocytopenia. Bone marrow examination is a valuable tool in the diagnosis of myelodysplastic syndromes.

7. The correct answer is A. Iron deficiency anemia. The combination of low serum iron, low ferritin, and high TIBC is diagnostic of iron deficiency anemia. Other causes of low serum iron and ferritin include thalassemia, myelodysplastic syndrome, and aplastic anemia. However, these conditions are typically associated with normal or low TIBC.

8. The correct answer is E.

Pure red cell aplasia. Pure red cell aplasia is a rare condition in which there is a failure of the bone marrow to produce red blood cells. This leads to a normocytic, normochromic anemia. Erythropoietin levels are typically low in pure red cell aplasia. Other causes of a normocytic, normochromic anemia with low erythropoietin levels include Aplastic anemia, Myelodysplastic syndrome, chronic kidney disease, HIV infection, Medications (eg., chemotherapy, immunosuppressants).

9. The correct answer is B.

Iron deficiency anemia. The combination of low serum iron, high TIBC, and low percent saturation is diagnostic of iron deficiency anemia. Other causes of microcytic anemia include thalassemia, myelodysplastic syndrome, and aplastic anemia. However, these conditions are typically associated with normal or high percent saturation. The reference intervals for serum iron (SI), total iron-binding capacity (TIBC), and percent saturation in cases of microcytic anemia are as follows: Serum iron: <30 mcg/dL, TIBC: >360 mcg/dL Percent saturation: <10%

10. The correct answer is C.

Sideroblastic anemia. Sideroblastic anemia is a rare condition that is characterized by the accumulation of iron in the mitochondria of red blood cells. This leads to a microcytic, hypochromic anemia with basophilic stippling. Other causes of microcytic anemia include iron deficiency anemia and thalassemia. However, these conditions are typically associated with low serum iron and ferritin levels.

11. The correct answer is A.

G6PD deficiency. G6PD deficiency is a genetic disorder that is characterized by the inability of red blood cells to effectively counteract oxidative stress. This can lead to hemolysis, or the destruction of red blood cells. Sulfamethoxazole/trimethoprim is a medication that can induce hemolysis in people with G6PD deficiency.

12. The correct answer is B.

Cold antibody immunohemolytic anemia. Cold antibody immunohemolytic anemia is a type of immunohemolytic anemia that is caused by antibodies that are activated at cold temperatures. These antibodies can bind to red blood cells and cause them to spherize. Spherocytes are red blood cells that are abnormally small and have a smooth surface. They are more likely to be destroyed by the spleen. Other causes of cold antibody immunohemolytic anemia include Mycoplasma infection, Infectious mononucleosis, Lymphoma, Idiopathic factors, Paroxysmal cold hemoglobinuria.

13. The correct answer is D.

Thalassemia. Thalassemia is a group of inherited blood disorders that are characterized by reduced production of globin chains. This leads to a microcytic, hypochromic anemia. Target cells and basophilic stippling are characteristic findings in thalassemia.

14. The correct answer is C. Paroxysmal nocturnal hemoglobinuria. PNH is a rare acquired clonal hematopoietic stem cell disorder that results in abnormal sensitivity of red blood cell membrane to lysis by complement, leading to hemolysis. Schistocytes and helmet cells are characteristic findings in PNH. Treatment options for PNH vary based on the severity of the condition and may include: Eculizumab (monoclonal antibody against complement protein C5), Iron replacement, Corticosteroids, Allogeneic hematopoietic stem cell transplantation.

15. The correct answer is A.

Aplastic anemia. Aplastic anemia is a rare bone marrow disorder that results in a decrease in the production of all three blood cell types: red blood cells, white blood cells, and platelets. This can lead to fatigue, increased risk of infections, and bleeding. The other answer choices are also possible causes of pancytopenia, but they are less likely given the clinical vignette. Myelodysplastic syndrome is a group of bone marrow disorders that are characterized by ineffective hematopoiesis. Leukemia is a cancer of the blood cells. Infection can also cause pancytopenia, but it is usually accompanied by other symptoms, such as fever, chills, and cough. Autoimmune disorders can also cause pancytopenia, but they are less common than the other causes. Treatment of pancytopenia focuses on addressing the underlying cause and may involve blood transfusions, medications, or bone marrow transplantation.

16. The correct answer is B.

Parenteral vitamin B12 100 mcg intramuscularly once daily for 7 days, then 100 mcg monthly. This is the most appropriate course of treatment for a patient with severe vitamin B12 deficiency anemia. The initial dose of 100 mcg intramuscularly once daily for 7 days will help to rapidly replenish the body's stores of vitamin B12. After the 7-day course, a maintenance dose of 100-1000 mcg monthly is usually prescribed to prevent recurrence.

17. The correct answer is (C).

Hydration is the most important initial step in managing a painful crisis in sickle cell anemia. This is because dehydration can lead to sickling of red blood cells and worsening of the pain. Oxygen, analgesics, and red blood cell transfusions may also be necessary in some cases. The other answer choices are not as appropriate for this patient. Increasing the dose of hydroxyurea may be considered if the patient is not responding to the current dose, but this is not the first step in management. Administering analgesics is important, but it is not the most important step. Transfusing red blood cells may be necessary in some cases, but it is not the first step in management.

18. The correct answer is (A).

Prednisone is a glucocorticoid that is generally used as a first-line treatment for autoimmune hemolysis. It works by suppressing the immune system and thereby reducing the destruction of red blood cells. The other answer choices are not as appropriate for this patient. Danazol is an androgen that has been shown to be effective in some patients with autoimmune hemolysis, but it is not as commonly used as prednisone. Plasmapheresis and rituximab are more advanced treatments that may be considered if prednisone is ineffective or cannot be used.

19. The correct answer is A.

Heparin-induced thrombocytopenia. HIT is a medical condition characterized by a decrease in platelet count caused by the administration of heparin. It is a type of immune-mediated thrombocytopenia, meaning that it is caused by the body's immune system reacting to heparin. The other answer choices are not as likely for this patient. Drug-induced thrombocytopenia is a decrease in platelet count caused by a medication other than heparin. Idiopathic thrombocytopenic purpura is a condition in which the body's immune system attacks its own platelets. Disseminated intravascular coagulation is a condition in which there is widespread clotting in the blood vessels. Thrombotic thrombocytopenic purpura is a rare condition characterized by the formation of blood clots and a decrease in platelet count.

20. The correct answer is D.

Pseudothrombocytopenia. Pseudothrombocytopenia is a medical condition characterized by the formation of platelet clumps, which commonly arises due to blood collection in ethylenediaminetetraacetic acid (EDTA) in a minority of patients (0.3%). The establishment of an accurate diagnosis can be achieved by means of examining a blood smear. The other answer choices are not as likely for this patient. Idiopathic thrombocytopenic purpura is a condition in which the body's immune system attacks its own platelets. Disseminated intravascular coagulation is a condition in which there is widespread clotting in the blood vessels. Thrombotic thrombocytopenic purpura is a rare condition characterized by the formation of blood clots and a decrease in platelet count. Heparin-induced thrombocytopenia is a decrease in platelet count caused by the administration of heparin.

21. The correct answer is B.

Liver disease. Liver disease can lead to deficiencies in all clotting factors except factor VIII. This can result in prolonged PT and PTT. The other answer choices are not as likely for this patient. Vitamin K deficiency can also lead to prolonged PT and PTT, but it is less common than liver disease. Disseminated intravascular coagulation is a condition in which there is widespread clotting in the blood vessels. Heparin-induced thrombocytopenia is a decrease in platelet count caused by the administration of heparin.

22. The correct answer is E.

Refer for splenectomy. Splenectomy is the most effective treatment for chronic ITP that is refractory to other treatments. The other answer choices are not as likely for this patient. Continuing prednisone or increasing the prednisone dose may be helpful in some patients, but they are not as effective as splenectomy. IVIg and rituximab are other treatments that may be considered, but they are not as effective as splenectomy.

23. The correct answer is E.

Manage the underlying cause of DIC. The most important step in managing DIC is to treat the underlying cause. In this case, the underlying cause is acute promyelocytic leukemia. Treatment for acute promyelocytic leukemia typically includes chemotherapy and supportive care. The other answer choices are not as appropriate for this patient. Administering platelets or fresh-frozen plasma may be helpful in some cases, but they are not the most important step in management. Administering heparin may be helpful in some cases of DIC, but it is not indicated in this case because the patient does not have thrombosis. Administering red blood cells may be necessary if the patient is bleeding, but it is not the most important step in management.

24. The correct answer is A.

Administer plasmapheresis. Plasmapheresis is the most effective treatment for TTP. It is a procedure that removes blood from the body, separates the plasma from the blood cells, and returns the blood cells to the body. This helps to remove the substances that are causing the TTP. The other answer choices are not as appropriate for this patient. Administering fresh frozen plasma or IV IgG may be helpful in some cases, but they are not as effective as plasmapheresis. Caplacizumab is a newer treatment that is not yet as widely available as plasmapheresis.

25. The correct answer is C.

Increase the dose of factor IX concentrate. If a patient with Hemophilia B is experiencing more frequent bleeding episodes, the first step is to increase the dose of factor IX concentrate. This will help to raise the level of factor IX in the blood and make it more difficult for the patient to bleed. The other answer choices are not as appropriate for this patient. Switching to recombinant factor IX may be helpful in some cases, but it is not as likely to be effective as increasing the dose of factor IX concentrate. Gene therapy is a newer treatment that is not yet as widely available as factor IX concentrate. Referring the patient to a hematologist is a good option if the patient is not responding to treatment.

26. The correct answer is C.

Switch to factor VIII concentrate. If a patient with Von Willebrand Disease is experiencing more frequent bleeding episodes, the first step is to switch to factor VIII concentrate. Factor VIII concentrate is a plasma product that contains factor VIII, which is the protein that is deficient in patients with Von Willebrand Disease. The other answer choices are not as appropriate for this patient. Increasing the dose of desmopressin may be helpful in some cases, but it is not as likely to be effective as switching to factor VIII concentrate. Cryoprecipitate is a plasma product that contains vWF, but it does not contain factor VIII. Referring to the patient to a hematologist is a good option if the patient is not responding to treatment.

27. The correct answer is B.

Stop unfractionated heparin therapy. The primary complication associated with unfractionated heparin therapy is hemorrhage. This patient is experiencing epistaxis, which is a sign of bleeding. The first step in management is to stop the unfractionated heparin therapy. This will help to stop the bleeding. The other answer choices are not as appropriate for this patient. Continuing unfractionated heparin therapy may make the bleeding worse. Administering protamine is a treatment for heparin-induced thrombocytopenia, not hemorrhage. Referring to the patient to a hematologist is a good option if the patient is not responding to treatment.

28. The correct answer is C.

Administer both vitamin K and FFP. Warfarin is a vitamin K antagonist, so it works by blocking the effects of vitamin K. Vitamin K is necessary for the production of clotting factors, so blocking its effects will lead to a decrease in clotting factors and an increased risk of bleeding. In this case, the patient has a head injury and a decreased level of consciousness, which are both signs of bleeding. The first step in management is to administer both vitamin K and FFP. Vitamin K will help to restore the levels of clotting factors, and FFP will provide the patient with immediate clotting factors. The other answer choices are not as appropriate for this patient. Administering vitamin K alone may not be enough to reverse the effects of warfarin. Administering FFP alone may not be enough to provide the patient with enough clotting factors. Referring to the patient to a hematologist is a good option if the patient is not responding to treatment.

29. The correct answer is B.

Switch to argatroban. Argatroban and lepirudin are both direct thrombin inhibitors, which means that they work by blocking the action of thrombin. Thrombin is a protein that is involved in the clotting cascade, so blocking its action will help to prevent clots from forming. In this case, the patient has developed heparin-induced thrombocytopenia, which is a condition in which the body's immune system attacks the heparin. This can lead to a decrease in the platelet count and an increased risk of bleeding. The first step in management is to switch the patient to a direct thrombin inhibitor. Argatroban and lepirudin are both effective in the treatment of heparin-induced thrombocytopenia, so either one would be a good option. The other answer choices are not as appropriate for this patient. Continuing heparin therapy may make the thrombocytopenia worse. Switching to low molecular weight heparin (LMWH) is not a good option because LMWH is also a type of heparin and can also cause heparin-induced thrombocytopenia. Referring to the patient to a hematologist is a good option if the patient is not responding to treatment.

30. The correct answer is D.

The efficacy of the new oral Xa and thrombin inhibitors in patients with heart valve abnormalities is still being studied. The new oral Xa and thrombin inhibitors are a promising new class of anticoagulants, but they have not yet been studied extensively in patients with heart valve abnormalities. Some studies have shown that these medications may be less effective than warfarin in preventing clots in patients with heart valve abnormalities, while other studies have shown that they may be equally effective.

31. The correct answer is B.

5-Azacytidine has been shown to significantly delay the progression to acute myeloid leukemia. 5-Azacytidine is a chemotherapy drug that has been shown to be effective in delaying the progression of Myelodysplastic Syndromes to acute myeloid leukemia. In some cases, 5-Azacytidine may also improve the quality of life in patients with Myelodysplastic Syndromes. However, 5-Azacytidine is not a cure for Myelodysplastic Syndromes. The other answer choices are not as accurate. 5-Azacytidine has not been shown to cure Myelodysplastic Syndromes, and it is not always safe and effective.

32. The correct answer is C.

Lenalidomide has been shown to induce transfusion independence in a significant proportion of patients diagnosed with the 5q- syndrome. Lenalidomide is a chemotherapy drug that has been shown to be effective in inducing transfusion independence in patients with Myelodysplastic Syndromes who have the 5q- syndrome. Transfusion independence means that the patient no longer needs blood transfusions to maintain their blood cell counts. This can improve the quality of life for patients with Myelodysplastic Syndromes.

33. The correct answer is B.

The JAK2 V617F mutation is a common finding in patients with polycythemia vera, and it is associated with a worse prognosis. The JAK2 V617F mutation is a genetic mutation that is found in about 90% of patients with polycythemia vera. This mutation leads to the activation of the JAK2 kinase, which is a protein that is involved in the signaling pathway that controls the production of blood cells. The activation of the JAK2 kinase leads to an increase in the production of blood cells, which can lead to the symptoms of polycythemia vera, such as a high red blood cell count, a high white blood cell count, and a high platelet count. The JAK2 V617F mutation is also associated with a worse prognosis in patients with polycythemia vera. Patients with this mutation are more likely to develop complications of polycythemia vera, such as heart disease, stroke, and blood clots. They are also more likely to progress to acute myeloid leukemia.

34. The correct answer is A.

Polycythemia vera. The patient in this case has several features that are consistent with polycythemia vera, including the presence of splenomegaly, leukocytosis, thrombocytosis, elevated levels of vitamin B12, decreased levels of erythropoietin, and the presence of a mutation in the JAK2 kinase (V617F). These features are not typically seen in secondary polycythemia. Secondary polycythemia is a condition in which the body produces too many red blood cells in response to a stimulus, such as high altitude or smoking. The symptoms of secondary polycythemia are similar to those of polycythemia vera, but the underlying cause is different. Essential thrombocytosis is a condition in which the body produces too many platelets. The symptoms of essential thrombocytosis are similar to those of polycythemia vera, but the underlying cause is different. Myelofibrosis is a condition in which the bone marrow is replaced by scar tissue. The symptoms of myelofibrosis are different from those of polycythemia vera.

35. The correct answer is D.

Observation. Idiopathic myelofibrosis is a chronic myeloproliferative neoplasm that is characterized by bone marrow fibrosis and splenomegaly. The disease is often asymptomatic in the early stages, and treatment is typically not necessary. However, as the disease progresses, patients may develop symptoms such as fatigue, weight loss, and bone pain. There is no cure for idiopathic myelofibrosis, and treatment is aimed at managing the symptoms and improving the quality of life. Supportive therapy, such as blood transfusions and pain medication, may be necessary. In some cases, targeted therapy with JAK2 inhibitors or telomerase inhibitors may be used to reduce splenomegaly and marrow fibrosis. However, these therapies have not been shown to improve overall survival. In the case of this patient, who is asymptomatic, the best management approach is observation. The patient should be monitored for the development of symptoms, and treatment can be initiated if necessary. The other answer choices are not as appropriate. Hydroxyurea, ruxolitinib, and lenalidomide are all targeted therapies that may be used to treat idiopathic myelofibrosis, but they are not typically used in asymptomatic patients.

36. The correct answer is B.

Ultrasound. In this case, the patient has an enlarged spleen, and the most appropriate imaging modality for further evaluation is ultrasound. Ultrasound is a non-invasive imaging test that uses sound waves to create images of the body. It is particularly useful for evaluating spleen size, detecting gross abnormalities, and guiding biopsies. CT is a more detailed imaging modality, but it is also more invasive and exposes the patient to radiation. MRI is a more specialized imaging modality that is not typically used for the evaluation of spleen conditions. PET scan is a nuclear medicine imaging test that is used to detect cancer. In this case, the patient does not have any specific symptoms that would suggest cancer, so a PET scan is not necessary. Ultrasound is the most appropriate imaging modality for further evaluation because it is a non-invasive, detailed imaging test that can be used to evaluate spleen size, detect gross abnormalities, and guide biopsies.

37. The correct answer is B.

The patient has a more unfavorable prognosis. CD38 is a protein that is expressed on the surface of B cells. In CLL, the percentage of CD38-positive tumors is often used as a prognostic marker. Patients with a high percentage of CD38-positive tumors are more likely to have a more aggressive form of CLL and a worse prognosis. The other answer choices are not as accurate. Patients with a high percentage of CD38-positive tumors are less likely to respond to treatment and have a worse prognosis.

38. The correct answer is A.

Administer supportive care. In the early stages of CLL, it is often possible to manage anemia and thrombocytopenia with supportive care. This may include blood transfusions, iron supplements, and platelet transfusions. If the patient's symptoms are severe or do not respond to supportive care, then other treatment options may be considered. Splenectomy is a surgical procedure that removes the spleen. The spleen is responsible for removing old red blood cells from the body. In some cases, splenectomy can help to improve anemia in patients with CLL. However, splenectomy is not a cure for CLL, and it may not be necessary in all cases. Chemotherapy is a treatment that uses drugs to kill cancer cells. Chemotherapy can be used to treat anemia and thrombocytopenia in patients with CLL. However, chemotherapy is not always effective, and it can have side effects. IVIg is a medication that is made from donated blood. IVIg can help to improve anemia and thrombocytopenia in patients with CLL. However, IVIg is not always effective, and it can be expensive.

39. The correct answer is 3 or D.

The FLIPI-2 score is a prognostic scoring system that is used to predict the risk of progression in patients with CLL. The score is calculated by adding up the points for each of the five risk factors. In this case, the patient's score is 3, which indicates that he is at a high risk of progression. The other answer choices are not as appropriate. A score of 0 indicates that the patient is at a low risk of progression, while a score of 1 indicates that the patient is at an intermediate risk of progression.

40. The correct answer is C.

Poor. The patient's prognosis is poor because he has a high LDH level, bulky disease, and an older age. The LDH level is a marker of tumor burden, and a high LDH level indicates that the tumor is large. Bulky disease refers to disease that is widespread throughout the body. An older age is also a poor prognostic factor for aggressive lymphomas. The other answer choices are not as appropriate. A good prognosis is associated with a low LDH level, limited disease, and a younger age. An intermediate prognosis is associated with a moderate LDH level, intermediate disease, and an older age.

41. The correct answer is C.

Dose-adjusted EPOCH is an infusional chemotherapy regimen that includes etoposide, prednisone, vincristine, cyclophosphamide, and doxorubicin. It is a more intensive regimen than R-CHOP or CHOP, and it has been shown to be more effective in the treatment of double-hit lymphomas. The other answer choices are not as appropriate. R-CHOP and CHOP are fewer intensive regimens than dose-adjusted EPOCH, and they have not been shown to be as effective in the treatment of double-hit lymphomas. Bendamustine is a targeted therapy that is not typically used in the treatment of double-hit lymphomas.

42. The correct answer is A.

Reed-Sternberg cells. Reed-Sternberg cells are large, atypical cells that are found in Hodgkin's lymphoma tumors. They are derived from B cells, but they have a very different appearance than normal B cells. Reed-Sternberg cells are responsible for the growth and spread of Hodgkin's lymphoma tumors. The other answer choices are not as appropriate. B cells, T cells, and plasma cells are all types of white blood cells, but they are not associated with the formation of Hodgkin's lymphoma tumors.

43. The correct answer is D.

Combined-modality therapy. Combined-modality therapy is the recommended treatment for patients presenting with any stage of disease accompanied by a sizable mediastinal mass. This treatment approach involves the administration of mechlorethamine, vincristine, procarbazine, and prednisone (MOPP)/ABVD or MOPP-ABV hybrid chemotherapy regimens, followed by mantle field radiation therapy. The other answer choices are not as appropriate. MOPP chemotherapy is a chemotherapy regimen that is not typically used to treat patients with a sizable mediastinal mass.

ABVD chemotherapy is a chemotherapy regimen that is typically used to treat patients with a sizable mediastinal mass, but it is not as effective as combined-modality therapy.

44. The correct answer is C.

Both bone marrow biopsy and peripheral blood smear. The diagnosis of acute myeloid leukemia (AML) can be established by assessing the presence of blasts in either peripheral blood or bone marrow samples. A bone marrow biopsy is a procedure in which a sample of bone marrow is removed from the hip bone. A peripheral blood smear is a test in which a sample of blood is examined under a microscope. Both bone marrow biopsy and peripheral blood smear are necessary to diagnose AML. The bone marrow biopsy is more sensitive than the peripheral blood smear, and it can help to determine the type of AML. The peripheral blood smear can help to assess the severity of the disease and to identify any other abnormalities. The other answer choices are not as appropriate. A peripheral blood smear alone is not sufficient to diagnose AML. Neither bone marrow biopsy nor peripheral blood smear is necessary if the patient does not have any symptoms of AML.

45. The correct answer is A.

3-4 cycles of cytarabine. Patients with low-risk acute myeloid leukemia who have successfully attained complete remission and have the t[8;21] genetic abnormality are typically treated with 3-4 cycles of cytarabine. This is a relatively short and less intensive treatment regimen, and it has been shown to be effective in preventing relapse. The other answer choices are not as appropriate. 7-8 cycles of cytarabine is a more intensive treatment regimen, and it is not necessary for patients with low-risk acute myeloid leukemia. Daunorubicin is a chemotherapy drug that is typically used in combination with cytarabine. However, it is not necessary for patients with low-risk acute myeloid leukemia who have successfully attained complete remission.

46. The correct answer is A.

Accelerated phase of chronic myeloid leukemia. The accelerated phase of chronic myeloid leukemia is a more advanced stage of the disease than the chronic phase. It is characterized by the presence of anemia that is not proportional to the disease activity or treatment, a decrease in platelet counts, and the occurrence of additional cytogenetic abnormalities. The other answer choices are not as appropriate. Blast crisis of chronic myeloid leukemia is a more advanced stage of the disease than the accelerated phase. Chronic phase of chronic myeloid leukemia is the earliest stage of the disease. Myelodysplastic syndrome is a group of diseases that are characterized by the production of abnormal blood cells.

47. The correct answer is A.

Within one year of diagnosis. The precise timing for transplantation in patients with CML is uncertain. However, it has been observed that transplantation during the chronic phase yields superior outcomes compared to transplantation during the accelerated phase or blast crisis. The effectiveness of transplantation is most pronounced in patients who receive treatment within one year of their diagnosis. A significant proportion of transplanted patients, ranging from 50% to 60%, have the potential to achieve long-term survival without the recurrence of disease. The other answer choices are not as appropriate. Transplantation within two years of diagnosis is not as effective as transplantation within one year of diagnosis. Transplantation within three years of diagnosis is not as effective as transplantation within two years of diagnosis. Transplantation after the disease progresses to the accelerated phase or blast crisis is not as effective as transplantation in the chronic phase.

48. The correct answer is A.

Glucocorticoids. Glucocorticoids are the most effective treatment for hypercalcemia in patients with ATL. They work by suppressing the production of calcium by the bones. Glucocorticoids can also help to reduce the size of the tumor and improve the patient's symptoms. The other answer choices are not as appropriate. Zidovudine and interferon (IFN) have been shown to have some palliative effects in patients with ATL, but they are not as effective as glucocorticoids for the treatment of hypercalcemia. Lenalidomide and mogamulizumab are newer treatments for ATL that have shown promise, but they are not yet widely available.

49. The correct answer is A.

The presence of an ill-defined tumor product hinders the migration of . Multiple myeloma is a cancer of , which are a type of white blood cell. Plasma cells produce , which help the body fight infection. In multiple myeloma, the tumor cells produce a protein that hinders the migration of granulocytes, which are another type of white blood cell that helps the body fight infection. This makes patients with multiple myeloma more vulnerable to bacterial infections. The other answer choices are not as appropriate. The patient does not necessarily have a decreased number of granulocytes or antibodies. The patient may have a decreased production of , but this is not the main reason for their increased vulnerability to bacterial infections.

50. The correct answer is A.

Lenalidomide, dexamethasone, and bortezomib. Lenalidomide, dexamethasone, and bortezomib is a combination therapy that has been shown to be effective in treating multiple myeloma. It is a relatively new treatment, but it has been shown to be effective in both the relapsed/refractory setting and in the frontline setting. The other answer choices are not as appropriate. Melphalan, prednisone, and thalidomide is an older combination therapy that is still used in some cases. However, it is not as effective as lenalidomide, dexamethasone, and bortezomib. CVAD and DBVD are chemotherapy regimens that are used to treat multiple myeloma. However, they are not as effective as combination therapies that include targeted agents, such as lenalidomide, dexamethasone, and bortezomib.

51. The correct answer is D.

Melphalan and prednisone is a combination therapy that has been shown to be effective in treating multiple myeloma in patients who are not eligible for transplantation. It is a relatively old treatment, but it is still effective in many cases. The other answer choices are not as appropriate. Bortezomib is a newer drug that can be used to enhance the efficacy of melphalan. However, it is not necessary in all cases. High dose melphalan followed by two autologous stem cell transplants is a more intensive treatment that is typically only used in younger patients who are eligible for transplantation.

52. The correct answer is B.

Folate deficiency. The patient's symptoms are consistent with a folate deficiency. , also known as folic acid or vitamin B9, is essential for the body's production and maintenance of cells, including red blood cells. It is required for DNA synthesis and repair. A diet low in leafy green vegetables and fruits, which are high in folate, can lead to a folate deficiency. With the absence of neurologic symptoms and normal methylmalonic acid levels, the patient is less likely to have a Vitamin B12 deficiency, as these are typically present with such a deficiency. Vitamin D deficiency is more associated with bone diseases like osteoporosis, falls and fractures, and rickets in children, due to its role in calcium absorption. Similarly, Vitamin E deficiency might affect vision, the immune system, and skin health, while Vitamin K deficiency could impact blood clotting. These symptoms are not present in the patient's case, making these options less likely.

53. The correct answer is D.

Vitamin B12 1 mg IM weekly and then monthly. This patient's symptoms and diet suggest a vitamin B12 deficiency. Neurologic deficits, megaloblastic macrocytic anemia, and increased methylmalonic acid are all indicative of this deficiency. Vitamin B12 is found in foods of animal origin, which the patient's vegan diet lacks. Therefore, the first line of treatment involves replenishing the body's vitamin B12 stores through injections (intramuscular, or IM), as the patient may have difficulty absorbing oral supplementation due to potential , a condition in which the body cannot absorb vitamin B12 from the gastrointestinal tract. Folic acid supplementation may be used in cases of folate deficiency, but this patient's symptoms are more consistent with a B12 deficiency. Vitamin D supplementation is typically used for bone health and deficiency symptoms include bone pain and muscle weakness. Iron supplementation is used in cases of iron deficiency anemia, which typically presents with microcytic anemia, not megaloblastic macrocytic anemia. Vitamin K supplementation is used to improve blood clotting but doesn't address the patient's symptoms.

54. The correct answer is C.

, Iron/TIBC <18%, ferritin 5 ng/mL. This patient's symptoms suggest iron deficiency anemia. (a craving to eat substances such as dirt or ice), (cracks and inflammation at the corners of the mouth), (a smooth, glossy tongue resulting from loss of the lingual papillae), and (indicating potential gastrointestinal bleeding) are all symptoms associated with iron deficiency anemia. In iron deficiency anemia, the percentage of transferrin saturation (Iron/TIBC) is usually less than 16%, and ferritin (a marker of iron stores in the body) levels are usually low (<30 ng/mL) as the body has used up its stored iron. Therefore, lab findings of Iron/TIBC <18% and ferritin 5 ng/mL would be consistent with a diagnosis of iron deficiency anemia. The patient should undergo a to screen for colon cancer as this could be a potential source of chronic blood loss leading to iron deficiency anemia. Treatment should involve replenishing the body's iron stores through oral or intravenous (IV) iron supplementation.

55. The correct answer is A.

Allogeneic stem cell transplant. For young patients with , allogeneic stem cell transplant offers an 80% long-term survival rate and significantly decreases the risk of malignant transformation. However, it does carry the risk of transplant-related morbidity and mortality. , such as with cyclosporine or tacrolimus, is associated with a response rate of 80% to 90% and a 5-year survival rate of 80% to 90%, but it is also linked to a 15% to 20% 10-year incidence of clonal disorders, including myelodysplastic syndrome, acute myelogenous leukemia, and paroxysmal nocturnal hemoglobinuria. are typically reserved for refractory disease, while supportive care with transfusions, antibiotics, and growth factors is more appropriate for an elderly or treatment refractory population. is not a suitable approach given the serious nature of aplastic anemia and the availability of effective treatments.

56. The correct answer is A.

Anemia of chronic inflammation. This patient's presentation is consistent with anemia of chronic inflammation, often seen in chronic illnesses such as lupus. Her worsening arthralgias and new oral ulcers would suggest a disease flare. The best management of her anemia would be to treat the underlying lupus. Iron deficiency anemia can coexist with anemia of chronic inflammation, but it's unlikely in this patient given the elevated ferritin levels. Her normal creatinine level argues against anemia of chronic kidney disease, while the normal Hgb last year and lack of offending exposures are not consistent with sideroblastic anemia or lead poisoning.

57. The correct answer is A.

Autoimmune hemolytic anemia (AIHA). This patient's clinical presentation is consistent with warm autoimmune hemolytic anemia. The patient's lymphadenopathy and absolute lymphocytosis suggest an underlying etiology of chronic lymphocytic leukemia for the AIHA. Although levofloxacin can cause drug-induced hemolytic anemia, it is less likely in this case due to the positive Coombs test. Similarly, there is no evidence of thrombocytopenia or schistocytosis that would suggest microangiopathic hemolytic anemia (MAHA). Hereditary spherocytosis would have likely presented at a much earlier age and is not typically associated with a positive Coombs test. Iron deficiency anemia is not consistent with the patient's symptoms and lab findings.

58. The correct answer is E.

Pure red cell aplasia. The symptoms provided suggest that the patient and her children were infected with , which can be associated with fevers and a "slapped cheek" appearance. Pure red cell aplasia occurs when a patient develops destructive antibodies or lymphocytes that target the bone marrow and lead to ineffective erythropoiesis. This condition can be associated with parvovirus infection, as well as with , , , and certain drugs. Aplastic anemia is less likely given the lack of evidence for thrombocytopenia or leukopenia. Chronic lymphocytic leukemia, thymoma, and autoimmune disease are also potential causes of pure red cell aplasia, but there's no specific information suggesting these conditions in this case.

59. The correct answer is C.

-Thalassemia minor. The long-standing, asymptomatic nature of the patient's anemia makes iron deficiency anemia unlikely, despite the low MCV. The correct diagnosis based on the low MCV, the normal transferrin saturation, and the hemoglobin electrophoresis results is -thalassemia minor. -Thalassemia minor results from the loss of two -chain genes. The genotype can be heterozygous for the -thalassemia-1 trait or homozygous for the -thalassemia-2 trait. Patients typically have mild anemia, hypochromia, and microcytosis, without other significant clinical manifestations, unlike -thalassemia intermedia or -thalassemia major. Other options like -Thalassemia minor, Anemia of chronic disease, and Sideroblastic anemia are less likely given the patient's clinical presentation and test results.

60. The correct answer is C.

This patient has acute chest syndrome (ACS), a leading cause of death in patients with sickle cell disease. ACS is characterized by pulmonary infiltrates on chest X-ray and at least two of the following: cough, fever, tachypnea, chest pain, and hypoxemia. Exchange transfusion is the most appropriate management for ACS because it rapidly decreases the percentage of hemoglobin S (HgbS) in the blood. This is important because HgbS is less soluble than oxygen, and it can sickle and block blood vessels in the lungs. Exchange transfusion also removes inflammatory mediators that can contribute to ACS. Simple transfusion may also be used to treat ACS, but it is not as effective as exchange transfusion. Simple transfusion can increase the risk of hyperviscosity, a condition in which the blood becomes too thick and can flow poorly. Steroids are not standard practice for ACS management in adults. Albuterol nebulizers may be used to treat bronchospasm in patients with ACS, but they will not reverse the underlying cause of the symptoms. Therefore, the most appropriate management for this patient is exchange transfusion.

61. The correct answer is B.

This patient has thrombotic thrombocytopenic purpura (TTP), a life-threatening condition characterized by the formation of blood clots in small blood vessels throughout the body. TTP is caused by a deficiency of the enzyme ADAMTS13, which is responsible for cleaving von Willebrand factor multimers. Plasma exchange is the first-line treatment for TTP. It removes inhibitory autoantibodies to ADAMTS13 and replaces low levels of ADAMTS13. Plasma exchange should be initiated immediately in patients with TTP, as it can significantly reduce mortality. Fresh frozen plasma can replace ADAMTS13, but it will not remove inhibitory autoantibodies. Red blood cell transfusion and platelet transfusion are not indicated in patients with TTP, as they will not address the underlying cause of the bleeding and may worsen the condition.

62. The correct answer is B.

Conduct Glucose-6-phosphate dehydrogenase (G6PD) testing. The patient's sudden onset of pallor and fatigue following the start of a new medication, trimethoprim-sulfamethoxazole, suggests drug-induced hemolytic anemia. This is a common complication in individuals with G6PD deficiency. Red blood cell transfusion should be given if the anemia is severe or the patient is symptomatic. Patients should also be advised to avoid oxidizing agents in the future.

63. The correct answer is A.

The patient's clinical presentation and imaging findings are consistent with warfarin-associated intracranial hemorrhage. 4F-PCC is the preferred treatment for warfarin-associated intracranial hemorrhage, as it leads to more rapid INR reversal than FFP. Vitamin K should also be administered to the patient, but it should be given as an intravenous infusion over 30 minutes.

64. The correct answer is A.

; Acquired platelet disorder; DDAVP (desmopressin acetate). This patient with uremia is experiencing an acquired platelet disorder. The most appropriate intervention in this case would be the administration of DDAVP. Dialysis would also be effective as it can correct the uremia. Platelet transfusion, however, would not be effective because the newly introduced platelets would become dysfunctional in the uremic plasma.

65. The correct answer is D.

The most likely diagnosis in this patient is immunoglobulin A (IgA) vasculitis, also known as Henoch-Schönlein purpura. The hallmark of IgA vasculitis is a rash of palpable purpura. The diagnosis of IgA vasculitis is based on the clinical presentation and the presence of IgA deposits in the skin or kidneys. Skin biopsy with direct immunofluorescence microscopy is the most sensitive and specific test for diagnosing IgA vasculitis. ANCA testing and anti-GBM antibody testing are used to diagnose other types of vasculitis, but they are not typically used to diagnose IgA vasculitis. Kidney biopsy is a more invasive test that is typically reserved for patients with severe renal failure or those who are not responding to treatment.

66. The correct answer is E. Thrombotic thrombocytopenic purpura.

Thrombotic thrombocytopenic purpura (TTP) is a condition characterized by microangiopathic hemolytic anemia (MAHA), thrombocytopenia, schistocytes on peripheral smear, elevated LDH, and elevated indirect bilirubin. MAHA is Coombs negative, and TTP is more common in women and African American patients. The patient's history of autoimmune hypothyroidism (Hashimoto thyroiditis) may increase her risk for autoimmune disorders like TTP. Early recognition of TTP is crucial as it necessitates emergent plasma exchange therapy. Primary immune thrombocytopenia is less likely due to the concurrent presence of hemolytic anemia. Evans syndrome, which presents with immune thrombocytopenia and hemolytic anemia, is also less likely due to the negative Coombs test. Drug-induced thrombocytopenia, which could be caused by drugs such as quinine, antimicrobials, quetiapine, and chemotherapy agents, is less likely due to the simultaneous presence of hemolytic anemia. Furthermore, the patient would not have required antimicrobial prophylaxis for her trip to Europe, making option D unlikely.

67. Answer: C

This patient most likely has immune (antibody)-mediated heparin-induced thrombocytopenia (HIT). HIT is a prothrombotic side effect of heparin therapy that is caused by antibodies against a complex of heparin and platelet factor 4 (PF4). The diagnosis of HIT is based on the clinical presentation and the results of laboratory tests. The most important test is the PF4-heparin ELISA, which is a highly sensitive and specific test for HIT. The management of HIT includes immediate discontinuation of heparin and initiation of an alternative anticoagulant. Bivalirudin is a direct thrombin inhibitor that is the preferred anticoagulant for patients with HIT. Corticosteroids and warfarin are not recommended for the initial treatment of HIT. Corticosteroids may delay the recovery of platelet counts, and warfarin can increase the risk of thrombosis in patients with HIT. Platelets are also not recommended for patients with HIT, as they may be consumed by the HIT antibodies. Aspirin is not effective in preventing thrombosis in patients with HIT. Therefore, the most appropriate management for this patient is to stop heparin, send PF4-heparin

ELISA, and start bivalirudin. Additional notes: The 4-T score is a clinical scoring system that can be used to assess the pretest probability of HIT. The patient in this case has a very high 4-T score, which further supports the diagnosis of HIT. Patients with HIT should be monitored closely for signs and symptoms of thrombosis, such as chest pain, shortness of breath, and leg pain and swelling. Most patients with HIT recover within 2-4 weeks of discontinuing heparin and starting an alternative anticoagulant.

68. The correct answer is: D. Immune Thrombocytopenic Purpura

This is a classic presentation of immune thrombocytopenia that has a bimodal age distribution for disease onset. In children and younger adults, the disease typically presents following a viral syndrome with sequelae from severe thrombocytopenia. The large morphology of platelets is also classic for immune thrombocytopenia. Despite the presence of low platelet count, the lack of constitutional symptoms, preserved Hemoglobin and White Blood Cell count, and absence of any abnormal leukocytes in the peripheral blood all argue against a diagnosis of Aleukemic Leukemia (choice A). Ehrlichiosis (choice B), a tick-borne disease often associated with thrombocytopenia, is unlikely in this case due to the absence of a clinical syndrome including constitutional symptoms, fevers, associated leukopenia, and Liver Function Test abnormalities. Although drug-associated thrombocytopenia (choice C) has to be considered, the overall clinical picture here is more consistent with immune thrombocytopenia. Lastly, while the disease often presents following a viral syndrome (choice E) in children and younger adults, this patient's lack of other symptoms makes a viral syndrome less likely.

69. Answer: D

This patient has from , , and . He is unlikely to have , as he does not have a history of easy bruising or bleeding, and his platelet count is not extremely low. The most effective way to rapidly increase the platelet count in this patient is with a . A platelet goal of >50,000/L is recommended for most surgical procedures. is a thrombopoietin receptor agonist that can be used to increase platelet counts in patients with immune thrombocytopenia. However, it is not as effective in patients with multifactorial thrombocytopenia. can be used to correct coagulopathy in patients with liver disease. However, the patient's INR is only mildly deranged, and he is unlikely to have significant coagulopathy. Therefore, vitamin K is not necessary in this case. contains platelets, but it is not as effective as a platelet transfusion for increasing platelet counts. Additionally, FFP can increase the risk of volume overload and other complications. Therefore, the most appropriate management of this patient's thrombocytopenia is a platelet transfusion with a platelet goal >50,000/L.

Additional notes: Patients with chronic liver disease and thrombocytopenia should be monitored closely for signs of bleeding, such as easy bruising, bleeding gums, and nosebleeds. If a patient with chronic liver disease and thrombocytopenia develops bleeding, they may require platelet transfusions or other treatments to stop the bleeding. In some cases, patients with chronic liver disease and thrombocytopenia may need to have surgery delayed until their platelet count is higher.

70. The correct answer is D. .

is a synthetic analogue of vasopressin that causes a transient release of von Willebrand factor (vWF) from storage granules in the vascular endothelium, leading to an increase in serum concentrations. Hence, it is a reasonable strategy for prophylaxis and treatment of minor bleeding in patients with mild type I vWD (Option A) and mild hemophilia A (factor VIII deficiency), because vWF increases the circulating half-life of factor VIII from approximately 30 minutes to 24 hours (Option B). It has also been seen to be effective in platelet dysfunction of end-stage renal disease (Option C). However, DDAVP is ineffective in type 3 vWD (Option D) because there is no vWF present in storage granules (which are Weibel-Palade bodies). Type 3 vWD is a rare variant of vWD characterized by a severe deficiency or near absence of any vWF, leading to a severe bleeding diathesis. Hence, DDAVP is ineffective as there is no vWF to be released from storage granules. Therefore, option D is the correct answer.

71. The correct answer is B. + .

This patient's condition is consistent with immune thrombocytopenia, an autoimmune disorder characterized by a low platelet count and increased risk of bleeding. The goal of treatment in these cases is to increase the patient's platelet count into a safe range, generally >30,000/L. Steroids are considered first-line therapy in the acute setting of immune thrombocytopenia and typically lead to a response in platelet count in 4 to 7 days after therapy is initiated. In cases of severe thrombocytopenia and high risk of CNS bleed, IVIG can also be added to the treatment regimen. IVIG typically induces a response in platelet count within 1 to 2 days. Other options such as platelet transfusion are generally not effective in this condition because the immune system will continue to destroy the transfused platelets. Similarly, while splenectomy and thrombopoietin agonist therapies can be effective for the management of immune thrombocytopenia, these are typically reserved for the chronic phase of the condition, not for initial management. Therefore, the combination of IVIG and steroids is the most appropriate initial management approach in this case.

72. Answer: D .

This patient has , which is an immune-mediated disorder that occurs after 5 days of exposure to heparin. It is caused by the formation of antibodies against a complex of heparin and platelet factor 4 (PF4). These antibodies activate platelets and lead to the formation of microthrombi. Type 1 HIT is a nonimmune thrombocytopenia that occurs within the first 2 days of heparin therapy. It is caused by the direct effect of heparin on platelets. Type 1 HIT is not prothrombotic and resolves with continued heparin therapy. IABP-induced thrombocytopenia is a mechanical thrombocytopenia that occurs in patients with intra-aortic balloon pumps. It is caused by the shearing of platelets as they pass through the IABP. All of the above diagnoses could contribute to the patient's thrombocytopenia. However, type 2 HIT is the most likely diagnosis because of the timing of the platelet count drop and the fact that the patient is on heparin. Type 2 HIT is a serious condition that can lead to thrombosis, ischemia, and death. It is important to diagnose and treat HIT early. The diagnosis of HIT is based on the clinical presentation and the results of laboratory tests. The most important test is the platelet factor 4 (PF4) heparin enzyme-linked immunosorbent assay (ELISA). The treatment of HIT includes immediate discontinuation of heparin and initiation of an alternative anticoagulant, such as bivalirudin or argatroban. Patients with HIT should be monitored closely for signs and symptoms of thrombosis.

73. Answer: B

This patient has acute promyelocytic leukemia (APL), which is a type of leukemia that is associated with disseminated intravascular coagulation (DIC). DIC is a condition in which blood clots form throughout the body, consuming clotting factors and platelets. However, this patient is not currently in a state of severe DIC. She is not actively bleeding, and her platelet count is not extremely low. Her PT and PTT are prolonged, but her fibrinogen level is relatively normal. Therefore, the most appropriate treatment at this time is intravenous vitamin K. Vitamin K is necessary for the production of clotting factors. This patient is likely deficient in vitamin K due to her APL and the antibiotic therapy that she is receiving. Platelet transfusions, cryoprecipitate transfusions, fresh frozen plasma transfusions, and PCC transfusions are not necessary at this time. These treatments may be indicated if the patient develops severe DIC with bleeding or if her laboratory parameters worsen. APL is a life-threatening condition, but it is highly curable with early diagnosis and treatment. DIC is a serious complication of APL, but it can be managed with supportive care, including vitamin K replacement and transfusions of blood products if necessary. Patients with APL should be monitored closely for signs and symptoms of DIC, such as bleeding, thrombosis, and organ failure.

74. The correct answer is D. Idarucizumab.

The patient is experiencing a major, potentially life-threatening bleed and is on dabigatran, a direct thrombin inhibitor. The most appropriate treatment in this situation is idarucizumab (Choice D), which is a monoclonal antibody specifically designed to reverse the anticoagulant effects of dabigatran. Fresh frozen plasma (Choice A) is generally avoided in bleeding associated with direct oral anticoagulants due to associated risks such as transfusion reactions, thrombosis, and volume overload, and the absence of data supporting its use except in the case of a coexisting coagulopathy. Andexanet (Choice B) is a reversal agent for factor Xa inhibitors (e.g., rivaroxaban, apixaban, edoxaban), not for dabigatran. An activated prothrombin complex concentrate (Choice C), such as Factor VIII inhibitor bypassing activity (FEIBA), could be administered instead if idarucizumab is not available, although this carries a significant prothrombotic risk. Factor VIII inhibitor bypassing activity (FEIBA) (Choice E) would not be the first choice in this situation. It's used if idarucizumab is not available but comes with a significant prothrombotic risk.

Answer: B

75. Emicizumab is a recombinant humanized bispecific monoclonal antibody that bridges activated factors IX and X, thereby mimicking the function of factor VIII. It is not inhibited by antibodies that bind to factor VIII, making it an ideal treatment for patients with hemophilia A and high titer inhibitors. Emicizumab is administered subcutaneously once weekly or once every 2 weeks. It is approved for prophylaxis in patients with hemophilia A and high titer inhibitors, but it can also be used to treat bleeding episodes. The other options are not as appropriate for this patient. Higher doses of recombinant factor VIII are unlikely to be effective due to the presence of high titer inhibitors. Recombinant factor IX is not effective in patients with hemophilia A, as it does not replace the missing factor VIII. Factor VIIa can be used to treat bleeding episodes in patients with hemophilia and high titer inhibitors, but it is associated with a high risk of thrombotic complications. Emicizumab is a relatively new medication, but it has been shown to be effective and safe in patients with hemophilia A and high titer inhibitors. Emicizumab can be used to prevent bleeding episodes (prophylaxis) or to treat bleeding episodes that have already occurred. Emicizumab is

administered subcutaneously once weekly or once every 2 weeks. Emicizumab is generally well-tolerated, but some side effects can occur, such as injection site reactions and allergic reactions. So, the best option for this patient is idarucizumab (Choice D), which is a specific reversal agent for dabigatran and does not carry the prothrombotic risk of activated prothrombin complex concentrates.

76. C. Flow cytometry for CD55 and CD59

This patient's presentation of hemolytic anemia, pancytopenia, and mesenteric venous thrombosis is suggestive of paroxysmal nocturnal hemoglobinuria. This is a rare, acquired hematopoietic stem cell disorder that results from a somatic mutation in a gene on the X chromosome. The diagnostic test of choice is flow cytometry for the glycophosphatidylinositol-linked proteins CD55 and CD59, which are characteristically decreased on RBCs and granulocytes. While Protein C and S and antithrombin III levels can be affected by acute thrombosis and anticoagulation, they are best assessed more than 2 weeks after completing anticoagulation. A positive activated protein C resistance assay would be consistent with factor V Leiden, but these other inherited thrombophilias would not explain this patient's hemolytic anemia or pancytopenia.

77. Answer: D

This patient has antiphospholipid syndrome, which is a condition that increases the risk of blood clots. Warfarin is the most effective long-term anticoagulant for preventing blood clots in patients with antiphospholipid syndrome. It is especially effective for preventing arterial thrombosis, which is the type of thrombosis that this patient has experienced. Enoxaparin, dabigatran, and rivaroxaban are direct oral anticoagulants (DOACs). DOACs are less effective than warfarin for preventing blood clots in patients with antiphospholipid syndrome, especially those with a history of arterial thrombosis. Enoxaparin can be used for short-term anticoagulation in patients with antiphospholipid syndrome, but it is not recommended for long-term use due to its high cost and the burden of daily injections. Antiphospholipid syndrome is a chronic condition, so patients typically need to take anticoagulants for life. Patients with antiphospholipid syndrome should be monitored closely for signs and symptoms of blood clots. If a patient with antiphospholipid syndrome develops a blood clot, they may need to be hospitalized for treatment.

78. The correct answer is: D. No anticoagulation Factor V Leiden is a mutation that increases the risk of developing abnormal blood clotting (venous thromboembolism). However, in this patient who is asymptomatic and does not have a history of clotting or high-risk circumstances (such as major surgery), there is no indication for anticoagulation. Anticoagulation therapy like Warfarin, Direct Oral Anticoagulants, or Heparin, is typically reserved for patients with a history of clotting or those who are undergoing a high-risk situation where clotting risk is increased. It's important to note that even though this patient has factor V Leiden, without any previous history of clots or high-risk circumstances, the risk of clotting is not high enough to justify the risks associated with anticoagulation therapy. However, venous thromboembolism prophylaxis should be considered at times of surgery or other high-risk situations. Aspirin is typically not used as a first-line treatment for preventing venous thromboembolism.

79. The correct answer is B.

No treatment. This patient's clinical presentation and lab findings suggest stage 0 chronic lymphocytic leukemia (CLL), characterized by an elevated white blood cell count primarily composed of lymphocytes. The stages of CLL are defined as follows:

- Stage 0: Only an elevated white blood cell count.
- Stage 1: Enlarged lymph nodes.
- Stage 2: Enlarged spleen.
- Stage 3: Anemia.
- Stage 4: Thrombocytopenia.

In CLL, treatment typically commences at stage 3, or if the patient is symptomatic from lymphadenopathy and/or splenomegaly. In the absence of these conditions, as in this patient's case, no treatment is required. Therefore, he should be monitored for any progression of the disease, but no active intervention is necessary at this time. The other options (A, C, D, E) are not appropriate because they represent treatments that are too aggressive for a patient at stage 0 CLL.

80. Answer: C

Microscopic cholesterol emboli are the most likely cause of eosinophilia in this patient. Cholesterol emboli can occur after cardiac catheterization, especially in patients with coronary artery disease. The emboli can travel to the kidneys and other organs, causing damage and inflammation. Eosinophilia is a common finding in patients with cholesterol emboli. The eosinophils are attracted to the inflamed tissue and help to clear the emboli. The other options are less likely causes of eosinophilia in this patient. Drug reactions and allergic reactions to the catheterization dye can cause eosinophilia, but they are usually accompanied by other symptoms, such as rash, itching, and swelling. Infection can also cause eosinophilia, but this patient does not have any other signs or symptoms of infection.

81. Answer: A

Solid organ transplant recipients, such as kidney transplant recipients, are at high risk for CMV infection due to their immunosuppressed state. CMV infection can be serious and even fatal in transplant recipients. Therefore, it is important to give them CMV-negative blood products. Leukoreduction is a process that removes white blood cells from blood products. Leukoreduction helps to reduce the risk of transfusion-related complications, such as febrile nonhemolytic transfusion reactions, human leukocyte antigen alloimmunization, and CMV transmission. Therefore, leukoreduced RBCs should be given to all patients, including transplant recipients. The other options are not as appropriate for this patient. CMV-positive blood products should not be given to transplant recipients due to the risk of CMV infection. Non-leukoreduced RBCs should not be given to any patients due to the increased risk of transfusion-related complications. CMV is a common virus that can cause a variety of symptoms, including fever, fatigue, and rash. CMV infection can be serious and even fatal in immunocompromised patients, such as transplant recipients. CMV is transmitted through contact with bodily fluids, such as blood, saliva, and urine. CMV can be prevented by avoiding contact with bodily fluids from infected people and by using condoms during sexual activity. Treatment for CMV infection includes antiviral medications. Microscopic cholesterol emboli can cause a variety of symptoms, including eosinophilia, acute kidney injury, skin lesions, and neurological symptoms. The diagnosis of cholesterol emboli is based on the clinical presentation and the results of laboratory tests. Treatment for cholesterol emboli is supportive and includes managing the underlying condition (e.g., coronary artery disease) and treating the symptoms. In some cases, patients with cholesterol emboli may need to be treated with corticosteroids or other medications to reduce inflammation.

82. Answer: B.

Chronic myelogenous leukemia. Basophilia is typically not an isolated finding but often associated with other symptoms or conditions. In this case, the patient presents with an elevated white blood cell count and excess mature granulocytes without symptoms of leukostasis or tumor lysis, which is characteristic of chronic myelogenous leukemia (CML). CML is a type of cancer that starts in the blood-forming cells of the bone marrow and invades the blood. It can spread to the organs and tissues of the body. Distinct from acute lymphoblastic leukemia, acute myeloid leukemia, chronic lymphocytic leukemia, and Hodgkin's lymphoma, CML often presents with an elevated white blood cell count and basophilia. Hence, in this clinical context, the most likely diagnosis is chronic myelogenous leukemia (option B).

83. Answer: A

This patient is experiencing a delayed hemolytic transfusion reaction, which is a type of transfusion reaction that occurs 1 or 2 weeks after a blood transfusion. It is caused by the development of antibodies against red blood cell antigens. Most delayed hemolytic transfusion reactions are mild and do not require treatment. However, patients with sickle cell disease are more likely to have severe reactions due to mild intravascular hemolysis. The first step in managing a delayed hemolytic transfusion reaction is to consult the blood bank. The blood bank can perform an antibody screen to identify the specific red blood cell antigen to which the patient has become sensitized. This information can then be used to select the appropriate blood products for future transfusions. Transfusing another unit of PRBCs before the antigen is identified could result in another hemolytic transfusion reaction. Therefore, it is important to wait for the results of the antibody screen before transfusing any more blood products. Antibiotics are not necessary for most delayed hemolytic transfusion reactions. However, if the patient develops signs or symptoms of infection, such as fever, chills, or hypotension, antibiotics may be necessary. Discharge home is not appropriate for this patient until the hemolysis has resolved. The patient should be monitored closely with serial blood tests to ensure that the hemolysis is not worsening. Delayed hemolytic transfusion reactions can be prevented by using antigen-matched blood products whenever possible. Patients who have had a delayed hemolytic transfusion reaction should be given antigen-matched blood products for future transfusions. Patients with sickle cell disease are at increased risk for delayed hemolytic transfusion reactions. Most delayed hemolytic transfusion reactions are mild and do not require treatment. However, patients with sickle cell disease are more likely to have severe reactions.

84. C. Transfusion-associated circulatory overload.

The patient's presentation suggests transfusion-associated circulatory overload (TACO). TACO is a complication of blood transfusion that can occur when the volume of blood transfused is too large or the transfusion is given too quickly, particularly in patients with preexisting heart disease or fluid balance issues. In this patient's case, she has several risk factors for developing TACO, including a history of heart failure and COPD, advanced age, being female, and having a small body habitus. To prevent this complication, measures such as slowing the transfusion rate, reducing the transfusion volume, and administering diuretics prior to the transfusion could have been taken. The other transfusion reactions listed as answer options typically occur during or soon after a transfusion rather than several hours later and are more likely to cause hypotension rather than hypertension, making them less likely in this patient's case.

85 A. Allogeneic stem cell transplant.

This patient has myelodysplastic syndrome with symptomatic anemia and neutropenia, which has led to recurrent cellulitis. However, her good cytogenetics and low blast count suggest that her disease is relatively indolent, and her low IPSS-R score indicates a prognosis of a median overall survival approaching 9 years. Given her overall good prognosis, the patient should be managed with supportive care measures, including antibiotics for her recurrent cellulitis and erythropoietin-stimulating agents to manage her anemia. Low-intensity therapies, such as azacitidine and decitabine, may also be beneficial. Allogeneic stem cell transplant, which is the only curative treatment for myelodysplastic syndrome, is generally reserved for patients with high or very high IPSS-R scores who have a good performance status. Despite being the correct answer, it should be noted that for this patient, an Allogeneic stem cell transplant might not be the first-line treatment due to her low IPSS-R score.

86. Answer: C

Patients with myelodysplastic syndrome (MDS) are at high risk for infections due to their suppressed immune system. Therefore, it is important to keep them up-to-date on all recommended vaccinations. The National Comprehensive Cancer Network (NCCN) guidelines recommend that patients with MDS receive the following vaccinations:

- Yearly influenza vaccine
- Pneumococcal vaccine every 5 years
- Age-appropriate vaccinations, such as the hepatitis B vaccine and the tetanus-diphtheria-pertussis vaccine
- Live vaccines, such as the measles-mumps-rubella (MMR) vaccine and the varicella-zoster virus (VZV) vaccine, should be avoided in patients with MDS. This is because live vaccines can cause serious infections in people with weakened immune systems. Prophylactic antibiotics and G-CSFs are not recommended for patients with MDS. Prophylactic antibiotics have not been shown to prevent infections in patients with MDS, and G-CSFs can increase the risk of serious infections.

87. Answer: A

Allogeneic stem cell transplant (ASCT) is the only curative treatment for MDS. It is especially recommended for patients with high-risk MDS, such as those with poor cytogenetics and a high IPSS-R score. Hypomethylating agents (HMAs) are another treatment option for MDS. However, they are generally more appropriate for patients with lower-risk MDS or patients who are not candidates for ASCT. Ivosidenib and enasidenib are targeted therapies that are approved for the treatment of MDS patients with IDH1 and IDH2 mutations, respectively. This patient does not have an IDH1 or IDH2 mutation, so these therapies are not appropriate for him. Intensive chemotherapy is associated with a high risk of toxicity and is not curative for MDS. It is generally only considered for patients with high-risk MDS who are not candidates for ASCT or targeted therapy.

88. answer is D. Low-dose aspirin and hydroxyurea.

The patient most likely has polycythemia vera, a condition characterized by the overproduction of red blood cells. Treatment for this condition typically involves phlebotomy to reduce the hematocrit to <45%, low-dose aspirin to reduce the risk of blood clots, and hydroxyurea for high-risk patients. High-risk patients include those who are aged 60 or older or who have a history of thrombus, both of which apply to this patient. Therefore, the correct treatment would be low-dose aspirin and hydroxyurea (Option D). Clopidogrel (Option B) is an antiplatelet medication used to prevent heart disease and stroke but is not typically the first line of treatment for polycythemia vera.

89. The correct answer is D.

RBC transfusion. The patient has primary myelofibrosis, which in this case is likely secondary to lupus. Primary myelofibrosis may also arise from other conditions such as polycythemia vera, essential thrombocythemia, other hematologic and solid cancers, and toxins. The symptoms are typically due to anemia and the subsequent splenomegaly. If the patient is asymptomatic and not anemic, there is no need for treatment. For younger patients with a poor prognosis, a more aggressive approach with an allogeneic stem cell transplant, which is the only potential cure, could be considered. However, for an older, symptomatic patient like this one, supportive care, including blood transfusions, is the standard treatment.

90 .Answer: D

Observation is the best course of action for this patient. He is young and has no history of thrombosis, so he is at low risk of complications. Aspirin and hydroxyurea are only recommended for patients with ET who are at high risk of complications, such as those with a history of thrombosis or those with a platelet count over 1,500,000/L. Interferon is rarely used in ET and is generally only reserved for patients who are not responding to other treatments. ET is a chronic blood disorder characterized by an elevated platelet count. Patients with ET are at increased risk of thrombosis, such as blood clots in the brain, heart, and lungs. Treatment for ET is aimed at reducing the platelet count and preventing thrombosis. Observation is the best course of action for patients with ET who are at low risk of complications. Aspirin and hydroxyurea are only recommended for patients with ET who are at high risk of complications. Interferon is rarely used in ET and is generally only reserved for patients who are not responding to other treatments.

91. Answer: C

The patient has acute myelogenous leukemia (AML) based on the presence of circulating blasts with myeloid markers. The translocation (8;21) and NPM1 gene mutation positivity confer a favorable prognosis in AML. AML is a cancer of the blood and bone marrow that develops when immature blood cells, called blasts, grow and multiply uncontrollably. AML is the most common type of acute leukemia in adults. The prognosis for AML varies depending on the subtype of AML and the presence of certain genetic markers. Patients with AML with a favorable prognosis have a better chance of survival than patients with AML with an unfavorable prognosis. Treatment for AML typically involves chemotherapy and stem cell transplantation.

92. Answer: A. Liposomal cytarabine and daunorubicin on days 1, 3, and 5.

This patient has most likely developed cytotoxic therapy-related acute myelogenous leukemia based on her history of breast cancer requiring chemotherapy. Therefore, the most appropriate induction therapy for this patient is liposomal cytarabine and daunorubicin on days 1, 3, and 5. Standard induction therapy (Choice B) would be indicated for patients who are under the age of 60 years, or who are over the age of 60 years but eligible for intensive chemotherapy, and who do not have targetable mutations. Choice E, with the addition of midostaurin, describes the appropriate induction therapy for patients with FLT3-mutated acute myelogenous leukemia. Choice D, with the addition of gemtuzumab ozogamicin, describes the appropriate induction therapy for patients with CD33-positive acute myelogenous leukemia. The reduced intensity therapy (Choice C) is indicated for patients who are over the age of 60 years and require nonintensive chemotherapy due to medical comorbidities or functional status. For patients under the age of 45 years, induction therapy includes standard therapy or high-dose cytarabine (HiDAC) for 6 days followed by idarubicin or daunorubicin for 3 days.

93. Answer: C

The patient is most likely experiencing differentiation syndrome, which is a life-threatening complication of ATRA therapy in patients with acute promyelocytic leukemia. Differentiation syndrome is characterized by fever, pulmonary infiltrates, shortness of breath, edema, hypotension, and acute kidney injury. The best treatment for differentiation syndrome is dexamethasone 10 mg twice daily and supportive care. Supportive care may include diuresis, vasopressors, oxygen support, and dialysis as needed. Additional chemotherapy agents are not indicated, and antibiotics are only indicated if an infectious source is identified. Differentiation syndrome is most likely to occur in the first 2 weeks of ATRA therapy. The mortality rate for differentiation syndrome is approximately 10%. Early diagnosis and treatment is essential to improve outcomes.

94. Answer: B.

If she discontinues the imatinib, she will have a 60% chance of recurrence in 24 months. Explanation: This patient achieved a complete molecular remission with imatinib-based chemotherapy, a result seen in approximately one-fourth of patients. The standard recommendation is to continue imatinib indefinitely due to its effectiveness in managing chronic myeloid leukemia. However, imatinib is teratogenic, posing a risk to conceiving women like the patient in the scenario. Data from several tyrosine kinase inhibitor discontinuation trials indicate that about 40% of patients remain free from molecular relapse at 2 years after discontinuing imatinib. Therefore, if she decides to discontinue imatinib, she faces a 60% chance of disease recurrence within 24 months. Following discontinuation, she would require intensive monitoring for the next 24 months to promptly detect any signs of disease recurrence.

95. The correct answer is A.Blinatumomab.

Blinatumomab is approved for patients with CD19 positive relapsed or refractory B-cell acute lymphoblastic leukemia and has been shown to be superior to standard chemotherapy options in terms of remission rates as well as improvements in overall survival. Option B, Inotuzumab , and option C, Tisagenlecleucel, are also new treatment options for patients with relapsed or refractory acute lymphoblastic leukemia. However, only a subset of the lymphoblasts are CD22 positive, making Inotuzumab less ideal. Additionally, the patient is over 26 years of age, making her ineligible to receive Tisagenlecleucel. Option D, Standard chemotherapy, has been shown to be less effective than Blinatumomab in terms of remission rates and overall survival. Option E, Watchful waiting, is not appropriate in this situation as the patient has a relapsed or refractory disease that requires active treatment.

96. Answer: A

The patient has acute myelogenous leukemia (AML) based on the presence of >20% circulating blasts in the peripheral blood with myeloid markers. Chronic myelogenous leukemia (CML) does not have high blast counts unless it is in accelerated phase or blast crisis. Acute lymphoblastic leukemia (ALL) is a cancer of lymphoid cells, not myeloid cells. Chronic lymphocytic leukemia (CLL) is a cancer of mature B lymphocytes, and multiple myeloma is a cancer of plasma cells. AML is the most common type of acute leukemia in adults. AML is a rapidly progressive cancer that requires prompt treatment. Treatment for AML typically involves chemotherapy and stem cell transplantation. The prognosis for AML depends on a number of factors, including the subtype of AML, the patient's age and overall health, and the presence of certain genetic markers.

97. Answer: D

This patient is most likely experiencing leukostasis, tumor lysis syndrome, and infection. Leukostasis is a life-threatening condition that occurs when there are too many white blood cells in the blood. This can block blood vessels and lead to organ damage. Tumor lysis syndrome is a complication of cancer that occurs when cancer cells release their contents into the blood too quickly. This can lead to electrolyte imbalances, kidney failure, and other complications. Infection is a common complication in patients with acute leukemia, as their immune system is weakened by the disease and its treatment. The patient's high white blood cell count, shortness of breath, and pulmonary infiltrates suggest leukostasis. The hyperkalemia, renal dysfunction, and elevated LDH suggest tumor lysis syndrome. The fever is a sign of infection. Treatment for leukostasis includes urgent cytoreductive therapy, leukapheresis, and intensive critical care. Treatment for tumor lysis syndrome includes hydration, electrolyte replacement, and allopurinol. Treatment for infection includes broad-spectrum antibiotics.

98. The correct answer is: B.

<50/mm3. Primary CNS lymphoma typically occurs when a patient's CD4 count drops below 50/mm3. Non-Hodgkin lymphoma (NHL) is an AIDS-defining malignancy. Patients are also typically co-infected with Epstein-Barr virus. Treatment involves intrathecal methotrexate, steroids, and possible radiation and/or temozolomide. The regimen may necessitate significant myeloablation, to the point of considering an autologous HSCT. Thus, in patients with AIDS, a significant drop in CD4 count (below 50/mm3) increases their susceptibility to primary CNS lymphoma.

99. Answer: B

Richter transformation is a progression of CLL to DLBCL. It occurs in roughly 5% of CLL patients and carries a poor prognosis. Patients are then treated for DLBCL, rather than for the initial CLL. The cause of Richter transformation is not fully understood, but it is thought to be caused by a combination of genetic and environmental factors. Richter transformation is typically diagnosed based on a biopsy of a new or enlarged lymph node. Treatment for Richter transformation typically involves R-CHOP chemotherapy, which is a combination of rituximab, cyclophosphamide, doxorubicin, vincristine, and prednisone. Radiation therapy may also be used. The prognosis for Richter transformation is poor, with a 5-year survival rate of 20-30%. The other answer choices are not as likely in this patient. CLL is a slow-growing cancer of B lymphocytes that does not typically cause rapidly worsening symptoms. Hodgkin lymphoma is a type of lymphoma that affects white blood cells, but it is not typically associated with CLL. Multiple myeloma is a type of cancer that affects plasma cells, not B lymphocytes.

100. The correct answer is: C.

Observation. This patient has asymptomatic chronic lymphocytic leukemia, which does not warrant treatment immediately. Chronic lymphocytic leukemia (CLL), a type of blood and bone marrow disease that usually gets worse slowly , is typically not treated unless patients have disease-related symptoms (e.g., pain from lymphadenopathy or hepatosplenomegaly) or have developed cytopenias (lower than normal counts of one or more types of blood cells).

If treatment becomes necessary, first-line therapy would typically be ibrutinib (option A). However, in this patient's case, the disease is asymptomatic, and hence, the best approach is a 'watch and wait' strategy, which is also known as observation. Allogeneic stem cell transplant (option B), chemotherapy (option D), and radiation therapy (option E) are more aggressive treatment options that would typically be reserved for patients with symptomatic or rapidly progressing disease.

101. Answer: A

The most appropriate treatment plan for this patient is ABVD (doxorubicin, bleomycin, vinblastine, dacarbazine) and repeat PET-CT after 2 cycles. ABVD is the first-line treatment for stage 1-2 Hodgkin lymphoma, and it has a cure rate of over 90%. BEACOPP is a more aggressive chemotherapy regimen that is typically used for patients with advanced Hodgkin lymphoma or for patients who have relapsed after ABVD. Brentuximab vedotin and pembrolizumab are immunotherapy agents that are active in Hodgkin lymphoma, but they are currently only approved for relapsed disease. Radiation therapy can be used in Hodgkin lymphoma, but it is typically used in combination with chemotherapy. Radiation therapy alone is not curative for Hodgkin lymphoma. The PET-CT scan after 2 cycles of ABVD is used to assess the response to treatment. Patients with a good response may be able to eliminate bleomycin from the remaining cycles of chemotherapy. Patients with a poor response to ABVD may need to be switched to a different chemotherapy regimen, such as BEACOPP. The prognosis for stage 1-2 Hodgkin lymphoma is excellent, with a 5-year survival rate of over 95%.

102. Answer: D.

Excisional lymph node biopsy, PET-CT scan, ESR, and bone marrow biopsy For suspected lymphoma, the most important next step in diagnostic workup is an excisional lymph node biopsy (not fine needle aspiration, as this will not reveal the surrounding architecture) with immunophenotyping and cytogenetics to confirm the diagnosis. For staging, which requires identification of the number of lymph node regions involved, the presence of disease on one or both sides of the diaphragm, and the presence or absence of involvement of extralymphatic organs, full-body imaging is necessary. A PET-CT scan is preferred over CT alone as it can more reliably detect spleen and liver involvement and the response to treatment, which can be prognostic and can guide treatment. Although CBC, complete metabolic profile, and LDH are not needed for staging, these lab values are used in predictive calculators to estimate the likelihood of response to therapy and overall survival. ESR is also used for this purpose. A bone marrow biopsy is indicated as this would be a site of extranodal disease. Head CT and/or MRI are not indicated in the absence of symptoms. HIV, human T-cell leukemia lymphoma virus, and Epstein-Barr virus serologies can be considered to rule out alternative etiologies of lymphadenopathy, but are not required for the diagnosis or risk stratification.

103. The correct answer is: A.

CXR, echocardiogram, pulmonary function tests. This patient is experiencing late effects from her treatment for Hodgkin lymphoma, which include an increased risk for second cancers, particularly lung, and hematologic malignancies. A complete blood count (CBC) with differential would be used to evaluate for hematologic malignancy. A Chest X-ray (CXR) should be performed to assess for possible lung cancer, given her symptoms. Further, because she received 6 cycles of both doxorubicin (which is cardiotoxic) and bleomycin (which can cause pulmonary toxicity), she should undergo an echocardiogram to evaluate her heart function and pulmonary function tests to assess her lung capacity and function. Option B (Mammography, Pap smear) is incorrect because, although these tests are used to screen for breast and cervical cancer respectively, this patient did not receive chest or neck radiation, so her risk of breast cancer is closer to average. Option C (Thyroid function tests) is incorrect because the risk of thyroid disease in this patient is similar to that of the general population, because the increased risk among patients with Hodgkin lymphoma applies only to those who receive neck radiation. Option D (Bone marrow biopsy) is not the most immediate step given the patient's presentation. Option E (Neck radiation) is not correct as this is a treatment modality and not a diagnostic step.

104. Answer: A

The most appropriate treatment plan for this patient is quadruple therapy for treatment of the H. pylori. H. pylori is a bacteria that is associated with the development of gastric MALT lymphoma. Eradication of H. pylori is curative in over 75% of patients with early-stage gastric MALT lymphoma. Radiation therapy and rituximab monotherapy are both options for patients with gastric MALT lymphoma who do not respond to H. pylori eradication or who have advanced disease. However, quadruple therapy is the first-line treatment for this patient, as he has early-stage disease and is H. pylori positive. Quadruple therapy is a combination of four medications: bismuth, metronidazole, tetracycline, and omeprazole. It is taken for 14 days. The side effects of quadruple therapy can include nausea, vomiting, diarrhea, and abdominal pain. If the patient's MALT lymphoma does not respond to H. pylori eradication, he will need to be treated with radiation therapy or rituximab monotherapy. The prognosis for patients with early-stage gastric MALT lymphoma is excellent, with a 5-year survival rate of over 95%.

105. Answer: B

The patient's clinical presentation and laboratory findings are highly suggestive of multiple myeloma. The next best step in management is to perform a bone marrow biopsy with cytogenetics and gene mutation analysis, as well as a skeletal survey. The bone marrow biopsy will confirm the diagnosis of multiple myeloma and provide information about the type and stage of the disease. The cytogenetics and gene mutation analysis will help to identify any high-risk features that may impact treatment and prognosis. The skeletal survey will evaluate for lytic bone lesions, which are a common complication of multiple myeloma. PET-CT is not a first-line diagnostic test for multiple myeloma. It is more commonly used in the diagnosis and staging of lymphoma. 2-microglobulin level and serum albumin are staging factors for multiple myeloma, but they are not necessary for diagnosis. Deferring further workup is not appropriate in this patient, as he has multiple myeloma-defining events and is at risk for serious complications, such as pathologic fracture. Multiple myeloma is a cancer of the plasma cells, which are a type of white blood cell. Multiple myeloma is the second most common blood cancer in adults. The prognosis for multiple myeloma depends on a number of factors, including the type and stage of the disease, the patient's age and overall health, and the presence of any high-risk features. Treatment for multiple myeloma typically involves a combination of chemotherapy, radiation therapy, and stem cell transplantation.

106. Answer: B.

1% per year risk of progression to a malignancy; 25% lifetime risk This patient likely has light chain monoclonal gammopathy of unknown significance (MGUS). MGUS is characterized by the presence of an abnormal free light chain ratio in the absence of symptoms or signs of multiple myeloma, such as lytic bone lesions, renal failure, or hypercalcemia. The prevalence of MGUS increases with age, being about 3% in patients over age 50, 5% in patients over age 70, and 7.5% in patients over age 85. Although MGUS itself is typically asymptomatic, it does carry a risk of progression to malignancy such as multiple myeloma or a malignant lymphoproliferative disease. This risk is estimated to be about 1% per year, and the lifetime risk of progression is about 25%. Therefore, patients diagnosed with MGUS should be monitored closely, with repeat serum protein electrophoresis (SPEP) every 6 months initially and then annually if stable, to detect any signs of progression to malignancy.

107. Answer: B

The most appropriate treatment plan for this patient is to start bendamustine + rituximab. Bendamustine + rituximab is a preferred regimen for initial treatment of Waldenstrom macroglobulinemia. It is effective in reducing tumor burden and improving symptoms. Observation is appropriate for asymptomatic patients with incidentally diagnosed Waldenstrom macroglobulinemia. However, this patient has symptoms of peripheral neuropathy, which is an indication for treatment. Bortezomib + dexamethasone + rituximab is another preferred regimen for initial treatment of Waldenstrom macroglobulinemia. However, bortezomib can worsen symptoms of neuropathy, so it is not the best choice for this patient. Autologous stem cell transplant is not indicated as first-line treatment for Waldenstrom macroglobulinemia. It is typically reserved for patients who have relapsed or refractory disease. Plasmapheresis is a procedure that removes plasma from the blood. It is sometimes used to treat Waldenstrom macroglobulinemia, but it is not typically used as first-line therapy. Waldenstrom macroglobulinemia is a rare type of lymphoma that affects the B cells. The prognosis for Waldenstrom macroglobulinemia is generally good. Most patients can live for many years with the disease. Treatment for Waldenstrom macroglobulinemia is typically aimed at reducing tumor burden and improving symptoms.

108. Answer: D.Hyperviscosity syndrome

The patient's symptoms are most consistent with hyperviscosity syndrome, which occurs in about 15% of patients with Waldenstrom macroglobulinemia. Symptoms will typically present when the relative serum viscosity is >5 or 6. The symptoms include blurred vision, headache, dizziness, change in mental status, congestive heart failure, and pulmonary infiltrates. The management is plasmapheresis. Raynaud phenomenon and vasculitis due to Type I cryoglobulinemia are also present in this patient, but do not explain the neurologic and pulmonary symptoms.

109. Answer: E.Smoldering multiple myeloma

This patient has smoldering multiple myeloma, which is diagnosed in patients with M protein >3 g/dL and/or 10% to 60% bone marrow clonal plasma cell infiltrate, without myeloma-related organ or tissue impairment or amyloidosis.

The findings are inconsistent with monoclonal gammopathy of unknown significance (MGUS), which requires M protein <3 g/dL and marrow plasmacytosis <10%. Nonsecretory multiple myeloma is diagnosed in patients with no M protein, but marrow plasmacytosis and myeloma-related organ or tissue impairment. The patient does not have clinical features or pathologic findings consistent with amyloidosis.

110. Answer: D

The patient has a solitary bone plasmacytoma, which is a localized form of plasma cell neoplasia. The most appropriate next step in management is radiation therapy to the right humerus lesion. Radiation therapy is effective in treating solitary bone plasmacytoma and can cure up to 80% of patients. The chemotherapy regimens listed in choices A, B, and C are typically used to treat multiple myeloma, which is a more disseminated form of plasma cell neoplasia. Although these regimens may be used to treat solitary bone plasmacytoma in certain cases, they are not the first-line therapy. Observation and referral to physical therapy are not appropriate in this case, as the patient is at risk for worsening pain and possibly pathologic fracture. Solitary bone plasmacytoma is a rare condition that accounts for about 5% of all plasma cell neoplasms. The prognosis for solitary bone plasmacytoma is generally good, with a 5-year survival rate of over 90%. Treatment for solitary bone plasmacytoma is typically aimed at curing the disease. This can be achieved with radiation therapy or surgery.

111. Answer: A

The most appropriate induction regimen for this patient is bortezomib/lenalidomide/dexamethasone. This is a triplet regimen that combines a proteasome inhibitor (bortezomib) with an immunomodulator (lenalidomide) and a steroid (dexamethasone). Triplet regimens have been shown to have the best response rates in patients with multiple myeloma. Bortezomib/cyclophosphamide/dexamethasone and carfilzomib/lenalidomide/dexamethasone are also triplet regimens that are commonly used in patients with multiple myeloma. However, bortezomib/lenalidomide/dexamethasone is generally considered to be the preferred regimen for patients who are eligible for autologous stem cell transplant. Pomalidomide/cyclophosphamide/dexamethasone is a quadruplet regimen that is used in patients with relapsed/refractory multiple myeloma. It is not typically used as first-line therapy. Induction therapy is the first phase of treatment for multiple myeloma. It is aimed at reducing the tumor burden and improving the patient's symptoms. Autologous stem cell transplant is a high-dose chemotherapy treatment followed by the reinfusion of the patient's own stem cells. It can be a curative treatment for multiple myeloma, but it is not appropriate for all patients. The prognosis for multiple myeloma has improved significantly in recent years, with many patients now living for many years with the disease.

112. The correct answer is: D.

Myeloablative conditioning followed by allogeneic transplant from his sibling. This patient has a high risk of relapse due to the presence of the FLT3-ITD mutation. Considering his age and the high risk of disease recurrence, along with the availability of a fully matched sibling donor, an allogeneic transplant would be the best choice for consolidation therapy. In a young patient with high-risk acute myelogenous leukemia without any comorbidities, myeloablative conditioning is tolerable and reduces the risk of leukemia recurrence in addition to the antileukemic effects from the graft versus leukemia effect of the allogeneic transplant itself. Option B is a reasonable approach for consolidation therapy for patients with good-risk acute myelogenous leukemia. FLT3 inhibitors have shown improvement in overall survival when added to standard induction chemotherapy followed by maintenance dosing. However, given the patient's age, availability of fully matched sibling donor, and high risk of disease recurrence, an allogeneic transplant would be the best choice for consolidation therapy.

113 The correct answer is: C.Steroids.

This patient has developed engraftment syndrome, which typically occurs 1 to 4 days after the absolute neutrophil count (ANC) exceeds 500. The major characteristics of this syndrome are fever, noncardiogenic pulmonary edema, and erythrodermatous rash. If only two of these criteria are present, the diagnosis can be supported by additional signs such as renal dysfunction, hepatic dysfunction, encephalopathy, or unexplained weight gain. The recommended treatment for engraftment syndrome is steroids at a dose of 1 mg/kg, which should be rapidly tapered over 3 to 4 days. Therefore, steroids (Option C) are the most appropriate treatment for this patient's condition.

114. Answer: A

The most likely diagnosis is acute graft-versus-host disease (GVHD). Acute GVHD is a common complication of allogeneic stem cell transplant, which occurs when the donor's immune cells attack the recipient's healthy tissues. The most common organs affected by acute GVHD are the skin, gastrointestinal tract, and liver. The patient's symptoms and laboratory findings are all consistent with acute GVHD. He has diarrhea, a maculopapular rash, and elevated liver enzymes. The fact that he underwent a mismatched related peripheral stem cell transplant also increases his risk for GVHD. Chronic GVHD is a less common complication of allogeneic stem cell transplant, which typically occurs more than 6 months after transplant. It can affect the skin, eyes, mouth, lungs, and liver. Sepsis is a life-threatening condition caused by a systemic inflammatory response to infection. The patient's symptoms and laboratory findings are not consistent with sepsis. He does not have a fever, hypotension, or tachycardia. Tumor lysis syndrome is a complication of cancer that occurs when cancer cells release their contents into the blood too quickly. This can lead to electrolyte imbalances, kidney failure, and other complications. The patient's symptoms and laboratory findings are not consistent with tumor lysis syndrome. He does not have hyperuricemia, hyperkalemia, hypophosphatemia, or hypercalcemia. Treatment for acute GVHD typically involves corticosteroids and other immunosuppressive medications. The prognosis for acute GVHD depends on the severity of the disease and the response to treatment. Most patients with acute GVHD can be cured with treatment, but some patients may develop chronic GVHD or other complications.

115. Answer: D

The most likely diagnosis is sinusoidal obstruction syndrome. Sinusoidal obstruction syndrome (SOS) is a condition in which the small blood vessels in the liver are blocked. This can lead to a buildup of fluid in the liver and other parts of the body, as well as damage to the liver cells. SOS is a common complication of hematopoietic cell transplant, especially in the first few weeks after the transplant. It is also associated with other conditions, such as certain medications, viral infections, and pregnancy. The patient's clinical presentation and laboratory findings are consistent with SOS. He has jaundice, ascites, and hepatomegaly, and his serum bilirubin is elevated. He recently underwent a hematopoietic cell transplant, which is a major risk factor for SOS. The other answer choices are less likely. Acute graft-versus-host disease (GVHD) is a condition in which the donor's immune cells attack the recipient's healthy tissues. It can affect the liver, but it is not typically associated with the sudden onset of jaundice and ascites. Budd-Chiari syndrome is a condition in which the veins that drain blood from the liver are blocked. It can also cause jaundice and ascites, but it is less common in patients who have undergone hematopoietic cell transplant. Hepatic ischemia is a condition in which the blood supply to the liver is reduced. It can cause liver damage, but it is not typically associated with jaundice and ascites. Treatment for SOS typically involves supportive care, such as fluid management and antibiotics. In some cases, medications may be used to try to improve blood flow to the liver. The prognosis for SOS depends on the severity of the condition and the underlying cause. In general, the prognosis is better for patients with SOS caused by hematopoietic cell transplant than for patients with SOS caused by other conditions.

Dr Rafael Zioni

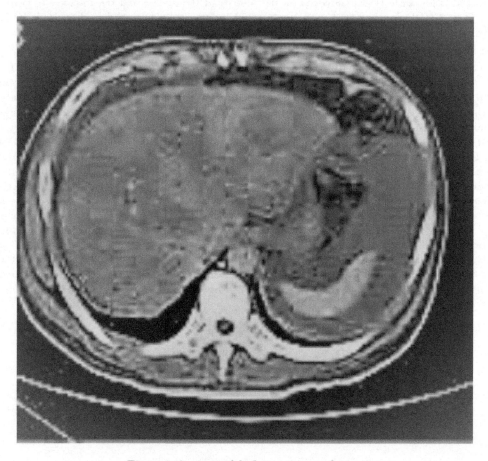

Figure 3.10: sinusoidal obstruction syndrome

Chapter 4

ONCOLOGY BOARD QUESTIONS

1. A 69-year-old man with a history of smoking presents with a cough and shortness of breath. He is found to have a lung mass on imaging. Biopsy of the mass reveals small-cell lung cancer (SCLC). Which of the following is the most likely treatment approach for this patient?

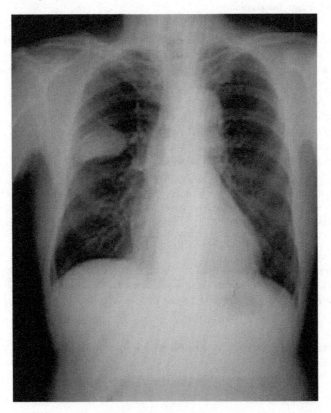

Figure 4.1: lung mass

- A. Surgery followed by chemotherapy and radiation therapy.
- B. Chemotherapy and radiation therapy alone
- C. Surgery alone
- D. Radiation therapy alone

127

- E. Palliative care only

2. Which of the following skeletal connective tissue syndromes is most commonly observed in association with lung cancer?

- A. Clubbing
- B. Hypertrophic pulmonary osteoarthropathy
- C. Sarcoidosis
- D. Osteoporosis
- E. Rheumatoid arthritis

3. A 43-year-old woman with no significant past medical history presents with a palpable breast lump. Mammogram and ultrasound reveal a 1.5 cm mass in the upper outer quadrant of the right breast. Biopsy of the mass reveals ductal carcinoma in situ (DCIS). Which of the following is the preferred treatment for this patient?

- A. Wide excision alone
- B. Wide excision and breast radiation therapy
- C. Wide excision, breast radiation therapy, and adjuvant tamoxifen
- D. Mastectomy
- E. Mastectomy and adjuvant tamoxifen

4. A 53-year-old woman with a history of breast cancer presents with a recurrence of the cancer in her left breast. Biopsy of the recurrent tumor reveals that it is Her2-positive. Which of the following statements is most accurate regarding the use of adjuvant trastuzumab in conjunction with chemotherapy for this patient?

- A. Adjuvant trastuzumab will not be effective in this patient because the cancer has already recurred.
- B. Adjuvant trastuzumab will reduce the risk of recurrence by 25%.
- C. Adjuvant trastuzumab will reduce the risk of recurrence by 50%.
- D. Adjuvant trastuzumab will reduce the risk of recurrence by 75%.
- E. Adjuvant trastuzumab will reduce the risk of recurrence by 100%.

5. A 71-year-old woman with a history of breast cancer presents for follow-up after surgery. She has no evidence of recurrence. Her tumor was estrogen receptor-positive and lymph no-positive. Which of the following is the recommended adjuvant therapy for this patient?

- A. Tamoxifen for 5 years
- B. Aromatase inhibitor for 5 years
- C. Tamoxifen for 2 years followed by an aromatase inhibitor for 3 years.
- D. Aromatase inhibitor for 2 years followed by tamoxifen for 3 years.
- E. Chemotherapy

6. What is the 5-year survival rate for patients diagnosed with esophageal carcinoma?

- A. 10%
- B. 20%
- C. 30%
- D. 40%
- E. 50%

7. A 50-year-old man with a history of atrophic gastritis presents with epigastric pain. He has no other significant past medical history. Which of the following risk factors is most strongly associated with his development of gastric carcinoma?

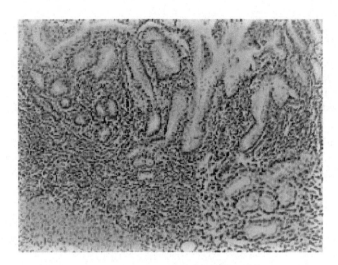

Figure 4.2: Atrophic gastritis

- A. Infection with Helicobacter pylori
- B. Undergoing a Billroth II gastrectomy or gastrojejunostomy.
- C. Having adenomatous gastric polyps.
- D. Pernicious anemia
- E. Hyperplastic gastric polyps

8. A 57-year-old man with a history of iron-deficiency anemia presents with epigastric pain. He has no other significant past medical history. He has been taking oral iron supplements for the past 6 months, but his anemia has not improved. Which of the following is the most likely diagnosis?

- A. Gastric carcinoma
- B. Pernicious anemia
- C. H. pylori infection
- D. Atrophic gastritis
- E. Zollinger-Ellison syndrome

9. What is the most common cause of low-grade MALT lymphoma?

- A. Helicobacter pylori infection
- B. Autoimmune diseases
- C. Radiation exposure
- D. Genetic mutations
- E. Environmental toxins

10. What is the rationale behind the need for proctoscopic surveillance subsequent to subsequent to subsequent to colectomy in patients with familial polyposis coli (FPC)?

- A. To remove any residual polyps that may have been missed during surgery.
- B. To monitor for the development of new polyps.
- C. To prevent the development of cancer in the remaining rectum.
- D. To all of the above.

11. Which of the following is the most likely diagnosis for a 26-year-old man with a family history of familial polyposis coli (FPC) who presents with multiple colorectal adenomatous polyps and a medulloblastoma?

- A. Turcot's syndrome
- B. Familial adenomatous polyposis (FAP)
- C. Gardner's syndrome
- D. Peutz-Jeghers syndrome
- E. Lynch syndrome

12. A 61-year-old man with stage C colorectal cancer is considering whether or not to undergo adjuvant chemotherapy. What are the benefits of adjuvant chemotherapy in this patient's case?

- A. Adjuvant chemotherapy can reduce the risk of recurrence by up to 50
- B. Adjuvant chemotherapy can improve overall survival by up to 20
- C. Adjuvant chemotherapy can delay the onset of recurrence.
- D. Adjuvant chemotherapy can improve the quality of life for patients with stage C colorectal cancer.
- E. All of the above.

13. What is the recommended therapeutic approach for alleviating symptoms associated with hepatic metastases from colorectal cancer?

- A. Intraarterial chemotherapy, specifically floxuridine (FUDR)
- B. Radiation therapy
- C. Both intraarterial chemotherapy and radiation therapy
- D. Surgery

E. None of the above 13. What are the therapeutic modalities available for the treatment of hepatocellular carcinoma (HCC)?

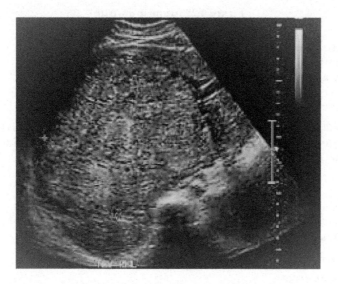

Figure 4.3: hepatocellular carcinoma

- A. Surgical resection
- B. Liver transplantation
- C. Radiofrequency ablation
- D. Transcatheter arterial embolization (TACE)
- E. All of the above

14. What is the most common anatomical site for pancreatic tumors?

- A. Head of the pancreas
- B. Body of the pancreas
- C. Tail of the pancreas
- D. None of the above

15. What is the most effective treatment for pancreatic cancer?

- A. Surgical resection
- B. Adjuvant chemotherapy
- C. Gemcitabine with erlotinib or capecitabine
- D. FOLFIRINOX

- E. None of the above

16. A 52-year-old man presents with symptoms of carcinoid syndrome. Which of the following is the most likely method to diagnose the tumor?

- A. CT scan of the abdomen and pelvis
- B. Urine 5-hydroxyindoleacetic acid (5-HIAA) test
- C. Octreotide scintigraphy
- D. Endoscopy with biopsy
- E. Magnetic resonance imaging (MRI) of the abdomen and pelvis

17. A 48-year-old woman presents with symptoms of hypoglycemia, including sweating, shakiness, and confusion. Her blood sugar level is 40 mg/dL. Which of the following is the most likely diagnostic criteria for insulinoma?

- A. Blood glucose level < 55 mg/dL with symptoms of hypoglycemia
- B. Increased levels of insulin in the bloodstream during fasting
- C. Decreased levels of C-peptide in the bloodstream during fasting.
- D. Increased levels of proinsulin in the bloodstream during fasting
- E. All of the above

18. A 53-year-old man presents with watery diarrhea, hypokalemia, achlorhydria, and renal failure. Which of the following is the most likely diagnosis?

- A. VIPoma
- B. Insulinoma
- C. Gastrinoma
- D. Pheochromocytoma
- E. Carcinoid tumor

19. A 44-year-old man presents with symptoms of necrolytic migratory erythema, weight loss, and diabetes mellitus. A fasting plasma glucagon level is 2000 ng/L. Which of the following is the most likely diagnosis?

- A. Glucagonoma
- B. Insulinoma
- C. Gastrinoma
- D. Pheochromocytoma
- E. Carcinoid tumor

20. A 73-year-old man with a history of bladder cancer presents with recurrent disease. He is found to have increased expression of epidermal growth factor receptors and HER2/neu receptors. Which of the following is the most likely treatment option?

- A. Chemotherapy
- B. Radiation therapy
- C. Targeted therapy with EGFR inhibitors
- D. Targeted therapy with HER2/neu inhibitors
- E. Immunotherapy

21. A 75-year-old man with muscle-invasive bladder cancer is not a candidate for radical surgery. Which of the following treatment options is most likely to offer him the best chance of survival?

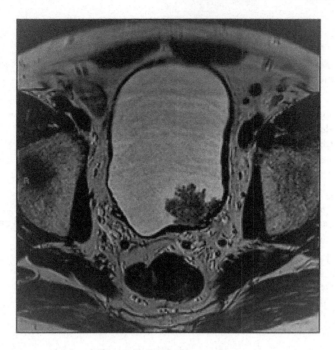

Figure 4.4: Bladder cancer

- A. External beam radiation therapy
- B. Chemotherapy with CMV
- C. Chemotherapy with cisplatin and radiation therapy
- D. Immunotherapy
- E. Bladder-preserving surgery

22. A 64-year-old man presents with a 2 cm mass in his right kidney. CT scan shows a solid mass with clear cell features. What is the most likely diagnosis?

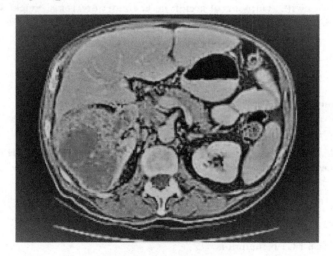

Figure 4.5: solid mass

- A. Clear cell renal cell carcinoma (RCC)
- B. Papillary RCC
- C. Chromophobe RCC

- D. Oncocytoma
- E. Collecting duct RCC.

23. A 72-year-old man with benign prostatic hyperplasia (BPH) presents with urinary retention. Which of the following is the most likely treatment option?

- A. Transurethral resection of the prostate (TURP)
- B. Medications to relax the prostate.
- C. Watchful waiting
- D. Radiation therapy
- E. Laser surgery

24. A 74-year-old man is diagnosed with prostate cancer. He has a palpable tumor in the right lobe of his prostate. What is the most likely stage of his cancer according to the Whitmore-Jewett staging system?

- A. Stage A
- B. Stage B1
- C. Stage B2
- D. Stage C
- E. Stage D

25. A 47-year-old man is diagnosed with a brain tumor. He also has papilledema. What is the most likely implication of the papilledema?

- A. The brain tumor is causing increased intracranial pressure.
- B. The brain tumor is causing decreased intracranial pressure.
- C. The brain tumor is causing hydrocephalus.
- D. The brain tumor is causing optic neuritis.
- E. The brain tumor is causing meningitis.

26. A 42-year-old man presents with a rapidly growing tumor in his mediastinum. He has elevated levels of serum tumor markers. What is the most likely diagnosis?

- A. Germ cell tumor
- B. Lymphoma
- C. Lung cancer
- D. Metastatic cancer
- E. Sarcoma

27. A 63-year-old man is diagnosed with squamous cell carcinoma of the lung. He presents with hypercalcemia. What is the most likely cause of his hypercalcemia?

- A. Hyperparathyroidism
- B. Addison's disease
- C. Multiple myeloma
- D. Hypercalcemia of malignancy
- E. Sarcoidosis

28. A 52-year-old woman presents with symptoms of Cushing's syndrome. She is found to have elevated levels of cortisol in her blood. What is the most likely diagnosis?

- A. Ectopic ACTH syndrome
- B. Adrenal adenoma
- C. Adrenal cancer
- D. Primary hyperaldosteronism
- E. Pheochromocytoma

29. A 60-year-old man presents with shortness of breath, facial swelling, and dilated neck veins. What is the most likely diagnosis?

- A. Superior vena cava syndrome
- B. Pneumonia
- C. Heart failure

- D. Pulmonary embolism
- E. Hyperthyroidism

30. A 71-year-old man with a history of lung cancer presents with back pain and weakness in his legs. What is the most likely diagnosis?

- A. Neoplastic spinal cord compression
- B. Spinal stenosis
- C. Herniated disc
- D. Osteoporosis
- E. Multiple sclerosis

31. A 50-year-old man with a history of heavy smoking presents with cough and hemoptysis. A CT scan reveals a suspicious mass in his lung. What is the best next step in the management of this patient?

- A. Chest X-ray and bronchoscopy
- B. CT-guided biopsy of the lung mass
- C. Thoracentesis
- D. Pulmonary function tests
- E. Fluorodeoxyglucose (FDG) PET/CT, and brain MRI; pending results, follow with mediastinal lymph node evaluation with endobronchial ultrasound, mediastinoscopy

32. A 58-year-old female with a history of smoking has recently been diagnosed with stage 4 non-small cell lung cancer. Molecular analysis of the tumor revealed that it harbors an EGFR-positive mutation, specifically a deletion in exon 19. What would be the most appropriate first-line therapy for this patient?

- A. Erlotinib
- B. Crizotinib
- C. Pembrolizumab alone
- D. Osimertinib alone
- E. Carboplatin and pemetrexed

33. A 67-year-old man presents with metastatic squamous cell carcinoma. His PD-L1 staining is 30%. What is the most appropriate first-line treatment?

- A. Carboplatin and paclitaxel
- B. Pembrolizumab alone
- C. Carboplatin, paclitaxel, and pembrolizumab
- D. Radiation therapy
- E. None of the above

34. A 66-year-old man with a history of smoking presents with nausea, vomiting, and fatigue. Physical exam reveals hypovolemia and hypotension. Laboratory studies reveal a serum sodium level of 125 mmol/L. What is the next best step in management?

- A. Order sodium studies, such as a urine sodium and a renin level.
- B. Order an MRI of the brain to rule out central pontine myelinolysis.
- C. Start intravenous fluids and monitor the patient's serum sodium level.
- D. Order a chest CT to rule out small cell lung cancer.
- E. None of the above

35. A 62-year-old man, who has a smoking history of 30-pack-years and has quit smoking 8 years ago, comes to your clinic asking about lung cancer screening. According to the US Preventive Services Task Force (USPSTF) recommendations, when should he stop his annual low-dose CT screening for lung cancer?

- A. Immediately
- B. In 5 years
- C. In 10 years
- D. In 15 years
- E. He should continue indefinitely

36. A 38-year-old premenopausal woman has been diagnosed with low-risk, early-stage ER+ breast cancer. She has no history of any other significant diseases. Considering her age and the nature of her cancer, what would be the

most appropriate first-line therapy?

- A. Anastrozole
- B. Combined aromatase inhibition and ovarian suppression
- C. Tamoxifen
- D. Chemotherapy
- E. Surgical ovarian suppression

37. Which of the following is NOT indicated for metastatic hormone receptor-positive, HER2-negative breast cancer?

- A. Aromatase inhibitors
- B. CDK 4/6 inhibitors
- C. Mammalian target of rapamycin (mTOR) inhibitors
- D. Lapatinib
- E. All of the above are indicated

38. 56-year-old woman presents with a new diagnosis of early-stage HER2-positive breast cancer. What is the most appropriate adjuvant therapy regimen?

- A. Docetaxel, cyclophosphamide, trastuzumab, pertuzumab (TCHP)
- B. Lapatinib, trastuzumab
- C. Trastuzumab emtansine (T-DM1)
- D. Letrozole, ribociclib
- E. None of the above

39. A patient has been diagnosed with metastatic breast cancer and is found to have a germline mutation. Considering the potential sensitivity to certain therapies, which gene mutation is more likely to be associated with this condition?

- A. MEN1
- B. BRCA2
- C. BRCA1
- D. Lynch syndrome
- E. BAP1

40. A patient has been newly diagnosed with hormone-sensitive metastatic prostate cancer. Considering the potential of an androgen burst with certain treatments, which of the following therapeutic combinations is most suitable for this patient?

- A. Leuprolide and bicalutamide
- B. Degarelix and bicalutamide
- C. Degarelix and abiraterone/prednisone
- D. Leuprolide alone
- E. Degarelix alone

41. A 67-year-old man with no major medical issues presents with a persistently elevated PSA. What is the next best step in management?

- A. Transrectal ultrasound (TRUS)-guided 12-core prostate biopsy
- B. Repeat PSA in 6 months
- C. Prostate MRI
- D. None of the above

42. A 25-year-old man presents with a family history of colorectal cancer. His father was diagnosed with colorectal cancer at age 45, his grandfather was diagnosed with colorectal cancer at age 52, and his aunt was diagnosed with colorectal cancer at age 48. The patient has no personal history of colorectal cancer. Genetic testing reveals a mutation in the PMS2 gene. What is the most appropriate screening schedule for colorectal cancer in this patient?

- A. Colonoscopy at age 20, then repeat screen yearly
- B. Colonoscopy at age 45, then repeat screen every 10 years
- C. Stool occult blood test (FOBT) at age 50, then repeat screen every 2 years
- D. No screening necessary
- E. None of the above

43. A patient has recently been diagnosed with colon cancer. Which of the following is the most appropriate next step in the management of this patient?

- A. Measure Carcinoembryonic antigen (CEA) level
- B. Perform CT of the chest, abdomen, and pelvis
- C. Perform brain imaging
- D. Both A and B
- E. None of the above

44. A 42-year-old man presents with a family history of breast cancer, ovarian cancer, and prostate cancer. His mother was diagnosed with breast cancer at age 45, his sister was diagnosed with ovarian cancer at age 35, and his father was diagnosed with prostate cancer at age 50. What is the most likely genetic syndrome causing this patient's family history of cancer?

- A. Hereditary nonpolyposis colorectal cancer (HNPCC)
- B. Familial breast/ovarian cancer BRCA2
- C. Lynch syndrome
- D. Li-Fraumeni syndrome
- E. None of the above

45. A patient with metastatic pancreatic cancer and a genomic BRCA2 mutation has recently completed a course of FOLFIRINOX therapy. The patient has an excellent response to the therapy but has developed significant neuropathy. What is the most appropriate next step in the management of this patient?

- A. Continue chemotherapy with FOLFOX (5FU/LV + oxaliplatin)
- B. Start a regimen consisting of abraxane
- C. Refer the patient for hospice care
- D. Initiate immunotherapy with PD-1 inhibitors
- E. Start therapy with Poly (ADP-ribose) polymerase (PARP) inhibitors

46. A patient presents with abdominal discomfort and weight loss. A physical examination shows slight jaundice. The doctor suspects a pancreatic condition. What would be the most appropriate next step in diagnosis?

- A. Checking CA 19-9 levels
- B. Abdominal ultrasound
- C. EUS-guided FNA without prior imaging
- D. Pancreatic protocol CT scan or MRI with contrast followed by endoscopic ultrasound (EUS)-guided fine needle aspiration (FNA)
- E. Magnetic resonance cholangiopancreatography (MRCP) without prior CT scan or MRI

47. A 23-year-old woman with leukemia presents with fever, abdominal pain, and diarrhea. She is neutropenic and thrombocytopenic. Her abdominal CT scan shows thickened bowel wall in the right lower quadrant. Which of the following is the most appropriate next step in management?

- A. Morphine
- B. Loperamide
- C. Nasogastric suction
- D. Surgery consult
- E. None of the above

48. A patient with unresectable locally advanced non-metastatic hepatocellular carcinoma with portal vein thrombosis of the main vein and several satellite nodules is looking for a reasonable approach to palliation. Which of the following treatment options is contraindicated in this patient?

- A. Liver transplantation
- B. Surgical resection
- C. Stereotactic body radiation therapy (SBRT)
- D. Transcatheter arterial chemoembolization (TACE)
- E. Systemic chemotherapy

49. A 52-year-old woman presents to the ER with nausea, vomiting, diarrhea, and severe fatigue a day after receiving her first cycle of FOLFOX (folinic acid, 5-Fluorouracil, and oxaliplatin) for metastatic colon cancer. She also has

a mild rash on her hands and feet. Her symptoms are severe and unexpected for a patient receiving the FOLFOX regimen. What is the most likely explanation for her symptoms?

- A. Dihydropyrimidine dehydrogenase deficiency
- B. Severe allergic reaction to oxaliplatin
- C. Adverse reaction to folinic acid
- D. Overdose of 5-Fluorouracil
- E. Immune reaction to the chemotherapy regimen

50. A 65-year-old man with metastatic melanoma is being treated with ipilimumab and nivolumab. He develops severe diarrhea 6 weeks after starting treatment. Colonoscopy shows active colitis, and biopsies are positive for checkpoint inhibitor-induced colitis. He has failed to respond to high-dose steroids. Which of the following is the most appropriate next step in management?

- A. Increase the dose of steroids
- B. Start vedolizumab
- C. Start infliximab
- D. Start chemotherapy
- E. None of the above

51. A 42-year-old woman with relapsed/refractory B-cell lymphoma undergoes chimeric antigen receptor (CAR) T-cell therapy. One day after CAR T-cell infusion, she develops fever, hypotension, and tachycardia. Her blood pressure responds to fluid resuscitation, but she remains tachycardic. What is the most appropriate next step in management?

- A. Methylprednisolone
- B. Infliximab
- C. Mycophenolate mofetil
- D. Tocilizumab
- E. None of the above

4.1 ANSWERS

1. The correct answer is (B).

SCLC is a highly aggressive cancer that is often treated with chemotherapy and radiation therapy. Surgery is rarely used in the treatment of SCLC due to its high degree of malignancy and propensity for early metastasis. (A) Surgery followed by chemotherapy and radiation therapy: This is not the most likely treatment approach for SCLC because surgery is rarely used to treat this cancer. (B) Chemotherapy and radiation therapy alone: This is the most likely treatment approach for SCLC. Chemotherapy and radiation therapy can help to control the cancer and prolong the patient's life. (C) Surgery alone: This is not the most likely treatment approach for SCLC because surgery is rarely used to treat this cancer. (D) Radiation therapy alone: Radiation therapy can be used to treat SCLC, but it is usually used in combination with chemotherapy. (E) Palliative care only: Palliative care is used to provide comfort and support to patients with advanced cancer. It is not the most likely treatment approach for SCLC, which is a treatable cancer.

2. The correct answer is (A), clubbing.

Clubbing is a condition in which the tips of the fingers and toes become enlarged and bulbous. It is a common sign of lung cancer, occurring in approximately 30% of cases. Clubbing is thought to be caused by increased levels of a hormone called parathyroid hormone-related protein (PTHrP), which is produced by some lung cancers. Hypertrophic pulmonary osteoarthropathy is another skeletal connective tissue syndrome that can be associated with lung cancer, but it is less common than clubbing. Hypertrophic pulmonary osteoarthropathy is characterized by pain, swelling, and redness in the joints, particularly the hands and feet. It is thought to be caused by increased levels of a substance called vascular endothelial growth factor (VEGF), which is produced by some lung cancers. The other answer choices are not associated with lung cancer. Sarcoidosis is a chronic inflammatory disease that can affect any organ in the body, but it does not typically involve the bones or joints. Osteoporosis is a condition in which the bones become weak and brittle, and it is not associated with lung cancer. Rheumatoid arthritis is an autoimmune disease that can cause inflammation in the joints, but it is not associated with lung cancer.

3. The correct answer is (C), wide excision, breast radiation therapy, and adjuvant tamoxifen.

DCIS is a noninvasive form of breast cancer, but it has the potential to become invasive if left untreated. The preferred treatment for DCIS is wide excision, which involves removing the entire area of DCIS and a margin of healthy tissue. Breast radiation therapy is then given to help prevent the cancer from recurring. Adjuvant tamoxifen is also often given to women with DCIS who are hormone receptor-positive, as it can help to reduce the risk of recurrence. (A) Wide excision alone: This is not the preferred treatment for DCIS because it does not provide the same level of protection against recurrence as wide excision with radiation therapy. (B) Wide excision and breast radiation therapy: This is the preferred treatment for DCIS. Wide excision removes the entire area of DCIS and a margin of healthy tissue, and breast radiation therapy helps to prevent the cancer from recurring. (C) Wide excision, breast radiation therapy, and adjuvant tamoxifen: This is also a good treatment option for DCIS. Adjuvant tamoxifen is often given to women with DCIS who are hormone receptor-positive, as it can help to reduce the risk of recurrence. (D) Mastectomy: Mastectomy is not the preferred treatment for DCIS unless the cancer is large or there is a high risk of recurrence. (E) Mastectomy and adjuvant tamoxifen: This is a good treatment option for DCIS if the cancer is large or there is a high risk of recurrence.

4. The correct answer is (C), adjuvant trastuzumab will reduce the risk of recurrence by 50%.

Trastuzumab is a monoclonal antibody that targets the HER2 protein, which is overexpressed in Her2-positive breast cancers. Adjuvant trastuzumab has been shown to reduce the risk of recurrence by 50% in patients with Her2-positive breast cancer. (A) Adjuvant trastuzumab will not be effective in this patient because the cancer has already recurred. This is not true. Adjuvant trastuzumab can be effective in patients with recurrent breast cancer, even if the cancer has already spread to other parts of the body. (B) Adjuvant trastuzumab will reduce the risk of recurrence by 25%. This is not as effective as the actual reduction in recurrence rate of 50%. (C) Adjuvant trastuzumab will reduce the risk of recurrence by 50%. This is the correct answer. Adjuvant trastuzumab has been shown to reduce the risk of recurrence by 50% in patients with Her2-positive breast cancer. (D) Adjuvant trastuzumab will reduce the risk of recurrence by 75%. This is not as effective as the actual reduction in recurrence rate of 50%. (E) Adjuvant trastuzumab will reduce the risk of recurrence by 100%. This is not possible, as no treatment is 100% effective in preventing recurrence.

5. The correct answer is (B), aromatase inhibitor for 5 years.

Aromatase inhibitors are recommended as adjuvant therapy for postmenopausal women with breast tumors that exhibit estrogen receptor expression. Aromatase inhibitors work by blocking the production of estrogen, which can help to prevent the growth of estrogen-dependent breast cancer cells. (A) Tamoxifen for 5 years: Tamoxifen is also a good option for adjuvant therapy for postmenopausal women with breast tumors that exhibit estrogen receptor expression. However, aromatase inhibitors are generally considered to be more effective than tamoxifen. (B) Aromatase inhibitor for 5 years: This is the correct answer. Aromatase inhibitors are recommended as adjuvant therapy for postmenopausal women with breast tumors that exhibit estrogen receptor expression. (C) Tamoxifen for 2 years followed by an aromatase inhibitor for 3 years: This is also a good option for adjuvant therapy. Tamoxifen can be used for the first 2 years of treatment, and then an aromatase inhibitor can be used for the remaining 3 years. (D) Aromatase inhibitor for 2 years followed by tamoxifen for 3 years: This is not the preferred option. It is better to use an aromatase inhibitor for the full 5 years of adjuvant therapy. (E) Chemotherapy: Chemotherapy is not the preferred option for adjuvant therapy for postmenopausal women with breast tumors that exhibit estrogen receptor expression. Chemotherapy is usually reserved for women with aggressive breast cancers that are not responsive to hormone therapy.

6. The correct answer is (A), 10%. The 5-year survival rate for esophageal carcinoma is below 10%.

This means that only about 10% of patients with esophageal carcinoma will survive for at least 5 years after diagnosis. The low 5-year survival rate for esophageal carcinoma is due to a number of factors, including: The cancer is often diagnosed at a late stage, when it has already spread to other parts of the body. There is no effective screening test for esophageal cancer. Treatment options for esophageal cancer are limited and often have significant side effects.

7. The correct answer is (A), infection with Helicobacter pylori.

Helicobacter pylori is a bacterium that can infect the stomach and cause a number of health problems, including atrophic gastritis, which is a major risk factor for gastric carcinoma. (A) Infection with Helicobacter pylori: This is the strongest risk factor for gastric carcinoma. (B) Undergoing a Billroth II gastrectomy or gastrojejunostomy: This is a risk factor for gastric carcinoma, but it is not as strong as infection with Helicobacter pylori. (C) Having adenomatous gastric polyps: This is a risk factor for gastric carcinoma, but it is not as strong as infection with Helicobacter pylori. (D) Pernicious anemia: This is a risk factor for gastric carcinoma, but it is not as strong as infection with Helicobacter pylori. (E) Hyperplastic gastric polyps: This is not a risk factor for gastric carcinoma.

8. The correct answer is (A), gastric carcinoma.

Iron deficiency anemia is observed in approximately two thirds of individuals diagnosed with gastric carcinoma. This finding is commonly observed in laboratory tests and can provide valuable assistance in the diagnosis of the disease. However, the symptom is non-specific and can also be observed in various other medical conditions, such as pernicious anemia, H. pylori infection, atrophic gastritis, and Zollinger-Ellison syndrome.(A) Gastric carcinoma: This is the most likely diagnosis, given the patient's history of iron-deficiency anemia and epigastric pain.(B) Pernicious anemia: Pernicious anemia is another cause of iron-deficiency anemia, but it is less common than gastric carcinoma.(C) H. pylori infection: H. pylori infection can cause iron-deficiency anemia, but it is less common than gastric carcinoma.(D) Atrophic gastritis: Atrophic gastritis can cause iron-deficiency anemia, but it is less common than gastric carcinoma.(E) Zollinger-Ellison syndrome: Zollinger-Ellison syndrome can cause iron-deficiency anemia, but it is rare.

9. The correct answer is (A), Helicobacter pylori infection.

Low-grade MALT lymphoma is a type of non-Hodgkin lymphoma that is often associated with infection with the Helicobacter pylori bacteria. H. pylori infection can cause inflammation in the stomach, which can lead to the development of MALT lymphoma. (A) Helicobacter pylori infection: This is the most common cause of low-grade MALT lymphoma.(B) Autoimmune diseases: Autoimmune diseases can sometimes lead to the development of MALT lymphoma, but they are not as common as H. pylori infection.(C) Radiation exposure: Radiation exposure can increase the risk of developing MALT lymphoma, but it is not as common as H. pylori infection.(D) Genetic mutations: Genetic mutations can increase the risk of developing MALT lymphoma, but they are not as common as H. pylori infection.(E) Environmental toxins: Environmental toxins can sometimes lead to the development of MALT lymphoma, but they are not as common as H. pylori infection.

10. The correct answer is (D), all of the above.

Proctoscopic surveillance is necessary subsequent to subtotal colectomy in patients with FPC for the following reasons: To remove any residual polyps that may have been missed during surgery. To monitor for the development of new polyps. To prevent the development of cancer in the remaining rectum. FPC is a genetic disorder that causes the development of numerous polyps in the colon. If left untreated, these polyps can eventually develop into cancer. Subtotal colectomy is a surgery that removes the entire colon except for the rectum. This surgery can prevent the development of cancer in the colon, but it does not remove the rectum. As a result, it is important to perform regular proctoscopic examinations of the rectum to remove any polyps that may develop and to monitor the development of cancer.

11.The correct answer is (A), Turcot's syndrome.

Turcot's syndrome is a rare hereditary disorder that is characterized by the presence of multiple colorectal adenomatous polyps and an increased risk of developing colorectal cancer. Additionally, individuals with Turcot's syndrome have a rare associated malignant tumor, known as medulloblastoma, which is a type of brain tumor. The other answer choices are all possible diagnoses for a 25-year-old man with a family history of FPC and multiple colorectal adenomatous polyps, but they do not include the presence of a medulloblastoma. Turcot's syndrome: This is the most likely diagnosis, given the patient's family history of FPC and the presence of a medulloblastoma. Familial adenomatous polyposis (FAP): FAP is another hereditary disorder that is characterized by the presence of multiple colorectal adenomatous polyps. However, FAP does not typically involve the development of brain tumors. Gardner's syndrome: Gardner's syndrome is a hereditary disorder that is similar to FAP, but it also involves the development of other benign tumors, such as desmoid tumors and osteomas. Gardner's syndrome does not typically involve the development of brain tumors. Peutz-Jeghers syndrome: Peutz-Jeghers syndrome is a hereditary disorder that is characterized by the presence of multiple polyps in the gastrointestinal tract, as well as mucocutaneous pigmentation. Peutz-Jeghers syndrome does not typically involve the development of brain tumors.Lynch syndrome: Lynch syndrome is a hereditary disorder that is characterized by an increased risk of developing colorectal cancer, as well as other types of cancer. Lynch syndrome does not typically involve the development of brain tumors.

12.The correct answer is (E), all of the above.

Adjuvant chemotherapy has been shown to effectively reduce the recurrence rate, improve overall survival, delay the onset of recurrence, and improve the quality of life for patients with stage C colorectal cancer.

13. The correct answer is (C), both intraarterial chemotherapy and radiation therapy.

Intraarterial chemotherapy, specifically floxuridine (FUDR), and radiation therapy have both been shown to provide palliative relief for symptoms associated with hepatic metastases from colorectal cancer. Intraarterial chemotherapy:

Dr Rafael Zioni

Intraarterial chemotherapy is a type of chemotherapy that is delivered directly to the liver. This type of chemotherapy can be more effective than systemic chemotherapy, which is delivered throughout the body, because it targets the cancer cells in the liver specifically. Radiation therapy: Radiation therapy is another treatment option for hepatic metastases from colorectal cancer. Radiation therapy can help to shrink the tumors and relieve symptoms such as pain and pressure. Surgery: Surgery is not usually an option for patients with hepatic metastases from colorectal cancer, as the cancer is often too advanced to be removed. However, surgery may be an option for patients with small, localized tumors. None of the above: There is no treatment that can cure hepatic metastases from colorectal cancer. However, the treatments mentioned above can help to alleviate symptoms and improve quality of life.

13. The correct answer is (E), all of the above.

Surgical resection, liver transplantation, radiofrequency ablation, transcatheter arterial embolization (TACE), and sorafenib or lenvatinib are all therapeutic modalities that can be used to treat HCC. Surgical resection: Surgical resection is the removal of the tumor and a margin of healthy tissue. This is the most effective treatment for HCC, but it is only possible for patients with small, localized tumors. Liver transplantation: Liver transplantation is the removal of the diseased liver and its replacement with a healthy liver from a deceased donor. This is an effective treatment for HCC, but it is not available to all patients. Radiofrequency ablation: Radiofrequency ablation is a minimally invasive procedure that uses heat to destroy the tumor. This is a good option for patients with small, localized tumors that are not suitable for surgery. Transcatheter arterial embolization (TACE): TACE is a procedure that blocks the blood supply to the tumor. This can help to shrink the tumor and relieve symptoms. Sorafenib or lenvatinib: Sorafenib and lenvatinib are targeted therapies that can inhibit the growth of HCC cells. These drugs can be used to treat patients with advanced HCC who are not eligible for surgery or liver transplantation.

14. The correct answer is (A), head of the pancreas.

Approximately 70% of pancreatic tumors are located in the head of the pancreas, while 20% are situated in the body, and the remaining 10% are found in the tail region. Head of the pancreas: The head of the pancreas is the most common site for pancreatic tumors. Pancreatic head tumors are located near the duodenum, which is the first part of the small intestine. This can cause symptoms such as jaundice, pain, and weight loss. Body of the pancreas: Pancreatic body tumors are less common than pancreatic head tumors. They are located behind the stomach and can cause symptoms such as pain, nausea, and vomiting. Tail of the pancreas: Pancreatic tail tumors are the least common type of pancreatic tumor. They are located near the spleen and can cause symptoms such as pain, weight loss, and fatigue. The location of the tumor can impact on the symptomatology, surgical approach, and management of pancreatic cancer. Imaging studies such as computed tomography (CT) or magnetic resonance imaging (MRI) can be used to precisely locate the tumor and determine its size and extent. The anatomical site where pancreatic tumors are found is an important factor to consider in the diagnosis and treatment of pancreatic cancer.

15. The correct answer is (D), FOLFIRINOX.

FOLFIRINOX is a combination therapy that comprises the chemotherapeutic agents 5-fluorouracil (5FU), irinotecan, and oxaliplatin. FOLFIRINOX has been shown to significantly increase the duration of disease-free survival following a complete resection. Surgical resection: Surgical resection is the removal of the tumor and a margin of healthy tissue. This is the most effective treatment for pancreatic cancer, but it is only possible for patients with small, localized tumors. Adjuvant chemotherapy: Adjuvant chemotherapy is chemotherapy that is given after surgery to help prevent the cancer from coming back. Adjuvant chemotherapy has been shown to improve survival for patients with pancreatic cancer who have undergone surgery. Gemcitabine with erlotinib or capecitabine: Gemcitabine with erlotinib or capecitabine are combination therapies that can be used to treat patients with advanced pancreatic cancer. These therapies have been shown to provide symptomatic relief and to prolong survival. FOLFIRINOX: FOLFIRINOX is a combination therapy that has been shown to be more effective than other chemotherapy options for patients with advanced pancreatic cancer. FOLFIRINOX has been shown to significantly increase the duration of disease-free survival following a complete resection.

16. The correct answer is B. Urine 5-hydroxyindoleacetic acid (5-HIAA) test.

5-HIAA is a serotonin metabolite that is produced by carcinoid tumors. A high level of 5-HIAA in the urine is a sensitive and specific test for carcinoid tumors. The other answer choices are also possible methods for diagnosing carcinoid tumors, but they are not as sensitive or specific as the urine 5-HIAA test. CT scan of the abdomen and pelvis can be used to identify the tumor's location, but it is not as good at detecting small tumors or tumors that have spread to other parts of the body. Octreotide scintigraphy is a more sensitive test than CT scan, but it is not as widely available. Endoscopy with biopsy can be used to confirm the diagnosis of carcinoid tumor, but it is not as sensitive as the urine 5-HIAA test. MRI of the abdomen and pelvis is not as good at detecting carcinoid tumors as CT scan or octreotide scintigraphy.

17. The correct answer is E. All of the above.

The diagnostic criteria for insulinoma include Blood glucose level < 55 mg/dL with symptoms of hypoglycemia. Increased levels of insulin in the bloodstream during fasting. Decreased levels of C-peptide in the bloodstream during fasting Increased levels of proinsulin in the bloodstream during fasting. The presence of all four of these criteria is highly suggestive of insulinoma.

18. The correct answer is A. VIPoma.

VIPoma is a rare neuroendocrine tumor that secretes vasoactive intestinal polypeptide (VIP). VIP is a hormone that causes the intestines to secrete fluids, leading to watery diarrhea. VIP also lowers potassium levels in the blood, which can cause hypokalemia. VIPomas can also cause achlorhydria (low stomach acid production) and renal failure. The other answer choices are also possible diagnoses for a patient with watery diarrhea, hypokalemia, achlorhydria, and renal failure, but they are less likely than VIPoma. Insulinoma is a tumor that secretes insulin, which can cause hypoglycemia (low blood sugar). Gastrinoma is a tumor that secretes gastrin, which can cause increased stomach acid production and ulcers. Pheochromocytoma is a tumor that secretes catecholamines, which can cause high blood pressure, sweating, and anxiety. Carcinoid tumor is a tumor that secretes serotonin and other hormones, which can cause a variety of symptoms, including flushing, diarrhea, and heart problems.

19. The correct answer is A. Glucagonoma.

Glucagonoma is a rare neuroendocrine tumor that secretes glucagon. Glucagon is a hormone that raises blood sugar levels. Symptoms of glucagonoma can include necrolytic migratory erythema, weight loss, and diabetes mellitus. A fasting plasma glucagon level of 2000 ng/L is diagnostic for glucagonoma. The other answer choices are also possible diagnoses for a patient with necrolytic migratory erythema, weight loss, and diabetes mellitus, but they are less likely than glucagonoma. Insulinoma is a tumor that secretes insulin, which lowers blood sugar levels. Gastrinoma is a tumor that secretes gastrin, which increases stomach acid production. Pheochromocytoma is a tumor that secretes catecholamines, which raise blood pressure and heart rate. Carcinoid tumor is a tumor that secretes serotonin and other hormones, which can cause a variety of symptoms, including flushing, diarrhea, and heart problems.

20. The correct answer is C. Targeted therapy with EGFR inhibitors. Epidermal growth factor receptors (EGFRs) and HER2/neu receptors are proteins that play a role in cell growth and division. Overexpression of these receptors in bladder cancer cells can make them more aggressive and resistant to treatment. Targeted therapy with EGFR inhibitors can block the activity of EGFRs, which can slow the growth of cancer cells and improve survival rates. The other answer choices are also possible treatments for bladder cancer, but they are less likely to be effective in patients with overexpression of EGFRs and HER2/neu receptors. Chemotherapy and radiation therapy can be used to kill cancer cells, but they are not as targeted as targeted therapy. Immunotherapy can help the body's immune system fight cancer, but it is not as effective in patients with overexpression of EGFRs and HER2/neu receptors.

21. The correct answer is C. Chemotherapy with cisplatin and radiation therapy.

Patients with muscle-invasive bladder cancer who are not candidates for radical surgery may benefit from chemotherapy with cisplatin and radiation therapy. This treatment can offer a 5-year survival rate of up to 45%. The other answer choices are also possible treatment options for patients with muscle-invasive bladder cancer who are not candidates for radical surgery, but they are less likely to be effective. External beam radiation therapy has a 5-year survival rate of 30% to 35%. Chemotherapy with CMV has a 5-year survival rate of 20% to 25%. Immunotherapy is still under investigation for the treatment of muscle-invasive bladder cancer. Bladder-preserving surgery is not an option for patients who are not candidates for radical surgery.

22. The correct answer is A. Clear cell RCC.

Clear cell RCC is the most common type of renal cancer, accounting for approximately 75% of cases. It is a tumor that develops from the clear cells of the kidney tubules. Clear cell RCCs are typically solid masses that can be seen on CT scan. They are often associated with high levels of calcium in the blood. The other answer choices are also possible diagnoses for a patient with a 2 cm mass in the kidney, but they are less likely than clear cell RCC. Papillary RCC is the second most common type of renal cancer, accounting for approximately 15% of cases. It is a tumor that develops from the papillary cells of the kidney tubules. Papillary RCCs are typically well-differentiated tumors that are less likely to spread than clear cell RCCs. Chromophobe RCC is the third most common type of renal cancer, accounting for approximately 5% of cases. It is a tumor that develops from the chromophobe cells of the kidney tubules. Chromophobe RCCs are typically slow-growing tumors that are less likely to spread than clear cell RCCs. Oncocytoma is a benign tumor that develops from the oncocytes of the kidney tubules. Oncocytomas are typically small, non-aggressive tumors that do not spread. Collecting duct RCC is a rare type of renal cancer that develops from the collecting ducts of the kidney. Collecting duct RCCs are typically aggressive tumors that are more likely to spread than other types of renal cancer.

23.The correct answer is A. Transurethral resection of the prostate (TURP).

TURP is the most common surgical procedure for BPH. It involves removing excess prostate tissue through the urethra. TURP is effective in relieving urinary retention and other complications of BPH. The other answer choices are also possible treatments for BPH, but they are less likely to be effective in patients with urinary retention. Medications to relax the prostate can be effective in relieving urinary symptoms, but they are not as effective as TURP in relieving urinary retention. Watchful waiting is a conservative approach that may be appropriate for patients with mild symptoms of BPH. Radiation therapy and laser surgery are fewer common treatments for BPH.

24. The correct answer is B. Stage B1.

The Whitmore-Jewett staging system for prostate cancer is based on the extent of tumor spread. Stage A tumors are not palpable, but they are detected during TURP. Stage B1 tumors are palpable in one lobe of the prostate. Stage B2 tumors are palpable in both lobes of the prostate. Stage C tumors are palpable outside the prostate capsule. Stage D tumors have metastasized to other parts of the body. In this case, the patient has a palpable tumor in the right lobe of his prostate. This is consistent with Stage B1 prostate cancer. Stage A tumors are not palpable, so this is not possible. Stage B2 tumors are palpable in both lobes of the prostate, so this is not possible. Stage C tumors are palpable outside the prostate capsule, so this is not possible. Stage D tumors have metastasized to other parts of the body, so this is not possible.

25.The correct answer is A.

The brain tumor is causing increased intracranial pressure. Papilledema is a swelling of the optic nerve that is caused by increased intracranial pressure. Increased intracranial pressure can be caused by a variety of conditions, including brain tumors. In the case of a patient with a brain tumor and papilledema, it is likely that the tumor is causing the increased intracranial pressure. Decreased intracranial pressure is not a common symptom of brain tumors. Hydrocephalus is a condition in which there is an excessive amount of cerebrospinal fluid (CSF) in the brain. It is not typically caused by brain tumors. Optic neuritis is an inflammation of the optic nerve. It is not typically caused by brain tumors. Meningitis is an inflammation of the meninges, the membranes that surround the brain and spinal cord. It is not typically caused by brain tumors. In conclusion, the most likely implication of papilledema in a patient diagnosed with a brain tumor is that the tumor is causing increased intracranial pressure.

26. The correct answer is A. Germ cell tumor.

The syndrome of unrecognized extragonadal germ cell cancer (SEGC) is a rare condition in which patients present with a tumor in the mediastinum, lung parenchyma, or lymph nodes. The tumors are typically aggressive and grow rapidly. Serum tumor markers may be elevated, but they may also be within normal range. Chemotherapy with cisplatin, etoposide, and bleomycin is the treatment of choice for SEGC. This regimen can produce complete responses in up to 25% of patients, and approximately 15% of patients may be cured. Lymphoma is a cancer of the lymphatic system. It is not typically associated with rapidly growing tumors in the mediastinum. Lung cancer is not typically associated with elevated serum tumor markers. Metastatic cancer is cancer that has spread from its original site to other parts of the body. It is not typically associated with rapidly growing tumors in the mediastinum. Sarcoma is a cancer of the connective tissue. It is not typically associated with elevated serum tumor markers.

27.The correct answer is D. Hypercalcemia of malignancy.

Hypercalcemia of malignancy is a paraneoplastic syndrome that is caused by the production of parathyroid hormone-related protein (PTHrP) by cancer cells. PTHrP is a hormone that acts like parathyroid hormone, and it causes the body to increase the amount of calcium in the blood. Squamous cell carcinomas of the head and neck, lung, and skin are all common tumor types that are associated with hypercalcemia of malignancy. Other types of tumor that can cause hypercalcemia of malignancy include breast, genitourinary, and gastrointestinal cancers.

28. The correct answer is A. Ectopic ACTH syndrome.

Ectopic ACTH syndrome is a paraneoplastic syndrome in which cancer cells produce adrenocorticotropic hormone (ACTH). ACTH is a hormone that stimulates the adrenal glands to produce cortisol. In patients with ectopic ACTH syndrome, the elevated levels of cortisol can lead to symptoms of Cushing's syndrome, such as weight gain, moon face, buffalo hump, and muscle weakness. Adrenal adenoma is a benign tumor of the adrenal glands. It can produce cortisol, but it is not typically associated with elevated levels of ACTH. Adrenal cancer is a malignant tumor of the adrenal glands. It can produce cortisol, but it is not typically associated with elevated levels of ACTH. Primary hyperaldosteronism is a condition in which the adrenal glands produce too much aldosterone. Aldosterone is a hormone that regulates blood pressure. It is not associated with elevated levels of ACTH. Pheochromocytoma is a tumor of the adrenal medulla. It produces catecholamines, such as epinephrine and norepinephrine. It is not associated with elevated levels of ACTH.

29.The correct answer is A. Superior vena cava syndrome.

Superior vena cava syndrome (SVCS) is a condition in which the superior vena cava (SVC), the large vein that carries blood from the head and neck to the heart, is compressed or obstructed. This can lead to a buildup of blood in the head and neck, causing symptoms such as shortness of breath, facial swelling, and dilated neck veins. Pneumonia is an infection of the lungs. It can cause shortness of breath, but it does not typically cause facial swelling or dilated neck veins. Heart failure is a condition in which the heart cannot pump blood effectively. It can cause shortness of breath, but it does not typically cause facial swelling or dilated neck veins. Pulmonary embolism is a blockage of a pulmonary artery. It can cause shortness of breath, but it does not typically cause facial swelling or dilated neck veins. Hyperthyroidism is a condition in which the thyroid gland produces too much thyroid hormone. It can cause a variety of symptoms, including shortness of breath, but it does not typically cause facial swelling or dilated neck veins.

30. The correct answer is A. Neoplastic spinal cord compression.

Neoplastic spinal cord compression (NSCC) is a serious condition that occurs when a tumor compresses the spinal cord. This can lead to pain, weakness, numbness, and paralysis in the arms and legs. NSCC is most commonly caused by metastases from lung cancer, prostate cancer, breast cancer, and lymphoma. Spinal stenosis is a narrowing of the spinal canal that can cause pain and numbness in the back and legs. However, it does not typically cause weakness or paralysis. Herniated disc is a condition in which a piece of cartilage in the spine ruptures and presses on a nerve. This can cause pain and numbness in the back and legs. However, it does not typically cause weakness or paralysis. Osteoporosis is a condition in which the bones become weak and brittle. This can lead to compression fractures in the spine, which can cause pain. However, it does not typically cause weakness or paralysis. Multiple sclerosis is a chronic disease that affects the central nervous system. It can cause a variety of symptoms, including weakness, numbness, and vision problems. However, it does not typically cause pain in the back or legs. In conclusion, the most likely diagnosis for a patient with back pain and weakness in his legs who has a history of lung cancer is neoplastic spinal cord compression.

31. Answer: E.

Fluorodeoxyglucose (FDG) PET/CT, and brain MRI; pending results, follow with mediastinal lymph node evaluation with endobronchial ultrasound, mediastinoscopy Explanation: The patient's presentation suggests a possible lung malignancy. The key determinant in treatment planning for lung cancer is the stage of the disease. Hence, the initial workup should focus on evaluating the presence of distant metastatic disease, which can be done with a PET/CT scan and brain MRI. If these tests are negative, it is then necessary to fully evaluate the local extent of the tumor within the mediastinum. This information is critical for determining the approach to treating locally advanced tumors, including the role of radiation therapy and the feasibility of surgical approaches. Therefore, after PET/CT and brain MRI, mediastinal lymph node evaluation should be done with endobronchial ultrasound and mediastinoscopy.

32. The correct answer is D. Osimertinib alone.

The patient has been diagnosed with stage 4 non-small cell lung cancer and the molecular analysis reveals an EGFR-positive mutation, specifically a deletion in exon 19. This type of mutation is an activating mutation predominantly found in nonsmokers with lung cancer, although it can also occur in smokers. The presence of EGFR mutations is predictive of response to EGFR inhibitors, which are more efficacious and less toxic than standard cytotoxic chemotherapy. Osimertinib, a third-generation EGFR tyrosine kinase inhibitor, is the most appropriate first-line therapy in this case. Osimertinib has shown more efficacy than earlier generation inhibitors, such as erlotinib (Choice A). The increased efficacy of osimertinib is thought to be related to its activity against both canonical EGFR mutations found in treatment-naïve patients (L858R and exon 19 deletions) and T790M resistance mutations found in almost 50% of patients who progress on early generation EGFR inhibitors. Additionally, osimertinib has better brain penetration than earlier generation EGFR inhibitors. Osimertinib should not be combined with carboplatin and pemetrexed as first-line therapy (Choice E). Crizotinib (Choice B) is also a tyrosine kinase inhibitor, but it targets ROS1 and should be used in patients with ROS1 mutation. Pembrolizumab alone (Choice C) and carboplatin/pemetrexed/pembrolizumab can be used for patients with PD-L1 staining >50% without other targetable mutations. Therefore, the most appropriate first-line therapy for this patient is osimertinib alone.

33. Answer: C

The most appropriate first-line treatment for this patient is carboplatin, paclitaxel, and pembrolizumab. This is a combination of chemotherapy and immunotherapy that has been shown to be effective in patients with metastatic squamous cell carcinoma. Carboplatin and paclitaxel are chemotherapy drugs that kill cancer cells. Pembrolizumab is an immunotherapy drug that helps the body's own immune system fight cancer. Pembrolizumab alone is a first-line therapy for patients with metastatic squamous cell carcinoma and PD-L1 staining greater than 50%. However, for patients with PD-L1 staining less than 50%, the first-line therapy is carboplatin/paclitaxel plus pembrolizumab. Radiation therapy may be used in combination with chemotherapy or immunotherapy for some patients with metastatic squamous cell carcinoma. However, it is not typically used as first-line therapy. The prognosis for metastatic squamous cell carcinoma has improved significantly in recent years with the advent of immunotherapy. Many patients with metastatic squamous cell carcinoma can now live for years with the disease. The choice of treatment for metastatic squamous cell carcinoma depends on a number of factors, including the stage of the disease, the patient's overall health, and the presence of any biomarkers.

34. Answer: D

The next best step in management is to order a chest CT to rule out small cell lung cancer. The patient's presentation is highly suggestive of the syndrome of inappropriate antidiuretic hormone secretion (SIADH), which is a paraneoplastic syndrome that can be associated with small cell lung cancer. SIADH is a condition in which the body produces too much of the hormone antidiuretic hormone (ADH), which causes the kidneys to retain water and excrete sodium. This can lead to hyponatremia, hypovolemia, and hypotension. A chest CT is the best way to rule out small cell lung cancer, which is the most common cause of SIADH in adults. Sodium studies, such as a urine sodium and a renin level, can be helpful in diagnosing SIADH, but they are not necessary in this patient because his presentation is so classic. An MRI of the brain is not necessary unless the patient has signs of central pontine myelinolysis, which is a rare complication of hyponatremia. Starting intravenous fluids and monitoring the patient's serum sodium level is important, but it is not the next best step in management because the patient's presentation is suggestive of a paraneoplastic syndrome. Small cell lung cancer is a type of cancer that is very aggressive and can spread quickly. SIADH is a relatively common complication of small cell lung cancer. It occurs in about 20% of patients with small cell lung cancer. Treatment for SIADH typically involves correcting the underlying cause, such as treating the small cell lung cancer. In some cases, medications may be used to reduce the production of ADH or to block the effects of ADH on the kidneys.

35. The correct answer is B.

In 5 years. According to the US Preventive Services Task Force (USPSTF), annual low-dose CT for lung cancer screening is recommended for individuals aged 55 to 80 who have a 30-pack-year smoking history and who currently smoke or have quit within the past 15 years . Our patient is 62 years old, has a 30-pack-year smoking history, and quit smoking 8 years ago, making him eligible for screening. However, since he quit smoking 8 years ago and the USPSTF recommends screening for 15 years post smoking cessation, he would be eligible for screening for another 7 years. Therefore, the annual low-dose CT screening should stop in 5 years when he reaches the age of 80, as per the USPSTF guidelines.

36. The correct answer is C. Tamoxifen.

Tamoxifen is the standard systemic therapy for low-risk, early-stage ER+ (estrogen receptor-positive) breast cancer in premenopausal women. An aromatase inhibitor like anastrozole would be first-line therapy for postmenopausal women. However, for a premenopausal woman like our patient, aromatase inhibitors do not block ovarian production of estrogen and so can only be used with concurrent medical or surgical ovarian suppression. Considering the patient's age and low-risk disease, tamoxifen would be the most appropriate first-line therapy. The choice of tamoxifen over other options takes into account the patient's age (premenopausal), the stage and risk of her disease (low-risk, early-stage), and the type of cancer (ER+). Extended therapy (up to 10 years) is generally superior to treatment for 5 years, but in low-risk patients, the benefits of extended therapy are small, so therapy could be stopped before 10 years if she experiences adverse effects.

37. Answer: D

Lapatinib is a reversible HER2 inhibitor, which is not indicated in HER2-negative breast cancer. Aromatase inhibitors, CDK 4/6 inhibitors, and mTOR inhibitors are all approved by the FDA for the treatment of metastatic hormone receptor-positive, HER2-negative breast cancer. Aromatase inhibitors work by blocking the production of estrogen, which is a hormone that can fuel the growth of breast cancer cells. CDK 4/6 inhibitors work by blocking cyclin-dependent kinases 4 and 6, which are proteins that are involved in the cell cycle. mTOR inhibitors work by blocking the mammalian target of rapamycin, which is a protein that is involved in cell growth and proliferation. The choice of treatment for metastatic hormone receptor-positive, HER2-negative breast cancer depends on a number of factors, including the patient's overall health, the stage of the disease, and the presence of any biomarkers.

38. Answer: A

The most appropriate adjuvant therapy regimen for this patient is docetaxel, cyclophosphamide, trastuzumab, pertuzumab (TCHP). TCHP is a combination of chemotherapy and targeted therapy that has been shown to be very effective in reducing the risk of recurrence and improving survival in patients with early-stage HER2-positive breast cancer. Lapatinib, trastuzumab, and trastuzumab emtansine (T-DM1) are all approved for the treatment of HER2-positive breast cancer, but they are not typically used as first-line adjuvant therapy. Letrozole and ribociclib are approved for the treatment of hormone receptor-positive, HER2-negative breast cancer. Adjuvant therapy is given after surgery to kill any remaining cancer cells and reduce the risk of recurrence. TCHP is a four-drug regimen that is given every three weeks for six months. TCHP is a very effective regimen, but it can cause side effects, such as hair loss, nausea, vomiting, and fatigue. The choice of adjuvant therapy regimen for HER2-positive breast cancer depends on a number of factors, including the stage of the disease, the patient's overall health, and the presence of any biomarkers.

39. The correct answer is B.

BRCA2, Both BRCA1 and BRCA2 increase the risk of breast and ovarian cancer, but there is a greater association of pancreatic cancer with BRCA2 mutations. BRCA mutated cancers are often more sensitive to therapies that target the homologous recombination repair pathway, including platinum therapy and poly (ADP-ribose) polymerase (PARP) inhibitors. PARP inhibitors are specifically approved for metastatic breast cancer with germline BRCA1/2 mutations. Therefore, considering the patient's diagnosis of metastatic breast cancer and the potential therapeutic implications, the BRCA2 mutation is more likely in this case.

40. The correct answer is C. Degarelix and abiraterone/prednisone

The backbone of therapy for hormone-sensitive metastatic prostate cancer is androgen deprivation therapy, either with a long-acting luteinizing hormone–releasing hormone (LHRH) agonist (eg, leuprolide) or LHRH antagonist (eg, degarelix). However, leuprolide alone is associated with a transient androgen burst, given its agonist activity on the LHRH receptor, and can worsen symptoms or precipitate crises in patients with high-volume disease. Hence, it is either phased into treatment after pretreating with an androgen receptor blocker (bicalutamide) for a couple of weeks or treatment is initiated with a direct antagonist of the LHRH receptor, which is not associated with the androgen surge. The latter approach, particularly in patients with a high volume of disease such as this patient, is often favored despite being more expensive. In this case, the combination of Degarelix (an LHRH antagonist) and abiraterone/prednisone is the most suitable.

41. Answer: C

The next best step in management is a prostate MRI. Prostate MRI is a non-invasive imaging test that can be used to visualize the prostate gland and identify any potential abnormalities. It is a more sensitive and specific test than TRUS-guided biopsy for detecting prostate cancer. In the study cited in the question, prostate MRI was able to identify clinically significant prostate cancer in a higher percentage of patients than standard TRUS-guided biopsy. This is because prostate MRI can be used to target a biopsy to specific areas of the prostate that are more likely to be cancerous. TRUS-guided biopsy is a more invasive procedure than prostate MRI and carries a risk of complications, such as bleeding and infection. Therefore, prostate MRI is now the recommended first-line test for patients with a persistently elevated PSA. A PSA level of 4.0 ng/mL or higher is considered elevated. A persistently elevated PSA is a risk factor for prostate cancer. Prostate cancer is the most common cancer in men after skin cancer. Most cases of prostate cancer are diagnosed in men over the age of 65. Early diagnosis and treatment of prostate cancer can improve survival.

42. Answer: A

This patient has a strong family history of colorectal cancer, and genetic testing has confirmed that he has a mutation in the PMS2 gene, which is a gene associated with hereditary nonpolyposis colorectal cancer (HNPCC). HNPCC is a genetic condition that increases the risk of developing colorectal cancer and other cancers, such as endometrial cancer and ovarian cancer. The most appropriate screening schedule for colorectal cancer in patients with HNPCC is to begin colonoscopy at age 20 and repeat the screening every 1 to 2 years. This is because patients with HNPCC are at a high risk of developing colorectal cancer at a young age. The other answer choices are not appropriate for patients with HNPCC. Colonoscopy at age 45, stool occult blood test (FOBT) at age 50, and no screening at all are all inadequate for detecting colorectal cancer in this high-risk population. HNPCC is caused by mutations in genes that are involved in the mismatch repair (MMR) pathway. The MMR pathway is responsible for repairing errors that occur when DNA is copied. When the MMR pathway is not working properly, these errors can accumulate and lead to cancer. HNPCC accounts for about 5% of all colorectal cancer cases. The lifetime risk of developing colorectal cancer in patients with HNPCC is 80-90%. Early detection and treatment of colorectal cancer can improve survival.

43. The correct answer is: D. Both A and B.

In patients with a known colon cancer diagnosis, Carcinoembryonic antigen (CEA) is often measured to subsequently track the patient's response to therapy. However, it's important to note that CEA is not used as a screening tool for colon cancer. After diagnosis, patients also undergo CT scans of the chest, abdomen, and pelvis to look for any signs of metastatic disease. Colon cancer often metastasizes to the liver, lungs, and peritoneum, in that order. Brain metastases are less common, therefore head imaging is not indicated unless the patient presents with neurologic symptoms. 44. Answer: B

The most likely genetic syndrome causing this patient's family history of cancer is familial breast/ovarian cancer BRCA2. BRCA2 is a gene that helps to repair damaged DNA. Mutations in the BRCA2 gene can increase the risk of developing breast cancer, ovarian cancer, prostate cancer, and other cancers. The patient's family history of breast cancer, ovarian cancer, and prostate cancer is consistent with BRCA2-related cancer. Additionally, the fact that the patient's mother and sister were diagnosed with cancer at a young age suggests that they may have a BRCA2 mutation. The other answer choices are less likely. HNPCC is a genetic syndrome that increases the risk of developing colorectal cancer, endometrial cancer, and other cancers. Lynch syndrome is another term for HNPCC. Li-Fraumeni syndrome is a genetic syndrome that increases the risk of developing breast cancer, sarcoma, and other cancers. The lifetime risk of developing breast cancer in women with a BRCA2 mutation is 45-70%. The lifetime risk of developing ovarian cancer in women with a BRCA2 mutation is 11-17%. The lifetime risk of developing prostate cancer in men with a BRCA2 mutation is 8-13%. Genetic testing can be used to determine if a person has a BRCA2 mutation. There are a number of options available for people who have a BRCA2 mutation to reduce their risk of cancer, such as increased screening and preventive surgery.

45. The correct answer is: E. Start therapy with Poly (ADP-ribose) polymerase (PARP) inhibitors.

Poly (ADP-ribose) polymerase (PARP) inhibitors are beneficial for patients with a BRCA2 mutation, as these tumors are exquisitely sensitive to the loss of PARP. This sensitivity is due to a phenomenon known as synthetic lethality, where a defect in either of two genes has little effect on the cell or organism, but a combination of defects in both genes results in cell death. In the case of this patient, continuing chemotherapy with FOLFOX (5FU/LV + oxaliplatin) or starting a regimen with abraxane could potentially worsen neuropathy symptoms, as these treatments are known to cause neurotoxicity. Immunotherapy with PD-1 inhibitors, on the other hand, has not shown efficacy in pancreatic cancers except for a very small subset of patients who have pancreas cancer secondary to Lynch syndrome, leading to microsatellite instability. Given the patient's good performance status and excellent response to initial therapy, referral for hospice care would not be appropriate at this point. Therefore, the best option is to start therapy with PARP inhibitors, which have been shown to prolong disease progression in metastatic pancreatic cancer patients with a genomic BRCA2 mutation.

46. The correct answer is D.

Pancreatic protocol CT scan or MRI with contrast followed by endoscopic ultrasound (EUS)-guided fine needle aspiration (FNA). For diagnosing suspected pancreatic conditions, a pancreatic protocol CT scan with intravenous contrast, including arterial and venous phase imaging or MRI with contrast, is the most important initial step. This helps in identifying the location and size of the lesion. If the lesion is not visible on these images, the next step would be EUS or MRCP. Following these imaging techniques, EUS-guided FNA is the preferred modality to obtain a tissue diagnosis. While it can be useful to check CA 19-9 levels preoperatively and trend them postoperatively to assess for recurrence (option A), this is not an essential test in the diagnosis process. Similarly, abdominal ultrasound (option B) is useful for assessing the liver, gallbladder, and kidneys but is less sensitive for pancreatic lesions. Performing

EUS-guided FNA (option C) without prior imaging could miss important contextual information about the lesion's size and location, and MRCP (option E) without prior CT scan or MRI might not provide enough detail about the lesion. Hence, these options are not the most appropriate next step.

47. Answer: C

The patient has neutropenic enterocolitis, which is a serious complication of neutropenia. Neutropenic enterocolitis is caused by infection of the bowel wall in patients with severe neutropenia. It can lead to necrosis of the bowel wall and perforation. The treatment for neutropenic enterocolitis includes supportive measures, such as bowel rest, intravenous fluids, nutritional support, and antibiotics. Morphine, loperamide, and prochlorperazine are all medications that can slow down the bowel and should be avoided in patients with neutropenic enterocolitis, as they can worsen ileus. Surgery is only necessary in cases where the patient is clinically deteriorating or develops perforation or persistent GI bleeding. Nasogastric suction is a supportive measure that can help to reduce the amount of work the bowel has to do and prevent further damage to the bowel wall. Neutropenic enterocolitis is a life-threatening condition and has a mortality rate of up to 50%. Early diagnosis and treatment is essential for improving survival. The prognosis for neutropenic enterocolitis depends on the severity of the disease, the underlying cause of the neutropenia, and the patient's overall health.

48. Correct Answer: D. Transcatheter arterial chemoembolization (TACE)

TACE is a minimally invasive technique that delivers chemotherapy locally into the hepatic artery branches feeding the tumor, and is generally a reasonable approach for palliation in patients with unresectable locally advanced nonmetastatic hepatocellular carcinoma. However, TACE is contraindicated in patients with portal vein thrombosis of the main vein or first order right or left branches due to the high risk of hepatic insufficiency from post-TACE ischemic liver injury. Patients with hepatocellular carcinoma and associated portal vein thrombosis have a worse overall prognosis and, in general, are not considered candidates for liver transplantation, surgical resection, and TACE. Stereotactic body radiation therapy (SBRT), a type of highly focused radiation therapy, can still be used in such cases, but is unlikely to be helpful given the multiple satellite nodules. In this particular case, TACE is not a suitable treatment option, making option D the correct answer.

49. Correct Answer: A. Dihydropyrimidine dehydrogenase deficiency

Dihydropyrimidine dehydrogenase (DPD) is the liver enzyme responsible for degrading up to 80% of 5-FU and capecitabine, its oral prodrug, into inactive metabolites. Polymorphisms in the DPD gene can lead to partial or complete deficiency of enzyme activity, resulting in increased exposure to 5-FU and its active metabolites. This can lead to serious toxicity, presenting with severe hematologic, gastrointestinal (GI), central nervous system (CNS), and dermatologic symptoms, as seen in this patient. These symptoms are not typically seen after FOLFOX treatment, which is usually administered on an outpatient basis without G-CSF support in most cases. Uridine triacetate, a pyrimidine derivative, can be used to competitively inhibit the incorporation of 5-FU into RNA and is an approved treatment for severe and unexpected toxicity from 5-FU or capecitabine, to be administered within 96 hours of completing chemotherapy. While severe allergic reactions to oxaliplatin (Option B) are possible, it is important to first consider DPD deficiency given the severity and rapid onset of the patient's symptoms.

50. Answer: C

The patient has severe checkpoint inhibitor-induced colitis that is refractory to steroids. The next best step in management is to start infliximab. Infliximab is a tumor necrosis factor (TNF) alpha inhibitor. TNF-alpha is a cytokine that plays a role in inflammation. Infliximab works by blocking the activity of TNF-alpha, which can reduce inflammation and improve symptoms in patients with checkpoint inhibitor-induced colitis. Vedolizumab is another biologic agent that can be used to treat checkpoint inhibitor-induced colitis. However, infliximab is typically the first-line treatment for severe checkpoint inhibitor-induced colitis that is refractory to steroids. Increasing the dose of steroids is not recommended, as this can increase the risk of side effects. Chemotherapy is not indicated for the treatment of checkpoint inhibitor-induced colitis. Checkpoint inhibitor-induced colitis is a rare but serious side effect of checkpoint inhibitor therapy. Checkpoint inhibitors are a type of immunotherapy that work by boosting the immune system's ability to fight cancer. However, checkpoint inhibitors can also cause the immune system to attack normal tissues, leading to autoimmune side effects. Checkpoint inhibitor-induced colitis can range from mild to severe. In severe cases, it can lead to life-threatening complications. Treatment for checkpoint inhibitor-induced colitis depends on the severity of the disease. Mild cases may be treated with supportive care, such as bowel rest and intravenous fluids. Severe cases may require treatment with biologic agents, such as infliximab or vedolizumab. The prognosis for checkpoint inhibitor-induced colitis is generally good. Most patients respond to treatment and are able to continue checkpoint inhibitor therapy. However, a small percentage of patients may develop severe complications, such as toxic megacolon or perforation. These patients may require surgery.

51. Answer: D

The patient has developed grade 3 cytokine release syndrome (CRS), a life-threatening complication of CAR T-cell therapy. CRS is caused by the massive release of inflammatory cytokines by CAR T-cells after they target and destroy cancer cells. Tocilizumab is an interleukin-6 (IL-6) inhibitor that is indicated for the treatment of grade 3 CRS. IL-6 is a key cytokine involved in inflammation. By blocking IL-6, tocilizumab can help to reduce inflammation and improve symptoms in patients with CRS. Methylprednisolone is a corticosteroid that is sometimes used to treat CRS. However, corticosteroids can suppress T-cell function, which can interfere with the efficacy of CAR T-cell therapy. Therefore, corticosteroids are avoided if possible in patients with CRS. Infliximab and mycophenolate mofetil are biologic agents that are sometimes used to treat specific complications of CAR T-cell therapy, such as colitis and hepatitis. However, they are not indicated for the treatment of CRS. CRS can range from mild to severe. Mild CRS is typically managed with supportive care, such as fever control and fluids. Severe CRS can be life-threatening and requires prompt treatment. Tocilizumab is the first-line treatment for grade 3 CRS. If tocilizumab is not effective, other treatments, such as corticosteroids or other biologic agents, may be considered. The prognosis for CRS is generally good. Most patients respond to treatment and are able to recover. However, a small percentage of patients may develop life-threatening complications, such as multiorgan failure. These patients may require intensive care support.

Chapter 5

CARDIOLOGY BOARD QUESTIONS

1. A 61-year-old man presents with shortness of breath and peripheral edema. On physical examination, he is found to have an elevated jugular venous pressure that increases with inspiration. What is the most likely diagnosis? Which of the following is the most appropriate answer?

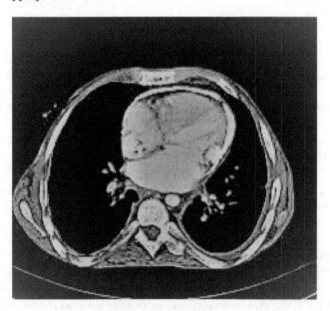

Figure 5.1: 61-year-old man

- A. Mitral stenosis
- B. Right heart failure
- C. Constrictive pericarditis
- D. Atrial fibrillation

2. A 69-year-old man presents with shortness of breath and peripheral edema. On physical examination, he is found to have a large "a" wave and a slow "y" descent in his jugular venous pulsation. What is the most likely diagnosis? Which of the following is the most appropriate answer?

- A. Tricuspid stenosis
- B. Constrictive pericarditis
- C. Atrial septal defect

149

- D. Tricuspid regurgitation

3. A 58-year-old man presents with shortness of breath and fatigue. On physical examination, he is found to have a holosystolic murmur that is loudest at the apex. What is the most likely diagnosis? Which of the following is the most appropriate answer?

- A. Pulmonic stenosis
- B. Tricuspid regurgitation
- C. Aortic stenosis
- D. Mitral regurgitation

4. A 42-year-old man with a history of hypertrophic cardiomyopathy presents with shortness of breath and chest pain. On physical examination, he is found to have a systolic murmur that is loudest at the left sternal border. What is the effect of the Valsalva maneuver on this murmur? Which of the following is the most appropriate answer?

- A. The murmur will become shorter and less intense.
- B. The murmur will become longer and louder.
- C. The murmur will not change in intensity or duration.
- D. The murmur will become softer and shorter.

5. A 33-year-old woman with a history of atrial septal defect (ASD) presents with shortness of breath and fatigue. On ECG, she is found to have incomplete right bundle branch block (RBBB). What is the most likely type of ASD? Which of the following is the most appropriate answer?

- A. Ostium primum defect
- B. Ostium secundum defect
- C. Sinus venosus defect
- D. None of the above

6. A 37-year-old man with a history of ventricular septal defect (VSD) presents with shortness of breath and fatigue. He has a Qp/Qs ratio of 1.5:1, but his pulmonary artery pressure and pulmonary vascular resistance are both below two-thirds of the systemic pressure and systemic resistance, respectively. Should he undergo percutaneous or surgical closure of his VSD? Which of the following is the most appropriate answer?

- A. No, he should not undergo percutaneous or surgical closure of his VSD.
- B. Yes, he should undergo percutaneous or surgical closure of his VSD.
- C. It is uncertain whether he should undergo percutaneous or surgical closure of his VSD.

7. A 51-year-old man with a history of tetralogy of Fallot presents to your office for a dental cleaning. He has never had antibiotic prophylaxis before dental procedures. Is antibiotic prophylaxis recommended for this patient? Which of the following is the most appropriate answer?

- A. Yes, antibiotic prophylaxis is recommended.
- B. No, antibiotic prophylaxis is not recommended.
- C. It is uncertain whether antibiotic prophylaxis is recommended.

8. A 53-year-old woman with a history of mitral stenosis presents with shortness of breath and fatigue. She has no other medical problems. What is the preferred procedure to manage her mitral stenosis? Which of the following is the most appropriate answer?

- A. Medical therapy
- B. Open surgical valvotomy
- C. Percutaneous balloon valvuloplasty
- D. Watchful waiting

9. A 71-year-old woman with a history of severe chronic primary mitral regurgitation (MR) presents with dyspnea on exertion. Her echocardiogram shows an LVEF of 55% and an end-systolic left ventricular diameter of 39 mm. Which of the following is the most appropriate treatment for this patient?

- A. Medical therapy with diuretics and ACE inhibitors
- B. Mitral valve repair
- C. Mitral valve replacement
- D. Transcatheter mitral valve repair

- E. Observation

10. A 75-year-old man presents with exertional dyspnea and syncope. Physical examination reveals a weak, delayed carotid pulse and a systolic murmur that is best heard at the second intercostal space on the right side. Which of the following findings are most likely to be present on this patient's physical examination?

- A. Soft or absent A2
- B. S4
- C. Pulsus paradoxus
- D. Midsystolic click.
- E. Diastolic murmur

11. A 74-year-old man with severe aortic stenosis is being evaluated for transcatheter aortic valve replacement (TAVR). What are some of the potential complications associated with this procedure?

- A. Stroke
- B. Permanent pacemaker
- C. Paravalvular aortic regurgitation
- D. All of the above

12. A 62-year-old woman with chronic aortic regurgitation (AR) presents with dyspnea on exertion. She is currently taking a beta-blocker. What is the rationale for avoiding beta-blockers in patients with chronic AR?

- A. Beta-blockers can worsen heart failure.
- B. Beta-blockers can increase the risk of stroke.
- C. Beta-blockers can prolong the duration of diastole.
- D. Beta-blockers can decrease cardiac output.

13. A 56-year-old man with a history of mitral valve prolapse presents with fever, chills, and fatigue. He has no recent dental work or other known risk factors for endocarditis. What are the most likely causative microorganisms associated with his native-valve endocarditis (NVE)?

- A. Viridans streptococci
- B. Staphylococci
- C. HACEK organisms
- D. Streptococcus gallolyticus subspecies gallolyticus

14. A 79-year-old man with a history of pacemaker implantation presents with fever, chills, and fatigue. He had his pacemaker implanted 6 months ago. What are the most likely causative microorganisms associated with his CIED-related endocarditis?

- A. Viridans streptococci
- B. CoNS
- C. S aureus
- D. HACEK organisms

15. A 68-year-old man with a history of mitral valve prolapse presents with fever, chills, and fatigue. He has no recent dental work or other known risk factors for endocarditis. An MRI scan is performed, which reveals the presence of multiple clinically asymptomatic emboli. What is the prevalence of clinically asymptomatic emboli detected on MRI in patients diagnosed with left-sided endocarditis?

- A. <5%
- B. 10-30%
- C. 5-10%
- D. 30-65%

16. A 67-year-old man with a history of mitral valve prolapse presents with fever, chills, and fatigue. He has no recent dental work or other known risk factors for endocarditis. A transesophageal echocardiogram (TEE) is performed, which is negative for any evidence of endocarditis. What is the next best step in management?

- A. Discharge the patient from the hospital
- B. Repeat the TEE examination in 7-10 days.
- C. Start antibiotic therapy.

- D. Refer the patient to a cardiologist for further evaluation.

17. A 64-year-old man with a history of prosthetic mitral valve replacement presents with fever, chills, and fatigue. He has no recent dental work or other known risk factors for endocarditis. An echocardiogram is performed, which reveals the presence of a vegetation on the prosthetic mitral valve. The patient is clinically stable and does not have any evidence of heart failure or other complications. What is the recommended duration of treatment for this patient?

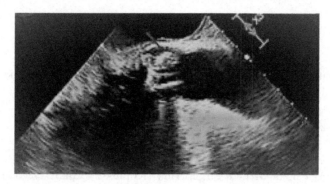

Figure 5.2: a vegetation on the prosthetic mitral valve

- A. 4 to 6 weeks
- B. 6 to 8 weeks
- C. 8 to 12 weeks
- D. 12 to 16 weeks

18. A 78-year-old woman with a history of dilated cardiomyopathy presents with dyspnea on exertion. She is currently in New York Heart Association (NYHA) class III heart failure. What is the role of aldosterone antagonist therapy in treating her condition?

- A. Aldosterone antagonist therapy is not indicated for patients with dilated cardiomyopathy.
- B. Aldosterone antagonist therapy may be considered for patients with dilated cardiomyopathy in NYHA class II heart failure.
- C. Aldosterone antagonist therapy is recommended for patients with dilated cardiomyopathy in NYHA class III heart failure.
- D. Aldosterone antagonist therapy is recommended for patients with dilated cardiomyopathy in NYHA class IV heart failure.

19. A 71-year-old man with a history of dilated cardiomyopathy presents with dyspnea on exertion. He is currently in NYHA class III heart failure. He has an LVEF of 30% and a QRS duration of 160 milliseconds. Is he a candidate for cardiac resynchronization therapy (CRT)?

- A. Yes, he is a candidate for CRT because he meets all of the criteria.
- B. No, he is not a candidate for CRT because his LVEF is above 35
- C. No, he is not a candidate for CRT because his QRS duration is below 150 milliseconds.
- D. It is unclear if he is a candidate for CRT because he does not have left bundle branch block.

20. A 69-year-old man with a history of systemic amyloidosis presents with dyspnea on exertion. He has no prior history of heart disease. What are the expected imaging findings in this patient?

- A. Normal echocardiogram
- B. Dilated left ventricle with decreased ejection fraction.
- C. Bilateral atrial enlargement with speckled pattern in the ventricles
- D. Thickened pericardium with pericardial effusion

21. A 49-year-old man presents with exertional dyspnea and chest pain. On physical examination, you note a brisk carotid upstroke with pulsus bisferiens, an S4 sound, and a harsh systolic murmur along the left sternal border. What is the most likely diagnosis?

- A. Hypertrophic cardiomyopathy

- B. Mitral stenosis
- C. Aortic stenosis
- D. Mitral regurgitation

22. A 52-year-old man with hypertrophic cardiomyopathy presents with a history of syncope. He has no other cardiac risk factors. His echocardiogram shows a left ventricular wall thickness of 3.2 cm. What is the indication for an implantable cardioverter-defibrillator (ICD) in this patient?

- A. Syncope
- B. Left ventricular wall thickness of 3.2 cm
- C. Family history of sudden death
- D. All of the above

23. A 56-year-old man presents with a 2-week history of progressive dyspnea and fatigue. He has no other medical history. His physical examination is unremarkable. His laboratory tests show an elevated white blood cell count and an elevated troponin level. His chest X-ray shows cardiomegaly. His echocardiogram shows an enlarged left ventricle with decreased ejection fraction. What is the next best step in the management of this patient?

- A. Endomyocardial biopsy
- B. Start empiric antibiotic therapy.
- C. Refer the patient to a cardiologist for further evaluation.
- D. Discharge the patient home with close follow-up.

24. A 39-year-old man presents with chest pain. His ECG shows widespread ST elevation with reciprocal ST depression. He has no history of heart disease. What is the most likely diagnosis?

- A. Acute pericarditis
- B. Acute ST elevation myocardial infarction (STEMI)
- C. Early repolarization
- D. Arrhythmogenic right ventricular

25. A 52-year-old man presents with chest pain and a pericardial rub. His ECG shows diffuse ST elevation with reciprocal ST depression. He has no history of heart disease. What is the most appropriate management for this patient?

- A. Start aspirin and clopidogrel.
- B. Start heparin.
- C. Start colchicine.
- D. Discharge the patient home with close follow-up.

26. A 57-year-old man presents with chest pain and shortness of breath. His ECG shown, Wwhat is the significance of this finding?

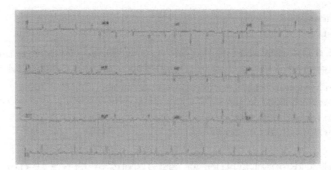

Figure 5.3: 57-year-old man

- A. Electrical alternans is a benign finding that is not associated with any significant pathology.
- B. Electrical alternans is a sign of cardiac tamponade.
- C. Electrical alternans is a sign of myocardial infarction.
- D. Electrical alternans is a sign of pericarditis.

27. A 67-year-old man presents with dyspnea on exertion and peripheral edema. He has no history of heart disease. His echocardiogram shows thickened pericardium with restricted diastolic filling. What is the next best step in the diagnosis of this patient?

- A. Cardiac catheterization
- B. Endomyocardial biopsy
- C. MRI
- D. CT

28. A 72-year-old man with hypertension presents with a serum creatinine level of 2.7 mg/dL. He is currently taking hydrochlorothiazide (HCTZ) for his hypertension. What is the next best step in his management?

- A. Increase the dose of HCTZ.
- B. Add a loop of diuretic to the regimen.
- C. Switch to a different thiazide diuretic.
- D. Discontinue HCTZ.

29. A 60-year-old man with hypertension is started on lisinopril. He also takes potassium chloride supplements for hypokalemia. What is the most important monitoring concern for this patient?

- A. Hypotension
- B. Hyperkalemia
- C. Renal insufficiency
- D. Hyperglycemia

30. A 25-year-old woman with chronic hypertension is planning to become pregnant. She is currently taking lisinopril for her hypertension. What is the most appropriate antihypertensive medication to switch her to in preparation for preg-nancy?

- A. Methyldopa
- B. Labetalol
- C. Hydralazine
- D. Nifedipine

31. A 58-year-old man presents with a blood pressure of 220/120 mmHg. He has no history of hypertension. His physi-cal examination is unremarkable. What is the most appropriate initial treatment for this patient? A. Nitroprusside B. Nicardipine C. Labetalol D. Enalaprilat 32. A 57-year-old man with a history of smoking, hypertension, and hypercholesterolemia presents with chest pain. He is referred to for an exercise stress test. Which of the following is a contraindication to exercise testing?

- A. Acute myocardial infarction (heart attack)
- B. Unstable angina
- C. Severe aortic stenosis
- D. Myocarditis or pericarditis
- E. Low exercise tolerance

33. A 58-year-old man with a history of smoking, hypertension, and hypercholesterolemia presents with chest pain. He is referred to for an exercise stress test. Which of the following is NOT a criterion for a positive exercise test?

- A. Chest pain or other symptoms that are consistent with angina.
- B. Diagnostic ST-segment changes on the ECG
- C. Failure to reach the target heart rate.
- D. A drop in blood pressure during exercise.
- E. A normal ECG

34. A 57-year-old man with a history of hypertension and diabetes presents with chest pain. He is prescribed a beta-blocker. Which of the following is a contraindication to beta-blockers?

- A. Congestive heart failure (CHF)
- B. Atrioventricular (AV) block
- C. Bronchospasm
- D. "Brittle" diabetes
- E. All of the above

35. A 55-year-old man with a history of coronary artery disease undergoes percutaneous coronary intervention (PCI) for a 50% stenosis of the left anterior descending artery. The procedure is performed with balloon dilatation alone. What is the rate of restenosis following this intervention?

- A. 10%
- B. 20%
- C. 30%
- D. 40%
- E. 50%

36. A 68-year-old man with a history of coronary artery disease presents with unstable angina. He has tried multiple medications, but his symptoms are not controlled. He has a left main coronary artery stenosis of 70% and a three-vessel disease. Which of the following is the most appropriate treatment for this patient?

- A. Percutaneous coronary intervention (PCI)
- B. Coronary artery bypass grafting (CABG)
- C. Medical therapy with nitrates and beta-blockers
- D. Medical therapy with calcium channel blockers
- E. Medical therapy with aspirin and clopidogrel

37. A 60-year-old man with a history of chronic stable angina presents to your clinic. He is currently taking medical therapy, but his symptoms are not well-controlled. He is considering PCI. Which of the following statements is most accurate?

- A. PCI is more effective than medical therapy in reducing the risk of MI or mortality in patients with chronic stable angina.
- B. PCI is more effective than medical therapy in providing relief from angina symptoms in patients with chronic stable angina.
- C. Medical therapy and PCI are equally effective in reducing the risk of MI or mortality in patients with chronic stable angina.
- D. Medical therapy and PCI are equally effective in providing relief from angina symptoms in patients with chronic stable angina.
- E. There is not enough evidence to determine which treatment is more effective in patients with chronic stable angina.

38. A 57-year-old man presents to the emergency department with chest pain. He has a history of ECG changes consistent with Prinzmetal's variant angina. Which of the following is the best way to confirm the diagnosis?

- A. Coronary angiography with provocative testing
- B. Coronary angiography without provocative testing
- C. Electrocardiography (ECG)
- D. Stress test
- E. Echocardiogram

39 A 61-year-old man presents to the emergency department with chest pain. He has a history of coronary artery disease. His ECG shows ST-segment depression. What is the most likely diagnosis?

- A. NSTEMI
- B. STEMI
- C. Unstable angina
- D. Prinzmetal's variant angina
- E. Pericarditis

40. A 67-year-old man with a history of coronary artery disease presents to the emergency department with unstable angina. He is taken to the cardiac catheterization laboratory for percutaneous coronary intervention (PCI). Which of the following is the recommended therapy for this patient?

- A. Tirofiban
- B. Eptifibatide
- C. Abciximab
- D. Aspirin

- E. Clopidogrel

41. A 61-year-old man with a history of coronary artery disease presents to the emergency department with chest pain. He has a troponin level that is elevated, but his ECG does not show ST-segment elevation. He is currently receiving medical therapy for his chest pain, but his pain is not controlled. Which of the following is the most appropriate management strategy for this patient?

- A. Immediate invasive strategy
- B. Selective invasive strategy
- C. Conservative medical therapy
- D. Observation

42. A 63-year-old man with a history of coronary artery disease presents to the emergency department with chest pain. He has a troponin level that is elevated, but his ECG does not show ST-segment elevation. He does not have any of the criteria for immediate invasive strategy. He does, however, have diabetes mellitus, renal insufficiency, and reduced left ventricular systolic function. Which of the following is the most appropriate management strategy for this patient?

- A. Immediate invasive strategy
- B. Selective invasive strategy
- C. Delayed invasive strategy.
- D. Conservative medical therapy

43. A 58-year-old man with a history of coronary artery disease presents to the emergency department with chest pain. He has an ECG that shows abnormal Q waves in leads V1-V2. What is the most likely diagnosis?

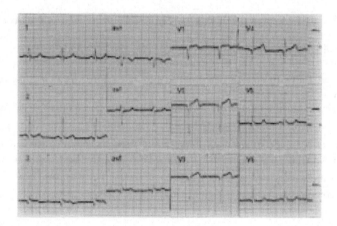

Figure 5.4: 58-year-old

- A. Anterolateral MI
- B. Inferior MI
- C. Apical MI
- D. True posterior MI
- E. Non-specific ST-T changes

44. A 56-year-old man with a history of coronary artery disease presents to the emergency department with chest pain. He has an ECG that shows ST-segment elevation in the anterior leads. The nearest PCI center is 150 minutes away. Which of the following is the most appropriate treatment option for this patient?

- A. Immediate PCI
- B. Intravenous fibrinolysis
- C. Medical therapy with aspirin and clopidogrel
- D. Observation

45. A 59-year-old man with a history of coronary artery disease presents to the emergency department with chest

pain. He has an ECG that shows ST-segment elevation in the anterior leads. He is also in hemodynamically unstable ventricular tachycardia. What is the most appropriate treatment option for this patient?

- A. Immediate electrical countershock
- B. Intravenous fibrinolysis
- C. Medical therapy with aspirin and clopidogrel
- D. Observation

46. A 71-year-old man with a history of coronary artery disease presents to the emergency department with chest pain. He has an ECG that shows ST-segment elevation in the anterior leads. He is also in acute heart failure. Which of the following is the most appropriate initial therapy for this patient?

- A. Furosemide
- B. Oxygen
- C. Nitrates
- D. Digitalis
- E. All of the above

47. A 65-year-old man with a history of coronary artery disease presents to the emergency department with chest pain. He has an ECG that shows ST-segment elevation in the anterior leads. He is also in cardiogenic shock. His systolic blood pressure is 80 mmHg, and his pulmonary capillary wedge pressure (PCWP) is 25 mmHg. What treatment options are available to maintain his systolic blood pressure above 90 mmHg and reduce his PCWP?

- A. Norepinephrine
- B. Dopamine
- C. Intraaortic balloon counterpulsation (IABP)
- D. All of the above

48. A 62-year-old man with a history of coronary artery disease presents to the emergency department with chest pain. He has an ECG that shows ST-segment elevation in the anterior leads. He is also hypothetical. His systolic blood pres-sure is 80 mmHg, and his heart rate is 120 beats per minute. An echocardiogram shows that he has a right ventricular MI. What is the treatment for his hypotension? A. Intravenous fluids B. Vasopressors C. Intraaortic balloon counterpulsation D. Mechanical ventilation 49. A 66-year-old man with a history of coronary artery disease presents to the emergency department with palpitations. He has an ECG that shows atrial flutter with a ventricular rate of 120 beats per minute. What is the initial treatment for this patient?

- A. Beta blockers
- B. Verapamil
- C. Diltiazem
- D. Digoxin
- E. All of the above

50. A 75-year-old man with a history of coronary artery disease presents to the emergency department with palpita-tions. He has an ECG that shows Torsade de pointes. What is the treatment for this patient?

- A. Intravenous magnesium
- B. Overdrive pacing
- C. Isoproterenol
- D. Lidocaine
- E. All of the above

51. A 61-year-old man with a history of coronary artery disease presents to the emergency department with palpita-tions. He has an ECG that shows supraventricular tachycardia with aberrant ventricular conduction. The ventricular rate is 200 beats per minute. What is the treatment for this patient?

- A. Beta blockers
- B. Verapamil
- C. Diltiazem
- D. Digoxin
- E. Electrical cardioversion

52. A 69-year-old man with a history of coronary artery disease presents to the cardiologist with complaints of fatigue

and lightheadedness. He has an ECG that shows sinus bradycardia with a heart rate of 40 beats per minute. He is also taking digoxin for his heart condition. What is the Class I indication for pacemaker implantation in this patient?

- A. Sinus bradycardia with a heart rate of 40 beats per minute
- B. Sinus bradycardia with symptoms
- C. Sinus bradycardia with symptoms that are refractory to medical therapy.
- D. Sinus bradycardia with symptoms that are refractory to medical therapy and are associated with an increased risk of syncope.
- E. All of the above

53. A 61-year-old man with a history of coronary artery disease presents to the emergency department with complaints of lightheadedness. He has an ECG that shows Mobitz II AV block with a 2:1 conduction pattern. What is the most appropriate next step in management?

- A. Observation
- B. Medications to increase the heart rate.
- C. Permanent pacemaker implantation
- D. Electrophysiology study

54. A 59-year-old man with a history of coronary artery disease presents to the cardiologist with complaints of palpitations and lightheadedness. He has an ECG that shows atrial fibrillation. What is the best approach to managing his AFib?

- A. Rhythm control with cardioversion
- B. Rate control with beta-blockers
- C. Rate control with calcium channel blockers
- D. Ibutilide

55. A 65-year-old man with a history of coronary artery disease and hypertension presents to the cardiologist with complaints of palpitations and lightheadedness. He has an ECG that shows chronic atrial fibrillation. He also has a history of rheumatic mitral stenosis. What is the best approach to managing his AFib?

- A. Rate control with beta-blockers
- B. Rate control with calcium channel blockers
- C. Rhythm control with cardioversion
- D. Anticoagulation with warfarin

56. A 67-year-old woman with a history of heart failure presents to the emergency department with complaints of nausea, vomiting, and visual disturbances. She is also taking digoxin for her heart condition. What is the most appropriate next step in management?

- A. Discontinue digoxin and monitor her symptoms.
- B. Administer atropine intravenously.
- C. Administer digoxin-specific antibody fragments.
- D. Admit to the hospital for observation.

57. A 81-year-old man with a history of heart failure presents to the cardiologist with complaints of shortness of breath and fatigue. He has an ejection fraction of 30% and is already taking the maximum tolerated dose of beta-blockers. What is the next best treatment option for this patient?

- A. Ivabradine
- B. Digoxin
- C. Ranolazine
- D. Hydralazine/isosorbide dinitrate
- E. Dobutamine

58. 63-year-old man with a history of diabetes mellitus presents to the emergency department with complaints of fever, shortness of breath, and altered mental status. He is found to be hypotensive and tachycardic. His initial laboratory workup shows leukocytosis and elevated serum lactate levels. His chest X-ray shows a diffuse infiltrate. What is the most appropriate vasopressor agent to initiate in this patient?

- A. Dopamine
- B. Norepinephrine

- C. Epinephrine
- D. Vasopressin
- E. Milrinone

59. A 68-year-old man presents to the emergency department with chest pain and shortness of breath. He is found to have a type A aortic dissection. What is the most appropriate initial treatment for this patient?

- A. Sodium nitroprusside
- B. Metoprolol
- C. Verapamil
- D. Diltiazem
- E. Hydralazine

60. A 55-year-old man with hypercholesterolemia is being evaluated for treatment. Which of the following is the most likely benefit of interventions aimed at lowering his LDL-C levels?

- A. Reduced risk of myocardial infarction
- B. Reduced risk of stroke.
- C. Reduced risk of overall mortality
- D. All of the above
- E. None of the above

61. A 38-year-old woman presents to the emergency department with chest pain that has lasted for 2 hours. She has no significant past medical history. An electrocardiogram shows no ST-segment elevations. Her troponin level is elevated. She undergoes a cardiac catheterization, which reveals no obstructive coronary disease. Her left ventricular function is found to be depressed. Which of the following is the most appropriate next step to confirm a potential diagnosis?

- A. Cardiac Magnetic Resonance Imaging (MRI)
- B. Pulmonary Function Tests
- C. Abdominal Ultrasound
- D. Chest X-ray
- E. Carotid Doppler Ultrasound

62. A patient with a left bundle branch block (LBBB) and poor exercise tolerance presents for evaluation of chest pain. Which of the following diagnostic tests is most appropriate?

- (A) Exercise stress test
- (B) Echocardiogram
- (C) Coronary CTA
- (D) Pharmacologic stress test with perfusion imaging
- (E) Cardiac catheterization

63. A 56-year-old man presents to the emergency department with chest pain that has been intermittent over the past few days. The pain is not associated with exertion and does not radiate. He has a family history of early coronary artery disease (CAD), hypertension, and hyperlipidemia. His chest pain is somewhat atypical, but given his risk factors, he has an intermediate probability of CAD. Which of the following is the most appropriate next step to exclude coronary disease?

- A. Cardiac Magnetic Resonance Imaging (MRI)
- B. Exercise Stress Test
- C. Coronary CT Angiography
- D. Cardiac Catheterization
- E. Echocardiogram

64. A 67-year-old man with a history of hypertension and hyperlipidemia presents with chest pain on exertion. He undergoes an exercise stress test, which is stopped after 7 minutes due to angina. His BP does not augment with exercise, and his ECG at 7 minutes into recovery shows diffuse ST depressions >2 mm and an ST elevation in aVR. Which of the following is the next most appropriate step in management?

- (A) Admit to the hospital for further monitoring
- (B) Perform coronary angiography

- (C) Start beta blocker therapy
- (D) Order a nuclear stress test
- (E) Refer to a cardiologist for follow-up

65. A 62-year-old man presents with a history of chest pain that occurs with exertion and is relieved by rest. His exercise stress test shows evidence of ischemia in a single territory, confirming the diagnosis of coronary artery disease (CAD). Assuming he is already on low-dose aspirin , what would be the next best step in management?

- A. Initiate -blocker and statin
- B. Proceed to coronary angiography
- C. Optimize lipid-lowering therapy only
- D. Consider coronary revascularization
- E. Perform a transthoracic echocardiogram

66. A 68-year-old man undergoes cardiac catheterization and receives a stent in his right coronary artery. Immediately after the procedure, he develops hypotension and a rapidly expanding hematoma at the access site. What is the most appropriate next step in management?

- (A) Start aspirin and P2Y12 inhibitor therapy
- (B) Administer blood products empirically
- (C) Order a CT of the abdomen
- (D) Apply manual compression to the access site
- (E) Consult the cardiologist

67. A 59-year-old male underwent stent placement for management of an acute coronary syndrome 10 months ago. He is currently on dual antiplatelet therapy with aspirin and clopidogrel. The patient now has severe knee pain and is considered for a knee replacement surgery. What is the best management of the patient's medication regimen considering the impending surgery?

- A. Continue dual antiplatelet therapy and proceed with knee replacement.
- B. Temporarily discontinue clopidogrel and proceed with knee replacement.
- C. Replace clopidogrel with intravenous P2Y12 inhibitor cangrelor.
- D. Continue dual antiplatelet therapy and delay knee replacement until 12 months have passed since stent placement.
- E. Conduct stress testing to guide the duration of dual antiplatelet therapy.

68. A 62-year-old male presents to the emergency department with intermittent chest pain over the last few days. He has a past medical history of hypertension and hyperlipidemia. His vitals are stable and his initial EKG and troponin levels are normal. His Thrombolysis in Myocardial Infarction (TIMI) score is 2. What is the most appropriate next step in the management of this patient?

- A. Initiate conservative therapy with aspirin, -blocker, and nitrates as needed, followed by noninvasive risk stratification (stress testing) to help determine if coronary angiography is appropriate, provided the patient remains asymptomatic.
- B. Perform immediate diagnostic angiography with the intent to revascularize.
- C. Perform early (within 24 hours) diagnostic angiography with the intent to revascularize.
- D. Immediately initiate dual antiplatelet therapy and proceed to coronary angiography.
- E. Initiate high dose statin therapy and order a coronary CT angiogram.

69. A patient with suspected acute coronary syndrome (ACS) is being evaluated for the appropriate timing of angiography. Which of the following is the most appropriate timing for angiography in this patient?

- A. within 6 hours
- Within 24 hours
- C. Within 48 hours
- D. Within 72 hours
- E. Immediately

70. A patient presents with a late presentation of a larger territory myocardial infarction (MI), especially of the anterior wall. He develops a harsh holosystolic murmur at the lower sternal border, especially in the presence of a palpable systolic thrill. What is the next best step in management?

- A. Initiate afterload reducing agents
- B. Start right heart catheterization
- C. Begin interventions with an intra-aortic balloon pump
- D. Urgent transthoracic echocardiography
- E. Wait and observe for further symptoms

71. Which of the following is the first-line therapy for vasospastic angina?

- A. Aspirin
- B. Beta-blocker
- C. Calcium channel blocker
- D. Nitrate
- E. None of the above

72. A 69-year-old woman is hospitalized due to severe shortness of breath. She has a history of congestive heart failure and has recently been diagnosed with sepsis. Despite being on inotropic support, her cardiac output remains reduced. Additionally, she is hypotensive and requires a vasopressor to maintain her systemic vascular resistance at a low end of normal. What is the most likely classification of her shock state?

- A. Mixed—cardiogenic and distributive
- B. Cardiogenic shock
- C. Distributive shock
- D. Obstructive shock
- E. Hypovolemic shock

73. A 68-year-old woman presents with symptoms suggestive of a heart failure exacerbation. She has acute kidney injury with normal mentation, normal perfusion, and normal pulse pressure. She has had a limited response to oral diuretics. What is the most appropriate next step in her management?

- A. Administer intravenous crystalloid.
- B. Administer intravenous furosemide.
- C. Start intravenous inotropic agents.
- D. Initiate renal replacement therapy.
- E. Arrange for an urgent cardiac transplantation.

74. What is a major risk of the intra-aortic balloon pump?

- A. Decreased aortic regurgitation
- B. Increased aortic regurgitation
- C. Decreased afterload
- D. Increased cardiac output
- E. None of the above

75. Which of the following medications is recommended for patients with heart failure with preserved ejection fraction (HFpEF) to reduce the risk of rehospitalization for HF?

- A. ACE inhibitor
- B. Phosphodiesterase type 5 inhibitor
- C. Aspirin
- D. Spironolactone
- E. SGLT2i

76. A patient is presented in cardiogenic shock due to profound acute decompensated heart failure (HF). The patient's condition is not improving with the current treatment plan. What would be the next appropriate step?

- A. Increase the dose of pressor
- B. Increase the dose of dobutamine
- C. Insert a percutaneous left ventricular assist device (eg, Impella or Tandem Heart)
- D. Use an intra-aortic balloon pump
- E. Continue with the current treatment plan

77. A 48-year-old male with a history of significant alcohol and cocaine use presents with symptoms of dilated cardiomyopathy. He also has recent influenza infection. Cardiac MRI does not support a diagnosis of acute myocarditis.

His ejection fraction (EF) is significantly decreased. What is the most appropriate next step in management?

- A. Initiate guideline-directed medical therapy, advise abstinence from alcohol and cocaine, and repeat transthoracic echocardiogram in 1 month.
- B. Initiate angiotensin-converting enzyme (ACE) inhibitor and -blocker; repeat transthoracic echocardiogram in 3 months.
- C. Perform a myocardial biopsy to determine the cause of the systolic dysfunction.
- D. Immediate placement of a primary prevention implantable cardiac defibrillator.
- E. Arrange for immediate referral for heart transplant evaluation.

78. What is the most likely diagnosis in a patient with low voltages on ECG and thick ventricular walls on transthoracic echocardiogram?

- A. Amyloidosis
- B. Sarcoidosis
- C. Long-standing hypertension
- D. Hypertrophic cardiomyopathy
- E. None of the above

79. A 52-year-old woman presents with a history of mitral valve prolapse. Echocardiography reveals an ejection fraction (EF) of 45% and a left ventricular end-systolic dimension (LVESD) of 42 mm. She is asymptomatic and without evidence of congestion. What should be the next step in the management of this patient's condition?

- A. Start furosemide
- B. Repeat echocardiography in 6 months
- C. Refer for mitral valve surgery
- D. Start ambulatory ECG monitoring
- E. Start beta-blocker therapy

80. A patient with a mechanical aortic valve and atrial fibrillation needs to have dental surgery. Which of the following is the best anticoagulation management strategy?

- A. Continue coumadin and monitor INR closely.
- B. Stop coumadin and start heparin 24 hours before surgery.
- C. Stop coumadin now and bridge with unfractionated heparin.
- D. Start a novel oral anticoagulant (NOAC) 24 hours before surgery.
- E. None of the above.

81. A 27-year-old woman with rheumatic mitral stenosis presents at 20 weeks gestation with symptoms of New York Heart Association (NYHA) class III heart failure. What is the best management strategy?

- A. Continue medical management and monitor closely.
- B. Schedule surgical mitral valve replacement.
- C. Perform percutaneous mitral balloon valvuloplasty (PMBV).
- D. Refer for PMBV as anatomy allows.
- E. Terminate the pregnancy.

82. A patient presents with distant heart sounds, elevated jugular vein pulsation, and hypotension, suggestive of Beck's triad. What is the most appropriate initial treatment step?

- A. Perform an emergent transthoracic echocardiogram
- B. Initiate pericardiocentesis
- C. Give 500 mL fluid bolus
- D. Conduct a pulmonary embolism CT scan
- E. Create a pericardial window

83. A 62-year-old man presents with a history of radiation therapy. He is found to have a jugular venous pulsation that does not decrease with inspiration and signs and symptoms of right-sided heart failure with clear lungs. An echocardiogram reveals respirophasic variation. What is the most likely diagnosis?

- A. Restrictive cardiomyopathy
- B. Constrictive pericarditis
- C. Acute myocarditis

- D. Dilated cardiomyopathy
- E. Hypertrophic cardiomyopathy

84. A 47-year-old man with no prior cardiovascular history presents with a blood pressure of 135/85 mmHg. What is the best management strategy?

- A. Calculating his atherosclerotic cardiovascular disease (ASCVD) risk score and, if >10%, starting an antihypertensive agent now.
- B. Starting an antihypertensive agent now.
- C. Monitoring his blood pressure closely and following up in 3 months.
- D. Recommending lifestyle changes only.
- E. None of the above.

85. 54-year-old woman with a history of type 2 diabetes mellitus visits your clinic for a routine check-up. She has been managing her diabetes with metformin. Recent laboratory results indicate the presence of microalbuminuria. Her blood pressure today is 150/90 mmHg. You decide to start her on antihypertensive therapy. Which of the following should be your first choice?

- A. Amlodipine (Calcium channel blocker)
- B. Hydrochlorothiazide (Diuretic)
- C. Metoprolol (Beta-blocker)
- D. Lisinopril (ACE inhibitor)
- E. Losartan (Angiotensin II receptor blocker)

86. A 69-year-old man presents to the emergency department with severe chest pain and blood pressure of 220/130 mmHg. He is tachycardic with a heart rate of 110 beats per minute. Chest X-ray shows a widened mediastinum. What is the best initial management strategy?

- A. Oral labetalol
- B. Intravenous labetalol
- C. Intravenous nitroglycerin
- D. Intravenous nitroprusside
- E. Intravenous esmolol

87. A 26-year-old woman presents with severe hypertension. On physical examination, an abdominal bruit is noted. What is the most appropriate next step in her diagnostic evaluation?

- A. MR angiography (MRA) of the renal arteries
- B. Duplex ultrasound of the renal arteries
- C. Noncontrast CT scan of the abdomen
- D. Renal angiography
- E. Percutaneous transluminal renal angioplasty

88. A 73-year-old man with a 5.2 cm abdominal aortic aneurysm (AAA) is referred to you for management. He has no symptoms related to the AAA. The AAA has grown by 0.5 cm in the past 6 months. What is the best management strategy?

- A. Observe the AAA with serial imaging.
- B. Start antihypertensive therapy to slow the growth of the AAA.
- C. Perform surgical repair of the AAA.
- D. Perform endovascular aneurysm repair (EVAR) of the AAA.
- E. None of the above.

89. A 26-year-old man presents with sudden onset severe chest and back pain. He stands at 6 feet 5 inches tall, with long arms and fingers, a high-arched palate, and a pectus excavatum deformity. On physical examination, you note a diastolic murmur and bilateral pulmonary rales. His blood pressure is elevated at 160/90 mmHg. Given this presentation, what would be the most appropriate next step in management?

- A. Administer a high-flow oxygen therapy
- B. Initiate anticoagulation treatment
- C. Prescribe analgesics for pain control
- D. Arrange for urgent surgical intervention

- E. Begin treatment with antihypertensive medications

90. A 37-year-old man presents with intermittent fevers, a recent history of a target-shaped rash, and travel to an endemic area for Lyme disease. He is hemodynamically unstable with a heart rate of 40 beats per minute and complete heart block with a slow escape rhythm. What is the best management strategy?

- A. Administer intravenous atropine.
- B. Perform transesophageal echocardiogram (TEE).
- C. Start intravenous antibiotics for Lyme disease and observe.
- D. Place a transvenous temporary pacemaker.
- E. Implant a permanent pacemaker.

91. A 72-year-old man with chronic obstructive pulmonary disease (COPD) presents with shortness of breath and a heart rate of 130 beats per minute. His ECG shows an irregular rhythm with three distinct P-wave morphologies. What is the most likely diagnosis?

- A. Atrial fibrillation
- B. Multifocal atrial tachycardia
- C. Atrioventricular nodal reentrant tachycardia
- D. Wolff-Parkinson-White syndrome

92. A 33-year-old patient presents to the emergency department with palpitations and dizziness. An ECG shows evidence of a pre-excitation syndrome, likely Wolff-Parkinson-White (WPW) syndrome, and he has now developed a rapid supraventricular tachycardia. What is the most appropriate initial management in this case?

- A) Adenosine
- B) Digoxin
- C) Direct current cardioversion
- D) Procainamide
- E) No treatment necessary

93. A 54-year-old woman with no prior cardiac history is admitted with pneumonia and started on broad-spectrum antibiotics. She suddenly goes into cardiac arrest with polymorphic ventricular tachycardia. Her ECG shows a pseudo-RBBB pattern with ST-segment elevation in V1 to V3. What is the most likely cause of her arrhythmia?

- A. Brugada syndrome
- B. Long QT interval
- C. Arrhythmogenic right ventricular cardiomyopathy
- D. Ischemia
- E. Left bundle branch block

94. A 52-year old woman with a history of hypertension presents with her fourth episode of monomorphic ventricular tachycardia over the past 2 months despite adequate medical therapy including -blockers, mexiletine, and amiodarone. Her most recent coronary angiogram suggests that her ventricular tachycardia is not driven by ischemia. What is the next most appropriate step in care?

- A. Increase dosage of -blockers
- B. Change mexiletine to another antiarrhythmic drug
- C. Initiate anticoagulation therapy
- D. Perform radiofrequency ablation
- E. Schedule for implantation of a cardiac defibrillator

95. A 68-year-old woman with a history of hypertension and atrial fibrillation (AF) presents with shortness of breath and fatigue. On examination, she is tachycardic with a heart rate of 130 beats per minute and her blood pressure is 160/90 mmHg. Transthoracic echocardiography (TTE) shows a dilated left ventricle with an ejection fraction of 30

- A. Increase her heart rate control medications.
- B. Start her on anticoagulation.
- C. Perform transesophageal echocardiogram (TEE); if no left atrial thrombus, perform cardioversion.
- D. Refer her for ablation of her AF.
- E. None of the above.

96. A 68-year old man with a history of ischemic cardiomyopathy presents with new-onset atrial fibrillation (AF). Which medication would be the most appropriate for the management of his condition?

- A. Amiodarone
- B. Flecainide
- C. Propafenone
- D. Diltiazem
- E. Metoprolol

97. A 72-year old woman presents to the emergency department following a mechanical fall. She has a life-threatening traumatic intracranial hemorrhage and is on both aspirin and apixaban. What would be the most appropriate intervention to manage her condition?

- A. Andexanet alfa
- B. Idarucizumab
- C. Fresh frozen plasma
- D. Vitamin K
- E. Platelet transfusion

98. A 69-year-old woman with rheumatic mitral stenosis and atrial fibrillation (AF) is currently taking warfarin for stroke prevention. She asks you about the possibility of switching to a direct-acting oral anticoagulant (DOAC). What is your response?

- A. DOACs are safe and effective alternatives to warfarin for stroke prevention in patients with AF and rheumatic mitral stenosis.
- B. DOACs are not indicated for stroke prevention in patients with AF and rheumatic mitral stenosis.
- C. DOACs are safe and effective alternatives to warfarin for stroke prevention in patients with AF and rheumatic mitral stenosis, but they require more frequent monitoring than warfarin.
- D. DOACs are safe and effective alternatives to warfarin for stroke prevention in patients with AF and rheumatic mitral stenosis, but they are more expensive than warfarin.
- E. DOACs are safe and effective alternatives to warfarin for stroke prevention in patients with AF and rheumatic mitral stenosis, but they are not as effective as warfarin in preventing thromboembolism.

99. A 58-year-old man presents with hypotension and elevated neck veins 6 hours after pacemaker implantation. He is also noted to have a blunted Y descent in his jugular veins. What is the most likely diagnosis?

- A. Pacemaker syndrome
- B. Lead perforation leading to cardiac tamponade
- C. Pacemaker-mediated tachycardia
- D. Flash pulmonary edema
- E. None of the above

100. A 63-year-old male patient presents with a fever, positive blood cultures showing S. aureus, and erythema around his pacemaker site. Despite a negative transesophageal echocardiogram (TEE), he has staphylococcal bacteremia. What would be the most appropriate treatment plan for this patient?

- A. Continue oral antibiotics
- B. Continue intravenous antibiotics
- C. Plan for pacemaker system removal
- D. Valve surgery
- E. Increase dosage of current medication

101. A 46-year-old man presents to the emergency department with sharp, central chest pain that worsens on lying down and improves on sitting forward. He also reports a low-grade fever. His ECG is shown below. Which of the following is the most likely diagnosis?

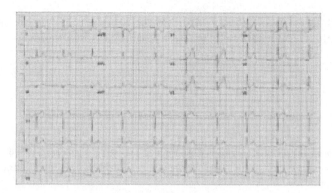

Figure 5.5: ECG of the patient

- A. Myocardial infarction
- B. Pulmonary embolism
- C. Pneumonia
- D. Pericardial effusion
- E. Acute pericarditis

102. A 53-year-old woman with a history of depression and anxiety presents to the clinic for a routine check-up. She is currently taking fluoxetine for her depression and lorazepam for her anxiety. She has no complaints and her physical examination is unremarkable. An ECG is performed as part of her routine check-up. Which of the following is the most appropriate next step in management?

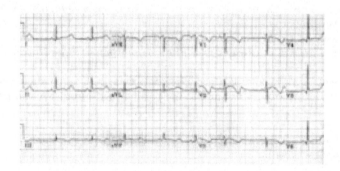

Figure 5.6: A 53-year-old woman ECG

- A. Discontinue fluoxetine and lorazepam immediately
- B. Start her on a beta-blocker
- C. Monitor her QT interval regularly
- D. Start her on a calcium channel blocker
- E. Refer her for an implantable cardioverter-defibrillator (ICD)

103. A 68-year-old man with a history of hypertension and type 2 diabetes presents to the emergency department with generalized weakness and muscle cramps. His medications include hydrochlorothiazide and metformin. His blood pressure is 140/90 mmHg, pulse is 80 beats per minute, and other vital signs are stable. Laboratory tests reveal a serum potassium level of 2.8 mEq/L (normal: 3.5-5.0 mEq/L). An ECG is performed, which is most likely to show which of the following?

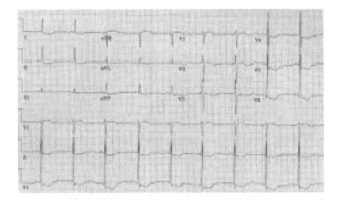

Figure 5.7: A 68-year-old man ECG

- A. T-wave flattening or inversion
- B. QRS widening
- C. ST-segment elevation
- D. PR segment elevation
- E. Absence of P waves

104. A 60-year-old man with a history of chronic kidney disease and hypertension presents to the emergency department with palpitations and weakness. His medications include lisinopril and amlodipine. His blood pressure is 130/80 mmHg, pulse is 90 beats per minute, and other vital signs are stable. Laboratory tests reveal a serum potassium level of 6.2 mEq/L (normal: 3.5-5.0 mEq/L). An ECG is performed, Which of the following is the most appropriate initial step in management?

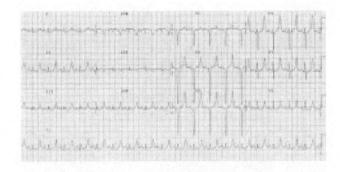

Figure 5.8: A 60-year-old man ECG

- A. Administer sodium polystyrene sulfonate
- B. Start him on a loop diuretic
- C. Administer intravenous calcium gluconate
- D. Discontinue lisinopril
- E. Start him on a beta-blocker

105. A 63year-old woman with a history of thyroidectomy for thyroid carcinoma presents to the emergency department with muscle twitches and spasms. She also reports numbness and tingling around her mouth and fingertips. Her blood pressure is 120/80 mmHg, pulse is 80 beats per minute, and other vital signs are stable. Laboratory tests reveal a serum calcium level of 6.8 mg/dL (normal: 8.5-10.2 mg/dL). An ECG is performed, which is most likely to show which of the following?

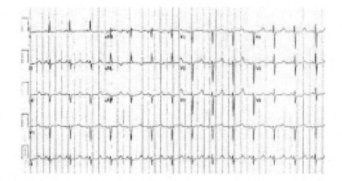

Figure 5.9: A 63year-old woman with a history of thyroidectomy

- A. Prolonged QT interval
- B. ST-segment elevation
- C. Shortened PR interval
- D. Absence of P waves
- E. QRS widening

106. A 67-year-old man with a history of hyperparathyroidism presents to the emergency department with consti-pation, polyuria, and confusion. His blood pressure is 140/90 mmHg, pulse is 80 beats per minute, and other vital signs are stable. Laboratory tests reveal a serum calcium level of 12.0 mg/dL (normal: 8.5-10.2 mg/dL). An ECG is performed, which is most likely to show which of the following findings?

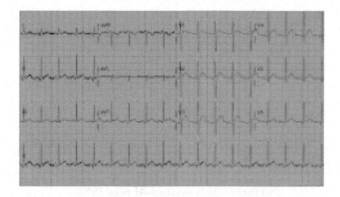

Figure 5.10: A 67-year-old man ECG

- A. Prolonged QT interval
- B. Shortened QT interval
- C. Prominent U waves
- D. PR segment elevation
- E. QRS narrowing

107. A 63-year-old man with a history of hypertension and smoking presents to the emergency department with severe chest pain radiating to his left arm. His blood pressure is 150/90 mmHg, pulse is 90 beats per minute, and other vital signs are stable. An ECG is performed, which of the following is the most likely diagnosis?

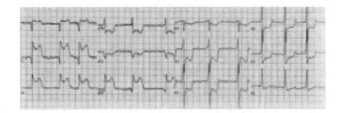

Figure 5.11: A 63-year-old man ECG

- A. Anterior ST-elevation myocardial infarction
- B. Pericarditis
- C. Inferior ST-elevation myocardial infarction
- D. Stable angina
- E. Unstable angina

108. A 61-year-old man with a history of ischemic heart disease suddenly collapses. On examination, he has no central pulse. The ECG shown here , What is the most appropriate initial management?

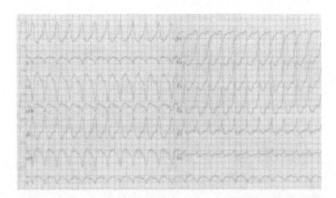

Figure 5.12: 67 year old

- A. Administer intravenous beta-blockers
- B. Begin chest compressions and prepare for defibrillation
- C. Administer intravenous amiodarone
- D. Perform immediate DC cardioversion
- E. Administer intravenous fluids

109. A 34-year-old woman presents to the emergency department with a sudden onset of palpitations. She has no history of heart disease but has been experiencing high levels of stress and anxiety recently. Her heart rate is 150 beats per minute, and the ECG shown here. What is the most likely diagnosis and initial treatment?

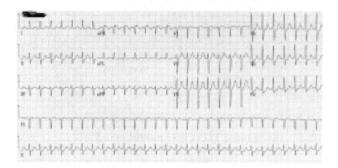

Figure 5.13: 34-year-old woman

- A. Sinus tachycardia; treat with beta-blockers
- B. Atrial flutter; treat with electrical cardioversion
- C. Ventricular tachycardia; treat with defibrillation
- D. Junctional supraventricular tachycardia (SVT); treat with vagal maneuvers and adenosine
- E. Atrial fibrillation; treat with anticoagulation

110. A 59-year-old man with a history of renal disease requiring dialysis presents to the emergency department. He missed his last dialysis session due to feeling dizzy and unwell. His ECG shown. What is the most likely diagnosis and immediate treatment?

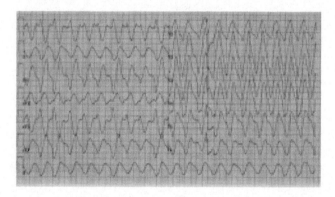

Figure 5.14: A 59-year-old man

- A. Hypokalemia; treat with oral potassium supplements
- B. Hyperkalemia; treat with calcium gluconate, insulin and dextrose, and urgent dialysis
- C. Hypocalkemia; treat with intravenous calcium
- D. Hypercalkemia; treat with intravenous fluids and furosemide
- E. Hyponatremia; treat with hypertonic saline

111. A 21-year-old man with a history of fainting episodes collapses during a basketball match. His ECG shown . What is the most likely diagnosis and the initial treatment?

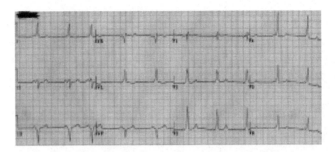

Figure 5.15: A 21-year-old

- A. Atrial fibrillation; treat with electrical cardioversion
- B. Ventricular tachycardia; treat with defibrillation
- C. Wolff-Parkinson-White (WPW) syndrome; treat with catheter ablation
- D. Long QT syndrome; treat with beta-blockers
- E. Brugada syndrome; treat with an implantable cardioverter-defibrillator (ICD).

112. A 56-year-old smoker presents with tight epigastric pain. His ECG shown, what is the most likely diagnosis and the initial treatment?

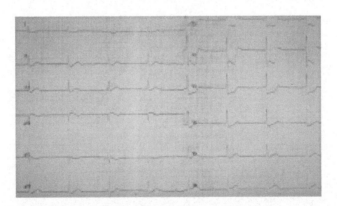

Figure 5.16: 56-year-old smoker

- A. Anterior myocardial infarction; treat with percutaneous coronary intervention (PCI)
- B. Posterior myocardial infarction; treat with thrombolytic therapy
- C. Posterior myocardial infarction; treat with percutaneous coronary intervention (PCI)
- D. Anterior myocardial infarction; treat with thrombolytic therapy
- E. Pericarditis; treat with nonsteroidal anti-inflammatory drugs (NSAIDs)

113. A 51-year-old man presents with a collapse. He has been recently unwell with a chest infection for which he has been prescribed clarithromycin. He also takes medication for his hayfever. His ECG shown, what is the most likely diagnosis and the initial treatment?

Dr Rafael Zioni

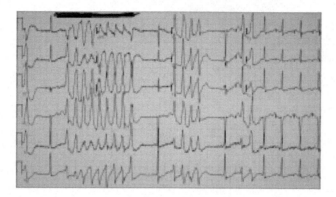

Figure 5.17: 51-year-old man

- A. Ventricular fibrillation; treat with defibrillation
- B. Atrial fibrillation; treat with electrical cardioversion
- C. Torsades de pointes; treat with intravenous magnesium
- D. Supraventricular tachycardia; treat with adenosine
- E. Sinus tachycardia; treat with beta-blockers

114. A 39-year-old man presents with palpitations after a weekend of heavy drinking. His ECG shown, what is the most likely diagnosis and the initial treatment?

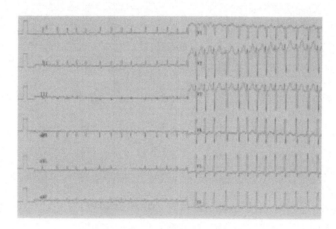

Figure 5.18: 39-year-old man

- A. Sinus tachycardia; treat with beta-blockers
- B. Atrial fibrillation; treat with rate control and anticoagulation
- C. Ventricular fibrillation; treat with defibrillation
- D. Supraventricular tachycardia; treat with adenosine
- E. Atrial flutter; treat with electrical cardioversion

115. A 42-year-old man presents with palpitations and shortness of breath after a weekend of heavy drinking. His ECG shown, what is the diagnosis and the initial treatment?

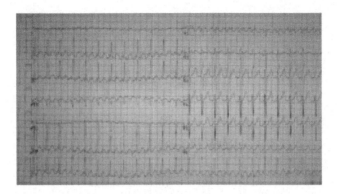

Figure 5.19: A 42-year-old man

- A. Atrial fibrillation; treat with rate control and anticoagulation
- B. Atrial flutter; treat with electrical cardioversion
- C. Ventricular tachycardia; treat with defibrillation
- D. Supraventricular tachycardia; treat with adenosine
- E. Sinus tachycardia; treat with beta-blockers

116. A 63-year-old man presents with occasional episodes of dizziness and syncope in the past. His ECG shown, what is the most likely diagnosis and the initial treatment?

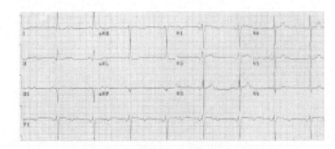

Figure 5.20: 62-year-old man

- A. Sinus bradycardia; treat with atropine
- B. Mobitz type 1 second-degree AV block; treat with observation
- C. Mobitz type 2 second-degree AV block; treat with pacemaker implantation
- D. Third-degree AV block; treat with pacemaker implantation
- E. Supraventricular tachycardia; treat with adenosine

117. A 71-year-old woman presents with episodes of dizziness and fatigue. Her ECG shows a regular atrial rate, but the ventricular rate is slower and not associated with the P waves. What is the most likely diagnosis and the initial treatment?

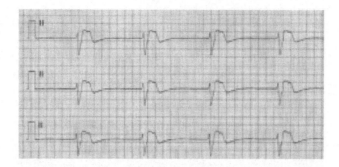

Figure 5.21: 71-year-old woman

- A. First-degree AV block; treat with observation
- B. Mobitz type 1 second-degree AV block; treat with observation
- C. Mobitz type 2 second-degree AV block; treat with pacemaker implantation
- D. Third-degree AV block; treat with pacemaker implantation
- E. Supraventricular tachycardia; treat with adenosine

118. A 77-year-old man presents with episodes of dizziness and occasional fainting. His ECG shown. What is the most likely diagnosis and the initial treatment?

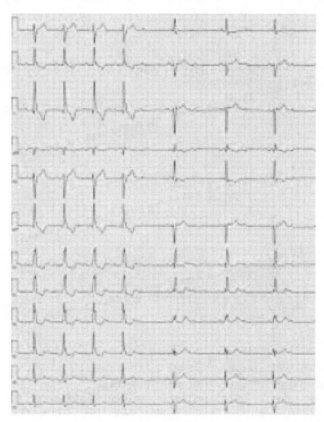

Figure 5.22: 77-year-old man

- A. First-degree AV block; treat with observation
- B. Mobitz type 1 second-degree AV block; treat with observation
- C. Mobitz type 2 second-degree AV block; treat with pacemaker implantation

- D. Trifascicular block; treat with pacemaker implantation
- E. Supraventricular tachycardia; treat with adenosine

5.1   ANSWERS

1. The correct answer is C.Constrictive pericarditis.

Kussmaul's sign is a clinical sign that is observed in constrictive pericarditis. It is characterized by an increase in jugular venous pressure (JVP) with inspiration. This is because the pericardium, which normally allows the heart to expand during inspiration, is stiff in constrictive pericarditis. This prevents the heart from expanding, which increases the JVP. The other answer choices are not as appropriate. Right heart failure can also cause an increase in JVP, but it does not typically increase with inspiration. Mitral stenosis and atrial fibrillation can also cause an increase in JVP, but they do not typically cause Kussmaul's sign.

2. The correct answer is A. Tricuspid stenosis.

A large "a" wave and a slow "y" descent are classic findings in tricuspid stenosis. The "a" wave is caused by the right atrium contracting against a closed tricuspid valve. The slow "y" descent is caused by the slow filling of the right ventricle. The other answer choices are not as appropriate. Constrictive pericarditis can also cause a large "a" wave, but it does not typically cause a slow "y" descent. Atrial septal defect and tricuspid regurgitation can cause a large "v" wave, but they do not typically cause a large "a" wave or a slow "y" descent.

3. The correct answer is D. Mitral regurgitation.

A holosystolic murmur is a heart murmur that lasts the entire time that the heart is in systole. This means that it is present during both the early and late phases of systole. Holosystolic murmurs are most commonly caused by mitral regurgitation or tricuspid regurgitation. In mitral regurgitation, the mitral valve does not close properly, which allows blood to leak back into the left atrium during systole. This causes a holosystolic murmur that is loudest at the apex. In tricuspid regurgitation, the tricuspid valve does not close properly, which allows blood to leak back into the right atrium during systole. This causes a holosystolic murmur that is loudest at the lower left sternal border. The other answer choices are not as appropriate. Aortic stenosis and pulmonic stenosis are both caused by narrowing of the aortic valve and pulmonic valve, respectively. These conditions can cause a systolic murmur, but they do not typically cause a holosystolic murmur.

4. The correct answer is B. The murmur will become longer and louder.

The Valsalva maneuver is a test that is used to assess the heart and lungs. It involves bearing down as if to have a bowel movement, which increases the pressure in the chest. This can have a number of effects on heart murmurs. In patients with hypertrophic cardiomyopathy, the Valsalva maneuver can cause the systolic murmur to become longer and louder. This is because the increased pressure in the chest can cause the mitral valve to close more tightly, which allows less blood to leak back into the left atrium during systole. This results in a louder murmur. The other answer choices are not as appropriate. The murmur will not change in intensity or duration in most patients. The murmur may become softer and shorter in patients with mitral valve prolapse.

5. The correct answer is A. Ostium primum defect.

Ostium primum defect is a type of ASD that is located in the lower part of the atrial septum. It is often associated with left-axis deviation on ECG. Incomplete RBBB can also be seen in patients with ostium primum defect, but it is not as common as left-axis deviation. Ostium secundum defect is a type of ASD that is located in the middle of the atrial septum. It is not typically associated with left-axis deviation or incomplete RBBB. Sinus venosus defect is a type of ASD that is located near the entry of the superior vena cava into the right atrium. It is not typically associated with left-axis deviation or incomplete RBBB. The other answer choices are not as appropriate. None of the other types of ASD are typically associated with left-axis deviation or incomplete RBBB.

6. The correct answer is B. Yes, he should undergo percutaneous or surgical closure of his VSD.

Percutaneous or surgical closure of VSD is indicated for patients who exhibit symptoms or experience volume overload, provided that irreversible pulmonary vascular disease is not present. This patient has a Qp/Qs ratio of 1.5:1, which is above the normal range of 1.0:1. This suggests that he is experiencing volume overload. Additionally, his pulmonary artery pressure and pulmonary vascular resistance are both below two-thirds of the systemic pressure and systemic resistance, respectively. This suggests that he does not have irreversible pulmonary vascular disease. Therefore, he should undergo percutaneous or surgical closure of his VSD. The other answer choices are not as appropriate. No, he should not undergo percutaneous or surgical closure of his VSD is not the correct answer because the patient is experiencing symptoms and volume overload. It is uncertain whether he should undergo percutaneous or surgical closure of his VSD is not the correct answer because the patient meets the criteria for closure of his VSD.

7. The correct answer is A. Yes, antibiotic prophylaxis is recommended.

Tetralogy of Fallot is a congenital heart defect that includes a ventricular septal defect, a right ventricular outflow tract obstruction, an overriding aorta, and right ventricular hypertrophy. This defect can cause a right-to-left shunt, which means that blood can flow from the right side of the heart to the left side of the heart. This can increase the risk of bacteria in the bloodstream from attaching to the heart valves and causing infective endocarditis. The American Heart Association recommends antibiotic prophylaxis for dental procedures in patients with tetralogy of Fallot. This is because the dental procedure can cause bacteremia, which is the presence of bacteria in the bloodstream. Antibiotic prophylaxis can help to prevent the bacteria from attaching to the heart valves and causing infective endocarditis. The other answer choices are not as appropriate. No, antibiotic prophylaxis is not recommended, but is not the correct answer because the patient has a congenital heart defect that increases the risk of infective endocarditis. It is uncertain whether antibiotic prophylaxis is recommended that is not the correct answer because the patient has a congenital heart defect that increases the risk of infective endocarditis.

8. The correct answer is C. Percutaneous balloon valvuloplasty.

Percutaneous balloon valvuloplasty is a minimally invasive procedure that is used to open a narrowed mitral valve. This procedure is usually performed under local anesthesia and does not require a large incision. Percutaneous balloon valvuloplasty is the preferred procedure for the management of uncomplicated mitral stenosis because it is less invasive and has a shorter recovery time than open surgical valvotomy. Open surgical valvotomy is a more invasive procedure that is performed under general anesthesia. This procedure involves making a large incision in the chest and opening the mitral valve with a scalpel. Open surgical valvotomy is typically only used if percutaneous balloon valvuloplasty is not an option. Medical therapy is not a long-term solution for mitral stenosis. Medical therapy can be used to relieve symptoms, but it will not open the mitral valve. Watchful waiting is not an appropriate option for this patient because she is already experiencing symptoms.

9. The patient is symptomatic with severe MR and has evidence of progressive left ventricular dysfunction. In cases where patients exhibit symptoms or experience progressive left ventricular dysfunction, such as a left ventricular ejection fraction (LVEF) below 60% or an end-systolic left ventricular diameter equal to or greater than 40 mm, surgical valve repair or replacement is considered an appropriate course of action. It is important to take into account valve repair as a potential treatment option for patients who are asymptomatic but have severe chronic mitral regurgitation (MR) and exhibit recent onset atrial fibrillation (AF), pulmonary hypertension, or a progressive decline in left ventricular ejection fraction (LVEF) or an increase in left ventricular end-systolic diameter on consecutive imaging. In this case, the patient's LVEF is still within the normal range, so valve repair is a viable option. Medical therapy with diuretics and ACE inhibitors may be used to manage the patient's symptoms, but it will not address the underlying problem of mitral regurgitation. Transcatheter mitral valve repair is a newer procedure that may be an option for some patients, but it is not yet as widely available as valve repair. Observation is not a reasonable option for this patient, as she is already symptomatic.

10. The answer to this question is A. Soft or absent A2.

This is because as the aortic valve narrows, it becomes more difficult for blood to flow out of the heart. This can cause the A2 heart sound to become softer or even absent. The other answer choices are also possible findings in patients with aortic stenosis, but they are not as specific as a soft or absent A2. For example, S4 is a heart sound that is often heard in patients with aortic stenosis, but it can also be heard in other conditions. Pulsus paradoxus is a decrease in systolic blood pressure during inspiration that is often seen in patients with severe heart failure, but it is not a specific finding for aortic stenosis. Midsystolic click is a heart sound that is often heard in patients with mitral valve prolapse, but it is not a finding in aortic stenosis. Diastolic murmur is a heart sound that is often heard in patients with aortic regurgitation, but it is not a finding in aortic stenosis.

11. The answer to this question is D. All of the above.

TAVR is a minimally invasive procedure, but it is not without risks. The most common complications associated with TAVR are stroke, the need for a permanent pacemaker, and paravalvular aortic regurgitation. Stroke occurs in about 1% of patients undergoing TAVR, and the need for a permanent pacemaker occurs in about 10% of patients. Paravalvular aortic regurgitation is a complication that occurs when there is a leak around the new valve. This can lead to heart failure and other complications. Other potential complications of TAVR include bleeding, infection, and vascular complications. However, these complications are less common than stroke, the need for a permanent pacemaker, and paravalvular aortic regurgitation.

12.The answer to this question is C. Beta-blockers can prolong the duration of diastole.

This is because beta-blockers work by slowing down the heart rate. A slower heart rate means that there is more time for blood to fill the left ventricle during diastole. In patients with chronic AR, this can lead to an increase in the amount of blood that regurgitates back into the left ventricle during diastole. This can worsen heart failure symptoms and increase the risk of stroke. The other answer choices are also possible reasons why beta-blockers should be avoided in patients with chronic AR, but they are not as likely as the prolongation of diastole. For example, beta-blockers can worsen heart failure by decreasing cardiac output. However, this is not as likely to happen in patients with chronic AR as it is in patients with other types of heart failure. Beta-blockers can also increase the risk of stroke by slowing down the heart rate. However, this risk is also relatively low in patients with chronic AR.

13. The answer to this question is A. Viridans streptococci.

Viridans streptococci are the most common causative microorganisms associated with NVE. They are found in the oral cavity and can enter the bloodstream through small breaks in the gums or other oral tissues. The other answer choices are also possible causative microorganisms for NVE, but they are less common than viridans streptococci. For example, staphylococci are another common causative microorganism for NVE, but they are more likely to be seen in patients who have a history of intravenous drug use or other risk factors for infection. HACEK organisms are a group of bacteria that are less common than viridans streptococci or staphylococci, but they can still cause NVE. Streptococcus gallolyticus subspecies gallolyticus is a less common causative microorganism for NVE, but it is more likely to be seen in patients who have colon cancer or polyp.

14. The answer to this question is C. S aureus.

S aureus is the most common causative microorganism associated with CIED-related endocarditis. It is found on the skin and can enter the bloodstream through small breaks in the skin. CoNS are also a common causative microorganism for CIED-related endocarditis. They are found in the skin and mucous membranes. Viridans streptococci and HACEK organisms are less common causative microorganisms for CIED-related endocarditis. The other answer choices are also possible causative microorganisms for CIED-related endocarditis, but they are less common than S aureus or CoNS. For example, viridans streptococci are another common causative microorganism for CIED-related endocarditis, but they are more likely to be seen in patients who have a history of dental work or other risk factors for infection. HACEK organisms are a group of bacteria that are less common than S aureus or CoNS, but they can still cause CIED-related endocarditis.

15. The answer to this question is D. 30-65%.

This is according to research findings that have revealed the presence of clinically asymptomatic emboli in approximately 30-65% of individuals diagnosed with left-sided endocarditis. The other answer choices are also possible prevalence rates for clinically asymptomatic emboli detected on MRI in patients diagnosed with left-sided endocarditis, but they are less likely than 30-65%. For example, 10-30% is the prevalence rate for clinically asymptomatic emboli detected on CT scans in patients diagnosed with left-sided endocarditis. 5-10% is the prevalence rate for clinically asymptomatic emboli detected on echocardiography in patients diagnosed with left-sided endocarditis. <5% is the prevalence rate for clinically asymptomatic emboli detected on physical examination in patients diagnosed with left-sided endocarditis.

16. The answer to this question is B. Repeat the TEE examination in 7-10 days.

This is because a negative TEE result does not definitively rule out the diagnosis of endocarditis, especially if there is a high likelihood of the disease. Repeating the TEE examination can help to confirm or rule out the diagnosis. The other answer choices are also possible next steps in management, but they are less likely than repeating the TEE examination. For example, discharging the patient from the hospital is not a reasonable option if there is a high likelihood of endocarditis. Starting with antibiotic therapy is a possible option, but it should only be done if there is a high likelihood of endocarditis, and the patient is symptomatic. Referring the patient to a cardiologist for further evaluation is a possible option, but it is not the best next step in management if the patient is already being seen by a cardiologist.

17. The answer to this question is B. 6 to 8 weeks.

This is because staphylococcal PVE is typically managed through a multidrug regimen lasting for a duration of 6 to 8 weeks. The other answer choices are also possible durations of treatment for staphylococcal PVE, but they are less

Dr Rafael Zioni

likely than 6 to 8 weeks. For example, 4 to 6 weeks is the recommended duration of treatment for non-staphylococcal PVE. 8 to 12 weeks is the recommended duration of treatment for staphylococcal PVE that is complicated by heart failure or other complications. 12 to 16 weeks is the recommended duration of treatment for staphylococcal PVE that is methicillin resistant.

18. The answer to this question is A. Hypertrophic cardiomyopathy.

The correct answer is C. Aldosterone antagonist therapy is recommended for patients with dilated cardiomyopathy in NYHA class III heart failure.

Aldosterone antagonists, such as spironolactone or eplerenone, are recommended in patients with NYHA class II-IV heart failure and who have symptoms of the condition, according to the American Heart Association and the American College of Cardiology. These medications have been shown to reduce both morbidity and mortality in these patients. In the case of the patient described, who has dilated cardiomyopathy and is in NYHA class III heart failure, aldosterone antagonist therapy would be a recommended part of her treatment plan. This is because aldosterone antagonists have been shown to improve symptoms and survival in patients with dilated cardiomyopathy. The other answer choices are also possible roles of aldosterone antagonist therapy in treating dilated cardiomyopathy, but they are less likely than for patients with NYHA class III heart failure. For example, aldosterone antagonist therapy is not indicated for patients with dilated cardiomyopathy who are not symptomatic. Aldosterone antagonist therapy may be considered for patients with dilated cardiomyopathy in NYHA class II heart failure, but it is not as effective as for patients in NYHA class III heart failure. Aldosterone antagonist therapy is not recommended for patients with dilated cardiomyopathy in NYHA class IV heart failure, as it has not been shown to be effective in this group of patients.

19. The answer to this question is A.

The patient meets all of the criteria for CRT, including heart failure of class III-IV severity, LVEF below 35%, and an extended QRS duration. Therefore, he is a candidate for CRT. The other answer choices are also possible, but they are less likely than for patients who meet all of the criteria for CRT. For example, a patient with LVEF above 35% is not a candidate for CRT. A patient with QRS duration below 150 milliseconds is not a candidate for CRT, unless they have left bundle branch block. A patient without left bundle branch block may still be a candidate for CRT, but it is less likely than for patients with left bundle branch block.

20. The answer to this question is C.

Bilateral atrial enlargement with speckled pattern in the ventricles. This is because infiltrative diseases, such as amyloidosis, can cause restrictive cardiomyopathy. Restrictive cardiomyopathy is characterized by a thickened myocardium that does not relax properly, which can lead to diastolic dysfunction and heart failure. The imaging findings of restrictive cardiomyopathy include bilateral atrial enlargement and a speckled pattern in the ventricles. The speckled pattern is caused by amyloid deposits in the myocardium. The other answer choices are also possible imaging findings in patients with heart disease, but they are less likely than bilateral atrial enlargement with speckled pattern in the ventricles. For example, a normal echocardiogram is not expected in a patient with restrictive cardiomyopathy. A dilated left ventricle with decreased ejection fraction is more likely to be seen in patients with dilated cardiomyopathy. A thickened pericardium with pericardial effusion is more likely to be seen in patients with constrictive pericarditis.

21. The answer to this question is A. Hypertrophic cardiomyopathy.

This is because the physical examination findings described are characteristic of hypertrophic cardiomyopathy. The brisk carotid upstroke with pulsus bisferiens is caused by the increased stroke volume that occurs in hypertrophic cardiomyopathy. The S4 sound is caused by the late diastolic closure of the mitral valve that occurs in hypertrophic cardiomyopathy. The harsh systolic murmur along the left sternal border is caused by the turbulent flow of blood through the narrowed left ventricular outflow tract that occurs in hypertrophic cardiomyopathy. The blowing murmur indicative of mitral regurgitation at the apex is caused by the backflow of blood through the mitral valve that occurs in hypertrophic cardiomyopathy. The other answer choices are also possible diagnoses, but they are less likely than hypertrophic cardiomyopathy. For example, mitral stenosis is characterized by a diastolic murmur that is heard best at the apex. Aortic stenosis is characterized by a systolic murmur that is heard best at the second right intercostal space. Mitral regurgitation is characterized by a holosystolic murmur that is heard best at the apex. 22. The answer to this question is D. All of the above.

This is because all of the factors listed are indications for an ICD in patients with hypertrophic cardiomyopathy. Syncope is a risk factor for sudden death in patients with hypertrophic cardiomyopathy. Left ventricular wall thickness of 3.2 cm is considered significant and is a risk factor for sudden death. Family history of sudden death is a risk factor for sudden death in patients with hypertrophic cardiomyopathy. The other answer choices are also possible indications for an ICD in patients with hypertrophic cardiomyopathy, but they are less likely than all of the factors listed. For example, nonsustained ventricular tachycardia (VT) is a risk factor for sudden death, but it is less likely than syncope in patients with hypertrophic cardiomyopathy. Exertional hypotension is a risk factor for sudden death, but it is less likely than left ventricular wall thickness of 3.2 cm in patients with hypertrophic cardiomyopathy.

23. The answer to this question is B. Start empiric antibiotic therapy.

This is because the patient's symptoms and laboratory findings are consistent with myocarditis. However, the diagnosis of myocarditis cannot be made definitively without endomyocardial biopsy. In most cases, the diagnosis of myocarditis can be made through non-invasive diagnostic methods, such as laboratory tests, imaging studies, and clinical evaluation. However, in this case, the patient's symptoms and laboratory findings are so suggestive of myocarditis that it is reasonable to start empiric antibiotic therapy while awaiting the results of the endomyocardial biopsy. The other answer choices are also possible next steps in the management of this patient, but they are less likely than starting empiric antibiotic therapy. For example, endomyocardial biopsy is not commonly used in the diagnostic evaluation of myocarditis and would only be performed if the diagnosis was uncertain after non-invasive testing. Refer the patient to a cardiologist for further evaluation is a reasonable next step, but it is not as likely as starting empiric antibiotic therapy in this case. Discharge the patient home with close follow-up is not a reasonable next step, as the patient's symptoms and laboratory findings are suggestive of a serious condition.

24. The answer to this question is A. Acute pericarditis.

This is because the ECG findings of widespread ST elevation with reciprocal ST depression are characteristic of acute pericarditis. In contrast, the ECG findings of acute STEMI are typically characterized by upwardly convex ST elevations accompanied by reciprocal ST depression in leads opposite to the affected area. Additionally, PR depression is not typically observed in acute pericarditis, but it is often seen in acute STEMI. T wave inversions may manifest in both acute pericarditis and acute STEMI, but they typically occur after the ST elevations have resolved in acute pericarditis. The other answer choices are also possible diagnoses, but they are less likely than acute pericarditis. For example, early repolarization is a benign condition that can cause ECG changes that mimic acute pericarditis. However, the ECG findings of early repolarization are typically seen in young, healthy individuals and are not associated with chest pain. ARVC is a rare genetic disorder that can cause ECG changes that mimic acute pericarditis. However, ARVC is typically associated with other symptoms, such as syncope and palpitations.

25. The answer to this question is C. Start colchicine.

This is because the administration of anticoagulants in cases of acute pericarditis is generally not recommended due to the potential risk of pericardial hemorrhage. Colchicine is a medication that is used to treat acute pericarditis and is not associated with the same risk of pericardial hemorrhage. The other answer choices are also possible treatments for acute pericarditis, but they are less likely than colchicine. For example, aspirin and clopidogrel are antiplatelet medications that can help to prevent the formation of blood clots. However, they can also increase the risk of pericardial hemorrhage. Heparin is an anticoagulant that can help to prevent the formation of blood clots. However, it is also associated with the risk of pericardial hemorrhage. Discharge the patient home with close follow-up is not a reasonable management option for this patient, as he has chest pain and a pericardial rub.

26. The answer to this question is B. Electrical alternans is a sign of cardiac tamponade.

This is because the swinging motion of the heart that causes electrical alternans is a consequence of the increased pressure in the pericardial sac that occurs in cardiac tamponade. The other answer choices are also possible interpretations of electrical alternans, but they are less likely than cardiac tamponade. For example, electrical alternans can be a benign finding that is not associated with any significant pathology. However, it is more likely to be a sign of cardiac tamponade in a patient with chest pain and shortness of breath. Myocardial infarction and pericarditis can also cause electrical alternans, but they are less likely than cardiac tamponade in this patient.

27. The answer to this question is A. Cardiac catheterization.

This is because cardiac catheterization is the most definitive way to diagnose constrictive pericarditis. During cardiac catheterization, the physician can measure the diastolic pressures in all chambers of the heart. If the diastolic pressures are equalized, then this is a sign of constrictive pericarditis. Additionally, the ventricular pressure tracings in constrictive pericarditis exhibit a characteristic "dip and plateau" appearance. The other answer choices are also possible diagnostic tests for constrictive pericarditis, but they are less definitive than cardiac catheterization. For example, endomyocardial biopsy can be used to diagnose constrictive pericarditis, but it is not as sensitive as cardiac catheterization. MRI and CT can also be used to diagnose constrictive pericarditis, but they are not as specific as cardiac catheterization.

28. The answer to this question is B. Add a loop diuretic to the regimen.

This is because the serum creatinine level of 2.7 mg/dL is above the level at which thiazides are typically effective. Loop diuretics are more potent than thiazides and can be effective in patients with higher serum creatinine levels. The other answer choices are also possible management options for this patient, but they are less likely than adding a loop diuretic. For example, increasing the dose of HCTZ may be effective in some patients, but it is less likely to be effective in a patient with a serum creatinine level of 2.7 mg/dL. Switching to a different thiazide diuretic may also be effective, but it is less likely to be effective than adding a loop diuretic. Discontinue HCTZ is not a reasonable management option for this patient, as he is currently taking HCTZ for his hypertension.

29. The answer to this question is B. Hyperkalemia.

This is because ACE inhibitors and ARBs can cause hyperkalemia, and potassium supplements and potassium-sparing diuretics can further increase the risk of hyperkalemia. The other answer choices are also possible monitoring concerns for this patient, but they are less likely than hyperkalemia. For example, hypotension is a possible side effect of ACE inhibitors and ARBs, but it is less likely in a patient who is also taking potassium supplements. Renal insufficiency is a possible side effect of ACE inhibitors and ARBs, but it is less likely in a patient who is otherwise healthy. Hyperglycemia is not a side effect of ACE inhibitors or ARBs.

30. The answer to this question is A. Methyldopa.

This is because methyldopa is the most commonly used antihypertensive medication in pregnancy. It is safe for both the mother and the fetus, and it has been shown to be effective in controlling blood pressure. The other answer choices are also possible antihypertensive medications that can be used in pregnancy, but they are less commonly used than methyldopa. For example, labetalol and hydralazine are also safe for use in pregnancy, but they are not as effective as methyldopa in controlling blood pressure. Nifedipine is a calcium channel blocker that is safe for use in pregnancy, but it is not as commonly used as methyldopa because it can cause fetal tachycardia.

31. The answer to this question is A. Nitroprusside.

This is because nitroprusside is the most effective antihypertensive agent for the treatment of hypertensive crisis. It is a short-acting agent that can be titrated to achieve the desired blood pressure response. The other answer choices are also possible antihypertensive agents that can be used for the treatment of hypertensive crisis, but they are not as effective as nitroprusside. For example, nicardipine and labetalol are also short-acting agents, but they are not as potent as nitroprusside. Enalaprilat is a longer-acting agent, but it takes longer to start working than nitroprusside. Hydralazine is a short-acting agent, but it can cause reflex tachycardia.

32. The correct answer is A.

Acute myocardial infarction is a contraindication to exercise testing because it is a condition in which the blood supply to the heart muscle is suddenly blocked. Exercise testing could worsen the condition and could lead to further damage to the heart muscle. The other answer choices are not contraindications to exercise testing. Unstable angina is a condition in which the patient experiences chest pain that is not relieved by rest or medication. However, exercise testing can be used to diagnose unstable angina and to determine the severity of the condition. Severe aortic stenosis is a narrowing of the aortic valve, which prevents blood from flowing smoothly from the heart to the rest of the body. However, exercise testing can be used to assess the patient's cardiovascular function and to determine the need for surgery. Myocarditis is an inflammation of the heart muscle. However, exercise testing can be used to diagnose myocarditis and to determine the severity of the condition. Pericarditis is an inflammation of the sac that surrounds the heart. However, exercise testing can be used to diagnose pericarditis and to determine the severity of the condition. Low exercise tolerance is the inability to exercise for a significant period of time due to a medical condition. However, exercise testing can be modified to accommodate patients with low exercise tolerance.

33. The correct answer is E.

A normal ECG is not a criterion for a positive exercise test. A positive exercise test is a sign that the patient may have coronary artery disease. However, a normal ECG does not rule out coronary artery disease. There are many patients with coronary artery disease who have a normal ECG. The other answer choices are all criteria for a positive exercise test. Chest pain or other symptoms that are consistent with angina are a sign that the patient is experiencing ischemia, which is a lack of blood flow to the heart muscle. Diagnostic ST-segment changes on the ECG are changes in the electrical activity of the heart that can be seen on an ECG. These changes are typically seen in patients with coronary artery disease. Failure to reach the target heart rate is a sign that the patient is not getting enough exercise. This could be due to a number of factors, such as poor exercise tolerance or a medical condition. A drop in blood pressure during exercise is a sign that the heart is not getting enough blood flow. This could be due to coronary artery disease or another medical condition.

34. The correct answer is E.

All of the above are contraindications to beta-blockers. Here are some additional details about the contraindications to beta-blockers: Congestive heart failure (CHF) is a condition in which the heart cannot pump blood effectively. Beta-blockers can worsen CHF by making the heart beat slower and weaker. Atrioventricular (AV) block is a condition in which the electrical signals that control the heart's rhythm are not transmitted properly. Beta-blockers can worsen AV block by slowing down the heart rate. Bronchospasm is a narrowing of the airways that can make it difficult to breathe. Beta-blockers can worsen bronchospasm by relaxing the airways. "Brittle" diabetes is a type of diabetes that is difficult to control. Beta-blockers can worsen "brittle" diabetes by making it more difficult to control blood sugar levels.

35. The rate of restenosis following balloon dilatation alone during PCI is approximately 30-45%.

This is because balloon dilatation can cause damage to the inner lining of the artery, which can lead to the formation of scar tissue. This scar tissue can narrow the artery again, resulting in restenosis. The other answer choices are incorrect. The rate of restenosis is lower than 10% in patients who undergo PCI with stenting. The rate of restenosis is higher than 50% in patients who have a high-risk lesion, such as a lesion that is heavily calcified or that has a long segment of stenosis. 36. The patient in this question has severe coronary artery disease (CAD) that is not responsive to medical treatment. He also has a left main coronary artery stenosis, which is a high-risk lesion that is associated with a high risk of death. In this case, CABG is the most appropriate treatment because it provides a more durable and effective way to improve blood flow to the heart. The other answer choices are incorrect. PCI is not a good option for this patient because his lesions are not suitable for this procedure. Medical therapy with nitrates and beta-blockers, calcium channel blockers, aspirin, and clopidogrel may help to control the patient's symptoms, but they will not provide a long-term solution to his CAD.

37. The answer is B.

PCI is more effective than medical therapy in providing relief from angina symptoms in patients with chronic stable angina. The available evidence shows that PCI does not reduce the risk of MI or mortality in patients with chronic stable angina. However, it does provide more effective relief from angina symptoms than medical therapy. This is because PCI opens up the narrowed coronary arteries, which improves blood flow to the heart. The other answer choices are incorrect. Medical therapy is not as effective as PCI in providing relief from angina symptoms. There is not enough evidence to determine which treatment is more effective in reducing the risk of MI or mortality in patients with chronic stable angina.

38. The answer is A.

Coronary angiography with provocative testing. Prinzmetal's variant angina is a type of angina that is caused by coronary artery vasospasm. This means that the coronary arteries narrow, which restricts blood flow to the heart. The diagnosis of Prinzmetal's variant angina can be confirmed by coronary angiography with provocative testing. This involves injecting a drug, such as acetylcholine, that can trigger coronary artery vasospasm. If the patient experiences chest pain and ECG changes consistently with Prinzmetal's variant angina, then the diagnosis is confirmed. The other answer choices are incorrect. Coronary angiography without provocative testing is not as sensitive for diagnosing Prinzmetal's variant angina. ECG, stress test, and echocardiogram can be used to support the diagnosis of Prinzmetal's variant angina, but they cannot confirm the diagnosis. 39. The answer is A. NSTEMI. NSTEMI and STEMI are both types of heart attacks, but they are distinguished by their ECG findings. In NSTEMI, the ECG shows ST-segment depression or T-wave inversion, but there is no ST-segment elevation. In STEMI, the ECG shows ST-segment elevation. The other answer choices are incorrect. Unstable angina is a condition that is similar to NSTEMI, but it does not involve the death of heart muscle tissue. Prinzmetal's variant angina is a type of angina that is caused by coronary artery vasospasm. Pericarditis is an inflammation of the pericardium, which is the sac that surrounds the heart.

40. The answer is A. Tirofiban.

High-risk unstable patients who undergo PCI are at an increased risk of developing a heart attack or stroke. In order to reduce this risk, these patients are often given an intravenous glycoprotein IIb/IIIa antagonist. Glycoprotein IIb/IIIa antagonists work by blocking the binding of platelets together, which helps to prevent the formation of blood clots. Tirofiban and eptifibatide are two of the most commonly used glycoprotein IIb/IIIa antagonists. Tirofiban is administered as a loading dose of 25 g/kg/min followed by a maintenance dose of 0.15 g/kg/min. Eptifibatide is administered as a loading dose of 180 g/kg followed by an infusion of 2 g/kg/min. The other answer choices are incorrect. Aspirin and clopidogrel are antiplatelet agents, but they are not as effective as glycoprotein IIb/IIIa antagonists in preventing heart attacks and strokes in high-risk unstable patients who undergo PCI.

41. The answer is A. Immediate invasive strategy.

Patients with NSTE-ACS who exhibit refractory angina, indications of heart failure or the development or exacerbation of mitral regurgitation, hemodynamic instability, recurrent angina or ischemia during periods of rest or with minimal exertion despite intensive medical treatment, and sustained episodes of ventricular tachycardia or ventricular fibrillation should be managed with an immediate invasive strategy. This means that they should undergo coronary angiography and revascularization as soon as possible. The other answer choices are incorrect. Selective invasive strategy is a management strategy that is used for patients with NSTE-ACS who do not meet the criteria for immediate invasive strategy. Conservative medical therapy is a management strategy that is used for patients with NSTE-ACS who do not meet the criteria for either immediate invasive strategy or selective invasive strategy. Observation is management strategies that is used for patients with NSTE-ACS who are stable and do not meet the criteria for any of the other management strategies.

42. The answer is C. Delayed invasive strategy.

Patients with NSTE-ACS who do not meet the criteria for immediate invasive strategy but have additional factors such as diabetes mellitus, renal insufficiency, reduced left ventricular systolic function, early postinfarction angina, a history of percutaneous coronary intervention within the past 6 months, prior coronary artery bypass graft surgery, or a GRACE risk score between 109 and 140 or a TIMI risk score of 2 or higher should be managed with a delayed invasive strategy. This means that they should undergo coronary angiography and revascularization after a period of observation and medical therapy. The other answer choices are incorrect. Immediate invasive strategy is a management strategy that is used for patients with NSTE-ACS who meet the criteria for immediate invasive strategy. Selective invasive strategy is a management strategy that is used for patients with NSTE-ACS who do not meet the criteria for immediate invasive strategy but do not have any of the additional factors listed above. Conservative medical therapy is a management strategy that is used for patients with NSTE-ACS who do not meet the criteria for either immediate invasive strategy or selective invasive strategy.

43. The answer is C. Apical MI.

Abnormal Q waves in leads V1-V2 are most commonly seen in apical MI. This is because the apical region of the heart is supplied by the left anterior descending artery (LAD), which is the most common site of coronary artery disease. The other answer choices are incorrect. Anterolateral MI typically involves leads I, aVL, V5, and V6. Inferior MI typically involves leads II, III, and aVF. True posterior MI is a rare type of MI that typically involves leads V1-V2. Non-specific ST-T changes can be seen in a variety of conditions, including MI, ischemia, and electrolyte imbalances.

44. The answer is B. Intravenous fibrinolysis. In patients with STEMI, the goal is to restore blood flow to the affected heart muscle as quickly as possible. If PCI is not available or if the delay between initial medical contact and PCI is more than 120 minutes, intravenous fibrinolysis is a viable treatment option. Intravenous fibrinolysis works by breaking up the blood clot that is blocking the coronary artery. The other answer choices are incorrect. Immediate PCI is the preferred treatment option for STEMI, but it is not available in this case. Medical therapy with aspirin and clopidogrel is a good option for patients who are not candidates for fibrinolysis, but it is not as effective as fibrinolysis in restoring blood flow to the heart muscle. Observation is not a recommended treatment option for STEMI.

45. The answer is A. Immediate electrical countershock.

Hemodynamically unstable ventricular tachycardia is a life-threatening arrhythmia that requires immediate treatment. for this arrhythmia. The recommended discharge for this procedure is an unsynchronized discharge of 200-300 J, or 50% less if a biphasic device is being used. The other answer choices are incorrect. Intravenous fibrinolysis is not a recommended treatment for hemodynamically unstable ventricular tachycardia. Medical therapy with aspirin and clopidogrel is a good option for patients who are not candidates for electrical countershock, but it is not as effective in treating this arrhythmia. Observation is not a recommended treatment option for hemodynamically unstable ventricular tachycardia.

46. The answer is E. All of the above.

The primary treatment for acute CHF post MI involves the administration of diuretics, such as furosemide, intravenously at a dosage of 10-20 mg. Inhaled oxygen and vasodilators, specifically nitrates, are recommended. Nitrates can be administered orally, topically, or intravenously, unless the patient is experiencing hypotension, indicated by a systolic blood pressure below 100 mmHg. The therapeutic efficacy of Digitalis in the context of acute myocardial infarction is generally limited. Diuretics help to reduce fluid overload, which is a major cause of CHF. Oxygen helps to improve oxygen delivery to the heart muscle. Nitrates help to dilate the blood vessels, which can improve blood flow to the heart muscle. Digitalis can help to strengthen the heart muscle, but it is not as effective as diuretics, oxygen, and nitrates in treating acute CHF.

47. The answer is D. All of the above.

Cardiogenic shock is a life-threatening condition that occurs when the heart is unable to pump enough blood to meet the body's needs. In cardiogenic shock, the systolic blood pressure is typically below 90 mmHg and the PCWP is elevated. There are a number of treatment options available for cardiogenic shock. These include the administration of vasopressors such as norepinephrine or dopamine, the use of intraaortic balloon counterpulsation (IABP), and mechanical ventilation. Vasopressors work by constricting the blood vessels, which increases the blood pressure. IABP works by inflating a balloon in the aorta during diastole, which increases the blood pressure during this phase of the cardiac cycle. Mechanical ventilation helps to improve the oxygen delivery to the tissues. The choice of treatment for cardiogenic shock depends on the severity of the condition and the patient's individual circumstances. In general, the goal of treatment is to maintain a systolic blood pressure above 90 mmHg and reduce the PCWP.

48. The answer is A. Intravenous fluids.

Right ventricular MI can cause hypotension because the right ventricle is unable to pump blood effectively. This can lead to a decrease in cardiac output and a decrease in blood pressure. The treatment for hypotension caused by right ventricular MI is the administration of intravenous fluids. This will increase the volume of blood in the circulation and help to improve cardiac output. Vasopressors and intraaortic balloon counterpulsation may also be used to treat hypotension caused by right ventricular MI. However, these treatments are typically used only if intravenous fluids are not effective. Mechanical ventilation is not typically used to treat hypotension caused by right ventricular MI. However, it may be used if the patient is also in cardiogenic shock.

49. The answer is E. All of the above.

Atrial flutter is a type of arrhythmia that occurs when the heart's atria (the upper chambers of the heart) beat very fast. This can cause the heart's ventricles (the lower chambers of the heart) to beat too fast, which can lead to symptoms such as palpitations, shortness of breath, and chest pain. The initial treatment for atrial flutter is to slow down the heart rate. This can be done with medications such as beta blockers, verapamil, diltiazem, or digoxin. These medications work by blocking the effects of adrenaline and noradrenaline, which are hormones that speed up the heart rate. If the patient is stable, the doctor may then consider trying to convert the heart back to normal sinus rhythm (NSR). This can be done with electrical cardioversion or with chemical cardioversion. Electrical cardioversion involves using a shock to the heart to stop the atrial flutter and start the heart beating normally again. Chemical cardioversion involves giving the patient a medication that will stop the atrial flutter and start the heart beating normally again.

50. The answer is E. All of the above.

Torsade de pointes is a type of arrhythmia that can be life-threatening. It occurs when the heart's ventricles beat very rapidly and irregularly. This can cause the heart to quiver, which can lead to a loss of consciousness or even death. The treatment for Torsade de pointes is to stop the arrhythmia and to prevent it from happening again. The first step is to give the patient intravenous magnesium. Magnesium helps to stabilize the heart's rhythm. If the magnesium is not effective, the doctor may then try overdrive pacing or the use of isoproterenol. Overdrive pacing involves using a pacemaker to artificially increase the heart rate. Isoproterenol is a medication that increases the heart rate. If the patient is still in Torsade de pointes after these treatments, the doctor may then give the patient lidocaine. Lidocaine is a medication that slows down the heart rate. Torsade de pointes are frequently linked to an extended QT interval, which may arise from congenital factors or drug-induced causes.

51. The answer is E. Electrical cardioversion.

Supraventricular tachycardia with aberrant ventricular conduction is a type of arrhythmia that occurs when the heart's atria beat very fast and the heart's ventricles beat irregularly. This can cause the heart to quiver, which can lead to a loss of consciousness or even death. The treatment for supraventricular tachycardia with aberrant ventricular conduction depends on the patient's individual circumstances. In general, the goal of treatment is to stop the arrhythmia and to prevent it from happening again. If the patient is stable, the doctor may try to slow down the heart rate with medications such as beta blockers, verapamil, diltiazem, or digoxin. However, if the patient is not stable or if the ventricular rate is very high, the doctor may need to use electrical cardioversion to stop the arrhythmia. Electrical cardioversion involves using a shock to the heart to stop the arrhythmia and start the heart beating normally again. In this case, the patient has a ventricular rate of 200 beats per minute, which is very high. Therefore, the doctor will likely recommend electrical cardioversion to stop the arrhythmia.

52. The answer is E. All of the above.

The Class I indications for pacemaker implantation in patients with SA node dysfunction are those that are considered to be the most clear-cut and for which there is the strongest evidence of benefit. These indications include Sinus bradycardia with a heart rate of <40 beats per minute: This is the most common indication for pacemaker implantation in patients with SA node dysfunction. Sinus bradycardia is a slow heart rate that can cause symptoms such as fatigue, lightheadedness, and syncope. Sinus bradycardia with symptoms: Even if the heart rate is >40 beats per minute, if the patient is symptomatic, a pacemaker may be indicated. Symptoms can include fatigue, lightheadedness, and syncope. Sinus bradycardia with symptoms that are refractory to medical therapy: If the patient is taking medications to treat their sinus bradycardia and the symptoms are not improving, a pacemaker may be indicated. Sinus bradycardia with symptoms that are refractory to medical therapy and are associated with an increased risk of syncope: If the patient is taking medications to treat their sinus bradycardia and the symptoms are not improving and the patient is at an increased risk of syncope, a pacemaker may be indicated.

53. The answer is C. Permanent pacemaker implantation.

Mobitz II AV block is a type of heart block that occurs when there is a delay in the conduction of electrical impulses from the atria to the ventricles. This can cause the heart rate to slow down and can lead to symptoms such as lightheadedness, syncope, and chest pain. Mobitz II AV block is a more serious type of heart block than Mobitz I AV block. This is because in Mobitz II AV block, the PR interval is not constant, which can lead to sudden progression to complete heart block. Complete heart block is a condition in which the atria and ventricles are no longer synchronized, which can lead to a very slow heart rate and can be life-threatening. The treatment for Mobitz II AV block is permanent pacemaker implantation. This is because pacemakers can help to regulate the heart rate and prevent sudden progression to complete heart block. In this case, the patient has Mobitz II AV block with a 2:1 conduction pattern. This means that for every two atrial beats, there is only one ventricular beat. This is a serious condition, and the patient should be referred to for permanent pacemaker implantation. The other answer choices are not appropriate for this patient. Observation is not appropriate because the patient is symptomatic. Medications to increase the heart rate may be helpful in some cases, but they are not a long-term solution. Electrophysiology study is a test that can be used to diagnose and evaluate heart block, but it is not necessary in this case.

54. The answer is B. Rate control with beta-blockers.

Atrial fibrillation (AFib) is a type of arrhythmia that occurs when the heart's atria (the upper chambers of the heart) beat very fast and irregularly. This can cause the heart's ventricles (the lower chambers of the heart) to beat too fast, which can lead to symptoms such as palpitations, shortness of breath, and chest pain. The two main approaches to managing AFib are rhythm control and rate control. Rhythm control aims to restore and maintain a normal heart rhythm, usually through medications or procedures such as cardioversion. Rate control seeks to keep the heart rate within a certain range, typically between 60 and 100 beats per minute. In this case, the patient is symptomatic with AFib. Therefore, the best approach is to manage his AFib with rate control. Beta-blockers are a good choice for rate control in patients with AFib because they can slow down the heart rate and reduce the risk of complications such as stroke. The other answer choices are not appropriate for this patient. Rhythm control with cardioversion is not an appropriate option for this patient because he is symptomatic. Rate control with calcium channel blockers is not an appropriate option because calcium channel blockers can worsen heart failure. Ibutilide is a medication that can be used to convert AFib to a normal heart rhythm, but it is not appropriate for patients who are not hemodynamically stable.

55. The answer is E. All of the above.

Atrial fibrillation (AFib) is a type of arrhythmia that occurs when the heart's atria (the upper chambers of the heart) beat very fast and irregularly. This can cause the heart's ventricles (the lower chambers of the heart) to beat too fast, which can lead to symptoms such as palpitations, shortness of breath, and chest pain. The patient in this case has a number of risk factors for stroke, including chronic atrial fibrillation, rheumatic mitral stenosis, and hypertension.

Therefore, he should be managed with a combination of rate control, rhythm control, and anticoagulation therapy. Rate control with beta-blockers or calcium channel blockers is important to slow down the heart rate and reduce the risk of complications such as stroke. Rhythm control with cardioversion may be used to restore a normal heart rhythm, but it is not always successful. Anticoagulation therapy with warfarin or a direct oral anticoagulant is important to reduce the risk of stroke. The other answer choices are not appropriate for this patient. Rate control with digoxin is not an appropriate option because digoxin can worsen heart failure. Rhythm control with ibutilide is not an appropriate option because ibutilide can cause serious side effects such as heart block.

56. The answer is C. Administer digoxin-specific antibody fragments.

Digitalis toxicity is a serious condition that can occur when a patient takes too much digoxin. Symptoms of digitalis toxicity can include nausea, vomiting, visual disturbances, confusion, and heart arrhythmias. The treatment for digitalis toxicity depends on the severity of the symptoms. In mild cases, the doctor may recommend discontinuing digoxin and monitoring the patient's symptoms. In more severe cases, the doctor may administer atropine intravenously or digoxin-specific antibody fragments. Digoxin-specific antibody fragments are a specific antidote for digoxin toxicity. They work by binding to digoxin in the bloodstream and preventing it from binding to its receptors in the heart. This can help to reverse the symptoms of digitalis toxicity. In this case, the patient is experiencing nausea, vomiting, and visual disturbances. These are all symptoms of digitalis toxicity. Therefore, the most appropriate next step in management is to administer digoxin-specific antibody fragments. The other answer choices are not appropriate for this patient. Discontinue digoxin and monitoring her symptoms is not an appropriate option because the patient is already experiencing symptoms of digitalis toxicity. Administering atropine intravenously may help to improve the heart rate, but it will not address the underlying cause of the toxicity. Admitting to the hospital for observation is a good option, but it is not the most appropriate next step in management.

57. The answer is A. Ivabradine.

Ivabradine is a medication that is used to treat heart failure. It works by slowing down the heart rate. This can help to improve the heart's ability to pump blood and reduce the symptoms of heart failure. In this case, the patient has a history of heart failure and an ejection fraction of 30%. He is already taking the maximum tolerated dose of beta-blockers. Therefore, the next best treatment option for this patient is ivabradine. The other answer choices are not appropriate for this patient. Digoxin is a medication that is used to treat heart failure, but it is not as effective as ivabradine in slowing down the heart rate. Ranolazine is a medication that is used to treat angina, but it is not as effective as ivabradine in treating heart failure. Hydralazine/isosorbide dinitrate is a combination medication that is used to treat heart failure, but it is not as effective as ivabradine in slowing down the heart rate. Dobutamine is a medication that is used to treat heart failure, but it is not as effective as ivabradine in improving the heart's ability to pump blood.

58. The answer is B. Norepinephrine.

Sepsis is a life-threatening condition that occurs when the body's response to an infection damages its own tissues and organs. Septic shock is a severe form of sepsis that is characterized by low blood pressure, high heart rate, and low oxygen levels. The treatment for septic shock includes fluids, antibiotics, and vasopressors. Vasopressors are medications that are used to raise blood pressure. Norepinephrine is a vasopressor that is generally preferred over dopamine as the first-line vasopressor agent in the treatment of septic shock. This is because norepinephrine is more selective for alpha-adrenergic receptors, which leads to a more pronounced increase in blood pressure. Dopamine, on the other hand, also activates beta-adrenergic receptors, which can lead to tachycardia and arrhythmias. In addition, norepinephrine has been shown to be more effective than dopamine in reducing mortality in patients with septic shock. The other answer choices are not as appropriate as norepinephrine in this case. Dopamine is a less selective vasopressor that can lead to tachycardia and arrhythmias. Epinephrine is a more potent vasopressor than norepinephrine, but it can also lead to tachycardia and arrhythmias. Vasopressin is a vasopressor that is often used in conjunction with norepinephrine, but it is not as effective as norepinephrine as a single agent. Milrinone is a medication that is used to improve cardiac function, but it is not a vasopressor.

59. The answer is A. Sodium nitroprusside.

Aortic dissection is a serious condition in which the wall of the aorta tears. This can cause blood to flow between the layers of the aorta, creating a false lumen. The false lumen can then expand and rupture, which can be fatal. The treatment for aortic dissection aims to stabilize the patient and prevent the dissection from progressing. This includes the following: Lowering blood pressure: This is done to reduce the pressure inside the aorta and prevent the dissection from expanding. Blood pressure is typically lowered to a target of 100-120 mmHg. Controlling heart rate: Heart rate is controlled to a rate of 60-80 beats per minute. This helps to reduce the workload on the heart and prevent the dissection from progressing. Preventing clot formation: Clots can form in the false lumen and block blood flow to the organs. This can be prevented by using medications such as heparin or aspirin. In the case of a type A aortic dissection, the initial treatment is to lower blood pressure with sodium nitroprusside. This is a medication that relaxes the blood vessels and lowers blood pressure. Metoprolol, verapamil, and diltiazem are also beta-blockers that can be used to lower blood pressure. However, they are not as effective as sodium nitroprusside in the acute setting. Hydralazine is a direct vasodilator that should not be used in patients with aortic dissection because it can increase the risk of aortic rupture. Once the patient's blood pressure is stabilized, other treatments may be considered, such as surgery or endovascular repair.

60. The answer is D, all of the above.

Interventions aimed at significantly lowering LDL-C levels in individuals with hypercholesterolemia can reduce the risk of cardiovascular disease, such as myocardial infarction and stroke, as well as overall mortality. This has been shown in numerous clinical trials, including the landmark Framingham Heart Study. The reason why interventions aimed at lowering LDL-C levels are so effective is because LDL cholesterol is a major risk factor for cardiovascular disease. LDL cholesterol is known as "bad" cholesterol because it can build up in the arteries and form plaques. These plaques can narrow the arteries, making it difficult for blood to flow through them. This can lead to a heart attack or stroke. By lowering LDL-C levels, interventions can help to reduce the risk of these complications. In addition, interventions can also help to improve overall cardiovascular health. For example, they can help to reduce the risk of heart failure and peripheral vascular disease.

61. The correct answer is : A. Cardiac Magnetic Resonance Imaging (MRI).

This patient's clinical presentation suggests a non-ST-elevation myocardial infarction (NSTEMI), yet her cardiac catheterization shows no obstructive coronary disease . This condition, known as myocardial infarction with no obstructive coronary artery disease (MINOCA), is more commonly seen in women. Patients with MINOCA continue to be at risk for major adverse cardiac events, thus it is crucial to investigate alternative causes for the patient's symptoms. Coronary films should be reviewed for any missed dissections, plaque erosion/disruption, emboli, or spasms. Additionally, assessing left ventricular (LV) function is a key step in evaluating such patients. In this case, the patient exhibits depressed LV function and elevated troponin levels. One possible diagnosis to consider given these findings is myocarditis, an inflammation of the myocardium that can result in impaired heart function and elevated cardiac biomarkers. Cardiac MRI is a non-invasive diagnostic tool that is particularly useful in the diagnosis of myocarditis, as it can reveal characteristic patterns of myocardial inflammation and edema. Therefore, it is the most appropriate next step to confirm the diagnosis in this patient. Other options listed, such as pulmonary function tests, abdominal ultrasound, chest X-ray, and carotid Doppler ultrasound, are less relevant in this clinical scenario as they do not directly aid in diagnosing the potential cause of this patient's symptoms.

62. Correct answer: D

Exercise stress testing is not recommended for patients with LBBB because the ECG changes associated with ischemia may be masked by the LBBB pattern. Echocardiography and coronary CTA can be used to evaluate for structural heart disease, but they cannot reliably diagnose ischemia. Cardiac catheterization is the most definitive test for diagnosing coronary artery disease, but it is invasive and should only be performed if the other noninvasive tests are inconclusive. Pharmacologic stress testing with perfusion imaging is the best diagnostic test for this patient. It is a noninvasive test that can reliably diagnose ischemia in patients with LBBB. The most common pharmacologic stress agents are dobutamine and adenosine. These agents dilate the coronary arteries and increase myocardial blood flow. If the patient has coronary artery disease, the areas of the heart that are supplied by the diseased arteries will not receive enough blood flow during stress, and this will show up on the perfusion images. LBBB causes a widening of the QRS complex on the ECG. This can make it difficult to see the ECG changes associated with ischemia. Pharmacologic stress testing with perfusion imaging is a noninvasive and accurate test for diagnosing ischemia in patients with LBBB. It is also relatively safe and well-tolerated. The most common risks of pharmacologic stress testing are mild and temporary, such as headache, flushing, and shortness of breath. More serious side effects, such as chest pain, arrhythmias, and heart attack, are rare. Patients with severe heart failure, unstable angina, or recent myocardial infarction should not undergo pharmacologic stress testing with perfusion imaging.

63. The correct answer is : C. Coronary CT Angiography.

In this patient who has atypical chest pain along with risk factors for coronary artery disease (CAD), a coronary CT angiography is a reasonable test to exclude coronary disease. It provides information about the anatomy of the coronary arteries as well as any stenoses. With its high negative predictive value, it can effectively rule out CAD in patients with an intermediate risk. If positive findings are observed, they may need to be confirmed with a coronary angiogram. Though Cardiac MRI can be used to examine the cardiac structure and function, it is not optimal in an emergency room setting due to the length of the test. Exercise stress testing can evaluate functional capacity and provoke symptoms with exercise, but this patient's chronic knee pain may limit his ability to reach 85% of the maximum predicted heart rate, thus limiting the test's diagnostic ability. Cardiac catheterization, while definitive, is invasive and usually reserved for when non-invasive tests are inconclusive or the patient is at high risk. An Echocardiogram is used mainly for assessing the heart's function and structure but is less sensitive and specific for detecting CAD. Therefore, given this patient's intermediate risk and the need for a relatively quick and reliable diagnostic method, a coronary CT angiography is the most appropriate next step.

64. Correct answer: B

The patient in this vignette has a high-risk stress test for several reasons. He achieved only 4 METs before stopping due to angina, his BP did not augment with exercise, and his ECG at 7 minutes into recovery showed diffuse ST depressions >2 mm and an ST elevation in aVR. These findings are highly concerning for significant coronary artery disease (CAD). Coronary angiography is the most definitive test for diagnosing CAD. It involves injecting a contrast dye into the coronary arteries and then taking X-rays to see how the blood flows through the arteries. Once the diagnosis of CAD is confirmed, coronary angiography can also be used to guide treatment, such as stenting or bypass surgery. The other options are not the best next steps in management. Admitting to the hospital for further monitoring is not necessary unless the patient is unstable or has other symptoms or findings that suggest an acute coronary syndrome. Starting beta blocker therapy is not enough to treat the underlying CAD. Ordering a nuclear stress test would not be as definitive as coronary angiography in this setting. Referring to a cardiologist for follow-up is appropriate, but the cardiologist would likely recommend coronary angiography as the next step in management.

65. The correct answer is: A. Initiate β-blocker and statin.

This patient presents with a syndrome consistent with stable angina. Once CAD is confirmed, optimal medical therapy should be initiated, which includes low-dose aspirin, β-blockers, and statin therapy. Coronary angiography (option B) is typically reserved for patients with refractory symptoms despite optimal medical therapy or those with high-risk stress test findings such as low ejection fraction, severe ischemia in more than one territory, or exercise-induced arrhythmias. While optimizing lipid-lowering therapy (option C) is also important, it's not the only therapy needed. Medical management of CAD requires a combination of antiplatelet, antihypertensive, and lipid-lowering medications. Coronary revascularization (option D) is usually considered after a trial of optimized medical therapy in patients with moderate to severe ischemia and in the absence of left main disease on coronary CT angiography, as per the ISCHEMIA trial. A transthoracic echocardiogram (option E) can identify structural heart disease but is not the next step in the management of this patient's CAD. Therefore, the next best step in managing this patient's CAD would be to initiate β-blocker and statin therapy, hence, the correct answer is option A.

66. Correct answer: D

Access site bleeding is a known complication of cardiac catheterization. The first step in managing active hemorrhage is manual compression of the access site. This should be done by pressing firmly on the common femoral artery, just above the groin. If manual compression is not successful, surgical or percutaneous intervention may be necessary. Starting aspirin and P2Y12 inhibitor therapy would not be helpful in the acute setting, as these medications take time to work. Administering blood products empirically may be necessary if the patient is hemodynamically unstable, but this should be done in consultation with a hematologist. Ordering a CT of the abdomen may be necessary to evaluate for hemoperitoneum, but this should be done after the bleeding has been controlled.

67. Correct Answer: B. Temporarily discontinue clopidogrel and proceed with knee replacement.

Patients who undergo stent placement for managing an acute coronary syndrome are at a higher risk for stent thrombosis and recurrent myocardial infarction. In such cases, dual antiplatelet therapy is recommended for a minimum of 12 months, regardless of the stent type. However, in this case, the patient's severe knee pain necessitates a knee replacement surgery, which may increase the risk of bleeding if dual antiplatelet therapy is continued. The optimal approach would be to temporarily discontinue clopidogrel, which is part of the dual antiplatelet therapy, to permit the knee replacement surgery. The use of intravenous P2Y12 inhibitor cangrelor (option C) is not typically indicated for elective procedures and is more applicable for semi-urgent procedures in patients at high risk of stent thrombosis. Continuing dual antiplatelet therapy and delaying the knee replacement (option D) may not be feasible due to the patient's severe knee pain. Lastly, there is no role for stress testing to guide the duration of dual antiplatelet therapy (option E). Therefore, option B is the most appropriate choice in this scenario.

68. The correct answer is A.

Initiate conservative therapy with aspirin, -blocker, and nitrates as needed, followed by noninvasive risk stratification (stress testing) to help determine if coronary angiography is appropriate, provided the patient remains asymptomatic. The patient in the question is presenting with symptoms suggestive of unstable angina. However, his TIMI score is low (2), indicating a low risk of adverse events. In such cases, a conservative strategy involving optimal medical treatment, followed by noninvasive risk stratification to assess the need for coronary angiography is typically recommended. This strategy is preferred over immediate or early diagnostic angiography for low-risk patients who remain asymptomatic on medical therapy.

69. The correct answer is B.

Within 24 hours. For high-risk patients with elevated troponin, ST-segment changes, or high Global Registry of Acute Coronary Events (GRACE) score (>140), early angiography within 24 hours is recommended[1]. Lower-risk patients (e.g., those without the above features, but with diabetes, chronic kidney disease, percutaneous coronary intervention in the past 6 months, prior coronary artery bypass grafting, or left ventricular ejection fraction <40%) can undergo angiography within 72 hours. Patients with refractory or recurrent angina or hemodynamic or electrical instability should undergo angiography immediately.

70.The correct answer is D. Urgent transthoracic echocardiography. The patient's presentation is suggestive of a ventricular septal defect, a mechanical complication that can develop after a myocardial infarction (MI), particularly in larger territory MIs and late presentations. The harsh holosystolic murmur at the lower sternal border, especially in the presence of a palpable systolic thrill, is pathognomonic for a ventricular septal defect. The diagnosis of a ventricular septal defect is typically made by a transthoracic echocardiogram, making option D the best next step in management. Although an increase of venous oxygen saturation between the right atrium and the pulmonary artery (PA) by right heart catheterization can be suggestive of a ventricular septal defect, it is not the first step in diagnosing this condition. Afterload reducing agents (option A) and interventions such as intra-aortic balloon pump (option C) can help decrease left to right shunting through the ventricular septal defect as a bridge to surgery but these interventions are done after the diagnosis is established. Waiting and observing for further symptoms (option E) is not appropriate in this scenario as the patient's condition requires urgent attention.

71. Answer: C. Calcium channel blocker

Vasospastic angina, also known as Prinzmetal angina, is a type of angina that is caused by a narrowing of the coronary arteries due to spasm. This spasm can be triggered by a variety of factors, including cold weather, stress, and smoking. Calcium channel blockers are the first-line therapy for vasospastic angina because they work to relax the smooth muscles in the coronary arteries, preventing spasm and widening the arteries to improve blood flow. Nitrates can also be effective in treating vasospastic angina, but they are less desirable as a first-line therapy because they can lead to nitrate tolerance, which means that they become less effective over time. Beta-blockers, particularly nonselective beta-blockers, can actually precipitate vasospasm and should therefore be avoided in patients with vasospastic angina. Aspirin should be used with caution in patients with vasospastic angina, as it can inhibit prostacyclin production at high doses, which can also precipitate vasospasm. Therefore, the correct answer is C. Calcium channel blocker.

72. The correct answer is A. Mixed—cardiogenic and distributive.

The patient's hypotension is indicative of a mixed shock state, including both cardiogenic (as evidenced by reduced cardiac output despite inotropic support due to diminished left ventricle [LV] function) and distributive (evidenced by low end of normal systemic vascular resistance but on vasopressor) shock. In pure cardiogenic shock and cardiac tamponade, we would typically expect high filling pressures. In pure distributive shock in a patient with sepsis, we would expect a normal or high cardiac output. Thus, this patient's clinical picture is most consistent with a mixed cardiogenic and distributive shock state.

73. The correct answer is B. Administer intravenous furosemide.

This patient's symptoms of heart failure exacerbation and acute kidney injury are likely due to cardiorenal syndrome, which is often driven by factors such as venous congestion. The initial treatment of choice in such cases is diuresis, which should not only improve the patient's symptoms of congestion but also likely improve her creatinine levels. Intravenous crystalloid, choice A, would likely worsen her heart failure exacerbation. Intravenous inotropic agents, choice C, are not indicated unless the patient's cardiac output is significantly reduced, which does not appear to be the case here. Renal replacement therapy, choice D, would not address the underlying cause of her symptoms, which is the heart failure exacerbation. Finally, urgent cardiac transplantation, choice E, is a drastic measure that would not be considered as an initial treatment in this scenario. Given her limited response to oral diuretics, it is possible that she is experiencing poor gut absorption due to bowel edema. Therefore, the most appropriate next step in her management is to administer intravenous furosemide or another intravenous diuretic, hence choice B is the correct answer.

74. Answer: B. Increased aortic regurgitation

One of the major risks of the intra-aortic balloon pump is that inflation during diastole can increase preexisting aortic regurgitation. This is because the inflated balloon partially obstructs the aortic valve, making it more difficult for the valve to close completely during diastole. Aortic aneurysms and aortic regurgitation are relative contraindications to balloon pump placement because they increase the risk of complications from the procedure. Therefore, the correct answer is B. Increased aortic regurgitation.

75. Answer: D. Spironolactone

Spironolactone is a mineralocorticoid receptor antagonist that is recommended for patients with HFpEF to reduce the risk of rehospitalization for HF. This is based on the results of the TOPCAT trial, which showed that spironolactone reduced the risk of HF hospitalization by 11% in patients with HFpEF. ACE inhibitors, phosphodiesterase type 5 inhibitors, and aspirin have not been shown in clinical trials to reduce the risk of HF hospitalization in patients with HFpEF. Trials of SGLT2i in HFpEF patients are ongoing. Therefore, the correct answer is D. Spironolactone.

76. answer: C.

Insert a percutaneous left ventricular assist device (eg, Impella or Tandem Heart) This patient is in cardiogenic shock due to profound acute decompensated HF. Increasing the dose of the pressor would not address his cardiogenic shock. Similarly, increasing the dose of dobutamine is unlikely to be sufficient and could risk further end-organ damage. An intra-aortic balloon pump is also unlikely to offer adequate support. A percutaneous left ventricular assist device can provide up to 5 L/min cardiac output and would be the next best step, as it can provide the necessary support to improve the patient's condition. It should be noted, however, that randomized trials supporting the use of assist devices are currently lacking, so their use should be carefully considered in the context of the patient's overall health and other treatment options.

77.Correct Answer: B. Initiate angiotensin-converting enzyme (ACE) inhibitor and -blocker; repeat transthoracic echocardiogram in 3 months.

This patient's systolic heart failure may be related to his influenza infection or his alcohol and cocaine use. Regardless of the cause, the first step in management should be to start guideline-directed medical therapy, including an ACE inhibitor and a -blocker, to promote positive left ventricle (LV) remodeling and possibly improve his EF. Additionally, he should be advised to abstain from alcohol and cocaine use, which can contribute to systolic dysfunction. A repeat transthoracic echocardiogram should be performed in 3 months to assess for recovery of function. One month may be too soon to expect significant improvement. If his LV function remains significantly impaired at that time, consideration can be given to placement of an implantable cardiac defibrillator for primary prevention of sudden cardiac death. A myocardial biopsy is not indicated in this case, as it is typically pursued in cases of hemodynamic or electrical instability when the pathology is expected to change the management. Immediate placement of a defibrillator or referral for transplant evaluation would be premature at this stage, as there is a reasonable expectation for recovery in LV function with appropriate therapy and lifestyle modifications.

78. Answer: A. Amyloidosis

Amyloidosis is a condition in which abnormal proteins are deposited in the organs and tissues of the body. This can damage the organs and tissues, including the heart. A classic ECG finding in cardiac amyloidosis is low voltages, despite thick ventricular walls on echocardiogram. This is because the amyloid deposits can interfere with the conduction of electrical signals through the heart. Sarcoidosis is another type of infiltrative cardiomyopathy, but it does not typically cause increased left ventricle (LV) wall thickness. Patients with sarcoidosis may have patchy involvement of the heart, which can lead to a variety of ECG abnormalities, but not typically low voltages. Long-standing hypertension and hypertrophic cardiomyopathy can both cause LV wall thickening, but they do not typically cause low voltages on ECG. Therefore, the most likely diagnosis in a patient with low voltages on ECG and thick ventricular walls on transthoracic echocardiogram is amyloidosis. Additional diagnostic tests for cardiac amyloidosis include:

- Serum and urine protein electrophoresis
- Quantification of serum free light chain ratio
- Possible fat pad biopsy
- Cardiac MRI

79. The correct answer is: C. Refer for mitral valve surgery.

Patients with chronic severe primary mitral regurgitation due to mitral valve prolapse should be referred for mitral valve replacement if they have an EF between 30% and 60% or a LVESD >40 mm, regardless of symptom status. In this case, the patient has an EF of 45% and LVESD of 42mm, meeting the criteria for referral. She has no evidence of congestion, so furosemide (Choice A) is not indicated. Since she already has an indication for mitral valve intervention, additional testing with ambulatory ECG monitoring (Choice D) or repeat echocardiography (Choice B) is not indicated. Beta-blocker therapy (Choice E) is not the primary intervention for her condition. Therefore, referral for mitral valve surgery (Choice C) is the most appropriate next step.

80. Answer: C. Stop coumadin now and bridge with unfractionated heparin.

Patients with mechanical heart valves are at high risk for thromboembolism, so it is important to maintain anticoagulation during and after surgery. Coumadin is a vitamin K antagonist that takes several days to reach its full therapeutic effect. Therefore, it is necessary to bridge patients from coumadin to heparin before surgery. Unfractionated heparin is a parenteral anticoagulant that has a rapid onset of action. It is the preferred bridging anticoagulant for patients with mechanical heart valves because it is effective and has a relatively low risk of hemorrhage. NOACs are contraindicated in patients with mechanical heart valves because they are not as effective at preventing thromboembolism in this population. Therefore, the best anticoagulation management strategy for this patient is to stop coumadin now and bridge with unfractionated heparin. The heparin should be started 24 hours before surgery and continued until the patient is back on coumadin with a therapeutic INR. The patient's INR should be checked at least 24 hours before surgery to ensure that it is within the therapeutic range. The patient's heparin dosage should be adjusted based on their INR. The patient should be monitored closely for signs of bleeding and thrombosis.

81. Answer: D. Refer for PMBV as anatomy allows.

Rheumatic mitral stenosis is a common valvular heart disease in pregnant women, and it can pose a significant risk to both the mother and the fetus. The increased cardiac output and blood volume of pregnancy can lead to decompensation of mitral stenosis and the development of heart failure. In pregnant women with moderate-to-severe mitral stenosis and heart failure, PMBV is the preferred treatment modality. PMBV is a minimally invasive procedure that can widen the mitral valve opening and improve cardiac function. It is safe and effective in pregnant women, and it can be performed at any stage of pregnancy. Surgical mitral valve replacement is a more invasive procedure and is typically reserved for pregnant women with severe mitral stenosis who do not respond to PMBV or who have other medical conditions that make PMBV high-risk. Termination of pregnancy is only recommended in pregnant women with severe mitral stenosis and heart failure who are not candidates for PMBV or surgery. Therefore, the best management strategy for this patient is to refer her for PMBV as anatomy allows. The patient's mitral valve anatomy should be assessed by echocardiography to determine if she is a candidate for PMBV. The patient's cardiac function and symptoms should be closely monitored during pregnancy. The patient should be counseled about the risks and benefits of PMBV and surgery.

82. Answer-C. Give 500 mL fluid bolus

The patient's presentation is suggestive of tamponade, which is characterized by Beck's triad (distant heart sounds, elevated jugular vein pulsation, and hypotension). The initial treatment for suspected tamponade involves volume expansion, hence the administration of a 500 mL fluid bolus. This is done while formulating a diagnostic and therapeutic plan. Performing an emergent transthoracic echocardiogram (Option A) is crucial to measure the size and location of the effusion, but it is typically done after initial fluid resuscitation. Similarly, initiating a pericardiocentesis (Option B) usually requires confirmation of the effusion's location and size, which is best done after volume expansion and echocardiogram. A pulmonary embolism CT scan (Option D) would not be the first step, as the history and physical are primarily suggestive of a pericardial effusion. A pericardial window (Option E) might be needed for posterior effusions not amenable to pericardiocentesis, but it's not the first step in management.

83. The correct answer is B. Constrictive pericarditis.

Constrictive pericarditis may occur in 1% to 2% of cases following pericarditis. In patients with tuberculosis, bacterial infections, neoplasm, or, as in this case, exposure to radiation therapy, the risk of developing constrictive pericarditis is higher. This condition occurs when there is adhesion between the visceral and parietal pericardium, resulting in a rigid pericardium limiting diastolic filling and increasing venous pressures. The limitation of venous return occurs only after the rapid filling stage following the opening of the tricuspid valve. These patients often present with the Kussmaul sign, which manifests as a jugular venous pulsation that does not decrease with inspiration. Sometimes, a pericardial knock may be present. ECG may show low voltages, but constrictive pericarditis does not cause conduction disease, which is more commonly seen with restrictive cardiomyopathy. Clinically, patients often have signs and symptoms of right-sided heart failure on examination with clear lungs. Diagnostically, a transthoracic echocardiogram reveals respirophasic variation, where during inspiration there is increased flow seen across the tricuspid valve and decreased flow across the mitral valve. Other findings include expiratory hepatic vein flow reversal. On simultaneous left and right heart catheterization, there is equalization of the ventricular end-diastolic pressures between the right and left ventricles and discordance of the right ventricular and left ventricular pressure peaks during the respiratory cycle.

84. Answer: A. Calculating his ASCVD risk score and, if >10%, starting an antihypertensive agent now.

The 2017 ACC/AHA blood pressure guidelines recommend starting antihypertensive therapy for adults with stage 1 hypertension (blood pressure of 130-139/80-89 mmHg) if they have clinical cardiovascular disease or a calculated AS-CVD risk score of >10%. ASCVD risk scores are calculated using a variety of factors, including age, sex, race/ethnicity, blood pressure, cholesterol levels, smoking status, and diabetes status. For this patient, it is important to calculate his ASCVD risk score to determine whether he should start antihypertensive therapy now. If his ASCVD risk score is >10%, then antihypertensive therapy should be initiated. If his ASCVD risk score is <10%, then lifestyle changes should be recommended and his blood pressure should be monitored closely. Follow-up in 3 months is appropriate to assess his blood pressure response to lifestyle changes and to determine if antihypertensive therapy is needed. The patient should be counseled on the importance of lifestyle changes, such as weight loss, healthy diet, exercise, and smoking cessation. The patient should be instructed to monitor his blood pressure at home and to keep a record of his readings. The patient should be scheduled for follow-up in 3 months to assess his blood pressure response and to determine if antihypertensive therapy is needed.

85. The correct answer is: D. Lisinopril (ACE inhibitor)

First-line antihypertensives include ACE inhibitors, calcium channel blockers, and diuretics. However, the choice of which antihypertensive to initiate depends on the presence of comorbidities. In patients with diabetes mellitus who have microalbuminuria, it's recommended to start with an ACE inhibitor, barring any contraindications. ACE inhibitors have been shown to provide specific renal benefits in diabetic patients, such as reducing proteinuria and slowing the progression of diabetic nephropathy, hence their first-line status in this patient population. Options A, B, C, and E may also be used to manage hypertension but they are not the first-line choice in this specific clinical scenario.

86. Answer: B. Intravenous labetalol

This patient is experiencing a hypertensive emergency complicated by aortic dissection. Aortic dissection is a life-threatening condition in which the inner layer of the aorta tears, allowing blood to flow between the layers of the aorta. This can lead to rupture of the aorta and death. Hypertensive emergency is defined as a severe elevation in blood pressure (greater than 220/120 mmHg) that is associated with end-organ damage. In this patient, the aortic dissection is evidence of end-organ damage. The goal of initial management is to rapidly lower blood pressure and heart rate to reduce the risk of aortic rupture. Intravenous labetalol is a beta-blocker with alpha-blocking properties. It is the preferred initial agent for hypertensive emergency complicated by aortic dissection. Labetalol blocks both beta-adrenergic and alpha-adrenergic receptors, resulting in a decrease in heart rate, blood pressure, and systemic vascular resistance. Oral labetalol is not preferred in this setting because it takes longer to take effect. Intravenous nitroglycerin is a vasodilator that can lead to reflex tachycardia, which is undesirable in this patient. Intravenous nitroprusside and esmolol are also vasodilators, but they are not preferred over labetalol in this setting because they do not provide the same degree of heart rate control. The patient should be admitted to the intensive care unit for close monitoring and management. After initial blood pressure and heart rate control, imaging studies such as a computed tomography (CT) scan or transesophageal echocardiogram (TEE) should be performed to confirm the diagnosis of aortic dissection and determine the extent of the dissection. Once the diagnosis is confirmed, the patient should be treated with definitive therapy, such as endovascular repair or open surgery.

87. The correct answer is: A. MR angiography (MRA) of the renal arteries.

In this young patient with severe hypertension and an abdominal bruit, renal artery stenosis secondary to fibromuscular dysplasia should be strongly suspected. An MRA of the renal arteries would be a reasonable first step in her diagnostic evaluation. Although a duplex ultrasound (option B) can be considered, it cannot definitively exclude fibromuscular dysplasia. A noncontrast CT scan (option C) will not visualize the vasculature adequately. In some instances, direct visualization with renal angiography (option D) may be required if clinical suspicion remains high, but a diagnosis cannot be made noninvasively. For patients with confirmed fibromuscular dysplasia in whom BP cannot be controlled, percutaneous transluminal renal angioplasty (option E) should be considered. However, these are subsequent steps after initial diagnosis, making option A the most appropriate initial step.

88. Answer: C. Perform surgical repair of the AAA.

The guidelines for the management of AAAs are based on the size and rate of growth of the aneurysm. Surgical repair is recommended for AAAs that are 5.5 cm in size or those that are growing at a rate of >0.5 cm/y. In this patient, the AAA is 5.2 cm in size and has grown by 0.5 cm in the past 6 months. Therefore, the best management strategy is to perform surgical repair of the AAA. EVAR is a less invasive alternative to open surgical repair, but it is not recommended for all patients with AAAs. EVAR is typically reserved for patients who are considered to be high risk for open surgery. The patient's risk factors for cardiovascular disease should be assessed and managed. The patient should be counseled on the risks and benefits of surgical repair. The patient should be prepared for surgery and managed postoperatively.

89. The correct answer is D. Arrange for urgent surgical intervention.

This patient's physical characteristics strongly suggest Marfan syndrome, a connective tissue disorder that makes him susceptible to aortic dissection. The acute chest and back pain, diastolic murmur suggestive of aortic regurgitation, and new signs of heart failure (bilateral pulmonary rales) are concerning for a proximal aortic dissection (type A). Type A dissections are a surgical emergency and require urgent intervention. In contrast, distal aortic dissections (type B) may be managed medically by decreasing the rate of change of pressure in the aorta over time (dP/dt) and targeting a heart rate of less than 60 beats per minute and a central systolic blood pressure less than 120 mmHg. While patients with Marfan syndrome are indeed at increased risk for pneumothorax, this patient's clinical presentation is much more consistent with aortic dissection, thus necessitating urgent surgical intervention.

90. Answer: D. Place a transvenous temporary pacemaker.

This patient has a clinical syndrome concerning for early disseminated Lyme disease, which can include complete heart block due to Lyme carditis. His hemodynamic instability is a contraindication to observation alone. Atropine is a temporary treatment for bradycardia that works by blocking the vagus nerve, which slows the heart rate. However, it is not a definitive treatment for complete heart block. TEE is an imaging test that can be used to assess cardiac function and to rule out other causes of heart block, such as structural heart disease. However, it is not necessary to perform TEE before placing a temporary pacemaker in a hemodynamically unstable patient with complete heart block. Intravenous antibiotics are the definitive treatment for Lyme disease, but they may not resolve the heart block completely. Therefore, a temporary pacemaker is needed to support the patient's heart rate while the antibiotics take effect. A permanent pacemaker is not immediately indicated in this patient because the heart block may resolve following a course of antibiotics. However, if the heart block does not resolve, a permanent pacemaker may be necessary. Therefore, the best management strategy is to place a transvenous temporary pacemaker.

91. Answer: B. Multifocal atrial tachycardia

The ECG findings in this patient are consistent with multifocal atrial tachycardia (MAT). MAT is an arrhythmia characterized by an irregular rhythm with three or more distinct P-wave morphologies. It is most commonly seen in patients with chronic lung disease, such as COPD. The other answer choices are less likely. Atrial fibrillation (AF) is an arrhythmia characterized by chaotic atrial activation, resulting in the absence of distinct P waves on ECG. Atrioventricular nodal reentrant tachycardia (AVNRT) and Wolff-Parkinson-White syndrome (WPW) are arrhythmias characterized by reentry through the atrioventricular node. These arrhythmias may have a retrograde P wave on ECG, but they typically have a regular rhythm. The treatment of MAT depends on the underlying cause and the severity of the patient's symptoms. In patients with COPD, treatment of the underlying lung disease is often sufficient to resolve the MAT. In other cases, medications such as beta-blockers, calcium channel blockers, or digoxin may be used to control the heart rate. If the MAT is severe or does not respond to medical therapy, ablation of the ectopic foci may be considered.

92. The correct answer is: D. Procainamide. In patients with WPW syndrome, a rapid supraventricular tachycardia can conduct through both the atrioventricular node and the accessory pathway. If a medication is administered that purely blocks the atrioventricular node, there is a risk that the rhythm might travel exclusively down the accessory

pathway and degenerate into ventricular fibrillation. For this reason, procainamide is the drug of choice as it will stabilize the atrial rhythm. Digoxin (Choice B) and adenosine (Choice A) will primarily target the atrioventricular node and are therefore contraindicated. Direct current cardioversion (Choice C) may eventually be required, but it is not emergent at this time if the patient is stable. Not treating the condition (Choice E) is not an option as it could lead to serious complications.

93. Answer: B. Long QT interval

The most likely cause of this patient's arrhythmia is an acquired long QT syndrome. Long QT syndrome is a condition in which the heart takes longer than normal to recharge between beats. This can lead to a variety of arrhythmias, including polymorphic ventricular tachycardia. Acquired long QT syndrome can be caused by a number of factors, including medications, electrolyte imbalances, and underlying medical conditions. In this patient, the most likely cause is the broad-spectrum antibiotics she is taking. Many antibiotics can prolong the QT interval, and this risk is increased in patients with other risk factors, such as female sex and hypokalemia. The other answer choices are less likely. Brugada syndrome is a rare genetic disorder that causes sudden cardiac death. It is typically associated with a different ECG pattern (type 1 Brugada pattern) and is more common in young men. Arrhythmogenic right ventricular cardiomyopathy is another rare condition that can cause sudden cardiac death. It is typically associated with monomorphic ventricular tachycardia and is more common in middle-aged men. Ischemia can cause polymorphic ventricular tachycardia, but this is more common in patients with underlying cardiovascular disease. Left bundle branch block is a conduction disorder that can be associated with ischemia, but it is not a direct cause of ventricular tachycardia. The treatment of acquired long QT syndrome is to discontinue any QT-prolonging medications and to correct any electrolyte imbalances. If the patient is hemodynamically unstable, cardioversion or defibrillation may be necessary. In some cases, medications such as beta-blockers or magnesium may be used to shorten the QT interval and prevent further arrhythmias. It is important to be aware of the medications that can prolong the QT interval and to use them with caution in patients with risk factors for long QT syndrome. It is also important to correct any electrolyte imbalances, such as hypokalemia, which can increase the risk of long QT syndrome.

94. The correct answer is: D. Perform radiofrequency ablation.

The patient presents with recurrent ventricular tachycardia, which has been occurring despite being on adequate medical therapy (-blockers, mexiletine, amiodarone). Her most recent coronary angiogram suggests that her ventricular tachycardia is not driven by ischemia. This indicates that the current medical therapy is not providing sufficient control of her arrhythmia. Option A is incorrect because simply increasing the dosage of -blockers may not address the underlying issue, as the patient's ventricular tachycardia has been recurring despite being on -blockers already. Option B is incorrect as changing mexiletine to another antiarrhythmic drug may not be effective, given that the patient's ventricular tachycardia is not responding to the current antiarrhythmic medications. Option C is incorrect as anticoagulation therapy is typically used for prevention of thromboembolic events in disorders such as atrial fibrillation or deep vein thrombosis, and it does not address the issue of recurrent ventricular tachycardia. Option E is incorrect because while implantation of a cardiac defibrillator can be useful in preventing sudden death from ventricular tachycardia, it does not treat or prevent the recurrence of the arrhythmia itself. Radiofrequency ablation (Option D) is a procedure that uses radio waves to destroy small areas of heart tissue that may be causing your heart's rhythm problems. This can be an effective therapy for recurrent ventricular tachycardia or ventricular tachycardia storm, making it the most appropriate next step in care for this patient.

95. Answer: C.

Perform transesophageal echocardiogram (TEE); if no left atrial thrombus, perform cardioversion. This patient has a tachycardia-induced cardiomyopathy, which is a reversible form of heart failure that can occur in patients with chronic tachycardia. The goal of treatment is to restore sinus rhythm and to control the heart rate. In this patient, increasing her heart rate control medications is unlikely to be sufficient to improve her left ventricular function. Starting her on anticoagulation is important to prevent thromboembolism, but it will not reverse her cardiomyopathy. Ablation of AF is a procedure that can be used to treat AF, but it is typically not recommended as a first-line therapy in patients with tachycardia-induced cardiomyopathy. Therefore, the best management strategy is to perform a TEE to rule out a left atrial thrombus. If there is no thrombus, then cardioversion can be performed to restore sinus rhythm. Once the patient is in sinus rhythm, her left ventricular function is likely to improve.

96. The correct answer is: A. Amiodarone.

The patient has new-onset AF and a history of an ischemic cardiomyopathy. Both flecainide (option B) and propafenone (option C) are class Ic antiarrhythmic drugs and can be useful for the management of AF. However, class

Ic drugs are contraindicated in patients with ischemia or structural heart disease because they can potentially worsen the condition. Although amiodarone (option A) has potential side effects, it can be used to maintain sinus rhythm in patients with structural heart disease. Amiodarone is a class III antiarrhythmic drug and is often used in patients with AF, especially those with structural heart disease. It acts by prolonging the action potential duration and refractory period in all cardiac tissues, thereby making it effective for both ventricular and supraventricular arrhythmias. A nondihydropyridine calcium channel blocker such as diltiazem (option D) may be helpful for rate control but is not typically considered to be an antiarrhythmic therapy and is contraindicated in heart failure (HF) as it might cause a decrease in cardiac output, exacerbating symptoms in patients with HF. Option E, metoprolol, is a ₋blocker that may be used for rate control in AF but it does not typically convert AF to sinus rhythm or prevent future episodes of AF. Therefore, it is less suitable than amiodarone in this context.

97. The correct answer is: A. Andexanet alfa.

This patient presents with a life-threatening traumatic intracranial hemorrhage following a mechanical fall. She is on both aspirin and apixaban, which increases her risk of bleeding. In the acute setting, reversal of the effect of both agents would be indicated with both platelet transfusion and andexanet alfa. Andexanet alfa (option A) is a recombinant factor Xa protein that reverses the effect of factor Xa inhibitors, including apixaban. This would be the most appropriate immediate intervention to manage her condition. Option B, Idarucizumab, is a monoclonal antibody that reverses the effect of the direct thrombin inhibitor dabigatran, not a factor Xa inhibitor like apixaban. Fresh frozen plasma (option C) contains all factors in the soluble coagulation system and can be utilized to restore factor deficiencies in patients who are bleeding or are planned to undergo procedures. However, it wouldn't be as effective or rapid in reversing the effects of apixaban as andexanet alfa. Vitamin K (option D) will reverse the effects of warfarin but not a factor Xa inhibitor like apixaban. Option E, Platelet transfusion, is also necessary given her use of aspirin, which inhibits platelet function. However, this alone would not reverse the anticoagulant effect of the apixaban.

98. Answer: B.

DOACs are not indicated for stroke prevention in patients with AF and rheumatic mitral stenosis. DOACs are not indicated for stroke prevention in patients with AF and rheumatic mitral stenosis because they have not been studied in this population and may not be as effective as warfarin. Warfarin remains the only recommended oral anticoagulant for stroke prevention in patients with AF and rheumatic mitral stenosis. Patients with rheumatic mitral stenosis are at very high risk for stroke. DOACs have been shown to be effective for stroke prevention in patients with AF without rheumatic mitral stenosis. DOACs have a lower risk of intracranial hemorrhage than warfarin. DOACs require less frequent monitoring than warfarin. Overall, DOACs are not indicated for stroke prevention in patients with AF and rheumatic mitral stenosis.

99. Answer: B. Lead perforation leading to cardiac tamponade

The patient's clinical presentation is most consistent with cardiac tamponade secondary to pacemaker lead perforation. Cardiac tamponade is a condition in which fluid accumulates in the pericardium, the sac that surrounds the heart. This can put pressure on the heart and make it difficult to pump blood effectively. Pacemaker lead perforation is a complication of pacemaker implantation that can occur when the lead perforates the heart wall. This can lead to bleeding into the pericardium and cardiac tamponade. The other answer choices are less likely. Pacemaker syndrome is a condition that can occur in patients with pacemakers that are not programmed properly. It is characterized by a feeling of pulsation in the neck and a decrease in blood pressure when the patient stands up. Pacemaker-mediated tachycardia is a type of arrhythmia that can occur in patients with pacemakers. It is characterized by a rapid, irregular heart rate. Flash pulmonary edema is a condition that can occur in patients with acute heart failure. It is characterized by a sudden onset of shortness of breath and cough. The diagnosis of cardiac tamponade is based on the patient's clinical presentation and imaging studies. Echocardiography is the most useful imaging study for diagnosing cardiac tamponade. It can show the presence of pericardial fluid and the collapse of the right atrium and right ventricle during diastole. The treatment of cardiac tamponade is to remove the fluid from the pericardium. This can be done with a pericardiocentesis, which is a minimally invasive procedure. In some cases, open heart surgery may be necessary. The prevention of pacemaker lead perforation is to use caution during pacemaker implantation and to avoid implanting pacemakers in patients with thin heart walls.

100. The correct answer is: C. Plan for pacemaker system removal.

This patient's presentation suggests pacemaker infection. The presence of fever, positive blood cultures growing S. aureus, and erythema around his device site are all indicative of this. Despite not having evidence of endocarditis on TEE, the presence of staphylococcal bacteremia necessitates definitive therapy with system removal. Options A (Continue oral antibiotics) and B (Continue intravenous antibiotics) would be inadequate therapy in this case. Even though antibiotics can treat the bacteremia, they cannot completely eradicate the infection that is likely attached to the pacemaker device. Option D (Valve surgery) is not appropriate as the patient does not have evidence of endocarditis. Finally, simply increasing the dosage of the current medication (option E) would not be sufficient to treat the source of infection - the infected pacemaker system. Therefore, the most appropriate treatment plan would be to remove the pacemaker system (option C).

101. The correct answer is E. Acute pericarditis.

The patient's symptoms and ECG findings are consistent with acute pericarditis. The classic ECG findings in pericarditis include PR segment depression, which is caused by inflammation of the pericardium interfering with electrical conduction between the atria and ventricles, and ST-segment elevation, which can be caused by irritation of the epicardium, the outer layer of the heart. Electrical alternans, seen in about 50% of cases of pericarditis, is caused by the swinging of the heart within the pericardial sac, which changes the distance between the electrodes and the heart muscle.

A. Myocardial infarction: While this can cause ST-segment elevation, it would also typically cause Q waves and T-wave inversion, which are not present in this case. B. Pulmonary embolism: This condition can cause chest pain and shortness of breath, but it would not typically cause an ECG with the findings seen in this case. C. Pneumonia: This can cause chest pain and fever, but it would not typically cause an ECG with the findings seen in this case. D. Pericardial effusion: This can cause ST-segment elevation, but it would not typically cause PR segment depression. Therefore, based on the patient's symptoms and ECG findings, acute pericarditis is the most likely diagnosis.

102. The correct answer is C. Monitor her QT interval regularly.

The patient's ECG shows a prolonged QT interval, which can increase the risk of a serious heart rhythm disorder called Torsades de Pointes (TdP). This can lead to fainting or even sudden death. Both fluoxetine and lorazepam can cause QT prolongation, but the risk is generally low and these medications are important for managing her mental health conditions.

Therefore, the most appropriate next step in management is to monitor her QT interval regularly, especially since she is taking medications that can prolong the QT interval. If her QT interval continues to increase or if she develops symptoms of TdP (such as fainting), then further action may be needed, such as adjusting her medications or considering other treatments.

The other options are less likely:

A. Discontinue fluoxetine and lorazepam immediately: This could worsen her mental health conditions and is not necessary unless her QT interval is significantly prolonged or she has symptoms of TdP. B. Start her on a beta-blocker: Beta-blockers can be used to treat some heart conditions, but they are not the first-line treatment for a prolonged QT interval without other heart conditions. D. Start her on a calcium channel blocker: Calcium channel blockers can be used to treat some heart conditions, but they are not the first-line treatment for a prolonged QT interval without other heart conditions. E. Refer her for an implantable cardioverter-defibrillator (ICD): An ICD can be used to treat serious heart rhythm disorders, but it is not necessary unless she has a very high risk of sudden cardiac death, such as a significantly prolonged QT interval with symptoms of TdP.

103. The correct answer is A. T-wave flattening or inversion.

The patient's symptoms and laboratory tests are consistent with hypokalemia, which is a common side effect of thiazide diuretics like hydrochlorothiazide. Hypokalemia can disrupt the electrical activity of the heart, leading to characteristic changes on an ECG. Early changes in hypokalemia often include T-wave flattening or slight inversion, typically seen in leads II, III, and aVF initially, and mild ST-segment depression, usually occurring in leads V5 and V6.

The other options are less likely:

B. QRS widening: This indicates prolonged conduction through the ventricles and is seen in extreme cases of hypokalemia, not typically at the level seen in this patient. C. ST-segment elevation: This is not a typical finding in hypokalemia. D. PR segment elevation: This is not a typical finding in hypokalemia. PR segment depression may occur with more severe hypokalemia. E. Absence of P waves: This is not a typical finding in hypokalemia. It is more commonly seen in atrial fibrillation or other atrial arrhythmias. Therefore, based on the patient's symptoms, laboratory tests, and the effects of hypokalemia on the ECG, T-wave flattening or inversion is the most likely ECG finding.

104. The correct answer is C. Administer intravenous calcium gluconate.

The patient's symptoms and laboratory tests are consistent with hyperkalemia, which can disrupt the electrical activity of the heart, leading to characteristic changes on an ECG such as tall peaked T waves. Hyperkalemia can be life-threatening due to the risk of cardiac arrhythmias and cardiac arrest.

The initial management of hyperkalemia involves counteracting the cardiac manifestations of hyperkalemia. Intravenous calcium gluconate is used to stabilize the cardiac membrane and reduce the risk of arrhythmias. It does not lower the potassium level but it helps to counteract the effects of hyperkalemia on the heart.

The other options are less likely: A. Administer sodium polystyrene sulfonate: This medication helps to eliminate potassium from the body and is usually used for chronic management of hyperkalemia, not for initial acute management. B. Start him on a loop diuretic: This can help to eliminate potassium from the body through the urine, but it is not the first-line treatment for acute hyperkalemia. D. Discontinue lisinopril: ACE inhibitors like lisinopril can cause hyperkalemia, so it may be appropriate to discontinue this medication. However, this is not the first-line treatment for acute hyperkalemia. E. Start him on a beta-blocker: Beta-blockers are not used in the management of hyperkalemia. Therefore, based on the patient's symptoms, laboratory tests, and the effects of hyperkalemia on the ECG, the most appropriate initial step in management is to administer intravenous calcium gluconate.

105. The correct answer is A. Prolonged QT interval.

The patient's symptoms, history of thyroidectomy (which can sometimes inadvertently result in removal or damage to the parathyroid glands leading to hypocalcemia), and laboratory tests are consistent with hypocalcemia. Hypocalcemia can disrupt the electrical activity of the heart, leading to characteristic changes on an ECG. The most consistent and characteristic ECG finding in hypocalcemia is a prolonged QT interval, which arises due to delayed ventricular repolarization caused by calcium's role in cell membrane stability. Hypocalcemia, characterized by low blood calcium levels, can leave its mark on your electrocardiogram (ECG). Recognizing these changes is crucial for prompt diagnosis and treatment. Here's a breakdown of the key findings:
The Hallmarks:

- Prolonged QT interval: This is the most consistent and characteristic ECG finding in hypocalcemia. It arises due to delayed ventricular repolarization caused by calcium's role in cell membrane stability.
- Lengthened ST segment: This often accompanies the prolonged QT interval, appearing as a subtle elevation of the baseline between the QRS complex and the T wave.
- Other potential findings:
-
- T-wave changes: T waves may be flattened or slightly inverted, initially in leads II, III, and aVF, and progress to deeper and more widespread inversion with worsening hypocalcemia.
- U waves: Prominent U waves may become evident, sometimes merging with the T wave.
- PR segment depression and QT-interval prolongation: These occur less frequently but can be seen in severe cases.
- QRS widening: In extreme cases, prolonged conduction through the ventricles can lead to widening of the QRS complex.

106. The correct answer is B. Shortened QT interval.

The patient's symptoms and laboratory tests are consistent with hypercalcemia, which is characterized by high blood calcium levels. One of the key ECG findings in hypercalcemia is a shortened QT interval. It arises due to accelerated ventricular repolarization caused by high calcium levels.
The other options are less likely:
A. Prolonged QT interval: This is a characteristic finding in hypocalcemia, not hypercalcemia. C. Prominent U waves: Prominent U waves may be seen in hypokalemia, but they are not a typical finding in hypercalcemia. D. PR segment elevation: PR segment elevation is not a typical finding in hypercalcemia. E. QRS narrowing: QRS widening may occur in extreme cases of hypocalcemia, indicating prolonged conduction through the ventricles, but it is not a typical finding in hypercalcemia. Therefore, based on the patient's symptoms, laboratory tests, and the ECG findings associated with hypercalcemia, the most likely finding on the ECG is a shortened QT interval.

107. The correct answer is C. Inferior ST-elevation myocardial infarction.

The patient's symptoms and ECG findings are consistent with an ST-elevation myocardial infarction (STEMI), a type of heart attack characterized by complete blockage of blood flow to a portion of the heart. The presence of ST elevations in leads III and aVF, which represent the inferior (or bottom) part of the heart, suggests an inferior STEMI.

The ST depressions in leads I and aVL are reciprocal changes often seen in inferior STEMI. The ST depressions in leads V2 and V3 may indicate posterior myocardial ischemia, and the T-wave inversions in V4 to V6 could suggest lateral wall ischemia. This patient meets STEMI criteria and requires urgent revascularization.

The other options are less likely:

A. Anterior ST-elevation myocardial infarction: This would typically present with ST elevations in the anterior leads (V1-V4), which is not the case here. B. Pericarditis: This condition typically presents with diffuse ST elevations in multiple leads, not the localized changes seen in this patient. D. Stable angina: This condition does not typically cause ST elevations on ECG. E. Unstable angina: This condition may cause ST depressions or T wave inversions, but not the ST elevations seen in this patient. Therefore, based on the patient's symptoms and ECG findings, the most likely diagnosis is an inferior ST-elevation myocardial infarction.

108. Answer: B. Begin chest compressions and prepare for defibrillation.

This patient's presentation is consistent with ventricular tachycardia (VT) leading to cardiac arrest. The absence of a central pulse indicates that the patient is in a state of hemodynamic compromise, and immediate intervention is required.

The most appropriate initial management in this case is to begin chest compressions and prepare for defibrillation (Option B) as per the Advanced Life Support (ALS) guidelines This is because VT is a shockable rhythm, and immediate defibrillation is the treatment of choice in a pulseless patient.

Option A (Administer intravenous beta-blockers): Beta-blockers are used in the management of stable VT or in cases of long QT syndrome to prevent torsade de pointes . However, in a cardiac arrest situation, immediate life-saving measures like chest compressions and defibrillation are needed. Option C (Administer intravenous amiodarone): Amiodarone is a Class III antiarrhythmic drug that can be used in the management of VT However, it is not the first-line treatment in a cardiac arrest situation. Defibrillation is the priority in this scenario. Option D (Perform immediate DC cardioversion): While DC cardioversion is indeed used in the management of VT, in a cardiac arrest situation, chest compressions should be initiated first. This is because the patient may be in a state of low perfusion, and chest compressions can help to improve perfusion and increase the chances of successful defibrillation. Option E (Administer intravenous fluids): Intravenous fluids are not the first-line treatment in a cardiac arrest situation. They may be used as part of the post-resuscitation care to maintain adequate perfusion, but they are not the immediate priority.

109. Answer: D. Junctional supraventricular tachycardia (SVT); treat with vagal maneuvers and adenosine.

The patient's presentation is consistent with junctional supraventricular tachycardia (SVT), a narrow-complex tachycardia originating from the AV node. This diagnosis is supported by the sudden onset of palpitations, the regular rhythm, the heart rate above 120 beats per minute, and the absence of visible P waves on the ECG. The initial treatment for SVT includes vagal maneuvers followed by adenosine. Vagal maneuvers, such as the Valsalva maneuver or carotid sinus massage, can help slow the heart rate and potentially terminate the tachycardia. If these maneuvers are unsuccessful, adenosine can be administered intravenously to block AV node conduction and terminate the tachycardia.

Option A (Sinus tachycardia; treat with beta-blockers): While sinus tachycardia can be caused by stress and anxiety, it rarely goes above 120 beats per minute. Also, sinus tachycardia typically presents with visible P waves on the ECG, which are not seen in this case. Option B (Atrial flutter; treat with electrical cardioversion): Atrial flutter typically presents with a "sawtooth" pattern on the ECG, which is not described here. Also, the heart rate in atrial flutter is usually closer to 300 beats per minute. Option C (Ventricular tachycardia; treat with defibrillation): Ventricular tachycardia is a wide-complex tachycardia, whereas the question describes a narrow-complex tachycardia. Also, ventricular tachycardia is typically associated with structural heart disease, which the patient does not have. Option E (Atrial fibrillation; treat with anticoagulation): Atrial fibrillation is characterized by an irregularly irregular rhythm, which is not described in this case. Also, anticoagulation is not the initial treatment for a new onset of atrial fibrillation; rate or rhythm control would be the first step. In summary, the most likely diagnosis for this patient is junctional SVT, and the initial treatment should include vagal maneuvers followed by adenosine.

110. Answer: B. Hyperkalemia; treat with calcium gluconate, insulin and dextrose, and urgent dialysis

The patient's presentation and ECG findings are consistent with severe hyperkalemia. The sine wave pattern on the ECG is a classic sign of severe hyperkalemia, which can quickly deteriorate into ventricular fibrillation. Other ECG changes in hyperkalemia can include peaking of the T-waves, a decrease in the height of the P-wave and an increase in the PR interval, and widening of the QRS complex. The immediate treatment for severe hyperkalemia includes administration of calcium gluconate for cardioprotection, insulin and dextrose to drive potassium into the intracellular space, and urgent dialysis to decrease total body potassium. Option A (Hypokalemia; treat with oral potassium supplements): Hypokalemia would present with different ECG changes, such as flattened T waves, prominent U waves, and ST segment depression. Option C (Hypocalcemia; treat with intravenous calcium): Hypocalcemia can cause prolonged QT interval on ECG, which is not described in this case. Option D (Hypercalcemia; treat with intravenous fluids and furosemide): Hypercalcemia can cause a shortened QT interval on ECG, which is not described in this case. Option E (Hyponatremia; treat with hypertonic saline): Hyponatremia does not typically cause specific ECG changes.

111. Answer: C. Wolff-Parkinson-White (WPW) syndrome; treat with catheter ablation.

The patient's presentation and ECG findings are consistent with Wolff-Parkinson-White (WPW) syndrome. This condition is characterized by the presence of an accessory pathway that bypasses the normal electrical conduction system of the heart, leading to a shortened PR interval and a 'delta wave' on the ECG. The initial treatment for WPW syndrome is typically catheter ablation. This procedure involves the use of radiofrequency energy to destroy the accessory pathway, thereby restoring normal electrical conduction in the heart.
Option A (Atrial fibrillation; treat with electrical cardioversion): Atrial fibrillation is characterized by an irregularly irregular rhythm and absence of P waves on the ECG, which is not described in this case.
Option B (Ventricular tachycardia; treat with defibrillation): Ventricular tachycardia is a wide-complex tachycardia, whereas the question describes a narrow-complex tachycardia. Also, ventricular tachycardia is typically associated with structural heart disease, which the patient does not have. Option D (Long QT syndrome; treat with beta-blockers): Long QT syndrome is characterized by a prolonged QT interval on the ECG, which is not described in this case. Option E (Brugada syndrome; treat with an implantable cardioverter-defibrillator (ICD)): Brugada syndrome is characterized by specific ST-segment elevation in the right precordial leads (V1-V3) on the ECG, which is not described in this case.

112. Answer: C. Posterior myocardial infarction; treat with percutaneous coronary intervention (PCI).

The patient's presentation and ECG findings are consistent with an acute posterior myocardial infarction (MI). The 'upside down' ST elevation seen in the anterior leads represents what is happening in the posterior region of the heart. This is a classic sign of a posterior MI. The bradycardia could be due to the involvement of the 'pacemaker' region of the SA node, which is often supplied by the same vessels that supply the posterior region of the heart. The initial treatment for an acute MI, whether it is anterior or posterior, is typically percutaneous coronary intervention (PCI), if it can be performed in a timely manner. This procedure involves the use of a catheter to open up the blocked coronary artery and restore blood flow to the heart muscle.
Option A (Anterior myocardial infarction; treat with PCI): The ECG findings are not consistent with an anterior MI, which would show ST elevation in the anterior leads. Option B (Posterior myocardial infarction; treat with thrombolytic therapy): While thrombolytic therapy can be used in the treatment of an acute MI, PCI is generally the preferred initial treatment if it can be performed in a timely manner. Option D (Anterior myocardial infarction; treat with thrombolytic therapy): Again, the ECG findings are not consistent with an anterior MI. Option E (Pericarditis; treat with NSAIDs): Pericarditis would typically present with diffuse ST elevation and PR depression on the ECG, which is not described in this case.

113. Answer: C. Torsades de pointes; treat with intravenous magnesium

The patient's presentation and ECG findings are consistent with Torsades de pointes, a type of polymorphic ventricular tachycardia. This condition can be precipitated by a number of causes, including medications and electrolyte imbalances, and is often associated with a prolonged QT interval. The initial treatment for Torsades de pointes is typically intravenous magnesium, regardless of the patient's serum magnesium concentration. This can help to stabilize the heart's electrical activity and prevent further episodes of this potentially life-threatening arrhythmia.
Option A (Ventricular fibrillation; treat with defibrillation): Ventricular fibrillation is a life-threatening condition that requires immediate defibrillation. However, the ECG findings described in the question are more consistent with Torsades de pointes. Option B (Atrial fibrillation; treat with electrical cardioversion): Atrial fibrillation is characterized by an irregularly irregular rhythm, which is not described in this case. Option D (Supraventricular tachycardia; treat with adenosine): Supraventricular tachycardia is a narrow-complex tachycardia, whereas the question describes a polymorphic ventricular tachycardia. Option E (Sinus tachycardia; treat with beta-blockers): Sinus tachycardia is a regular tachycardia originating from the sinus node, which is not described in this case.

114. Answer: B. Atrial fibrillation; treat with rate control and anticoagulation

The patient's presentation and ECG findings are consistent with atrial fibrillation (AF). This condition is characterized by an irregularly irregular rhythm and the absence of P waves on the ECG. AF can be triggered by a number of factors, including heavy alcohol consumption, which is often referred to as 'holiday heart' syndrome. The initial treatment for AF typically involves rate control and anticoagulation. Rate control can be achieved with medications such as beta-blockers or calcium channel blockers, while anticoagulation is used to reduce the risk of stroke.

Option A (Sinus tachycardia; treat with beta-blockers): Sinus tachycardia is characterized by a regular rhythm with a rate above 100 beats per minute, which is not described in this case. Option C (Ventricular fibrillation; treat with defibrillation): Ventricular fibrillation is a life-threatening condition that requires immediate defibrillation. However, the ECG findings described in the question are more consistent with AF. Option D (Supraventricular tachycardia; treat with adenosine): Supraventricular tachycardia is a narrow-complex tachycardia with a regular rhythm, which is not described in this case. Option E (Atrial flutter; treat with electrical cardioversion): Atrial flutter is characterized by a regular rhythm with a 'sawtooth' pattern on the ECG, which is not described in this case.

115. Answer:B. Atrial flutter; treat with electrical cardioversion.

The patient's presentation and ECG findings are consistent with atrial flutter. This condition is characterized by a regular rhythm with a rate typically around 150 beats per minute and a 'seesaw' baseline on the ECG. Atrial flutter can be triggered by a number of factors, including heavy alcohol consumption.

The initial treatment for atrial flutter is typically electrical cardioversion. This procedure involves the use of a controlled electric shock to restore the heart's normal rhythm.

Option A (Atrial fibrillation; treat with rate control and anticoagulation): Atrial fibrillation is characterized by an irregularly irregular rhythm, which is not described in this case.

Option C (Ventricular tachycardia; treat with defibrillation): Ventricular tachycardia is a life-threatening condition that requires immediate defibrillation. However, the ECG findings described in the question are more consistent with atrial flutter.

Option D (Supraventricular tachycardia; treat with adenosine): Supraventricular tachycardia is a narrow-complex tachycardia with a regular rhythm, which is not described in this case.

Option E (Sinus tachycardia; treat with beta-blockers): Sinus tachycardia is characterized by a regular rhythm with a rate above 100 beats per minute, which is not described in this case.

116. Answer:C. Mobitz type 2 second-degree AV block; treat with pacemaker implantation.

The patient's presentation and ECG findings are consistent with Mobitz type 2 second-degree AV block. This condition is characterized by a constant PR interval with occasional non-conducted beats. It can lead to episodes of dizziness due to the intermittent drop in heart rate. The initial treatment for Mobitz type 2 second-degree AV block is typically pacemaker implantation. This is because this type of block can unpredictably progress to complete heart block, which can be life-threatening.

Option A (Sinus bradycardia; treat with atropine): Sinus bradycardia is characterized by a regular rhythm with a rate below 60 beats per minute, which is not described in this case. Option B (Mobitz type 1 second-degree AV block; treat with observation): Mobitz type 1 second-degree AV block, also known as Wenckebach block, is characterized by a progressively lengthening PR interval until a beat is dropped. This is not described in this case. Option D (Third-degree AV block; treat with pacemaker implantation): Third-degree AV block, or complete heart block, is characterized by a complete dissociation between the atrial and ventricular rhythms. This is not described in this case. Option E (Supraventricular tachycardia; treat with adenosine): Supraventricular tachycardia is characterized by a regular, rapid rhythm, which is not described in this case.

117. D. Third-degree AV block; treat with pacemaker implantation.

The patient's presentation and ECG findings are consistent with third-degree AV block, also known as complete heart block. This condition is characterized by a complete loss of communication between the atria and the ventricles. The atrial rate continues as normal, but the ventricular rate is slower and not associated with the P waves. The initial treatment for third-degree AV block is typically pacemaker implantation. This is because this type of block can lead to a dangerously slow heart rate, causing symptoms such as dizziness and fatigue. Option A (First-degree AV block; treat with observation): First-degree AV block is characterized by a prolonged PR interval, which is not described in this case. Option B (Mobitz type 1 second-degree AV block; treat with observation): Mobitz type 1 second-degree AV block, also known as Wenckebach block, is characterized by a progressively lengthening PR interval until a beat is dropped. This is not described in this case. Option C (Mobitz type 2 second-degree AV block; treat with pacemaker implantation): Mobitz type 2 second-degree AV block is characterized by a constant PR interval with occasional non-conducted beats. This is not described in this case. Option E (Supraventricular tachycardia; treat with adenosine): Supraventricular tachycardia is characterized by a regular, rapid rhythm, which is not described in this case.

118. Answer:D. Trifascicular block; treat with pacemaker implantation

The patient's presentation and ECG findings are consistent with trifascicular block. This condition is characterized by a block in two fascicles and a delay in the third, which is indicated by a bifascicular block with a prolonged PR interval. Trifascicular block can lead to episodes of dizziness and fainting due to the intermittent drop in heart rate. The initial treatment for trifascicular block is typically pacemaker implantation. This is because this type of block can unpredictably progress to complete heart block, which can be life-threatening.

Chapter 6

PULMONOLOGY BOARD QUESTIONS

1. A 58-year-old woman presents to the emergency department with complaints of shortness of breath and cyanosis. On physical examination, she is found to have bluish discoloration of her lips, tongue, and oral mucosa. Which of the following is the most likely diagnosis?

- A. Peripheral cyanosis
- B. Central cyanosis
- C. Methemoglobinemia
- D. Carbon monoxide poisoning
- E. Hypoxia

2. A 57-year-old woman with hypertension presents to her doctor with a complaint of a persistent dry cough. She has been taking an ACE inhibitor for the past 6 months. Which of the following is the most likely etiology of her cough?

- A. ACE inhibitor-induced cough
- B. Postnasal drip
- C. Asthma
- D. Lung cancer
- E. Pneumonia

3. A 62-year-old man presents to the emergency department with hemoptysis. He reports coughing up a large amount of blood, approximately 300 mL, over the past hour. He has no other medical problems and takes no medications. His vital signs are within normal limits. Which of the following is the most appropriate definition of massive hemoptysis?

- A. Hemoptysis that is greater than 100 mL in a 24-hour period
- B. Hemoptysis that is greater than 150 mL in a single episode
- C. Hemoptysis that is greater than 400 mL in a 24-hour period
- D. Hemoptysis that is greater than 600 mL in a 24-hour period
- E. Hemoptysis is greater than 800 mL in a 24-hour period.

4. A 59-year-old man with a history of smoking presents to his doctor with complaints of shortness of breath and wheezing. He has been experiencing these symptoms for the past few months and they have been getting worse. His physical examination is significant for decreased breath sounds on auscultation. A chest X-ray shows hyperinflation of the lungs. Spirometry shows a reduced FEV1/FVC ratio of 0.6. Which of the following is the most likely diagnosis?

Dr Rafael Zioni

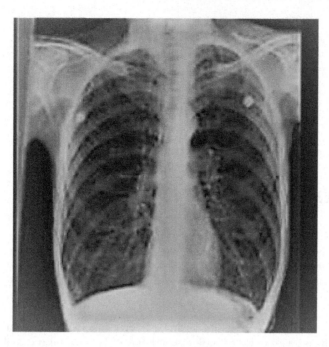

Figure 6.1: hyperinflation

- A. Asthma
- B. Chronic obstructive pulmonary disease (COPD)
- C. Emphysema
- D. Bronchiectasis
- E. Pulmonary fibrosis

5. A 71-year-old woman with a history of rheumatoid arthritis presents to her doctor with complaints of shortness of breath and dry cough. She has been experiencing these symptoms for the past few months and they have been getting worse. Her physical examination is significant for decreased breath sounds on auscultation. A chest X-ray shows decreased lung volumes. Spirometry shows a reduced TLC of 60% predicted. Which of the following is the most likely diagnosis?

- A. Asthma
- B. Chronic obstructive pulmonary disease (COPD)
- C. Emphysema
- D. Pulmonary fibrosis

6. A 48-year-old woman with a history of asthma presents to her doctor with complaints of shortness of breath and wheezing. She has been experiencing these symptoms for the past few months and they have been getting worse. Her physical examination is significant for decreased breath sounds on auscultation. A chest X-ray shows hyperinflation of the lungs. Spirometry shows a FEV1 of 2.0 L and a FEV1/FVC ratio of 0.7. After the administration of albuterol, her FEV1 increases to 2.4 L and her FEV1/FVC ratio increases to 0.8. Which of the following is the most likely diagnosis?

- A. Asthma
- B. Chronic obstructive pulmonary disease (COPD)
- C. Emphysema
- D. Bronchiectasis
- E. Pulmonary fibrosis

7. A 53-year-old woman with a history of asthma presents to her doctor with complaints of shortness of breath and wheezing. She has been experiencing these symptoms for the past few months and they have been getting worse. She has been taking a short-acting 2-adrenergic agonist inhaler, but she has been experiencing tremors and palpitations.

Which of the following is the most likely explanation for her symptoms?

- A. Her asthma is getting worse.
- B. She is taking too much of the 2-adrenergic agonist inhaler.
- C. She is experiencing side effects from the 2-adrenergic agonist inhaler.
- D. She has a different underlying medical condition.
- E. She is not taking the 2-adrenergic agonist inhaler correctly.

8. A 38-year-old woman with a history of asthma presents to her doctor with complaints of shortness of breath and wheezing. She has been experiencing these symptoms for the past few months and they have been getting worse. She has been taking a long-acting 2-adrenergic agonist (LABA) inhaler, but she has not been taking any inhaled corticosteroids. Which of the following is the most likely explanation for her symptoms?

- A. Her asthma is getting worse.
- B. She is taking too much of the LABA inhaler.
- C. She is experiencing side effects from the LABA inhaler.
- D. She needs to be taking inhaled corticosteroids in addition to the LABA inhaler.
- E. She is not taking the LABA inhaler correctly.

9. A 49-year-old woman with a history of asthma presents to the emergency department with shortness of breath. She has been experiencing these symptoms for the past few hours and they have been getting worse. Her physical examination is significant for decreased breath sounds on auscultation. A chest X-ray shows hyperinflation of the lungs. Her blood gas analysis shows a decreased oxygen saturation of 88%. Which of the following is the most likely outcome of this patient's asthma exacerbation?

- A. Hypoxemia
- B. Hypercapnia
- C. Respiratory failure
- D. Death
- E. All of the above

10. A 41-year-old woman with a history of asthma presents to the emergency department with shortness of breath. She has been experiencing these symptoms for the past few hours and they have been getting worse. Her physical examination is significant for decreased breath sounds on auscultation. A chest X-ray shows hyperinflation of the lungs. Her blood gas analysis shows a decreased oxygen saturation of 88%. Which of the following is the most appropriate modality for the administration of corticosteroids in this patient?

- A. Oral prednisone
- B. Intravenous methylprednisolone
- C. Both oral prednisone and intravenous methylprednisolone
- D. Neither oral prednisone nor intravenous methylprednisolone

11. A 57-year-old woman presents to her doctor with complaints of shortness of breath and wheezing. She has been working as a hair stylist for the past 20 years and has noticed that her symptoms are worse at work. She has been taking a short-acting 2-agonist inhaler, but it is not providing adequate relief. Her doctor suspects that she may have occupational asthma. Which of the following is the most appropriate test to help diagnose occupational asthma?

- A. Spirometry
- B. Chest X-ray
- C. Skin prick test
- D. Methacholine challenge test
- E. All of the above

12. A 72-year-old man with a history of asbestos exposure presents to his doctor with complaints of shortness of breath and a dry cough. He has been experiencing these symptoms for the past few months and they have been getting worse. His physical examination is significant for decreased breath sounds on auscultation. A chest X-ray shows diffuse interstitial infiltrates. Which of the following is the most likely diagnosis?

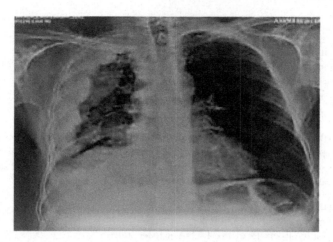

Figure 6.2: 72-year-old man

- A. Pleural plaques
- B. Interstitial lung disease
- C. Benign pleural effusion
- D. Lung cancer
- E. Mesothelioma

13. A 76-year-old man with a 20-pack-year smoking history presents to his doctor with complaints of shortness of breath. He has been experiencing these symptoms for the past few months and they have been getting worse. His physical examination is significant for decreased breath sounds on auscultation. A chest X-ray shows small, rounded opacities throughout both lungs. Which of the following is the most likely diagnosis?

- A. Simple coal workers' pneumoconiosis (CWP)
- B. Progressive massive fibrosis (PMF)
- C. Sarcoidosis
- D. Tuberculosis
- E. Lung cancer

14. A 58-year-old man with a history of beryllium exposure presents to his doctor with complaints of shortness of breath and a dry cough. He has been experiencing these symptoms for the past few months and they have been getting worse. His physical examination is significant for decreased breath sounds on auscultation. A chest X-ray shows diffuse interstitial infiltrates. Which of the following tests is most likely to help differentiate between chronic beryllium disease (CBD) and sarcoidosis?

- A. Lymphocyte proliferation test
- B. Chest CT scan
- C. Pulmonary function tests
- D. Skin biopsy
- E. All of the above

15. A 59-year-old man with a history of COPD presents to his doctor with complaints of shortness of breath. He has been experiencing these symptoms for the past few months and they have been getting worse. His physical examination is significant for decreased breath sounds on auscultation. A chest X-ray shows hyperinflation of the lungs. Arterial blood gas analysis shows a partial pressure of oxygen (PaO2) of 57 mmHg and a saturation of arterial oxygen (SaO2) of 87%. Which of the following is the most appropriate recommendation for oxygen therapy?

- A. Oxygen therapy is not indicated.
- B. Oxygen therapy should be initiated to increase the SaO2 level to at least 90
- C. Oxygen therapy should be initiated only if the patient develops clinical manifestations of pulmonary hypertension or cor pulmonale.
- D. Oxygen therapy should be initiated only if the patient develops shortness of breath at rest.

• E. Oxygen therapy should be initiated only if the patient develops shortness of breath with exertion.

16. A 66-year-old man with a history of COPD presents to his doctor with complaints of shortness of breath. He has been experiencing these symptoms for the past few years and they have been getting worse. His physical examination is significant for decreased breath sounds on auscultation. A chest X-ray shows hyperinflation of the lungs. Pulmonary function tests show a forced expiratory volume in 1 second (FEV1) of 1.2 L (20% predicted) and a diffusing capacity of the lungs for carbon monoxide (DLCO) of 0.8 mL/min/mmHg (20% of predicted). Which of the following is the most appropriate recommendation for lung volume reduction surgery?

• A. The patient should be considered for lung volume reduction surgery.
• B. The patient should not be considered for lung volume reduction surgery because his FEV1 is too low.
• C. The patient should not be considered for lung volume reduction surgery because his DLCO is too low.
• D. The patient should not be considered for lung volume reduction surgery because he has a diffuse distribution of emphysema.
• E. The patient should not be considered for lung volume reduction surgery because he has both a low FEV1 and a low DLCO.

17. A 44-year-old woman presents with a deep vein thrombosis in her right leg. She has no personal or family history of venous thromboembolism. Which of the following genetic risk factors is most likely to be present?

• A. Factor V Leiden
• B. Prothrombin G20210A mutation
• C. Deficiency of antithrombin
• D. Deficiency of protein C
• E. Deficiency of protein S

18. A 53-year-old man presents to the emergency department with shortness of breath, chest pain, and syncope. He has a history of deep vein thrombosis 6 months ago. His vital signs are: blood pressure 90/60 mmHg, heart rate 120 beats per minute, respiratory rate 30 breaths per minute, and oxygen saturation 88% on room air. His physical exam is notable for jugular venous distension, rales on lung exam, and cyanosis of the lips and nail beds. Which of the following is the most likely diagnosis?

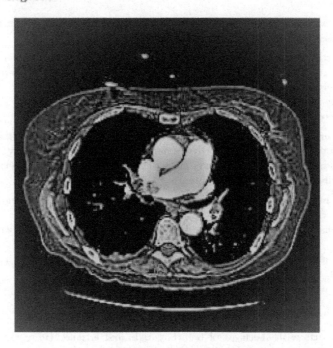

Figure 6.3: CT scan

• A. Massive pulmonary embolism

- B. Acute myocardial infarction
- C. Pneumonia
- D. Aortic dissection
- E. Tension pneumothorax

19. A 65-year-old woman presents to the emergency department with shortness of breath and chest pain. She has a heart rate of 110 beats per minute, and her oxygen saturation is 92% on room air. She has no history of deep vein thrombosis or pulmonary embolism. She has been immobilized in bed for the past 3 days due to a recent surgery. On physical exam, she has no clinical signs of deep vein thrombosis. She does have hemoptysis. Which of the following is the most likely Wells score for this patient?

- A. 0
- B. 1
- C. 2
- D. 3
- E. 4

20. A 70-year-old woman with a history of deep vein thrombosis is admitted to the hospital with a suspected pulmonary embolism. She is started on unfractionated heparin (UFH). Which of the following is the correct dosing strategy for UFH?

- A. Initial bolus dose of 80 units per kilogram, followed by a continuous infusion at a rate of 12 units per kilogram per hour.
- B. Initial bolus dose of 80 units per kilogram, followed by a continuous infusion at a rate of 18 units per kilogram per hour.
- C. Initial bolus dose of 100 units per kilogram, followed by a continuous infusion at a rate of 20 units per kilogram per hour.
- D. Initial bolus dose of 120 units per kilogram, followed by a continuous infusion at a rate of 24 units per kilogram per hour.
- E. Initial bolus dose of 140 units per kilogram, followed by a continuous infusion at a rate of 28 units per kilogram per hour.

21. A 68-year-old woman with metastatic breast cancer is diagnosed with a deep vein thrombosis in her left leg. Which of the following is the standard treatment protocol for this patient?

- A. Low molecular weight heparin (LMWH) for 3 months, followed by warfarin for 6 months.
- B. Low molecular weight heparin (LMWH) indefinitely unless the patient achieves a state of cancer remission.
- C. Warfarin indefinitely unless the patient achieves a state of cancer remission.
- D. Aspirin indefinitely unless the patient achieves a state of cancer remission.
- E. No treatment is necessary, as the VTE is likely to resolve on its own.

22. A 64-year-old man presents to the emergency department with shortness of breath and chest pain. He has a history of deep vein thrombosis 6 months ago. His computed tomography pulmonary angiogram (CTPA) shows a large pulmonary embolism in the right main pulmonary artery. Which of the following is the best definition of low-dose, ultrasound-facilitated, catheter-directed thrombolysis?

- A. A treatment that uses a low dose of a thrombolytic agent, such as tissue plasminogen activator (tPA), and ultrasound to help break up a blood clot.
- B. A treatment that uses a high dose of a thrombolytic agent, such as tPA, and ultrasound to help break up a blood clot.
- C. A treatment that uses a low dose of a thrombolytic agent, such as tPA, and a mechanical device to help break up a blood clot.
- D. A treatment that uses a high dose of a thrombolytic agent, such as tPA, and a mechanical device to help break up a blood clot.
- E. None of the above.

23. A 36-year-old man presents with shortness of breath, cough, and fatigue. He works as a farmer and has been exposed to dust from moldy hay. Which of the following is the most likely diagnosis?

- A. Hypersensitivity pneumonitis
- B. Pneumoconiosis

- C. Asthma
- D. Chronic obstructive pulmonary disease (COPD)
- E. Lung cancer

24. A 54-year-old man presents with shortness of breath, cough, and fatigue. He has no history of smoking or other lung diseases. His chest X-ray shows diffuse ground-glass opacities. His pulmonary function tests show a restrictive pattern. A bronchoalveolar lavage (BAL) is performed and shows milky fluid with foamy macrophages. Which of the following is the most likely diagnosis?

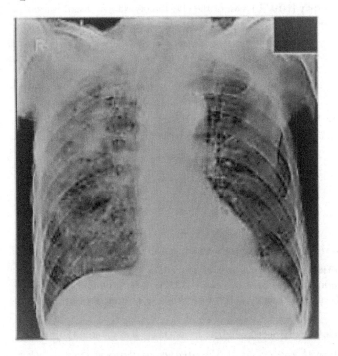

Figure 6.4: 54-year-old man

- A. Acquired pulmonary alveolar proteinosis (PAP)
- B. Pneumonia
- C. Interstitial lung disease (ILD)
- D. Sarcoidosis
- E. Lymphangioleiomyomatosis (LAM)

25. A 68-year-old woman presents with shortness of breath and dry cough. She has a history of smoking for 40 years. Her chest X-ray shows diffuse interstitial markings. Her pulmonary function tests show a restrictive pattern with a decreased forced vital capacity (FVC) and forced expiratory volume in 1 second (FEV1). Which of the following is the most likely diagnosis?

- A. Interstitial lung disease (ILD)
- B. Asthma
- C. Chronic obstructive pulmonary disease (COPD)
- D. Pneumonia
- E. Heart failure

26. A 58-year-old man presents with shortness of breath, cough, and fatigue. He has a history of asthma and is a smoker. His chest X-ray shows diffuse interstitial markings. His pulmonary function tests show a restrictive pattern with a decreased forced vital capacity (FVC) and forced expiratory volume in 1 second (FEV1). Which of the following ILDs are most amenable to treatment with glucocorticoids?

- A. Eosinophilic pneumonia

- B. Chronic obstructive pulmonary disease (COPD)
- C. Hypersensitivity pneumonitis (HP)
- D. Acute radiation pneumonitis
- E. Drug-induced interstitial lung disease (ILD)

27. A 62-year-old man presents with shortness of breath, cough, and fatigue. He has no history of smoking or other lung diseases. His chest X-ray shows diffuse interstitial markings. His pulmonary function tests show a restrictive pattern with a decreased forced vital capacity (FVC) and forced expiratory volume in 1 second (FEV1). A high-resolution computed tomography (HRCT) scan of the chest shows classic usual interstitial pneumonia (UIP) patterns. Is a surgical lung biopsy typically necessary in order to definitively establish the diagnosis of IPF?

- A. Yes, in most cases, a surgical lung biopsy is necessary to definitively establish the diagnosis of IPF.
- B. No, a surgical lung biopsy is not necessary in this case, as the patient has classic UIP patterns on HRCT scan.
- C. It is difficult to say without further testing, such as bronchoalveolar lavage (BAL).
- D. It is difficult to say without further testing, such as a transbronchial biopsy.
- E. It is difficult to say without further testing, such as a serum blood test.

28. What is the typical pulmonary manifestation observed in granulomatous vasculitides, such as granulomatosis with polyangiitis (GPA)?

- A. Nodules
- B. Infiltrates
- C. Hemoptysis
- D. Pleural effusion
- E. All of the above

29. What are the three established criteria for diagnosing an exudative pleural effusion?

- A. Pleural fluid to serum protein ratio greater than 0.5.
- B. Pleural fluid to serum lactate dehydrogenase (LDH) ratio greater than 0.6.
- C. Pleural fluid LDH greater than 2/3 the upper limit of normal serum LDH.
- D. All of the above.

30. What distinguishes spontaneous pneumothorax from traumatic pneumothorax?

- A. Spontaneous pneumothorax occurs in the absence of thoracic trauma, whereas traumatic pneumothorax arises from either penetrating or nonpenetrating chest trauma.
- B. Spontaneous pneumothorax is more common in men, whereas traumatic pneumothorax is more common in women.
- C. Spontaneous pneumothorax is more likely to be recurrent, whereas traumatic pneumothorax is less likely to be recurrent.
- D. Spontaneous pneumothorax is more likely to be associated with underlying lung disease, whereas traumatic pneumothorax is less likely to be associated with underlying lung disease.

31. What additional conditions are correlated with obstructive sleep apnea-hypopnea syndrome (OSAHS)?

- A. Depression
- B. Hypertension
- C. Diabetes
- D. All of the above

32. A 55-year-old man presents with shortness of breath, fatigue, and chest pain. He has a history of hypertension and hyperlipidemia. His physical exam is notable for jugular venous distension, peripheral edema, and a right ventricular heave. His chest X-ray shows cardiomegaly and pulmonary vascular congestion. What are the most likely manifestations of pulmonary hypertension in this patient?

- A. Exertional dyspnea, fatigue, angina, syncope, and peripheral edema.
- B. Exertional dyspnea, fatigue, and syncope.
- C. Exertional dyspnea and fatigue.
- D. Fatigue and syncope.
- E. None of the above.

33. What are the primary laboratory findings and diagnostic tests employed for the evaluation and diagnosis of pulmonary hypertension?

- A. Chest X-ray (CXR), electrocardiogram (ECG), echocardiogram, pulmonary function tests (PFTs), and chest computed tomography (CT).
- B. CXR, ECG, echocardiogram, PFTs, CT, ANA titer assessment, rheumatoid factor evaluation, anti-Scl-70 antibody testing, and HIV screening.
- C. CXR, ECG, echocardiogram, PFTs, CT, BNP and NT-proBNP levels, and right heart catheterization.
- D. All of the above.

34. What are some therapeutic interventions that have received approval for the treatment of pulmonary arterial hypertension (PAH)?

- A. Endothelin receptor antagonists like bosentan, macitentan, and ambrisentan.
- B. Phosphodiesterase type 5 inhibitors such as sildenafil and tadalafil.
- C. Prostaglandins like iloprost, epoprostenol, and treprostinil.
- D. The oral soluble guanylyl cyclase stimulator riociguat.
- E. All of the above.

35. Under what circumstances is lung transplantation a potential treatment option for pulmonary arterial hypertension (PAH)?

- A. Persistent right heart failure.
- B. Failure of medical therapies.
- C. Both A and B.
- D. Neither A nor B.

36. What are the findings on a chest X-ray in cases of acute pulmonary edema?

- A. Pulmonary vascular redistribution.
- B. Diffuse haziness in the lung fields.
- C. Perihilar "butterfly" appearance.
- D. All of the above.

37. What are the indicated inotropic agents for the treatment of cardiogenic pulmonary edema and severe left ventricular dysfunction?

- A. Dopamine.
- B. Dobutamine.
- C. Milrinone.
- D. All of the above

38. What are the primary diagnostic criteria for Acute Respiratory Distress Syndrome (ARDS)?

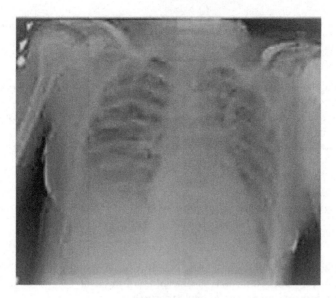

Figure 6.5: ARDS

- A. The presence of diffuse bilateral pulmonary infiltrates as observed on chest X-ray.
- B. A ratio of arterial partial pressure of oxygen (PaO2) to inspired oxygen fraction (FIO2) equal to or less than 300 mmHg.
- C. The absence of elevated pressure in the left atrium.
- D. All of the above.

39. What is the presently endorsed ventilator strategy for patients with acute respiratory distress syndrome (ARDS)?

- A. Low tidal volumes (equal to or less than 6 milliliters per kilogram of predicted body weight) in combination with positive end-expiratory pressure (PEEP) set at levels that minimize alveolar collapse and achieve adequate oxygenation with the lowest possible fraction of inspired oxygen (FIO2) requirement.
- B. High tidal volumes (greater than 10 milliliters per kilogram of predicted body weight) in combination with low positive end-expiratory pressure (PEEP) levels.
- C. High tidal volumes (greater than 10 milliliters per kilogram of predicted body weight) in combination with high positive end-expiratory pressure (PEEP) levels.
- D. Low tidal volumes (equal to or less than 6 milliliters per kilogram of predicted body weight) in combination with low positive end-expiratory pressure (PEEP) levels.

40. What threshold value of the ratio f/VT, measured at the conclusion of the spontaneous breathing test, indicates the need for a trial of extubation?

- A. Less than 105.
- B. Greater than 105.
- C. Between 90 and 105.
- D. Cannot be determined from the information provided.

41. A patient presents with a reduced diffusion capacity on PFTs. Which of the following is the least likely cause?

- (A) Pulmonary embolism
- (B) Neuromuscular disease
- (C) Pulmonary fibrosis
- (D) Anemia
- (E) Interstitial lung disease

42. A patient with a history of asthma presents with evidence of acutely worsened airflow obstruction in the setting of a likely viral exacerbation of asthma. There is no evidence of pneumonia or anaphylaxis. What is the best initial step in the management of this patient?

- A) Administer albuterol nebulizers and IV methylprednisolone.
- B) Administer epinephrine.
- C) Administer magnesium.
- D) Administer noninvasive positive-pressure ventilation.
- E) Administer antibiotics.

43. A 46-year-old woman with a history of asthma presents with a sudden worsening of her symptoms. She has recently been exposed to a basement renovation. On examination, she has wheezing and crackles in her lungs. Her chest X-ray shows central bronchiectasis. Her laboratory results are as follows:

- Total IgE: 1,000 IU/mL
- Aspergillus-specific IgE: 20 IU/mL
- Aspergillus-specific IgG: 40 IU/mL
- Absolute eosinophil count: 1,000 cells/L

Which of the following tests is most necessary to confirm the diagnosis of allergic bronchopulmonary aspergillosis (ABPA)?

- (A) Pulmonary function tests
- (B) Bronchoscopy with bronchoalveolar lavage
- (C) High-resolution chest CT scan
- (D) Total IgE and Aspergillus-specific IgE
- (E) Absolute eosinophil count

44. A patient with chronic obstructive pulmonary disease (COPD) presents with altered mental status and hypercarbia. What is the most appropriate next step in management?

- A) Administer ipratropium nebulizers and steroids.
- B) Administer high-flow nasal cannula oxygen therapy.
- C) Initiate noninvasive positive-pressure ventilation.
- D) Administer antibiotics.
- E) Administer basic ventilator settings and sedation.

45. A patient with bronchiectasis presents with massive hemoptysis (>500 mL of expectorated blood in 24 hours). What is the most appropriate initial step in managing this patient?

- A) Administer cough suppressants.
- B) Perform a chest CT scan.
- C) Place the patient R-side down.
- D) Administer a blood transfusion.
- E) Intubate the patient.

46. A 34-year-old woman presents with shortness of breath on exertion and a painful red rash on her shin. She has no other significant medical history. On examination, she has bilateral crackles in her lungs. Her chest X-ray shows hilar lymphadenopathy. Her pulmonary function tests show a mixed obstructive and restrictive pattern. Which of the following is the most likely diagnosis?

- (A) Hypersensitivity pneumonitis
- (B) Collagen vascular disease
- (C) Sarcoidosis
- (D) Idiopathic interstitial pneumonia
- (E) None of the above

47. A 57-year-old man presents with shortness of breath and a cough. He also has a history of hearing loss, bloody nasal discharge, and hematuria. A chest X-ray shows cavitating peripheral lung nodules and masses. Which of the following tests is most likely to confirm the diagnosis of granulomatosis with polyangiitis (GPA)?

- (A) Antineutrophilic cytoplasmic antibody (ANCA)
- (B) Bronchoscopy with bronchoalveolar lavage
- (C) Lung biopsy
- (D) Infectious disease workup
- (E) None of the above

48. Which of the following findings is NOT characteristic of idiopathic pulmonary fibrosis?

- A) Apical cystic changes.
- B) Subpleural, bibasilar distribution of reticular opacities.
- C) Honeycombing.
- D) Traction bronchiectasis.
- E) Ground-glass opacities.

49. A 52-year-old male with a smoking history of 35 pack-years presents with dyspnea upon exertion. Pulmonary function testing reveals a decreased FEV1/FEV ratio and reduced DLCO. Exercise testing shows a decreased peak VO2 and maximum O2 pulse. Right heart catheterization shows a mean pulmonary artery pressure >25 mmHg, normal pulmonary capillary wedge pressure, and a transpulmonary gradient of 22 mmHg. Which of the following is the most likely diagnosis?

- A) Chronic obstructive pulmonary disease (COPD).
- B) Group 3 pulmonary hypertension.
- C) Idiopathic pulmonary arterial hypertension (PAH).
- D) Interstitial lung disease.
- E) Anorexigen-associated pulmonary arterial hypertension.

50. A 67-year-old man with severe ARDS is on mechanical ventilation. His FiO2 is 0.6 and his PEEP is 5 cmH2O. His SpO2 is 86What is the most appropriate next step?

- (A) Increase respiratory rate
- (B) Increase positive end-expiratory pressure
- (C) Decrease respiratory rate
- (D) Decrease positive end-expiratory pressure
- (E) None of the above

6.1 ANSWERS

1. Correct answer: B

The patient's presentation is consistent with central cyanosis, which is a bluish discoloration of the lips, tongue, and oral mucosa. Central cyanosis occurs when there is a decrease in the amount of oxygen carried by arterial blood. This can be caused by a number of conditions, including heart disease, lung disease, and anemia. Peripheral cyanosis, on the other hand, is a bluish discoloration of the extremities, specifically the fingers, toes, ears, and nose. Peripheral cyanosis is caused by the constriction of blood vessels in a specific area, leading to a bluish discoloration. This can be caused by a number of conditions, including cold exposure, Raynaud's phenomenon, and vasoconstriction due to medications. The other answer choices are not as likely. Methemoglobinemia is a condition in which there is an increase in the amount of methemoglobin in the blood. Methemoglobin is a form of hemoglobin that cannot carry oxygen, so it can lead to cyanosis. However, methemoglobinemia typically causes a more generalized cyanosis, rather than the localized cyanosis that is seen in this patient. Carbon monoxide poisoning can also cause cyanosis, but it typically causes a more severe cyanosis than what is seen in this patient. Hypoxia is a condition in which there is a decrease in the amount of oxygen in the blood. Hypoxia can cause cyanosis, but it typically causes a more generalized cyanosis, rather than the localized cyanosis that is seen in this patient.

2. Correct answer: A

The patient's presentation is consistent with ACE inhibitor-induced cough. ACE inhibitor-induced cough is a dry, non-productive cough that occurs in approximately 20% of patients who take ACE inhibitors. The cough typically starts within the first few weeks of starting ACE inhibitor therapy and can persist for as long as the medication is taken. The other answer choices are not as likely. Postnasal drip can cause a cough, but it is usually accompanied by other symptoms, such as a runny nose and sore throat. Asthma can also cause a cough, but it is usually accompanied by other symptoms, such as wheezing and shortness of breath. Lung cancer and pneumonia can cause a cough, but they are typically accompanied by other symptoms, such as chest pain, fever, and shortness of breath.

3. Correct answer: C

The patient's presentation is consistent with massive hemoptysis. Massive hemoptysis is defined as the expectoration of more than 400 mL of blood in a 24-hour period. However, some experts define massive hemoptysis as the expectoration of more than 100 mL of blood in a 24-hour period or more than 150 mL in a single episode. The other answer choices are not as accurate. Hemoptysis that is less than 400 mL in a 24-hour period is not considered to be massive hemoptysis. Hemoptysis that is greater than 800 mL in a 24-hour period is extremely rare and is considered to be life-threatening.

4. Correct answer: B

The patient's presentation is consistent with COPD. COPD is a chronic lung disease that is characterized by airway obstruction and inflammation. The obstruction of the airways can cause shortness of breath, wheezing, and a cough. The inflammation of the airways can cause mucus production and further obstruction of the airways. The other answer choices are not as likely. Asthma is a chronic lung disease that is characterized by airway inflammation and bronchospasm. The bronchospasm can cause shortness of breath, wheezing, and a cough. However, asthma is not typically associated with hyperinflation of the lungs. Emphysema is a type of COPD that is characterized by destruction of the alveoli, which are the small air sacs in the lungs. Bronchiectasis is a chronic lung disease that is characterized by dilation of the bronchi, which are the airways that carry air to the lungs. Pulmonary fibrosis is a chronic lung disease that is characterized by scarring of the lungs.

5. Correct answer: D

The patient's presentation is consistent with pulmonary fibrosis. Pulmonary fibrosis is a lung condition characterized by the formation of scar tissue in the lungs, leading to stiffness and reduced lung compliance. This results in restricted lung expansion and impaired gas exchange. Spirometry can help assess the severity of pulmonary fibrosis and monitor disease progression. The other answer choices are not as likely. Asthma is a chronic lung disease that is characterized by airway inflammation and bronchospasm. The bronchospasm can cause shortness of breath, wheezing, and a cough. However, asthma is not typically associated with decreased lung volumes. COPD is a chronic lung disease that is characterized by airway obstruction and inflammation. The obstruction of the airways can cause shortness of breath, wheezing, and a cough. However, COPD is not typically associated with decreased lung volumes. Emphysema is a type of COPD that is characterized by destruction of the alveoli, which are the small air sacs in the lungs. Sarcoidosis is a multisystem disorder that primarily affects the lungs, causing inflammation and the formation of granulomas. This inflammatory response can lead to a reduction in lung volume and restrictive lung function. However, sarcoidosis is less likely than pulmonary fibrosis in this patient given her history of rheumatoid arthritis.

6. Correct answer: A

The patient's presentation is consistent with asthma. Asthma is a chronic lung disease that is characterized by airway inflammation and bronchospasm. The bronchospasm can cause short breath, wheezing, and a cough. The reversibility of the bronchospasm is a hallmark of asthma. In this patient, the administration of albuterol resulted in a significant increase in her FEV1 and FEV1/FVC ratio, which confirms the diagnosis of asthma. The other answer choices are not as likely. COPD is a chronic lung disease that is characterized by airway obstruction and inflammation. The obstruction of the airways can cause shortness of breath, wheezing, and a cough. However, COPD is not typically reversible with bronchodilators. Emphysema is a type of COPD that is characterized by destruction of the alveoli, which are the small air sacs in the lungs. Bronchiectasis is a chronic lung disease that is characterized by dilation of the bronchi, which are the airways that carry air to the lungs. Pulmonary fibrosis is a chronic lung disease that is characterized by scarring of the lungs.

7. Correct answer: C

The patient's symptoms of shortness of breath and wheezing are consistent with asthma. However, her symptoms of tremors and palpitations are also consistent with side effects of 2-adrenergic agonists. The prevalence of these adverse effects is more pronounced in oral formulations, which the patient is not taking. Therefore, the most likely explanation for her symptoms is that she is experiencing side effects from the 2-adrenergic agonist inhaler. The other answer choices are not as likely. The patient's asthma is not likely to be getting worse if she is already taking a short-acting 2-adrenergic agonist inhaler. She is also not likely to be taking too much of the inhaler, as this would typically cause more severe side effects, such as chest pain and anxiety. The patient is not likely to have a different underlying medical condition, as her symptoms are consistent with asthma. Finally, the patient is likely to be taking the inhaler correctly, as she has been experiencing these symptoms for several months.

8. Correct answer: D

The patient's symptoms of shortness of breath and wheezing are consistent with asthma. However, her symptoms are not likely to be getting worse if she is already taking a LABA inhaler. She is also not likely to be taking too much of the inhaler, as this would typically cause more severe side effects, such as chest pain and anxiety. The patient is not likely to have a different underlying medical condition, as her symptoms are consistent with asthma. Finally, the patient is likely to be taking the inhaler correctly, as she has been experiencing these symptoms for several months. Therefore, the most likely explanation for the patient's symptoms is that she needs to be taking inhaled corticosteroids in addition to the LABA inhaler. The use of LABAs without concurrent inhaled corticosteroids has been associated with an elevated likelihood of mortality. This is because LABAs can relax the muscles in the airways too much, which can lead to a decrease in blood pressure and heart rate. Inhaled corticosteroids, on the other hand, help to reduce inflammation in the airways, which can help to prevent these adverse effects.

9. Correct answer: E

The patient's presentation is consistent with an asthma exacerbation. Asthma exacerbations can lead to a number of potential outcomes, including hypoxemia, hypercapnia, respiratory failure, and death. Hypoxemia is a condition in which the level of oxygen in the blood is decreased. This can be caused by a number of factors, including asthma exacerbations. Hypoxemia can lead to a number of symptoms, including shortness of breath, cyanosis, and confusion. Hypercapnia is a condition in which the level of carbon dioxide in the blood is increased. This can also be caused by asthma exacerbations. Hypercapnia can lead to a number of symptoms, including headache, dizziness, and drowsiness. Respiratory failure is a condition in which the lungs are unable to adequately oxygenate the blood. This can be caused by a number of factors, including asthma exacerbations. Respiratory failure can be fatal. Death is the most serious outcome of an asthma exacerbation. Asthma exacerbations can be fatal, especially if they are not treated promptly. Therefore, the most likely outcome of this patient's asthma exacerbation is all of the above. The patient is at risk for hypoxemia, hypercapnia, respiratory failure, and death.

10. Correct answer: B

The patient's presentation is consistent with an asthma exacerbation. Asthma exacerbations are typically treated with corticosteroids. Corticosteroids can be administered orally or intravenously. In this patient, the most appropriate modality for the administration of corticosteroids is intravenous methylprednisolone. This is because the patient's asthma exacerbation is severe, and she is at risk for respiratory failure. Intravenous methyl prednisolone will provide more rapid relief of symptoms than oral prednisone. Oral prednisone can be used as an alternative to intravenous methylprednisolone. However, oral prednisone takes longer to take effect and is not as effective as intravenous methylprednisolone in severe asthma exacerbations. Therefore, the most appropriate modality for the administration of corticosteroids in this patient is intravenous methylprednisolone.

11. Correct answer: A

The patient's presentation is consistent with occupational asthma. Occupational asthma is a type of asthma that is caused by exposure to an allergen or irritant in the workplace. Spirometry is a test that measures the amount of air that can be breathed in and out of the lungs. It is a useful test for diagnosing occupational asthma because it can show a decrease in lung function after exposure to the suspected allergen or irritant. Chest X-ray is not a very useful test for diagnosing occupational asthma. It can show changes in the lungs, but these changes are not specific for occupational asthma. Skin prick test is a test that is used to measure the allergic response to a specific allergen. It is not a very useful test for diagnosing occupational asthma because there are many allergens that can cause occupational asthma and it is not always possible to identify the specific allergen that is causing the patient's symptoms. Methacholine challenge test is a test that is used to measure the airway responsiveness to a bronchoconstrictor. It is a more sensitive test than spirometry for diagnosing occupational asthma, but it is also more invasive.

12. Correct answer: E

The patient's presentation is consistent with mesothelioma. Mesothelioma is a rare cancer that is caused by exposure to asbestos. It typically affects the lining of the lungs (pleural mesothelioma) or the lining of the abdomen (peritoneal mesothelioma). Pleural plaques are benign lesions that are caused by exposure to asbestos. They do not typically cause any symptoms. Interstitial lung disease is a chronic lung disease that is caused by inflammation of the lung tissue. It can be caused by a number of factors, including asbestos exposure. Benign pleural effusion is a collection of fluid in the space between the lung and the chest wall. It is a common finding in people who have been exposed to asbestos, but it does not typically cause any symptoms. Lung cancer is a common cancer that can be caused by a number of factors, including asbestos exposure. It typically presents with symptoms such as shortness of breath, cough, and chest pain.

13. Correct answer: A

The patient's presentation is consistent with simple coal workers' pneumoconiosis (CWP). CWP is a lung disease that is caused by the inhalation of coal dust. It is characterized by the presence of small, rounded opacities in the lungs. These opacities are called "coal macules" and they are typically located in the upper parts of the lungs. Progressive massive fibrosis (PMF) is a more advanced form of CWP. It is characterized by the presence of large, irregular opacities in the lungs. These opacities can cause significant lung damage and can lead to respiratory failure. Sarcoidosis is a chronic inflammatory disease that can affect any organ in the body. It is characterized by the formation of small, non-necrotic granulomas. These granulomas can be seen in the lungs, but they can also be seen in other organs, such as the liver, spleen, and skin. Tuberculosis is a bacterial infection that can affect the lungs. It is characterized by the formation of small, round lesions in the lungs. These lesions can cause significant lung damage and can lead to respiratory failure. Lung cancer is a common cancer that can affect the lungs. It is characterized by the formation of a tumor in the lungs. These tumors can grow and spread to other parts of the body, such as the brain and bone. Therefore, the most likely diagnosis in this patient is simple coal workers' pneumoconiosis (CWP).

14. Correct answer: A

The patient's presentation is consistent with both chronic beryllium disease (CBD) and sarcoidosis. However, the lymphocyte proliferation test is the most likely test to help differentiate between the two diseases. This is because the test measures T-lymphocyte responses to beryllium. Delayed hypersensitivity to beryllium is detected in CBD but not in sarcoidosis; thus, the test can be used to differentiate between the two diseases. Chest CT scan can be used to visualize the lungs and help to identify the presence of any abnormalities. However, it is not as specific as the lymphocyte proliferation test for differentiating between CBD and sarcoidosis. Pulmonary function tests can be used to assess the function of the lungs. However, they are not specific for either CBD or sarcoidosis. Skin biopsy can be used to identify the presence of granulomas, which are characteristic of sarcoidosis. However, granulomas can also be seen in other diseases, such as tuberculosis. Therefore, the lymphocyte proliferation test is the most likely test to help differentiate between chronic beryllium disease (CBD) and sarcoidosis.

15.Correct answer: B

The patient's presentation is consistent with COPD. The arterial blood gas analysis shows a PaO2 of 57 mmHg and a SaO2 of 87%. These values are below the recommended guidelines for oxygen therapy in COPD. Therefore, the most appropriate recommendation is to initiate oxygen therapy to increase the SaO2 level to at least 90%. Oxygen therapy is not indicated for patients with COPD who have a PaO2 of 57 mmHg and a SaO2 of 87% if they do not have clinical manifestations of pulmonary hypertension or cor pulmonale. Oxygen therapy should be initiated only if the patient develops shortness of breath at rest or with exertion. Therefore, the most appropriate recommendation is to initiate oxygen therapy to increase the SaO2 level to at least 90%.

16. Correct answer: E

The patient's presentation is consistent with COPD. However, his FEV1 and DLCO are both below 20% predicted. This indicates that he is in the high-risk category for lung volume reduction surgery. Therefore, the patient should not be considered for lung volume reduction surgery. The other answer choices are incorrect because they do not take into account the patient's FEV1 and DLCO values.

17. The correct answer is A

Factor V Leiden is a mutation in the factor V gene that causes resistance to activated protein C. This results in an increased risk of blood clots. Prothrombin G20210A mutation is a mutation in the prothrombin gene that causes an increased production of prothrombin. Prothrombin is a clotting factor, so this mutation also increases the risk of blood clots. Deficiency of antithrombin is a rare genetic disorder that causes a deficiency of antithrombin, a protein that helps to regulate blood clotting. This results in an increased risk of blood clots. Deficiency of protein C is a rare genetic disorder that causes a deficiency of protein C, a protein that helps to regulate blood clotting. This results in an increased risk of blood clots. Deficiency of protein S is a rare genetic disorder that causes a deficiency of protein S, a protein that helps to regulate blood clotting. This results in an increased risk of blood clots.

18. The correct answer is A.

Massive pulmonary embolism. Massive pulmonary embolism is a life threatening condition that occurs when a large blood clot blocks a major pulmonary artery. This can lead to sudden shortness of breath, chest pain, syncope, hypotension, and cyanosis. The patient in this question has all of the classic symptoms of massive pulmonary embolism, and he has a history of deep vein thrombosis, which is a risk factor for pulmonary embolism. The other answer choices are less likely in this case. Acute myocardial infarction can cause chest pain, but it is less likely to cause shortness of breath, syncope, or cyanosis. Pneumonia can cause shortness of breath, but it is less likely to cause chest pain or syncope. Aortic dissection can cause chest pain, but it is less likely to cause shortness of breath, syncope, or cyanosis. Tension pneumothorax can cause shortness of breath, but it is less likely to cause chest pain or syncope.

19. The correct answer is C. 2.

The Wells score for this patient is 2. She has a heart rate of 110 beats per minute, and she has hemoptysis. She does not have any other risk factors for pulmonary embolism, such as a recent surgery or immobilization, or a history of deep vein thrombosis or pulmonary embolism. The other answer choices are incorrect. A score of 0 indicates that the patient is very unlikely to have pulmonary embolism. A score of 1 indicates that the patient is unlikely to have pulmonary embolism. A score of 3 indicates that the patient is more likely to have pulmonary embolism. A score of 4 indicates that the patient is very likely to have pulmonary embolism.

20. The correct answer is B.

Initial bolus dose of 80 units per kilogram, followed by a continuous infusion at a rate of 18 units per kilogram per hour. This is the conventional therapeutic strategy for UFH, which aims to achieve an activated partial thromboplastin time (aPTT) within the range of 60-80 seconds. The other answer choices are incorrect. Option A uses a lower initial bolus dose and a lower continuous infusion rate, which is unlikely to achieve a therapeutic aPTT. Option C uses a higher initial bolus dose and a higher continuous infusion rate, which is more likely to cause bleeding complications. Option D and Option E use even higher initial bolus doses and continuous infusion rates, which are even more likely to cause bleeding complications.

21. The correct answer is B.

Low molecular weight heparin (LMWH) indefinitely, unless the patient achieves a state of cancer remission. This is the standard treatment protocol for patients with cancer and VTE, as it is effective in preventing recurrent VTE and has a lower risk of bleeding complications than warfarin. The other answer choices are incorrect. Option A recommends a shorter duration of treatment with LMWH, which is not recommended for patients with cancer and VTE. Option C recommends warfarin indefinitely, which is not recommended as it has a higher risk of bleeding complications than LMWH. Option D recommends aspirin indefinitely, which is not an effective treatment for VTE. Option E recommends no treatment, which is not recommended as it increases the risk of recurrent VTE.

22. The correct answer is A.

A treatment that uses a low dose of a thrombolytic agent, such as tissue plasminogen activator (tPA), and ultrasound to help break up a blood clot. Low-dose, ultrasound-facilitated, catheter-directed thrombolysis is a minimally invasive procedure that uses a catheter to deliver a thrombolytic agent, such as tPA, directly to the blood clot. The ultrasound helps to break up the clot and improve blood flow. This treatment is typically used for patients with submassive or massive pulmonary embolism, or those with extensive femoral, iliofemoral, or upper extremity deep vein thrombosis. The other answer choices are incorrect. Option B describes high-dose, ultrasound-facilitated, catheter-directed thrombolysis, which is not as commonly used as low-dose thrombolysis. Option C describes a treatment that uses a low dose of a thrombolytic agent and a mechanical device to help break up a blood clot. This is called mechanical thrombectomy, and it is not the same as low-dose, ultrasound-facilitated, catheter-directed thrombolysis. Option D describes a treatment that uses a high dose of a thrombolytic agent and a mechanical device to help break up a blood clot. This is also called mechanical thrombectomy, and it is not the same as low-dose, ultrasound-facilitated, catheter-directed thrombolysis. Option E is the incorrect answer.

23. The correct answer is A.

Hypersensitivity pneumonitis. Hypersensitivity pneumonitis is an inflammatory lung disease that is caused by repeated exposure to an inhaled allergen. The most common allergens that cause hypersensitivity pneumonitis are moldy hay, bird droppings, and animal dander. The patient in this question has a history of exposure to moldy hay, which is a known risk factor for hypersensitivity pneumonitis.

24. The correct answer is A.

Acquired pulmonary alveolar proteinosis (PAP). PAP is a rare lung disease that is characterized by the accumulation of surfactant in the alveoli. Surfactant is a substance that helps to keep the lungs inflated. When surfactant is not produced properly, the alveoli can collapse, which can lead to shortness of breath, cough, and fatigue. The other answer choices are incorrect. Pneumonia is an infection of the lungs that can cause similar symptoms to PAP. However, pneumonia is usually associated with fever, chills, and sputum production. ILD is a group of lung diseases that can cause similar symptoms to PAP. However, ILD is usually associated with other findings on chest X-ray or pulmonary function tests. Sarcoidosis is a chronic inflammatory disease that can affect many organs in the body, including the lungs. LAM is a rare lung disease that affects women.

25. The correct answer is A.

Interstitial lung disease (ILD). ILD is a group of lung diseases that is characterized by inflammation and scarring of the lungs. The pulmonary function tests in patients with ILD typically show a restrictive pattern, which means that the lungs are not able to expand as much as they should. The FVC and FEV1 are both decreased in patients with ILD. The other answer choices are incorrect. Asthma is a chronic lung disease that is characterized by inflammation of the airways. The pulmonary function tests in patients with asthma typically show an obstructive pattern, which means that the airways are narrowed. COPD is a progressive lung disease that is caused by smoking. The pulmonary function tests in patients with COPD typically shows an obstructive pattern. Pneumonia is an infection of the lungs that can cause shortness of breath and cough. The pulmonary function tests in patients with pneumonia are usually normal. Heart failure is a condition in which the heart is not able to pump blood efficiently. The pulmonary function tests in patients with heart failure are usually normal.

26. The correct answer is C.

Hypersensitivity pneumonitis (HP). HP is an inflammatory lung disease that is caused by repeated exposure to an inhaled allergen. Glucocorticoids are the first-line treatment for HP and are often very effective in reducing inflammation and improving symptoms. The other answer choices are incorrect. Eosinophilic pneumonia is a rare lung disease that is characterized by an accumulation of eosinophils in the lungs. Glucocorticoids are not the first-line treatment for eosinophilic pneumonia, but they may be used in combination with other medications. COPD is a progressive lung disease that is caused by smoking. Glucocorticoids are not effective in treating COPD. Acute radiation pneumonitis is a lung injury that can occur after radiation therapy. Glucocorticoids are the first-line treatment for acute radiation pneumonitis. Drug-induced interstitial lung disease is a lung disease that is caused by certain medications. Glucocorticoids are often used to treat drug-induced interstitial lung disease, but they may not be effective in all cases.

27. The correct answer is A.

Yes, in most cases, a surgical lung biopsy is necessary to definitively establish the diagnosis of IPF. IPF is a progressive lung disease that is characterized by scarring of the lungs. The diagnosis of IPF can be difficult to make, as there is no single test that can definitively diagnose the disease. However, a surgical lung biopsy is often necessary to confirm the diagnosis of IPF. The other answer choices are incorrect. Option B is incorrect because even patients with classic UIP patterns on HRCT scan may not have IPF. Option C is incorrect because BAL is not a reliable test for diagnosing IPF. Option D is incorrect because transbronchial biopsy is not a reliable test for diagnosing IPF. Option E is incorrect because serum blood tests are not reliable tests for diagnosing IPF.

28. The correct answer is E.

All of the above. Granulomatous vasculitides, such as GPA, can cause a variety of pulmonary manifestations, including nodules, infiltrates, hemoptysis, and pleural effusion.

29. The correct answer is D.

All of the above. Exudative pleural effusions are defined by the presence of one or more of three established criteria. The first criterion is a pleural fluid to serum protein ratio greater than 0.5. This means that if the ratio of pleural fluid protein to serum protein is greater than 0.5, then the effusion is categorized as an exudate. The second criterion is a pleural fluid to serum lactate dehydrogenase (LDH) ratio greater than 0.6. This means that if the ratio of pleural fluid LDH to serum LDH is greater than 0.6, then the effusion is categorized as an exudate. The third criterion is a pleural fluid LDH greater than 2/3 the upper limit of normal serum LDH. This means that if the pleural fluid LDH is greater than 2/3 the upper limit of normal serum LDH, then the effusion is categorized as an exudate. Exudative pleural effusions are typically caused by inflammatory conditions, such as pneumonia, cancer, or tuberculosis. They can also be caused by infections, such as empyema or pyothorax. Exudative pleural effusions can also be caused by non-infectious causes, such as heart failure or pancreatitis.

30. The correct answer is A.

Spontaneous pneumothorax occurs in the absence of thoracic trauma, whereas traumatic pneumothorax arises from either penetrating or nonpenetrating chest trauma. Spontaneous pneumothorax is a condition in which air leaks into the space between the lung and the chest wall. This can happen spontaneously, in the absence of any trauma, or it can be caused by trauma. Traumatic pneumothorax is a pneumothorax that is caused by trauma to the chest. This can be caused by penetrating trauma, such as a gunshot wound or stab wound, or it can be caused by nonpenetrating trauma, such as a rib fracture.

31. The correct answer is D. All of the above.

Obstructive sleep apnea-hypopnea syndrome (OSAHS) is a sleep disorder that is characterized by recurrent episodes of complete or partial obstruction of the upper airway during sleep. OSAHS is correlated with a number of other conditions, including Depression: People with OSAHS are more likely to have depression than people without OSAHS. Hypertension: People with OSAHS are more likely to have hypertension than people without OSAHS. Diabetes: People with OSAHS are more likely to have diabetes than people without OSAHS. Heart disease: People with OSAHS are more likely to have heart disease than people without OSAHS. Stroke: People with OSAHS are more likely to have a stroke than people without OSAHS. Accidents: People with OSAHS are more likely to have accidents than people without OSAHS.

32. The correct answer is A.

Exertional dyspnea, fatigue, angina, syncope, and peripheral edema. Pulmonary hypertension is a condition in which the blood pressure in the lungs is abnormally high. This can lead to a number of symptoms, including exertional dyspnea, fatigue, angina, syncope, and peripheral edema. Exertional dyspnea is shortness of breath that occurs with exertion. This is because the heart has to work harder to pump blood through the lungs, which can lead to shortness of breath. Fatigue is a feeling of tiredness that is not relieved by rest. This can be caused by a number of factors, including pulmonary hypertension. Angina is chest pain that is caused by restricted blood flow to the heart. This can occur in people with pulmonary hypertension because the right ventricle has to work harder to pump blood through the lungs, which can restrict blood flow to the heart. Syncope is a sudden loss of consciousness. This can occur in people with pulmonary hypertension because the heart may not be able to pump enough blood to the brain. Peripheral edema is swelling in the hands and feet. This can occur in people with pulmonary hypertension because the heart may not be able to pump enough blood to the extremities. The other answer choices are incorrect because they do not include all of the typical manifestations of pulmonary hypertension.

33. The correct answer is D. All of the above.

The primary laboratory findings and diagnostic tests employed for the evaluation and diagnosis of pulmonary hypertension encompass a range of procedures, such as chest X-ray (CXR), electrocardiogram (ECG), echocardiogram, pulmonary function tests (PFTs), chest computed tomography (CT), antinuclear antibody (ANA) titer assessment, rheumatoid factor evaluation, anti-Scl-70 antibody testing, human immunodeficiency virus (HIV) screening, cardiopulmonary exercise testing, right heart catheterization, and measurement of serum brain natriuretic peptide (BNP) and NT-proBNP levels.

34. The correct answer is E. All of the above.

The therapeutic interventions that have received approval for the treatment of PAH encompass a range of medications targeting specific molecular pathways. These include endothelin receptor antagonists like bosentan, macitentan, and ambrisentan; phosphodiesterase type 5 inhibitors such as sildenafil and tadalafil; prostaglandins like iloprost, epoprostenol, and treprostinil; the oral soluble guanylyl cyclase stimulator riociguat; and the oral prostaglandin I2 receptor selexipag.

35. The correct answer is C. Both A and B.

Lung transplantation is a potential treatment option for patients with PAH who are experiencing persistent right heart failure and have failed medical therapies. PAH is a progressive disease that can lead to right heart failure over time. When medical therapies for PAH are no longer effective in managing the condition and the right heart failure is severe and progressive, lung transplantation may be considered to improve overall heart and lung function. In addition to persistent right heart failure and failure of medical therapies, other factors that may be considered in the decision to pursue lung transplantation for PAH include: The patient's age and overall health. The severity of the patient's PAH. The availability of suitable donor lungs. The patient's willingness to undergo the risks and challenges of lung transplantation. Lung transplantation is a major surgery with significant risks, but it can be a life-saving treatment for patients with PAH who have exhausted other treatment options.

36. The correct answer is D. All of the above.

Acute pulmonary edema is a condition in which fluid leaks from the blood vessels into the lungs. This can lead to a number of changes on a chest X-ray, including: Pulmonary vascular redistribution: This refers to a shift of blood flow from the periphery of the lungs to the central regions. This is seen on a chest X-ray as increased prominence of the pulmonary arteries in the hilar regions. Diffuse haziness in the lung fields: This refers to the presence of fluid in the lungs. This is seen on a chest X-ray as a hazy appearance to the lungs. Perihilar "butterfly" appearance: This refers to a specific pattern of haziness that is seen in acute pulmonary edema. It is typically seen in the central regions of the lungs, and it has a butterfly-like appearance.

37. The correct answer is D. All of the above.

Inotropic agents are medications that increase the contractility of the heart. This can be helpful in cases of cardiogenic pulmonary edema and severe left ventricular dysfunction, as it can help to improve the pumping action of the heart and reduce the amount of fluid that leaks into the lungs. The three inotropic agents that are most commonly used for the treatment of cardiogenic pulmonary edema and severe left ventricular dysfunction are dopamine, dobutamine, and milrinone. Dopamine is a general inotropic agent that can also have vasoconstrictive effects. Dobutamine is a more selective inotropic agent that has fewer vasoconstrictive effects. Milrinone is a phosphodiesterase inhibitor that has both inotropic and vasodilatory effects. The choice of inotropic agent will depend on the individual patient's clinical presentation and other factors, such as the patient's blood pressure and heart rate. In general, dopamine is a good choice for patients who have low blood pressure, while dobutamine is a good choice for patients who have high blood pressure. Milrinone is a good choice for patients who have both low blood pressure and high heart rate.

38. The correct answer is D. All of the above.

The primary diagnostic criteria for ARDS are: The presence of diffuse bilateral pulmonary infiltrates as observed on chest X-ray. A ratio of arterial partial pressure of oxygen (PaO2) to inspired oxygen fraction (FIO2) equal to or less than 300 mmHg. The absence of elevated pressure in the left atrium. The occurrence of acute onset within one week following a clinical insult or the emergence of new or aggravated respiratory symptoms.

39. The correct answer is A.

Low tidal volumes (equal to or less than 6 milliliters per kilogram of predicted body weight) in combination with positive end-expiratory pressure (PEEP) set at levels that minimize alveolar collapse and achieve adequate oxygenation with the lowest possible fraction of inspired oxygen (FIO2) requirement. This ventilator strategy is based on the concept of lung protective ventilation, which aims to reduce ventilator-induced lung injury (VILI). VILI is a major cause of morbidity and mortality in patients with ARDS. It is caused by the mechanical forces generated by the ventilator, such as high tidal volumes and low positive end-expiratory pressure (PEEP) levels. Low tidal volumes and high positive end-expiratory pressure (PEEP) levels help to reduce VILI by limiting the amount of stretch and shear stress that is applied to the alveoli. This helps to prevent the alveoli from collapsing and minimizes the amount of damage that is caused to the lung tissue. The fraction of inspired oxygen (FIO2) requirement should be kept as low as possible to further reduce the risk of VILI. High FIO2 levels can cause oxygen toxicity, which can also damage the lung tissue.

40. The correct answer is A. Less than 105.

A spontaneous breathing test (SBT) is a test that is used to assess a patient's readiness for extubation. The SBT is performed by gradually reducing the ventilator settings until the patient is breathing spontaneously. The f/VT ratio is a measure of the patient's respiratory workload. A low f/VT ratio indicates that the patient is not working hard to breathe. A threshold value of f/VT of less than 105 is considered to be a good predictor of successful extubation. This means that if the patient's f/VT ratio is less than 105 at the conclusion of the SBT, they are likely to be able to breathe spontaneously without the ventilator. A f/VT ratio of greater than 105 indicates that the patient is working hard to breathe and may not be ready for extubation.

41. Answer: B

Neuromuscular disease would not affect diffusion capacity. Instead, it would result in progressive restriction and reduced forces generated during inspiration and expiration. This is because neuromuscular disease weakens the muscles that control breathing. The other answer choices are all possible causes of reduced diffusion capacity: Pulmonary embolism: A blood clot in the lung that blocks the flow of blood to the alveoli. This can reduce the surface area of lung participating in gas exchange. Pulmonary fibrosis: A scarring of the lung tissue that thickens the barrier between the alveoli and the capillaries. This can make it more difficult for oxygen and carbon dioxide to diffuse across the barrier. Anemia: A condition in which the blood does not have enough red blood cells. This can reduce the amount of oxygen that can be carried in the blood. Interstitial lung disease: A group of diseases that affect the interstitium, the tissue that surrounds the alveoli. These diseases can thicken the interstitium and make it more difficult for oxygen and carbon dioxide to diffuse across the barrier. Therefore, the best answer is B. Neuromuscular disease.

42. The best answer is A) Administer albuterol nebulizers and IV methylprednisolone.

In the acute setting of asthma exacerbation, the mainstays of treatment include short-acting -agonist therapy at frequent intervals, corticosteroids, and supportive care. Albuterol nebulizers provide short-acting -agonist therapy to relieve bronchospasm and improve airflow. IV methylprednisolone is a corticosteroid that helps reduce airway inflammation. These treatments are the first-line therapies for acute asthma exacerbation. Epinephrine is not the best initial step in the management of this patient because there is no evidence of anaphylaxis. Epinephrine is typically used in the treatment of anaphylaxis, not asthma exacerbation. Magnesium may be considered in patients who fail to respond to first-line therapies, but it is not the best initial step. It is not recommended as the first-line treatment for acute asthma exacerbation. Noninvasive positive-pressure ventilation is controversial in asthma as it cannot reverse the inflammatory lung process and may contribute to complications such as pneumothorax and hemodynamic instability. It is not the best initial step in the management of this patient. Antibiotics are not indicated in this case because there is no evidence of pneumonia. Antibiotics are only used when there is a bacterial infection present. Therefore, the best initial step in the management of this patient is to administer albuterol nebulizers and IV methylprednisolone.

43. Answer: D

The diagnosis of ABPA is based on the following criteria:

- Asthma or cystic fibrosis
- Elevated total IgE
- Elevated Aspergillus-specific IgE or immediate cutaneous reactivity to Aspergillus
- At least two of the following additional criteria:
- Radiographic pulmonary opacities consistent with ABPA (central bronchiectasis in the absence of distal bronchiectasis)
- Eosinophilia

Precipitating serum antibodies to Aspergillus or elevated levels of Aspergillus-specific serum IgG In this case, the patient meets all of the criteria for ABPA except for elevated Aspergillus-specific IgE. Therefore, the most necessary test to confirm the diagnosis is a total IgE and Aspergillus-specific IgE test. The other answer choices are not as necessary to confirm the diagnosis of ABPA: Pulmonary function tests may show airflow obstruction, but this is not specific for ABPA. Bronchoscopy with bronchoalveolar lavage may show evidence of Aspergillus colonization, but this is not necessary for the diagnosis of ABPA. High-resolution chest CT scan may show central bronchiectasis, but this is not specific for ABPA and is not required for the diagnosis. Absolute eosinophil count is a supportive finding for ABPA, but it is not necessary for the diagnosis. Therefore, the best answer is D. Total IgE and Aspergillus-specific IgE.

44. The best answer is C) Initiate noninvasive positive-pressure ventilation.

In this patient with altered mental status and hypercarbia, the most appropriate next step in management is to initiate noninvasive positive-pressure ventilation (NPPV). NPPV helps improve ventilation and breathe off the excess carbon dioxide (CO_2). The patient likely needs NPPV to improve ventilation and prevent further CO_2 retention. Administering ipratropium nebulizers and steroids, (choice A) is important in managing acute COPD exacerbations, but they are unlikely to improve the patient's CO_2 levels and mental status once CO_2 retention has already begun. High-flow nasal cannula oxygen therapy (choice B) may be effective in providing respiratory support in some cases, but it may not be sufficient to address the underlying issue of hypercarbia and altered mental status. NPPV is a more appropriate intervention in this scenario.

Administering antibiotics (choice D) is not indicated in this case unless there is evidence of a bacterial infection. The patient's altered mental status and hypercarbia are more likely related to the COPD exacerbation rather than an infectious process. Administering basic ventilator settings and sedation (choice E) may be necessary in some cases, but it does not specifically address the need for noninvasive positive-pressure ventilation to improve ventilation and CO_2 elimination. Therefore, the most appropriate next step in management for this patient is to initiate noninvasive positive-pressure ventilation.

45. The best answer is C) Place the patient R-side down.

In a patient experiencing massive hemoptysis, the initial step in management is to stabilize the patient and prevent asphyxiation. Placing the patient with the affected side down helps to minimize the risk of blood pooling in the unaffected lung and potentially causing asphyxiation. This position can help to redirect blood away from the unaffected lung and reduce the risk of further bleeding. Administering cough suppressants (choice A) is not recommended in this scenario, as it may increase the risk of asphyxiation by suppressing the cough reflex and preventing the clearance of blood from the airways. Performing a chest CT scan (choice B) may be useful in determining the location or source of the bleeding, but it is not the initial step in managing a patient with massive hemoptysis. Stabilizing the patient and preventing asphyxiation take precedence. Administering a blood transfusion (choice D) is not necessary at this time, as the patient is hemodynamically stable. The immediate concern is to prevent asphyxiation rather than addressing potential blood loss. Intubating the patient (choice E) may be necessary if the patient becomes unstable from a respiratory perspective, but it is not the initial step in managing massive hemoptysis. Intubation should be selectively performed on the non-affected lung to maintain ventilation while awaiting definitive treatment. Therefore, the most appropriate initial step in managing this patient with massive hemoptysis is to place the patient R-side down.

46. Answer: C

The patient's demographics, clinical presentation, and pulmonary function tests are most consistent with sarcoidosis. Sarcoidosis is a multisystem granulomatous disease that can affect many organs, including the lungs. It is most common in young women. Erythema nodosum is a common skin manifestation of sarcoidosis. Hilar lymphadenopathy is a common finding on chest imaging in patients with sarcoidosis. A mixed obstructive and restrictive pattern on pulmonary function tests is also common in sarcoidosis. The other answer choices are less likely: Hypersensitivity pneumonitis is a lung disease caused by an allergic reaction to inhaled antigens. It is typically more common in patients with occupational exposures to antigens such as mold, dust, or bird droppings. This patient does not have any exposures to suggest hypersensitivity pneumonitis. Collagen vascular disease is a group of autoimmune diseases that can affect many organs, including the lungs. Scleroderma is a type of collagen vascular disease that can cause interstitial lung disease. However, this patient does not have any other features of scleroderma, such as skin, joint, or muscle involvement. Idiopathic interstitial pneumonia is a group of lung diseases that cause interstitial lung disease. However, it is considered a diagnosis of exclusion, meaning that other possible causes of the patient's interstitial lung disease, such as sarcoidosis, hypersensitivity pneumonitis, and collagen vascular disease, must first be ruled out. Therefore, the best answer is C. Sarcoidosis.

47. Answer: A

ANCA is a type of autoantibody that is directed against neutrophils or their cytoplasmic components. It is highly specific for GPA and other ANCA-associated vasculitis. Bronchoscopy with bronchoalveolar lavage may show evidence of inflammation, but it is not specific for GPA. Lung biopsy is the gold standard for diagnosing GPA, but it is not necessary in all cases. Infectious disease workup is important to rule out other possible causes of the patient's symptoms, but it is not likely to be diagnostic of GPA. Therefore, the best answer is A. Antineutrophilic cytoplasmic antibody (ANCA). GPA is a systemic vasculitis that typically affects the kidneys and lungs. The most common pulmonary manifestations of GPA include cavitating nodules and masses, as well as waxing-and-waning pulmonary opacities and lymphadenopathy. ANCA testing is the most important test for diagnosing GPA. ANCA is highly specific for GPA and other ANCA-associated vasculitis. If ANCA testing is positive, other tests, such as bronchoscopy with bronchoalveolar lavage and lung biopsy, may be performed to confirm the diagnosis and rule out other possible causes of the patient's symptoms. Treatment for GPA typically involves corticosteroids and other immunosuppressive medications.

48. The correct answer is A) Apical cystic changes.

Idiopathic pulmonary fibrosis (IPF) is a chronic and progressive interstitial lung disease characterized by specific radiographic findings. The characteristic features of IPF include a subpleural, bibasilar distribution of reticular opacities, honeycombing, and traction bronchiectasis. These findings are typically seen on imaging studies such as high-resolution computed tomography (HRCT). Ground-glass opacities are classically absent in idiopathic pulmonary fibrosis, although their presence does not completely exclude the diagnosis. Ground-glass opacities are more commonly associated with other interstitial lung diseases. Apical cystic changes, on the other hand, are not seen as part of idiopathic pulmonary fibrosis. This finding is not characteristic of the disease and may suggest an alternative diagnosis or coexisting condition. Therefore, among the given options, the finding that is NOT characteristic of idiopathic pulmonary fibrosis is A) Apical cystic changes.

49. The correct answer is C) Idiopathic pulmonary arterial hypertension (PAH).

The patient's clinical presentation and diagnostic findings are suggestive of pulmonary hypertension. The mean pulmonary artery pressure >25 mmHg, normal pulmonary capillary wedge pressure, and elevated transpulmonary gradient (mean pulmonary artery pressure - pulmonary capillary wedge pressure) of 22 mmHg indicate precapillary pulmonary hypertension. Given that the patient has no evidence of chronic obstructive pulmonary disease (COPD) on pulmonary function testing (decreased FEV1/FEV ratio) or interstitial lung disease on imaging, these conditions are less likely to be the cause of the patient's symptoms. Group 3 pulmonary hypertension refers to pulmonary hypertension associated with lung diseases and/or hypoxia. However, in this case, there is no evidence of lung disease or hypoxia, ruling out group 3 pulmonary hypertension. Anorexigen-associated pulmonary arterial hypertension is a specific subtype of pulmonary arterial hypertension associated with the use of appetite suppressant medications. There is no mention of the patient using such medications in the provided information, making this diagnosis less likely. Therefore, the most likely diagnosis based on the clinical presentation and diagnostic findings is C) Idiopathic pulmonary arterial hypertension (PAH).

50. Answer: B

The patient's SpO2 is below goal, so the goal is to increase his oxygenation. Increasing the FiO2 is the first step, but the patient is already on a high FiO2. Therefore, the next step is to increase the positive end-expiratory pressure (PEEP). PEEP helps to keep the alveoli open, which can improve oxygenation. Increasing the respiratory rate and tidal volume can also improve ventilation, but this should be done cautiously in patients with ARDS, as it can lead to hyperinflation and barotrauma. Therefore, the best answer is B. Increase positive end-expiratory pressure. Acute respiratory distress syndrome (ARDS) is a severe lung condition that can be caused by a variety of factors, such as pneumonia, sepsis, and trauma. ARDS is characterized by diffuse alveolar damage, which leads to decreased lung compliance and impaired oxygenation. Mechanical ventilation is the mainstay of treatment for ARDS. The goal of mechanical ventilation is to support ventilation and oxygenation while minimizing lung injury. PEEP is a key component of mechanical ventilation in ARDS. PEEP helps to keep the alveoli open, which can improve oxygenation and reduce the risk of lung collapse. PEEP is typically set at 5-10 cmH2O in patients with ARDS. Other important settings on mechanical ventilation in ARDS include: Respiratory rate: The respiratory rate should be set to maintain a normal end-tidal carbon dioxide level (35-45 mmHg), Tidal volume: The tidal volume should be set to maintain a normal pH (7.35-7.45). It is important to note that there is no one-size-fits-all approach to mechanical ventilation in ARDS. The optimal settings will vary depending on the individual patient's condition.

Chapter 7

GASTROENTEROLOGY BOARD QUESTIONS

1. A 33-year-old man presents to the emergency room with sudden, forceful vomiting of stomach contents that occurs without any preceding nausea. He also complains of severe headaches and blurred vision. His past medical history is unremarkable. What is the most likely clinical implication of his projectile vomiting?

- A. Gastrointestinal obstruction
- B. Elevated intracranial pressure.
- C. Esophageal varices
- D. Acute gastritis
- E. Peptic ulcer disease

2. A 54-year-old woman with a past medical history of hypertension and type 2 diabetes presents to her primary care physician with a 2-week history of upper abdominal pain. She describes the pain as a burning sensation that's exacerbated by eating. She denies weight loss, difficulty swallowing, and any changes in bowel habits. As a clinician, which of the following symptoms, if present, would be considered an alarm symptom necessitating further diagnostic evaluation?

- A. Recent onset dyspepsia
- B. Odynophagia
- C. Progressive dysphagia
- D. Upper gastrointestinal bleeding
- E. All of the above

3. A 63-year-old man presents to your office with complaints of hoarseness and difficulty swallowing. He has been experiencing these symptoms for the past few weeks. His physical examination is notable for decreased vocal fold movement and difficulty swallowing liquids. A barium swallow study reveals a narrowing of the esophagus at the level of the cricoid cartilage. The patient is diagnosed with laryngeal cancer. What is the most likely association between the patient's hoarseness and dysphagia?

- A. The hoarseness is a result of the tumor obstructing the vocal cords.
- B. The dysphagia is a result of the tumor obstructing the esophagus.
- C. The hoarseness and dysphagia are both a result of the tumor's involvement of the recurrent laryngeal nerve.
- D. The hoarseness and dysphagia are both a result of the tumor's involvement of the vagus nerve.
- E. The hoarseness and dysphagia are not associated with each other.

4. A 52-year-old woman presents to your office with complaints of difficulty swallowing solid foods. She has been experiencing these symptoms for the past few months. Her physical examination is notable for a smooth, red tongue and a white, web-like membrane at the back of her throat. A blood test reveals iron deficiency anemia. The patient is diagnosed with Plummer-Vinson syndrome. What is the clinical manifestation known as Plummer-Vinson syndrome?

223

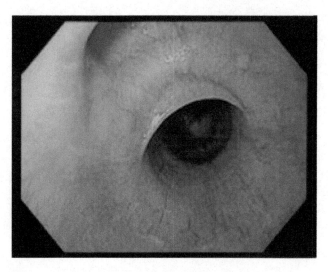

Figure 7.1: 52-year-old woman

- A. Difficulty swallowing solid foods.
- B. Iron deficiency anemia
- C. A smooth, red tongue
- D. A white, web-like membrane at the back of the throat
- E. All of the above

5. A 47-year-old woman presents to your clinic with complaints of difficulty swallowing, both solids and liquids, which has been progressively worsening over the past 6 months. She also reports occasional regurgitation of undigested food. Barium swallow reveals a dilated esophagus with a distal tapering, often referred to as a "bird's beak" appearance. Which of the following medications can be used to manage her condition by inducing relaxation of the Lower Esophageal Sphincter (LES)?

- A. Nifedipine
- B. Isosorbide dinitrate
- C. Sildenafil
- D. Metformin
- E. All of the above except D

6. A 46-year-old woman comes to the clinic with complaints of chest pain and difficulty swallowing. She has a history of recurrent peptic ulcer disease for which she takes over-the-counter medications. She denies any history of heart disease. She has been otherwise healthy and does not smoke or consume alcohol. The pain is described as a burning sensation and is not related to physical activity. She also mentions a recent weight loss. Which of the following medications might be taking could have potentially caused the symptoms?

- A. Doxycycline
- B. Tetracycline
- C. Aspirin
- D. Potassium chloride (KCl)
- E. All of the above

7. A 61-year-old man presents to the emergency department with severe epigastric pain and melena. The patient has a history of rheumatoid arthritis, for which he has been taking over the counter NSAIDs regularly for the past two years. He has no prior history of gastrointestinal disorders. On examination, he appears pale, and his abdomen is tender on palpation in the epigastric area. Lab tests show a decreased hemoglobin level. The patient is suspected of having a gastric ulcer. What is the likelihood that this patient's gastric ulcer is attributable to his chronic use of nonsteroidal anti-inflammatory drugs (NSAIDs)?

- A. Less than 5%
- B. 5-15%

- C. 15-30%
- D. 30-45%
- E. More than 45%

8. A 47-year-old woman presents to your clinic with recurrent peptic ulcers and severe diarrhea. She reports no history of NSAID use and she does not consume alcohol. She has been previously treated with multiple courses of antibiotics for H. pylori infection, but her symptoms continue to persist. Based on her clinical presentation, you suspect Zollinger-Ellison Syndrome (ZES). What is the preferred therapeutic approach for managing this patient's condition?

- A. Administration of antibiotics to treat H. pylori infection.
- B. High-dose omeprazole or lansoprazole until the maximum gastric acid output is less than 10 mmol/h before the next dose.
- C. Surgical resection of the gastrinoma
- D. Strict dietary modifications
- E. Administration of histamine H2-receptor antagonists

9. A 32-year-old woman presents to your clinic with a 2-week history of diarrhea. She describes her stools as watery and voluminous. She has attempted to fast for a day, but this did not change the nature of her stools. She denies any recent travel, use of antibiotics, or consumption of questionable food or water. Her vital signs are within normal limits, she appears well hydrated, and abdominal examination is unremarkable. Which of the following is most likely to be found on laboratory analysis of her stool in this scenario?

- A. Increased concentration of sodium and potassium
- B. Decreased osmolal gap.
- C. Positive Clostridium difficile toxin
- D. Presence of fecal leukocytes
- E. Positive ova and parasites

10. A 46-year-old man presents to your office with complaints of diarrhea, weight loss, and fatigue. He has been experiencing these symptoms for the past few months. His physical examination is notable for pale skin and abdominal distension. A blood test reveals low levels of vitamin B12. The patient is diagnosed with malabsorption. What is the purpose of the d-Xylose absorption test?

- A. To diagnose malabsorption.
- B. To determine the cause of malabsorption.
- C. To monitor the response to treatment for malabsorption.
- D. To assess the risk of malabsorption.
- E. To determine the severity of malabsorption.

11. A 68-year-old man presents with unexplained weight loss, abdominal pain, and chronic diarrhea. He has a medical history of coronary artery disease, chronic obstructive pulmonary disease, and congestive heart failure. You suspect his symptoms may be due to malabsorption resulting from a vascular disease. Which of the following vascular diseases is MOST likely associated with malabsorption in this patient?

- A. Constrictive pericarditis
- B. Left-sided heart failure
- C. Carotid artery stenosis
- D. Abdominal aortic aneurysm
- E. Peripheral artery disease

12. A 36-year-old man with a history of ulcerative colitis presents to your office with complaints of abdominal pain, bloody diarrhea, and fever. He has been experiencing these symptoms for the past few days. His physical examination is notable for abdominal distension and tenderness. A blood test reveals elevated white blood cell count and C-reactive protein. A CT scan of the abdomen reveals colonic wall thickening and dilation. The patient is diagnosed with toxic megacolon. What are the possible complications associated with ulcerative colitis?

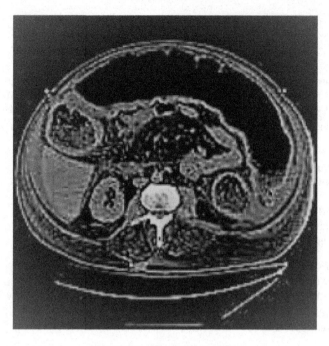

Figure 7.2: Toxic megacolon

- A. Toxic megacolon
- B. Colonic perforation
- C. Colon cancer
- D. All of the above
- E. None of the above

13. A 28-year-old woman presents to your clinic with a 6-month history of recurring abdominal pain and diarrhea. Recently, she has also begun to experience joint pain in her wrists and ankles. She has no prior medical history and takes no medications. Laboratory investigations reveal signs of inflammation, and a colonoscopy shows evidence of chronic inflammation, suggestive of inflammatory bowel disease (IBD). In this patient, which of the following best describes the relationship between her joint symptoms and her suspected IBD?

- A. The joint symptoms are an unrelated coincidence.
- B. The joint symptoms are a direct result of the bowel inflammation.
- C. The joint symptoms are a type of extra-intestinal manifestation of IBD.
- D. The joint symptoms are caused by medications for IBD.
- E. The joint symptoms are indicative of a separate, co-existing autoimmune disease.

14. A 52-year-old man with a history of ulcerative colitis presents to your office with complaints of diarrhea and rectal bleeding. He has been experiencing these symptoms for the past few months. His physical examination is notable for abdominal pain and tenderness. A blood test reveals elevated white blood cell count and C-reactive protein. A colonoscopy reveals ulcerative colitis. The patient has not responded to standard treatments. Which of the following biologics would be the most appropriate first-line treatment option for this patient?

- A. Adalimumab
- B. Infliximab
- C. Vedolizumab
- D. Tofacitinib
- E. None of the above

15. A 37-year-old woman presents with recurring abdominal pain and changes in bowel habits. She reports her symptoms have been ongoing for about 8 months and are causing significant distress. You suspect irritable bowel syndrome (IBS). Which of the following best describes the criteria for diagnosing this condition?

- A. Frequent abdominal pain for at least 1 month, associated with a change in stool frequency or appearance.
- B. Constant abdominal pain for at least 3 months, not associated with defecation or changes in stool.
- C. Recurring abdominal pain weekly for at least 3 months, associated with defecation or changes in stool frequency or appearance.
- D. Intermittent abdominal pain for at least 6 months, unassociated with changes in bowel habits
- E. Continuous abdominal pain for 6 months, relieved with defecation or related to stool changes.

16. A 76-year-old man presents to the emergency department with complaints of periumbilical pain that is disproportionate to tenderness. He has also been experiencing nausea, vomiting, distention, and altered bowel habits. His physical examination is notable for abdominal distention and tenderness. An abdominal x-ray shows signs of bowel distention and air-fluid levels. What is the most likely diagnosis for this patient?

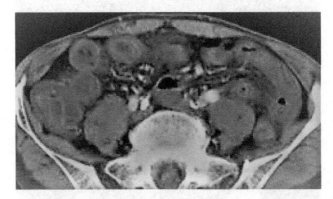

Figure 7.3: 76-year-old man

- A. Acute mesenteric ischemia
- B. Acute appendicitis
- C. Gastroenteritis
- D. Pancreatitis
- E. None of the above

17. A 47-year-old man with a history of intravenous drug use presents with jaundice, pruritus, and fatigue. His laboratory results show elevated liver enzymes and bilirubin. A liver biopsy reveals fibrosing cholestatic hepatitis. Which viral infections should be primarily considered in this case?

- A. Hepatitis A and Hepatitis E
- B. Hepatitis B and Hepatitis C
- C. Hepatitis D and Hepatitis E
- D. Hepatitis A and Hepatitis B
- E. Hepatitis C and Hepatitis E

18. A 34-year-old woman presents to your office with complaints of jaundice and pruritus. She has been experiencing these symptoms for the past few months. Her physical examination is notable for jaundice and excoriations from scratching. A blood test reveals elevated liver enzymes and bile acids. An abdominal ultrasound shows dilated bile ducts. A liver biopsy shows the loss of bile ducts. What is the most likely diagnosis for this patient?

- A. Vanishing bile duct syndrome
- B. Primary biliary cholangitis
- C. Drug-induced liver injury
- D. Autoimmune hepatitis
- E. None of the above

19. A 58-year-old woman presents with right upper quadrant pain, fever, and nausea. An ultrasound reveals an inflamed gallbladder without the presence of gallstones. What is the most likely etiological factor contributing to the development of this patient's acute cholecystitis?

- A. Gallstones

- B. Gallbladder stasis due to fasting or hyperalimentation.
- C. Gallbladder carcinoma
- D. Vasculitis
- E. Common bile duct carcinoma

20. A 48-year-old man presents to your office with complaints of fatigue, pruritus, and jaundice. He has been experiencing these symptoms for the past few months. His physical examination is notable for jaundice and excoriations from scratching. A blood test reveals elevated liver enzymes and bile acids. An abdominal ultrasound shows dilated bile ducts. A liver biopsy shows the loss of bile ducts. What are the associations of primary sclerosing cholangitis (PSC)?

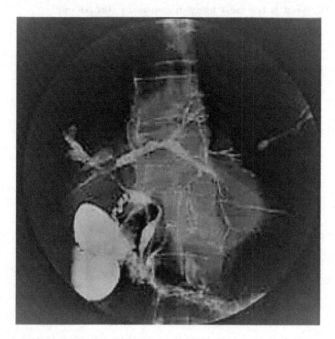

Figure 7.4: PSC

- A. Inflammatory bowel disease
- B. Autoimmune pancreatitis
- C. AIDS
- D. Multifocal fibrosclerosis syndromes
- E. All of the above

21. A 52-year-old man presents to the emergency department with severe, persistent discomfort in the epigastric area that radiates to his back. He also reports nausea and vomiting. On physical examination, he is found to have tachycardia, hypotension, and abdominal tenderness. There is also a blue discoloration in the periumbilical area. Which clinical sign is most likely associated with the patient's presentation?

- A. Cullen's sign
- B. Turner's sign
- C. Murphy's sign
- D. Kehr's sign
- E. Rovsing's sign

22. A 58-year-old man presents to the emergency department with complaints of severe abdominal pain, nausea, and vomiting. He has been experiencing these symptoms for the past few hours. His physical examination is notable for fever, tachycardia, and hypotension. A blood test reveals elevated lipase and amylase levels. An abdominal ultrasound shows an enlarged pancreas with fluid collections. What are the potential systemic complications associated with this patient's acute pancreatitis?

- A. Shock
- B. Gastrointestinal bleeding
- C. Obstruction of the common duct
- D. Ileus
- E. All of the above

23. A 38-year-old male with a history of chronic alcoholism presents with recurrent abdominal pain, weight loss, and chronic diarrhea. His diagnosis of chronic pancreatitis is confirmed. What is the primary therapeutic approach for managing his symptoms?

- A. Pancreatic enzyme replacement therapy
- B. Gastric acid suppression therapy
- C. Prokinetic agents
- D. Bile acid sequestrants
- E. Antibiotics

24. A 50-year-old man with a history of chronic hepatitis C presents to your office for a routine checkup. He has been stable on his current treatment regimen for the past few years. His physical examination is unremarkable. A blood test reveals a normal serum albumin level. What are the implications of this patient's normal serum albumin level?

- A. The patient has a favorable prognosis.
- B. The patient does not have chronic hepatocellular disease.
- C. The patient's liver is functioning normally.
- D. The patient's liver is not functioning normally.
- E. None of the above

25. A 56-year-old man presents with abdominal distention and discomfort. On physical examination, ascites is noted. Lab tests reveal a serum albumin level of 3.0 g/dL and an ascitic fluid albumin level of 1.5 g/dL. Based on the serum-ascites albumin gradient (SAAG), what is the most likely cause of his ascites?

- A. Cirrhosis
- B. Peritonitis
- C. Pancreatitis
- D. Nephrotic syndrome
- E. Malignancy

26. 59-year-old man with a history of cirrhosis and ascites presents to the emergency department with complaints of fever, abdominal pain, and worsening ascites. He has been experiencing these symptoms for the past few days. His physical examination is notable for fever, abdominal distension, and tenderness. A blood test reveals elevated white blood cell count and C-reactive protein. An abdominal ultrasound shows ascites. A diagnostic paracentesis is performed, and the ascitic fluid analysis reveals a polymorphonuclear (PMN) cell count of 300 cells per microliter (L). What is the most likely diagnosis for this patient?

- A. Spontaneous Bacterial Peritonitis (SBP)
- B. Cirrhosis
- C. Ascites
- D. Upper gastrointestinal bleeding
- E. None of the above

27. A 62-year-old man with a known history of advanced cirrhosis presents with an abrupt decline in renal function over the last week. His serum creatinine has increased significantly, and his ascites have become refractory. Imaging and urinalysis show no significant renal pathology. Which of the following is the most likely diagnosis?

- A. Acute tubular necrosis
- B. Glomerulonephritis
- C. Nephrotic syndrome
- D. Type 1 Hepatorenal Syndrome
- E. Type 2 Hepatorenal Syndrome

28. 25-year-old woman presents to your office with complaints of fatigue, nausea, and jaundice. She has been experiencing these symptoms for the past few weeks. Her physical examination is notable for jaundice and hepatomegaly. A

blood test reveals elevated liver enzymes and anti-HAV IgM antibodies. What is the most likely mode of transmission for this patient's HAV infection?

- A. Fecal-oral route
- B. Blood transfusion
- C. Sexual contact
- D. Vertical transmission
- E. None of the above

29. A 38-year-old woman presents with jaundice, fatigue, and abdominal discomfort. You suspect hepatitis B infection and order tests to confirm the diagnosis.Which of the following is NOT typically necessary for routine diagnosis of Hepatitis B Virus (HBV) infection?

- A. Serum HBsAg
- B. IgM anti-HBc
- C. HBV DNA in serum
- D. Anti-HBs
- E. Liver function tests

30. A 24-year-old pregnant woman presents to your office with complaints of fatigue, nausea, and jaundice. She has been experiencing these symptoms for the past few weeks. Her physical examination is notable for jaundice and hepatomegaly. A blood test reveals elevated liver enzymes and anti-HEV IgM antibodies. What is the mortality rate for this patient?

- A. 10%
- B. 20%
- C. 30%
- D. 40%
- E. 50%

31 A 41-year-old woman is admitted to the hospital with signs of acute liver injury. She admits to taking an excessive amount of acetaminophen two days ago. Her laboratory tests confirm the diagnosis of acute liver injury due to acetaminophen overdose. Which of the following is the most appropriate next step in management?

- A. Gastric lavage
- B. Oral administration of charcoal
- C. Administration of N-acetylcysteine
- D. Liver transplantation
- E. Administration of cholestyramine

32. A 27-year-old man presents to the emergency department with complaints of fatigue, nausea, and jaundice. He has been experiencing these symptoms for the past few weeks. His physical examination is notable for jaundice, hepatomegaly, and encephalopathy. A blood test reveals elevated liver enzymes and anti-HAV IgM antibodies. What is the objective of therapy for this patient's fulminant hepatitis?

- A. To provide patient support through the maintenance of fluid balance, circulation and respiration support, bleeding control, hypoglycemia correction, and treatment of additional complications associated with the comatose state, with the aim of facilitating liver regeneration and repair.
- B. To cure the underlying viral infection.
- C. To prevent the development of cirrhosis.
- D. To prevent the development of hepatocellular carcinoma.
- E. To prevent the development of liver failure.

33. A 53-year-old man with a known diagnosis of Hepatitis B is in your clinic for a follow-up visit. He complains of significant side effects from his current treatment regimen. Which of the following treatments for Hepatitis B is known to exhibit limited tolerability?

- A. Lamivudine
- B. Tenofovir
- C. Entecavir
- D. Pegylated Interferon (PEG IFN)

- E. Adefovir

34. A 42-year-old man is diagnosed with chronic hepatitis B. He tests negative for hepatitis B e antigen (HBeAg), exhibits a hepatitis B virus (HBV) DNA level ranging from 1 to greater than 2 times the upper limit of normal, and has an alanine aminotransferase (ALT) level equal to or below the upper limit of normal. What is the recommended therapeutic approach for this patient?

- A. Treatment is not deemed necessary. The patient should be classified as an individual who carries the infection but does not exhibit active symptoms.
- B. Treatment with antiviral medication is recommended to suppress the virus and prevent progression of liver disease.
- C. Treatment with liver transplant is recommended to replace the damaged liver with a healthy one.
- D. Treatment with lifestyle modifications, such as abstaining from alcohol and maintaining a healthy weight, is recommended to reduce the risk of complications.
- E. Treatment with a combination of antiviral medication and lifestyle modifications is recommended.

35. A 41-year-old woman presents with fatigue, jaundice, and right upper quadrant pain. Workup reveals elevated liver enzymes. She has no history of alcohol abuse or unsafe sexual practices. Further serologic testing is planned to determine the cause. Which of the following serologic abnormalities is MOST commonly observed in individuals with autoimmune hepatitis?

- A. Antimitochondrial antibody
- B. Anti-liver-kidney microsomal (anti-LKM) antibodies
- C. False-positive anti-HCV enzyme immunoassay
- D. Smooth muscle antibody
- E. Atypical p-ANCA

36. A 55-year-old man with a history of cirrhosis presents to your office with complaints of fatigue, nausea, and jaundice. He has been experiencing these symptoms for the past few weeks. His physical examination is notable for jaundice, hepatomegaly, and splenomegaly. A blood test reveals elevated liver enzymes and a prothrombin time (PT) that is twice the normal value. What are the potential complications associated with this patient's cirrhosis?

- A. Coagulopathy
- B. Gastroesophageal varices
- C. Factor deficiency
- D. Portal hypertensive gastropathy
- E. All of the above

37. A 47-year-old man with a known history of heavy alcohol use presents to the emergency department with jaundice, fatigue, and abdominal discomfort. His laboratory results reveal elevated bilirubin and prothrombin time. Which of the following is a defining factor of severe alcoholic hepatitis?

- A. Prothrombin time (PT) that is more than five times higher than the control value.
- B. Bilirubin levels below 137 mol/L (or 8 mg/dL)
- C. Elevated levels of albumin in the blood
- D. Absence of azotemia
- E. Hemoglobin levels above 13 g/dL

38. A 64-year-old woman with a history of Primary Biliary Cirrhosis presents to your office with complaints of severe itching. She has been experiencing this symptom for the past few weeks. Her physical examination is notable for jaundice and excoriations from scratching. A blood test reveals elevated liver enzymes and positive anti-mitochondrial antibodies. What is the treatment of choice for this patient's pruritus?

- A. Cholestyramine
- B. Rifampin
- C. Naltrexone
- D. Plasmapheresis

39. A 60-year-old man with cirrhosis undergoes liver transplantation and is in stable condition postoperatively. The transplant team plans to start immunosuppressive therapy to prevent organ rejection. Which of the following pharmaceutical agents is commonly employed for the purpose of immunosuppression subsequent to liver transplantation?

- A. Tacrolimus
- B. Aspirin
- C. Metformin
- D. Furosemide
- E. Atorvastatin

40. A 58-year-old man presents to the emergency department with complaints of fatigue, nausea, and jaundice. He has been experiencing these symptoms for the past few weeks. His physical examination is notable for jaundice, hepatomegaly, and splenomegaly. A blood test reveals elevated liver enzymes and a prothrombin time (PT) that is twice the normal value. An ultrasound of the abdomen shows ascites and portosystemic collaterals. What is the most likely etiology of this patient's portal hypertension?

- A. Prehepatic
- B. Post herpetic
- C. Both prehepatic and post hepatic
- D. Neither prehepatic nor post hepatic.

41. A 51-year-old man with a history of liver cirrhosis presents with hematemesis. You suspect variceal bleeding. Which of the following factors is correlated with the risk of variceal bleeding?

- A. The size and location of the varices
- B. The presence of peptic ulcers
- C. The level of serum sodium
- D. The presence of gastroenteritis
- E. The level of serum creatinine

42. A 59-year-old man with a history of liver cirrhosis presents to the emergency department with complaints of confusion, slurred speech, and irritability. He has been experiencing these symptoms for the past few days. His physical examination is notable for asterixis and a decreased level of consciousness. What is the most likely diagnosis for this patient?

- A. Hepatic encephalopathy
- B. Liver failure
- C. Subdural hematoma
- D. Cerebral edema
- E. Seizure disorder

43. A 61-year-old female with a history of hepatic encephalopathy is experiencing intolerance to lactulose. Which of the following is an alternative treatment option that can be used in this patient?

- A. Neomycin
- B. Amoxicillin
- C. Ciprofloxacin
- D. Levofloxacin
- E. Azithromycin

44. A 36-year-old woman with a history of Acute Intermittent Porphyria presents to the emergency department with complaints of abdominal pain, nausea, and vomiting. She has been experiencing these symptoms for the past few days. Her physical examination is notable for abdominal tenderness and distension. A blood test reveals elevated liver enzymes and a low hemoglobin level. What is the recommended therapeutic approach for this patient?

- A. Administration of heme arginate, heme albumin, or hematin at a dosage of 3-4 mg per day over a period of 4 consecutive days.
- B. Administration of narcotic analgesics for abdominal pain.
- C. Administration of phenothiazines for nausea, vomiting, anxiety, and restlessness.
- D. Administration of intravenous glucose at rates of up to 20 g/h or the use of parenteral nutrition when oral feeding is not feasible for extended durations.
- E. All of the above.

45. A 22-year-old male presents with tremors, dysarthria, and hepatomegaly. You suspect Wilson's Disease. Which of the following diagnostic methods is commonly employed for the identification of Wilson's Disease?

- A. Serum ceruloplasmin levels
- B. Serum calcium levels
- C. Serum albumin levels
- D. Blood urea nitrogen levels
- E. Serum potassium levels

46. 49-year-old man with a history of Wilson's disease is prescribed trientine. He is concerned about the potential side effects of the medication. What are the potential adverse effects associated with the administration of trientine?

- A. Bone marrow suppression
- B. Proteinuria
- C. Hepatic injury
- D. All of the above
- E. None of the above

47. A 58-year-old male presents with a 6-month history of difficulty swallowing. He reports no associated pain but mentions that the problem seems to be getting worse. Which of the following diagnostic procedures would be most appropriate for evaluating his condition?

- A. Esophagogastroduodenoscopy (EGD)
- B. Colonoscopy
- C. Bronchoscopy
- D. Cystoscopy
- E. Laryngoscopy

48. 47-year-old man presents to the gastroenterology clinic with complaints of chest pain and dysphagia. He has been experiencing these symptoms for the past few months. The doctor performs an upper endoscopy and does not see any abnormalities. The doctor suspects that the patient has diffuse esophageal spasm (DES). What pharmaceutical agents can be used to induce spasm during the assessment of DES?

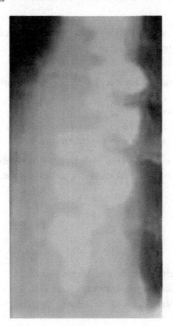

Figure 7.5: DES

- A. Edrophonium
- B. Ergonovine
- C. Bethanechol
- D. All of the above

- E. None of the above

49. A 43-year-old man presents to his doctor with complaints of fatigue, pale skin, and numbness and tingling in his hands and feet. He has been experiencing these symptoms for the past few months. The doctor suspects that the patient has pernicious anemia, which is a condition caused by a deficiency of vitamin B12. What is the purpose of the Schilling test?

- A. To assess B12 malabsorption.
- B. To diagnose pernicious anemia.
- C. To measure the level of vitamin B12 in the blood.
- D. To determine the cause of vitamin B12 deficiency.
- E. To assess the effectiveness of vitamin B12 therapy.

50. A 72-year-old woman presents with chronic diarrhea and weight loss. You suspect a malabsorption disorder. Which of the following findings can be inferred from barium contrast x-ray studies?

- A. Thickened bowel folds
- B. Decreased liver enzymes.
- C. Elevated serum calcium levels
- D. High blood urea nitrogen levels
- E. Increased serum potassium levels

51. A 46-year-old man presents to the emergency department with a complaint of severe chest pain after a bout of forceful vomiting. He has a history of alcohol abuse. Which of the following complications is most likely in this patient?

- A. Aspiration pneumonitis
- B. Boerhaave's syndrome
- C. Dental caries
- D. Metabolic alkalosis
- E. Hypokalemia

52. A 38-year-old woman with a history of Multiple Endocrine Neoplasia type 1 (MEN 1) and Zollinger-Ellison Syndrome (ZES) presents with persistent hypercalcemia and peptic ulcer disease. Which of the following is the most appropriate next step in managing her condition?

- A. Start treatment with a proton pump inhibitor for hypergastrinemia.
- B. Perform total parathyroidectomy.
- C. Surgical resection of the gastrin-secreting tumor
- D. Start treatment with a calcium channel blocker for hypercalcemia.
- E. Start treatment with a bisphosphonate for hypercalcemia.

53. A 52-year-old man presents with chronic diarrhea, weight loss, and abdominal discomfort. Investigations reveal malabsorption. Which of the following is a potential cause of bile salt insufficiency leading to his condition?

- A. Use of Proton Pump Inhibitors
- B. Impaired ileal reabsorption
- C. Regular use of antacids
- D. Lactose intolerance
- E. Pancreatic enzyme deficiency

54. A 46-year-old man presents with pruritus, jaundice, and fatigue. His laboratory results show increased alkaline phosphatase levels. An MRCP reveals multifocal strictures and dilations of the intrahepatic and extrahepatic bile ducts. Which of the following conditions should be included in the differential diagnosis?

- A. Cholangiocarcinoma
- B. Caroli disease
- C. Fasciola hepatica infection
- D. IgG4-associated cholangitis
- E. All of the above

55. A 54-year-old woman with a history of chronic pancreatitis presents with persistent abdominal pain. She has been using various pain medications with little relief. Her physician decides to try a different approach to managing her

pain. Which of the following medications could improve her pain management and potentially reduce the necessity for other pain medications?

- A. Metformin
- B. Pregabalin
- C. Omeprazole
- D. Atorvastatin
- E. Hydrochlorothiazide

56. A 57-year-old male with a history of alcohol abuse presents with jaundice, ascites, and lethargy. Labs show elevated bilirubin, decreased serum albumin, and prolonged prothrombin time. Based on the Child-Pugh classification, which of the following categories best describes the severity of his liver disease?

- A) Child-Pugh class A
- B) Child-Pugh class B
- C) Child-Pugh class C
- D) Child-Pugh class D
- E) Child-Pugh class E

57. A 56-year-old man with a history of hypertension and hyperlipidemia presents to the emergency department with a 2-day history of dysphagia and dysarthria. He reports difficulty initiating a swallow and sometimes coughs or chokes when eating or drinking. His speech is slurred and indistinct. Physical examination reveals weakness of the right facial muscles and decreased sensation on the right side of his body. Which of the following is the most likely diagnosis?

- A. Esophageal stricture
- B. Gastroesophageal reflux disease (GERD)
- C. Stroke
- D. Myasthenia gravis
- E. Amyotrophic lateral sclerosis (ALS)

58. A 56-year-old male patient with a history of long-standing GERD, central adiposity, and smoking presents with new-onset dysphagia. He denies any weight loss or excessive vomiting. Physical examination is normal. What is the most appropriate next step in managing this patient?

- A. Wait and watch for further symptoms
- B. Refer for esophagogastroduodenoscopy (EGD)
- C. Start on proton pump inhibitors (PPIs)
- D. Refer for barium swallow
- E. Advise lifestyle modifications

59. A 45-year-old man presents with epigastric pain that worsens with meals. He has been using nonsteroidal anti-inflammatory drugs (NSAIDs) for arthritis. The patient denies any weight loss, vomiting, or difficulty swallowing. Physical examination reveals mild epigastric tenderness. There is no family history of peptic ulcer disease or gastric cancer. What is the most appropriate next step in managing this patient?

- A. Start a proton pump inhibitor
- B. Refer for esophagogastroduodenoscopy (EGD)
- C. Start empiric treatment for H. pylori
- D. Advise to stop NSAIDs
- E. Reassure and monitor for symptom resolution

60. A 72-year-old man with a history of hypertension, diabetes, and chronic kidney disease presents to the emergency department with hematemesis and melena. He has been taking ibuprofen and aspirin for his arthritis and prednisone for his asthma. On physical examination, he is hypotensive and tachycardic. His hemoglobin is 8 g/dL. Which of the following is the most important initial step in the management of this patient?

- A. Red blood cell transfusion
- B. IV proton pump inhibitor
- C. Esophagogastroduodenoscopy (EGD)
- D. Volume resuscitation with crystalloid fluids
- E. IV antibiotics

61. A 57-year-old woman with cirrhosis, ascites, and splenomegaly presents to the emergency department with hematemesis and melena. She is hemodynamically stable and has received appropriate medical management. Which of the following is the next best step in management?

- A. Gastroenterology consultation for esophagogastroduodenoscopy (EGD)
- B. Sengstaken-Blakemore tube placement
- C. Transjugular intrahepatic portosystemic shunt (TIPS) placement
- D. Gastric variceal sclerotherapy
- E. Observation

62. A 67-year-old obese man presents with a sudden onset of painless, bright red blood per rectum. The bleeding was significant but stopped abruptly. The patient remains hemodynamically stable. His medical history is unremarkable. What is the most probable diagnosis?

- A. Ischemic colitis
- B. Diverticular bleeding
- C. Gastrointestinal malignancy
- D. Upper gastrointestinal bleeding
- E. Hemorrhoidal bleeding

63. A 61-year-old man presents to the clinic with a 6-month history of diarrhea. He reports having 3-4 loose, foul-smelling, floating stools per day. He has also lost 10 pounds of weight unintentionally over the past 6 months. His physical exam is unremarkable. Which of the following is the most likely diagnosis?

- A. Acute infectious diarrhea
- B. Chronic secretory diarrhea
- C. Chronic malabsorptive diarrhea
- D. Irritable bowel syndrome with diarrhea (IBS-D)
- E. Microscopic colitis

64. A 72-year-old woman presents with tiredness and pallor. Laboratory tests reveal a low mean corpuscular volume and an elevated red cell distribution width. She has no overt symptoms of bleeding, but her fecal occult blood test is positive. What is the most appropriate next step in the management of this patient?

- A. Reassure the patient
- B. Perform a CT arteriography
- C. Order a tagged white blood cell (WBC) scan
- D. Conduct a video capsule endoscopy
- E. Initiate iron supplementation

65. A 73-year-old woman is admitted to the hospital for pneumonia and is started on antibiotics. She has a history of chronic constipation for which she takes MiraLAX daily. On hospital day 3, she reports having 4 to 5 loose bowel movements per day. She denies abdominal pain, nausea, vomiting, or fever. Her white blood cell count is 8,000/μL. Stool testing is positive for C. difficile by PCR but negative for C. difficile toxin. What is the most appropriate next step in management?

- A) Discontinue the MiraLAX
- B) Start treatment for C. difficile infection
- C) Continue MiraLAX and monitor the patient clinically
- D) Perform glutamate dehydrogenase testing
- E) Increase the dosage of MiraLAX

66. A 20-year-old man presents to the emergency department with a 2-day history of diarrhea and vomiting. He reports having 3-4 loose, watery stools per day and has vomited once. He has no other significant medical history. On physical examination, he is well-appearing and has a normal vital signs. Which of the following groups of patients is most likely to benefit from antibiotic treatment for nontyphoidal Salmonella infection?

- A. Patients with prior exposure to Salmonella
- B. Immunocompromised patients
- C. Patients with a nontoxic examination and normal PO intake
- D. All patients with nontyphoidal Salmonella infection

- E. None of the above

67. A 65-year-old man with a history of pancreatitis is admitted to the hospital with acute pancreatitis. He develops paralytic ileus of the colon. Which of the following is the most important initial step in management?

- A. Bowel rest
- B. Bowel decompression
- C. Restoring normal intestinal peristalsis
- D. All of the above

68. A 28-year-old man presents with a 2-year history of recurrent episodic vomiting. He says the vomiting episodes are intense and last for 24-48 hours, followed by symptom-free periods. He also mentions that taking hot showers or baths seems to temporarily alleviate his symptoms. On further questioning, he admits to using marijuana daily for the last 4 years. His laboratory tests are all within normal ranges. What is the best management strategy for this patient?

- A. Advise cessation of marijuana use.
- B. Commence ondansetron therapy.
- C. Commence lorazepam therapy.
- D. Order an esophagogastroduodenoscopy.
- E. Start therapy with a tricyclic antidepressant.

69. A 62-year-old woman is recovering in the hospital following a complicated surgery. Despite being on peripheral IV D5NS, she hasn't been meeting her caloric needs. She suffered from colonic pseudo-obstruction post-surgery but she has recently shown signs of recovery as evidenced by the spontaneous passage of stool and flatus and the ability for the rectal tube to be discontinued. What is the most appropriate next step in managing this patient's nutrition?

- A. Begin enteral nutrition.
- B. Start total parenteral nutrition.
- C. Continue with peripheral IV D5NS.
- D. Initiate peripheral parenteral nutrition.
- E. No additional nutritional support is needed.

70. A 56-year-old obese man presents to the emergency department with left lower quadrant abdominal pain and fever. He has no significant medical history. Physical examination reveals left lower quadrant tenderness and guarding. Laboratory studies show a white blood cell count of 12,000/L. A CT scan of the abdomen and pelvis shows diverticulitis without abscess, perforation, or fistula. Which of the following is the most appropriate management plan for this patient?

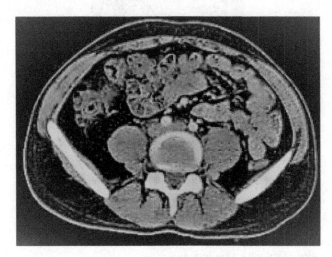

Figure 7.6: Diverticulitis

- A. Hospitalization with intravenous antibiotics

- B. Surgical resection of the sigmoid colon
- C. Outpatient therapy with PO metronidazole and ciprofloxacin for 7 days
- D. Interventional radiology consultation for drain placement
- E. None of the above

71. A 54-year-old man presents to the emergency department with left lower quadrant abdominal pain and fever. He is diagnosed with mild, uncomplicated diverticulitis. Which of the following is the most accurate statement about the risk of recurrence after a first episode of diverticulitis?

- A. The risk of recurrence is low, regardless of the patient's risk factors.
- B. The risk of recurrence is high, and all patients should be treated with prophylactic antibiotics.
- C. The risk of recurrence is low in patients with no risk factors, but higher in patients with obesity, smoking, and a family history of diverticulitis.
- D. The risk of recurrence is 10-30
- E. The risk of recurrence is high in patients with a first episode of diverticulitis, and all patients should be referred for surgery.

72. A 50-year-old woman comes to the clinic for a routine check-up. She discloses that her mother was diagnosed with colorectal cancer at the age of 50. The patient also has a history of hypertension and mentions that her cousin has ulcerative colitis. She also says she regularly takes aspirin for headache relief. Which of the following factors increases her risk of colorectal cancer?

- A. Personal history of hypertension
- B. Family history of colorectal cancer in a first-degree relative
- C. Ulcerative colitis in a cousin
- D. Regular aspirin use
- E. None of the above

73. A 36-year-old woman presents with a 6-month history of recurrent bouts of diarrhea, abdominal pain, and occasional rectal bleeding. She reports up to 10 bowel movements daily, often containing blood and mucus. She is about to undergo a colonoscopy. Given her symptoms and suspected diagnosis of ulcerative colitis, what would you expect to observe during the colonoscopy?

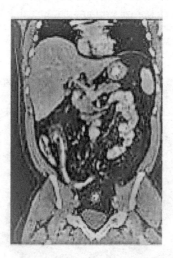

Figure 7.7: Ulcerative Colitis

- A. Grossly normal-appearing colonoscopy.
- B. Deep cobble-stoning ulceration with skip lesions.
- C. Inflammation of the colonic mucosa in a contiguous pattern starting at the rectum and progressing proximally.
- D. Pseudomembranes.
- E. Focal areas of inflammation and ulceration in the ascending colon only.

74. A 46-year-old man is diagnosed with left-sided ulcerative colitis. Which of the following is true about his risk of colorectal cancer?

- A. He has a decreased risk of colorectal cancer compared to the baseline population rate.
- B. He has an increased risk of colorectal cancer compared to the baseline population rate.
- C. He has the same risk of colorectal cancer as the baseline population rate.
- D. His risk of colorectal cancer is unaffected by his diagnosis of ulcerative colitis.
- E. It is impossible to predict his risk of colorectal cancer based on his diagnosis alone.

75. A 50-year-old man with a 20-year history of Crohn's disease involving the ileum and colon presents to the clinic for routine follow-up. He has had several previous hospitalizations for Crohn's flares, but his disease has been relatively well-controlled for the past few years. He is currently taking mesalamine and azathioprine. Which of the following complications is he at risk for?

- A. Biliary obstruction
- B. Fatty liver disease
- C. Osteopenia or osteoporosis
- D. All of the above

76. A 31-year-old female patient has been diagnosed with severe acute ulcerative colitis after going through clinical, endoscopic, and histologic examinations. She has responded positively to IV steroids. Now, she needs to be transitioned to an agent for long-term maintenance of remission. Which among the following is the best treatment option for maintenance of remission in her condition?

- A. Oral Prednisone
- B. Methotrexate
- C. Infliximab
- D. Cyclosporine
- E. Hydroxychloroquine

77. A 78-year-old man with a history of atrial fibrillation (not on anticoagulation) presents with severe abdominal pain that started suddenly 6 hours ago. The pain is diffuse, constant, and severe. He has nausea but no vomiting, diarrhea, or fever. Physical examination reveals a mildly distended, diffusely tender abdomen with no signs of peritonitis. Heart rate is 88/min and regular, and blood pressure is 130/70 mm Hg. Laboratory studies show a lactate level of 4.1 mmol/L (N=0.5–2.2) and a white blood cell count of 14,500/μL (N=4500–11,000). What is the most appropriate next step in diagnosis?

- A. Abdominal ultrasound
- B. Colonoscopy
- C. CT angiography of the abdomen
- D. Magnetic resonance imaging of the abdomen
- E. Upper gastrointestinal series

78. A 72-year-old man with a history of coronary artery disease and carotid artery stenosis presents to the emergency department with postprandial abdominal pain, early satiety, and weight loss. Physical examination reveals no abdominal tenderness or guarding. Laboratory studies are within normal limits. Which of the following is the most likely diagnosis?

- A. Chronic mesenteric ischemia
- B. Crohn's disease
- C. Ulcerative colitis
- D. Ischemic colitis
- E. Diverticulitis

79. A 72-year-old man with a history of coronary artery disease, carotid artery stenosis, and chronic kidney disease presents to the emergency department with postprandial abdominal pain, early satiety, and weight loss. Physical examination reveals no abdominal tenderness or guarding. Laboratory studies are within normal limits. Which of the following imaging tests is the most appropriate initial step in the diagnosis of chronic mesenteric ischemia?

- A. Invasive angiography
- B. CT angiography with venous phase contrast

- C. Ultrasonography without Dopplers of the mesenteric vessels
- D. Ultrasonography with Dopplers of the mesenteric vessels
- E. MR angiography

80. A 46-year-old female with a history of alcohol abuse presents to the emergency department with severe epigastric pain radiating to the back, associated with nausea and vomiting. She reports having multiple prior episodes of acute pancreatitis and states that she had several alcoholic drinks earlier in the day. On examination, she appears uncomfortable and has signs of volume depletion. Lipase level is normal. What is the most appropriate next step in management?

- A) IV lactated Ringer's solution and pain management
- B) Immediate alcohol withdrawal treatment
- C) IV normal saline solution and pain management
- D) Invasive angiography
- E) Administration of prophylactic antibiotics

81. A 47-year-old woman with a history of alcoholism presents to the emergency department with intense epigastric pain, nausea, and vomiting. She reports drinking heavily on the day of admission. On examination, she appears dehydrated, and her blood pressure is low. Her lipase level is normal, but she has a history of multiple prior episodes of acute pancreatitis. What is the best treatment option for this patient?

- A) IV lactated Ringer's solution and pain management
- B) Fluid restriction and alcohol withdrawal management
- C) Parenteral nutrition and analgesics
- D) Surgical intervention
- E) Alcohol abstinence counseling

82. A 22-year-old man presents with steatorrhea and abdominal pain. He has no significant medical history, and his physical exam is unremarkable. Laboratory studies show elevated liver enzymes and pancreatic enzymes. Which of the following is the next best step in laboratory workup?

- A. Antinuclear antibody and IgG subtypes
- B. Cultures for bacteria and viruses
- C. HIV and H. pylori testing
- D. Serum alcohol level
- E. Glucocorticoids

83. A 31-year-old woman presents to the clinic with a 1-week history of jaundice and dark urine. She has no other significant medical history and denies any recent travel or sick contacts. She is taking azithromycin for a sinus infection. Physical examination reveals scleral icterus and dark urine. Laboratory studies show elevated liver enzymes (AST 150 U/L, ALT 200 U/L, ALP 300 U/L) and alkaline phosphatase (300 U/L). Bilirubin is elevated at 4 mg/dL (direct 2 mg/dL, indirect 2 mg/dL). Which of the following is the most likely cause of her liver injury?

- A. Acetaminophen
- B. Azithromycin
- C. Hydralazine
- D. Nitrofurantoin
- E. Penicillin

84. A 28-year-old man presents with jaundice. His liver enzymes are normal, and he has normal liver synthetic function. He does not have any symptoms, medications, or alcohol use. His lab results show an elevated unconjugated bilirubin. What should be the next step in managing this patient's condition?

- A. Order genetic testing for Gilbert syndrome.
- B. Begin treatment with ursodeoxycholic acid.
- C. Review prior lab results and ask about a current illness or stressor.
- D. Request a liver biopsy to rule out other causes of jaundice.
- E. Order an abdominal ultrasound to assess for possible gallstones.

85. A 46-year-old woman presents to the clinic with a 2-month history of pruritus. She has no other significant medical history and denies any recent travel or sick contacts. She is not taking any medications. Physical examination reveals

no jaundice or abdominal tenderness. Laboratory studies show an isolated elevated alkaline phosphatase (ALP) of 150 U/L (normal range 40-120 U/L). All other liver function tests are normal. Which of the following is the next best step in management?

- A. Order antioxidants
- B. Order ultrasonography of the abdomen
- C. Order gamma-glutamyl transpeptidase (GGT) level
- D. Order antimitochondrial antibodies
- E. Refer the patient to a gastroenterologist

86. 25-year-old man who has sex with men presents to the clinic with a 1-week history of nausea, vomiting, jaundice, and right upper quadrant pain. He has no other significant medical history and denies any recent travel or sick contacts. Physical examination reveals scleral icterus and tenderness in the right upper quadrant. Laboratory studies show elevated liver enzymes (AST 1000 U/L, ALT 1500 U/L, ALP 500 U/L) and bilirubin (total 10 mg/dL, direct 5 mg/dL). Which of the following is the most likely cause of his liver injury?

- A. Hepatitis A virus (HAV)
- B. Hepatitis B virus (HBV)
- C. Hepatitis C virus (HCV)
- D. Alcoholic hepatitis
- E. Drug-induced hepatitis

87. A 38-year-old man presents with a positive Hepatitis B envelope Antigen (HBeAg) and a high level of Hepatitis B Virus (HBV) DNA (>20,000 IU/mL). His liver function tests show an elevated alanine aminotransferase (ALT) level. Anti-HBe is negative. What is the most appropriate next step in managing this patient's condition?

- A. Monitor and retest in six months.
- B. Begin tenofovir.
- C. Start interferon therapy.
- D. Initiate lamivudine.
- E. Order a liver biopsy to assess the degree of fibrosis.

88. A 43-year-old man with a history of chronic alcohol abuse is admitted to the hospital with severe alcoholic hepatitis and spontaneous bacterial peritonitis (SBP). His Maddrey discriminant function score is 34, suggesting a high 1-month mortality rate. He has had multiple admissions for alcohol-associated hepatitis in the past. What is the most appropriate next step in the management of this patient's condition?

- A. Administer IV ceftriaxone.
- B. Start oral glucocorticoids.
- C. Begin therapy with pentoxifylline.
- D. Refer for liver transplantation.
- E. Start interferon therapy.

89. A 62-year-old man with chronic kidney disease (eGFR 25 mL/min) is found to have hepatitis C virus (HCV) RNA on routine blood work. He has no significant medical history and denies any recent travel or sick contacts. He is not taking any medications. He has no signs or symptoms of liver disease, and his physical exam is unremarkable. Laboratory studies show an elevated AST (100 U/L) and ALT (150 U/L). All other liver function tests are normal. Vibration-controlled transient elastography shows normal liver stiffness. Which of the following is the most appropriate management for this patient?

- A. Suggest treatment with elbasvir-grazoprevir (a direct-acting antiviral regimen)
- B. Perform a liver biopsy to confirm or exclude cirrhosis
- C. Start treatment with pegylated interferon and ribavirin
- D. Refer the patient to a hepatologist
- E. Observe the patient without treatment

90. A 23-year-old woman presents to the emergency department with a 1-day history of right upper quadrant pain, nausea, and vomiting. She admits to taking an unknown amount of acetaminophen tablets 12 hours ago following a breakup with her boyfriend. Physical examination reveals a lethargic patient with right upper quadrant tenderness. Laboratory studies show an ALT of 5000 U/L, AST of 4600 U/L, and an acetaminophen level is pending. What is the most appropriate next step in management?

- A. Activated charcoal
- B. N-acetylcysteine
- C. Hemodialysis
- D. Pentoxifylline
- E. Observation

91. A 47-year-old man with acute liver failure due to acetaminophen overdose presents to the emergency department with grade 3 encephalopathy. He is intubated and mechanically ventilated. His vital signs are stable, but he is unresponsive to verbal commands. Which of the following is the most appropriate treatment for his encephalopathy?

- A. Lactulose
- B. IV fluids
- C. IV mannitol
- D. Prophylactic antibiotics
- E. Liver transplantation

92. A 50-year-old man with acute liver failure due to acetaminophen overdose is scheduled for a liver transplant. His INR is 1.5 and his platelet count is 10,000/mm3. Which of the following blood products should be administered to the patient prior to the transplant?

- (A) Fresh frozen plasma
- (B) Cryoprecipitate
- (C) Platelets
- (D) Vitamin K
- (E) None of the above

93. A 56-year-old man with a history of cirrhosis due to alcohol use presents to the emergency department with increasing abdominal girth, fever, and mild confusion. On physical examination, his abdomen is distended and diffusely tender to palpation. Diagnostic paracentesis reveals 1500 polymorphonuclear cells/μL. Considering his presentation, which of the following is the most appropriate next step in the management of this patient?

- A. Administer IV ceftriaxone
- B. Administer IV fluoroquinolone
- C. Start amoxicillin-clavulanic acid therapy
- D. Administer IV fourth-generation cephalosporin
- E. Start carbapenem therapy

94. A 60-year-old patient with a known history of liver cirrhosis presents with rapid deterioration in renal function. The patient has been on diuretics and a -blocker. No signs of infection or gastrointestinal bleeding are noted. What is the most appropriate next step in the management of this patient?

- A. Continue the -blocker and increase the dose of diuretics.
- B. Hold diuretics and give IV albumin 1 g/kg.
- C. Start treatment for sepsis.
- D. Start on a trial of midodrine and octreotide.
- E. Increase the dose of -blocker.

95. A 38-year-old man with Child class A cirrhosis and medium-to-large esophageal varices that have not yet bled presents to the clinic. He has no other significant medical history and denies any recent travel or sick contacts. Which of the following is the next most appropriate management step?

- (A) Endoscopic variceal ligation and nonselective -blocker
- (B) Transjugular intrahepatic portosystemic shunt (TIPS)
- (C) Sengstaken-Blakemore tube placement
- (D) Observation without treatment

96. A 61-year-old woman with end-stage renal disease on hemodialysis presents with right upper quadrant abdominal pain and hepatomegaly. She has a history of oral contraceptive pill use and hypertension. Her laboratory studies show elevated liver enzymes (AST 100 U/L, ALT 150 U/L, ALP 500 U/L) and bilirubin (total 10 mg/dL, direct 5 mg/dL). Which of the following imaging tests is the most appropriate initial step in the diagnosis of Budd-Chiari syndrome?

- (A) Abdominal ultrasonography with Dopplers
- (B) MRI with gadolinium
- (C) CT of the abdomen and pelvis with IV contrast
- (D) MRV of the abdomen and pelvis
- (E) Liver biopsy

97. A patient undergoing hematopoietic stem cell transplantation (HSCT) presents with hepatomegaly, right upper quadrant pain, jaundice, and ascites. The patient's condition is associated with a 20% mortality rate. What is the most likely diagnosis?

- A. Hepatocellular carcinoma
- B. Chronic hepatitis B infection
- C. Alcoholic liver disease
- D. Sinusoidal obstruction syndrome
- E. Cirrhosis

98. A 58-year-old man with a history of cirrhosis presents with new-onset ascites. A diagnostic paracentesis reveals a serum-ascites albumin gradient of 2.5. What is the most likely cause of ascites in this patient?

- A. Nephrotic syndrome
- B. Congestive heart failure
- C. Portal hypertension
- D. Tuberculous peritonitis
- E. Malignancy

99. A 60-year-old man with a history of diabetes mellitus presents to the emergency department with fever, abdominal pain, and distention. He had a laparotomy for acute appendicitis 3 days ago. His vital signs are: temperature 39.5°C, heart rate 110 beats/min, respiratory rate 24 breaths/min, and blood pressure 100/60 mmHg. His physical examination reveals tenderness and rebound tenderness in the right upper quadrant of the abdomen. Which of the following imaging tests is the most appropriate next step in management?

- (A) CT of the abdomen and pelvis
- (B) Abdominal ultrasonography
- (C) MRI of the abdomen and pelvis
- (D) X-ray of the abdomen
- (E) Liver biopsy

100. A 64-year-old woman with end-stage renal disease on peritoneal dialysis presents with abdominal pain, fever, and cloudy peritoneal dialysis effluent. Her vital signs are: temperature 39°C, heart rate 120 beats/min, respiratory rate 24 breaths/min, and blood pressure 100/60 mmHg. Her physical examination reveals tenderness and rebound tenderness in the right lower quadrant of the abdomen. Which of the following antibiotic regimens is the most appropriate initial treatment?

- (A) IV ceftriaxone and doxycycline
- (B) IV ciprofloxacin and vancomycin
- (C) IV ampicillin and gentamicin
- (D) IV vancomycin and gentamicin
- (E) Oral amoxicillin-clavulanate

101. A 68-year-old woman presents with right upper quadrant (RUQ) pain, jaundice, fever, chills, confusion, and shock. Ultrasonography reveals dilation of the bile duct but no visible stones. What is the most appropriate initial management for this patient?

- A. Administer broad-spectrum antibiotics only
- B. Administer broad-spectrum antibiotics and perform an urgent liver transplant
- C. Administer broad-spectrum antibiotics and perform an urgent endoscopic retrograde cholangiopancreatography (ERCP)
- D. Administer broad-spectrum antibiotics and perform an urgent laparoscopic cholecystectomy
- E. Administer broad-spectrum antibiotics and perform an urgent percutaneous transhepatic cholangiography (PTC)

102. A 46-year-old obese pregnant woman presents to your clinic with episodic right upper quadrant pain that begins abruptly, lasts for about an hour, and is associated with nausea and belching. She has been experiencing these symptoms for a few weeks now. She has no history of any significant medical conditions. What is the most appropriate next step in the management of this patient's condition?

- A. Initiate therapy for GERD.
- B. Start treatment for gastritis.
- C. Begin a regimen for peptic ulcer disease.
- D. Request a transabdominal ultrasonography.
- E. Schedule immediate surgical intervention.

103. A critically ill patient presents with a persistent fever and shock. Ultrasonography reveals gas in the gallbladder wall, lack of gallbladder wall enhancement, and edema around the gallbladder, but no gallstones are detected. What is the most appropriate course of action?

- A. Cholecystectomy
- B. Trial of a cholecystostomy tube
- C. Initiate total parenteral nutrition
- D. Administer broad-spectrum antibiotics
- E. Continue supportive care and monitor

7.1   ANSWERS

1. The best answer is B. Elevated intracranial pressure.

Projectile vomiting with no preceding nausea, combined with severe headaches and blurred vision, is highly suggestive of elevated intracranial pressure (ICP). Conditions such as traumatic brain injury, brain tumors, intracranial hemorrhage, hydrocephalus, or infections can increase ICP, resulting in these symptoms. Option A, gastrointestinal obstruction, can cause vomiting, but it usually doesn't result in projectile vomiting. Besides, the presence of severe headaches and changes in vision suggest a neurological cause. Option C, esophageal varices, primarily present with upper gastrointestinal bleeding and not usually with projectile vomiting. Option D, acute gastritis, and E, peptic ulcer disease, can cause vomiting, but they are usually associated with abdominal pain and don't typically present with severe headaches and blurred vision. These symptoms are more consistent with a neurological issue, like elevated ICP. In this case, the patient's symptoms warrant immediate investigation and management to identify the cause of the elevated ICP and prevent further complications.

2.The best answer is E. All of the above.

Alarm symptoms in the evaluation of gastrointestinal disorders are symptoms that suggest a serious underlying condition, necessitating further diagnostic evaluation such as endoscopy or imaging. These include: A. Recent onset dyspepsia: Dyspepsia, or upper abdominal pain, is a common symptom. However, its recent onset in individuals aged 45 years and older is considered an alarm symptom because it could be indicative of an underlying condition like gastric cancer. B. Odynophagia: This refers to painful swallowing. It can be a sign of severe esophagitis, stricture, or esophageal cancer. C. Progressive dysphagia: This refers to an increasing difficulty in swallowing. The progression can suggest a narrowing of the esophagus, possibly due to conditions like esophageal cancer. D. Upper gastrointestinal bleeding: Symptoms such as hematemesis (vomiting blood) or melena (black, tarry stools) can indicate upper gastrointestinal bleeding, which can be due to various severe conditions like peptic ulcer disease, esophageal varices, or gastric cancer. Given the woman's age and symptoms, the presence of any of these alarm symptoms would necessitate further diagnostic evaluation to rule out serious conditions.

3. The correct answer is C: the hoarseness and dysphagia are both a result of the tumor's involvement of the recurrent laryngeal nerve.

The recurrent laryngeal nerve is responsible for innervating the vocal cords. When the nerve is damaged, it can lead to hoarseness and difficulty swallowing. In the patient in the question, the tumor is obstructing the recurrent laryngeal nerve, which is causing both his hoarseness and dysphagia. Here are some other potential associations between hoarseness and dysphagia: Laryngitis: Inflammation of the larynx can cause hoarseness and, in some cases, dysphagia. Gastroesophageal reflux disease (GERD): GERD can cause inflammation of the larynx, which can lead to hoarseness and dysphagia. Neuromuscular disorders: Neuromuscular disorders, such as myasthenia gravis, can affect the muscles of the larynx and esophagus, leading to hoarseness and dysphagia.

4.The correct answer is E: all of the above.

Plummer-Vinson syndrome is a rare condition that is characterized by difficulty swallowing solid foods (oropharyngeal dysphagia), iron deficiency anemia, a smooth, red tongue, and a white, web-like membrane at the back of the throat. The exact cause of Plummer-Vinson syndrome is unknown, but it is thought to be related to a deficiency of vitamin B12 or iron. Plummer-Vinson syndrome can be a precursor to esophageal cancer.

5. The correct answer is E: all of the above.

Nifedipine and isosorbide dinitrate are calcium channel blockers that can induce relaxation of the LES. Sildenafil is a phosphodiesterase-5 inhibitor that can enhance the relaxation of the LES that occurs during swallowing. All of these medications can be used to manage achalasia, and they can help to prevent the necessity of dilation or surgery. Here are some other medications that can be used to manage achalasia: Botulinum toxin injections: Botulinum toxin can be injected into the LES to relax it. Balloon dilation: A balloon can be inflated in the LES to stretch it open. Surgery: Surgery can be used to create a new opening between the esophagus and stomach.

6.The best answer is E. All of the above.

All the medications listed, including Doxycycline (A), Tetracycline (B), Aspirin (C), and Potassium chloride (KCl) (D), have the potential to cause localized inflammation in the esophagus, which can manifest esophagitis. This condition can present symptoms such as chest pain and difficulty swallowing, which the patient is experiencing. Doxycycline and tetracycline are antibiotics that can cause esophagitis, especially when taken without adequate amounts of water or right before bedtime. Aspirin and other nonsteroidal anti-inflammatory drugs (NSAIDs) can also cause inflammation of the esophagus and exacerbate symptoms in patients with pre-existing esophageal disorders. Potassium chloride (KCl) is known to cause esophageal ulcers, particularly when a pill gets stuck in the esophagus. Given the patient's history of peptic ulcer disease and the use of over-the-counter medications (which may include NSAIDs), her symptoms could be attributed to one of these medications causing esophageal inflammation. Therefore, the best answer is E. All of the above.

7. The best answer is C. 15-30%.

Chronic use of salicylates or nonsteroidal anti-inflammatory drugs (NSAIDs) is a known risk factor for the development of gastric ulcers. It has been estimated that approximately 15-30% of gastric ulcers can be attributed to the chronic use of these medications. The patient in the question has been taking over the counter NSAIDs regularly for the past two years, which increases his risk of developing a gastric ulcer. Other symptoms such as severe epigastric pain, melena, and decreased hemoglobin level further support this diagnosis. Therefore, the best answer is C. 15-30%

8. The best answer is B. High-dose omeprazole or lansoprazole until the maximum gastric acid output is less than 10 mmol/h before the next dose.

Zollinger-Ellison Syndrome (ZES) is a condition characterized by the development of gastrin-secreting tumors (gastrinomas) in the pancreas and duodenum, leading to severe peptic ulcers and diarrhea. The preferred initial treatment for patients with ZES who candidates for surgical tumor resection are not the administration of proton pump inhibitors (PPIs) like omeprazole or lansoprazole. These medications are given in high doses and the dosage is adjusted gradually until the maximum gastric acid output is less than 10 mmol/h before the next dose. This approach helps control the symptoms and complications of ZES by reducing gastric acid secretion. Therefore, the best answer is B. High-dose omeprazole or lansoprazole until the maximum gastric acid output is less than 10 mmol/h before the next dose.

9.The best answer is A. Increased concentration of sodium and potassium.

This patient's symptoms are consistent with secretory diarrhea, which is characterized by watery, voluminous stools that persist even with fasting. This type of diarrhea occurs when there is an active secretion or inhibition of absorption of electrolytes and water in the gut, leading to an increase in stool water content. The electrolytes sodium and potassium are typically increased in the stool in secretory diarrhea. The osmolal gap, which is the difference between the measured stool osmolality and the osmolality accounted for by sodium and potassium, usually remains below 40 in secretory diarrhea because most of the osmolality can be accounted for by these electrolytes. Therefore, the best answer is A. Increased concentration of sodium and potassium.

10. The d-Xylose absorption test is a convenient method for evaluating the functionality of small-bowel absorption.

D-Xylose is a simple sugar that is not metabolized by the body. It is absorbed in the small intestine and excreted in the urine. The d-Xylose absorption test measures the amount of d-Xylose that is absorbed in the small intestine and excreted in the urine. A low d-Xylose absorption rate indicates that there is a problem with small-bowel absorption. The d-Xylose absorption test can be used to diagnose malabsorption and to monitor the response to treatment for malabsorption. Here are some other tests that can be used to diagnose malabsorption: Stool analysis: Stool can be analyzed for the presence of fat, undigested food particles, and bacteria. Intestinal biopsy: A small piece of tissue can be removed from the intestine for examination under a microscope. Breath test: A breath test can be used to measure the amount of a certain gas that is produced after eating a specific food.

11. The best answer is A. Constrictive pericarditis.

In the clinical context of malabsorption, certain vascular diseases can be associated. Constrictive pericarditis, right-sided heart failure, and mesenteric arterial or venous insufficiency can lead to malabsorption. These conditions can cause decreased blood flow or congestion in the intestinal tract, disrupting the normal absorption of nutrients. In this patient with a history of heart disease, constrictive pericarditis could be a possible cause of his symptoms. Constrictive pericarditis can lead to elevated venous pressures, including in the portal system, which can, in turn, lead to protein-losing enteropathy and malabsorption. Right-sided heart failure can cause similar symptoms but is less likely in the absence of other signs of systemic congestion. Therefore, the best answer is A. Constrictive pericarditis.

12. The correct answer is D: all of the above.

Ulcerative colitis is a chronic inflammatory bowel disease that affects the lining of the colon. It can cause a variety of symptoms, including diarrhea, rectal bleeding, abdominal pain, and weight loss. In severe cases, ulcerative colitis can lead to complications such as toxic megacolon, colonic perforation, and colon cancer. Toxic megacolon is a life-threatening condition that occurs when the colon becomes dilated and inflamed. Colonic perforation is a hole in the colon wall that can lead to peritonitis, a serious infection of the lining of the abdomen. Colon cancer is a risk for people with ulcerative colitis, especially those who have had the disease for many years. The presence of dysplasia can be identified through the examination of surveillance colonoscopic biopsies, which may occur before or concurrently with the development of cancer. Dysplasia is an abnormal growth of cells in the colon that can be a precursor to cancer.

13. The best answer is C. The joint symptoms are a type of extra-intestinal manifestation of IBD.

This patient's joint symptoms are likely an example of peripheral arthritis, a known extra-intestinal manifestation of inflammatory bowel disease (IBD). Peripheral arthritis typically affects large joints like the knees, ankles, and wrists, and its activity often correlates with the activity of the bowel disease. Therefore, it's not a direct result of bowel inflammation (as in choice B), nor is it caused by IBD medications (as in choice D) or suggestive of a separate autoimmune disease (as in choice E). It's also not an unrelated coincidence (as in choice A). Therefore, the best answer is C. The joint symptoms are a type of extra-intestinal manifestation of IBD.

14. The correct answer is C: vedolizumab.

Vedolizumab is a biologic that is often used as a first-line option for ulcerative colitis, particularly in older patients with comorbidities or those with a higher risk of infection. This drug has been shown to be a cost-effective option when included in health plan formularies. Adalimumab and infliximab are also biologics that are used to treat ulcerative colitis, but they are not as commonly used as first-line agents. Tofacitinib is a small molecule that is approved for use in ulcerative colitis, but it is not a biologic. The selection of the most appropriate biologic treatment for ulcerative colitis is a complex decision that should be made in consultation with a healthcare provider. Factors that may be considered include the specific type of IBD (Crohn's Disease or Ulcerative Colitis), the patient's individual characteristics, and the patient's response to previous treatments.

15. The best answer is C. Recurring abdominal pain weekly for at least 3 months, associated with defecation or changes in stool frequency or appearance.

The Rome IV criteria are commonly used for the diagnosis of irritable bowel syndrome (IBS). The criteria specify that the patient should have recurred abdominal pain on average at least 1 day per week in the last 3 months, and it must be associated with two or more of the following criteria: related to defecation, associated with a change in stool frequency, or associated with a change in form (appearance) of stool. The symptoms should have started at least 6 months before diagnosis. Therefore, the best answer is C. Recurring abdominal pain weekly for at least 3 months, associated with defecation or changes in stool frequency or appearance. Other options do not match the Rome IV criteria for the diagnosis of IBS.

16. The correct answer is A: acute mesenteric ischemia.

The clinical manifestations of acute mesenteric ischemia are typically periumbilical pain that is disproportionate to tenderness, along with symptoms such as nausea, vomiting, distention, gastrointestinal bleeding, and altered bowel habits. The abdominal x-ray may show signs of bowel distention, air-fluid levels, and thumbprinting. The presence of peritoneal signs is indicative of bowel infarction, which necessitates surgical resection. The other answer choices are less likely diagnoses for this patient. Acute appendicitis typically presents with right lower quadrant pain that is associated with nausea, vomiting, and fever. Gastroenteritis typically presents with nausea, vomiting, diarrhea, and abdominal cramps. Pancreatitis typically presents with epigastric pain that is associated with nausea, vomiting, and fever.

17. The best answer is B. Hepatitis B and Hepatitis C.

Fibrosing cholestatic hepatitis (FCH) is a severe form of liver disease that is often seen in patients with viral hepatitis. The condition is characterized by rapid progression of fibrosis and cholestasis, and it is most commonly associated with Hepatitis B and Hepatitis C infections, particularly in immunocompromised individuals. Therefore, in the context of a patient with a history of intravenous drug use (a risk factor for Hepatitis B and C) presenting with signs of advanced liver disease, Hepatitis B and Hepatitis C (choice B) would be the most likely viral causes to consider. Other forms of viral hepatitis, such as Hepatitis A, D, and E (choices A, C, and E), are less commonly associated with FCH. Although Hepatitis B can coexist with Hepatitis D (choice D), Hepatitis D alone is not a common cause of FCH.

18. The correct answer is A: vanishing bile duct syndrome.

The clinical presentation of VBDS is typically jaundice and pruritus. Other symptoms may include fatigue, right upper quadrant pain, and weight loss. Diagnosis is typically made on the basis of these clinical symptoms, biochemical tests showing elevated bile acid levels in the blood, imaging studies, and liver biopsy demonstrating the loss or reduction of bile ducts. The other answer choices are less likely diagnoses for this patient. Primary biliary cholangitis is a chronic autoimmune disease that affects the small bile ducts in the liver. Drug-induced liver injury can cause jaundice and pruritus, but it is usually accompanied by other symptoms, such as fever, rash, and muscle pain. Autoimmune hepatitis is another chronic autoimmune disease that affects the liver, but it usually presents with symptoms of liver inflammation, such as fever, fatigue, and right upper quadrant pain.

19. The best answer is B. Gallbladder stasis due to fasting or hyperalimentation.

The majority of acute cholecystitis cases are attributed to gallstones (around 90%). However, in this patient, the ultrasound reveals an inflamed gallbladder without the presence of gallstones, indicating acalculous cholecystitis which accounts for 5-10% of cases. Acalculous cholecystitis can be due to a variety of etiological factors, including gallbladder stasis resulting from fasting or hyperalimentation, which is the most common etiology in this scenario (choice B). Gallbladder or common bile duct carcinoma (choices C and E) are less common causes. Vasculitis (choice D) is a rare cause. Though gallstones (choice A) are the most common cause of acute cholecystitis, the ultrasound in this case did not reveal any gallstones, making this option unlikely in this particular patient.

20. The correct answer is E: all of the above.

Primary sclerosing cholangitis (PSC) is a chronic inflammatory disease of the bile ducts. It is frequently associated with inflammatory bowel disease, particularly ulcerative colitis. Other associations of PSC include autoimmune pancreatitis, AIDS, and multifocal fibrosclerosis syndromes. Inflammatory bowel disease is a group of chronic diseases that involve inflammation of the digestive tract. Ulcerative colitis is a type of inflammatory bowel disease that causes inflammation of the lining of the colon. Autoimmune pancreatitis is a rare condition that causes inflammation of the pancreas. AIDS is a chronic condition caused by the human immunodeficiency virus (HIV). Multifocal fibrosclerosis syndromes are a group of rare conditions that involve the development of scar tissue in multiple organs. The association between PSC and inflammatory bowel disease is thought to be due to an underlying autoimmune process. The association between PSC and other conditions is not fully understood.

21. The best answer is A. Cullen's sign.

The patient's symptoms and physical examination findings are consistent with acute pancreatitis. Cullen's sign, which is characterized by periumbilical blue discoloration due to hemoperitoneum, is a rare but recognized clinical sign of severe acute pancreatitis (choice A). Turner's sign (choice B) is also associated with acute pancreatitis, but it is characterized by a blue-red-purple or green-brown discoloration of the flanks, not the periumbilical area. Murphy's sign (choice C) is a clinical sign of acute cholecystitis, characterized by sudden cessation of inspiration due to pain when the gallbladder is palpated. Kehr's sign (choice D) is left shoulder pain due to diaphragmatic or spleen irritation, often associated with ruptured spleen, ectopic pregnancy, or referred pain from the phrenic nerve. Rovsing's sign (choice E) is elicited in acute appendicitis when palpation of the left lower quadrant causes pain in the right lower quadrant.

22. The correct answer is E: all of the above.

Acute pancreatitis is a serious medical condition that can lead to a number of systemic complications. Some of the potential systemic complications associated with acute pancreatitis include: Shock: This is a life-threatening condition that occurs when the body's organs do not receive enough blood flow. Gastrointestinal bleeding: This can occur due to erosion of the lining of the stomach or intestines. Obstruction of the common duct: This can occur if the pancreas becomes swollen and blocks the duct that carries bile from the liver to the small intestine. Ileus: This is a condition in which the bowel stops moving. Splenic infarction or rupture: This can occur if the spleen becomes damaged by the inflammation from pancreatitis. Disseminated intravascular coagulation: This is a serious condition in which the blood clots abnormally. Subcutaneous fat necrosis: This can occur when the fat under the skin becomes inflamed. Acute respiratory distress syndrome: This is a life-threatening condition in which the lungs do not get enough oxygen. Pleural effusion: This is a build-up of fluid in the space between the lungs and the chest wall. Acute renal failure: This is a condition in which the kidneys stop working properly. Sudden onset of blindness: This is a rare complication of pancreatitis that can occur due to inflammation of the optic nerve.

23.The best answer is A. Pancreatic enzyme replacement therapy.

Chronic pancreatitis often results in malabsorption and pain symptoms, primarily due to the loss of pancreatic enzyme function. The fundamental approach to treating these symptoms in chronic pancreatitis is the administration of pancreatic enzyme replacement therapy (choice A). This therapy typically manages symptoms of diarrhea and improves fat absorption to a satisfactory extent, which in turn facilitates weight restoration. Gastric acid suppression therapy (choice B) is used to treat conditions like gastroesophageal reflux disease (GERD) and peptic ulcer disease, not chronic pancreatitis. Prokinetic agents (choice C) are used to enhance gastrointestinal motility, and while they might help with some symptoms, they do not address the underlying issue in chronic pancreatitis. Bile acid sequestrants (choice D) are primarily used in the management of dyslipidemia. Antibiotics (choice E) are used to treat bacterial infections and do not play a role in the management of chronic pancreatitis unless there is a concomitant infection.

24. The correct answer is A: the patient has a favorable prognosis.

Serum albumin is a protein that is produced by the liver. It is an important marker of liver function. A normal serum albumin level indicates that the liver is functioning normally. In patients with chronic hepatocellular disorders, a normal serum albumin level is a good prognostic sign. A low serum albumin level can be a sign of liver damage or dysfunction. It can also be a sign of malnutrition or other medical conditions. If you have a low serum albumin level, it is important to see a doctor to determine the cause and get treatment. Here are some other implications of a typical albumin level in cases of chronic hepatocellular disorders: A normal serum albumin level can help to differentiate between chronic hepatocellular disorders and other medical conditions that can cause liver damage, such as alcoholism or non-alcoholic fatty liver disease. A normal serum albumin level can also help to predict the long-term prognosis of patients with chronic hepatocellular disorders. Patients with a normal serum albumin level are more likely to have a favorable prognosis than patients with a low serum albumin level.

25. The best answer is A. Cirrhosis.

The serum-ascites albumin gradient (SAAG) is calculated by subtracting the ascitic fluid albumin level from the serum albumin level. In this case, the SAAG is 3.0 g/dL - 1.5 g/dL = 1.5 g/dL. A SAAG value of 1.1 g/dL or greater is indicative of ascites due to portal hypertension, most commonly due to cirrhosis (choice A). Peritonitis (choice B), pancreatitis (choice C), nephrotic syndrome (choice D), and malignancy (choice E) typically result in a SAAG of less than 1.1 g/dL, as these conditions cause ascites due to increased capillary permeability rather than portal hypertension. 26. 55-year-old man with a history of cirrhosis and ascites presents to the emergency department with complaints of fever, abdominal pain, and worsening ascites. He has been experiencing these symptoms for the past few days. His physical examination is notable for fever, abdominal distension, and tenderness. A blood test reveals elevated white blood cell count and C-reactive protein. An abdominal ultrasound shows ascites. A diagnostic paracentesis is performed, and the ascitic fluid analysis reveals a polymorphonuclear (PMN) cell count of 300 cells per microliter (L).

26. The correct answer is A: Spontaneous Bacterial Peritonitis (SBP).

The clinical presentation of SBP is typically fever, abdominal pain, and worsening ascites. Other symptoms may include nausea, vomiting, diarrhea, and weight loss. Diagnosis is typically made on the basis of these clinical symptoms, biochemical tests showing elevated white blood cell count and C-reactive protein, ascitic fluid analysis revealing a

PMN cell count of greater than 250 cells per microliter (L), and diagnostic paracentesis with positive culture. The other answer choices are less likely diagnoses for this patient. Cirrhosis is a chronic liver disease that can cause ascites, but it does not typically cause fever or abdominal pain. Ascites is a buildup of fluid in the abdomen, but it does not typically cause fever or abdominal pain. Upper gastrointestinal bleeding is a potential complication of cirrhosis, but it does not typically cause ascites. None of the other answer choices are associated with the clinical presentation of SBP.

27. The best answer is D. Type 1 Hepatorenal Syndrome.

The patient's rapid decline in renal function over the course of a week, in the context of advanced cirrhosis and refractory ascites, and in the absence of any clear renal pathology, is suggestive of Type 1 Hepatorenal Syndrome (HRS) (choice D). This condition is characterized by a notable decline in renal function within a timeframe of 1-2 weeks. Acute tubular necrosis (choice A) typically occurs as a result of severe injury or acute renal ischemia and would show evidence of renal pathology. Glomerulonephritis (choice B) and nephrotic syndrome (choice C) would also show specific signs on urinalysis and possibly on renal imaging, which are absent in this case. Type 2 HRS (choice E) is characterized by a slower, progressive renal impairment and is typically associated with a more stable clinical course compared to Type 1 HRS. Given the patient's rapid decline in renal function, Type 1 HRS is more likely in this case.

28. The correct answer is A: fecal-oral route.

Hepatitis A virus (HAV) is predominantly transmitted through the fecal-oral route. This means that the virus is found in the feces of an infected person and can be transmitted through contact with contaminated food or water, or through close personal contact with an infected person. The other answer choices are less likely modes of transmission for HAV infection. Blood transfusion is a possible mode of transmission, but it is less common than fecal-oral transmission. Sexual contact is not a recognized mode of transmission for HAV infection. Vertical transmission (from mother to child) is possible, but it is also rare.

29. The best answer is C. HBV DNA in serum.

The diagnosis of hepatitis B infection typically involves testing for serum HBsAg (choice A) and IgM anti-HBc (choice B). The presence of HBsAg in the serum is indicative of both acute and chronic infection. Additionally, the presence of IgM anti-HBc can provide insights into acute or recent infection. Although the detection of HBV DNA in serum (choice C) can be useful in certain situations, such as measuring response to antiviral therapy or determining the infectivity of a patient, it is not typically necessary for routine diagnosis of HBV infection. Anti-HBs (choice D') is not used in the initial diagnosis of HBV; however, it is used in determining immunity to HBV, either from vaccination or past infection. Liver function tests (choice E) can provide information on the level of liver damage or inflammation but do not directly diagnose HBV infection.

30. The correct answer is A: 10% to 20%.

Pregnant women are at an increased risk of developing severe complications from hepatitis E virus (HEV) infection. The mortality rate among pregnant women with HEV infection ranges from 10% to 20%. This is significantly higher than the mortality rate among non-pregnant adults with HEV infection, which is less than 1%. The reason for the increased risk of severe complications in pregnant women with HEV infection is not fully understood. However, it is thought to be due to a combination of factors, including the hormonal changes that occur during pregnancy, the decreased immune function that occurs during pregnancy, and the increased demands that pregnancy places on the liver.

31. The best answer is C. Administration of N-acetylcysteine.

In the case of acetaminophen overdose, a targeted therapeutic approach exists in the utilization of sulfhydryl compounds, such as N-acetylcysteine (choice C). The administration of therapy should ideally commence within a time frame of 8 hours following ingestion, although it is noteworthy that therapeutic interventions may still yield positive outcomes if initiated within a period of 24-36 hours subsequent to the occurrence of overdose. Gastric lavage (choice A) and oral administration of charcoal (choice B) are interventions typically used immediately following ingestion of a toxic substance to prevent absorption. However, given that the patient ingested the acetaminophen two days ago, these interventions are unlikely to be beneficial. Liver transplantation (choice D) is an option in instances of significant severity, but it is generally considered after medical treatments have failed or in cases of fulminant liver failure. Cholestyramine (choice E) is a bile acid sequestrant that can be used in certain types of drug toxicity, but it is not the treatment of choice in acetaminophen overdose.

32. The correct answer is A: to provide patient support through the maintenance of fluid balance, circulation and respiration support, bleeding control, hypoglycemia correction, and treatment of additional complications associated with the comatose state, with the aim of facilitating liver regeneration and repair.

Fulminant hepatitis is a life-threatening condition that occurs when there is rapid and extensive liver damage. The objective of therapy for fulminant hepatitis is to provide patient support and facilitate liver regeneration and repair. This includes:

- Maintaining fluid balance
- Supporting circulation and respiration
- Controlling bleeding
- Correcting hypoglycemia
- Treating additional complications associated with the comatose state.

There is no specific treatment for the underlying viral infection that causes fulminant hepatitis. However, supportive therapy can help to improve the chances of survival and prevent complications.

33. The best answer is D. Pegylated Interferon (PEG IFN).

Pegylated Interferon (PEG IFN) (choice D) is a treatment for Hepatitis B that is known to exhibit limited tolerability. Patients taking PEG IFN may experience side effects such as flu-like symptoms, depression, and cytopenias, which can limit its use in certain patient populations. Lamivudine (choice A), Tenofovir (choice B), Entecavir (choice C), and Adefovir (choice E) are all antiviral medications used in the treatment of Hepatitis B. While these medications can have side effects, they are generally better tolerated than PEG IFN.

34. The correct answer is A: treatment is not deemed necessary.

In this case, the patient is HBeAg negative, which means that the virus is not actively replicating. The HBV DNA level is also only mildly elevated, and the ALT level is normal. This suggests that the patient is not experiencing any active liver damage. In general, treatment for chronic hepatitis B is not recommended for patients who are HBeAg negative and have normal ALT levels. These patients are considered to be carriers of the virus, but they do not exhibit active symptoms. Treatment with antiviral medication can be associated with side effects, and it is not clear that it provides any benefit in this setting. The patient should be monitored regularly with blood tests to assess the level of the virus and the liver function. If the virus becomes more active or if the ALT level begins to rise, then treatment with antiviral medication may be recommended.

35.The best answer is D. Smooth muscle antibody.

Autoimmune hepatitis is often characterized by the presence of several serologic abnormalities. Among them, smooth muscle antibody (choice D) is observed with a prevalence of 40-80%, making it one of the most common findings in individuals with this condition. Antimitochondrial antibodies (choice A) are present in 10-20% of cases and are more commonly associated with primary biliary cholangitis. Anti-liver-kidney microsomal (anti-LKM) antibodies (choice B) are typically associated with Type II autoimmune hepatitis, but this is less common than Type I, which is associated with smooth muscle antibodies. False-positive anti-HCV enzyme immunoassay (choice C) can occur but is not a typical finding in autoimmune hepatitis. Atypical p-ANCA (choice E) may be present in autoimmune hepatitis, but it is less commonly observed than smooth muscle antibodies.

36. The correct answer is E: all of the above.

Cirrhosis is a chronic liver disease that is characterized by the formation of scar tissue in the liver. This scar tissue can block the flow of blood through the liver, leading to portal hypertension. Portal hypertension is a condition in which the blood pressure in the portal vein is increased. This can lead to a number of complications, including: Coagulopathy: This is a condition in which the blood does not clot properly. This can be caused by a deficiency of clotting factors, which are produced by the liver. Gastroesophageal varices: These are dilated veins that form in the esophagus or stomach. They can rupture and bleed, which can be a life-threatening complication. Factor deficiency: This is a condition in which there is a deficiency of one or more clotting factors. This can be caused by liver damage or by other conditions. Portal hypertensive gastropathy: This is a condition in which the lining of the stomach becomes inflamed. It can cause bleeding and other complications. Splenomegaly: This is an enlargement of the spleen. The spleen is an organ that helps to filter the blood. Splenomegaly can cause a number of complications, including thrombocytopenia (low platelet count).

37. The best answer is A. Prothrombin time (PT) that is more than five times higher than the control value. Severe alcoholic hepatitis is a serious condition that is characterized by a number of specific lab abnormalities. One defining

factor of severe alcoholic hepatitis is a prothrombin time (PT) that is more than five times higher than the control value (choice A).

Bilirubin levels in severe alcoholic hepatitis typically exceed 137 mol/L (or 8 mg/dL) (choice B is incorrect because it states that the levels are below this value). Hypoalbuminemia, or reduced levels of albumin in the blood, is another characteristic (choice C is incorrect because it states that the levels are elevated). The presence of azotemia, or high levels of nitrogen compounds in the blood, is another defining factor (choice D is incorrect because it states the absence of azotemia). Hemoglobin levels above 13 g/dL (choice E) are not a defining factor of severe alcoholic hepatitis.

38. The correct answer is A: cholestyramine.

Cholestyramine is a bile acid sequestrant that is typically administered alongside meals. It works by binding to bile acids in the intestine, which helps to reduce their absorption. This can help to relieve pruritus in patients with Primary Biliary Cirrhosis. If cholestyramine is not effective, other treatment options may be considered. These include rifampin, naltrexone, and plasmapheresis. Rifampin: This is an antibiotic that has been shown to be effective in some patients with Primary Biliary Cirrhosis. It works by reducing the production of bile acids. Naltrexone: This is a medication that is typically used to treat addiction. It has also been shown to be effective in some patients with Primary Biliary Cirrhosis. It works by blocking the effects of endorphins, which are hormones that can cause itching. Plaspheresis: This is a procedure in which the blood is removed from the body, the plasma is separated from the cells, and the plasma is then returned to the body. Plasmapheresis can help to remove antibodies and other substances that may be causing the itching.

39. The best answer is A. Tacrolimus.

Immunosuppression is crucial after liver transplantation to prevent organ rejection. Tacrolimus (choice A) is commonly used in conjunction with other agents such as glucocorticoids, sirolimus, everolimus, mycophenolate mofetil, or OKT3 (monoclonal antithymocyte globulin). Aspirin (choice B) is an antiplatelet drug and, while it may be used in some post-transplant patients for cardiovascular disease prevention, it is not typically used for post-transplant immunosuppression. Metformin (choice C) is an antidiabetic medication, Furosemide (choice D) is a diuretic used to treat fluid overload conditions like heart failure or liver disease, and Atorvastatin (choice E) is a statin used for cholesterol control. None of these are primary agents used for immunosuppression after liver transplantation.

40. The correct answer is B: posthepatic.

Portal hypertension is a condition in which the blood pressure in the portal vein is increased. The portal vein is a large vein that carries blood from the intestines and spleen to the liver. There are two main types of portal hypertension: prehepatic and posthepatic. Prehepatic portal hypertension arises from conditions that impede the circulation of blood prior to its arrival at the liver. This can be caused by conditions such as portal vein thrombosis, congenital abnormalities of the portal vein, and splenic vein thrombosis. Posthepatic portal hypertension arises due to the presence of certain conditions that impede the normal flow of blood after it has exited the liver. This can be caused by conditions such as liver cirrhosis, Budd-Chiari syndrome, and right-sided heart failure. In this patient, the presence of ascites and portosystemic collaterals suggests that he has portal hypertension. The fact that he has liver cirrhosis makes posthepatic portal hypertension the most likely etiology.

41. The best answer is A. The size and location of the varices.

The risk of variceal bleeding in patients with liver cirrhosis is associated with several factors. These include the size and location of the varices (choice A), the level of portal hypertension (typically when the portal venous pressure exceeds 12 mmHg), and the severity of cirrhosis, as determined by the Child-Pugh classification. The presence of peptic ulcers (choice B), the level of serum sodium (choice C), the presence of gastroenteritis (choice D), and the level of serum creatinine (choice E) are not directly correlated with the risk of variceal bleeding, although they could be associated with other complications in patients with liver disease.

42. The correct answer is A: hepatic encephalopathy.

Hepatic encephalopathy is a condition that occurs when there is a buildup of toxins in the brain due to liver disease. It is a serious condition that can lead to coma and death. The clinical manifestations of hepatic encephalopathy can vary depending on the severity of the condition. In mild cases, symptoms may include confusion, slurred speech, and irritability. In more severe cases, symptoms may include drowsiness, coma, and seizures. Asterixis is a classic sign of hepatic encephalopathy. It is a tremor that occurs when the hands are extended, and the wrists are dorsiflexed.

43. The best answer is A. Neomycin.

For patients who experience intolerance to lactulose, a common alternative treatment involves the use of poorly absorbed antibiotics. Neomycin (choice A) is often used, sometimes in alternation with metronidazole, to mitigate specific side effects associated with each antibiotic. Rifaximin is another such antibiotic used in recent times. Amoxicillin (choice B), Ciprofloxacin (choice C), Levofloxacin (choice D), and Azithromycin (choice E) are all well-absorbed systemic antibiotics and are not typically used as primary therapy for hepatic encephalopathy. Their systemic absorption makes them less effective at reducing gut ammonia production compared to poorly absorbed antibiotics like Neomycin and Rifaximin.

44. The correct answer is E: all of the above.

Acute Intermittent Porphyria is a rare inherited disorder that affects the production of heme, a component of hemoglobin. Heme is essential for the production of red blood cells. An acute episode of Acute Intermittent Porphyria can be triggered by a number of factors, including stress, alcohol, certain medications, and infections. The symptoms of an acute episode of Acute Intermittent Porphyria can vary depending on the severity of the episode. Common symptoms include abdominal pain, nausea, vomiting, constipation, anxiety, restlessness, and seizures. The recommended therapeutic approach for managing an acute episode of Acute Intermittent Porphyria involves the administration of heme, specifically heme arginate, heme albumin, or hematin. Heme provides the body with the building blocks it needs to produce new red blood cells. In addition to heme, other medications that may be helpful in managing an acute episode of Acute Intermittent Porphyria include narcotic analgesics for abdominal pain, phenothiazines for nausea, vomiting, anxiety, and restlessness, and intravenous glucose at rates of up to 20 g/h or the use of parenteral nutrition when oral feeding is not feasible for extended durations.

45. The best answer is A. Serum ceruloplasmin levels.

Wilson's Disease is a genetic disorder characterized by excessive copper accumulation in the body, particularly in the liver and brain. Several diagnostic methods are employed for its identification. Serum ceruloplasmin levels (choice A) frequently exhibit a deficiency in patients with Wilson's Disease, although it's worth noting that approximately 10% of patients may present with normal levels. Serum calcium levels (choice B), serum albumin levels (choice C), blood urea nitrogen levels (choice D), and serum potassium levels (choice E) are not typically used as primary diagnostic markers for Wilson's Disease. The levels of copper in the urine exhibit an increase, and the diagnostic criterion considered as the benchmark is the presence of an increased copper level observed through liver biopsy. In cases where genetic testing is accessible, it can serve as a reliable means to ascertain the diagnosis due to the genetic etiology of the disorder.

46. The correct answer is D: all of the above.

Trientine is a medication used to treat Wilson's disease, a rare genetic disorder that causes copper to build up in the body. Trientine works by helping the body to remove copper from the body. Trientine can cause a number of side effects, including: Bone marrow suppression: This is one of the most serious side effects associated with trientine. Bone marrow suppression, also known as myelosuppression, can lead to a decrease in the number of red blood cells, white blood cells, and platelets. This can increase the risk of infection, bleeding, and bruising. Proteinuria: Trientine may cause proteinuria, which is the presence of excess proteins in urine. This can lead to kidney damage. Hepatic injury: Trientine can cause hepatic injury, which is damage to the liver. This can lead to jaundice, liver failure, and death.

47. The best answer is A. Esophagogastroduodenoscopy (EGD).

The patient's symptoms suggest dysphagia, which could be due to a variety of structural or functional problems in the esophagus. Esophagogastroduodenoscopy (EGD) (choice A) is a diagnostic procedure that allows direct visualization of the esophageal lining, stomach, and duodenum. It can detect structural abnormalities, inflammation, ulcers, or other lesions that may contribute to dysphagia. During EGD, biopsies can also be taken for further evaluation to rule out conditions like esophageal cancer or eosinophilic esophagitis. Colonoscopy (choice B) is used to examine the colon and is not typically used in the evaluation of swallowing difficulties. Bronchoscopy (choice C) is used to examine the airways and lungs and would not be useful in this case. Cystoscopy (choice D) is used to examine the urinary bladder and urethra, and laryngoscopy (choice E) examines the larynx, or voice box. While a laryngoscopy could potentially identify some causes of dysphagia, it would not provide as comprehensive a view of the esophagus as an EGD.

48. The correct answer is D: all of the above.

Diffuse esophageal spasm is a condition that causes involuntary contractions of the esophagus. These contractions can make it difficult to swallow and can cause chest pain. There are no specific diagnostic tests for DES. The diagnosis is often made based on the patient's symptoms and the results of an upper endoscopy. In some cases, the doctor may induce spasms in the esophagus to confirm the diagnosis of DES. This can be done by administering one of the following pharmaceutical agents: Edrophonium: This is a medication that mimics the effects of the neurotransmitter acetylcholine. Acetylcholine is a chemical that helps to relax the muscles in the esophagus. Ergotamine: This is a medication that constricts blood vessels. Constricting the blood vessels in the esophagus can cause spasms. Bethanechol: This is a medication that stimulates the production of acetylcholine. As mentioned above, acetylcholine helps to relax the muscles in the esophagus. If the patient experiences spasms after receiving one of these medications, it is likely that they have DES.

49. The correct answer is A: to assess B12 malabsorption.

The Schilling test is a three-part test that is used to assess B12 malabsorption. The first part of the test involves giving the patient a radioactive form of vitamin B12. The second part of the test involves giving the patient intrinsic factor, a protein that is necessary for the absorption of vitamin B12. The third part of the test involves measuring the amount of radioactive vitamin B12 that is absorbed from the intestine. If the patient absorbs a significant amount of radioactive vitamin B12 when intrinsic factor is given, then the problem is not with B12 absorption. If the patient does not absorb a significant amount of radioactive vitamin B12 when intrinsic factor is given, then the problem is with B12 absorption. The Schilling test is a valuable tool for diagnosing B12 malabsorption. If the test is positive, then the patient will need to receive treatment with vitamin B12 injections or oral supplements.

50. The best answer is A. Thickened bowel folds.

Barium contrast radiographic examinations are often used to assess the gastrointestinal tract. These studies can indicate various conditions depending on the findings. Thickened bowel folds (choice A) can be seen in conditions like malabsorption, which is consistent with this patient's symptoms of chronic diarrhea and weight loss. Decreased liver enzymes (choice B), elevated serum calcium levels (choice C), high blood urea nitrogen levels (choice D), and increased serum potassium levels (choice E) are not typically findings inferred from barium contrast x-ray studies. These are blood test findings and would not be visible on a barium contrast x-ray. Other potential findings on barium contrast studies could indicate conditions such as inflammatory bowel disease, tuberculosis, neoplasms, intestinal fistulas, or motility disorders.

51. Best Answer: B. Boerhaave's syndrome

This patient's severe chest pain following an episode of forceful vomiting suggests a diagnosis of Boerhaave's syndrome, a spontaneous rupture of the esophagus. It is a serious condition often associated with forceful or prolonged vomiting. The symptoms typically include severe chest pain, and it can lead to severe complications if not treated promptly. Option A, Aspiration pneumonitis, is a possible consequence of vomiting, specifically when gastric contents are aspirated into the lungs. However, this complication typically presents with respiratory symptoms such as coughing, wheezing, or shortness of breath rather than chest pain. Option C, Dental caries, is a long-term complication associated with frequent vomiting, particularly seen in conditions such as bulimia nervosa. It is unlikely to be the cause of acute chest pain. Option D, Metabolic alkalosis, can occur due to excessive loss of gastric acid from chronic vomiting. However, it doesn't cause severe chest pain. Option E, Hypokalemia, can result from chronic vomiting due to the loss of potassium. While hypokalemia can cause muscle weakness and cramps, it does not typically present as severe chest pain. Therefore, given this patient's presentation and history, the most likely complication is Boerhaave's syndrome.

52. Best Answer: B. Perform total parathyroidectomy.

In patients with Multiple Endocrine Neoplasia type 1 (MEN 1) and Zollinger-Ellison Syndrome (ZES), the therapeutic approach often involves addressing hyperparathyroidism before treating hypergastrinemia. Hyperparathyroidism, characterized by hypercalcemia, is often the first endocrinopathy to manifest in MEN 1 and can exacerbate the gastric acid hypersecretion seen in ZES, leading to severe peptic ulcer disease. Option A, starting treatment with a proton pump inhibitor, would address the hypergastrinemia associated with ZES. However, this should not be the first-line treatment in this context due to the potential amelioration of hypergastrinemia following the treatment of hyperparathyroidism. Option C, surgical resection of the gastrin-secreting tumor, may not always be feasible due to the multifocal nature of these tumors in MEN 1. Options D and E, starting treatment with a calcium channel blocker or bisphosphonate for hypercalcemia, would not address the root cause of the hypercalcemia in this case, which is hyperparathyroidism. Therefore, the most appropriate next step in managing her condition would be to perform a total parathyroidectomy (Option B) to treat the hyperparathyroidism, potentially improving the hypergastrinemia and associated peptic ulcer disease.

53. Best Answer: B. Impaired ileal reabsorption

Bile salts are essential for the digestion and absorption of dietary fats in the small intestine. Bile salt insufficiency can lead to malabsorption, resulting in symptoms such as chronic diarrhea, weight loss, and abdominal discomfort. Option A, use of Proton Pump Inhibitors, primarily affects stomach acid production and is not directly related to bile salt production or absorption. Option B, impaired ileal reabsorption, can indeed lead to bile salt insufficiency. The ileum is the primary site of bile salt absorption in the intestine. Any disease or condition that impairs the function of the ileum can result in bile salt deficiency and subsequent malabsorption. Option C, regular use of antacids, would mainly affect stomach acid levels and not directly cause bile salt insufficiency. Option D, lactose intolerance, causes malabsorption due to the inability to digest lactose, a sugar found in milk and dairy products. It does not directly affect bile salt production or absorption. Option E, pancreatic enzyme deficiency, would affect the digestion of fats, proteins, and carbohydrates but does not directly impact bile salt production or absorption. Therefore, the most appropriate next step in managing her condition would be to perform a total parathyroidectomy (Option B) to treat the hyperparathyroidism, potentially improving the hypergastrinemia and associated peptic ulcer disease.

54. Best Answer: E. All of the above

The patient's presentation and imaging findings are suggestive of primary sclerosing cholangitis (PSC). However, other conditions can mimic the clinical and radiographic findings of PSC, so it's important to consider a broad differential diagnosis. Option A, cholangiocarcinoma, is a type of bile duct cancer that can present with similar symptoms and radiographic findings to PSC. Option B, Caroli disease, is characterized by cystic dilation of the bile ducts and can mimic the radiographic findings of PSC. Option C, Fasciola hepatica infection (a type of parasitic infection), can cause bile duct inflammation and strictures, similar to PSC. Option D, IgG4-associated cholangitis, is an autoimmune condition that can cause bile duct inflammation and strictures, similar to PSC.

55. Best Answer: B. Pregabalin

Chronic pancreatitis often results in persistent abdominal pain, which can be challenging to manage. Traditional pain medications may not always provide adequate relief, necessitating exploration of alternative pharmaceutical interventions. Option A, Metformin, is a medication used primarily for the management of type 2 diabetes and does not directly affect pain pathways. Option B, Pregabalin, is a medication that reduces neuropathic pain by decreasing the release of certain neurotransmitters in the brain and spinal cord. Recent research indicates that it may be effective in improving pain management in individuals with chronic pancreatitis, thereby reducing the necessity for other pain medications. Option C, Omeprazole, is a proton pump inhibitor used primarily to reduce stomach acid production and treat conditions like gastroesophageal reflux disease (GERD). It does not directly affect pain pathways. Option D, Atorvastatin, is a statin medication used to lower cholesterol levels and reduce the risk of cardiovascular disease. It doesn't have a direct role in pain management. Option E, Hydrochlorothiazide, is a diuretic medication used in the management of hypertension and edema. It doesn't have a direct role in pain management. Therefore, among the options given, Pregabalin (Option B) is the most appropriate choice for this patient.

56.Answer: C) Child-Pugh class C

The Child-Pugh classification is used to assess the severity and prognosis of chronic liver disease, primarily cirrhosis. The system uses five clinical measures of liver disease, including serum bilirubin levels, serum albumin levels, prothrombin time, and the presence and severity of ascites and hepatic encephalopathy. Each of these measures is scored 1-3 points, with 3 indicating most severe dysfunction. In the case of this patient, his symptoms and lab findings (jaundice, ascites, lethargy, elevated bilirubin, decreased serum albumin, and prolonged prothrombin time) point to severe liver disease. The scores are added together to give a total score, which is then classified as class A (5-6 points), class B (7-9 points), or class C (10-15 points). Given the severity of this patient's symptoms and lab findings, his score would likely fall into the Class C range (10-15 points), indicating severe liver disease.

57. Answer: C

The patient's presentation is most consistent with a stroke. The combination of dysphagia, dysarthria, and right-sided weakness suggests a lesion in the left hemisphere of the brain, where the centers for speech and swallowing are located. The patient's vascular risk factors also increase the likelihood of stroke. Esophageal stricture, GERD, myasthenia gravis, and ALS are all possible causes of dysphagia, but they are less likely than stroke in this patient. Esophageal stricture is typically characterized by progressive dysphagia to solids and liquids. GERD is often associated with heartburn and regurgitation. Myasthenia gravis is a neuromuscular disorder that can cause weakness in a variety of muscles, including those involved in swallowing. However, it is typically characterized by fluctuating weakness that is worse with exertion and improves with rest. ALS is a progressive neurodegenerative disease that causes weakness and wasting in all muscles, including those involved in swallowing. However, it is typically associated with other symptoms such as fasciculations (muscle twitches) and atrophy (muscle wasting). In conclusion, the most likely diagnosis in this patient is a stroke.

58. Correct Answer: B. Refer for esophagogastroduodenoscopy (EGD)

The patient has long-standing GERD and risk factors for Barrett's esophagus and esophageal adenocarcinoma including age over 50 years, central adiposity, and smoking. The new onset of dysphagia is considered an alarm symptom, which warrants further investigation for potential malignancy. Other alarm symptoms include excessive vomiting, weight loss, and anemia. While GERD can lead to complications such as esophagitis and strictures that may cause dysphagia, it's essential to first exclude the possibility of malignancy given the patient's risk profile and alarm symptom. The most appropriate next step is to refer the patient for an esophagogastroduodenoscopy (EGD). EGD is more sensitive and specific for diagnosing Barrett's esophagus and malignancy compared to a barium swallow, making it the preferred initial diagnostic approach in this scenario. Options A, C, D, and E may be considered in different contexts but are not the most appropriate immediate actions given the patient's risk factors and presentation. Proton pump inhibitors (Option C) can alleviate symptoms but wouldn't address the potential underlying cause of the dysphagia. Similarly, lifestyle modifications (Option E) may help manage GERD but do not investigate the cause of the new symptom. A 'wait and watch' approach (Option A) is not advised given the alarm symptom. Lastly, a barium swallow (Option D) is less sensitive and specific than EGD for detecting Barrett's esophagus and malignancy.

59. Correct Answer: A. Start a proton pump inhibitor

This patient's symptoms are typical for peptic ulcer disease, specifically a gastric ulcer, as the pain worsens with meals (pain from a duodenal ulcer is typically relieved with food). His use of NSAIDs is the most likely cause of the presumed peptic ulcer disease. Given the patient's history of NSAID use, absence of alarm symptoms (such as weight loss, vomiting, or difficulty swallowing), and a reassuring physical examination, it is reasonable to start empiric treatment with a proton pump inhibitor while he continues on NSAIDs, and closely monitor him for symptom resolution. Option B (refer for EGD) is not needed at this point but should be considered if his symptoms prove refractory to proton pump inhibitor therapy. Empiric treatment for H. pylori (Option C) without testing is not recommended. Advising to stop NSAIDs (Option D) might reduce the risk of peptic ulcer disease, but it doesn't address the current presumptive ulcer. Reassurance alone (Option E) would be inappropriate given the patient's symptoms and NSAID use.

60. Answer: D

The patient is presenting with several risk factors for peptic ulcer disease (PUD), such as ibuprofen and aspirin use in combination with prednisone use. He also has signs and symptoms of a rapid upper GI bleed, such as hematemesis, melena, hypotension, and tachycardia. Volume resuscitation with crystalloid fluids is the most important initial step in the management of a brisk upper GI bleed. This is because the patient is at risk of hypovolemic shock, which can be fatal. Red blood cell transfusion, IV proton pump inhibitor, and EGD are all important steps in the management of upper GI bleeding, but they can be done after the patient has been resuscitated. IV antibiotics are not typically used unless there is evidence of infection. In conclusion, the most important initial step in the management of this patient is volume resuscitation with crystalloid fluids.

61. Answer: A

The patient is at high risk for variceal bleeding, given her cirrhosis, portal hypertension, and upper GI bleed. The next best step in management is to perform an EGD to confirm the source of the bleeding and initiate endoscopic band ligation if varices are found. A Sengstaken-Blakemore tube is not necessary at this time, since the patient is hemodynamically stable and the bleeding is not uncontrollable. A TIPS is not an appropriate first management step without first attempting EGD. Gastric varices are possible, but they must first be confirmed by EGD. Observation is not appropriate, since the patient has a high risk for rebleeding. In conclusion, the next best step in management is gastroenterology consultation for EGD.

62. Correct Answer: B. Diverticular bleeding

This patient's symptoms of overt hematochezia, sudden onset and abrupt cessation of bleeding, and stable hemodynamics suggest a lower gastrointestinal (GI) bleed, specifically a diverticular bleed. Diverticular bleeding typically presents with painless bleeding. The patient's age and obesity are risk factors for diverticulosis. Option A (Ischemic colitis) is less likely as it is usually accompanied by abdominal pain and bloody stool. Option C (Gastrointestinal malignancy) often presents with more chronic symptoms such as weight loss, anemia, or changes in bowel habits. An upper GI source (Option D) is unlikely in a patient who is hemodynamically stable, as upper GI bleeding is usually more rapid and can lead to hemodynamic instability. Hemorrhoidal bleeding (Option E) is typically associated with pain and the blood is often noticed on the toilet paper rather than as blood per rectum.

63. Answer: C

The patient's presentation is most consistent with chronic malabsorptive diarrhea. This is because he has had diarrhea for more than 4 weeks, his stools are foul-smelling and floating, and he has lost weight unintentionally. Fecal fat testing is the most important test to distinguish between malabsorptive and secretory diarrhea. In malabsorptive diarrhea, the body is unable to absorb nutrients from food, which leads to elevated levels of fat in the stool. In secretory diarrhea, the body produces excessive amounts of fluid, which leads to watery stools. Chronic secretory diarrhea is less likely in this patient because it typically does not improve with fasting. IBS-D and microscopic colitis are also less likely because they are not typically associated with foul-smelling, floating stools. In conclusion, the most likely diagnosis in this patient is chronic malabsorptive diarrhea. Other causes of chronic malabsorptive diarrhea include celiac disease, Crohn's disease, ulcerative colitis, and pancreatic insufficiency. Treatment for chronic malabsorptive diarrhea depends on the underlying cause.

64. Correct Answer:D. Conduct a video capsule endoscopy

This patient presents with a new, symptomatic anemia suggestive of iron deficiency (low MCV, elevated red cell distribution width). Although she doesn't display overt symptoms of bleeding, her positive fecal occult blood test suggests occult gastrointestinal (GI) blood loss. Therefore, a full evaluation should be performed to identify potential sources of GI bleeding. The most appropriate next step in this case would be a video capsule endoscopy (Option D), as it could identify small bowel lesions that may account for her blood loss. Option A (Reassure the patient) is inappropriate as her lab results and positive fecal occult blood test demand further investigation. Option B (Perform a CT arteriography) is unlikely to be helpful because this imaging modality requires a bleeding rate of about 0.5 mL./min or more to detect bleeding from the culprit vessel. Since this patient has no overt signs of bleeding, it is unlikely that she is losing blood at a rate greater than 0.5 mL./min. Option C (Order a tagged WBC scan) is not suitable because this modality is used to detect inflammation and does not help localize occult GI bleeding. Option E (Initiate iron supplementation) may be part of the treatment once the cause of the iron deficiency anemia is identified and treated, but it's not the immediate next step.

65. The correct answer is A. Discontinue the MiraLAX.

The patient's stool testing results likely represent C. difficile colonization rather than C. difficile-associated diarrhea (CDAD), as evidenced by her lack of fever, absence of leukocytosis, the presence of an alternative explanation for loose stools (MiraLAX use), and negative C. difficile toxin result. Up to 20% of hospitalized patients who receive antibiotics may have asymptomatic C. difficile colonization (as determined by positive C. difficile PCR testing) without clinical CDAD. Therefore, the likely culprit for her loose stools, laxative use, should be addressed first, and she should be monitored clinically. Treatment of C. difficile infection should not be implemented at this time. Glutamate dehydrogenase testing would not yield additional clarity to the question of colonization versus CDAD.

66. Answer: B

Immunocompromised patients are at increased risk for severe complications from nontyphoidal Salmonella infection, such as sepsis and meningitis. Therefore, they should be considered for antibiotic treatment, even if they have a nontoxic examination and normal PO intake. Patients with a nontoxic examination and normal PO intake can typically be managed with supportive care alone. Prior exposure to Salmonella does not impact treatment decisions for a subsequent episode. In conclusion, the group of patients most likely to benefit from antibiotic treatment for nontyphoidal Salmonella infection is immunocompromised patients. Other groups of patients who may benefit from antibiotic treatment for nontyphoidal Salmonella infection include:

- Infants and young children
- Older adults
- Patients with chronic medical conditions such as diabetes and kidney disease

Patients with invasive Salmonella infection (e.g., bloodstream infection, meningitis) The choice of antibiotic for nontyphoidal Salmonella infection depends on the patient's age, underlying medical conditions, and the susceptibility of the Salmonella strain to different antibiotics. Fluoroquinolones are typically the first-line treatment for nontyphoidal Salmonella infection in adults. Patients who are being treated with antibiotics should have their stool cultures repeated in 48-72 hours to ensure that the infection has cleared.

67. Answer: D

All of the above are important initial steps in the management of paralytic ileus of the colon. Bowel rest can be achieved by making the patient NPO and discontinuing offending medications. Bowel decompression can be attempted with either nasogastric tube or rectal tube placement (or both). Restoring normal intestinal peristalsis can be attempted with methylnaltrexone or neostigmine. The patient's critical illness, pancreatitis, hospitalization, and opiate administration are all risk factors for colonic pseudo-obstruction. In conclusion, the most important initial step in the management of paralytic ileus of the colon is all of the above.

68. The correct answer is A. Advise cessation of marijuana use.

This patient's history of recurrent, intense episodes of vomiting, alleviated by hot showers or baths, and heavy marijuana use is suggestive of cannabinoid hyperemesis syndrome. While IV fluids, antiemetics, and benzodiazepines may be used to control acute symptoms, these agents are not recommended for long-term use due to their risk and side effect profiles. The most effective treatment strategy for this syndrome is cessation of marijuana use. Starting therapy with a tricyclic antidepressant might be considered for refractory symptoms, but it is not the initial step. Given the self-limited nature of the patient's episodes and a history consistent with cannabinoid hyperemesis syndrome, an esophagogastroduodenoscopy is not needed at this time.

69. Answer- A. Begin enteral nutrition.

This patient is not meeting her caloric needs on peripheral IV D5NS alone. At this point, more aggressive nutritional support should be attempted. Enteral nutrition is the preferred route of nutritional support in the absence of a contraindication. Since the colonic pseudo-obstruction has resolved (as evidenced by the spontaneous passage of stool and flatus and ability for the rectal tube to be discontinued), enteral nutrition should be attempted first. The patient should be monitored closely. If she is unable to tolerate enteral nutrition due to nausea, vomiting, or recurrence of colonic pseudo-obstruction, alternative forms of nutritional support such as peripheral parenteral nutrition and total parenteral nutrition should then be considered.

70. Answer: C

The patient has mild, uncomplicated diverticulitis. He is able to tolerate PO intake, has pain that is well-controlled with acetaminophen, and has no significant medical comorbidities. Therefore, outpatient therapy with PO antibiotics is the most appropriate management plan. Antibiotic regimens for outpatient treatment of mild, uncomplicated diverticulitis typically include metronidazole along with a fluoroquinolone antibiotic (e.g., ciprofloxacin) or amoxicillin/clavulanic acid for a duration of 7-10 days. Hospitalization is indicated for patients with severe diverticulitis or those with complications such as abscess, perforation, or fistula. Surgery is typically reserved for patients with recurrent diverticulitis or those with complications. Interventional radiology consultation for drain placement is indicated for patients with abscess formation. In conclusion, the most appropriate management plan for this patient is outpatient therapy with PO metronidazole and ciprofloxacin for 7 days.

71. Answer: D

The risk of recurrence after a first episode of diverticulitis is 10-30% within 10 years. The risk is higher in patients with obesity, smoking, and a family history of diverticulitis. Choices A, B, and E are incorrect. The risk of recurrence is not low, regardless of the patient's risk factors. Prophylactic antibiotics are not recommended for all patients with diverticulitis. Surgery is typically reserved for patients with recurrent diverticulitis or those with complications. Choice C is partially correct. The risk of recurrence is lower in patients with no risk factors, but it is not possible to accurately predict which patients will and will not have a recurrence. In conclusion, the most accurate statement about the risk of recurrence after a first episode of diverticulitis is that the risk is 10-30% within 10 years.

72. Answer: B. Family history of colorectal cancer in a first-degree relative

This patient's family history of colorectal cancer in a first-degree relative (her mother), particularly a relative diagnosed before the age of 60, significantly increases her risk of colorectal cancer. Current guidelines recommend that individuals with such a family history should begin colorectal cancer screening at age 40, or 10 years before the earliest age of colorectal cancer diagnosis in the family member, whichever comes first. As such, this patient should have begun screening at age 40. The other factors listed - personal history of hypertension, a cousin with ulcerative colitis, and regular aspirin use - are not recognized as risk factors for colorectal cancer. In fact, regular use of aspirin may have a protective effect against colorectal cancer, though this is not a reason to initiate aspirin use in individuals not otherwise indicated for it due to potential side effects.

73. Answer: C. Inflammation of the colonic mucosa in a contiguous pattern starting at the rectum and progressing proximally.

The patient's symptoms of recurrent diarrhea, abdominal pain, and rectal bleeding are consistent with a diagnosis of ulcerative colitis. During colonoscopy, it would be expected to observe inflammation of the colonic mucosa in a contiguous pattern starting at the rectum and progressing proximally. This is characteristic of ulcerative colitis, which is an inflammatory bowel disease that affects the colon and rectum. Option A is unlikely as with this patient's degree of symptoms, including grossly bloody diarrhea, one would not generally expect a grossly normal-appearing colonoscopy. Option B suggests a feature seen in Crohn's colitis, another form of inflammatory bowel disease. However, Crohn's typically presents with "skip lesions" (areas of inflammation separated by healthy tissue), which is not consistent with the patient's presumed diagnosis of ulcerative colitis. Option D, pseudomembranes, are a feature typical of C. difficile infection, not ulcerative colitis. In option E, ulcerative colitis typically begins in the rectum and extends proximally in a continuous manner, so it would be unusual to see inflammation and ulceration only in the ascending colon.

74. Answer: B

Patients with ulcerative colitis have an increased risk of colorectal cancer, especially those with pancolitis and those with disease duration of more than 8 years. The risk is highest in patients with left-sided ulcerative colitis. The patient in the question has left-sided ulcerative colitis, which puts him at an increased risk of colorectal cancer. He should be informed of this increased risk and should undergo a more aggressive colorectal cancer screening strategy. The other answer choices are incorrect. Patients with ulcerative colitis do not have a decreased risk of colorectal cancer. Patients with ulcerative colitis do not have the same risk of colorectal cancer as the baseline population. The patient's risk of colorectal cancer is not unaffected by his diagnosis of ulcerative colitis. It is possible to predict a patient's risk of colorectal cancer based on their diagnosis of ulcerative colitis and other risk factors. In conclusion, the patient has an increased risk of colorectal cancer compared to the baseline population rate.

75. Answer: D

The patient in the question is at risk for all of the complications listed. Biliary obstruction: Patients with Crohn's disease are at increased risk for gallstone formation. This is because Crohn's disease can damage the small intestine and lead to impaired bile acid absorption. Bile acids are essential for fat digestion, and when they are not absorbed properly, they can clump together and form gallstones. Fatty liver disease: Crohn's disease can also lead to fatty liver disease. This is because the disease can damage the liver cells and make it difficult for them to process fat. Osteopenia or osteoporosis: Patients with Crohn's disease are at increased risk for osteopenia or osteoporosis. This is because Crohn's disease can lead to malnutrition and malabsorption of vitamin D, both of which are important for bone health. In conclusion, the patient is at risk for all of the complications listed.

76. Answer: C. Infliximab

Infliximab is the best treatment option from the list provided for maintenance of remission in patients presenting with severe acute ulcerative colitis. The goal should be to transition patients to a steroid-sparing agent for maintenance of remission, given the adverse effects of long-term steroid use. This rules out Oral Prednisone (Option A). Methotrexate (Option B) is incorrect, as this therapy is only approved for Crohn disease and not for ulcerative colitis. Cyclosporine (Option D) is incorrect as this is a therapy used for the management of acute severe ulcerative colitis but is not used as a long-term maintenance therapy. Hydroxychloroquine (Option E) is typically used in rheumatologic conditions and has no known benefit for ulcerative colitis. Therefore, Infliximab (Option C) is the most appropriate choice for this patient's long-term maintenance therapy after achieving remission from severe acute ulcerative colitis.

77. Correct Answer: C. CT angiography of the abdomen

This elderly patient who is not anticoagulated for atrial fibrillation is at risk for arterial embolism. The "pain out of proportion to physical examination findings" is classic for acute mesenteric ischemia. The elevated lactate and white blood cell count are likely due to bowel infarction. Of the possibilities listed, CT angiography (arterial phase) is the noninvasive test of choice (the venous phase is used for the diagnosis of mesenteric venous thrombosis). Invasive angiography is the gold standard. This can be potentially therapeutic (e.g., embolectomy) and would be the next step if CT angiography is suggestive of vascular occlusion.

78. Answer: A

The patient's presentation is classic for chronic mesenteric ischemia, which is a condition in which decreased blood flow to the gut causes abdominal pain after eating. The pain is intermittent (postprandial) and resolves with rest. The other answer choices are less likely based on the patient's presentation. Crohn's disease is a chronic inflammatory bowel disease that typically causes crampy abdominal pain, diarrhea, and rectal bleeding. Ulcerative colitis is another chronic inflammatory bowel disease that typically causes crampy abdominal pain, diarrhea, and rectal bleeding.

Ischemic colitis is a condition in which decreased blood flow to the gut causes sudden, severe abdominal pain and other symptoms such as diarrhea and rectal bleeding. Diverticulitis is a condition in which inflammation or infection of small pouches in the colon causes abdominal pain, tenderness, and fever. In conclusion, the most likely diagnosis is chronic mesenteric ischemia.

79. Answer: D

Ultrasonography with Dopplers of the mesenteric vessels is the most appropriate initial step in the diagnosis of chronic mesenteric ischemia in this patient. It is a non-invasive test that can provide valuable information about the blood flow to the gut. CT angiography with arterial phase contrast is another reasonable first-line imaging test. However, it exposes the patient to contrast, which is a risk factor for kidney failure in patients with chronic kidney disease. Invasive angiography is the gold standard test for diagnosing chronic mesenteric ischemia, but it is a more invasive test and is typically reserved for patients who have not responded to other treatments or who are considering surgery. MR angiography is a newer imaging test that can be used to diagnose chronic mesenteric ischemia, but it is not as widely available as ultrasonography or CT angiography. Tonometry, spectroscopic oximetry, and MR angiography are still under investigation for the diagnosis of chronic mesenteric ischemia. In conclusion, the most appropriate initial step in the diagnosis of chronic mesenteric ischemia in this patient is ultrasonography with Dopplers of the mesenteric vessels.

80. Correct Answer: A) IV lactated Ringer's solution and pain management

This patient is presenting with a likely episode of acute pancreatitis, evidenced by her classic symptoms of epigastric pain radiating to the back and a history of multiple prior similar episodes. Despite her normal lipase level, which can occur in patients with a history of recurrent acute pancreatitis, her symptoms are highly suggestive of this diagnosis. The mainstay of treatment for pancreatitis is aggressive fluid resuscitation within the first 24 hours. An initial IV bolus of 20 mL/kg should be followed by 3 mL/kg/h. Lactated Ringer's solution is often preferred over normal saline as it may be superior in this context. Pain management is also an essential part of the treatment protocol. Alcohol withdrawal treatment (Option B) is not indicated at this stage as she had alcohol intake earlier in the day and it is likely too early for withdrawal symptoms to occur. Normal saline (Option C) could be used for fluid resuscitation, but Lactated Ringer's solution is often preferred. Invasive angiography (Option D) is not indicated in this case as there's no suggestion of vascular occlusion. Prophylactic antibiotics (Option E) are not routinely recommended in the management of acute pancreatitis unless there are signs of infection or sepsis.

81. The correct answer is A) IV lactated Ringer's solution and pain management.

The patient appears to be experiencing another episode of acute pancreatitis, likely due to her heavy alcohol consumption. Despite her normal lipase level, her clinical presentation is classic for pancreatitis, and her history of multiple episodes supports this diagnosis. Proper management involves aggressive fluid resuscitation (using a solution like lactated Ringer's), which can help to restore her fluid balance and reduce the risk of systemic complications. Pain management is also crucial as pancreatitis can be highly painful. Contrary to choice B, it is likely too early for alcohol withdrawal to be a significant issue, and fluid restriction would not be appropriate given her dehydration. Parenteral nutrition (choice C) may be used in certain situations, but fluid resuscitation and pain management are more immediate concerns. Surgical intervention (choice D) is generally reserved for complications of pancreatitis, such as abscess or necrosis, which does not seem to be the case here. Finally, while alcohol abstinence counseling (choice E) would certainly be beneficial for this patient in the long term, it is not the immediate treatment required for her acute condition.

82. Answer: A

The patient's presentation is suggestive of chronic pancreatitis. Autoimmune pancreatitis is a type of chronic pancreatitis that is caused by inflammation of the pancreas. It is more common in young adults, and it can be difficult to distinguish from other types of chronic pancreatitis. Antinuclear antibody and IgG subtypes are tests that can be used to diagnose autoimmune pancreatitis. Glucocorticoids are the first-line treatment for autoimmune pancreatitis. The other answer choices are less likely to be helpful in the diagnosis or treatment of chronic pancreatitis. Cultures for bacteria and viruses are typically not necessary in patients with chronic pancreatitis, unless there is evidence of infection. HIV and H. pylori testing are not routinely indicated in patients with chronic pancreatitis. Serum alcohol level is not helpful in diagnosing chronic pancreatitis, as only a minority of cases are caused by alcohol abuse. In conclusion, the next best step in laboratory workup is antinuclear antibody and IgG subtypes to assess for autoimmune pancreatitis.

83. Answer: B

Azithromycin is a macrolide antibiotic that can cause a pure cholestatic pattern of abnormal liver chemistries. This type of liver injury is characterized by elevated alkaline phosphatase and bilirubin, with relatively normal liver enzymes. Acetaminophen can cause hepatocellular injury, which is characterized by elevated liver enzymes. Hydralazine can also cause hepatocellular injury, but it is less common. Nitrofurantoin, amoxicillin-clavulanic acid, azathioprine, carbamazepine, mirtazapine, and penicillin can cause a mixed pattern of liver injury, with elevated liver enzymes and alkaline phosphatase. In conclusion, the most likely cause of the patient's liver injury is azithromycin. The patient should discontinue azithromycin and her liver function tests should be monitored closely. If her liver function tests do not improve, liver imaging may be considered to rule out other causes of liver injury, such as cholangitis or choledocholithiasis. Most patients recover from azithromycin-induced liver injury within a few weeks of discontinuing the medication.

84. The correct answer is C. Review prior lab results and ask about a current illness or stressor.

This patient likely has Gilbert syndrome, which is characterized by an elevated unconjugated bilirubin with normal liver enzymes, normal liver synthetic function, and no symptoms, medications, or alcohol use. In Gilbert syndrome, the patient's prior lab work would reveal previous elevated indirect bilirubin levels, which improved after a period of illness or stress. This syndrome is the most common inherited disorder of bilirubin glucuronidation and is a benign condition. It is characterized by recurrent episodes of jaundice that may be triggered by, among other things, dehydration, fasting, intercurrent disease, menstruation, and overexertion. Patients are typically asymptomatic other than jaundice. The diagnosis is made by excluding other causes of unconjugated hyperbilirubinemia, although genetic testing is available. A presumptive diagnosis can be made in patients with the following features: Unconjugated hyperbilirubinemia on repeated testing, a normal CBC, blood smear, and reticulocyte count, and normal serum aminotransferase and alkaline phosphatase levels. Option A (Order genetic testing for Gilbert syndrome) is not the best next step in managing this patient's condition because Gilbert syndrome is typically diagnosed by excluding other causes of unconjugated hyperbilirubinemia. While genetic testing is available, it is not usually necessary. Option B (Begin treatment with ursodeoxycholic acid) is not correct because Gilbert syndrome is a benign condition that typically does not require treatment. Option D (Request a liver biopsy to rule out other causes of jaundice) is also not correct because the patient's normal liver enzymes and synthetic function make other causes of jaundice unlikely. Option E (Order an abdominal ultrasound to assess for possible gallstones) is not the best next step because this patient's jaundice is likely due to Gilbert syndrome, not gallstones.

85. Answer: C

The patient has an isolated elevated ALP, which is a nonspecific finding. It can be caused by a variety of conditions, including bone disorders, liver diseases, and medications. The first step in working up an isolated elevated ALP is to repeat the test fasting, as postprandial levels can be elevated. If the repeat fasting ALP is still elevated, the next step is to determine whether the ALP is of bone or liver origin. GGT is a more specific marker of liver injury than ALP. If the GGT is elevated, it suggests that the ALP is of liver origin. In this case, ultrasonography of the abdomen should be done to look for bile ductal dilatation, and antimitochondrial antibodies should be tested for primary biliary cholangitis (PBC). Antioxidants are not indicated at this time, as there is no evidence of oxidative stress. The patient should be referred to a gastroenterologist for further evaluation and management. If the GGT is normal, it suggests that the ALP is of bone origin. In this case, further evaluation of the patient's bone health may be warranted. Other causes of an isolated elevated ALP include hyperparathyroidism, hypothyroidism, and Paget's disease. These conditions should be considered in the differential diagnosis.

86. Answer: A

The patient's presentation is most consistent with acute hepatitis A. HAV is a highly contagious virus that is transmitted through the fecal-oral route. It is common in men who have sex with men, and it can also be spread through contact with contaminated food or water. The patient's elevated liver enzymes and bilirubin levels are consistent with acute hepatitis. The AST/ALT ratio is less than 1, which is also consistent with HAV. HBV, HCV, and alcoholic hepatitis are less likely, given the patient's presentation and lack of risk factors. Drug-induced hepatitis is a possibility, but the patient is not taking any known hepatotoxic medications. HAV infection is typically self-limited and resolves within a few weeks. Treatment for HAV infection is supportive and includes rest and hydration. There is a vaccine available for HAV, which is recommended for men who have sex with men and other high-risk groups. In conclusion, the most likely cause of the patient's liver injury is HAV infection.

87. The correct answer is B. Begin tenofovir.

This patient has HBeAg-positive chronic HBV (immunoreactive phase), indicated by his HBeAg-positive result, elevated ALT level, and high HBV DNA level. A liver biopsy would likely show moderate-to-severe inflammation and possible fibrosis. Chronic HBV infection should be treated in the immunoreactive and immune reactivation phases, and in cirrhotic patients with an elevated HBV DNA level or decompensation. First-line treatment is with a nucleo(s/t)ide analog, such as entecavir or tenofovir, which are well-tolerated and associated with a low rate of resistance at 5 years. HBeAg seroconversion occurs in 30% to 40% of treated patients, with loss of HBsAg in 5% to 10%. Tenofovir is preferred if there is a history of lamivudine resistance. Option A (Monitor and retest in six months) is not the best step as this patient's current condition merits treatment, not observation. Option C (Start interferon therapy) is not the first-line treatment for this condition. Nucleo(s/t)ide analogs like tenofovir are the preferred choice. Option D (Initiate lamivudine) is not the best option due to the risk of lamivudine resistance. Tenofovir is preferred in such cases. Option E (Order a liver biopsy to assess the degree of fibrosis) is not the best immediate step. Although a biopsy might reveal inflammation and fibrosis, it doesn't change the immediate management, which is to begin antiviral therapy.

88. The correct answer is A. Administer IV ceftriaxone.

The patient's severe alcohol-associated hepatitis and high Maddrey discriminant function score indicate a high short-term mortality risk. While oral glucocorticoids might be considered, an ongoing spontaneous bacterial peritonitis (SBP) infection contraindicates their use. Similarly, pentoxifylline might be considered if glucocorticoids were contraindicated, but it's not recommended in conjunction with glucocorticoids. Liver transplantation is currently not a viable option due to his multiple past admissions for alcohol-associated hepatitis. Therefore, the best immediate step is to manage his SBP, which can be effectively treated with IV ceftriaxone. Option B (Start oral glucocorticoids) is contraindicated due to the patient's ongoing SBP. Option C (Begin therapy with pentoxifylline) is not recommended in conjunction with glucocorticoids, and it's not the primary treatment for SBP. Option D (Refer for liver transplantation) is not currently feasible due to the patient's history of multiple admissions for alcohol-associated hepatitis. Option E (Start interferon therapy) is not applicable as this therapy is more typically used in the management of viral hepatitis, not alcoholic hepatitis or SBP.

89. Answer: A

The patient has chronic HCV infection, which is a preventable cause of liver disease. Treatment with direct-acting antiviral therapy is recommended for all patients with chronic HCV infection, regardless of the presence or absence of cirrhosis. Elbasvir-grazoprevir is a direct-acting antiviral regimen that has been shown to be effective and safe in patients with chronic kidney disease, including those on dialysis. Pegylated interferon and ribavirin are rarely used to treat HCV infection due to their inferior efficacy and worse side effect profile compared to direct-acting antiviral regimens. Liver biopsy is not necessary in this patient, as there is no evidence of cirrhosis on imaging or vibration-controlled transient elastography. Therefore, the most appropriate management for this patient is to suggest treatment with elbasvir-grazoprevir. Treatment with direct-acting antiviral regimens is typically short-course (12-24 weeks) and well-tolerated. The sustained virologic response rate for direct-acting antiviral regimens is greater than 95%. Treatment with direct-acting antiviral regimens has been shown to improve mortality in patients with chronic HCV infection, even in the absence of cirrhosis.

90. The correct answer is B. N-acetylcysteine.

This patient presents with symptoms of acute liver injury following a significant acetaminophen ingestion. While activated charcoal is beneficial if given within 4 hours of a potentially toxic ingestion, this patient's presentation is too delayed and she is too lethargic for administration of charcoal. Hemodialysis does not effectively remove acetaminophen, and pentoxifylline is not useful in the treatment of acute liver failure due to acetaminophen. N-acetylcysteine is the accepted antidote for acetaminophen poisoning and is given to all patients at significant risk for hepatotoxicity. Although the acetaminophen level is not yet back, she has evidence of liver damage and a history of acetaminophen ingestion, making N-acetylcysteine the best treatment option.

91. Answer: C

The patient has grade 3 encephalopathy, which is a serious complication of acute liver failure. The goal of treatment is to reduce intracranial pressure and prevent further brain damage. IV mannitol is a hypertonic osmotic diuretic that can be used to reduce intracranial pressure. It is the first-line treatment for grade 3 or 4 encephalopathy in patients with acute liver failure. Lactulose is a laxative that can be used to reduce ammonia levels in the blood. However, it can also cause volume depletion, which is a risk in patients with acute liver failure. Therefore, lactulose is generally avoided in this setting. IV fluids are important to maintain hydration and prevent renal failure. However, they should be given cautiously in patients with acute liver failure, as they can worsen cerebral edema. Prophylactic antibiotics are not routinely recommended for patients with acute liver failure. They should only be used if there is evidence of infection. Liver transplantation is the definitive treatment for acute liver failure. However, it is not always available or appropriate. Other treatments that may be considered for refractory encephalopathy in patients with acute liver failure include barbiturates and therapeutic hypothermia. The prognosis for patients with acute liver failure is poor, especially those with grade 3 or 4 encephalopathy. However, with aggressive treatment, some patients can survive.

92. Answer: (C)

Patients with acute liver failure are at risk for bleeding due to multiple hematologic abnormalities. One of the most important risk factors for bleeding is thrombocytopenia. A platelet count of 10,000/mm3 is considered to be severly thrombocytopenic. In this setting, it is reasonable to aim for a platelet count of 50,000/mm3 prior to a procedure such as a liver transplant. Fresh frozen plasma and cryoprecipitate are not routinely recommended for patients with acute liver failure. Fresh frozen plasma contains coagulation factors, but it also contains protein C and S, which are decreased in patients with acute liver failure. This can make it difficult to predict the effect of fresh frozen plasma on the INR. Cryoprecipitate contains fibrinogen, but it is only recommended for patients with bleeding and a fibrinogen level of 100 to 120 mg/dL. Vitamin K can be given if there is concern for vitamin K deficiency. However, it takes 6 to 8 hours to be effective and would not be useful right before a procedure. In conclusion, the most appropriate blood product to administer to the patient prior to the liver transplant is platelets. The INR is not a reliable measure of bleeding risk in patients with acute liver failure due to the decrease in protein C and S production. Platelet administration should be avoided in patients with acute liver failure unless the platelet count is <10,000 to 15,000 or there is bleeding or an imminent procedure.

93. Answer: A. Administer IV ceftriaxone

This patient has developed spontaneous bacterial peritonitis (SBP), a bacterial infection of the ascitic fluid, common in patients with cirrhosis. Empiric antibiotic therapy for SPB should begin immediately and pending culture results, include a third-generation cephalosporin, such as ceftriaxone, or amoxicillin-clavulanic acid for 5 days (choice A). Fluoroquinolones (choice B) are generally avoided in areas with high fluoroquinolone resistance or in patients already taking a fluoroquinolone for SBP prophylaxis. Amoxicillin-clavulanic acid (choice C) is an alternative, but not the first choice. Fourth-generation cephalosporin (choice D) or a carbapenem (choice E) would be considered for broader empiric coverage but are typically reserved for patients with a history of resistant infections, multiple recent hospitalizations, or systemic illness, none of which are indicated in this patient's history. 94. Answer=B. Hold diuretics and give IV albumin 1 g/kg. This patient's clinical scenario suggests a possible hepatorenal syndrome, a type of kidney failure seen in patients with advanced liver disease, often precipitated by overdiuresis, infection, or certain medications like NSAIDs. When hepatorenal syndrome is suspected, the first step is to rule out prerenal acute kidney injury. This can be achieved through volume expansion, which involves withholding diuretics and administering IV albumin at a dosage of 1 g/kg/d for 2 days. This approach helps increase circulating blood volume, potentially improving renal perfusion and function. In this case, discontinuing the -blocker would also be appropriate. The other options mentioned—treatment for sepsis, a trial of midodrine and octreotide, or increasing the dose of -blocker—are not indicated based on the current findings. Thus, the best answer is to hold diuretics and administer IV albumin (Option B), aiming to improve the patient's renal function through volume expansion.

95. Answer: (A)

Primary prevention of variceal bleeding in patients with medium-to-large esophageal varices that have not yet bled includes either a nonselective -blocker or endoscopic variceal ligation. Both of these therapies have been shown to be effective in reducing the risk of variceal bleeding. TIPS is a minimally invasive procedure that can be used to create a shunt between the portal vein and hepatic vein. This can reduce portal vein pressure and help to prevent variceal bleeding. However, TIPS is typically reserved for patients who have already bled from esophageal varices or who have failed to respond to other treatments. Sengstaken-Blakemore tube placement is a last-resort treatment for variceal bleeding that is not controlled by other means. This tube is inserted through the nose and into the esophagus. It has three balloons that can be inflated to compress the esophageal varices and stop the bleeding. However, the Sengstaken-Blakemore tube is associated with a number of complications, including esophageal perforation and aspiration. In conclusion, the next most appropriate management step for this patient is endoscopic variceal ligation and nonselective -blocker therapy. The patient's Child class A cirrhosis indicates that he is at relatively low risk of complications from endoscopic variceal ligation and nonselective -blocker therapy. The patient should be monitored closely for signs of variceal bleeding, and his treatment should be adjusted as needed.

96. Answer: (A)

Budd-Chiari syndrome (BCS) is a rare disorder characterized by occlusion of the hepatic veins or inferior vena cava. It can be caused by a variety of factors, including oral contraceptive pill use, prior venous thrombosis, myeloproliferative disorders, and malignancies. Abdominal ultrasonography with Dopplers is the most appropriate initial step in the diagnosis of BCS. It is a non-invasive test that can visualize the hepatic veins and inferior vena cava and identify any obstructions. MRI with gadolinium should be avoided in patients with end-stage renal disease due to the risk of nephrogenic systemic fibrosis. CT of the abdomen and pelvis with IV contrast can be used to diagnose BCS, but it is more invasive than ultrasonography and exposes the patient to radiation. MRV of the abdomen and pelvis is another option, but it is not as widely available as ultrasonography. Liver biopsy is not necessary to diagnose BCS, and it is not recommended in patients with elevated liver enzymes and bilirubin, as it could worsen their condition. In conclusion, the most appropriate initial step in the diagnosis of BCS in this patient is abdominal ultrasonography with Dopplers.

97. The correct answer is D. Sinusoidal obstruction syndrome.

Sinusoidal obstruction syndrome (formerly known as hepatic veno-occlusive disease) is characterized by the occlusion of hepatic venules and sinusoids due to a toxic insult to hepatic vein endothelium. This syndrome often occurs in patients undergoing HSCT and less commonly following the use of certain chemotherapeutic agents in nontransplant settings, ingestion of alkaloid toxins, high-dose radiation therapy, or liver transplantation. The condition is characterized by hepatomegaly, right upper quadrant (RUQ) pain, jaundice, and ascites. Treatment is largely supportive and consists mainly of fluid management with diuretics. The other options are less likely because: A. Hepatocellular carcinoma usually presents with a liver mass, weight loss, and a history of chronic liver disease. B. Chronic hepatitis B infection usually presents with symptoms of chronic liver disease such as fatigue, mild right upper quadrant pain, and jaundice. It doesn't typically cause hepatomegaly and ascites. C. Alcoholic liver disease usually presents with a history of heavy alcohol use, and the presence of cirrhosis, ascites, and portal hypertension. E. Cirrhosis presents with a history of liver disease, including jaundice, ascites, and variceal bleeding. While cirrhosis can have many of the same symptoms as sinusoidal obstruction syndrome, the history of HSCT makes sinusoidal obstruction syndrome a more likely diagnosis.

98. Answer: C. Portal hypertension

The serum-ascites albumin gradient is calculated as the serum albumin concentration minus the ascites albumin concentration (in g/dL). A serum-ascites albumin gradient 1.1 strongly suggests portal hypertension with about 97% accuracy. In this patient's case, the serum-ascites albumin gradient is 2.5, which is highly suggestive of portal hypertension, most likely due to his known history of cirrhosis. The other options listed (nephrotic syndrome, congestive heart failure, tuberculous peritonitis, and malignancy) would typically present with a serum-ascites albumin gradient of <1.1.

99. Answer: (A)

The patient's presentation is suggestive of secondary bacterial peritonitis, which is a serious complication of intra-abdominal surgery. The most likely cause of the peritonitis is an intra-abdominal abscess or perforation. CT of the abdomen and pelvis is the most appropriate next step in management. It is a sensitive and specific test for diagnosing intra-abdominal abscesses and perforations. Abdominal ultrasonography is less sensitive than CT for diagnosing intra-abdominal abscesses and perforations. It may be helpful in identifying ascites and hepatosplenomegaly, but it is not reliable for detecting intra-abdominal abscesses or perforations. MRI of the abdomen and pelvis is another option, but it is not as widely available as CT and it takes longer to perform. X-ray of the abdomen is not helpful in diagnosing intra-abdominal abscesses or perforations. Liver biopsy is not necessary and is not recommended in this setting. In conclusion, the most appropriate next step in management is CT of the abdomen and pelvis. The patient should also be started on broad-spectrum antibiotics, such as a third-generation cephalosporin and metronidazole. If the CT scan shows an intra-abdominal abscess, the patient may require an exploratory laparotomy to drain the abscess. If the CT scan shows a perforation, the patient may require surgery to repair the perforation.

100. Answer: (D)

Peritonitis in the setting of peritoneal dialysis is usually caused by intraluminal contamination. The most common causative organisms are gram-positive bacteria, such as coagulase-negative staphylococci and methicillin-resistant Staphylococcus aureus. Gram-negative bacteria, such as Escherichia coli and Klebsiella pneumoniae, can also cause peritonitis in this setting. The initial antibiotic regimen should cover both gram-positive and gram-negative bacteria. IV vancomycin and gentamicin is a broad-spectrum antibiotic regimen that is effective against both gram-positive and gram-negative bacteria. Ceftriaxone and doxycycline is a good regimen for community-acquired pneumonia, but it is not as broad-spectrum as vancomycin and gentamicin. Ciprofloxacin is a good regimen for urinary tract infections, but it is not as effective against gram-positive bacteria as vancomycin. Ampicillin and gentamicin is a good regimen for sepsis in the general population, but it is not as effective against methicillin-resistant Staphylococcus aureus as vancomycin. Amoxicillin-clavulanate is a good regimen for community-acquired infections, but it is not as broad-spectrum as vancomycin and gentamicin. In conclusion, the most appropriate initial antibiotic regimen for peritonitis in the setting of peritoneal dialysis is IV vancomycin and gentamicin. The patient should also be admitted to the hospital for close monitoring and management. The peritoneal dialysis catheter should be removed and the patient should be switched to hemodialysis until the peritonitis is resolved. The patient's peritoneal dialysis effluent should be cultured to identify the causative organism and to guide further antibiotic therapy.

101. Answer: C. Administer broad-spectrum antibiotics and perform an urgent endoscopic retrograde cholangiopancreatography (ERCP)

The patient's symptoms (RUQ pain, jaundice, fever and chills, confusion, and shock) are indicative of Reynolds pentad, a syndrome associated with severe, acute ("ascending") cholangitis, which is most likely due to a bile duct stone. Although the stone is not visible on ultrasonography, the dilation of the bile duct suggests possible choledocholithiasis. Immediate initiation of broad-spectrum antibiotics to cover common bile pathogens is necessary. However, approximately 20% of patients, likely including this one given her severity of illness, require urgent biliary decompression. This is most effectively achieved via ERCP, which can provide papillotomy, stone extraction, and/or stent insertion. The other management options listed either lack the necessary urgency (A), are too aggressive (B), or are not as effective or appropriate as ERCP (D, E) in this setting.

102. Answer: D. Request a transabdominal ultrasonography.

The patient's symptoms are typical of biliary pain, likely due to cholelithiasis. Risk factors for cholelithiasis include being female, obese, pregnant, and over 40 years old, all of which apply to this patient. Biliary pain or "colic" is characterized by episodic right upper quadrant or epigastric abdominal pain that begins abruptly, is continuous, resolves slowly, lasts from 30 minutes to 3 hours, and may radiate to the scapula. It is often accompanied by nausea and belching. Transabdominal ultrasonography is the first-line diagnostic tool for suspected gallstones, particularly in the setting of typical biliary symptoms. Therefore, although the patient could potentially have GERD, gastritis, or peptic ulcer disease, her symptoms and risk factors make cholelithiasis the most likely diagnosis, and ultrasonography would be the most appropriate next step. Options A, B, and C (initiating therapy for GERD, starting treatment for gastritis, starting a regimen for peptic ulcer disease) may not address the likely cause of the patient's symptoms, and are therefore not the best immediate steps. Option E (scheduling immediate surgical intervention) is not indicated without a confirmed diagnosis and consideration of the patient's pregnancy status. It's generally preferred to manage biliary pain conservatively in pregnant women, and surgery is only considered if bouts of biliary pain are frequent and recurrent.

103. Correct Answer: A. Cholecystectomy

This patient is suffering from acalculous cholecystitis, a condition that often occurs in critically ill or hospitalized patients and is typically caused by gallbladder stasis and ischemia. In this case, the presence of gas in the gallbladder wall, lack of gallbladder wall enhancement, and edema around the gallbladder are all highly specific indicators of this condition. Given that the patient's condition includes features such as gallbladder necrosis and emphysematous cholecystitis due to a gas-forming organism, emergency cholecystectomy is indicated. Although in acalculous cholecystitis without these features, a trial of a cholecystostomy tube may be the appropriate initial treatment, this patient's critical condition warrants immediate surgical intervention

Chapter 8

ALLERGY, RHEUMATOLOGY BOARD QUESTIONS

1. A 48-year-old patient presents skin lesions that have been present for 48 hours. The lesions are causing pain rather than pruritus and there are signs of potential scarring. What should be the next step in diagnosing the patient's condition?

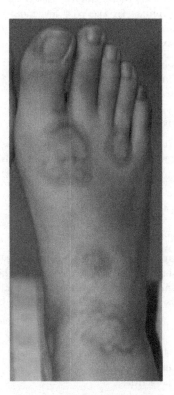

Figure 8.1: 48-year-old patient

- A. Administer opioid painkillers.
- B. Start a course in antibiotics.
- C. Advise the patient to avoid alcohol.
- D. Conduct a skin biopsy.
- E. Refer the patient for a colonoscopy.

2. 38-year-old woman presents to her doctor with complaints of chronic hives. She has been experiencing these symptoms for the past 6 months. She has tried taking long-acting H1 antihistamines four times daily, as well as a CysLT1 receptor antagonist, but her symptoms have not improved. The doctor diagnoses the patient with chronic urticaria and prescribes omalizumab. What is the rationale behind the use of omalizumab in this patient?

- A. Omalizumab is a monoclonal anti-IgE antibody that binds to IgE, preventing it from binding to mast cells and basophils.
- B. Omalizumab is a long-acting H1 antihistamine that is more effective than traditional H1 antihistamines.
- C. Omalizumab is a CysLT1 receptor antagonist that is more effective than traditional CysLT1 receptor antagonists.
- D. Omalizumab is a combination of a long-acting H1 antihistamine and a CysLT1 receptor antagonist.
- E. Omalizumab is a new medication that has not been proven to be effective in the treatment of chronic urticaria.

3. A 32-year-old patient presents with signs of a severe anaphylactic reaction. What is the preferred initial therapeutic intervention?

- A. Administer 2.0 mL of 1:1000 (1.0 mg/mL) epinephrine intramuscularly.
- B. Administer 0.3-0.5 mL of 1:1000 (1.0 mg/mL) epinephrine intramuscularly.
- C. Administer a course of broad-spectrum antibiotics.
- D. Advise the patient to drink plenty of water.
- E. Refer the patient for a skin biopsy.

4. 24-year-old African American woman presents to her doctor with complaints of fatigue, fever, malaise, and weight loss. She has been experiencing these symptoms for the past few months. The doctor diagnoses the patient with systemic lupus erythematosus (SLE), a chronic autoimmune disease that can affect many parts of the body. Which ethnic group exhibits the highest prevalence of SLE?

- A. African American and Afro-Caribbean women
- B. Hispanic and Latin American women
- C. Asian and Pacific Islander women
- D. White women
- E. Native American and Alaska Native women

5. A 58-year-old patient presents with symptoms suggestive of lupus and a history of long-term drug use. In the context of suspecting drug-induced lupus, which of the following is less likely to be observed?

- A. Presence of anti-nuclear antibodies (ANA)
- B. Presence of antibodies to histones
- C. Presence of antibodies to double-stranded DNA (dsDNA)
- D. Photosensitivity
- E. Arthralgias

6. A 33-year-old woman with a history of systemic lupus erythematosus (SLE) presents to the emergency department with complaints of fatigue, fever, and rash. She has been experiencing these symptoms for the past few days. The doctor diagnoses the patient with severe nephritis, a life-threatening complication of SLE. What is the method of administration for cyclophosphamide in the treatment of severe nephritis in SLE?

- A. Intravenous infusion
- B. Oral ingestion
- C. Both intravenous infusion and oral ingestion
- D. Neither intravenous infusion nor oral ingestion
- E. It depends on the severity of the nephritis.

7. A 41-year-old patient is being evaluated for persistent joint pain and stiffness. The physician suspects rheumatoid arthritis (RA) and is considering ordering a test for antibodies. Which of the following statements is most accurate concerning antibodies targeting cyclic citrullinated protein (anti-CCP)?

- A. Anti-CCP antibodies are less sensitive than rheumatoid factor (RF) for detecting RA.
- B. Anti-CCP antibodies have lower specificity than RF for detecting RA.
- C. Anti-CCP antibodies are particularly advantageous in the late stages of RA.
- D. Anti-CCP antibodies are often found in patients exhibiting mild disease characteristics.

- E. Anti-CCP antibodies are often found in patients with aggressive RA and a propensity for the development of bone erosions.

8. A 37-year-old woman presents to her doctor with complaints of joint pain and stiffness. She has been experiencing these symptoms for the past few months. The doctor performs a physical examination and finds that the patient has swelling and tenderness in her hands, wrists, and knees. What evaluation is typically recommended for this patient?

- A. Complete blood count (CBC)
- B. Erythrocyte sedimentation rate (ESR)
- C. Rheumatoid factor (RF)
- D. A chest X-ray (CXR)
- E. All of the above

9. A 34-year-old patient presents with chronic back pain. The clinician considers a diagnosis of axial spondyloarthritis and intends to apply the ASAS criteria. Which of the following sets of features is included in the ASAS criteria for diagnosing axial spondyloarthritis?

- A. Inflammatory back pain, osteoarthritis, anterior uveitis, psoriasis, positive response to corticosteroids, presence of HLA-B27 antigen
- B. Inflammatory back pain, arthritis, heel enthesitis, anterior uveitis, dactylitis, psoriasis, Crohn's disease or ulcerative colitis, positive response to NSAIDs, family history of spondyloarthritis, presence of HLA-B27 antigen, elevated CRP levels
- C. Non-inflammatory back pain, arthritis, heel enthesitis, posterior uveitis, dactylitis, psoriasis, Crohn's disease or ulcerative colitis, positive response to NSAIDs, family history of osteoarthritis, presence of HLA-B27 antigen, elevated CRP levels
- D. Inflammatory back pain, osteoarthritis, heel enthesitis, anterior uveitis, dactylitis, psoriasis, Crohn's disease or ulcerative colitis, positive response to corticosteroids, family history of spondyloarthritis, absence of HLA-B27 antigen, normal CRP levels
- E. Inflammatory back pain, arthritis, heel enthesitis, anterior uveitis, absence of dactylitis, absence of psoriasis, absence of Crohn's disease or ulcerative colitis, negative response to NSAIDs, family history of spondyloarthritis, presence of HLA-B27 antigen, elevated CRP levels

10. A 40-year-old man presents to his doctor with complaints of back pain and stiffness. He has been experiencing these symptoms for the past few months. The doctor performs a physical examination and finds that the patient has decreased range of motion in his lumbar spine. The doctor performs the Schober test to quantify the patient's range of motion. What is the Schober test?

- A. A clinical assessment tool employed to ascertain the presence of diminished flexion range of motion in the lumbar spine, primarily attributable to Ankylosing Spondylitis.
- B. A laboratory test that measures the level of inflammation in the body.
- C. A radiographic test that images the lumbar spine.
- D. A magnetic resonance imaging (MRI) scan of the lumbar spine.
- E. A computed tomography (CT) scan of the lumbar spine.

11. A 27-year-old male patient presents to your clinic with joint pain and inflammation in his knees and ankles. You suspect reactive arthritis. Which of the following is an important step in the evaluation of this patient?

- A. Screening for HIV
- B. Screening for Hepatitis A
- C. Screening for Influenza
- D. Screening for Tuberculosis
- E. Screening for Lyme disease

12. A 51-year-old man presents to his doctor with complaints of joint pain and deformity. He has been experiencing these symptoms for the past few years. The doctor performs a physical examination and finds that the patient has severe joint deformities in his hands and feet. The doctor diagnoses the patient with arthritis mutilans. What is arthritis mutilans?

- A. A highly aggressive manifestation of arthritis characterized by pronounced joint deformities and extensive bone erosion.
- B. A type of arthritis that is caused by an overactive immune system.

- C. A type of arthritis that is caused by a genetic defect.
- D. A type of arthritis that is caused by an infection.
- E. None of the above

13. A 37-year-old female patient with a known history of inflammatory bowel disease presents to your clinic with complaints of joint pain. You suspect enteropathic arthritis. Which of the following is a potential treatment option for her condition?

- A. Anti-tumor necrosis factor (anti-TNF) agents
- B. Nonsteroidal anti-inflammatory drugs (NSAIDs)
- C. Sulfasalazine
- D. Azathioprine
- E. All of the above

14. 39-year-old woman presents to her doctor with complaints of Raynaud's phenomenon, fatigue, and shortness of breath. She has been experiencing these symptoms for the past few years.The doctor performs a physical examination and finds that the patient has skin thickening on her fingers and toes. The doctor diagnoses the patient with systemic sclerosis.

Figure 8.2: 39-year-old woman

- A. Diffuse cutaneous SSc and Limited cutaneous SSc
- B. CREST syndrome and Raynaud's phenomenon
- C. Pulmonary arterial hypertension and esophageal dysmotility
- D. Calcinosis and telangiectasias
- E. None of the above

15. A 38-year-old woman presents with a history of recurrent miscarriages. You suspect antiphospholipid syndrome (APS). Which of the following is a crucial step in the evaluation of this patient?

- A. Measuring Prothrombin Time (PT)
- B. Assessing the presence of antibodies targeting cardiolipin.
- C. Conducting a dilute Russell viper venom test.
- D. Measuring Partial Thromboplastin Time (PTT)
- E. All of the above

16. A 31-year-old woman presents to her doctor with complaints of recurrent miscarriages. She has had two miscarriages in the past year. The doctor performs a physical examination and finds that the patient has no other significant medical problems. The doctor orders blood tests, and the patient is found to have antiphospholipid antibodies. What is the recommended therapeutic approach for this patient?

- A. Warfarin therapy with an international normalized ratio (INR) ranging from 2.5 to 3.5.
- B. Heparin in combination with a daily dose of 80 mg of aspirin

- C. Intravenous immunoglobulins (IVIG)
- D. Glucocorticoids
- E. All of the above

17. A 44-year-old male presents with persistent nasal discharge, cough, and hemoptysis. He also reports occasional shortness of breath. On examination, you notice a saddlenose deformity. Which of the following is the most likely diagnosis?

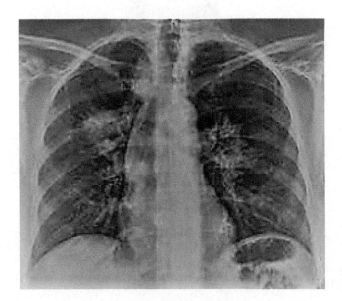

Figure 8.3: 44-year-old male

- A. Allergic Rhinitis
- B. Nasal Polyps
- C. Granulomatosis with Polyangiitis (Wegener's)
- D. Chronic Sinusitis
- E. Tuberculosis

18. A 53-year-old man presents to his doctor with complaints of fever, fatigue, and weight loss. He also reports having had a rash on his legs for the past few weeks. The doctor performs a physical examination and finds that the patient has decreased peripheral pulses and a palpable abdominal mass. The doctor orders blood tests and the patient is found to have elevated levels of C-reactive protein and erythrocyte sedimentation rate. What are the clinical manifestations associated with Polyarteritis Nodosa?

- A. Fever, fatigue, weight loss, rash, decreased peripheral pulses, and palpable abdominal mass.
- B. Fever, fatigue, weight loss, rash, and decreased peripheral pulses.
- C. Fever, fatigue, weight loss, and palpable abdominal mass
- D. Fever, fatigue, weight loss, and rash
- E. None of the above

19. A 79-year-old woman presents with a rash on her legs, arms, joint pain, and weakness. Blood tests reveal the presence of cryoglobulins. Which of the following could be a potential underlying cause of her condition?

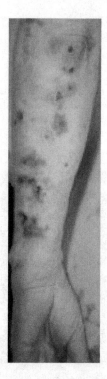

Figure 8.4: 79-year-old woman

- A. Hepatitis C infection
- B. Rheumatoid arthritis
- C. Lung cancer
- D. Diabetes mellitus
- E. All of the above

20. What is the definition and classification of Secondary Vasculitis Syndromes?

- A. Secondary Vasculitis Syndromes are a range of conditions caused by an underlying disease or condition, such as infection, malignancy, or rheumatic disease.
- B. Secondary Vasculitis Syndromes are a range of conditions caused by exposure to drugs or other environmental factors.
- C. Secondary Vasculitis Syndromes are a range of conditions that are not caused by an underlying disease or condition.
- D. Secondary Vasculitis Syndromes are a range of conditions that are caused by an autoimmune response.
- E. None of the above

21. A 60-year-old man presents with severe pain and swelling in the big toe. His serum uric acid levels are found to be within normal limits. Which of the following is the most appropriate next step in diagnosing his condition?

- A. Dismiss the possibility of gout due to normal serum uric acid levels.
- B. Conduct a urine test to check for uric acid excretion.
- C. Perform a synovial fluid analysis.
- D. Recommend a dietary change.
- E. Initiate treatment for osteoarthritis

22. What are the therapeutic interventions employed for the management of relapsing polychondritis?

- A. Glucocorticoids, such as prednisone administered at a dosage of 40-60 mg per day with subsequent tapering, have the potential to inhibit acute manifestations and mitigate the intensity and frequency of subsequent episodes.

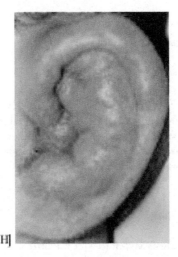

[H]

Figure 8.5: relapsing polychondritis

- B. Cytotoxic and other immunosuppressive agents should be allocated exclusively for cases of unresponsive disease or for patients who necessitate high doses of glucocorticoids.
- C. In cases of significant airway obstruction, the implementation of a tracheostomy procedure may become necessary.
- D. All of the above
- E. None of the above

23. A 68-year-old woman presents with severe shoulder and hip pain. She also reports on experiencing unexplained weight loss and fatigue. Which of the following is the most likely diagnosis and what other condition should be considered?

- A. Polymyalgia Rheumatica (PMR) and Giant Cell Arteritis (GCA)
- B. Fibromyalgia and Chronic Fatigue Syndrome
- C. Osteoarthritis and Rheumatoid Arthritis
- D. Lupus and Vasculitis
- E. Systemic Sclerosis and Sjogren's Syndrome

24. What are the characteristics of pulmonary involvement in sarcoidosis?

- A. Hilar adenopathy, infiltrates, interstitial pneumonitis, and fibrosis
- B. Airway obstruction and pulmonary hypertension
- C. Direct vascular involvement and lung fibrosis
- D. All of the above
- E. None of the above

25. A 69-year-old man presents with symptoms of fatigue, weight loss, and swelling around his eyes and ankles. He also reports feeling an irregular heartbeat. His health history indicates a long-standing issue with kidney function. The doctor suspects amyloidosis. Which of the following would be the most effective diagnostic technique to confirm this suspicion?

- A. Echocardiogram
- B. Chest X-ray
- C. Blood test for kidney function
- D. Congo red staining of abdominal fat
- E. Lung function test

26. A 46-year-old male with a history of hepatitis B infection presents with new onset of fever, weight loss, muscle and joint aches, and a rash consisting of small red spots on the lower extremities. On examination, the spots are palpable and spread across the lower limbs. Further investigation reveals the presence of vasculitis. What is the most

appropriate next step in the management of this patient?

- A) Immediate initiation of high-dose corticosteroids
- B) Angioplasty
- C) Administration of antiviral agents
- D) Observation and rest
- E) Administration of nonsteroidal anti-inflammatory drugs (NSAIDs)

27. A 70-year-old woman presents with a three-month history of bilateral shoulder and hip pain and stiffness, particularly in the morning. She also reports low-grade fever and unintended weight loss. Lab tests show an elevated erythrocyte sedimentation rate. Based on these symptoms, she is diagnosed with polymyalgia rheumatica (PMR). Which of the following is the most appropriate initial therapeutic intervention for this patient?

- A) High-dose ibuprofen
- B) Physical therapy
- C) Prednisone 10 to 20 milligrams daily
- D) Methotrexate
- E) Biologic therapy with tumor necrosis factor (TNF) inhibitors

28. A 33-year-old woman presents with a one-month history of persistent skin lesions on her face, particularly around the nasal bridge, eyes, and cheeks. The lesions are indurated, blue-purple, and shiny. She also reports occasional fatigue and dry cough. Based on these symptoms, what is the most likely cutaneous manifestation of sarcoidosis present in this patient?

- A) Erythema nodosum
- B) Maculopapular lesions
- C) Subcutaneous nodules
- D) Lupus pernio
- E) Psoriasis

29. A 67-year-old man presents with fatigue, weight loss, and edema of the lower extremities. After a series of tests, he is diagnosed with AL amyloidosis. Considering the condition and his overall health status, what is the likelihood of him being eligible for aggressive treatment of AL amyloidosis through the utilization of high-dose intravenous melphalan followed by autologous stem-cell transplantation?

- A) Less than 10%
- B) Approximately 25%
- C) Approximately 50%
- D) Approximately 75%
- E) More than 90%

30. A 28-year-old woman presents with a 3-month history of pain and stiffness in her hands and wrists, especially in the morning. She also reports progressive fatigue and occasional low-grade fever. On physical examination, she has tender, swollen metacarpophalangeal and proximal interphalangeal joints bilaterally without any deformities. The rest of her examination is unremarkable. What is the most appropriate diagnostic test to perform next?

- A. Anti-neutrophil cytoplasmic antibody assay
- B. Anti-nuclear antibody assay
- C. Erythrocyte sedimentation rate
- D. C-reactive protein
- E. Rheumatoid factor (RF) and anti-cyclic citrullinated peptide (anti-CCP) antibodies

31. A 37-year-old woman with rheumatoid arthritis presents to the clinic with persistent joint pain and swelling despite treatment with methotrexate. She has a history of intolerance to methotrexate, including nausea, vomiting, and hair loss. She also has a history of a severe reaction to a sulfa-containing medication and is planning to have children in the next year. Which of the following is the next best step in management?

- (A) Biologic disease-modifying antirheumatic drug (DMARD)
- (B) Conventional synthetic DMARD
- (C) Targeted synthetic DMARD
- (D) Glucocorticoids

- (E) Surgery

32. A 23-year-old man presents with a 2-week history of daily fevers, night sweats, unintentional weight loss, lymphadenopathy, and a salmon-colored rash on his trunk and extremities. He is otherwise healthy and has no significant past medical history. Which of the following is the most appropriate next step in management?

- (A) Start prednisone 0.5 mg/kg.
- (B) Order an excisional biopsy of a cervical lymph node.
- (C) Order a chest X-ray, abdominal ultrasound, and pelvic ultrasound.
- (D) Order a chest X-ray, abdominal and pelvic CT scan, and excisional biopsy of a cervical lymph node.
- (E) Refer the patient to a rheumatologist for evaluation of adult-onset Still disease.

33. A 53-year old man presents with recurrent episodes of acute inflammatory asymmetric oligoarthritis that resolve completely with anti-inflammatory therapy. Upon examination, evidence of firm nodules in the olecranon bursa are observed. The patient has no extra-articular or axial features. What is the most likely diagnosis?

- A. Acute gouty arthritis
- B. Seronegative spondyloarthropathy
- C. Rheumatoid arthritis
- D. Osteoarthritis
- E. Infectious arthritis

34. A 63-year-old male patient with a history of chronic kidney disease, type 1 diabetes mellitus (T1DM), and ischemic cardiomyopathy presents with an acute inflammatory polyarthritis. He has multiple risk factors for hyperuricemia, and bilateral tophi are observed on examination. He has been on diuresis with loop diuretics. His uric acid level is within the normal range. Given his comorbidities, which of the following would be the most appropriate treatment for this patient's likely condition of acute polyarticular gouty arthritis?

- A. NSAIDs
- B. Intra-articular steroids
- C. Systemic steroids
- D. Colchicine
- E. Anakinra 100 mg QD SQ

35. A 40-year-old woman presents with a 1-day history of severe pain, swelling, and erythema of her left knee. She has no fever or other systemic symptoms. Her medical history is unremarkable, and she is not taking any medications. Physical examination reveals a hot, swollen, and erythematous left knee with significant tenderness and limited range of motion. Which of the following is the least likely diagnosis?

- (A) Gout
- (B) Pseudogout
- (C) Bacterial septic arthritis
- (D) Acute monoarticular presentation of rheumatoid arthritis
- (E) All of the above are equally likely diagnoses.

36. A 31-year-old woman presents with a 6-month history of low back pain and stiffness. The pain is worse in the morning and improves with activity. She has no other systemic symptoms. Her physical examination reveals tenderness over the sacroiliac joints. Which of the following is the next best step in the evaluation?

- (A) Complete blood count (CBC)
- (B) Erythrocyte sedimentation rate (ESR)
- (C) C-reactive protein (CRP) level
- (D) Sacroiliac (SI) joint radiographs
- (E) MRI of the SI joints

37. A 43-year-old man from India, who has been diagnosed with severe rheumatoid arthritis, is being considered for anti-TNF therapy. Given his background and the associated risk of reactivation of latent tuberculosis with anti-TNF therapy, which of the following is the most appropriate test to perform prior to initiating therapy?

- A. Complete blood count (CBC)
- B. Liver function tests
- C. Interferon release assay (IGRA)

- D. Chest X-ray
- E. Erythrocyte sedimentation rate (ESR)

38. A 30-year-old man presents with a 2-week history of acute onset of arthritis in his knees, ankles, and wrists. He also has a 3-day history of dysuria and urethral discharge. His medical history is unremarkable and he is not taking any medications. Physical examination reveals warm, swollen, and erythematous knees, ankles, and wrists. He also has a purulent urethral discharge. Which of the following is the most likely diagnosis?

- (A) Rheumatoid arthritis
- (B) Osteoarthritis
- (C) Reactive arthritis
- (D) Gout
- (E) Pseudogout

39. A 62-year-old woman with a history of Raynaud phenomenon presents with a blood pressure of 180/110 mm Hg. She has been feeling fatigued lately and has noticed some mild abdominal pain. Laboratory studies show a creatinine of 2.5 mg/dL (baseline 0.8), hemoglobin of 9.5 g/dL, platelet count of 100,000/L, and an indirect bilirubin of 1.5 mg/dL. Urinalysis shows trace protein but is otherwise unremarkable. On physical examination, you notice several telangiectasias and dilated capillary loops with dropout. What is the best next step in the management of this patient?

- A. Initiate hemodialysis
- B. Start prednisone
- C. Initiate plasmapheresis
- D. Start captopril
- E. Continue to monitor and recheck labs in one week

40. A patient with scleroderma presents with symptoms suggestive of an impending scleroderma renal crisis (SRC). Which of the following antibodies, if present, would indicate a higher risk of developing SRC in this patient?

- A. Antinuclear antibody (ANA)
- B. Anti-double-stranded DNA (anti-dsDNA)
- C. Anti-histone
- D. Anti-RNA polymerase III
- E. Anti-Jo1

41. A 56-year-old woman presents with a 3-month history of progressive weakness in her arms and legs. She also has a rash on her face and hands. Her medical history is unremarkable and she is not taking any medications. Physical examination reveals proximal muscle weakness in the upper and lower extremities. She also has a violaceous rash on her upper eyelids and a rash on the extensor surfaces of her joints. Which of the following is the most likely diagnosis?

- (A) Rheumatoid arthritis
- (B) Systemic lupus erythematosus
- (C) Scleroderma
- (D) Dermatomyositis
- (E) Polymyositis

42. A 42-year-old woman presents with a 2-year history of fatigue, arthralgias, myalgias, Raynaud's phenomenon, and hand edema. She also has a puffy appearance to her fingers. Her physical examination is unremarkable except for mild synovitis in her wrists and ankles. Laboratory studies show a positive antinuclear antibody (ANA) with a speckled pattern, a positive anti-U1 RNP antibody, and a negative rheumatoid factor. Which of the following is the most likely diagnosis?

- (A) Rheumatoid arthritis
- (B) Mixed connective tissue disease (MCTD)
- (C) Systemic lupus erythematosus (SLE)
- (D) Systemic sclerosis (SSc)
- (E) Polymyositis

43. A 47-year-old male patient presents with symptoms of fevers, arthralgia, rash, and chest pain upon inspiration, consistent with pleuritis. Laboratory testing is notable for a positive antinuclear antibody, positive anti-dsDNA,

and a positive anti-histone antibody. The patient's medication list includes the following: adalimumab, atorvastatin, amlodipine, and aspirin. Which of the following medications is most likely associated with the patient's presentation?

- A. Adalimumab
- B. Atorvastatin
- C. Amlodipine
- D. Aspirin
- E. None of the above

44. A 62-year-old male patient presents with symptoms of fever, malaise, arthritis, rash, and serositis. Laboratory testing reveals a positive antinuclear antibody, positive anti-dsDNA, and a positive anti-histone antibody. The patient's symptoms and lab results are most consistent with a diagnosis of drug-induced lupus. Which of the following would be the most reliable way to differentiate drug-induced lupus from systemic lupus erythematosus?

- A. Presence of anti-dsDNA antibodies
- B. Presence of anti-histone antibodies
- C. Clinical history
- D. Skin biopsy results
- E. Gender of the patient

45. A 26-year-old woman with known lupus presents with fatigue, low-grade fevers, rash, and synovitis. She is taking hydroxychloroquine but has not taken any other medications for her lupus in the past year. Her laboratory studies show an elevated white blood cell count, elevated erythrocyte sedimentation rate, and elevated C-reactive protein level. Which of the following medications is the most appropriate initial treatment for this patient?

- (A) Hydroxychloroquine
- (B) Prednisone
- (C) Cyclophosphamide
- (D) Mycophenolate mofetil
- (E) Rituximab

46. A 58-year-old man with a history of allergic rhinitis and asthma presents with fevers, unintentional weight loss, hemoptysis, petechial rash, and mononeuritis multiplex. His laboratory studies show a white blood cell count of 12,000 cells/mm³ with 10% eosinophils. Which of the following tests is most appropriate to diagnose his underlying condition?

- (A) Complete blood count (CBC) with differential
- (B) Antinuclear antibody (ANA) test
- (C) Rheumatoid factor test
- (D) Electromyography (EMG) and nerve conduction study (NCS)
- (E) Lung biopsy

47. A 43-year-old woman with a history of systemic lupus erythematosus is being treated with hydroxychloroquine. She has been on this medication for the past 4 years. What is the most appropriate step in the management of this patient?

- A. Start her on anti-TNF therapy
- B. Stop hydroxychloroquine immediately
- C. Perform renal biopsy
- D. Screening ophthalmologic examinations
- E. Order anti-dsDNA antibody testing

48. A 46-year-old male presents with a three-week history of fever, malaise, weight loss, abdominal pain, and bloody stools. He also reports muscle aches and pain in his hands and feet. On physical examination, he has purpura on his legs and decreased sensation and strength in his right hand and left foot. Laboratory testing shows an elevated erythrocyte sedimentation rate, C-reactive protein, and creatinine. Imaging reveals renal artery aneurysms. What is the most likely diagnosis?

- A. Giant cell arteritis
- B. Granulomatosis with polyangiitis
- C. Microscopic polyangiitis

- D. Eosinophilic granulomatosis with polyangiitis
- E. Polyarteritis nodosa

49. A 51-year-old man presents with painless obstructive jaundice. He is found to have a 3-cm mass in the pancreatic head, widespread lymphadenopathy, and elevated serum IgG4 levels. Which of the following is the most appropriate next step in management?

- (A) Endoscopic ultrasound with biopsy
- (B) Pancreaticoduodenectomy (Whipple procedure)
- (C) Chemotherapy
- (D) Radiation therapy
- (E) Observation

50. A 47-year-old male patient with a history of Hepatitis C presents to your clinic. He complains of general malaise, joint pain, and has developed a palpable purpuric rash on his lower limbs. He also reports experiencing some numbness and tingling in his hands and feet recently. His lab testing reveals a positive rheumatoid factor and low C4 levels. Which of the following is the next best step in the management of this patient?

- A. Kidney biopsy
- B. Skin biopsy
- C. Liver function tests
- D. Cryoglobulin testing
- E. Platelet count

51. A 66-year-old man presents with peripheral neuropathy, recent onset of carpal tunnel, increased fluid retention, and easy bruising. On physical examination, you notice an enlargement of the anterior shoulder ("shoulder pad sign"), hepatosplenomegaly, and periorbital bruising. Laboratory testing reveals an elevated creatinine with significant proteinuria. What would be the most appropriate initial diagnostic test to confirm your suspected diagnosis?

- A. Renal biopsy
- B. Liver biopsy
- C. Bone marrow biopsy
- D. Abdominal fat pad biopsy
- E. Serum protein electrophoresis (SPEP) and urine protein electrophoresis (UPEP) with immunofixation

52. 57-year-old man with a history of asthma presents with a 2-week history of fever, night sweats, weight loss, and a rash on his trunk and extremities. He also has a history of multiple episodes of sinusitis and pneumonia. Physical examination reveals a papular rash on the patient's trunk and extremities, as well as wheezing on lung auscultation. Laboratory studies show an elevated white blood cell count with eosinophilia, elevated erythrocyte sedimentation rate, and elevated C-reactive protein level. Chest X-ray shows bilateral infiltrates. What is the most likely diagnosis?

- (A) Eosinophilic granulomatosis with polyangiitis
- (B) Allergic bronchopulmonary aspergillosis
- (C) Chronic obstructive pulmonary disease (COPD)
- (D) Bronchiectasis
- (E) Cystic fibrosis

53. A 51-year-old woman presents with a 3-month history of progressive weakness in her arms and legs. She also has a rash on her face and hands. Her medical history is unremarkable and she is not taking any medications. Physical examination reveals proximal muscle weakness in the upper and lower extremities. She also has a violaceous rash on her upper eyelids and a rash on the extensor surfaces of her joints. Laboratory studies show elevated muscle enzymes and a positive antinuclear antibody (ANA) test with a speckled pattern. What is the most appropriate next step in management?

- (A) Start corticosteroids
- (B) Start methotrexate
- (C) Refer to a physical therapist
- (D) Order a colonoscopy
- (E) Order a transvaginal ultrasound

54. A 36-year-old woman presents with a history of atraumatic radial wrist pain, fullness and tenderness over the

dorsal radial wrist. She reports that she has been working from home for the past few months and uses her computer for extended periods. On examination, you find a positive Finkelstein maneuver. What is the most likely diagnosis?

- A. Scaphoid fracture
- B. De Quervain tenosynovitis
- C. Carpal tunnel syndrome
- D. Ganglion cyst
- E. Rheumatoid arthritis

8.1 ANSWERS

1. The correct answer is D. Conduct a skin biopsy.

In the context of skin lesions that have a duration exceeding 36 hours, are causing pain rather than pruritus (itching), and show signs of potential scarring, a skin biopsy should be considered to investigate the possibility of urticarial vasculitis. Option A, administering opioid painkillers, is not the best choice as it only treats the symptom (pain), but it does not address the underlying cause of the condition. Option B, starting a course of antibiotics, would be more appropriate if there were signs of infection, but the question does not provide information suggesting this. Option C, advising the patient to avoid alcohol, is a general health advice but it doesn't directly relate to the patient's presenting symptoms or potential urticarial vasculitis. Option E, referring to the patient for a colonoscopy, would be relevant for gastrointestinal issues or concerns about colorectal conditions, but not in the case of skin lesions potentially indicative of urticarial vasculitis. Therefore, conducting a skin biopsy (Option D) is the most appropriate next step as it would allow for further investigation of the skin lesions and the potential diagnosis of urticarial vasculitis.

2. The correct answer is A: omalizumab is a monoclonal anti-IgE antibody that binds to IgE, preventing it from binding to mast cells and basophils.

Chronic urticaria is a condition that is caused by the release of histamine and other inflammatory mediators from mast cells and basophils. IgE is a protein that binds to mast cells and basophils, triggering their activation and the release of these mediators. Omalizumab is a monoclonal anti-IgE antibody that binds to IgE, preventing it from binding to mast cells and basophils. This prevents the activation of mast cells and basophils and the release of histamine and other inflammatory mediators, which can help to improve the symptoms of chronic urticaria. Omalizumab has been shown to be effective in the treatment of chronic urticaria that has not responded to other treatments. It is administered by injection every 4 weeks.

3. The correct answer is B. Administer 0.3-0.5 mL of 1:1000 (1.0 mg/mL) epinephrine intramuscularly.

In the context of a severe anaphylactic reaction, the preferred initial therapeutic intervention is to administer 0.3-0.5 mL of 1:1000 (1.0 mg/mL) epinephrine intramuscularly, with subsequent doses administered as needed at intervals ranging from 5 to 20 minutes (Option B). Option A, administering 2.0 mL of 1:1000 (1.0 mg/mL) epinephrine intramuscularly, provides an excessive dose which may cause unnecessary side effects or complications. Option C, administering a course of broad-spectrum antibiotics, is not the appropriate treatment for anaphylaxis as this is an immune-mediated reaction, not an infection. Option D, advising the patient to drink plenty of water, can be a part of general health advice but it does not address the immediate life-threatening condition. Option E, referring to the patient for a skin biopsy, is not relevant in the context of an anaphylactic reaction as a skin biopsy is used to investigate dermatological conditions, not allergic reactions. Therefore, the preferred initial therapeutic intervention for a severe anaphylactic reaction is to administer 0.3-0.5 mL of 1:1000 (1.0 mg/mL) epinephrine intramuscularly (Option B).

4. The correct answer is A: African American and Afro-Caribbean women.

SLE is a chronic autoimmune disease that is more common in women than in men. The prevalence of SLE varies by ethnicity. African American and Afro-Caribbean women have the highest prevalence of SLE, followed by Hispanic and Latin American women, Asian and Pacific Islander women, white women, and Native American and Alaska Native women. The reason for the higher prevalence of SLE in African American and Afro-Caribbean women is not fully understood. However, it is thought to be due to a combination of genetic and environmental factors. The constitutional symptoms of SLE can include fatigue, fever, malaise, and weight loss. These symptoms can be nonspecific and can be caused by other conditions. However, they are often the first symptoms of SLE.

5. The correct answer is C. Presence of antibodies to double-stranded DNA (dsDNA).

In cases of drug-induced lupus, the presence of antibodies to double-stranded DNA (dsDNA) and hypocomplementemia is infrequent (Option C). Option A, the presence of anti-nuclear antibodies (ANA), is frequently observed in drug-induced lupus. Option B, the presence of antibodies to histones, is also commonly seen in drug-induced lupus, with a high proportion of patients testing positive for anti-histone antibodies. Option D, photosensitivity, and Option E, arthralgias, are common clinical manifestations in drug-induced lupus. Therefore, the presence of antibodies to double-stranded DNA (dsDNA) (Option C) is less likely to be observed in cases of drug-induced lupus.

6. The correct answer is A: intravenous infusion.

Cyclophosphamide is a chemotherapy medication that is used to treat a variety of conditions, including SLE. In the treatment of SLE, cyclophosphamide is typically administered intravenously. This means that it is given through a needle in the vein. There are two main intravenous (IV) treatment protocols for cyclophosphamide in the treatment of severe nephritis or other life-threatening SLE. High-dose cyclophosphamide: This protocol involves the administration of cyclophosphamide at a dosage range of 500-1000 mg/m2 IV over a period of six months. Low-dose cyclophosphamide: This protocol involves the administration of cyclophosphamide at a dosage of 500 mg administered every two weeks for a total of six doses. E. Anti-CCP antibodies are often found in patients with aggressive RA and a propensity for the development of bone erosions.

7. The correct answer is E. Anti-CCP antibodies are often found in patients with aggressive RA and a propensity for the development of bone erosions.

Antibodies targeting cyclic citrullinated protein (anti-CCP) are comparable in sensitivity to rheumatoid factor (RF) and have superior specificity, making option A and B incorrect (Options A and B). These antibodies are particularly advantageous in the early stages of rheumatoid arthritis (RA), not the late stages, making option C incorrect. The prevalence of anti-CCP antibodies is highest among patients exhibiting aggressive disease characteristics, often accompanied by a propensity for the development of bone erosions, making option E the correct answer. Therefore, the most accurate statement concerning anti-CCP antibodies is that they are often found in patients with aggressive RA and a propensity for the development of bone erosions (Option E).

8. The correct answer is E: all of the above.

The evaluation that is typically recommended for RA includes a complete blood count (CBC), erythrocyte sedimentation rate (ESR), rheumatoid factor (RF), and a chest X-ray (CXR). CBC: This test helps to rule out other conditions that can cause joint pain, such as anemia or infection. ESR: This test is a measure of inflammation. An elevated ESR can be a sign of RA. RF: This antibody is present in most people with RA. CXR: This test can help to rule out lung involvement in RA. In addition to these tests, they may also recommend an examination of synovial fluid from an affected joint. This can help to rule out the presence of crystalline disease or infection. Radiographs of the affected joints may also be helpful. These can show changes such as juxta-articular osteopenia, joint space constriction, and marginal erosions.

9. The correct answer is B. Inflammatory back pain, arthritis, heel enthesitis, anterior uveitis, dactylitis, psoriasis, Crohn's disease or ulcerative colitis, positive response to NSAIDs, family history of spondyloarthritis, presence of HLA-B27 antigen, elevated CRP levels.

The ASAS criteria for the diagnosis of axial spondyloarthritis includes a list of features such as inflammatory back pain, arthritis, enthesitis (specifically in the heel), anterior uveitis, dactylitis, psoriasis, Crohn's disease or ulcerative colitis, positive response to nonsteroidal anti-inflammatory drugs (NSAIDs), family history of spondyloarthritis, presence of HLA-B27 antigen, and elevated C-reactive protein (CRP) levels (Option B). Option A, C, D, and E variously include features not part of the ASAS criteria (such as osteoarthritis, non-inflammatory back pain, posterior uveitis, positive response to corticosteroids, family history of osteoarthritis, absence of HLA-B27 antigen, normal CRP levels, absence of dactylitis, absence of psoriasis, absence of Crohn's disease or ulcerative colitis, and negative response to NSAIDs). Therefore, the correct answer is Option B, which accurately lists the features included in the ASAS criteria for diagnosing axial spondyloarthritis.

10. The correct answer is A: a clinical assessment tool employed to ascertain the presence of diminished flexion range of motion in the lumbar spine, primarily attributable to Ankylosing Spondylitis.

The Schober test is a clinical assessment tool that is used to measure the range of motion in the lumbar spine. The test is performed by marking two points on the patient's back, one 10 cm below the lumbosacral junction and the other 5 cm above this point. The patient is then asked to bend forward as far as possible. The distance between the two marks is then measured. A decrease in the distance between the two marks indicates a decrease in the range of motion in the lumbar spine. This can be a sign of a number of conditions, including Ankylosing Spondylitis. The Schober test is a simple and easy-to-perform test that can be used to assess the range of motion in the lumbar spine. It is a useful tool for diagnosing and monitoring a number of conditions that affect the spine.

11. The correct answer is A. Screening for HIV.

Reactive arthritis is often triggered by an infection in another part of your body, often the urinary tract, genitals, or intestines. While various infections can lead to reactive arthritis, HIV is a significant trigger. Therefore, it is imperative to conduct HIV screening in all patients during the assessment of reactive arthritis. Option B (Hepatitis A), C (Influenza), D (Tuberculosis), and E (Lyme disease) do not routinely require screening in the evaluation of reactive arthritis. While these conditions can potentially be associated with joint symptoms, they are not typically implicated as triggers for reactive arthritis. Therefore, the correct answer is Option A, which accurately identifies the need for HIV screening in the evaluation of reactive arthritis.

12. The correct answer is A: a highly aggressive manifestation of arthritis characterized by pronounced joint deformities and extensive bone erosion.

Arthritis mutilans is a rare and severe form of arthritis that is characterized by the rapid destruction of joints. The condition is most commonly seen in people with psoriatic arthritis, but it can also occur in people with rheumatoid arthritis and other types of arthritis. The symptoms of arthritis mutilans typically begin in the hands and feet, and they can progress to involve other joints in the body. The most common symptoms include joint pain, swelling, deformity, and loss of function. The cause of arthritis mutilans is not fully understood, but it is thought to be caused by a combination of genetic and environmental factors. There is no cure for arthritis mutilans, but there are treatments that can help to manage the symptoms and slow the progression of the disease. Treatment typically includes medications, physical therapy, and surgery.

13. The correct answer is E. All of the above.

Enteropathic arthritis is a type of arthritis associated with inflammatory bowel disease (IBD). The management of enteropathic arthritis primarily involves treating the underlying IBD. Anti-tumor necrosis factor (anti-TNF) agents have been shown to be effective in reducing arthritis symptoms (Option A). Nonsteroidal anti-inflammatory drugs (NSAIDs) can also help alleviate joint symptoms, but they may exacerbate the IBD, so their use must be carefully considered (Option B). Sulfasalazine, azathioprine, and methotrexate are also used for peripheral arthritis and can have potential therapeutic benefits (Options C and D). Therefore, all of the mentioned options (Option E) are potential treatment options for enteropathic arthritis. However, the exact treatment plan would depend on the individual patient's disease severity, response to previous treatments, and overall health status among other factors.

14. The correct answer is A: Diffuse cutaneous SSc and Limited cutaneous SSc.

Systemic sclerosis (SSc) is a chronic autoimmune disease that affects the skin, joints, and internal organs. The condition is characterized by the buildup of collagen in the skin and other tissues. There are two main subsets of SSc: diffuse cutaneous SSc and limited cutaneous SSc. Diffuse cutaneous SSc: This subset is characterized by the rapid development of symmetrical skin thickening in various areas of the body, including the proximal and distal extremities, face, and trunk. Limited cutaneous SSc: This subset typically presents with long-standing Raynaud's phenomenon before other symptoms manifest. In this subset, skin involvement is limited to the fingers (sclerodactyly), the extremities distal to the elbows, and the face. Generally, limited cutaneous SSc is associated with a more favorable prognosis, although it can also be linked to pulmonary arterial hypertension. Additionally, a subset of limited cutaneous SSc may exhibit features of CREST syndrome, which includes calcinosis, Raynaud's phenomenon, esophageal dysmotility, sclerodactyly, and telangiectasias.

15. The correct answer is E. All of the above.

Antiphospholipid syndrome (APS) is a disorder of the immune system that results in an increased risk of blood clots. The diagnosis of APS typically involves a combination of clinical findings and laboratory tests. Prothrombin Time (PT) and Partial Thromboplastin Time (PTT) are basic laboratory tests that assess the clotting parameters of the blood and are usually prolonged in APS (Options A and D). The presence of antibodies targeting cardiolipin is a characteristic feature of APS. These antibodies can be identified through specific laboratory tests (Option B). The dilute Russell viper venom test is another laboratory test used to detect the presence of lupus anticoagulant; an antibody often found in APS (Option C). To confirm the diagnosis of APS, it is recommended to measure the levels of these antibodies on two separate occasions, with a time interval of 12 weeks between each measurement. This is because the presence of these antibodies can sometimes be transient, and a single positive test does not necessarily confirm the diagnosis. Therefore, all of these steps (Option E) are crucial in the evaluation of a patient suspected of having APS.

16. The correct answer is E: all of the above.

Antiphospholipid syndrome (APS) is an autoimmune disorder that can cause blood clots to form in the blood vessels. It can also increase the risk of pregnancy complications, such as miscarriage. The recommended therapeutic approach for APS involves the use of anticoagulation therapy, such as warfarin or heparin. This helps to prevent blood clots from forming. In addition, patients with APS may also be prescribed aspirin or other medications to reduce inflammation. For women with APS who are planning a pregnancy, it is important to take steps to reduce the risk of pregnancy complications. This may include the use of anticoagulation therapy, aspirin, and intravenous immunoglobulins (IVIG). IVIG is a blood product that contains antibodies from healthy donors. It can help to suppress the immune system and reduce the risk of blood clots. Glucocorticoids are another type of medication that can be used to treat APS. They can help to reduce inflammation and suppress the immune system.

17. The correct answer is C. Granulomatosis with Polyangiitis (Wegener's).

Granulomatosis with Polyangiitis (Wegener's) is characterized by the concurrent involvement of the upper and lower respiratory tracts, often with renal involvement in the form of glomerulonephritis. The patient's symptoms of persistent nasal discharge, possibly purulent or bloody, along with cough and hemoptysis, and the physical finding of a saddlenose deformity are all suggestive of this disease (Option C). Allergic rhinitis (Option A) and nasal polyps (Option B) can cause nasal symptoms but would not typically cause a cough with hemoptysis or the deformity seen in this patient. Chronic sinusitis (Option D) could explain the nasal discharge and saddlenose deformity but is less likely to cause hemoptysis and cough. Tuberculosis (Option E) can cause a chronic cough with hemoptysis, but it would not typically cause a saddlenose deformity or the nasal symptoms seen in this patient. This patient's presentation is most consistent with Granulomatosis with Polyangiitis (Wegener's), making Option C the best answer.

18. The correct answer is A: fever, fatigue, weight loss, rash, decreased peripheral pulses, and palpable abdominal mass.

Polyarteritis nodosa (PAN) is a rare systemic vasculitis that affects medium-sized arteries. The condition can affect any organ in the body, but it most commonly affects the kidneys, liver, gastrointestinal tract, nerves, and skin. The clinical manifestations of PAN vary depending on the organs that are affected. Common symptoms include fever, fatigue, weight loss, rash, decreased peripheral pulses, abdominal pain, and neurological problems. PAN is diagnosed based on a combination of clinical findings, laboratory tests, and imaging studies. Treatment typically involves the use of immunosuppressive medications, such as steroids and cyclophosphamide.

19. The correct answer is E. All of the above.

Cryoglobulinemic Vasculitis is a condition characterized by inflammation and damage to small and medium-sized blood vessels due to the presence of abnormal proteins called cryoglobulins in the blood. These cryoglobulins can result in a variety of symptoms, including skin rashes, joint pain, muscle pain, weakness, and numbness in the hands and feet. Cryoglobulinemic Vasculitis is often associated with viral infections, particularly Hepatitis C (Option A), but it can also occur in people with other underlying health conditions. Rheumatoid arthritis (Option B) is an autoimmune disorder that can lead to the production of cryoglobulins. Certain forms of cancer, such as lung cancer (Option C), can cause paraneoplastic syndromes that result in cryoglobulin production. While Diabetes mellitus (Option D) is not typically associated with cryoglobulinemia, it is a systemic disease that can lead to immune dysregulation and, in rare cases, may be associated with cryoglobulinemia. Therefore, all of these conditions (Option E) could potentially be underlying causes of the patient's condition, making E the best answer.

20. The correct answer is A: Secondary Vasculitis Syndromes are a range of conditions caused by an underlying disease or condition, such as infection, malignancy, or rheumatic disease.

Secondary Vasculitis Syndromes are a group of disorders that are characterized by inflammation of the blood vessels. These disorders can be caused by a variety of underlying diseases or conditions, including: Infection: Some infections, such as hepatitis B and C, can trigger vasculitis. Malignancy: Cancers, such as lymphoma and leukemia, can also cause vasculitis. Rheumatic diseases: Conditions such as rheumatoid arthritis and systemic lupus erythematosus can lead to vasculitis. Drugs: Some drugs, such as hydralazine and propylthiouracil, can cause vasculitis as a side effect. Environmental factors: Exposure to certain chemicals or toxins can also trigger vasculitis.

21. The correct answer is C. Perform a synovial fluid analysis.

Gout is a form of inflammatory arthritis that is often characterized by severe pain and swelling in the joints, especially the big toe. Although elevated serum uric acid levels can be indicative of gout, normal serum uric acid levels do not definitively exclude the possibility of gout. Hence, option A is not correct. Urine testing for uric acid excretion (Option B) can be a part of the diagnostic process, especially in cases of suspected uric acid overproduction, but it is not the most definitive diagnostic method. A synovial fluid analysis (Option C) is a more conclusive diagnostic test for gout. It involves joint aspiration and the identification of monosodium urate (MSU) crystals through polarizing microscopy. This is the gold standard for diagnosing gout and is the most appropriate next step in this case. A dietary change (Option D) can be part of the management of gout, but it is not a diagnostic step. Initiating treatment for osteoarthritis (Option E) without a definitive diagnosis would not be appropriate. Therefore, option C is the best answer.

22. The correct answer is D: all of the above.

Relapsing polychondritis is a rare autoimmune disorder that affects the cartilage in the body. The condition can affect any cartilage in the body, but it most commonly affects the ears, nose, and joints. The symptoms of relapsing polychondritis can vary depending on the affected cartilage. Common symptoms may include:

- Ear pain, redness, and swelling.
- Nasal congestion, obstruction, and collapse
- Joint pain and swelling
- Eye inflammation
- Respiratory problems
- Heart problems
- Kidney problems

The diagnosis of relapsing polychondritis is based on a combination of clinical findings, laboratory tests, and imaging studies. Treatment typically involves the use of corticosteroids, such as prednisone. In some cases, other immunosuppressive medications may be necessary. In cases of significant airway obstruction, a tracheostomy procedure may be necessary to help the patient breathe.

23. The correct answer is A. Polymyalgia Rheumatica (PMR) and Giant Cell Arteritis (GCA).

The patient's symptoms of severe shoulder and hip pain, along with systemic symptoms like unexplained weight loss and fatigue, are characteristic of Polymyalgia Rheumatica (PMR) (Option A). PMR is an inflammatory condition that often affects older adults, causing pain and stiffness in the shoulder and hip girdles. Additionally, there is a known correlation between PMR and Giant Cell Arteritis (GCA), an inflammatory disease that affects medium and large arteries. Patients with PMR may develop GCA, and vice versa. Therefore, in a patient presenting with symptoms of PMR, it is important to consider the possibility of GCA as well. The other options listed (B-E) don't fit the patient's symptoms as well as PMR and GCA. Fibromyalgia and Chronic Fatigue Syndrome (Option B) typically present with widespread pain and fatigue, but do not typically cause the shoulder and hip pain seen in PMR. Osteoarthritis and Rheumatoid Arthritis (Option C) typically cause joint pain, but not the systemic symptoms seen in PMR. Lupus and Vasculitis (Option D), and Systemic Sclerosis and Sjogren's Syndrome (Option E) are all systemic autoimmune conditions that can cause a variety of symptoms, but the patient's symptoms are more specifically indicative of PMR. Therefore, option A is the best answer.

24. The correct answer is D: all of the above.

Sarcoidosis is a chronic inflammatory disorder that can affect any organ in the body, but it most commonly affects the lungs. The pulmonary manifestations of sarcoidosis can vary depending on the stage of the disease. In the early stages of sarcoidosis, the lungs may be affected by hilar adenopathy, which is a swelling of the lymph nodes in the chest. This can be seen on a chest X-ray or CT scan. As the disease progresses, the lungs may develop infiltrates, which are areas of inflammation. This can also be seen on a chest X-ray or CT scan. In some cases, the inflammation in the lungs can lead to interstitial pneumonitis, which is a type of lung inflammation that affects the small airways and the lung tissue. This can cause shortness of breath, coughing, and chest pain. In the late stages of sarcoidosis, the lungs may develop fibrosis, which is a type of scarring. This can cause severe shortness of breath and can lead to respiratory failure. Airway obstruction can also occur in sarcoidosis, due to inflammation of the airways. This can cause short breathing and wheezing. Pulmonary hypertension can also occur in sarcoidosis, due to either direct vascular involvement or lung fibrosis. This can cause shortness of breath and chest pain.

25. The correct answer is D. Congo red staining of abdominal fat.

Amyloidosis is a condition that results from the abnormal deposition of amyloid proteins in various tissues and organs throughout the body. It can affect different parts of the body (like the heart and kidneys) and cause a wide range of symptoms, including fatigue, weight loss, swelling, and irregular heartbeat, as described in this patient's case. While all of the listed diagnostic techniques (A-E) could potentially provide useful information, the most definitive way to diagnose amyloidosis is through the detection of amyloid deposits in tissue. This is most commonly done through the Congo red staining of abdominal fat (Option D), which has been found to be effective in over 80% of patients with systemic amyloidosis. The stained tissue is then examined under a microscope for the presence of the characteristic apple-green birefringence of amyloid deposits when viewed under polarized light. Echocardiogram (Option A), chest X-ray (Option B), and lung function test (Option E) can provide evidence of organ involvement by amyloidosis but cannot definitively diagnose the disease. Blood tests for kidney function (Option C) can indicate kidney damage, which may occur in amyloidosis, but again, they do not directly detect amyloid deposits. Therefore, Congo red staining of abdominal fat (Option D) is the most effective diagnostic technique for confirming a diagnosis of amyloidosis in this case.

26. Best Answer: C) Administration of antiviral agents

The patient's symptoms and history of hepatitis B infection suggest he may be suffering from polyarteritis nodosa (PAN) or cryoglobulinemic vasculitis, both of which are forms of vasculitis associated with hepatitis B virus (HBV). Antiviral agents play a crucial role in the management of HBV-related vasculitis. They work by suppressing the viral load and preventing further damage to the vascular system.

27. Best Answer: C) Prednisone 10 to 20 milligrams daily

The recommended initial treatment for polymyalgia rheumatica (PMR) is prednisone, usually in a daily dosage between 10 to 20 milligrams. This dosage effectively reduces the pain, stiffness, and inflammation associated with PMR. While nonsteroidal anti-inflammatory drugs (NSAIDs) like ibuprofen (Option A) can relieve pain and inflammation, they are not typically the first line of treatment for PMR due to their lower efficacy and higher risk of side effects compared to low-dose prednisone. Physical therapy (Option B) can be a part of the management plan for PMR but is not the first-line treatment. Methotrexate (Option D) and tumor necrosis factor (TNF) inhibitors (Option E) are typically reserved for patients who do not respond to or cannot tolerate glucocorticoids. Therefore, the most appropriate initial therapeutic intervention for this patient would be prednisone 10 to 20 milligrams daily (Option C).

28. Best Answer: D) Lupus pernio

Sarcoidosis can present with several types of cutaneous manifestations. Erythema nodosum (Option A), maculopapular lesions (Option B), and subcutaneous nodules (Option C) can all occur in sarcoidosis. However, the description of indurated, blue-purple, shiny lesions specifically located around the nasal bridge, eyes, and cheeks fits the description of lupus pernio, which is a specific cutaneous manifestation of sarcoidosis. Psoriasis (Option E) can cause skin lesions, but these typically consist of red, scaly patches rather than the indurated, blue-purple, shiny lesions described in this case. Therefore, given the patient's symptoms and the nature of the skin lesions, lupus pernio (Option D) is the most likely cutaneous manifestation of sarcoidosis.

29. Best Answer: C) Approximately 50%

In patients diagnosed with AL amyloidosis, approximately half are found to meet the criteria for receiving intensive therapeutic interventions such as high-dose intravenous melphalan followed by autologous stem-cell transplantation. While this treatment can be effective, it comes with a relatively high risk of mortality due to the procedure itself, especially considering the compromised organ functionality often seen in these patients. This sets AL amyloidosis apart from other hematologic disorders where such aggressive treatment might be more commonly indicated. Therefore, given the patient's diagnosis and the general statistics for this treatment, it can be estimated that there is approximately a 50% chance (Option C) that he would be eligible for this aggressive treatment approach.

30. Answer: E. Rheumatoid factor (RF) and anti-cyclic citrullinated peptide (anti-CCP) antibodies.

This patient's presentation of symmetric polyarthritis involving small joints of the hands, morning stiffness, fatigue, and low-grade fever is suggestive of rheumatoid arthritis (RA). The most appropriate diagnostic tests to perform next are rheumatoid factor (RF) and anti-cyclic citrullinated peptide (anti-CCP) antibodies. These are the two most common serologic markers for RA, with RF being positive in about 70-80% of patients and anti-CCP being positive in about 60-70% of patients. The presence of these antibodies helps confirm the diagnosis of RA, although a negative result does not rule it out, as these tests can be negative in early disease or in seronegative RA. Anti-CCP antibodies are particularly useful because they are very specific for RA and are often present early in the disease, sometimes even before clinical symptoms develop.

31. Answer: (A)

Given the patient's intolerance to methotrexate and history of a severe reaction to a sulfa-containing medication, biologic DMARD therapy is the next best step in management. Biologic DMARDs are highly effective in treating rheumatoid arthritis and have a relatively good safety profile. Conventional synthetic DMARDs, such as sulfasalazine and hydroxychloroquine, are typically not used as first-line therapy in patients with moderate to severe rheumatoid arthritis. Targeted synthetic DMARDs, such as JAK/STAT inhibitors, are a newer class of medications that have been shown to be effective in treating rheumatoid arthritis. However, they are more expensive than biologic DMARDs and have not been as well-studied in terms of long-term safety. Glucocorticoids can be used to control inflammation in patients with rheumatoid arthritis, but they are not typically used as first-line therapy due to their potential for side effects. Surgery is an option for patients with severe rheumatoid arthritis that does not respond to medical therapy. However, it is usually considered a last resort. In conclusion, the next best step in management for this patient is to initiate biologic DMARD therapy. Some examples of biologic DMARDs include adalimumab (Humira), etanercept (Enbrel), and infliximab (Remicade). Biologic DMARDs are typically administered by injection once or twice a month. The patient should be monitored for side effects of biologic DMARD therapy, such as infections, allergic reactions, and blood count changes.

32. Answer: (D)

The patient's presentation is concerning for a systemic inflammatory disorder, such as adult-onset Still disease. However, it is important to exclude other possible diagnoses, such as malignancy and infectious etiologies, before initiating empiric treatment with prednisone. The most appropriate next step in management is to order a chest X-ray, abdominal and pelvic CT scan, and excisional biopsy of a cervical lymph node. The chest X-ray and CT scan will help to evaluate for localizing pathology in the chest, abdomen, and pelvis. The excisional biopsy of the lymph node will help to rule out malignancy and other atypical infections etiologies. Judicious use of NSAIDs may be pursued for symptomatic control while additional evaluation is pursued. However, empiric treatment with steroids is not recommended at this stage, as it could obscure underlying pathology. Once the results of the evaluation are available, the patient can be referred to a rheumatologist for further evaluation and management of adult-onset Still disease, if indicated. Adult-onset Still disease is a rare systemic inflammatory disorder that is characterized by a triad of fever, rash, and polyarthritis. The diagnosis of adult-onset Still disease is made after other possible diagnoses, such as malignancy and infectious etiologies, have been excluded. The treatment of adult-onset Still disease typically involves the use of nonsteroidal anti-inflammatory drugs (NSAIDs) and corticosteroids. In some cases, biologic disease-modifying antirheumatic drugs (DMARDs) may be necessary.

33. The correct answer is A. Acute gouty arthritis.

The patient's recurrent acute intermittent inflammatory asymmetric oligoarthritis that resolves completely with anti-inflammatory therapy, and the presence of firm nodules in the olecranon bursa (tophi), suggest a crystal-induced arthritis, specifically gout. The intermittent, resolving nature of these episodes and the absence of extra-articular or axial features make peripheral arthritis associated with seronegative spondyloarthropathies less likely. Therefore, the best answer is A. Acute gouty arthritis.

34. Correct answer: E. Anakinra 100 mg QD SQ

This patient's symptoms and risk factors point to a diagnosis of acute polyarticular gouty arthritis. Treatment options for acute gout include NSAIDs, intra-articular steroids, colchicine, systemic steroids, or anti-IL-1 therapy. However, this patient's comorbidities contraindicate several of these options. NSAIDs are not advisable due to his chronic kidney disease and peptic ulcer disease. Intra-articular or systemic steroids could cause acute blood sugar elevations, which would be harmful given his T1DM. Colchicine is relatively contraindicated due to severe renal insufficiency. Anakinra, an IL-1R antagonist, is effective for treating severe gouty arthritis flares and is not contraindicated given the patient's comorbidities. Therefore, Anakinra 100 mg QD SQ is the best treatment option for this patient.

35. Answer: (D)

An acute presentation of rheumatoid arthritis is the least likely diagnosis in this patient. Rheumatoid arthritis is a chronic inflammatory arthritis that typically presents with a gradual onset of polyarticular joint pain and stiffness. Acute monoarticular presentations of rheumatoid arthritis are rare, and they typically occur in patients with established disease. Gout, pseudogout, and bacterial septic arthritis are all more likely diagnoses in this patient. Gout is a common type of inflammatory arthritis caused by the deposition of uric acid crystals in the joints. Pseudogout is a similar condition caused by the deposition of calcium pyrophosphate dihydrate crystals in the joints. Bacterial septic arthritis is a serious infection of a joint that can lead to joint damage and sepsis. All of these conditions can present with acute monoarthritis, which is characterized by the sudden onset of pain, swelling, and redness in a single joint. The patient in this case should be evaluated for gout, pseudogout, and bacterial septic arthritis. This may include laboratory tests, such as a complete blood count, erythrocyte sedimentation rate, C-reactive protein level, and synovial fluid analysis. Imaging studies, such as X-rays and MRI, may also be helpful.

36. Answer: (D)

The patient's presentation is suggestive of sacroiliitis, which is inflammation of the sacroiliac joints. Sacroiliitis is a common cause of low back pain in adults. The next best step in the evaluation is to obtain plain radiographs of the sacroiliac joints. These radiographs can help to identify abnormalities in the sacroiliac joints that are suggestive of sacroiliitis. CBC, ESR, and CRP level are laboratory tests that can be used to assess for inflammation. However, these tests are not specific for sacroiliitis and can be elevated in other conditions, such as infection and other types of inflammatory arthritis. MRI of the SI joints is a more sensitive test for detecting sacroiliitis than plain radiographs. However, it is more expensive and not always necessary. MRI of the SI joints is typically reserved for patients with clinical suspicion of sacroiliitis who have negative or non-diagnostic plain radiographs. In conclusion, the next best step in the evaluation of this patient is to obtain plain radiographs of the sacroiliac joints. Once the diagnosis is established, the patient can be treated appropriately. Gout and pseudogout are typically treated with anti-inflammatory medications. Bacterial septic arthritis requires treatment with antibiotics and, in some cases, drainage of the infected joint. The patient's lack of systemic symptoms, such as fever, suggests that she is less likely to have bacterial septic arthritis. However, it is important to rule out this diagnosis, as it is a serious condition. The patient's acute presentation makes it less likely that she has rheumatoid arthritis. However, it is important to keep this diagnosis in mind, as it is a chronic condition that can have a significant impact on a patient's life.

37. Answer: C. Interferon release assay (IGRA)

Anti-TNF therapy is associated with a high risk of Mycobacterium tuberculosis reactivation in patients with a history of latent TB. Therefore, excluding latent TB infection before initiating anti-TNF therapy is crucial. This patient, originating from India where TB is endemic, is at high risk for TB infection. The Interferon release assay (IGRA), measures T-cell release of interferon- following stimulation by antigens from MTb, hence making it the most appropriate test for this patient. The other tests (A, B, D, E) are not necessarily required prior to initiation of anti-TNF therapy, but may be checked depending on additional risk factors or age-appropriate screening.

38. Answer: (C)

The patient's presentation is most suggestive of reactive arthritis. Reactive arthritis is a type of inflammatory arthritis that occurs in response to an infection. It is most commonly triggered by infections of the gastrointestinal or urogenital tract. The patient's history of dysuria and urethral discharge is suggestive of a urogenital infection, such as chlamydia or gonorrhea. These infections are common triggers of reactive arthritis. The patient's arthritis is also consistent with reactive arthritis. Reactive arthritis typically affects multiple joints, including the knees, ankles, and wrists. The joints are typically warm, swollen, and erythematous. Rheumatoid arthritis is a chronic inflammatory arthritis that typically presents with a gradual onset of polyarticular joint pain and stiffness. Osteoarthritis is a degenerative arthritis that typically affects the weight-bearing joints, such as the knees and hips. Gout is a type of inflammatory arthritis caused by the deposition of uric acid crystals in the joints. Pseudogout is a similar condition caused by the deposition of calcium pyrophosphate dihydrate crystals in the joints. In conclusion, the most likely diagnosis in this patient is reactive arthritis. The diagnosis of reactive arthritis is based on clinical suspicion and exclusion of other possible diagnoses. Treatment for reactive arthritis typically involves the use of nonsteroidal anti-inflammatory drugs (NSAIDs). In some cases, antibiotics may be necessary to treat the underlying infection. Most cases of reactive arthritis resolve within 1 year of diagnosis. However, some patients may develop chronic arthritis.

39. Answer: The correct answer is D. Start captopril.

The patient's presentation of new-onset hypertension, acute kidney injury, anemia, thrombocytopenia, and elevated indirect bilirubin is suggestive of thrombotic microangiopathy (TMA). Given the patient's history of Raynaud phenomenon and physical examination findings of telangiectasias and dilated capillary loops with dropout, the most likely diagnosis is scleroderma renal crisis (SRC). SRC is a TMA that can occur in patients with systemic sclerosis, particularly those with diffuse cutaneous systemic sclerosis (DcSSc). It often presents early in the disease course and requires immediate treatment due to its severity. While other causes of TMA, including thrombotic thrombocytopenic purpura and hemolytic uremic syndrome, should be considered, the patient's clinical presentation and history are most suggestive of SRC. The mainstay of treatment for SRC is an angiotensin-converting enzyme (ACE) inhibitor such as captopril (Choice D). Steroids, such as prednisone (Choice B), are generally avoided as they can provoke SRC. Hemodialysis (Choice A) and plasmapheresis (Choice C) may be required in severe cases, but there is no current indication for these treatments in this patient. Monitoring and rechecking labs in one week (Choice E) would not be appropriate given the severity and urgency of this patient's presentation.

40. Answer: D. Anti-RNA polymerase III v

Patients with scleroderma who have antibodies against RNA polymerase III have an increased risk of developing scleroderma renal crisis (SRC). While antinuclear antibody (ANA) is often positive in scleroderma, a positive ANA does not specifically increase the risk of SRC. Anti-double-stranded DNA (anti-dsDNA) antibodies are associated with lupus, not scleroderma. Anti-histone antibodies are typically found in patients with drug-induced lupus, and anti-Jo1 antibodies are seen in dermatomyositis. Therefore, among the options provided, anti-RNA polymerase III is the best answer because it is specifically associated with an increased risk of SRC in patients with scleroderma.

41. Answer: (D)

The patient's clinical presentation is most suggestive of dermatomyositis. Dermatomyositis is a chronic inflammatory disease that affects the muscles and skin. It is characterized by proximal muscle weakness and a characteristic skin rash. The patient's proximal muscle weakness is the most characteristic finding of dermatomyositis. Proximal muscle weakness is the weakness of the muscles that are closest to the body's center. In dermatomyositis, proximal muscle weakness typically affects the arms and legs. The patient's skin rash is also consistent with dermatomyositis. The rash of dermatomyositis can vary in appearance, but it is often violaceous and affects the face, hands, and extensor surfaces of the joints. Rheumatoid arthritis, systemic lupus erythematosus, and scleroderma are other autoimmune diseases that can cause muscle weakness and skin rash. However, these diseases have different clinical presentations than dermatomyositis. In conclusion, the most likely diagnosis in this patient is dermatomyositis. The diagnosis of dermatomyositis is based on clinical suspicion and a variety of laboratory tests, including blood tests, muscle biopsy, and electromyography. Treatment for dermatomyositis typically involves the use of corticosteroids and other immunosuppressive medications. The prognosis for dermatomyositis is variable. Some patients go into remission, while others develop chronic muscle weakness.

42. Answer: (B)

The patient's presentation is most suggestive of mixed connective tissue disease (MCTD). MCTD is a rare autoimmune disease that is characterized by an overlap of features from lupus, systemic sclerosis, and inflammatory myopathy. The patient's positive ANA with a speckled pattern and positive anti-U1 RNP antibody are both consistent with MCTD. The patient's fatigue, arthralgias, myalgias, Raynaud's phenomenon, hand edema, and synovitis are all common features of MCTD. Rheumatoid arthritis, SLE, SSc, and polymyositis are other autoimmune diseases that can cause similar symptoms to MCTD. However, these diseases have different clinical presentations and laboratory findings. In conclusion, the most likely diagnosis in this patient is MCTD. The diagnosis of MCTD is based on clinical suspicion and a variety of laboratory tests, including ANA, anti-U1 RNP antibody, rheumatoid factor, and muscle biopsy. Treatment for MCTD is typically supportive and may involve the use of nonsteroidal anti-inflammatory drugs (NSAIDs), corticosteroids, and other immunosuppressive medications. The prognosis for MCTD is variable. Some patients go into remission, while others develop chronic symptoms.

43. Correct Answer: A. Adalimumab

The patient's symptoms and laboratory findings are most consistent with drug-induced lupus, an autoimmune response triggered by certain medications. Adalimumab, a TNF- inhibitor, is known to be associated with drug-induced lupus. Atorvastatin, amlodipine, and aspirin are not typically associated with this condition. Hence, adalimumab is the most likely cause of this patient's presentation. Anti-histone antibodies are commonly positive in drug-induced lupus, differentiating it from systemic lupus erythematosus, which is more associated with anti-dsDNA antibodies.

44. Answer: C. Clinical history

Drug-induced lupus and systemic lupus erythematosus have many overlapping features, making differentiation between the two challenging. However, the clinical history can provide some distinguishing elements. Unlike systemic lupus erythematosus, which has a female predominance, drug-induced lupus occurs with equal frequency in males and females. Additionally, drug-induced lupus often occurs in older adults due to increased exposure to causative medications and generally has a more abrupt onset. The presence of anti-dsDNA antibodies and anti-histone antibodies can be seen in both conditions, making them less useful for differentiation. While anti-dsDNA positivity rates are lower in drug-induced lupus than in systemic lupus erythematosus, they do not provide a definitive distinction.

Both conditions can show interface dermatitis on skin biopsy, hence, skin biopsy results also do not provide a clear distinction. The diagnosis of drug-induced lupus relies on a plausible clinical syndrome, consistent laboratory testing, and a clear medication exposure. Therefore, the clinical history is the most reliable way to differentiate drug-induced lupus from systemic lupus erythematosus.

45. Answer: (B)

The patient's presentation is most consistent with a mild-to-moderate lupus flare. Lupus flares are characterized by the recurrence of symptoms of lupus, such as fatigue, fever, rash, and joint pain. The most appropriate initial treatment for a mild-to-moderate lupus flare is a short course of prednisone. Prednisone is a corticosteroid that can help to reduce inflammation and improve symptoms. Hydroxychloroquine is a disease-modifying antirheumatic drug (DMARD) that is used to treat lupus and prevent flares. However, it is not effective in treating acute flares. Cyclophosphamide is a more potent immunosuppressive medication that is used to treat severe lupus flares and lupus nephritis. It is not typically used as first-line therapy for mild-to-moderate flares. Mycophenolate mofetil is another DMARD that is used to treat lupus. It is sometimes used as first-line therapy for severe flares, but it is not as effective as prednisone for treating mild-to-moderate flares. Rituximab is a biologic DMARD that is used to treat certain autoimmune diseases, including lupus. It is not typically used as first-line therapy for mild-to-moderate flares. In conclusion, the most appropriate initial treatment for this patient is a short course of prednisone. The patient should be monitored closely during treatment for the flare. If her symptoms do not improve with prednisone, or if she develops organ involvement, she may need to be hospitalized and treated with IV steroids and/or other immunosuppressive medications. The patient should also be continued on hydroxychloroquine for long-term prevention of flares.

46. Answer: (D)

The patient's clinical presentation is most suggestive of eosinophilic granulomatosis with polyangiitis (EGPA), formerly known as Churg-Strauss syndrome. EGPA is a rare form of vasculitis that is characterized by granulomatous inflammation of small- and medium-sized vessels. The patient's history of allergic rhinitis and asthma, peripheral eosinophilia, and mononeuritis multiplex are all consistent with EGPA. EMG and NCS can be used to diagnose mononeuritis multiplex and to assess the severity of nerve damage. EMG and NCS can also be used to distinguish EGPA from other types of vasculitis. CBC with differential is a routine blood test that is used to screen for a variety of conditions. However, it is not specific for EGPA. ANA test is used to screen for systemic lupus erythematosus and other autoimmune diseases. However, it is not specific for EGPA. Rheumatoid factor test is used to screen for rheumatoid arthritis. However, it is not specific for EGPA. Lung biopsy is a definitive test for EGPA. However, it is not typically performed until other diagnostic tests have been done. In conclusion, the most appropriate test to diagnose this patient's underlying condition is EMG and NCS. If the EMG and NCS are consistent with EGPA, the patient should be tested for antineutrophil cytoplasmic antibodies (ANCA). ANCA are positive in about 30% to 60% of patients with EGPA. If the patient has a positive ANCA test and clinical features of EGPA, a lung biopsy may not be necessary to make a diagnosis. Treatment for EGPA typically involves corticosteroids and other immunosuppressive medications.

47. The correct answer is D. Screening ophthalmologic examinations.

Hydroxychloroquine, often used in the management of systemic lupus erythematosus, may cause retinopathy as a side effect. Therefore, patients receiving this medication should have a baseline screening fundoscopic examination with an ophthalmologist to rule out preexisting retinal disease and then regular screening with fundoscopic examination and visual field testing. Spectral-domain optical coherence therapy (SD OCT) should be performed, especially after 5 years of receiving hydroxychloroquine therapy. Regular ophthalmologic examinations can help identify hydroxychloroquine-induced retinopathy before vision changes occur. In many cases, further damage can be prevented by stopping hydroxychloroquine therapy, although retinopathy may also progress despite stopping the therapy. Starting anti-TNF therapy (option A) is not indicated in this context. Stopping hydroxychloroquine immediately (option B) is not necessary unless there are signs of retinopathy or other serious side effects. A renal biopsy (option C) is not warranted unless there are signs of lupus nephritis, such as proteinuria or hematuria. Anti-dsDNA antibody testing (option E) may be used in the diagnosis of lupus but is not necessary in this patient who already has a confirmed diagnosis.

48. Correct Answer: E. Polyarteritis nodosa

The patient's presentation of systemic symptoms, hypertension due to renal artery disease, abdominal pain, gastrointestinal bleeding, asymmetric sensory and motor deficits (indicative of mononeuritis multiplex), and muscle aches along with the identification of renal artery aneurysms on imaging strongly suggest Polyarteritis nodosa (PAN). PAN is a medium-vessel vasculitis that often involves the renal and visceral arteries but spares the lungs, which differentiates it from other vasculitides. The diagnosis of PAN is further supported by the presence of elevated inflammatory markers and acute kidney injury. Among the other options, PAN is the only condition that typically presents with these combined findings.

49. Answer: (A)

The patient's presentation is most suggestive of IgG4-related disease (IgG4-RD). IgG4-RD is a systemic inflammatory disease that can affect the pancreas, bile ducts, salivary glands, and other organs. The most appropriate next step in management is to perform an endoscopic ultrasound with biopsy. Endoscopic ultrasound is a minimally invasive procedure that can be used to visualize the pancreas and obtain tissue samples for biopsy. Pancreaticoduodenectomy (Whipple procedure) is a major surgery that is typically used to treat pancreatic cancer. It is not typically performed in patients with IgG4-RD, unless the patient has failed other treatments or has a high suspicion of malignancy. Chemotherapy and radiation therapy are not typically used to treat IgG4-RD. However, they may be used in patients with severe or refractory disease. Observation is an option for patients with early-stage IgG4-RD and mild symptoms. However, most patients will eventually need treatment, as the disease can progress and lead to organ damage. In conclusion, the most appropriate next step in management of this patient is to perform an endoscopic ultrasound with biopsy. If the biopsy confirms the diagnosis of IgG4-RD, the patient will need to be treated with corticosteroids or other immunosuppressive medications. Most patients with IgG4-RD respond well to treatment and have a good prognosis. However, some patients may experience relapses, and a small number of patients may develop chronic organ damage.

50. Answer: The correct answer is D. Cryoglobulin testing.

This patient's symptoms, including general malaise, joint pain (arthralgias), palpable purpura, and peripheral neuropathy, along with his history of Hepatitis C and lab findings of a positive rheumatoid factor and low C4 levels, are suggestive of mixed cryoglobulinemia syndrome. This condition is a small-vessel vasculitis caused by immune complex deposition, often associated with Hepatitis C infection. Cryoglobulin testing is used to confirm the diagnosis. It is important to note that cryoglobulins can precipitate at room temperature, so blood samples for this test must be collected in warmed tubes and remain warm until processed by the lab to prevent false-negative results. Other diagnostic methods, like skin or kidney biopsy, may be used if there are relevant symptoms or findings, but this patient does not have signs of renal disease at present, making kidney biopsy inappropriate at this time.

51. Correct Answer: E. Serum protein electrophoresis (SPEP) and urine protein electrophoresis (UPEP) with immunofixation

The patient's presentation is highly suggestive of amyloid light-chain (AL) amyloidosis. AL amyloidosis is a systemic condition characterized by the deposition of monoclonal light-chain antibodies in various tissues, leading to organ dysfunction. The wide range of potential presentations reflects the diversity of possible sites of amyloid deposition. In this case, the patient's symptoms like peripheral neuropathy, kidney disease (manifested as proteinuria and elevated creatinine), easy bruising, and specific physical signs (shoulder pad sign, hepatosplenomegaly, periorbital bruising) are indicative of AL amyloidosis. SPEP and UPEP with immunofixation are the initial tests of choice in these patients as they can detect the monoclonal light chains characteristic of this disease. Other potential confirmatory tests, such as biopsy of various sites (e.g., abdominal fat pad, bone marrow), may be performed based on the clinical scenario and the results of the initial screening tests.

52. Answer: (A)

The patient's presentation is most suggestive of eosinophilic granulomatosis with polyangiitis (EGPA), formerly known as Churg-Strauss syndrome. EGPA is a rare systemic vasculitis that is characterized by granulomatous inflammation of small- and medium-sized vessels. It is characterized by a triad of asthma, eosinophilia, and systemic vasculitis. The patient's history of asthma, eosinophilia, multiple episodes of sinusitis and pneumonia, and rash are all consistent with EGPA. Allergic bronchopulmonary aspergillosis (ABPA) is a hypersensitivity reaction to the fungus Aspergillus fumigatus. It can cause asthma, eosinophilia, and pulmonary infiltrates. However, ABPA is less likely to cause skin rash and systemic vasculitis. COPD is a chronic inflammatory lung disease that is characterized by airflow obstruction. It is not associated with eosinophilia or systemic vasculitis. Bronchiectasis is a chronic lung disease that is characterized by dilated bronchi. It is also not associated with eosinophilia or systemic vasculitis. Cystic fibrosis is a genetic disorder that affects the lungs and other organs. It is not associated with eosinophilia or systemic vasculitis. In conclusion, the most likely diagnosis in this patient is eosinophilic granulomatosis with polyangiitis. EGPA is a rare disease, with an estimated prevalence of 10-13 per million people. The diagnosis of EGPA is based on clinical and laboratory findings. There is no single test that can definitively diagnose EGPA. Treatment for EGPA typically involves the use of corticosteroids and other immunosuppressive medications.

53. Answer: (D)

The patient's presentation is most suggestive of dermatomyositis. Dermatomyositis is a chronic inflammatory disease that affects the muscles and skin. It is characterized by proximal muscle weakness and a characteristic skin rash. Patients with dermatomyositis have an increased risk of developing cancer. Therefore, all patients with a new diagnosis of dermatomyositis should undergo thorough cancer screening. Colonoscopy is the most appropriate next step in cancer screening for this patient. Colonoscopy is a minimally invasive procedure that allows the doctor to examine the colon for signs of cancer. Corticosteroids and methotrexate are medications that are used to treat dermatomyositis. However, they should not be started until after cancer screening has been completed. Physical therapy can be helpful for patients with dermatomyositis. However, it is not the most important next step in management. Transvaginal ultrasound is sometimes used to screen for ovarian cancer in patients with dermatomyositis. However, it is not the most important next step in management. In conclusion, the most appropriate next step in management of this patient is to order a colonoscopy. Other cancer screening tests that may be recommended for patients with dermatomyositis include low-dose chest CT (for lung cancer screening), mammogram, and Pap smear. The frequency of cancer screening in patients with dermatomyositis is not well established. However, it is generally recommended that patients be screened annually for the first 3-5 years after diagnosis. Treatment for dermatomyositis typically involves the use of corticosteroids and other immunosuppressive medications.

54. The correct answer is B. De Quervain tenosynovitis.

De Quervain tenosynovitis is characterized by pain and swelling over the radial aspect of the wrist and tenderness over the first dorsal compartment of the wrist. It is often due to repetitive activities that maintain the thumb in extension and abduction, which might be the case for this patient who uses her computer for extended periods. The positive Finkelstein maneuver, which involves the patient making a fist with the thumb tucked inside the fingers and then deviating the wrist towards the ulnar side, is highly suggestive of this condition. Option A (Scaphoid fracture) is less likely because our patient doesn't have a history of trauma, and the pain is not localized to the anatomical snuffbox, a key feature of scaphoid fractures. Option C (Carpal tunnel syndrome) causes numbness, tingling, and pain in the distribution of the median nerve (thumb, index, middle, and half of the ring finger), and is typically associated with night-time symptoms and positive Tinel's or Phalen's signs. Option D (Ganglion cyst) would present as a palpable mass and wouldn't necessarily be painful unless it's pressing on a nerve. Option E (Rheumatoid arthritis) typically presents with symmetrical joint involvement and systemic symptoms such as fatigue, weight loss, and low-grade fever, which our patient does not report. Therefore, the patient's symptoms and occupational history, along with the physical exam findings, make De Quervain tenosynovitis the most likely diagnosis.

Chapter 9

INFECTIOUS DISEASES BOARD QUESTIONS

1. A 62-year-old man with a history of chronic kidney disease and end-stage renal disease has had a urinary catheter in place for the past 3 months. He presents to your office with complaints of fever, chills, and cloudy urine. What measures should be taken in this case?

- A. Replace the catheter and collect a freshly voided urine specimen for culture.
- B. Collect a urine specimen from the catheter and send it for culture.
- C. Treat the patient with antibiotics without collecting a urine specimen.
- D. Remove the catheter and observe the patient.
- E. Send the patient to the hospital for further evaluation.

2. What are the potential risk factors associated with the development of pneumonia?

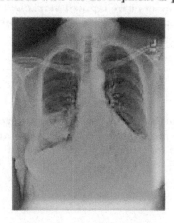

Figure 9.1: Pneumonia

- A. Previous utilization of antibiotics
- B. Utilization of ventilator equipment that has been contaminated.
- C. Decrease in gastric acidity
- D. Factors that elevate the risk of aspiration
- E. All of the above

3. A 51-year-old man undergoes a colon resection for colon cancer. He develops a surgical wound infection 5 days after surgery. What are the most likely pathogens responsible for this infection?

- A. Staphylococcus aureus
- B. Coagulase-negative staphylococci
- C. Enteric bacteria

289

- D. Anaerobic bacteria

4. A 40-year-old man with HIV infection presents to the emergency department with headache, fever, and neck stiffness. He has no history of meningitis. On physical examination, you note a normal mental status, photophobia, and nuchal rigidity. Which of the following is the most likely diagnosis?

- A. Cryptococcal meningitis
- B Listeria meningitis
- C Bacterial meningitis
- D Viral meningitis
- E Tuberculous meningitis

5. Which individuals are more susceptible to developing a brain abscess?

- A. Individuals with prolonged neutropenia
- B. Individuals with impaired cellular immunity
- C. Both individuals with prolonged neutropenia and individuals with impaired cellular immunity
- D. Neither individuals with prolonged neutropenia nor individuals with impaired cellular immunity
- E. Cannot be determined from the information provided.

6. A 46-year-old man with acute myeloid leukemia (AML) presents with fever, abdominal pain, and diarrhea. He has a white blood cell count of 100 cells/L and a platelet count of 20,000 cells/L. A CT scan of the abdomen shows cecal thickening and inflammation. Which of the following is the most appropriate therapeutic intervention for this patient?

- A. Intravenous antibiotics
- B. Intravenous antibiotics and bowel rest
- C. Intravenous antibiotics, bowel rest, and surgical resection
- D. Intravenous antibiotics and surgical resection
- E. Surgical resection

7. Which of the following pharmaceutical agents have replaced amphotericin B deoxycholate as the preferred choice for empirical antifungal therapy in individuals experiencing febrile neutropenia?

- A. Liposomal amphotericin B
- B. Voriconazole
- C. Posaconazole
- D. Caspofungin
- E. All of the above

8. A 31-year-old woman with acute lymphoblastic leukemia (ALL) undergoes an allogeneic HSCT. She is started on broad-spectrum antibiotics and fluconazole prophylaxis. On day 21 post-transplant, she develops fever and respiratory symptoms. What is the most likely type of fungal infection in this patient?

- A. Candida
- B. Aspergillus
- C. Fusarium
- D. Cryptococcus
- E. Zygomycetes

9. A 27-year-old man with acute lymphoblastic leukemia (ALL) undergoes an allogeneic HSCT. He is engrafted after 20 days and is started on maintenance immunosuppression. What is the most appropriate maintenance prophylaxis for this patient to prevent Pneumocystis jirovecii pneumonia (PCP)?

- A. Trimethoprim-sulfamethoxazole (TMPSMX) at a dosage of 160/800 mg per day
- B. Dapsone 100 mg per day
- C. Atovaquone 1500 mg per day
- D. Pentamidine isethionate 300 mg every month by intramuscular injection
- E. None of the above

10. A 25-year-old woman with acute myeloid leukemia (AML) undergoes an allogeneic HSCT. She is engrafted after 20 days and develops fever and cough. What are the respiratory viral infections that should be considered in this patient?

- A. Respiratory syncytial virus
- B. Parainfluenza virus
- C. Metapneumovirus
- D. Influenza virus
- E. All of the above

11. A 51-year-old man with end-stage renal disease undergoes a kidney transplant. What is the recommended prophylactic treatment for this patient during the initial 4-6 months after surgery?

- A. TMP-SMX
- B. Acyclovir
- C. Fluconazole
- D. Pentamidine
- E. None of the above

12. A 68-year-old man with a history of chronic obstructive pulmonary disease (COPD) presents to the emergency department with fever, cough, and shortness of breath. He is found to have pneumonia on chest X-ray. Blood cultures are positive for Streptococcus pneumoniae. What are the predominant causative agents of PBP in this patient?

- A. Enteric gram-negative bacilli
- B. Gram-positive organisms
- C. Both enteric gram-negative bacilli and gram-positive organisms
- D. Neither enteric gram-negative bacilli nor gram-positive organisms
- E. Cannot be determined

13. A 62-year-old woman with a history of diabetes mellitus presents with fever, abdominal pain, and nausea. She is found to have cloudy peritoneal fluid on paracentesis. What are the diagnostic methods for determining PBP in this patient?

- A. Examination of peritoneal fluid for more than 250 polymorphonuclear leukocytes (PMNs) per microliter
- B. Introduction of a 10-mL quantity of peritoneal fluid directly into blood culture bottles
- C. Performance of blood cultures
- D. All of the above
- E. None of the above

14. A 42-year-old man attends a barbecue and consumes a large amount of grilled chicken. He develops diarrhea and abdominal cramps 8 hours later. What is the most likely cause of his illness?

- A. Salmonella
- B. Campylobacter
- C. Clostridium perfringens
- D. Escherichia coli
- E. Norovirus

15. A 36-year-old man presents with watery diarrhea, vomiting, and abdominal cramps. He has been experiencing these symptoms for 24 hours. What interventions can be employed to reduce the duration and volume of stool in this patient?

- A. Azithromycin (administered as a single 1-g dose)
- B. Erythromycin (250 mg orally four times daily for a duration of three days)
- C. Tetracycline (500 mg orally four times daily for a duration of three days)
- D. Ciprofloxacin (500 mg orally twice daily for a duration of three days)
- E. All of the above

16. A 24-year-old woman presents with watery diarrhea, abdominal cramps, and weight loss. She has been experiencing these symptoms for 2 weeks. What are the diagnostic methods for Cryptosporidiosis in this patient?

- A. Fecal examination for oocysts
- B. Modified acid-fast staining
- C. Direct immunofluorescent techniques
- D. Enzyme immunoassays (EIAs)
- E. All of the above

17. A 57-year-old man with a history of chronic gastritis presents with fever, diarrhea, and abdominal cramps. He has been experiencing these symptoms for 24 hours. What are the factors that contribute to this patient's increased susceptibility to Salmonella infection?

- A. Decreased gastric acidity
- B. Compromised intestinal integrity
- C. Both decreased gastric acidity and compromised intestinal integrity
- D. Neither decreased gastric acidity nor compromised intestinal integrity
- E. Cannot be determined

18. A 28-year-old woman presents with fever, diarrhea, and abdominal cramps. She has been experiencing these symptoms for 24 hours. What are the potential complications associated with this patient's Nontyphoidal salmonellosis (NTS)?

- A. Bacteremia
- B. Hepatosplenic abscesses
- C. Meningitis
- D. Pneumonia
- E. All of the above

19. A 25-year-old woman presents with fever, diarrhea, and abdominal cramps. She has been experiencing these symptoms for 24 hours. Is the administration of antibiotics advised for the management of this patient's yersiniosis?

- A. Yes
- B. No
- C. Cannot be determined

20. A 23-year-old woman presents with fever, right upper quadrant pain, and weight loss. She has been experiencing these symptoms for 2 weeks. A serological test for Entamoeba histolytica is negative. What is the next best course of action?

- A. Administer metronidazole
- B. Repeat the serological test after one week
- C. Obtain an ultrasound or CT scan of the liver
- D. Observe the patient and repeat the serological test in 2 weeks
- E. Refer the patient to a hepatologist

21. A 54-year-old man is admitted to the hospital with fever, diarrhea, and abdominal cramps. He has been taking amoxicillin for 10 days for a sinus infection. What is the most likely mode of acquisition for this patient's Clostridioides difficile infection (CDI)?

- A. Contact with an infected person
- B. Ingestion of contaminated food or water
- C. A break in the skin
- D. Antimicrobial therapy
- E. None of the above

22. A 59-year-old man is treated for C. difficile infection with a course of metronidazole. He continues to have diarrhea after completing the course of antibiotics. What is the most likely explanation for the patient's persistent diarrhea?

- A. The patient is not responding to treatment.
- B. The patient has developed a resistance to metronidazole.
- C. The patient has developed a new infection.
- D. The patient is experiencing a side effect of the antibiotics.
- E. The patient is experiencing a recurrence of C. difficile infection.

23. A 37-year-old man presents to the clinic with dysuria, urethral discharge, and urinary frequency. What are the predominant etiological agents responsible for this patient's urethritis?

- A. Neisseria gonorrhoeae
- B. Chlamydia trachomatis
- C. Mycoplasma genitalium
- D. Ureaplasma urealyticum

- E. Trichomonas vaginalis

24. A 22-year-old woman presents to the clinic with vaginal discharge and odor. What are the clinical presentations that suggest that this patient may have trichomoniasis or bacterial vaginosis (BV)?

- A. Vulvar irritation and a copious white or yellow homogeneous vaginal discharge with a pH level that is typically equal to or greater than 5.
- B. The presence of an unpleasant odor in the vaginal region, accompanied by a mild to moderate elevation in the amount of white or gray homogeneous discharge that evenly covers the walls of the vagina. This discharge typically exhibits a pH level exceeding 4.5.
- C. Both A. and B.
- D. Neither A. nor B.
- E. Cannot be determined

25. A 26-year-old woman presents to the clinic with vaginal discharge and odor. She is diagnosed with trichomoniasis. What is the most efficacious treatment for this patient?

- A. Metronidazole, administered orally at a dosage of 2 grams once
- B. Metronidazole, administered orally at a dosage of 500 milligrams twice daily for duration of 7 days
- C. Secnidazole, administered orally at a dosage of 2 grams once
- D. Tinidazole, administered orally at a dosage of 2 grams once
- E. None of the above

26. A 24-year-old woman presents to the clinic with pelvic pain, fever, and vaginal discharge. She is diagnosed with pelvic inflammatory disease (PID). What types of specimens should be collected for nucleic acid amplification tests (NAATs) in this patient?

- A. Vaginal swab
- B. Endocervical swab
- C. Cervical swab
- D. Both A. and B.
- E. None of the above

27. What are the applications of treponemal tests and what are the limitations that render them unsuitable for screening purposes?

- A. Treponemal tests are used to validate the outcomes obtained from lipoidal tests.
- B. Treponemal tests are used to screen for syphilis.
- C. Treponemal tests are used to diagnose syphilis.
- D. Treponemal tests are used to monitor the effectiveness of treatment for syphilis.
- E. All of the above.

28. What is the recommended course of treatment for patients with confirmed penicillin allergy who are diagnosed with primary, secondary, or early latent syphilis?

- A. Benzathine penicillin G
- B. Doxycycline
- C. Tetracycline hydrochloride
- D. Ceftriaxone
- E. None of the above

29. What is the recommended therapeutic approach for initial occurrences of genital infections caused by the herpes simplex virus (HSV)?

- A. Oral acyclovir at a dosage of 400 mg three times daily for 7-14 days
- B. Oral valacyclovir at a dosage of 1 g twice daily for 7-14 days
- C. Oral famciclovir at a dosage of 250 mg twice daily for 7-14 days
- D. All of the above
- E. None of the above

30. What is the impact of chancroid on the vulnerability to HIV transmission?

- A. Chancroid does not increase the vulnerability to HIV transmission.

- B. Chancroid increases the vulnerability to HIV transmission by providing a portal of entry for the virus.
- C. Chancroid decreases the vulnerability to HIV transmission by increasing the body's immune response.
- D. Chancroid has no impact on the vulnerability to HIV transmission.
- E. The impact of chancroid on the vulnerability to HIV transmission is unknown.

31. What is the main therapeutic approach for necrotizing fasciitis caused by group A streptococcus?

- A. Administration of Clindamycin (600-900 mg IV every 6-8 hours)
- B. Administration of penicillin G (4 million units IV every 4 hours)
- C. Administration of both Clindamycin and penicillin G
- D. Administration of surgery
- E. Both C and D

32. What are the diagnostic methods employed for the identification of necrotizing fasciitis?

- A. Evaluation of the patient's clinical presentation
- B. Identification of gas within deep tissues through imaging investigations
- C. Significantly heightened levels of serum CPK
- D. All of the above
- E. None of the above

33. A 28-year-old woman presents to the emergency department with a 2-day history of fever, chills, rash, and migratory arthritis. Which of the following is the most likely diagnosis?

- A. Disseminated gonococcal infection.
- B. Reactive arthritis
- C. Lyme disease
- D. Reiter syndrome
- E. Septic arthritis

34. A 47-year-old man with no history of prior antibiotic use presents to the emergency department with a 1-week history of pain and swelling in his left ankle. Physical examination reveals erythema, warmth, and tenderness over the lateral aspect of the left ankle. Laboratory tests show an elevated white blood cell count and C-reactive protein. A bone biopsy is performed, and cultures grow Methicillin-susceptible Staphylococcus aureus. What is the optimal antibiotic treatment for this patient?

- A. Nafcillin 2 grams IV every 6 hours
- B. Oxacillin 2 grams IV every 6 hours
- C. Rifampin 300-450 milligrams PO every 12 hours
- D. Levofloxacin 750 milligrams PO every 24 hours
- E. Levofloxacin 500 milligrams PO every 12 hours

35. A 68-year-old man presents to the emergency department with a 3-day history of fever, cough, and shortness of breath. On physical examination, he is found to have a temperature of 102 degrees Fahrenheit, a respiratory rate of 24 breaths per minute, and an oxygen saturation of 90% on room air. His chest X-ray shows a right lower lobe infiltrate. What are the most likely bacterial pathogens associated with this patient's community-acquired pneumonia?

- A. Streptococcus pneumoniae
- B. Haemophilus influenzae
- C. Staphylococcus aureus
- D. Klebsiella pneumoniae
- E. Pseudomonas aeruginosa

36. A 53-year-old man presents to the emergency department with a 2-day history of fever, cough, and shortness of breath. On physical examination, he is found to have a temperature of 101 degrees Fahrenheit, a respiratory rate of 22 breaths per minute, and an oxygen saturation of 92% on room air. His chest X-ray shows a right lower lobe infiltrate. What is the CURB-65 score for this patient?

- A. 0
- B. 1
- C. 2
- D. 3

- E. 4

37. A 35-year-old woman presents to her doctor's office with a 2-day history of fever, cough, and shortness of breath. She has no history of prior antibiotic use and is otherwise in good health. What is the suggested antibiotic treatment for this patient?

- A. Clarithromycin 500 mg orally twice daily
- B. Azithromycin 500 mg orally once, followed by 250 mg daily.
- C. Doxycycline 100 mg orally twice daily
- D. Amoxicillin 500 mg orally three times daily
- E. Trimethoprim-sulfamethoxazole (TMP-SMX) 1 double-strength tablet orally twice daily

38. A 72-year-old man with a history of chronic obstructive pulmonary disease (COPD) is admitted to the ICU with a diagnosis of VAP. He is started on empiric antimicrobial therapy. How long would you typically wait before expecting to see clinical improvement in this patient?

- A. 24 hours
- B. 48 hours
- C. 72 hours
- D. 96 hours
- E. 120 hours

39. A 59-year-old man presents to the emergency department with a 5-day history of fever, cough, and shortness of breath. On physical examination, he is found to have a temperature of 102 degrees Fahrenheit, a respiratory rate of 24 breaths per minute, and an oxygen saturation of 90% on room air. His chest X-ray shows a right upper lobe infiltrate with a cavity. What is the optimal treatment approach for this patient?

- A. Clindamycin 600 mg IV three times a day
- B. Amoxicillin/clavulanate 500/125 mg orally three times a day
- C. Metronidazole 500 mg IV three times a day
- D. Imipenem/cilastatin 500 mg IV every 6 hours
- E. Ceftriaxone 2 g IV every 24 hours

40. A 37-year-old man presents to his doctor's office with a 2-week history of cough, fever, and weight loss. He has a history of prior tuberculosis treatment that was unsuccessful. What is the most likely diagnosis for this patient?

- A. Multidrug-resistant tuberculosis (MDR-TB)
- B. Extensively drug-resistant tuberculosis (XDR-TB)
- C. Latent tuberculosis infection (LTBI)
- D. Active tuberculosis (TB)
- E. Nontuberculous mycobacterial infection

41. A 41-year-old woman presents to the emergency department with a 2-week history of cough, fever, and shortness of breath. She also has a history of right upper lobe pneumonia that was treated with antibiotics 6 months ago. Her chest X-ray shows a right pleural effusion. What is the most likely diagnostic test for tuberculosis in this patient?

- A. Direct smear of pleural fluid
- B. Culture of pleural fluid
- C. Polymerase chain reaction (PCR) assay of pleural fluid
- D. Pleural biopsy
- E. Quantiferon Gold test

42. A 23-year-old man presents to the emergency department with a 2-week history of fever, cough, and shortness of breath. He also has a history of right upper lobe pneumonia that was treated with antibiotics 6 months ago. His chest X-ray shows a diffuse miliary infiltrate. What is the most likely etiology of miliary tuberculosis in this patient?

- A. Hematogenous spread from a primary pulmonary focus
- B. Hematogenous spread from a site of extrapulmonary tuberculosis.
- C. Direct extension from a contiguous focus of infection
- D. Inhalation of bacilli
- E. Iatrogenic

43. A 34-year-old man with HIV and tuberculosis presents to his doctor's office with a 2-week history of worsening

cough, fever, and shortness of breath. He has been taking antiretroviral therapy for 6 months. What is the most likely diagnosis for this patient?

- A. Immune reconstitution inflammatory syndrome (IRIS)
- B. Active tuberculosis (TB)
- C. Latent tuberculosis infection (LTBI)
- D. Drug-resistant tuberculosis (TB)
- E. Exacerbation of HIV

44. A 39-year-old man presents to his doctor's office with a 2-week history of cough, fever, and shortness of breath. He has a history of latent tuberculosis infection (LTBI). What is the least efficacious initial treatment option for this patient?

- A. Ethambutol
- B. Isoniazid
- C. Rifampin
- D. Pyrazinamide
- E. Streptomycin

45. A 29-year-old man presents to his doctor's office with a 3-day history of fever, headache, and a rash. His rash is initially located on his ankles and wrists, and it has progressed to involve his palms and soles. What is the most beneficial diagnostic test for this patient?

- A. Immunohistologic examination of a cutaneous biopsy sample obtained from a rash lesion.
- B. Enzyme-linked immunosorbent assay (ELISA) for Rocky Mountain spotted fever.
- C. Polymerase chain reaction (PCR) assay for Rocky Mountain spotted fever.
- D. Blood culture
- E. Chest X-ray

46. A 32-year-old man presents to the emergency department with a 3-day history of fever, headache, and chills. He is also complaining of shortness of breath and generalized weakness. On physical examination, he is found to have a temperature of 104 degrees Fahrenheit, a respiratory rate of 24 breaths per minute, and a blood pressure of 90/60 mmHg. His peripheral blood smear shows a parasitemia of 20 What is the most likely diagnosis for this patient?

- A. Severe falciparum malaria
- B. Acute respiratory distress syndrome (ARDS)
- C. Disseminated intravascular coagulation (DIC)
- D. Spontaneous hemorrhaging
- E. Acute kidney injury

47. A 69-year-old man with atrial fibrillation and malaria is started on quinidine therapy. His baseline QTc interval is 0.4 seconds. After 3 days of therapy, his total plasma quinidine level is 10 g/mL and his QTc interval is 0.6 seconds. What should the next step be in this patient's management?

- A. Decrease the quinidine dose.
- B. Temporarily halt the quinidine infusion.
- C. Continue the quinidine infusion without change.
- D. Obtain an ECG
- E. Obtain a serum potassium level.

48. A 51-year-old man with HIV infection presents to his doctor's office with a 2-week history of fever, weight loss, and diarrhea. His CD4+ T cell count is 150/L. What is the most likely diagnosis for this patient?

- A. Acquired Immunodeficiency Syndrome (AIDS)
- B. HIV infection
- C. Opportunistic infection
- D. Tuberculosis
- E. Pneumocystis jirovecii pneumonia

49. A 39-year-old man with HIV infection presents to his doctor's office with a 2-week history of a painless skin rash. The rash is initially located on his feet and hands, and it has progressed to involve his trunk and face. What is the most likely diagnosis for this patient?

- A. Kaposi's sarcoma
- B. Lymphoma
- C. Multicentric Castleman's disease
- D. Basal cell carcinoma
- E. Squamous cell carcinoma

50. A 62-year-old man with HIV infection presents to his doctor's office with a CD4+ T cell count of 150 cells/L. What is the indication for primary prophylaxis of Pneumocystis jiroveci pneumonia in this patient?

- A. CD4+ T cell count below 200 cells/L
- B. History of Pneumocystis jiroveci pneumonia
- C. HIV infection
- D. Age greater than 65 years
- E. None of the above

51. 59-year-old man presents to the emergency department with a 2-day history of fever, cough, and shortness of breath. On physical examination, he is found to have a temperature of 101 degrees Fahrenheit, a respiratory rate of 24 breaths per minute, and a blood pressure of 90/60 mmHg. His chest X-ray shows a right lower lobe infiltrate. What are the additional anomalies that are likely to be present in this patient?

- A. Ileus
- B. Disseminated intravascular coagulation (DIC)
- C. Sick euthyroid syndrome
- D. All of the above
- E. None of the above

52. A 58-year-old man presents to the emergency department with a 2-day history of fever, cough, and shortness of breath. On physical examination, he is found to have a temperature of 101 degrees Fahrenheit, a respiratory rate of 24 breaths per minute, and a blood pressure of 90/60 mmHg. His chest X-ray shows a right lower lobe infiltrate. What are distinct care protocols for the early management of this patient?

- A. Administration of antibiotics and fluids
- B. Administration of antibiotics and vasopressors
- C. Administration of fluids and vasopressors
- D. Administration of antibiotics, fluids, and vasopressors
- E. None of the above

53. A 22-year-old woman presents with a 2-day history of fever, rash, and joint pain. She also has a purulent vaginal discharge. Physical examination reveals a fever of 39°C, a maculopapular rash on her trunk and extremities, and a tender right knee joint. Laboratory studies show an elevated white blood cell count with neutrophilia, elevated erythrocyte sedimentation rate, and elevated C-reactive protein level. Blood cultures are negative. What is the most appropriate next step in management?

- (A) Order serologic testing for disseminated gonococcal infection (DGI)
- (B) Order an MRI of the right knee joint
- (C) Order nucleic acid amplification testing (NAAT) on bodily fluid from multiple sources
- (D) Start empiric treatment for DGI
- (E) Observe the patient and repeat laboratory studies in 24 hours

54. A 26-year-old sexually active woman presents with sudden onset of left ankle pain and swelling. On examination, you find that her left ankle is warm, red, and tender. She also has flexor tenosynovial involvement of the second flexor tendon and a pustular eruption on her palms. Her lab results show leukocytosis and pyuria. What is the most likely diagnosis?

- A. Disseminated gonococcal infection
- B. Reactive arthritis
- C. Rheumatoid arthritis
- D. Gout
- E. Lyme disease

55. A 60-year-old man with a history of gout presents with acute right knee pain and swelling. Synovial fluid analysis

shows 49,000 WBCs/L with 95% neutrophils. The fluid also contains urate crystals, but the Gram stain is negative. What is the most appropriate next step in management?

- A. Administer an intra-articular corticosteroid injection
- B. Obtain blood cultures and start intravenous vancomycin/ceftriaxone
- C. Start oral colchicine
- D. Start oral NSAIDs
- E. Refer for orthopedic surgery

56. A 56-year-old woman presents with a 3-day history of fever, cough, and shortness of breath. She also has a history of chronic obstructive pulmonary disease (COPD). Physical examination reveals a temperature of 39°C, a respiratory rate of 32 breaths/min, and a blood pressure of 100/60 mmHg. Lung auscultation reveals crackles in both lungs. Laboratory studies show a white blood cell count of 15,000 cells/mm^3 with neutrophilia, a platelet count of 100,000 cells/mm^3, and a chest X-ray that shows multilobular infiltrates. What is the most appropriate next step in management?

- (A) Admit the patient to the hospital and start intravenous antibiotics
- (B) Discharge the patient home with oral antibiotics and follow-up in 24 hours
- (C) Order a sputum culture and start oral antibiotics
- (D) Order a bronchoscopy
- (E) Observe the patient in the emergency department and repeat laboratory studies in 2 hours

57. A 68-year-old woman has been admitted to the hospital for 5 days due to an episode of congestive heart failure. She was initially doing well, but today she has developed a fever and a new cough. A chest radiograph shows a new infiltrate in the right lower lobe. The patient received intravenous antibiotics for a urinary tract infection about 75 days ago. Which of the following is the most appropriate empiric treatment?

- A. Cefepime and vancomycin
- B. Amoxicillin-clavulanate
- C. Azithromycin
- D. Doxycycline
- E. Ceftriaxone and azithromycin

58. 54-year-old immunocompromised man presents to the emergency department with symptoms of community-acquired pneumonia. His medical history is significant for recent IV antibiotic treatment. In addition to sputum Gram stain and culture, blood cultures, S. pneumoniae urinary antigen, and viral testing, which of the following would NOT be advisable to help direct the use of antibiotics in this patient?

- A. C-reactive protein
- B. Procalcitonin
- C. Erythrocyte sedimentation rate
- D. Chest X-ray
- E. Complete blood count

59. A 33-year-old woman presents with a 2-day history of fever, cough, and shortness of breath. She is otherwise healthy with no known drug allergies. On examination, she is afebrile with a respiratory rate of 28 breaths per minute and an oxygen saturation of 90% on room air. Chest X-ray shows right lower lobe consolidation. Influenza testing is positive. Which of the following is the best treatment for this patient's influenza pneumonia?

- (A) Oseltamivir 75 mg once daily for 5 days
- (B) Amantadine 100 mg twice daily for 5 days
- (C) Oseltamivir 75 mg twice daily for 5 days
- (D) Zanamivir 10 mg twice daily for 5 days
- (E) None of the above

60. A 67-year-old female post-heart transplant patient presents with fever and malaise. Blood cultures return positive for Candida species. She has a peripherally inserted central catheter line and a Foley catheter in place. What is the most likely source of her candidemia?

- A. Hematologic malignancy
- B. Foley catheter

- C. Peripherally inserted central catheter line
- D. Total parenteral nutrition
- E. TNF- inhibitor therapy

61. A 36-year-old woman, who recently underwent a heart transplant, is admitted to the hospital with persistent fever. She has been receiving total parenteral nutrition via a peripherally inserted central catheter line. Additionally, she has a Foley catheter in place. Blood cultures are ordered and come back positive for Candida species. Which of the following is most likely the source of her candidemia?

- A. Hematologic malignancy
- B. Total parenteral nutrition
- C. Biologic therapies
- D. IV drug use
- E. Foley catheter

62. Which of the following statements about the galactomannan assay is TRUE?

- (A) It is a specific test for Aspergillus galactomannan antigen.
- (B) It is not useful in the diagnosis of invasive aspergillosis in patients with hematologic malignancies.
- (C) It can be positive in the setting of infections with other fungi, such as Fusarium spp and Penicillium spp.
- (D) It can be falsely positive in the setting of intravenous immunoglobulin (IVIG) and piperacillin-tazobactam.
- (E) All of the above.

63. A 59-year-old female who recently underwent a heart transplant presents with fever and malaise. Blood cultures reveal yeast. In the context of this patient's condition and the presence of yeast in the blood cultures, which of the following is the most likely source of her infection?

- A. Heart transplant
- B. Foley catheter
- C. Surgical wound
- D. Peripherally inserted central catheter line
- E. Recent IV drug use

64. A 57-year-old man with acute myeloid leukemia presents with fever and yeast in his blood. He has a peripherally inserted central catheter line (PICC line). Which of the following is the best management for this patient?

- (A) Remove the PICC line and start empiric antifungal therapy with fluconazole.
- (B) Remove the PICC line and start empiric antifungal therapy with micafungin.
- (C) Obtain an infectious disease consult.
- (D) A and C.
- (E) All of the above.

65. A 52-year-old man presents with a 2-week history of fever and cough. He has a history of acute myeloid leukemia and underwent a stem cell transplant 6 months ago. He has also been on high-dose steroids for the past month due to graft-versus-host disease. On examination, he is febrile and tachycardic. His respiratory rate is 28 breaths per minute and his oxygen saturation is 90% on room air. Chest X-ray shows a right upper lobe infiltrate. Serum galactomannan is positive. Which of the following is the most likely diagnosis?

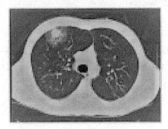

Figure 9.2: 52-year-old man

- (A) Pneumonia due to Streptococcus pneumoniae

- (B) Invasive pulmonary aspergillosis
- (C) Pneumocystis jirovecii pneumonia
- (D) Viral pneumonia
- (E) None of the above

66. A 33-year-old woman presents with dysuria, frequency, and suprapubic pain for 2 days. She denies flank pain, fever, or nausea. Her past medical history is unremarkable except for nephrolithiasis 2 years ago. What is the most likely diagnosis?

- A. Complicated urinary tract infection (UTI)
- B. Acute uncomplicated cystitis
- C. Kidney stone
- D. Interstitial cystitis
- E. Bladder cancer

67. A 35-year-old woman with a renal transplant presents with dysuria, frequency, and urgency. Urinalysis reveals pyuria and bacteriuria. Which of the following is the best classification for this patient's UTI?

- (A) Complicated UTI
- (B) Uncomplicated UTI
- (C) Asymptomatic bacteriuria
- (D) Pyelonephritis
- (E) Urosepsis

68. A 28-year-old woman presents with frequency, dysuria, and suprapubic pain. Her symptoms started 48 hours ago. She denies nausea, vomiting, fever, or flank pain. She is sexually active with one partner and uses condoms consistently. She denies penicillin allergy. What's the next best step in the management of this patient?

- A. Test for N. gonorrhoeae and C. trachomatis
- B. CT abdomen and pelvis
- C. Urinalysis, urine culture, and CBC
- D. Start empiric antibiotics without further workup
- E. MRI abdomen and pelvis

69. A 66-year-old man with a history of diabetes mellitus presents with a painful, swollen, erythematous left foot. He has a history of peripheral neuropathy and poor glycemic control. His foot radiograph does not show any abnormalities. What is the most likely diagnosis?

- A. Acute gouty arthritis
- B. Diabetic foot infection
- C. Chronic osteomyelitis
- D. Peripheral vascular disease
- E. Cellulitis

70. Which of the following clinical findings is most supportive of a diagnosis of osteomyelitis?

- (A) Probing to bone or grossly visible bone
- (B) Ulcer size >2 cm
- (C) Ulcer duration longer than 1 to 2 weeks
- (D) ESR >70 mm/h
- (E) All of the above

71. A 71-year-old man with a history of diabetes and peripheral neuropathy presents with a moderately severe diabetic foot infection. Which antibiotic regimen is most appropriate for his condition?

- A. Vancomycin and ampicillin-sulbactam
- B. Linezolid and ertapenem
- C. Daptomycin and fluoroquinolones
- D. Cefepime and metronidazole
- E. Vancomycin, cefepime, and metronidazole

72. A 37-year-old man presents with a 2-day history of fever and back pain. He has no known medical history and is not taking any medications. On examination, he is febrile and tachycardic. His back pain is localized to the lumbar

spine and is exacerbated by movement. He has no motor or sensory deficits. Which of the following is the most likely diagnosis?

- (A) Spinal stenosis
- (B) Epidural abscess
- (C) Lumbar radiculopathy
- (D) Degenerative disc disease
- (E) Osteoarthritis

73. A 42-year-old man presents with a 12-hour history of severe pain, swelling, and redness in his left leg. He had been fishing the day before and had sustained a small cut on his leg. On examination, his leg is swollen and erythematous. There is crepitus on palpation. He is febrile and tachycardic. Which of the following is the most likely diagnosis?

- (A) Necrotizing fasciitis
- (B) Cellulitis
- (C) Lymphangitis
- (D) Deep vein thrombosis
- (E) Erysipelas

74. A 61-year-old patient presents with sudden onset of facial paralysis on one side, ear pain, decreased hearing, and tinnitus. You also notice vesicles in the patient's auditory canal. What is the most likely diagnosis?

- A. Bell's Palsy
- B. Meniere's Disease
- C. Otitis Media
- D. Stroke
- E. Ramsay Hunt Syndrome

75. A 48-year-old patient presents with symptoms suggestive of varicella zoster virus reactivation. What is the optimal test to confirm this diagnosis?

- A. Complete blood count (CBC)
- B. Varicella zoster virus IgG
- C. Direct fluorescent antigen testing
- D. Varicella zoster virus viral culture
- E. Viral PCR for varicella zoster virus

76. A 53-year-old man presents with a 2-day history of fever, confusion, and ataxia. He has a rash on his right chest and back that has been present for 5 days. The rash is vesicular and crusted. Lumbar puncture reveals a cerebrospinal fluid (CSF) white blood cell count of 30 cells/mm3, a red blood cell count of 10 cells/mm3, and a glucose level of 60 mg/dL (normal 50-80 mg/dL). Protein level is normal. CSF PCR for herpes simplex virus (HSV) and enterovirus is negative. Which of the following is the most likely diagnosis?

- (A) Herpes simplex encephalitis
- (B) Enteroviral encephalitis
- (C) Bacterial meningitis
- (D) Varicella zoster encephalitis
- (E) Lyme meningitis

77. A patient presents with elevated WBC count, low glucose, and high total protein in CSF studies post neurosurgical procedure. What is the most likely diagnosis?

- A. Bacterial meningitis
- B. Fungal meningitis
- C. Tuberculous meningitis
- D. Viral meningitis
- E. Non-infectious inflammatory disease

78. A 32-year-old woman with a history of intravenous drug use presents with a 2-week history of fever, cough, and shortness of breath. On examination, she is febrile and tachycardic. She has a murmur and palmar Janeway lesions. Chest X-ray shows multiple small nodules in both lungs. Which of the following is the best initial management for this patient?

- (A) Blood cultures and empiric antibiotics with coverage for MRSA
- (B) ECG and echocardiogram
- (C) Transthoracic echocardiogram only
- (D) Transesophageal echocardiogram only
- (E) All of the above

79. A 59-year-old man who was born in a country where tuberculosis (TB) is endemic presents with a positive tuberculin skin test (TST). He has no respiratory symptoms and is otherwise healthy. He received the BCG vaccine as a child. Which of the following is the best next step in the management of this patient? A) Induced sputum and chest X-ray (CXR) (B) Interferon release assay (IGRA) (C) Empiric anti-tuberculosis therapy (D) None of the above 80. A patient with a history of travel to a tuberculosis-endemic area undergoes an interferon release assay, but the results are indeterminate due to a strong negative control response. What is the most appropriate next step in management?

- A. Assure the patient that this is a normal response to the BCG vaccine
- B. Proceed with the tuberculin skin test
- C. Repeat interferon release assay
- D. Start the patient on tuberculosis treatment
- E. Discontinue further testing for tuberculosis

81. A 54-year-old man with no known risk factors for tuberculosis (TB) presents for a routine physical examination. His tuberculin skin test (TST) is positive and his chest X-ray is normal. He has no respiratory symptoms. Which of the following is the best treatment option for this patient?

- (A) Rifampin daily for 4 months
- (B) Isoniazid daily (with vitamin B6) for 9 months
- (C) Isoniazid and rifapentine weekly for 12 weeks
- (D) Either A or B
- (E) None of the above

82. A 37-year-old man was recently diagnosed with HIV infection. As part of the routine workup, which of the following tests are NOT advised?

- A. CD4 cell count
- B. Glucan and galactomannan
- C. HIV viral load and genotype
- D. Hepatitis (A, B, and C) serologies
- E. Tuberculin skin test or an interferon release assay

83. A 38-year-old man presents with a CD4 cell count of 150 cells/L. He has no symptoms of opportunistic infections. Which of the following is the best recommendation for this patient?

- (A) Start antiretroviral therapy (ART) at this visit, if patient is agreeable to start.
- (B) Wait for the results of all laboratory tests and genotype before starting ART.
- (C) Start ART only if the patient develops symptoms of opportunistic infections.
- (D) Start ART if the CD4 cell count drops below 200 cells/L.
- (E) Start ART if the viral load is greater than 100,000 copies/mL.

84. A 31-year-old man with HIV infection has been on ART for 6 months and has been tolerating it well. His CD4 cell count is now 300 cells/L. Which of the following is the best recommendation for this patient's Pneumocystis jiroveci pneumonia (PCP) prophylaxis?

- (A) He can stop TMP-SMX at this time.
- (B) He should continue TMP-SMX until his CD4 cell count is >400 cells/L.
- (C) He should continue TMP-SMX indefinitely.
- (D) He should switch to dapsone for PCP prophylaxis.
- (E) He should switch to atovaquone for PCP prophylaxis.

85. A 30-year-old man is in a serodiscordant relationship with his partner who is HIV positive. They report consistent condom use during sexual activity. He is negative for HIV based on the recent testing. What is the most appropriate next step in management?

- A. Continue condom use only
- B. Start pre-exposure prophylaxis after each sexual encounter
- C. Start tenofovir and emtricitabine daily
- D. Start on-demand use of tenofovir and emtricitabine
- E. No action needed as the partner is HIV positive

86. A 37-year-old man presents with a 2-week history of fever, fatigue, and a rash on his left arm. The rash is red and ring-shaped. He also reports having chest pain and shortness of breath. On examination, he has a heart rate of 120 beats per minute and a blood pressure of 90/60 mmHg. He has a loud murmur on auscultation. His electrocardiogram shows first-degree atrioventricular block. Which of the following is the best management for this patient?

- (A) Start IV ceftriaxone and switch to oral doxycycline upon clinical improvement.
- (B) Start a temporary pacemaker.
- (C) Order blood cultures to confirm the diagnosis.
- (D) Start lifelong antibiotics.
- (E) None of the above.

87. A 68-year-old male patient from Massachusetts with recent rash typical for erythema migrans, anemia with evidence of hemolysis, and pancytopenia and transaminitis is suspected to have tick-borne illness. Which of the following is the best next step in the management of this patient?

- A. Check Lyme ELISA screen, blood parasite smear, human granulocytic anaplasmosis PCR.
- B. Start empiric treatment without further testing.
- C. Check for Ehrlichiosis (Ehrlichia chaffeensis).
- D. Test for Babesia microti only.
- E. Hospitalize and observe without further intervention.

88. A 32-year-old man presents to the clinic 2 weeks after returning from a 3-week trip to sub-Saharan Africa. He is afebrile with a normal physical examination. He reports feeling well, but requests to be evaluated for fever in the setting of recent travel. Which of the following is the most appropriate next step in management?

- (A) Order basic metabolic panel, CBC and differential, LFTs, and blood cultures.
- (B) Reassure the patient and discharge him home.
- (C) Prescribe antibiotics and schedule a follow-up appointment in 1 week.
- (D) Perform rapid diagnostic testing for malaria.
- (E) All of the above.

89. A 67-year-old woman presents with a 3-week history of fever, fatigue, and a localized headache in the temporal region. She also reports jaw pain while eating. On examination, her temporal arteries are tender and thickened. Laboratory findings show an elevated erythrocyte sedimentation rate (ESR). What is the most appropriate next step in the management of this patient's condition?

- A. Order a brain MRI
- B. Perform a lumbar puncture
- C. Wait for further symptoms to manifest
- D. Initiate high-dose prednisone
- E. Schedule a temporal artery biopsy

9.1 ANSWERS

1. The correct answer is A: replace the catheter and collect a freshly voided urine specimen for culture. When there is suspicion of infection in the context of chronic catheterization, it is important to definitively confirm the presence of an infection.

This can be done by replacing the catheter and collecting a freshly voided urine specimen for culture. The urine specimen should be collected before the catheter is replaced. If the culture is positive for bacteria, then the patient has a urinary tract infection. The patient should be treated with antibiotics for the infection. If the culture is negative for bacteria, then the patient may have a catheter-associated urinary tract colonization. This is a condition in which bacteria are present on the catheter but do not cause an infection. In this case, the patient may not need treatment.

2. All of the answer choices are potential risk factors for the development of pneumonia. Previous utilization of antibiotics can lead to the development of antibiotic resistance, which can make it more difficult to treat pneumonia.

Utilization of ventilator equipment that has been contaminated can introduce bacteria into the lungs, increasing the risk of infection. Decrease in gastric acidity can make it easier for bacteria to travel from the stomach to the lungs. Factors that elevate the risk of aspiration, such as nasogastric or endotracheal intubation, can also increase the risk of pneumonia. Finally, conditions that compromise the lung's host defense mechanisms, such as chronic obstructive pulmonary disease, extremes of age, or upper abdominal surgery, can also increase the risk of infection. Therefore, the correct answer is E. All of the above.

3. The correct answer is E: all of the above.

The predominant pathogens responsible for surgical wound infections are S. aureus, coagulase-negative staphylococci, enteric bacteria, and anaerobic bacteria. These organisms are commonly encountered in surgical wound infections. S. aureus is a major pathogen that causes a wide variety of clinical manifestations, including surgical wound infections. Coagulase-negative staphylococci are also common pathogens of surgical wound infections. Enteric bacteria, such as Escherichia coli and Klebsiella pneumoniae, are also common pathogens of surgical wound infections. Anaerobic bacteria, such as Bacteroides fragilis, are also common pathogens of surgical wound infections.

4. The correct answer is A: Cryptococcal meningitis.

Patients with deficiencies in cellular immunity are at increased risk for infection with Cryptococcus, a fungus that can cause meningitis. Listeria is another fungus that can cause meningitis, but it is less common in patients with cellular immunodeficiency. Bacterial meningitis is the most common type of meningitis, but it is less likely in this case given the patient's HIV infection. Viral meningitis is also less common in this case, and tuberculous meningitis is rare in HIV-infected patients. In conclusion, the most likely diagnosis in this case is Cryptococcal meningitis based on the patient's presentation and physical examination findings. Patients with deficiencies in cellular immunity who exhibit symptoms of meningitis should be evaluated for potential infection with Cryptococcus or Listeria.

5. The answer is C. Both individuals with prolonged neutropenia and individuals with impaired cellular immunity.

Individuals with prolonged neutropenia are more susceptible to developing brain abscesses caused by pathogens such as Aspergillus, Nocardia, or Cryptococcus. This is because neutropenia impairs the body's ability to fight off infection. Individuals with impaired cellular immunity are also more susceptible to developing brain abscesses, especially those caused by Toxoplasma and Epstein-Barr virus (EBV). This is because cellular immunity plays a role in clearing Toxoplasma and EBV from the body. It is important to note that not all individuals with prolonged neutropenia or impaired cellular immunity will develop a brain abscess. However, they are at an increased risk of doing so.

6. The best answer is C.

The recommended approach for managing typhlitis involves the administration of antibiotics targeting the microorganisms present in the bowel, along with surgical intervention if perforation occurs. In this case, the patient has risk factors for typhlitis, including AML and low white blood cell and platelet counts. The CT scan findings are consistent with typhlitis. Therefore, the most appropriate treatment is intravenous antibiotics, bowel rest, and surgical resection if perforation occurs.

7. The best answer is E.

Empirical antifungal treatment has seen a shift in preference towards liposomal formulations of amphotericin B, newer azoles such as voriconazole or posaconazole, and echinocandins like caspofungin, thereby replacing amphotericin B deoxycholate. A. Liposomal amphotericin B is a lipid-based formulation of amphotericin B that is less nephrotoxic than amphotericin B deoxycholate. B. Voriconazole is an azole antifungal agent that is active against a wide range of fungal pathogens, including Candida and Aspergillus species. C. Posaconazole is another azole antifungal agent that is similar to voriconazole in terms of its spectrum of activity. D. Caspofungin is an echinocandin antifungal agent that is active against Candida and Aspergillus species. E. All of the above pharmaceutical agents have replaced amphotericin B deoxycholate as the preferred choice for empirical antifungal therapy in individuals experiencing febrile neutropenia.

8. The best answer is B.

Fungal infections, specifically those caused by Candida species, are becoming more prevalent in patients undergoing HSCT beyond the initial week, particularly in individuals who are administered broad-spectrum antibiotics. The prevalence of resilient fungi such as Aspergillus and Fusarium is also on the rise, which can be attributed to the escalated utilization of prophylactic fluconazole. In the case of the patient in the question, she is at risk for developing a fungal infection because she has undergone HSCT and is being administered broad-spectrum antibiotics. The most likely type of fungal infection in this patient is Aspergillus, followed by Fusarium.

9. The best answer is A.

Maintenance prophylaxis for the prevention of PCP is advised to be initiated after engraftment and continued for a minimum duration of one year, utilizing TMPSMX at a dosage of 160/800 mg per day. TMPSMX is the most effective agent for preventing PCP and is well-tolerated by most patients. A. TMPSMX is the most effective agent for preventing PCP and is well-tolerated by most patients. The recommended dosage is 160/800 mg per day. B. Dapsone is an alternative agent for preventing PCP. The recommended dosage is 100 mg per day. C. Atovaquone is another alternative agent for preventing PCP. The recommended dosage is 1500 mg per day. D. Pentamidine isethionate is an alternative agent for preventing PCP. The recommended dosage is 300 mg every month by intramuscular injection. E. None of the above is the not the correct answer.

10. The best answer is E.

Respiratory viral infections, including respiratory syncytial virus, parainfluenza virus, metapneumovirus, influenza virus, and adenovirus, have the potential to manifest following hematopoietic stem cell transplantation (HSCT). These infections can be serious, especially in patients who are immunocompromised. A. Respiratory syncytial virus (RSV) is a common respiratory virus that can cause serious infections in young children and adults with weakened immune systems. B. Parainfluenza virus is a common respiratory virus that can cause serious infections in young children and adults with weakened immune systems. C. Metapneumovirus is a respiratory virus that is becoming increasingly common. It can cause serious infections in young children and adults with weakened immune systems. D. Influenza virus is a common respiratory virus that can cause serious infections in people of all ages, but is especially dangerous for young children, the elderly, and people with weakened immune systems. E. All of the above respiratory viruses can cause serious infections in patients who have undergone HSCT. In the case of the patient in the question, she is at risk for developing a respiratory viral infection because she has undergone HSCT and is immunocompromised. The most likely respiratory viral infections in this patient are RSV, parainfluenza virus, metapneumovirus, influenza virus, and adenovirus.

11. The best answer is A.

It is recommended to administer TMP-SMX prophylaxis for a duration of 4-6 months after kidney transplantation, as this practice has been shown to reduce the occurrence of infections during the early and middle stages post-surgery. This is particularly effective in preventing urinary tract infections that may arise due to anatomical changes resulting from the transplantation procedure. A. TMP-SMX is a combination antibiotic that is effective against a wide range of bacteria, including those that can cause urinary tract infections. B. Acyclovir is an antiviral medication that is used to prevent and treat infections caused by the herpes virus. C. Fluconazole is an antifungal medication that is used to prevent and treat infections caused by fungi. D. Pentamidine is an antiprotozoal medication that is used to prevent and treat infections caused by Pneumocystis jirovecii. E. None of the above medications is recommended for the initial 4-6 months after kidney transplantation. In the case of the patient in the question, he is at risk for developing urinary tract infections because he has undergone kidney transplantation and is immunocompromised. The most likely infection in this patient is a urinary tract infection, and TMP-SMX is the most effective medication for preventing and treating this type of infection.

12. The best answer is C.

The most prevalent causative agents of infection in PBP are enteric gram-negative bacilli, such as Escherichia coli, as well as gram-positive organisms, including streptococci, enterococci, and pneumococci. In this patient, the causative agent is Streptococcus pneumoniae, which is a gram-positive organism.

13. The best answer is D. The diagnostic methods for determining PBP in this patient are: Examination of peritoneal fluid for more than 250 polymorphonuclear leukocytes (PMNs) per microliter. Introduction of a 10-mL quantity of peritoneal fluid directly into blood culture bottles. Performance of blood cultures. The presence of more than 250 PMNs per microliter in peritoneal fluid is a sensitive but not specific finding for PBP. The introduction of a 10-mL quantity of peritoneal fluid directly into blood culture bottles can enhance the cultural yield of bacteria. Blood cultures are recommended due to the high prevalence of bacteremia in patients with PBP.

14. The best answer is C.

Clostridium perfringens is a bacterium that is acquired through the consumption of heat-resistant spores present in insufficiently cooked meat, poultry, or legumes. When these spores are ingested, they germinate in the gastrointestinal tract and produce toxins that cause diarrhea and abdominal cramps. The incubation period typically spans from 8 to 14 hours, and symptoms typically resolve within 24 hours. Vomiting or fever are not commonly observed symptoms. A. Salmonella is a bacterium that can also cause foodborne illness. However, the incubation period for salmonella is typically 12 to 72 hours, and symptoms can include diarrhea, fever, and abdominal cramps. B. Campylobacter is another bacterium that can cause foodborne illness. The incubation period for campylobacter is typically 2 to 5 days, and symptoms can include diarrhea, fever, and abdominal cramps. C. Clostridium perfringens is the most likely cause of the patient's illness in this case because the symptoms are consistent with those caused by this bacterium. D. Escherichia coli is a bacterium that can also cause foodborne illness. However, the incubation period for E. coli is typically 1 to 3 days, and symptoms can include diarrhea, fever, and abdominal cramps. E. Norovirus is a virus that can cause foodborne illness. However, the incubation period for norovirus is typically 12 to 48 hours, and symptoms can include vomiting, diarrhea, and abdominal cramps.

15. The best answer is E.

All of the interventions listed above can be employed to reduce the duration and volume of stool in individuals affected by Cholera. Azithromycin, erythromycin, tetracycline, and ciprofloxacin are all antibiotics that are effective against the bacterium Vibrio cholerae, which causes Cholera. These antibiotics can help to reduce the number of bacteria in the intestines, which can help to reduce the amount of diarrhea. A. Azithromycin (administered as a single 1-g dose) is an antibiotic that is effective against Vibrio cholerae. It can be administered as a single dose, which is convenient for patients. B. Erythromycin (250 mg orally four times daily for a duration of three days) is another antibiotic that is effective against Vibrio cholerae. It is a slightly older antibiotic than azithromycin, but it is still effective. C. Tetracycline (500 mg orally four times daily for a duration of three days) is a third antibiotic that is effective against Vibrio cholerae. It is also an older antibiotic, but it is still effective. D. Ciprofloxacin (500 mg orally twice daily for a duration of three days) is a newer antibiotic that is effective against Vibrio cholerae. It is often used as a first-line treatment for Cholera because it is effective and has few side effects. E. All of the above can be employed to reduce the duration and volume of stool in individuals affected by Cholera.

16. The best answer is E.

All of the diagnostic methods listed above can be used to diagnose Cryptosporidiosis in this patient. Fecal examination for oocysts is the most sensitive diagnostic method, but it is also the most technically demanding. Modified acid-fast staining, direct immunofluorescent techniques, and enzyme immunoassays (EIAs) are all less sensitive than fecal examination for oocysts, but they are more rapid and easier to perform. A. Fecal examination for oocysts: This is the most sensitive diagnostic method for Cryptosporidiosis. Oocysts are the infective form of Cryptosporidium, and they are typically 4-5 m in diameter. They can be difficult to see on a routine stool examination, but they can be detected using modified acid-fast staining or direct immunofluorescent techniques. B. Modified acid-fast staining: This is a laboratory technique that can be used to detect Cryptosporidium oocysts in stool samples. The oocysts are stained with a modified acid-fast stain, which makes them more visible under a microscope. C. Direct immunofluorescent techniques: This is another laboratory technique that can be used to detect Cryptosporidium oocysts in stool samples. The oocysts are stained with a fluorescent antibody, which makes them glow under a special microscope. D. Enzyme immunoassays (EIAs): These are rapid and easy-to-use tests that can be used to detect Cryptosporidium antigens in stool samples. EIAs are not as sensitive as fecal examination for oocysts, but they are more convenient and can be performed in a doctor's office or clinic. E. All of the above: All of the diagnostic methods listed above can be used to diagnose Cryptosporidiosis in this patient. The most appropriate diagnostic method will depend on the availability of testing and the clinical presentation of the patient.

17. The best answer is C.

Decreased gastric acidity and compromised intestinal integrity are two factors that can contribute to an increased susceptibility to Salmonella infection. Gastric acidity helps to kill Salmonella bacteria, so decreased gastric acidity can make it more likely that Salmonella bacteria will survive and cause an infection. Compromised intestinal integrity can also make it more likely that Salmonella bacteria will be able to invade the bloodstream and cause a systemic infection.

18. The best answer is E.

All of the potential complications listed above can be associated with Nontyphoidal salmonellosis (NTS). Bacteremia is the most common complication, occurring in about 8% of cases. Hepatosplenic abscesses, meningitis, pneumonia, and osteomyelitis are all fewer common complications, but they can occur in patients with NTS. Reactive arthritis is a rare complication that can occur after Salmonella gastroenteritis, particularly in patients who possess the HLA-B27 histocompatibility antigen.

19. The best answer is B.

Antibiotics are not recommended for the treatment of diarrhea caused by yersiniae. In fact, antibiotics can actually prolong the course of the illness. Supportive measures, such as fluids and electrolytes, are sufficient to treat most cases of yersiniosis. A. Yes: Antibiotics are not recommended for the treatment of diarrhea caused by yersiniae. In fact, antibiotics can actually prolong the course of the illness. Supportive measures, such as fluids and electrolytes, are sufficient to treat most cases of yersiniosis. B. No: Antibiotics are not recommended for the treatment of diarrhea caused by yersiniae. In fact, antibiotics can actually prolong the course of the illness. Supportive measures, such as fluids and electrolytes, are sufficient to treat most cases of yersiniosis. C. Cannot be determined: The answer cannot be determined without more information. For example, if the patient has a severe case of yersiniosis or if they are immunocompromised, antibiotics may be necessary.

20. The best answer is B.

If a patient diagnosed with acute amebic liver abscess exhibits negative serological results, it is recommended to conduct a repeat test after one week if there is a persistent high clinical suspicion. This is because serological tests can be negative in up to 20% of patients with acute amebic liver abscess. A repeat serological test after one week is more likely to be positive if the patient actually has acute amebic liver abscess.

21. The best answer is D.

Clostridioides difficile infection (CDI) is commonly acquired in conjunction with antimicrobial therapy, as nearly all antibiotics pose a potential risk for CDI. This is because antibiotics can disrupt the normal balance of bacteria in the gut, allowing Clostridioides difficile to overgrow. A. Contact with an infected person: This is not a common mode of acquisition for CDI. B. Ingestion of contaminated food or water: This is a possible mode of acquisition for CDI, but it is not as common as acquisition through antimicrobial therapy. C. A break in the skin: This is not a common mode of acquisition for CDI. D. Antimicrobial therapy: This is the most common mode of acquisition for CDI. E. None of the above: This is not a correct answer. CDI can be acquired through any of the modes listed above.

22. The best answer is E.

C. difficile infection has a recurrence rate of approximately 15-30% following treatment. Persistent diarrhea following treatment for C. difficile can be indicative of a recurring infection. In such cases, patients may require further treatment with antibiotics, such as metronidazole or oral vancomycin, as well as modifications to underlying risk factors such as avoiding unnecessary use of antibiotics. It's important to follow the guidance and recommendations of healthcare providers for the management of recurrent C. difficile infections, to minimize the risk of complications associated with the infection.

23. The best answer is A. Neisseria gonorrhoeae and Chlamydia trachomatis are the two most common causes of urethritis in males. Together, they account for about 80% of cases. Mycoplasma genitalium, Ureaplasma urealyticum, Trichomonas vaginalis, and herpes simplex virus (HSV) are fewer common causes of urethritis in males. A. Neisseria gonorrhoeae: This is the most common cause of urethritis in males. It is a bacterium that can be transmitted through sexual contact. B. Chlamydia trachomatis: This is the second most common cause of urethritis in males. It is also a bacterium that can be transmitted through sexual contact. C. Mycoplasma genitalium: This is a less common cause of urethritis in males. It is a bacterium that can be transmitted through sexual contact. D. Ureaplasma urealyticum: This is another less common cause of urethritis in males. It is a bacterium that can be transmitted through sexual contact. E. Trichomonas vaginalis: This is a protozoan parasite that can cause urethritis in both males and females. It is transmitted through sexual contact.

24. The best answer is C.

Both trichomoniasis and bacterial vaginosis (BV) can present with vaginal discharge and odor. Trichomoniasis is distinguished by vulvar irritation and a copious white or yellow homogeneous vaginal discharge with a pH level that is typically equal to or greater than 5. Bacterial vaginosis (BV) is distinguished by the presence of an unpleasant odor in the vaginal region, accompanied by a mild to moderate elevation in the amount of white or gray homogeneous discharge that evenly covers the walls of the vagina. This discharge typically exhibits a pH level exceeding 4.5.

25. The best answer is B.

Metronidazole, administered orally at a dosage of 500 milligrams twice daily for duration of 7 days, has been demonstrated as an efficacious therapeutic intervention for trichomoniasis. A. Metronidazole, administered orally at a dosage of 2 grams once: This is an effective treatment for trichomoniasis, but it is not the most efficacious treatment. B. Metronidazole, administered orally at a dosage of 500 milligrams twice daily for duration of 7 days: This is the most efficacious treatment for trichomoniasis. C. Secnidazole, administered orally at a dosage of 2 grams once: Secnidazole is another effective treatment for trichomoniasis, but it is not as efficacious as metronidazole. D. Tinidazole, administered orally at a dosage of 2 grams once: Tinidazole is another effective treatment for trichomoniasis, but it is not as efficacious as metronidazole. E. None of the above: None of the other answer choices are effective treatments for trichomoniasis.

26. The best answer is D.

It is recommended to collect vaginal or endocervical swab specimens for nucleic acid amplification tests (NAATs) targeting Neisseria gonorrhoene and C. trachomatis. These are the two most common causes of PID. A. Vaginal swab: This is a good specimen for NAATs targeting Neisseria gonorrhoene and C. trachomatis. B. Endocervical swab: This is also a good specimen for NAATs targeting Neisseria gonorrhoene and C. trachomatis. C. Cervical swab: This is not a good specimen for NAATs targeting Neisseria gonorrhoene and C. trachomatis. D. Both A. and B.: Both vaginal and endocervical swab specimens are good for NAATs targeting Neisseria gonorrhoene and C. trachomatis. E. None of the above: None of the other answer choices are good specimens for NAATs targeting Neisseria gonorrhoene and C. trachomatis.

27. The best answer is A.

Treponemal tests are used to validate the outcomes obtained from lipoidal tests. Lipoidal tests are used to screen for syphilis, but they can sometimes produce false-positive results. Treponemal tests can be used to confirm a positive lipoidal test result. Treponemal tests are not used to screen for syphilis because they can produce a significant number of false-positive results. False-positive results can occur in people who have never been infected with syphilis. Treponemal tests can also produce positive results for several years after successful treatment for syphilis. Therefore, treponemal tests are not recommended for screening purposes. They are most useful for confirming positive lipoidal test results and for monitoring the effectiveness of treatment for syphilis. 28. The best answer is C. The recommended course of treatment for patients with confirmed penicillin allergy who are diagnosed with primary, secondary, or early latent syphilis is doxycycline 100 mg orally twice daily for two weeks. Benzathine penicillin G is the preferred treatment for syphilis, but it is not recommended for patients with a confirmed penicillin allergy. Ceftriaxone is an alternative treatment for penicillin-allergic patients, but it is not as effective as doxycycline. Tetracycline hydrochloride is another alternative treatment for penicillin-allergic patients, but it is not as effective as doxycycline. If the patient has an abnormal cerebrospinal fluid (CSF) analysis, then it is advisable to consider the possibility of neurosyphilis and initiate appropriate treatment. This may include intravenous penicillin G or ceftriaxone.

29. The best answer is D.

All of the above are recommended therapeutic approaches for initial occurrences of genital infections caused by the herpes simplex virus (HSV). Oral acyclovir at a dosage of 400 mg three times daily, valacyclovir at a dosage of 1 g twice daily, and famciclovir at a dosage of 250 mg twice daily have all been demonstrated to be efficacious in the treatment of initial episodes of genital infections caused by HSV. These treatments are also well-tolerated and have few side effects.

30. The best answer is B.

Chancroid increases the vulnerability to HIV transmission by providing a portal of entry for the virus. The open sores caused by chancroid can allow HIV to enter the bloodstream more easily during sexual intercourse. Chancroid is a sexually transmitted infection (STI) that is caused by the bacterium Haemophilus ducreyi. It can cause painful genital ulcers, as well as fever, swollen lymph nodes, and pain in the rectum.

31. The best answer is E.

The main therapeutic approach for necrotizing fasciitis caused by group A streptococcus involves the administration of both Clindamycin and penicillin G. Surgery is often necessary to remove the dead tissue and to prevent the spread of infection. Supportive care may include fluids, electrolytes, pain medication, and respiratory support. Necrotizing fasciitis is a serious bacterial infection that can rapidly destroy the skin, fat, and muscle tissue. It is caused by a variety of bacteria, but group A streptococcus is the most common cause. Early diagnosis and treatment are essential for preventing death from necrotizing fasciitis. The treatment typically involves the administration of antibiotics, surgery, and supportive care. Clindamycin and penicillin G are both effective antibiotics against group A streptococcus. They are usually given together to provide a broad spectrum of coverage and to prevent the development of antibiotic resistance. With early diagnosis and treatment, the mortality rate for necrotizing fasciitis is about 20%. However, the mortality rate can be as high as 80% if the infection is not diagnosed and treated early.

32. The best answer is D.

All of the above are diagnostic methods employed for the identification of necrotizing fasciitis. Necrotizing fasciitis is a serious bacterial infection that can rapidly destroy the skin, fat, and muscle tissue. It is caused by a variety of bacteria, but the most common causes are group A streptococcus and clostridium species. The diagnosis of necrotizing fasciitis is often made based on the patient's clinical presentation. Patients typically present with fever, pain, and swelling at the site of infection. The skin may appear red and mottled, and there may be blisters or bullae. In some cases, gas may be seen within the tissues on imaging studies. This is more common with clostridial infections, but it can also be seen with group A streptococcus infections. Significantly heightened levels of serum CPK may also be seen in cases of necrotizing fasciitis. This is due to the damage to muscle tissue that can occur with this infection.

33. The correct answer is A.

Disseminated gonococcal infection. DGI is a sexually transmitted infection that can spread to the bloodstream and cause a variety of symptoms, including fever, chills, rash, and arthritis. The arthritis in DGI is typically migratory, meaning that it moves from joint to joint. Cultures of synovial fluid from affected joints are usually negative for gonococci, but the diagnosis can be confirmed by blood cultures. The other answer choices are less likely in this case. Reactive arthritis is a condition that can occur after a bacterial infection, such as an STI, but it does not typically cause fever or rash. Lyme disease can cause a rash, but it is usually not accompanied by fever or arthritis. Reiter syndrome is a condition that is characterized by arthritis, conjunctivitis, and urethritis, but it is not typically associated with a rash. Septic arthritis is a serious infection of the joint, but it is usually caused by bacteria other than gonococci.

34. The correct answer is A.

Nafcillin and oxacillin are both beta-lactam antibiotics that are highly effective against Methicillin-susceptible Staphylococcus aureus. They are typically given intravenously for the first 2-4 weeks of treatment, followed by oral antibiotics for an additional 4-6 weeks. Rifampin and levofloxacin are both antibiotics that have activity against Methicillin-susceptible Staphylococcus aureus. However, they are not typically used as first-line agents because they are more expensive and have more side effects than beta-lactam antibiotics. In this case, the patient does not have any implants, so there is no need to use a combination of antibiotics to prevent the development of antibiotic resistance. Therefore, the optimal antibiotic treatment for this patient is intravenous nafcillin 2 grams every 6 hours.

35. The correct answer is A.

Streptococcus pneumoniae is the most common bacterial pathogen associated with community-acquired pneumonia, accounting for approximately 50% of cases. Haemophilus influenzae is the second most common bacterial pathogen, accounting for approximately 20% of cases. Staphylococcus aureus is the third most common bacterial pathogen, accounting for approximately 10% of cases. Klebsiella pneumoniae and Pseudomonas aeruginosa are less common bacterial pathogens, accounting for approximately 5% of cases each.

36. To calculate the CURB-65 score, you should first assign 1 point for each of the following criteria: Confusion

- Urea nitrogen greater than 7 mmol/L (19 mg/dL)
- Respiratory rate of 30 breaths per minute or greater
- Blood pressure less than 90 mmHg systolic or diastolic blood pressure 60 mmHg or less
- Age 65 or older.

In this case, the patient has a score of 1 because he meets the criteria for respiratory rate greater than 30 breaths per minute. Patients with a CURB-65 score of 0 may be eligible for home-based treatment, while patients with a score of 1 or 2 should be admitted to a hospital. Patients with a score of 3 may necessitate intensive care unit (ICU) intervention. Therefore, the correct answer is B.

37. The correct answer is B.

Azithromycin is a macrolide antibiotic that is effective against a wide range of bacteria, including the most likely pathogens associated with community-acquired pneumonia in this patient. It is also a once-daily medication, which is convenient for patients. The other answer choices are also effective antibiotics for community-acquired pneumonia, but they are not as preferred in this case because they are not as effective against the most likely pathogens, or they are not as convenient for patients (e.g., amoxicillin requires three daily doses).

38. The correct answer is C.

Clinical improvement, if observed, typically becomes apparent within a span of 48 to 72 hours following the commencement of antimicrobial therapy for VAP. The other answer choices are incorrect because they are either too short or too long. For example, clinical improvement is unlikely to be observed within 24 hours of starting antimicrobial therapy, and it is also unlikely to take 96 hours or more for clinical improvement to be observed.

39. The correct answer is A.

Clindamycin is a broad-spectrum antibiotic that is effective against the most likely pathogens associated with primary lung abscesses, including Streptococcus pneumoniae, Haemophilus influenzae, and Staphylococcus aureus. It is also relatively inexpensive and well-tolerated by patients. The other answer choices are also effective antibiotics for primary lung abscesses, but they are not as preferred in this case because they are either more expensive, less well-tolerated, or not as effective against the most likely pathogens.

40. The correct answer is A.

MDR-TB is a strain of tuberculosis that exhibits resistance to at least two key drugs, namely isoniazid and rifampin. It is a serious condition that can be difficult to treat. The other answer choices are incorrect. XDR-TB is a rare form of MDR-TB that is resistant to even more drugs. LTBI is an infection with tuberculosis bacteria that does not cause symptoms. Active TB is an infection with tuberculosis bacteria that is causing symptoms. Nontuberculous mycobacterial infections are caused by bacteria that are not tuberculosis.

41. The correct answer is D.

Pleural biopsy is the most likely diagnostic test for tuberculosis in this patient. Direct smears, cultures, and PCR assays of pleural fluid have reduced sensitivity in the diagnosis of tuberculosis, with positive rates of up to 50%, 30%, and 25%, respectively. Pleural biopsy, on the other hand, has a positive rate of up to 80% for cultures and 75% for PCR assays. The other answer choices are incorrect. Direct smears, cultures, and PCR assays of pleural fluid are not as sensitive as pleural biopsy for the diagnosis of tuberculosis. The Quantiferon Gold test is a blood test that can be used to diagnose latent tuberculosis infection, but it is not as sensitive as pleural biopsy for the diagnosis of active tuberculosis.

42. The correct answer is A.

Miliary tuberculosis is caused by the hematogenous spread of Mycobacterium tuberculosis from a primary pulmonary focus or from a site of extrapulmonary tuberculosis. The bacilli are disseminated through the bloodstream and lodge in various organs, where they form small granulomas. The other answer choices are incorrect. Direct extension from a contiguous focus of infection is a less common mode of spread of tuberculosis. Inhalation of bacilli is the most common mode of transmission of tuberculosis, but it does not typically lead to miliary tuberculosis. Iatrogenic miliary tuberculosis can occur as a complication of tuberculosis treatment, but it is rare.

43. The correct answer is A.

Immune reconstitution inflammatory syndrome (IRIS) is a phenomenon that can manifest in HIV patients with tuberculosis (TB) approximately 1 to 3 months after the commencement of antiretroviral therapy. IRIS is caused by the immune system's exaggerated response to tuberculosis bacteria that were previously suppressed by HIV. This can lead to worsening of the symptoms and signs of tuberculosis. The other answer choices are incorrect. Active tuberculosis is a condition in which tuberculosis bacteria are actively replicating and causing symptoms. Latent tuberculosis infection is a condition in which tuberculosis bacteria are present in the body but are not actively replicating and are not causing symptoms. Drug-resistant tuberculosis is a condition in which tuberculosis bacteria are resistant to one or more anti-tuberculosis drugs. Exacerbation of HIV is a worsening of HIV symptoms that can occur due to a number of factors, including infection with tuberculosis.

44. The correct answer is A.

Ethambutol is considered to be the least efficacious among the primary therapeutic agents used in the treatment of tuberculosis. It is often used in combination with other drugs to prevent the development of drug resistance and enhance treatment effectiveness. However, Ethambutol's efficacy can be limited due to various factors, including its minimal activity against dormant bacterial populations and the relatively easy emergence of bacterial strains with resistance to Ethambutol. The other answer choices are incorrect. Isoniazid, rifampin, pyrazinamide, and streptomycin are all considered to be more efficacious initial treatment options for tuberculosis than ethambutol.

45. The correct answer is A.

Immunohistologic examination of a cutaneous biopsy sample obtained from a rash lesion is the only diagnostic test that is considered beneficial for the identification of Rocky Mountain spotted fever (RMSF) during the acute phase of illness. It has a sensitivity of 70% and a specificity of 100%. The other answer choices are incorrect. ELISA and PCR assays for RMSF are not as sensitive as immunohistologic examination of a cutaneous biopsy sample. Blood culture is not a sensitive test for RMSF, and it can take several days to obtain results. Chest X-ray is not a sensitive test for RMSF, and it is not typically used to diagnose RMSF.

46. The correct answer is A.

Severe falciparum malaria is a life-threatening condition that is caused by the Plasmodium falciparum parasite. It is characterized by one or more of the following clinical manifestations: compromised consciousness or coma, severe normocytic anemia, renal dysfunction, pulmonary edema, acute respiratory distress syndrome (ARDS), circulatory shock, disseminated intravascular coagulation (DIC), spontaneous hemorrhaging, acidosis, hemoglobinuria, jaundice, recurrent generalized convulsions, and a parasitemia level exceeding 5%. The other answer choices are incorrect. Acute respiratory distress syndrome (ARDS) disseminated intravascular coagulation (DIC), spontaneous hemorrhaging, and acute kidney injury are all possible complications of severe falciparum malaria, but they are not the defining features of the disease.

47. The correct answer is B.

The patient's total plasma quinidine level is above the therapeutic range and his QTc interval is prolonged. These are both indications for decelerating and temporarily halting the quinidine infusion. The other answer choices are incorrect. Decreasing the quinidine dose would be appropriate if the patient's QTc interval was only slightly prolonged. Continuing the quinidine infusion without change would be inappropriate as it could lead to further prolongation of the QTc interval and an increased risk of arrhythmias. Obtaining an ECG and a serum potassium level would be helpful, but they would not be the next step in management.

48. The correct answer is A.

The patient's CD4+ T cell count is below 200/L, which is the diagnostic criteria for AIDS. He also has symptoms that are consistent with an opportunistic infection, which is a type of infection that only occurs in people with severely weakened immune systems. The other answer choices are incorrect. HIV infection is the presence of the HIV virus in the body, but it does not necessarily mean that the person has AIDS. Opportunistic infections can occur in people with HIV infection, but they do not automatically mean that the person has AIDS. Tuberculosis and Pneumocystis jirovecii pneumonia are both opportunistic infections, but they are not the only opportunistic infections that can occur in people with AIDS.

49. The correct answer is A.

Kaposi's sarcoma is a type of cancer that is commonly associated with HIV infection. It is characterized by the formation of purplish or reddish skin lesions. The lesions can occur anywhere on the body, but they are most common on the feet, hands, trunk, and face. The other answer choices are incorrect. Lymphoma is a type of cancer that can occur in people with HIV infection, but it is not as common as Kaposi's sarcoma. Multicentric Castleman's disease is a rare disorder that is characterized by the growth of abnormal lymph nodes. Basal cell carcinoma and squamous cell carcinoma are types of skin cancer that can occur in people with HIV infection, but they are not as common as Kaposi's sarcoma.

50. The correct answer is A.

The administration of primary prophylaxis is strongly recommended for the prevention of Pneumocystis jiroveci pneumonia in cases where the count of CD4+ T cells decreases to below 200 cells/L. The other answer choices are incorrect. History of Pneumocystis jiroveci pneumonia, HIV infection, and age greater than 65 years are all risk factors for Pneumocystis jiroveci pneumonia, but they are not indications for primary prophylaxis.

51. The correct answer is D.

Sepsis is a systemic inflammatory response syndrome that can cause a variety of abnormalities, including ileus, disseminated intravascular coagulation (DIC), and sick euthyroid syndrome. Ileus is a condition in which the bowel stops moving, DIC is a condition in which the blood clots abnormally, and sick euthyroid syndrome is a condition in which the body's metabolism is altered. The other answer choices are incorrect. Respiratory and cardiovascular impairment are the two most common manifestations of sepsis, but they are not the only manifestations.

52. The correct answer is D.

The three distinct care protocols for the early management of sepsis and septic shock are the administration of antibiotics, fluids, and vasopressors. The first protocol, administration of antibiotics, is aimed at targeting the suspected infection and reducing the risk of complications. The second protocol, administration of fluids, is aimed at improving tissue perfusion and oxygen delivery. The third protocol, administration of vasopressors, is aimed at maintaining blood pressure and organ perfusion. All three protocols are essential for the early management of sepsis and septic shock and should be initiated as soon as possible after patient presentation.

53. Answer: (C)

The patient's presentation is most suggestive of DGI. DGI is a rare but serious complication of gonorrhea. It occurs when the bacteria that cause gonorrhea (Neisseria gonorrhoeae) spread through the bloodstream to other parts of the body. The diagnosis of DGI is based on clinical suspicion and laboratory findings. Blood cultures are often negative in patients with DGI, so nucleic acid amplification testing (NAAT) on bodily fluid from multiple sources is the most appropriate next step in management. Serologic testing does not have a role in the diagnosis of DGI. MRI does not show specific findings for DGI. Empiric treatment for DGI should be started if the patient has a high clinical suspicion and NAAT results are not yet available. However, it is best to wait for NAAT results to confirm the diagnosis before starting treatment. In conclusion, the most appropriate next step in management of this patient is to order NAAT on bodily fluid from multiple sources. NAAT is a highly sensitive and specific test for the diagnosis of DGI. Bodily fluids that should be tested for NAAT in patients with suspected DGI include oropharyngeal secretions, rectal secretions, urethral secretions, and synovial fluid. Empiric treatment for DGI typically involves the use of ceftriaxone or cefotaxime. Patients with DGI should be hospitalized for treatment and monitoring.

54. The correct answer is A. Disseminated gonococcal infection.

The clinical presentation of an acute inflammatory monoarthritis on the left ankle, flexor tenosynovial involvement of the second flexor tendon, the pustular eruption on the palms, leukocytosis, and pyuria in a sexually active patient is highly suggestive of disseminated gonococcal infection. Option B (Reactive arthritis) could present with an acute monoarthritis, but it wouldn't account for the pustular rash seen in this patient. Option C (Rheumatoid arthritis) typically presents with symmetrical polyarticular joint involvement and systemic symptoms like fatigue, weight loss, and fever. Option D (Gout) generally affects the big toe joint, and it is less common in young women. It presents with severe pain, redness, and swelling but would not cause a pustular rash or pyuria. Option E (Lyme disease) could cause arthritis, but it typically presents with a "bull's eye" rash (erythema migrans), and the patient would commonly have a history of tick exposure, which isn't mentioned here. Therefore, the patient's symptoms and sexual history, along with the physical exam findings, make disseminated gonococcal infection the most likely diagnosis.

55. The correct answer is B.

Obtain blood cultures and start intravenous vancomycin/ceftriaxone. In this scenario, the patient's presentation and synovial fluid analysis are concerning for septic arthritis, despite his history of gout. Septic arthritis due to most bacterial organisms is associated with high synovial fluid WBC counts, often >50,000 cells/L. Lower cell counts may be observed, and thus the results of the fluid must be interpreted in the clinical context. In this case, a cell count of 49,000 cells/L does not rule out a septic process. Furthermore, a neutrophil percentage >90% is concerning for a septic process. Although Gram stain is often used to identify the causative organism in septic arthritis, it only has a sensitivity of 30% to 50%. Thus, a negative Gram stain does not exclude the diagnosis. Additionally, the presence of crystals in the fluid does not rule out the presence of a concomitant septic process. Given the overall high pretest probability of septic arthritis and the results of the synovial fluid analysis, the next most appropriate step would be to start empiric antibiotics after obtaining blood cultures. Intravenous vancomycin and ceftriaxone would provide broad coverage for the most common organisms that cause septic arthritis, including Staphylococcus aureus (including MRSA), Streptococcus species, and gram-negative rods. If a septic process is excluded based on culture results, then antibiotics can be discontinued, and the patient can be treated for a flare of gouty arthritis.

56. Answer: (A)

The patient's presentation is most suggestive of severe community-acquired pneumonia (CAP). Severe CAP is defined as CAP that requires hospitalization. The patient's respiratory rate of 32 breaths/min, thrombocytopenia, and multilobular infiltrates meet the criteria for severe CAP. The most appropriate next step in management is to admit the patient to the hospital and start intravenous antibiotics. Discharging the patient home with oral antibiotics is not appropriate, as she has severe CAP. Ordering a sputum culture is not necessary before starting antibiotics, as the patient has severe CAP. Ordering a bronchoscopy is not necessary in this patient, as the diagnosis of CAP is clear and she does not have any risk factors for aspiration. Observing the patient in the emergency department and repeating laboratory studies in 2 hours is not appropriate, as the patient has severe CAP and needs to be admitted to the hospital immediately. In conclusion, the most appropriate next step in management of this patient is to admit her to the hospital and start intravenous antibiotics. The choice of intravenous antibiotics for severe CAP should be based on the patient's risk factors for multidrug-resistant organisms. Empiric antibiotic coverage should include a beta-lactam antibiotic, such as ceftriaxone or cefotaxime, and a macrolide antibiotic, such as azithromycin or clarithromycin.

57. Answer: A. Cefepime and vancomycin

The patient's clinical picture is suggestive of hospital-acquired pneumonia. Empiric treatment for this condition depends on various factors, the most important of which is the presence of risk factors for multidrug-resistant pathogens. Having received IV antibiotics within the past 90 days is a significant risk factor, making it necessary to consider multidrug-resistant organisms such as Pseudomonas aeruginosa and Methicillin-Resistant Staphylococcus aureus (MRSA) in the treatment plan. The combination of cefepime (effective against Pseudomonas) and vancomycin (effective against MRSA) is the most suitable empiric treatment option in this case. Other options may not cover these multidrug-resistant organisms effectively, making them less suitable. 58. Answer: B. Procalcitonin Procalcitonin is a biomarker that is upregulated in acute respiratory infections caused by bacterial, but not viral, etiologies. It is often used to help guide the use of antibiotics in patients with community-acquired pneumonia. However, it is not validated in immunocompromised hosts such as this patient, and therefore would not be advisable in this case. The other options listed (C-reactive protein, erythrocyte sedimentation rate, chest X-ray, and complete blood count) can still provide valuable information in an immunocompromised patient with suspected pneumonia.

59. Answer: (C) Oseltamivir 75 mg twice daily for 5 days

Oseltamivir is the first-line antiviral treatment for influenza. It is most effective when started within 48 hours of symptom onset. Oseltamivir can reduce the duration of illness by about one day and the risk of complications such as pneumonia. Amantadine is no longer recommended for the treatment of influenza due to high rates of resistance. Zanamivir is an inhaled antiviral medication that can be used to treat influenza in patients who are unable to take oseltamivir. However, it is not as effective as oseltamivir and is not recommended for patients with pneumonia. Therefore, the best treatment for this patient's influenza pneumonia is oseltamivir 75 mg twice daily for 5 days. 60. Answer: The correct answer is C. Peripherally inserted central catheter line. This patient is immunosuppressed because of her recent heart transplant, which increases her risk for invasive fungal infections. Other risk factors for fungemia include administration of total parenteral nutrition, hematologic malignancy, solid organ transplant, biologic therapies (including TNF- inhibitors), and IV drug use. In this case, the source was likely her peripherally inserted central catheter line, which should be removed immediately. The Foley catheter is unlikely to be a source of her candidemia. Therefore, the most likely source of her candidemia is the peripherally inserted central catheter line.

61. Correct Answer: B. Total parenteral nutrition

The patient's recent heart transplant has made her immunosuppressed, thereby increasing her risk for invasive fungal infections. Among the risk factors for fungemia are total parenteral nutrition administration, hematologic malignancy, solid organ transplant, biologic therapies (including TNF- inhibitors), and IV drug use. In this case, her peripherally inserted central catheter line, which has been used for total parenteral nutrition administration, is likely the source of her candidemia. While a Foley catheter could theoretically introduce infection, it is less likely to be the source of her candidemia in this context.

62. Answer: (E) All of the above

All of the statements in the answer choices are true. The galactomannan assay is a sensitive test for the diagnosis of invasive aspergillosis, but it is not specific. It can be positive in the setting of infections with other fungi, such as Fusarium spp and Penicillium spp, and it can be falsely positive in the setting of intravenous immunoglobulin (IVIG) and piperacillin-tazobactam. However, it is still a valuable tool for the diagnosis of invasive aspergillosis, especially in patients with hematologic malignancies. The galactomannan assay is a sandwich enzyme immunoassay that detects galactomannan antigen in blood and bronchoalveolar lavage fluid. It is most sensitive in patients with invasive aspergillosis, but it can also be positive in patients with non-invasive aspergillosis and in patients with other fungal infections. The test can also be falsely positive in patients with IVIG administration and in patients receiving piperacillin-tazobactam. Despite its limitations, the galactomannan assay is a valuable tool for the diagnosis of invasive aspergillosis, especially in patients with hematologic malignancies. It is a non-invasive test that can be performed quickly and easily. It can also be used to monitor patients with invasive aspergillosis during treatment.

63. Answer: B. Foley catheter

Explanation: This patient is immunosuppressed due to her recent heart transplant, which puts her at an increased risk for invasive fungal infections. Other risk factors for fungemia include administration of total parenteral nutrition, hematologic malignancy, solid organ transplant, biologic therapies (including TNF- inhibitors), and IV drug use. In this case, the source was likely her peripherally inserted central catheter line, which should be removed immediately. The Foley catheter is unlikely to be a source of her candidemia. Therefore, the most likely source of infection in this patient is her Foley catheter.

64. Answer: (D) A and C.

The most likely cause of yeast in this patient's blood is Candida species. Candida glabrata and Candida krusei can have resistance against azole antifungals, such as fluconazole, so it is important to start empiric antifungal therapy with an echinocandin, such as micafungin. The PICC line should also be removed, as it is a potential source of infection. Once the patient's condition is stable and the Candida species has been identified, the antifungal therapy can be adjusted based on the susceptibility testing results. If the patient has Candida albicans, which is the most common Candida species and has little resistance in the absence of prior exposure to azoles, the patient could be transitioned to fluconazole. However, even if the patient has Candida albicans, it is important to obtain an infectious disease consult, as candidemia in immunocompromised hosts is associated with high mortality. The infectious disease specialist can help to guide the patient's management and ensure that they are receiving the best possible care. Therefore, the best management for this patient is to remove the PICC line and start empiric antifungal therapy with micafungin, and to obtain an infectious disease consult.

65. Answer: (B) Invasive pulmonary aspergillosis

This patient is at high risk for invasive pulmonary aspergillosis due to his prolonged and profound neutropenia and immunosuppression. He has a history of stem cell transplant and has been on high-dose steroids. His positive serum galactomannan and CT findings are also highly suggestive of aspergillosis. Streptococcus pneumoniae is a common cause of pneumonia, but it is less likely in this patient due to his immunosuppression. Pneumocystis jirovecii pneumonia is another common cause of pneumonia in immunosuppressed patients, but it is less likely in this patient due to his negative serum galactomannan. Viral pneumonia is also a possibility, but it is difficult to distinguish from aspergillosis on clinical grounds alone. Therefore, the most likely diagnosis in this patient is invasive pulmonary aspergillosis. Invasive pulmonary aspergillosis is a serious fungal infection that can be fatal in immunosuppressed patients. It is typically caused by the fungus Aspergillus fumigatus. The most common symptoms are fever, cough, and shortness of breath. Chest X-ray may show a pulmonary infiltrate. Serum galactomannan is a sensitive but not specific test for invasive aspergillosis. A positive test result should be interpreted in the context of the patient's clinical presentation and other risk factors. Treatment for invasive pulmonary aspergillosis typically involves antifungal medications such as voriconazole or micafungin. In some cases, surgery may be necessary to remove infected tissue.

66. Answer: B. Acute uncomplicated cystitis

This patient most likely has acute uncomplicated cystitis, given her symptoms are confined to the bladder without evidence of upper tract involvement or systemic signs. It's important to note that a history of nephrolithiasis, poorly controlled diabetes, HIV, urinary strictures with stents, and immunocompromised patients are not automatically considered complicated UTIs. However, there should be a lower threshold to treat these individuals as complicated infections. The answer is not A (Complicated UTI) because there are no symptoms or signs suggesting upper urinary tract involvement or systemic signs. Also, her past history of nephrolithiasis alone doesn't qualify the infection as complicated. The answer is not C (Kidney stone) because the patient does not present with symptoms typical of a kidney stone such as flank pain or hematuria. The answer is not D (Interstitial cystitis) because this condition typically presents with chronic symptoms. Finally, the answer is not E (Bladder cancer) because the patient does not present with hematuria or risk factors for bladder cancer such as smoking or exposure to certain industrial chemicals.

67. Answer: (A) Complicated UTI

Individuals with renal transplants are considered to have complicated UTIs, regardless of whether the infection extends beyond the bladder. This is because they are at increased risk for complications from UTIs, such as sepsis and graft rejection. Uncomplicated UTIs are infections of the lower urinary tract in otherwise healthy individuals. Asymptomatic bacteriuria is the presence of bacteria in the urine without any symptoms. Pyelonephritis is an infection of the kidneys. Urosepsis is a systemic infection caused by bacteria from the urinary tract. Therefore, the best classification for this patient's UTI is complicated UTI. Complicated UTIs are typically treated with longer courses of antibiotics than uncomplicated UTIs. Antibiotics are also chosen based on the patient's risk factors and the results of urine culture and susceptibility testing. Patients with complicated UTIs should be closely monitored for complications. If the patient develops signs or symptoms of sepsis, such as fever, chills, hypotension, or confusion, they should be hospitalized immediately.

68. Answer: C. Urinalysis, urine culture, and CBC

The patient's symptoms are suggestive of a urinary tract infection (UTI). The next best step in the management is to confirm the diagnosis with a urinalysis and urine culture, and also to perform a CBC to assess for any systemic signs of infection. Pyuria on urinalysis would provide further evidence of a UTI. CT abdomen and pelvis (option B) is not necessary in this patient at this time as she is not severely ill, her symptoms have not persisted despite antibiotics (she hasn't started any yet), and there is no suspicion for obstruction from stones, renal abscess, or recurrent symptoms within a few weeks of treatment. Option A (test for N. gonorrhoeae and C. trachomatis) could be considered in sexually active patients with UTI symptoms and sterile pyuria, but this patient's urinalysis results are not yet known. Option D (start empiric antibiotics without further workup) is not ideal because it's important to confirm the diagnosis and obtain a urine culture before initiating antibiotics to guide therapy. MRI abdomen and pelvis (option E) is not typically necessary in the initial workup of uncomplicated UTI.

69. Answer: B. Diabetic foot infection

Explanation: This patient's presentation is consistent with a diabetic foot infection. Risk factors for diabetic foot infections include peripheral neuropathy (which can lead to decreased awareness of injury), peripheral vascular disease (which can impair necessary blood flow for healing), and poor glycemic control (which can impair neutrophil function). If the patient had chronic osteomyelitis (option C), there would likely be findings on the foot radiograph, which can typically demonstrate abnormalities by 2 weeks after infection. In this case, the foot radiograph does not show any abnormalities, making chronic osteomyelitis less likely. Acute gouty arthritis (option A), peripheral vascular disease (option D), and cellulitis (option E) are less likely given the patient's history of diabetes with peripheral neuropathy and the absence of other typical features of these conditions.

70. Answer: (E) All of the above

All of the clinical findings listed in the answer choices are supportive of a diagnosis of osteomyelitis. Probing to bone or grossly visible bone is a sign that the infection has extended to the bone. Ulcers that are larger than 2 cm and have been present for more than 1 to 2 weeks are more likely to be infected. An ESR greater than 70 mm/h is a sign of inflammation, which could be due to osteomyelitis. MRI is the most sensitive imaging study to detect osteomyelitis, but it is not always necessary. If the patient has a high clinical suspicion of osteomyelitis and a negative plain radiograph, MRI can be ordered to confirm the diagnosis. Therefore, the best answer is (E) All of the above. Osteomyelitis is a serious infection of the bone. It can be caused by bacteria, fungi, or viruses. The most common symptoms of osteomyelitis are pain, swelling, and redness over the affected area. The patient may also have fever, chills, and fatigue. Osteomyelitis is often diagnosed based on a combination of clinical findings and imaging studies. Plain radiographs may show signs of osteomyelitis, such as bone destruction or periosteal elevation. However, plain radiographs can be negative in the early stages of osteomyelitis. If the plain radiograph is negative but the patient has a high clinical suspicion of osteomyelitis, MRI can be ordered to confirm the diagnosis. MRI is the most sensitive imaging study to detect osteomyelitis. It can show signs of infection, such as bone marrow edema and abscesses. Osteomyelitis is treated with antibiotics. The type of antibiotic and the duration of treatment will depend on the type of infection and the patient's overall health. In some cases, surgery may be necessary to remove infected tissue or to drain an abscess.

71. Answer: E. Vancomycin, cefepime, and metronidazole

Explanation: The patient's diabetic foot infection should be treated with antibiotics that target gram-positive organisms (like vancomycin), gram-negative bacilli (like cefepime), and anaerobic organisms (like metronidazole). Pseudomonas aeruginosa is a common pathogen in diabetic foot infections, and ertapenem would not be an appropriate agent to use for this reason. The recommended antibiotic regimen in this case would therefore be a combination of vancomycin, cefepime, and metronidazole (option E). Other treatments for this patient's condition would include limb elevation, non-weight-bearing status, wound care, tight glycemic control, and potentially surgical consultation for debridement and revascularization.

72. Answer: (B) Epidural abscess

The patient's clinical presentation is most suggestive of an epidural abscess. Epidural abscesses are rare but serious infections of the space between the spinal cord and the dura mater. They can be caused by bacteria, fungi, or viruses. The most common symptoms of epidural abscesses are back pain, fever, and neurologic deficits. Spinal stenosis is a narrowing of the spinal canal that can cause back pain, leg pain, and numbness and tingling in the legs. Lumbar radiculopathy is inflammation of a nerve root in the lumbar spine. Degenerative disc disease is a condition in which the discs between the vertebrae in the spine degenerate. Osteoarthritis is a degenerative joint disease that can affect the joints of the spine. All of these conditions can cause back pain, but they are less likely than an epidural abscess to cause fever and neurologic deficits. In addition, the patient's history of fever and the localization of his back pain to the lumbar spine are both risk factors for epidural abscess. Therefore, the most likely diagnosis is epidural abscess. Epidural abscesses are a medical emergency. Early diagnosis and treatment are essential to prevent neurologic complications. The diagnosis of epidural abscess is typically made based on a combination of clinical findings and imaging studies. MRI is the most sensitive imaging study for detecting epidural abscesses. Treatment for epidural abscesses typically involves antibiotics and surgery. The type of antibiotic and the duration of treatment will depend on the type of infection and the patient's overall health. Surgery is necessary to drain the abscess and relieve pressure on the spinal cord. The prognosis for epidural abscesses is generally good with early diagnosis and treatment. However, patients who develop neurologic complications may have long-term disability.

73. Answer: (A) Necrotizing fasciitis

The patient's clinical presentation is most suggestive of necrotizing fasciitis. Necrotizing fasciitis is a rare but serious infection of the skin and soft tissues. It is caused by bacteria that spread quickly and destroy the fascia, the layer of tissue that separates the muscles from the skin. The most common symptoms of necrotizing fasciitis are severe pain, swelling, and redness in the affected area. The skin may also be discolored and may have blisters. In some cases, there may be crepitus, which is the sound of gas under the skin. Necrotizing fasciitis is a medical emergency. Early diagnosis and treatment are essential to prevent death and disability. The diagnosis of necrotizing fasciitis is typically made based on a combination of clinical findings and imaging studies. MRI is the most sensitive imaging study for detecting necrotizing fasciitis. Treatment for necrotizing fasciitis typically involves antibiotics and surgery. The type of antibiotic and the duration of treatment will depend on the type of infection and the patient's overall health. Surgery is necessary to remove infected tissue and relieve pressure on the muscles. The patient's history of water exposure suggests that he may have been exposed to Aeromonas or Pseudomonas species. These bacteria are less common causes of necrotizing fasciitis than group A streptococcus, but they should be considered in patients with water exposure. Therefore, the most likely diagnosis is necrotizing fasciitis. Necrotizing fasciitis has a high mortality rate, but it is treatable with early diagnosis and aggressive treatment. The prognosis is better for patients who are diagnosed and treated early. Patients with necrotizing fasciitis are typically admitted to the hospital and treated in the intensive care unit. They are given broad-spectrum antibiotics to cover a wide range of bacteria. Surgery is typically performed to remove infected tissue and relieve pressure on the muscles. Patients with necrotizing fasciitis may require multiple surgeries to remove all of the infected tissue. They may also require skin grafts to cover the areas where the infected tissue has been removed. The prognosis for patients with necrotizing fasciitis depends on the severity of the infection and the patient's overall health. Patients who are diagnosed and treated early have a better prognosis.

74. Answer: E. Ramsay Hunt Syndrome

This patient's symptoms are indicative of Ramsay Hunt Syndrome, otherwise known as herpes zoster oticus. This condition is caused by a reactivation of the varicella zoster virus within the eighth cranial nerve. It typically presents with ipsilateral facial paralysis, hearing abnormalities (including ear pain, decreased hearing, and tinnitus), and vesicles within the auditory canal. The patient may also experience changes in taste perception, tongue lesions, and lacrimation. Given the combination of symptoms presented in the question, Ramsay Hunt Syndrome (option E) is the most likely diagnosis.

75. Answer: E. Viral PCR for varicella zoster virus

Explanation: Viral PCR yields the highest sensitivity for diagnosing varicella zoster virus reactivation, making it the best option in this situation (option E). Although direct fluorescent antigen testing from scrapings of an active vesicular lesion is the second-best diagnostic study, it is not as sensitive as viral PCR. Isolating the virus via culture (option D) can take up to a week for results and yields only 50% to 75% compared with PCR-positive samples, making it less optimal. Varicella zoster virus IgG (option B) would not be useful in diagnosing active infection in this patient. Therefore, the answer is E. Viral PCR for varicella zoster virus.

76. Answer: (D) Varicella zoster encephalitis

The patient's clinical presentation is most suggestive of varicella zoster encephalitis. Varicella zoster encephalitis is a rare but serious complication of varicella-zoster virus (VZV) infection. VZV is the virus that causes chickenpox and shingles. The most common symptoms of varicella zoster encephalitis are fever, headache, confusion, and seizures. The patient may also have other neurologic symptoms, such as ataxia, weakness, and paralysis. The diagnosis of varicella zoster encephalitis is typically made based on a combination of clinical findings, CSF findings, and PCR testing of the CSF for VZV. In this patient, the CSF findings are consistent with viral encephalitis. The negative CSF PCR for HSV and enterovirus suggests that VZV is the most likely cause of the encephalitis. The patient's rash is also consistent with VZV infection. However, it is important to note that the rash may be absent or resolved in patients with varicella zoster encephalitis. Therefore, the most likely diagnosis is varicella zoster encephalitis. Varicella zoster encephalitis is treated with antiviral medications, such as acyclovir or famciclovir. Early treatment is important to improve the outcome. The prognosis for varicella zoster encephalitis is variable. Some patients make a full recovery, while others may have long-term neurologic sequelae.

77. Answer: A. Bacterial meningitis

Explanation: Given the elevated WBC count, low glucose, and high total protein, the CSF studies suggest bacterial, fungal, or tuberculous etiologies. However, since the WBC count is particularly high and predominantly polymorphonuclear cells, a bacterial meningitis would be most likely (option A). After a recent neurosurgical procedure, this patient is at risk for Staphylococcus aureus, coagulase-negative staphylococci, and gram-negative bacilli, which are common pathogens in bacterial meningitis. Although fungal and tuberculous meningitis (options B and C) could present with similar CSF findings, the high WBC count and patient's recent surgical history make bacterial meningitis more likely. Viral meningitis (option D) typically presents with a lymphocytic predominance and normal or slightly reduced glucose in the CSF, making it a less likely diagnosis. Non-infectious inflammatory diseases (option E) also do not align with the patient's symptomatology and CSF findings. Therefore, the answer is A. Bacterial meningitis.

78. Answer: (E) All of the above

This patient's presentation is highly suggestive of infectious endocarditis. She has a history of intravenous drug use, which is a major risk factor for infectious endocarditis. She also has a murmur, which could be due to valvular damage from infectious endocarditis. The palmar Janeway lesions and possible septic pulmonary emboli on chest X-ray are also suggestive of infectious endocarditis. The initial management of infectious endocarditis includes blood cultures and empiric antibiotics with coverage for MRSA. At least two sets of blood cultures should be drawn with two bottles per set. After blood cultures are drawn, the patient should be started on empiric broad-spectrum antibiotics, such as intravenous vancomycin and cefepime. An ECG should be obtained to assess for any conduction abnormalities. An echocardiogram should be obtained to assess for valvular vegetations. It is reasonable to start with a transthoracic echocardiogram, although the patient may also need a transesophageal echocardiogram (TEE), depending on the transthoracic echocardiogram quality and findings. Therefore, the best initial management for this patient is all of the above: blood cultures, empiric antibiotics with coverage for MRSA, ECG, and echocardiogram.

79. Answer: (B) Interferon release assay (IGRA)

The TST is a test that is used to screen for TB infection. It is a good screening test, but it can be false-positive in some people, such as those who have been vaccinated with the BCG vaccine. The BCG vaccine is a live vaccine that is used to prevent TB. It is given to children in countries where TB is endemic. The IGRA is a newer test that is used to screen for TB infection. It is more specific than the TST and is not affected by the BCG vaccine. Therefore, the best next step in the management of this patient is to perform an IGRA. If the IGRA is positive, the patient will need to be further evaluated to determine if they have active TB. This may involve additional tests, such as a sputum smear and culture, and a chest X-ray. If the patient is found to have active TB, they will need to be treated with anti-tuberculosis therapy. The IGRA is a blood test that measures the amount of interferon that is produced by the body's T cells when they are exposed to TB antigens. Interferon is a cytokine that is involved in the immune response to TB. The IGRA has two commercially available tests: the QuantiFERON-TB Gold In-Tube test and the T-SPOT.TB test. Both tests are highly sensitive and specific for TB infection. The IGRA is the preferred test for TB screening in people who have been vaccinated with the BCG vaccine. It is also the preferred test for TB screening in people who are at high risk for TB, such as those who have been exposed to someone with TB or who have traveled to a country where TB is endemic. If a person has a positive IGRA, they will need to be further evaluated to determine if they have active TB. This may involve additional tests, such as a sputum smear and culture, and a chest X-ray. If the patient is found to have active TB, they will need to be treated with anti-tuberculosis therapy.

80. Answer: C. Repeat interferon release assay

Explanation: Interferon release assay tests, such as QuantiFERON and T spot, are commonly used to identify latent tuberculosis infection. If the initial test results are indeterminate, either due to a strong negative control response or a weak response to positive control, the appropriate next step is to repeat the interferon release assay (option C). If the repeat test is also indeterminate, then proceeding with the tuberculin skin test could be considered. The indeterminate result is not expected from the BCG vaccine (option A), hence providing reassurance would be incorrect. Starting the patient on tuberculosis treatment (option D) is not indicated without a positive test result or clear clinical signs of active disease. Similarly, discontinuing further testing for tuberculosis (option E) would be inappropriate given the patient's history and the potential public health implications of untreated latent tuberculosis infection. Therefore, the best answer is C. Repeat interferon release assay.

81. Answer: (D) Either A or B

The patient has latent TB. Latent TB is a condition in which a person is infected with the TB bacteria but does not have active TB disease. Latent TB is not contagious. Treatment for latent TB is recommended to prevent the development of active TB disease. The two most common treatment regimens for latent TB are rifampin daily for 4 months and isoniazid daily (with vitamin B6) for 9 months. Isoniazid and rifapentine weekly for 12 weeks is also an option. The choice of treatment regimen for latent TB depends on a number of factors, including the patient's age, medical history, and risk factors for developing active TB. In this case, the patient is healthy and has no known risk factors for developing active TB. Therefore, either rifampin daily for 4 months or isoniazid daily (with vitamin B6) for 9 months would be an appropriate treatment option. Latent TB is treated with antibiotics to kill the TB bacteria and prevent them from becoming active. Treatment for latent TB is usually very successful. However, it is important to complete the full course of treatment, even if the patient feels better. Patients who are being treated for latent TB should be monitored for side effects from the antibiotics. The most common side effects from rifampin are nausea, vomiting, and diarrhea. The most common side effects from isoniazid are liver problems and peripheral neuropathy (nerve damage). Patients who complete the full course of treatment for latent TB have a very low risk of developing active TB disease

82. The correct answer is B. Glucan and galactomannan.

Typically, patients with a newly diagnosed HIV infection should have the following labs checked: CD4 cell count, HIV viral load and genotype, CBC with differential, basic metabolic panel, LFTs, fasting lipids, HbA1c, syphilis screen, hepatitis (A, B, and C) serologies, and routine gonorrhea and chlamydia screening. Depending on the patient's CD4 cell count, toxoplasmosis IgG and cytomegalovirus IgG may also be done. Patients should also have a tuberculin skin test or an interferon release assay to assess for TB infection. However, glucan and galactomannan are not typically advised in the routine workup for a new diagnosis of HIV as they are more commonly associated with diagnosing invasive fungal infections, such as invasive aspergillosis or other fungal diseases.

83. Answer: (A) Start antiretroviral therapy (ART) at this visit, if patient is agreeable to start.

Current guidelines recommend that all people with HIV infection start ART, regardless of CD4 cell count or viral load. Early initiation of ART has been shown to improve survival and reduce the risk of developing opportunistic infections. In this case, the patient has a CD4 cell count of 150 cells/L, which is below the threshold for starting ART in the past. However, current guidelines recommend starting ART for all people with HIV infection, regardless of CD4 cell count. The patient should be counseled about the benefits and risks of ART. If the patient is agreeable to start ART, it should be started at this visit. There is no need to wait for the results of all laboratory tests and genotype before starting ART. ART is a combination of antiretroviral drugs that are used to suppress the replication of HIV. ART can help to improve the health of people with HIV and reduce the risk of transmitting HIV to others. The most common side effects of ART are nausea, vomiting, and diarrhea. These side effects are usually mild and go away on their own. However, some people may experience more serious side effects.

84. Answer: (A) He can stop TMP-SMX at this time.

Pneumocystis jiroveci pneumonia (PCP) is a serious opportunistic infection that can occur in people with HIV infection. PCP prophylaxis is recommended for all people with HIV infection who have a CD4 cell count of less than 200 cells/L. The most common PCP prophylaxis regimen is TMP-SMX. TMP-SMX is a combination of two antibiotics that are effective in preventing PCP. PCP prophylaxis can be stopped once a patient's CD4 cell count is >200 cells/L for 3 to 6 months while on suppressive ART. This patient's CD4 cell count is now 300 cells/L and he has been on suppressive ART for 6 months. Therefore, he can stop TMP-SMX at this time. It is important to note that PCP prophylaxis should be restarted if the patient's CD4 cell count drops below 200 cells/L or if they stop taking ART. Patients with HIV infection should also be vaccinated against other opportunistic infections, such as Streptococcus pneumoniae, Haemophilus influenzae type b, and hepatitis B virus.

85. Answer: C. Start tenofovir and emtricitabine daily

Preexposure prophylaxis (PrEP) is highly effective at preventing HIV transmission in HIV serodiscordant couples. This involves the HIV-uninfected partner taking tenofovir and emtricitabine (TDF-FTC) daily. It's important to note that taking PrEP only after a sexual encounter is not currently advised. Despite the patient's use of condoms, he is still at high risk of acquiring HIV infection, therefore, PrEP should be advised. Option A is not the best choice because despite the use of condoms, there's still a risk of transmission. Option B is not recommended because PrEP is not advised to be taken only after a sexual encounter. Option D might be less effective than daily use of PrEP. Option E is incorrect because even if the partner is HIV positive, the risk of transmission still exists. Therefore, option C is the best answer in this scenario.

86. Answer: (A) Start IV ceftriaxone and switch to oral doxycycline upon clinical improvement.

This patient has Lyme carditis, a complication of Lyme disease that can cause inflammation of the heart muscle. Lyme carditis is most commonly caused by the bacteria Borrelia burgdorferi, which is transmitted by deer ticks. The most common symptoms of Lyme carditis are fever, chest pain, shortness of breath, and palpitations. Lyme carditis can also cause heart block, a condition in which the electrical signals between the upper and lower chambers of the heart are disrupted. The diagnosis of Lyme carditis is based on a combination of clinical presentation, laboratory findings, and imaging studies. Blood cultures are not useful for diagnosing Lyme carditis, as the bacteria are rarely cultured from the blood. The treatment for Lyme carditis is antibiotics. Ceftriaxone is the antibiotic of choice for Lyme carditis. Patients are typically started on IV ceftriaxone and switched to oral doxycycline upon clinical improvement. Treatment is typically for 14 to 21 days. Temporary pacemakers may be needed in some patients with Lyme carditis who develop severe heart block. However, most patients with Lyme carditis make a full recovery with antibiotic treatment and do not require a permanent pacemaker. Lyme carditis is a serious complication of Lyme disease, but it is treatable with antibiotics. Early diagnosis and treatment are essential to prevent permanent heart damage. Patients with Lyme carditis should be followed closely by a cardiologist. Once they have completed their course of antibiotics, they should be evaluated to see if they have any residual heart damage.

87. A. Check Lyme ELISA screen, blood parasite smear, human granulocytic anaplasmosis PCR.

This patient's geographical location and his symptoms (recent rash typical for erythema migrans) raise a high concern for tick-borne illness, especially Lyme disease. The ELISA (enzyme-linked immunosorbent assay) is often the first step in testing for Lyme disease. In addition, his lab abnormalities (anemia with evidence of hemolysis, pancytopenia, and transaminitis) suggest possible coinfection with other tick-borne diseases. Babesia microti, which can cause babesiosis, is one such disease that can lead to anemia and hemolysis. A blood smear would help identify intracellular parasites and measure parasitemia. Another disease to consider is anaplasmosis (caused by Anaplasma phagocytophilum), which can also cause pancytopenia and transaminitis. Ehrlichiosis (caused by Ehrlichia chaffeensis) is relatively uncommon in Massachusetts, and while it should be considered, it is more crucial to test for anaplasmosis due to the listed symptoms. Thus, the best next step for this patient would be to conduct a Lyme ELISA screen, blood parasite smear, and human granulocytic anaplasmosis PCR.

88. Answer: (D) Perform rapid diagnostic testing for malaria.

In a traveler returning from sub-Saharan Africa, malaria is the most likely diagnosis, even if the patient is afebrile at the time of evaluation. Malaria is a serious and potentially life-threatening infection that is caused by a parasite. The parasite is transmitted to humans through the bite of an infected mosquito. The symptoms of malaria typically begin 7 to 30 days after being bitten by an infected mosquito. The most common symptoms of malaria are fever, chills, headache, and muscle aches. However, some people with malaria may not have any symptoms. The diagnosis of malaria is made by identifying the malaria parasite in the blood. Rapid diagnostic tests for malaria are available and can be performed in the clinic setting. If the rapid diagnostic test for malaria is positive, the patient should be started on antiparasitic treatment immediately. Antiparasitic treatment for malaria is typically given for 1 to 3 weeks. The other answer choices are not the most appropriate next steps in management. Basic metabolic panel, CBC and differential, LFTs, and blood cultures are not necessary for the diagnosis of malaria. Antibiotics are not effective against the malaria parasite. Reassuring the patient and discharging him home without further evaluation is not appropriate, as malaria can be a serious and life-threatening infection. 89. Answer: D. Initiate high-dose prednisone

The patient's clinical presentation suggests Giant Cell Arteritis (GCA), a vasculitis involving large and medium-sized arteries, particularly the temporal arteries. Key clinical features include new-onset localized headache, scalp tenderness, jaw claudication, and markedly elevated ESR. Given the risk of irreversible vision loss due to anterior ischemic optic neuropathy, immediate treatment with high-dose prednisone is indicated when clinical suspicion of GCA is high. Temporal artery biopsy can help confirm the diagnosis, but therapy should not be delayed while awaiting biopsy results. Brain MRI (option A) and lumbar puncture (option B) are not typically indicated in the initial evaluation of suspected GCA. Waiting for further symptoms to manifest (option C) could result in serious complications, including blindness.

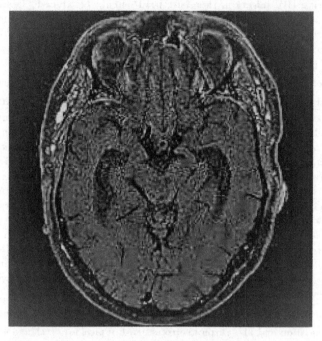

Figure 9.3: Giant Cell Arteritis (GCA)

Chapter 10

NEUROLOGY BOARD QUESTIONS

1. A 68-year-old woman, with a history of breast cancer, presents with severe headache and on examination, she exhibits papilledema. The physician decides to perform a lumbar puncture. In order to follow best practice, which of the following imaging studies should be conducted prior to the lumbar puncture?

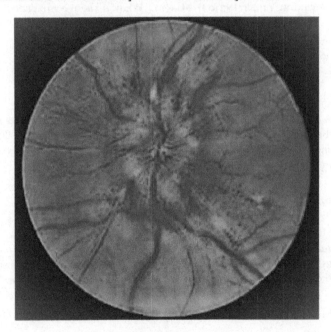

Figure 10.1: 68-year-old woman

- A. Chest X-ray
- B. Abdominal ultrasound
- C. Brain MRI or CT scan
- D. Lumbar spine MRI
- E. Echocardiogram

2. Is it advisable to initiate empirical antibiotic therapy before performing neuroimaging and lumbar puncture (LP) in cases where bacterial meningitis is suspected?

- A. Yes
- B. No

- C. It depends on the patient's clinical presentation.
- D. It depends on the results of the neuroimaging study.
- E. It depends on the results of the LP.

3. A 44-year-old immunocompetent male presents with sudden onset of severe headache, fever, and neck stiffness. The physician suspects acute bacterial meningitis. Which of the following pathogens are most likely to be implicated in this case?

- A. Escherichia coli and Staphylococcus aureus
- B. Streptococcus pneumoniae and Neisseria meningitidis
- C. Klebsiella pneumoniae and Pseudomonas aeruginosa
- D. Haemophilus influenzae and Listeria monocytogenes
- E. Staphylococcus epidermidis and Streptococcus pyogenes

4. What percentage of patients will exhibit organisms in the cerebrospinal fluid (CSF) Gram's stain?

- A. 20%
- B. 40%
- C. 60%
- D. 80%
- E. 100%

5. A 20-year-old college student has been diagnosed with meningococcal meningitis. His roommate, a healthy 21-year-old male, seeks advice regarding prophylactic treatment. What is the recommended prophylactic treatment for the roommate?

- A. Rifampin 600 mg every 12 hours for two days
- B. Azithromycin 500 mg single dose
- C. Ceftriaxone 250 mg single intramuscular dose
- D. All of the above
- E. None of the above

6. A 23-year-old woman presents with headache, fever, and neck stiffness. Lumbar puncture is performed, and the following CSF results are obtained: White blood cell count: 200 cells/μL (lymphocytes 90Protein: 0.5 g/L Glucose: 4.0 mmol/L Opening pressure: 15 cmH2O Which of the following is the most likely diagnosis?

- A. Bacterial meningitis
- B. Viral meningitis
- C. Tuberculous meningitis
- D. Fungal meningitis
- E. Syphilitic meningitis

7. A 37-year-old woman presents with a severe headache that is localized to the right side of her head. The headache is throbbing and is associated with nausea and vomiting. She also reports having had a visual disturbance before the headache started, which she describes as a blind spot in her left visual field. Which of the following is the most likely diagnosis?

- A. Migraine headache
- B. Cluster headache
- C. Tension headache
- D. Sinus headache
- E. Brain tumor

8. A 49-year-old woman presents to her primary care physician with a history of frequent headaches. She describes them as a constant pressure-like sensation around her forehead and at the back of her head, often lasting the entire day. She has tried over-the-counter analgesics with limited success. Which of the following medications could be considered for the prevention of this patient's chronic tension-type headaches?

- A. Topiramate
- B. Propranolol
- C. Amitriptyline
- D. Sumatriptan

- E. Aspirin

9. A 68-year-old man presents to the emergency department with recurrent episodes of sudden loss of consciousness, each lasting for a few seconds. He describes feeling lightheaded and dizzy before each episode. He has a history of hypertension and diabetes. Which of the following conditions should be considered in the differential diagnosis of his symptoms?

- A. Hypertrophic cardiomyopathy
- B. Simple febrile seizures
- C. Transient ischemic attacks
- D. Fibrostenotic disease
- E. Well-differentiated thyroid cancer

10. A 72-year-old man presents to your clinic with a complaint of dizziness and feeling faint when he stands up from a seated or lying down position. His blood pressure drops significantly when moving to an upright position. He has been diagnosed with orthostatic hypotension. What is the initial step in the management of this patient's condition?

- A. Administer fludrocortisone.
- B. Provide educational resources on changing positions.
- C. Increase fluid and salt intake
- D. Discontinue the use of vasoactive medications.
- E. Administer midodrine.

11. A 25-year-old woman presents with recurrent episodes of fainting. She reports that the episodes occur when she stands up quickly, after prolonged standing, or when she is in hot weather. She has no other medical problems, and her physical examination is normal. Which of the following interventions is the most appropriate for this patient?

- A. Reassurance and avoidance of triggers
- B. Fluid and salt replacement
- C. Pharmacological therapy
- D. Tilt-table testing
- E. Electrocardiography

12. A patient with narcolepsy experiences an abrupt partial or complete loss of muscular tone often triggered by strong emotions. What is this symptom called and how long does it typically last?

- A. Cataplexy lasts between 30 seconds and 2 minutes.
- B. Syncope lasts between 30 seconds and 2 minutes.
- C. Narcolepsy lasts between 30 seconds and 2 minutes.
- D. Hypnagogic hallucinations last between 30 seconds and 2 minutes.
- E. Sleep paralysis lasts between 30 seconds and 2 minutes.

13. A 52-year-old man presents to your clinic complaining of recurrent episodes of vertigo, especially when he gets out of bed in the morning or when he tilts his head back to look up. The episodes last for less than a minute and are associated with nausea but no hearing loss or tinnitus. Which of the following is the most appropriate next step in the evaluation of this patient?

- A. Brain MRI
- B. Electronystagmography
- C. Audiometry testing
- D. Dix-Hallpike maneuver
- E. CT scan of the head

14. A patient presents with benign paroxysmal positional vertigo (BPPV). What is the most effective treatment for this condition?

- A. Repositioning exercises, such as the Epley maneuver.
- B. Antihistamines.
- C. Benzodiazepines.
- D. Vestibular suppressants.
- E. Surgery.

15. A 47-year-old woman presents with a history of recurrent episodes of vertigo, hearing loss, and tinnitus. She has

tried a low-salt diet and diuretics, but her symptoms have not improved. What is the next best treatment option for this patient?

- A. Vestibular rehabilitation therapy
- B. Anti-nausea medication
- C. Endolymphatic sac decompression surgery
- D. Vestibular nerve sectioning

16. A 67-year-old woman presents to the emergency department with sudden onset of right-sided weakness and difficulty speaking. She has a history of hypertension and hyperlipidemia. A CT scan of her head shows no evidence of hemorrhage. Based on the most common causes of neurologic deficits resulting from vascular mechanisms, which type of event is most likely responsible for this patient's symptoms?

- A. Subarachnoid hemorrhage
- B. Intracerebral hemorrhage
- C. Cerebral infarction
- D. Transient ischemic attack
- E. Migraine

17. A 58-year-old man presents with sudden onset weakness on the right side of his body. The weakness started 30 minutes ago and has not improved. He has no other symptoms. What is the most likely diagnosis?

- A. Transient ischemic attack (TIA)
- B. Stroke
- C. Migraine headache
- D. Seizure
- E. Brain tumor

18. A patient presents with transient ischemic attack (TIA). What is the most commonly used classification system for TIAs and how many subtypes does it categorize TIAs into?

- A. The Trial of ORG 10172 in Acute Stroke Treatment (TOAST) classification, five subtypes.
- B. The Modified Rankin Scale (MRS), three subtypes.
- C. The National Institutes of Health Stroke Scale (NIHSS), four subtypes.
- D. The Canadian Neurological Scale (CNS), six subtypes.
- E. The Barthel Index (BI), two subtypes.

19. A 68-year-old man presents to the emergency department with a sudden onset of left-sided weakness and slurred speech. His symptoms began approximately an hour ago. He has a history of hypertension and diabetes. Upon investigation, you suspect an acute ischemic stroke (AIS). Which of the following would be a contraindication for the administration of intravenous recombinant tissue plasminogen activator (rtPA) in this patient?

- A. Recent head injury two weeks ago
- B. Major surgery performed twenty days ago.
- C. Gastrointestinal bleeding episode that occurred a month ago
- D. Myocardial infarction that occurred last year
- E. None of the above

20. A patient with severe hydrocephalus may require urgent intervention. What is the recommended intervention for such patients?

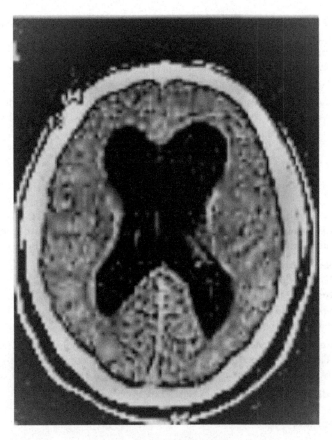

Figure 10.2: Hydrocephalus

- A. Placement of a ventricular catheter for external CSF drainage.
- B. Repeat CT scanning to evaluate ventricular size.
- C. Permanent shunt placement.
- D. MRI to evaluate ventricular size.
- E. Administration of diuretics

21. A 50-year-old man presents with a headache that is worse in the morning. He also reports nausea, vomiting, and double vision. On examination, his pupils are dilated and unresponsive to light. He has no other focal neurological deficits. What is the most likely diagnosis?

- A. Increased intracranial pressure (ICP)
- B. Subarachnoid hemorrhage (SAH)
- C. Stroke
- D. Meningitis
- E. Brain tumor

22. A 57-year-old woman is brought to the emergency department following a severe head trauma due to a motor vehicle accident. Imaging suggests the presence of cytotoxic edema. Which of the following would be an appropriate early step in the management of this patient's condition?

- A. Administering a beta-blocker.
- B. Starting an antibiotic.
- C. Administering an osmotic diuretic.
- D. Infusing a dopamine agonist.
- E. Starting an antiviral medication.

23. What is the definition of an absence seizure?

- A. A sudden and brief impairment of consciousness, while maintaining postural control.
- B. A seizure lasting longer than 30 minutes.
- C. A seizure characterized by loss of consciousness and convulsions.
- D. A seizure characterized by abnormal electrical activity in one cerebral hemisphere.
- E. A seizure characterized by sudden loss of postural control.

24. A 51-year-old man with a history of cardiac arrest presents with involuntary muscle jerks that are worse when he is stressed or fatigued. He has no other neurological deficits. What is the best treatment option for this patient?

- A. Clonazepam
- B. Valproate
- C. Levetiracetam
- D. Topiramate
- E. Primidone

25. A 35-year-old woman is brought to the emergency department by her husband, who reports that she has been experiencing episodes of unresponsiveness and shaking. No lab abnormalities or neuroimaging findings are identified. Which of the following features would be most suggestive of a psychogenic seizure rather than an epileptic seizure?

- A. Abrupt commencement and cessation of the seizure
- B. A predictable pattern of seizure episodes
- C. The seizure episodes are not associated with stress or trauma.
- D. The absence of a predictable pattern of the seizures
- E. The seizures are related to aberrant cerebral electrical activity.

26. A 70-year-old woman presents with progressive memory disturbance, dressing difficulty, urinary incontinence, and gait ataxia over 12 weeks. There was no past history of stroke, stroke-like events or seizures, or measles in childhood. On examination, she has myoclonus and decreased muscle tone. What is the most likely diagnosis?

- A. Creutzfeldt-Jakob disease (CJD)
- B. Alzheimer's disease
- C. Frontotemporal dementia
- D. Vascular dementia
- E. Parkinson's disease

27. What are the potential initial symptoms of dementia with Lewy bodies (DLB)?

- A. Sudden appearance of a parkinsonian syndrome, characterized by symptoms such as resting tremor, cogwheel rigidity, bradykinesia, and festinating gait.
- B. Loss of consciousness and convulsions.
- C. Abnormal electrical activity in one cerebral hemisphere.
- D. Sudden loss of postural control.
- E. Spontaneous changes in attention and alertness.

28. A 76-year-old man presents to your clinic with his daughter, who reports that her father has been showing signs of memory loss and difficulty with daily tasks. His symptoms are not severe enough to interfere significantly with his daily activities, but they are noticeable and concerning his family. Given the patient's symptoms and the family's concerns, which of the following diagnoses would most appropriately describe his condition?

- A. Severe Alzheimer's disease
- B. Late symptomatic Alzheimer's disease
- C. Mild Cognitive Impairment
- D. Early symptomatic Alzheimer's disease
- E. Normal aging process

29. A 62-year-old man presents with a tremor in his right hand that is worse when he is at rest. He also has difficulty initiating movements and has a slow, shuffling gait. What is the most likely diagnosis?

- A. Parkinson's disease
- B. Essential tremor
- C. Multiple sclerosis
- D. Alzheimer's disease

- E. Huntington's disease

30. What are the potential etiological factors contributing to the development of secondary Parkinsonism?

- A. Use of certain medications, such as neuroleptics and gastrointestinal drugs like metoclopramide, which inhibit dopamine. Infections or exposure to toxins like carbon monoxide or manganese.
- B. Exposure to asbestos and other industrial chemicals.
- C. Genetic mutations.
- D. Head trauma.
- E. Chronic alcohol abuse.

31. A 46-year-old woman presents to the clinic with a 6-month history of progressively worsening imbalance and unsteady gait. She has no significant past medical history but mentions that her father had similar symptoms in his late 40s. Based on her symptoms and family history, which of the following is the most likely cause of her chronic cerebellar ataxia?

- A. Autosomal dominant spinocerebellar ataxias (SCAs)
- B. Acute cerebellar stroke
- C. Cerebellar tumor
- D. Drug-induced cerebellar toxicity
- E. Multiple sclerosis

32. A 53-year-old man is diagnosed with amyotrophic lateral sclerosis (ALS). He is considering treatment with edaravone. What is the pharmacological profile of edaravone and what is its mechanism of action in the treatment of ALS?

- A. Edaravone is a free radical scavenger that can protect neurons from damage.
- B. Edaravone is a nitric oxide synthase inhibitor that can reduce inflammation.
- C. Edaravone is a glutamate receptor antagonist that can prevent excitotoxicity.
- D. Edaravone is a microtubule stabilizer that can prevent neuronal degeneration.
- E. Edaravone is a neurotransmitter precursor that can improve nerve function.

33. What alternative pharmacological interventions may be considered for patients with Trigeminal Neuralgia who exhibit inadequate response to Carbamazepine or Oxcarbazepine?

- A. Lamotrigine (at a daily dosage of 400 mg), Phenytoin (at a dosage range of 300-400 mg per day), or Baclofen (initially administered at a dosage of 5-10 mg three times a day).
- B. Aspirin (at a daily dosage of 81 mg), Ibuprofen (at a dosage range of 400-800 mg per day), or Acetaminophen (at a dosage range of 500-1000 mg per day).
- C. Morphine (at a daily dosage of 10 mg), Oxycodone (at a dosage range of 5-10 mg per day), or Fentanyl (initially administered at a dosage of 25 mcg per hour).
- D. Gabapentin (at a daily dosage of 300 mg), Pregabalin (at a dosage range of 75-150 mg per day), or Duloxetine (initially administered at a dosage of 30 mg per day).
- E. Diazepam (at a daily dosage of 5 mg), Alprazolam (at a dosage range of 0.25-0.5 mg per day), or Lorazepam (initially administered at a dosage of 1 mg per day).

34. A 50-year-old woman with myasthenia gravis (MG) is prescribed ciprofloxacin for a urinary tract infection. What is the most likely outcome of this treatment?

- A. The ciprofloxacin will worsen her MG symptoms.
- B. The ciprofloxacin will have no effect on her MG symptoms.
- C. The ciprofloxacin will improve her MG symptoms.
- D. The ciprofloxacin will cause her to develop a new autoimmune disease.
- E. The ciprofloxacin is contraindicated in patients with MG.

35. A 28-year-old woman comes to your office with a year-long history of progressive unsteady gait and numbness in her right leg. She denies any other systemic symptoms. An MRI of the brain and spinal cord shows multiple T2+ lesions in the periventricular region and two T2+ lesions in the spinal cord. Cerebrospinal fluid analysis reveals oligoclonal bands. Based on these findings, which of the following is the most likely diagnosis?

- A. Neuromyelitis optica
- B. Primary progressive multiple sclerosis (PPMS)

- C. Amyotrophic lateral sclerosis (ALS)
- D. Guillain-Barre syndrome
- E. Transverse myelitis

36. 75-year-old woman presents with a 2-day history of fever, confusion, and agitation. She is unable to name the days of the week backward. Which of the following is the most likely diagnosis?

- (A) Alcohol-induced mood disorder
- (B) Bipolar disorder, manic
- (C) Brief psychotic disorder
- (D) Delirium
- (E) Schizophrenia, paranoid type

37. A 78-year-old woman with a history of Alzheimer's disease and type 2 diabetes mellitus on insulin therapy presents to the emergency department with an acute change in mental status. Her daughter, who is her primary caregiver, reports that her mother has been more confused than usual for the past few hours. The patient is not able to provide her own history due to her cognitive decline. Her vitals are within normal limits. The physical examination is non-revealing. What is the next best step in the management of this patient?

- A. Obtain a basic metabolic panel
- B. Obtain a complete blood count
- C. Obtain a urinalysis
- D. Perform a blood glucose fingerstick
- E. Order a noncontrast head CT scan

38. A 68-year-old man presents with a 1-year history of a progressive behavioral syndrome. He was previously known to be calm and pleasant, but recently he has been displaying inappropriate behavior, anger, and impulsivity, which are seriously impacting his social and occupational functioning. MRI revealed atrophy primarily involving the frontal and temporal lobes. Which of the following is the most likely diagnosis?

- A. Alzheimer's disease
- B. Behavioral variant of frontotemporal dementia
- C. Lewy body disease
- D. Corticobasal degeneration

E. Primary progressive aphasia

39. A 36-year-old man presents with a generalized tonic-clonic seizure. He is unconscious and unresponsive. Which of the following is the most important initial management step? (A) Administer lorazepam (B) Obtain a head CT (C) Perform a lumbar puncture (D) Ensure proper oxygenation (E) Administer phenytoin 40. A 26-year-old woman presents with a history of recurrent episodes of loss of consciousness. She describes the episodes as lasting for a few seconds to a few minutes, and during these episodes, she is unaware of her surroundings and does not respond to stimuli. She does not have any other symptoms, such as tonic-clonic movements, tongue biting, or urinary incontinence. A routine EEG is performed and is normal. What is the most appropriate next step in the management of this patient?

- (A) Reassure the patient that her symptoms are unlikely to be due to a seizure disorder.
- (B) Order a 24-hour Holter monitor.
- (C) Schedule a tilt table test.
- (D) Order a long-term EEG.
- (E) Start anticonvulsant therapy.

41. A 44-year-old man with a history of major depressive disorder, including a prior suicide attempt, has been recently diagnosed with epilepsy. His neurologist is deciding on an appropriate antiepileptic medication for him. Which of the following medications should be avoided in this patient due to his history?

- A. Valproic Acid
- B. Lacosamide
- C. Carbamazepine
- D. Levetiracetam
- E. Oxcarbazepine

42. A 67-year-old male with a known history of alcohol use disorder presents with the sudden onset of ataxia, ophthalmoparesis, and altered mental status. His wife reports that he has been drinking heavily for the past few weeks and has not been eating well. She is concerned about his declining health. Which of the following is the most appropriate treatment for this patient?

- A. Riboflavin
- B. Pyridoxine
- C. Cyanocobalamin
- D. Folate
- E. Thiamine

43. A 58-year-old man with a history of alcohol abuse presents to the emergency department with a 3-day history of hallucinations, hypertension, shivering, sweating, and tachycardia. What is the most likely diagnosis?

- (A) Delirium tremens
- (B) Schizoaffective disorder
- (C) Posttraumatic stress disorder
- (D) Depression
- (E) None of the above

44. A 52-year-old man with a history of alcohol abuse presents to the emergency department with a 3-day history of hallucinations, hypertension, shivering, sweating, and tachycardia. He is diagnosed with delirium tremens. Which of the following medications is NOT appropriate for the management of delirium tremens?

- (A) Alprazolam
- (B) Chlordiazepoxide
- (C) Diazepam
- (D) Lorazepam
- (E) Propofol

45. A 42-year-old woman presents to the emergency department with continuous dizziness for the past 5 hours. She denies any hearing loss, fever, headache, or any change in her vision. Her examination reveals a positive head thrust test, unilaterally beating nystagmus, and no skew. Which of the following is the most likely diagnosis?

- A) Benign paroxysmal positional vertigo
- B) Labyrinthitis
- C) Posterior circulation stroke
- D) Vestibular neuritis
- E) Central nystagmus

46. A 27-year-old woman presents with a history of brief episodes of dizziness that occur when she changes head position. The episodes last for a few seconds to a few minutes and resolve on their own. She does not have any other symptoms, such as headache, nausea, or vomiting. Which of the following is the most likely diagnosis?

- (A) Benign paroxysmal positional vertigo
- (B) Vestibular neuritis
- (C) Migraine
- (D) Concussion
- (E) Vertebrobasilar insufficiency

47. A 38-year-old man presents with a history of sudden onset of vertigo, nausea, and vomiting. He has no other medical history and is not taking any medications. On physical examination, he has nystagmus with horizontal components. Which of the following tests is NOT a component of the HINTS test?

- (A) Finger-to-nose coordination test
- (B) Head impulse test
- (C) Nystagmus test
- (D) Test of skew
- (E) None of the above

48. A 69-year-old man is brought to the emergency department with acute onset of inability to speak and move the right side of his body. His gaze is deviated to the left. Which of the following is the most likely site of the lesion?

- A. Left middle cerebral artery (MCA)
- B. Right anterior cerebral artery
- C. Right middle cerebral artery (MCA)
- D. Left posterior cerebral artery
- E. Right posterior inferior cerebellar artery

49. A 70-year-old woman with a history of hypertension and diabetes presents to the hospital with sudden onset of left face and arm weakness that started 4 hours ago. Which of the following is the most appropriate next step in management?

- A. Wait for 6 hours to administer tissue plasminogen activator
- B. Administer tissue plasminogen activator immediately, despite her recent surgery
- C. Administer tissue plasminogen activator immediately, despite her recent intracerebral hemorrhage
- D. Administer tissue plasminogen activator immediately
- E. Refer the patient to a neurologist for further management

50. A 66-year-old man with end-stage renal disease presents to the emergency department with a 2-hour history of right-sided hemiplegia and aphasia. He has a history of hypertension and hyperlipidemia. He is not taking any medications. Which of the following imaging studies is the most appropriate for this patient?

- (A) Non-contrast CT head
- (B) Contrast-enhanced CT head
- (C) MRI brain
- (D) CT angiography
- (E) Carotid duplex ultrasound

51. A 67-year-old man with a history of hypertension presents to the emergency department with a 2-hour history of left-sided hemiplegia and aphasia. On physical examination, he has a blood pressure of 180/110 mmHg. MRI brain showing hemorrhage in the right basal ganglia Which of the following is the most likely cause of the patient's intracerebral hemorrhage?

- (A) Arteriovenous malformation
- (B) Cerebral amyloid angiopathy
- (C) Intracranial aneurysm
- (D) Neoplastic lesion
- (E) Hypertension

52. A 49-year-old man presents with rapidly progressing weakness in his limbs over a few days. He also complains about back pain and numbness in his extremities. On examination, symmetric proximal and distal limb weakness, areflexia, and distal paresthesias/sensory loss are noted. Lumbar puncture reveals elevated protein without cerebrospinal fluid (CSF) pleocytosis. Which of the following is the best initial treatment for his condition?

- A. Intravenous antibiotics
- B. Antiviral therapy
- C. Intravenous immunoglobulin (IVIG)
- D. Steroids
- E. MRI of the spine

53. A 62-year-old female patient presents with complaints of chronic, burning pain in her lower extremities. The pain is described as a constant burning sensation, worse at night, and is accompanied by tingling and numbness. Her past medical history is significant for type 2 diabetes mellitus. In light of her symptoms and history, you suspect she is suffering from diabetic neuropathy. Which of the following would be the least appropriate initial treatment for her condition?

- A. Nonsteroidal anti-inflammatory drugs (NSAIDs)
- B. Gabapentin
- C. Pregabalin
- D. Amitriptyline
- E. Duloxetine

54. A 64-year-old man presents to the clinic with a 3-month history of progressive weakness in his legs. He reports

difficulty climbing stairs and getting out of a chair. He also reports feeling tired easily. On physical examination, he has decreased muscle strength in his legs and hyporeflexia. Which of the following medications is the most effective symptomatic treatment for this patient?

- (A) 3,4-Diaminopyridine (3,4-DAP)
- (B) Edrophonium
- (C) Pyridostigmine
- (D) Prednisone
- (E) Rituximab

55. A 57-year-old woman presents to the clinic with a 2-month history of progressive weakness in her legs and arms. She also reports difficulty climbing stairs, getting out of low chairs, and combing her hair. On physical examination, she has proximal weakness in all four extremities and mild weakness in the neck flexors. She also has erythematous papules over the extensor surfaces of her elbows and knees (Gottron papules) and a maculopapular rash over her upper back (shawl sign). Which of the following histopathological findings is most suggestive of the diagnosis of dermatomyositis?

- (A) Eosinophilic myositis
- (B) Perifascicular atrophy and perivascular inflammation
- (C) Vacuolar myopathy
- (D) Necrotizing myopathy
- (E) Granulomatous myositis

56. A 47-year-old man presents with unilateral, severe, periorbital headaches that occur in clusters, often in the evening. He reports that the pain is excruciating and is associated with restlessness and feelings of panic. He also experiences lacrimation, conjunctival injection, and rhinorrhea on the same side as the headache. Each attack can last up to three hours and he can have up to eight attacks a day. These clusters of headaches can last for weeks to months, followed by headache-free periods. What is the most likely diagnosis?

- A) Cluster headache
- B) Short-lasting unilateral neuralgiform pain with conjunctival injection and tearing syndrome
- C) Trigeminal neuralgia
- D) Tension headache
- E) Secondary headache

57. A 46-year-old man presents with a chronic headache of severe attacks with autonomic features superimposed on a continuous headache of at least 3 months' duration. After a thorough evaluation, including brain imaging to exclude a structural lesion and dedicated venous imaging to exclude venous sinus thrombosis, he is diagnosed with hemicrania continua. Which of the following is the most appropriate treatment?

- A. Indomethacin
- B. Tricyclic antidepressants
- C. Topiramate
- D. Verapamil
- E. Triptans

58. A 30-year-old woman presents with a 2-week history of worsening headaches. The headaches are described as throbbing and are located in the frontal and occipital regions. She has also been experiencing nausea and vomiting. She reports that the headaches are worse when she is lying down and that they wake her up from sleep. On physical examination, the patient has bilateral papilledema. Cranial imaging is performed and shows nonvisualization of the right transverse, sigmoid, and jugular venous system on magnetic resonance venogram. What is the most appropriate next step in the management of this patient?

- (A) Order an electroencephalogram (EEG).
- (B) Order a lumbar puncture.
- (C) Admit the patient to the hospital for observation.
- (D) Start the patient on anticonvulsant medication.
- (E) Send thrombophilia workup and start therapeutic anticoagulation with heparin.

59. A 59-year-old woman presents with a 2-week history of pain and numbness in her right leg. The pain is described as shooting and radiates from her lower back down the lateral aspect of her thigh and leg. She also reports numbness

over the lateral calf and great toe. She has difficulty lifting her right foot and dragging her toes when she walks. On physical examination, the patient has weakness of the dorsiflexion of her right foot. Her patellar and Achilles reflexes are normal. Which nerve root is most likely affected?

- (A) L4
- (B) L5
- (C) S1
- (D) Thoracic spinal cord
- (E) Peroneal

60. A 68-year-old woman presents with symptoms of rapidly progressing weakness and numbness of her bilateral lower extremities. On examination, she has evidence of a thoracic myelopathy based on her pattern of weakness (involving the lower but sparing the upper extremities), hyperreflexia, upgoing toes, and T4 sensory level to pinprick. Her imaging reveals an epidural mass lesion compressing the spinal cord at the level of the T5 vertebra. Which of the following is the most appropriate next step in management?

- A. Administer dexamethasone 10 mg IV, with urgent evaluation for thoracic spine decompression
- B. Administer a high dose of morphine for pain control
- C. Immediate referral to a physical therapist
- D. Initiate aggressive chemotherapy regimen
- E. Start radiation therapy

10.1 ANSWERS

1. The correct answer is C. Brain MRI or CT scan.

In patients presenting certain conditions such as head trauma, immunocompromised states, established malignancies, or focal neurologic abnormalities such as papilledema or stupor/coma, it is recommended that a neuroimaging examination of the brain be conducted prior to performing a lumbar puncture. This is to rule out any existing intracranial mass effect, which if present, may lead to brain herniation following the lumbar puncture due to the sudden change in cerebrospinal fluid pressure. A brain MRI or CT scan (Option C). Keynote is that MRI is the preferred imaging study in such scenarios, as it provides a more detailed view of the brain tissues and can be more sensitive in detecting lesions, compared to a CT scan. Chest X-ray (Option A), abdominal ultrasound (Option B), lumbar spine MRI (Option D), and echocardiogram (Option E) are not the recommended imaging studies in this situation as they do not provide the necessary information about the brain that is needed before a lumbar puncture.

2. The correct answer is A: yes.

Bacterial meningitis is a serious infection of the meninges, the membranes that surround the brain and spinal cord. It can be life-threatening, so it is important to start treatment as soon as possible. The diagnosis of bacterial meningitis is made by performing a lumbar puncture (LP). This is a procedure in which a needle is inserted into the spinal canal to collect cerebrospinal fluid (CSF). The CSF is then analyzed for the presence of bacteria. However, LP can be risky in patients with suspected bacterial meningitis. The procedure can introduce bacteria into the CSF, which can worsen the infection. For this reason, it is advisable to start empirical antibiotic therapy before performing LP in cases where bacterial meningitis is suspected. This will help to protect the patient from the risk of further infection. The antibiotics can be adjusted after the LP, based on the results of the CSF analysis.

3. The correct answer is B. Streptococcus pneumoniae and Neisseria meningitidis.

Acute bacterial meningitis is a severe and life-threatening condition characterized by inflammation of the meninges, which are the protective membranes surrounding the brain and spinal cord. The condition is most often caused by a bacterial infection, although it can also be caused by viruses, fungi, parasites, or non-infectious causes. In immunocompetent adults, the most common causative agents of acute bacterial meningitis are Streptococcus pneumoniae, also known as pneumococcus, and Neisseria meningitidis, also known as meningococcus. Streptococcus pneumoniae is responsible for approximately 50% of cases, and Neisseria meningitidis is responsible for approximately 25% of cases. The other options listed (A, C, D, and E) include bacteria that can cause infections in humans, but they are not the most common causes of acute bacterial meningitis in immunocompetent adults. For instance, Escherichia coli (Option A) is more frequently implicated in neonatal meningitis, and Listeria monocytogenes (Option D) is more common in neonates, older adults, pregnant women, and immunocompromised individuals. Therefore, Option B is the best answer in this case.

4. The correct answer is C: 60%.

The sensitivity of the CSF Gram's stain for detecting organisms in bacterial meningitis is approximately 60%. This means that approximately 60% of patients with bacterial meningitis will have organisms visible on CSF Gram's stain. The reason for the low sensitivity of the CSF Gram's stain is that bacteria are not always present in the CSF in large enough numbers to be visible on a Gram stain. Additionally, the presence of cells in the CSF, such as white blood cells, can make it difficult to see bacteria on a Gram stain. If the CSF Gram's stain is negative for organisms, but the patient is still suspected of having bacterial meningitis, then a CSF pathogen panel may be ordered. A CSF pathogen panel is a molecular diagnostic test that can detect the DNA of bacteria in the CSF. The CSF pathogen panel is more sensitive than the CSF Gram's stain for detecting bacteria in bacterial meningitis. The sensitivity of the CSF pathogen panel is approximately 90%. This means that approximately 90% of patients with bacterial meningitis will have bacteria detected on a CSF pathogen panel. If the CSF pathogen panel is positive for bacteria, then the patient can be treated with antibiotics. If the CSF pathogen panel is negative for bacteria, then other causes of the patient's symptoms should be investigated.

5. The correct answer is D. All of the above.

In the context of meningococcal meningitis, close contacts of the infected individual are at a higher risk of contracting the disease. Prophylactic treatment is recommended for these individuals to prevent the spread of the infection. The prophylactic treatment options for an adult include: Rifampin 600 mg every 12 hours for two days (Option A) A single dose of Azithromycin 500 mg (Option B) A single intramuscular dose of Ceftriaxone 250 mg (Option C) All of these options (Option D) are recommended for adults, including the roommate in the scenario, who is a healthy 21-year-old male. Therefore, all of the options listed are appropriate and the correct answer is D. Option E is incorrect since prophylaxis is indeed recommended for close contacts of patients diagnosed with meningococcal meningitis.

6. The correct answer is B: viral meningitis.

Viral meningitis is characterized by a lymphocytic pleocytosis (increase in the number of lymphocytes in the CSF) in the range of 25-500 cells/µL, a normal or slightly elevated protein concentration, a normal glucose concentration, and a normal or slightly elevated opening pressure. Bacterial meningitis, tuberculous meningitis, fungal meningitis, and syphilitic meningitis are all characterized by a different combination of CSF findings.

7. The correct answer is A: migraine headache.

The traditional triad of migraine headache consists of unilateral throbbing headache, nausea, and vomiting. In this case, the patient has all three of these symptoms, as well as a visual disturbance that is consistent with migraine aura. Cluster headache is characterized by severe, unilateral headaches that occur in clusters over a period of weeks or months. Tension headaches are typically less severe than migraine headaches and are not associated with nausea or vomiting. Sinus headaches are caused by inflammation of the sinuses and are often associated with facial pain, congestion, and rhinorrhea. Brain tumors can cause headaches, but they are usually accompanied by other symptoms such as seizures, weakness, or vision problems.

8. Best Answer: C. Amitriptyline.

Each of the medications listed might be used in the management of different types of headaches, but the specific type of headache described here aligns most closely with chronic tension-type headaches. A. Topiramate is primarily used in the prevention of migraines, not tension-type headaches. B. Propranolol, a beta-blocker, is also more commonly used in the prevention of migraines. C. Amitriptyline, a tricyclic antidepressant, has been shown to be effective in the prevention of chronic tension-type headaches. It helps to reduce the frequency and severity of these headaches. D. Sumatriptan is a triptan, typically used for acute treatment of migraine attacks, not for the prevention of tension-type headaches. E. Aspirin is an over-the-counter analgesic that can be used for acute relief of various types of headaches, but it is not typically used for the prevention of chronic tension-type headaches. So, given this patient's symptoms and the lack of success with over-the-counter analgesics, amitriptyline could be a suitable option for preventing her chronic tension-type headaches.

9. Best Answer: C. Transient ischemic attacks.

While all of these conditions can theoretically present with a loss of consciousness, the patient's age, symptomatology, and medical history make some diagnoses more plausible than others. A. Hypertrophic cardiomyopathy usually presents symptoms like chest pain, dyspnea, or palpitations, rather than loss of consciousness. B. Simple febrile seizures are primarily a pediatric condition. C. Transient ischemic attacks (TIAs) can present transient loss of consciousness and are particularly plausible given the patient's age and history of hypertension, which is a risk factor for TIAs. D. Fibrostenotic disease relates to persistent symptoms from a stricture, typically involving the gastrointestinal tract. It's not typically associated with loss of consciousness. E. Well-differentiated thyroid cancer generally doesn't present with loss of consciousness. Therefore, among the choices given, transient ischemic attacks are the most plausible condition that this patient's syncope needs to be distinguished from. However, it's important to note that the differential for syncope is broad and many other conditions such as orthostatic hypotension, cardiac arrhythmias, and others could also be potential causes.

10. Best Answer: D. Discontinue the use of vasoactive medications.

While all of the options listed could potentially be part of managing a patient with orthostatic hypotension, the initial step should be: D. Discontinuing the use of vasoactive medications. These medications can cause or exacerbate orthostatic hypotension, so if the patient is on any such medications, they should be discontinued if possible. After that initial step, other interventions can be considered, such as: B. Providing the patient with educational resources on how to change positions slowly to mitigate symptoms. C. Recommending an increase in fluid and salt intake to increase blood volume. A. and E. Administering pharmacological interventions like fludrocortisone or midodrine could be considered if nonpharmacological interventions are insufficient, but typically these would not be the initial step in management. So, among the options given, discontinuing the use of vasoactive medications is the best initial step in managing this patient's orthostatic hypotension.

11. The correct answer is A: reassurance and avoidance of triggers.

Neurally mediated syncope is a common condition that is caused by a sudden drop in blood pressure when a person stands up. The most important intervention for this condition is to reassure the patient that it is not a serious condition and to teach them how to avoid the triggers that cause their episodes. These triggers can include standing up quickly, prolonged standing, hot weather, and emotional stress. Fluid and salt replacement may be helpful for patients who have frequent or severe episodes of neurally mediated syncope. Pharmacological therapy may be necessary for patients who do not respond to conventional treatment. Tilt-table testing, and electrocardiography are diagnostic tests that can be used to rule out other causes of syncope.

12. Answer: A) Cataplexy, lasts between 30 seconds and 2 minutes. Cataplexy is an abrupt partial or complete loss of muscular tone often triggered by strong emotions, seen in 60-75% of narcolepsy patients. Unlike syncope, consciousness is maintained throughout the attacks, which typically last between 30 seconds and 2 minutes. Also confirms that cataplexy is a brief and sudden loss of muscle tone and represents REM sleep intrusion during wakefulness.

13. Best Answer: D. Dix-Hallpike maneuver.

The patient's symptoms are suggestive of benign positional vertigo (BPV), a common cause of vertigo that is triggered by changes in head position relative to gravity. A. A Brain MRI is typically not the first step in the evaluation of a patient with suspected BPV, as the condition is diagnosed clinically. B. Electronystagmography is a test used to evaluate involuntary eye movement (nystagmus), but it is not typically the first step in diagnosing BPV. C. Audiometry testing is used to evaluate hearing and is more relevant in conditions such as Meniere's disease where there is associated hearing loss. D. The Dix-Hallpike maneuver is the most appropriate next step in this case. It is a diagnostic test for BPV. If the maneuver reproduces the patient's vertigo and provokes characteristic nystagmus, the diagnosis of BPV is confirmed. E. A CT scan of the head is not typically necessary in the evaluation of a patient with suspected BPV, as the condition is diagnosed clinically. So, among the options given, performing the Dix-Hallpike maneuver is the best next step in the evaluation of this patient's condition.

14. Answer: A. Repositioning exercises, such as the Epley maneuver.

BPPV is caused by small crystals of calcium carbonate becoming dislodged and repositioned within the structures of the inner ear, leading to symptoms of vertigo when the head is moved in certain ways. Also states that BPPV has been observed to exhibit significant improvement when treated with repositioning exercises, such as the Epley maneuver, which is specifically designed to dislodge particulate debris from the posterior semicircular canal. Therefore, the most effective treatment for BPPV is repositioning exercises, such as the Epley maneuver.

15. The correct answer is A: vestibular rehabilitation therapy.

Vestibular rehabilitation therapy is a non-invasive treatment option that can be effective in reducing the severity and frequency of vertigo attacks in patients with Ménière's disease.

This therapy involves a series of exercises designed to promote balance and reduce the severity of vertigo attacks. Anti-nausea medication, such as dimenhydrinate, meclizine, or promethazine, may be prescribed to alleviate nausea and vomiting associated with vertigo attacks. However, these medications do not address the underlying cause of the vertigo and may not be effective in preventing future attacks. Endolymphatic sac decompression surgery and vestibular nerve sectioning are surgical interventions that may be necessary in patients with Ménière's disease who have not responded to other treatment options. However, these surgeries are associated with risks and side effects, and should only be considered after careful consideration of all treatment options.

16. Best Answer: C. Cerebral infarction

The patient's symptoms of sudden onset right-sided weakness and difficulty speaking are suggestive of a cerebrovascular event. Given that her CT scan does not show any evidence of hemorrhage, her symptoms are most likely due to an ischemic event rather than a hemorrhagic one. A. Subarachnoid hemorrhage is a type of stroke caused by bleeding into the space surrounding the brain. It accounts for only a small percentage of all strokes and is less common than ischemic stroke. B. Intracerebral hemorrhage is a type of stroke caused by bleeding within the brain tissue itself. Like subarachnoid hemorrhage, it is also less common than ischemic stroke. C. Cerebral infarction, or ischemic stroke, is the most common cause of neurologic deficits resulting from vascular mechanisms, accounting for approximately 85% of cases. This is the most likely cause of this patient's symptoms. D. A transient ischemic attack (TIA) is a temporary blockage of a blood vessel in the brain that doesn't cause permanent damage. Symptoms of a TIA are similar to those of a stroke but resolve within a few minutes to 24 hours. Given the ongoing nature of this patient's symptoms, a TIA is less likely. E. Migraine is a type of headache that can cause severe throbbing pain or a pulsing sensation, usually on one side of the head. It is not typically associated with the acute neurologic deficits seen in this patient. Therefore, among the options given, a cerebral infarction is the most likely cause of this patient's symptoms.

17. The correct answer is A: transient ischemic attack (TIA). TIAs are temporary episodes of neurological dysfunction caused by a lack of blood flow to the brain.

They are often called "mini strokes" because they can have the same symptoms as a stroke, but the symptoms resolve within 24 hours. The majority of TIAs have a duration ranging from 5 to 15 minutes. Strokes, on the other hand, are permanent damage to brain tissue caused by a lack of blood flow. The symptoms of a stroke do not resolve and can lead to long-term disability or death. Migraine headaches are a common neurological disorder that can cause a variety of symptoms, including headache, nausea, vomiting, and sensitivity to light and sound. Seizures are a sudden change in brain activity that can cause a variety of symptoms, including loss of consciousness, convulsions, and sensory disturbances. Brain tumors are abnormal growths of tissue in the brain that can cause a variety of symptoms, depending on their location and size. In this case, the patient's symptoms are consistent with a TIA. The weakness started suddenly and has not improved. The symptoms are also limited to one side of the body, which is another characteristic of TIAs. The patient does not have any other symptoms that would suggest a stroke, migraine headache, seizure, or brain tumor.

18. Answer: A. The Trial of ORG 10172 in Acute Stroke Treatment (TOAST) classification, five subtypes.

the most commonly used classification system for TIAs is the Trial of ORG 10172 in Acute Stroke Treatment (TOAST) classification, which categorizes TIAs into one of five subtypes. Therefore, the best answer is A) The Trial of ORG 10172 in Acute Stroke Treatment (TOAST) classification, five subtypes. This system categorizes TIAs into one of five subtypes based on their underlying etiology or cause. The five subtypes are: Large artery atherosclerosis: caused by the build-up of fatty deposits in the arteries leading to the brain, which can lead to narrowing or blockage of these vessels. Cardioembolism: the result of blood clots that have formed in the heart and subsequently travel to the brain, leading to transient neurological symptoms. Small vessel occlusion: caused by the blockage of small blood vessels in the brain, leading to transient ischemia. Other determined etiology includes those caused by factors such as dissections or vasculitis. Undetermined etiology: those for which the underlying cause cannot be determined despite thorough evaluation.

19. Best Answer: A. Recent head injury two weeks ago. The administration of intravenous recombinant tissue plasminogen activator (rtPA) is an effective treatment for acute ischemic stroke (AIS), but it has several contraindications.

A. A recent head injury is a contraindication to the administration of rtPA. If the patient had a head injury within the preceding 14 days, it increases the risk of hemorrhagic complications. Therefore, rtPA should not be administered. B. Major surgery performed twenty days ago is close to the cutoff, but falls outside of the 14-day window, and thus, would not necessarily preclude the use of rtPA. C. Gastrointestinal bleeding that occurred a month ago (or 30 days ago) is beyond the 21-day window that is typically considered a contraindication for the administration of rtPA.

D. A myocardial infarction that occurred last year is not recent enough to be considered a contraindication for the administration of rtPA. E. "None of the above" would not be the best answer in this case because option A represents a contraindication for rtPA administration. Therefore, among the options given, a recent head injury two weeks ago would be a contraindication for the administration of rtPA in this patient.

20.   Answer: A) Placement of a ventricular catheter for external CSF drainage. Hydrocephalus is a condition characterized by the accumulation of cerebrospinal fluid in the brain, which can lead to increased pressure and damage to brain tissue. The most appropriate intervention for severe cases of hydrocephalus is surgical intervention.

The following are the most common surgical interventions for hydrocephalus: Placement of a ventricular shunt: This is the most common treatment for hydrocephalus. A shunt is a long, flexible tube with a valve that keeps fluid from the brain flowing in the right direction and at the proper rate. The shunt drains excess cerebrospinal fluid from the brain to another part of the body, such as the abdomen, where it can be more easily absorbed.

21. The correct answer is A: increased intracranial pressure (ICP). The symptoms of increased ICP are consistent with the patient's presentation. The headache is worse in the morning because the brain is more swollen when the patient is lying down. The nausea, vomiting, and double vision are also common symptoms of increased ICP. The dilated and unresponsive pupils are a sign of increased pressure on the brainstem. Subarachnoid hemorrhage (SAH) is a serious condition that can cause a sudden onset of headache, stiff neck, and vomiting.

Stroke is a condition that occurs when there is a blockage or rupture of a blood vessel in the brain. Meningitis is an infection of the meninges, the membranes that surround the brain and spinal cord. Brain tumor is a growth of abnormal tissue in the brain. In this case, the patient's symptoms are most consistent with increased ICP. The other conditions are less likely because they do not typically cause all of the symptoms that the patient is experiencing. Therefore, the most likely diagnosis is increased intracranial pressure (ICP). The patient should be evaluated by a neurologist to determine the cause of the increased ICP and to start treatment.

22. Best Answer: C. Administering an osmotic diuretic:

In the case of cytotoxic edema, which is often a result of traumatic brain injury (TBI) or stroke, management typically includes the use of osmotic diuretics, such as mannitol or hypertonic saline. These agents work by creating an osmotic gradient that draws fluid out of the brain tissue, reducing the edema and potentially decreasing intracranial pressure. A. Beta-blockers are commonly used for managing conditions such as hypertension, arrhythmias, and heart failure, but they do not have a direct role in the management of cytotoxic edema B. Antibiotics would be used if there were a concern for infection, but they do not directly address the issue of cytotoxic edema D. Dopamine agonists have a variety of uses, including in the treatment of Parkinson's disease and certain pituitary tumors, but they are not used in the management of cytotoxic edema. E. Antiviral medications would not be helpful in this context unless there was a specific concern for a viral infection, which is not indicated by the information given. Therefore, among the options given, administering an osmotic diuretic like mannitol or hypertonic saline is the most appropriate early step in managing a patient with cytotoxic edema due to head trauma or stroke.

23. Answer: A. A sudden and brief impairment of consciousness, while maintaining postural control.

An absence seizure is a generalized seizure characterized by a sudden and brief impairment of consciousness, while maintaining postural control. The seizure typically lasts for a short duration, ranging from 5 to 10 seconds, but has the potential to repeat numerous times within a single day. Therefore, the best answer is A) A sudden and brief impairment of consciousness, while maintaining postural control.

24. The correct answer is A: clonazepam.

Clonazepam is a benzodiazepine that is effective in controlling myoclonus. It usually started at a dose of 1.5 mg once daily and can be increased up to 10 mg daily as needed. Valproate is an anticonvulsant that is also effective in controlling myoclonus. It is usually started at a dose of 300 mg once daily and can be increased to 1200 mg daily as needed. Levetiracetam, topiramate, and primidone are other anticonvulsants that can be used to treat myoclonus. However, they are not as effective as clonazepam or valproate. In this case, the patient's symptoms are consistent with posthypoxic myoclonus. Clonazepam is the best treatment option because it is effective and has a good safety profile.

25. Best Answer: D. The absence of a predictable pattern of the seizures.

Psychogenic non-epileptic seizures (PNES), also known as psychogenic seizures, are paroxysmal behaviors that mimic epileptic seizures but are not associated with abnormal electrical discharges in the brain. They are often associated with psychological factors such as stress or trauma. A distinguishing feature of psychogenic seizures is that they often lack the characteristic attributes commonly associated with epileptic seizures. A. Abrupt commencement and cessation of the seizure is more suggestive of an epileptic seizure, not a psychogenic seizure. B. A predictable pattern of seizure episodes is more indicative of epileptic seizures, which often have a stereotyped pattern, not psychogenic seizures. C. The fact that seizure episodes are not associated with stress or trauma would be more suggestive of epileptic seizures. Psychogenic seizures are often related to psychological factors such as stress or trauma. D. The absence of a predictable pattern of the seizures is more characteristic of psychogenic seizures, making this the best answer among the options. E. Seizures related to aberrant cerebral electrical activity are indicative of epileptic seizures, not psychogenic seizures.

26. The correct answer is A: Creutzfeldt-Jakob disease (CJD).

The presence of myoclonus and the rapid advancement of dementia are indicative of a prion disease, specifically CJD. CJD is a rare and fatal neurodegenerative disease that is caused by the misfolding of a protein called prion protein. The misfolded prion protein can spread to other cells in the brain, causing damage and eventually death. Alzheimer's disease is the most common type of dementia. It is characterized by a gradual decline in cognitive function, including memory, thinking, and language skills. Frontotemporal dementia is a type of dementia that affects the frontal and temporal lobes of the brain. It is characterized by changes in personality, behavior, and language skills. Vascular dementia is caused by damage to blood vessels in the brain. It is characterized by a gradual decline in cognitive function, as well as problems with gait and balance. Parkinson's disease is a neurodegenerative disease that affects the motor system. It is characterized by tremor, rigidity, slowness of movement, and balance problems. In this case, the patient's symptoms are most consistent with CJD. The rapid advancement of dementia and the presence of myoclonus are characteristic of CJD. The other conditions are less likely because they do not typically cause all of the symptoms that the patient is experiencing. Therefore, the most likely diagnosis is Creutzfeldt-Jakob disease (CJD). The patient should be referred to as a neurologist for further evaluation and treatment.

27. Answer: A. Sudden appearance of a parkinsonian syndrome, characterized by symptoms such as resting tremor, cogwheel rigidity, bradykinesia, and festinating gait. According to the primary indications of dementia with Lewy bodies (DLB) may manifest as the sudden appearance of a parkinsonian syndrome, characterized by symptoms such as resting tremor, cogwheel rigidity, bradykinesia, and festinating gait. Other potential symptoms of DLB may include spontaneous changes in attention and alertness, recurrent visual hallucinations, REM sleep behavior disorder, and slow movement. Therefore, the best answer is A. Sudden appearance of a parkinsonian syndrome, characterized by symptoms such as resting tremor, cogwheel rigidity, bradykinesia, and festinating gait.

28. Best Answer: D. Early symptomatic Alzheimer's disease

The concept of "Early symptomatic Alzheimer's disease" is being adopted as a replacement for the Mild Cognitive Impairment (MCI) framework. This is because it better represents Alzheimer's disease as the primary pathological condition. In this stage, individuals experience noticeable symptoms such as memory loss and difficulty with daily tasks, but these symptoms are not severe enough to interfere significantly with their daily activities. A. Severe Alzheimer's disease is characterized by profound memory loss, inability to recognize loved ones, inability to communicate coherently, and inability to care for oneself. This does not match the patient's symptoms. B. Late symptomatic Alzheimer's disease would involve more severe cognitive and functional deficits than those described by the patient's daughter. C) The term "Mild Cognitive Impairment" has been largely replaced by "Early symptomatic Alzheimer's disease" as it better represents Alzheimer's disease as the primary pathological condition. E. While memory loss can be a part of the normal aging process, the reported symptoms are concerning and go beyond what would be expected for normal aging. Therefore, the most appropriate description of the patient's condition would be symptomatic Alzheimer's disease early. This recognizes the presence of noticeable but not severe cognitive symptoms that are likely due to Alzheimer's disease.

29. The correct answer is A: Parkinson's disease.

The combination of a resting tremor, slowness of movement, and gait disturbance are classic features of Parkinson's disease. Essential tremor is another movement disorder that can cause tremor, but it does not typically cause slowness of movement or gait disturbance. Multiple sclerosis is a demyelinating disease that can cause a variety of symptoms, including tremor, but it does not typically cause the classic features of Parkinson's disease. Alzheimer's disease is a neurodegenerative disease that causes dementia, but it does not typically cause tremor or other movement disorders. Huntington's disease is a genetic disorder that causes chorea, which is a type of involuntary movement, but it does not typically cause tremor or other movement disorders. In this case, the patient's symptoms are most consistent with Parkinson's disease. He should be referred to a neurologist for further evaluation and treatment.

30. Answer: A. Use of certain medications, such as neuroleptics and gastrointestinal drugs like metoclopramide, which inhibit dopamine. Infections or exposure to toxins like carbon monoxide or manganese. Secondary Parkinsonism can be linked to the use of certain medications, such as neuroleptics and gastrointestinal drugs like metoclopramide, which inhibit dopamine. Additionally, it can be caused by infections or exposure to toxins like carbon monoxide or manganese. Therefore, the best answer is A) Use of certain medications, such as neuroleptics and gastrointestinal drugs like metoclopramide, which inhibit dopamine. Infections or exposure to toxins like carbon monoxide or manganese.

31. Best Answer: A. Autosomal dominant spinocerebellar ataxias (SCAs) Chronic cerebellar ataxia can have various underlying causes, but in the context of a family history and progressive symptoms, inherited diseases are a likely cause.

A. Autosomal dominant spinocerebellar ataxias (SCAs) are a group of genetic disorders characterized by progressive problems with movement. They are typically inherited in an autosomal dominant manner, meaning that an affected person has a 50% chance of passing the disorder to each of their children. The patient's symptoms and family history make this the most likely diagnosis. B. Acute cerebellar stroke usually presents with sudden onset of symptoms, not progressively worsening symptoms over six months. C. While a cerebellar tumor could potentially cause ataxia, it would typically present with other symptoms such as headache, nausea, or vomiting. The patient's family history also suggests a genetic disorder. D. Drug-induced cerebellar toxicity tends to occur in the context of specific medication use, which is not mentioned in this case. E. Multiple sclerosis could potentially cause ataxia, but it would typically present with other neurological symptoms and has no known direct genetic inheritance pattern. Therefore, given the patient's symptoms and family history, autosomal dominant spinocerebellar ataxias (SCAs) are the most likely cause of her chronic cerebellar ataxia.

32. The correct answer is A: Edaravone is a free radical scavenger that can protect neurons from damage.

Edaravone is a small molecule that can cross the blood-brain barrier and enter the brain. It is a free radical scavenger, which means that it can neutralize free radicals, which are unstable molecules that can damage cells. Edaravone has been shown to slow the progression of ALS in clinical trials. However, it is important to note that survival was not considered as a primary outcome in these trials. The other answer choices are incorrect. Edaravone is not a nitric oxide synthase inhibitor, a glutamate receptor antagonist, a microtubule stabilizer, or a neurotransmitter precursor.

33. Answer: A.

Lamotrigine (at a daily dosage of 400 mg), Phenytoin (at a dosage range of 300-400 mg per day), or Baclofen (initially administered at a dosage of 5-10 mg three times a day). If a patient with Trigeminal Neuralgia does not exhibit a response to Carbamazepine or Oxcarbazepine, alternative medications such as Lamotrigine (at a daily dosage of 400 mg), Phenytoin (at a dosage range of 300-400 mg per day), or Baclofen (initially administered at a dosage of 5-10 mg three times a day) may be considered as potential therapeutic options. Therefore, the best answer is A. Lamotrigine (at a daily dosage of 400 mg), Phenytoin (at a dosage range of 300-400 mg per day), or Baclofen (initially administered at a dosage of 5-10 mg three times a day). 34. The correct answer is A: The ciprofloxacin is likely to worsen her MG symptoms. Ciprofloxacin is a quinolone antibiotic that can block the function of acetylcholine receptors, which are essential for muscle contraction. This can worsen the symptoms of MG, which is an autoimmune disorder that causes muscle weakness. The other answer choices are incorrect. The ciprofloxacin is not likely to have no effect, improve, or cause a new autoimmune disease in patients with MG. Ciprofloxacin is not contraindicated in patients with MG, but it should be used with caution.

35. Best Answer: B. Primary progressive multiple sclerosis (PPMS).

The diagnostic criteria for primary progressive multiple sclerosis (PPMS) include a minimum of one year of disease progression, determined either retrospectively or prospectively. Furthermore, at least two out of the three following criteria must be fulfilled: One or more T2+ lesions in the periventricular, juxtacortical, or infratentorial regions of the brain. Two or more T2+ lesions in the spinal cord. Detection of oligoclonal bands and/or elevated IgG index in the cerebrospinal fluid. In this case, the woman has shown a year-long history of progressive symptoms, and her MRI findings and cerebrospinal fluid analysis match the criteria. Therefore, the most likely diagnosis is Primary progressive multiple sclerosis (PPMS). Other options such as Neuromyelitis optica A., Amyotrophic lateral sclerosis (ALS) C., Guillain-Barre syndrome D., and Transverse myelitis E. can also cause progressive neurological symptoms, but the specific combination of imaging findings and cerebrospinal fluid analysis in this case is more consistent with PPMS.

36. Answer: (D) Delirium

The patient's presentation is most suggestive of delirium. Delirium is a sudden, often temporary change in mental function that is characterized by confusion, difficulty paying attention, and other changes in thinking and behavior. Delirium is a common complication of hospitalization, especially in older adults. It can also be caused by a variety of other medical conditions, including infections, metabolic abnormalities, toxin exposure/medications, and physiologic stressors (such as pain or constipation). The patient's confusion, agitation, and inability to name the days of the week backward are all hallmark features of delirium. Additionally, her fever suggests that she may have an underlying infection. The other answer choices are less likely diagnoses. Alcohol-induced mood disorder, bipolar disorder, brief psychotic disorder, and schizophrenia are all chronic mental health conditions that would not typically present with a sudden change in mental function. Delirium is a serious condition that can lead to complications such as falls, injuries, and pneumonia. Early diagnosis and treatment are essential to improve outcomes. Treatment for delirium typically involves addressing the underlying medical cause. In some cases, medications may be used to manage the symptoms of delirium, such as anxiety, agitation, and sleep disturbances. Most patients with delirium make a full recovery, but some may experience long-term cognitive impairment.

37. Answer: D. Perform a blood glucose fingerstick

This patient's presentation of acute change in mental status superimposed on chronic cognitive decline due to Alzheimer's disease raises concern for multiple potential causes, including metabolic, infectious, and neurologic etiologies. However, given the patient's history of insulin use for type 2 diabetes, the immediate step should be to check her blood glucose. Hypoglycemia, which is a common side effect of insulin use, can present with altered mental status and is a rapidly reversible cause of altered mental status that can be diagnosed and treated at the bedside. Therefore, a blood glucose fingerstick is the next best step in this patient's management. Other tests such as a basic metabolic panel, complete blood count, and urinalysis should also be considered as part of the workup for encephalopathy, but can be done subsequently. A noncontrast head CT may be necessary if there is concern for acute cerebral pathology, such as hemorrhage or stroke, but given the patient's presentation and history, hypoglycemia should be ruled out first.

38. The correct answer is B.

The patient's symptoms of progressive behavioral changes, including disinhibition and a dramatic shift in personality, along with the MRI findings of atrophy in the frontal and temporal lobes, are indicative of the behavioral variant of frontotemporal dementia. This condition is a tauopathy, and typical pathology findings include rounded intracytoplasmic structures that show immunoreactivity to tau immunostains. Alzheimer's disease (choice A) can also present with behavioral changes, but these typically occur in the later stages of the disease and early frontal atrophy is not a characteristic feature. Lewy body disease (choice C) and corticobasal degeneration (choice D) can present with psychosis, but they do not typically cause dramatic behavioral changes without other Parkinsonian features. Lastly, there is no language involvement in this patient to suggest primary progressive aphasia (choice E).

39. Answer: (D) Ensure proper oxygenation

The first step in managing a seizure is to ensure the patient's airway, breathing, and circulation (ABCs). This means checking to make sure that the patient's airway is open, that they are breathing adequately, and that their circulation is intact. If the patient is unconscious or unresponsive, it is important to open their airway by tilting their head back and lifting their chin. If the patient is not breathing, artificial respiration may be necessary. Once the patient's ABCs have been secured, the next step is to assess the severity of the seizure and to determine if further treatment is necessary. If the seizure is brief and self-limited, no further treatment may be necessary. However, if the seizure is prolonged or if the patient has multiple seizures in a short period of time, further treatment may be necessary to prevent status epilepticus. Lorazepam is a benzodiazepine that is used to treat status epilepticus. Phenytoin is an anticonvulsant that is used to prevent seizures. However, phenytoin is not effective in treating status epilepticus. A head CT may be obtained to rule out any underlying structural abnormalities that may be causing the seizures. A lumbar puncture may also be performed to rule out any infectious or inflammatory causes of the seizures. However, these tests are not necessary for the initial management of a seizure. Status epilepticus is a medical emergency. It is defined as a seizure that lasts longer than 5 minutes or two or more seizures without full recovery of consciousness in between. Status epilepticus can be life-threatening and requires immediate treatment. The goal of treatment is to stop the seizure as quickly as possible. There are a variety of treatments available for status epilepticus, including benzodiazepines, anticonvulsants, and propofol. The specific treatment will depend on the patient's individual situation.

40. Answer: (D) Order a long-term EEG.

A normal routine EEG does not exclude the possibility of an underlying seizure disorder. In fact, the sensitivity of a routine EEG for detecting an underlying seizure disorder is only about 50%. This means that half of all patients with a seizure disorder will have a normal routine EEG. If suspicion remains high for seizures after a normal routine EEG, the next step is to order a long-term EEG. A long-term EEG is an EEG that is performed over a longer period of time, typically 24 hours or more. This allows for a greater chance of capturing a seizure on EEG. The other answer choices are not the most appropriate next step in the management of this patient. Reassuring the patient that her symptoms are unlikely to be due to a seizure disorder is not appropriate, as there is still a significant possibility that she has a seizure disorder. Ordering a 24-hour Holter monitor or scheduling a tilt table test is not appropriate, as these tests are used to evaluate for syncope, not seizures. Starting anticonvulsant therapy without a definitive diagnosis of a seizure disorder is also not appropriate. It is important to note that a long-term EEG can also be normal in some patients with a seizure disorder. This is because seizures can occur at any time, and it is possible that a seizure does not occur during the time that the EEG is being performed. If a long-term EEG is normal, but suspicion for a seizure disorder remains high, the patient may need to be referred to a neurologist for further evaluation. The neurologist may recommend additional tests, such as video EEG monitoring or magnetic resonance imaging (MRI) of the brain. Video EEG monitoring is a type of EEG that is performed while the patient is also being video recorded. This allows the neurologist to see what the patient is doing during the EEG and to correlate any clinical events with the EEG findings. MRI of the brain is a type of imaging that can be used to identify any structural abnormalities in the brain that may be causing the seizures.

41. The correct answer is D. Levetiracetam.

This patient has a history of major depressive disorder, including a prior suicide attempt. Levetiracetam, an antiepileptic medication, has been reported in 10% to 20% of patients to cause mood symptoms ranging from depression to irritability and, in severe cases, rage and agitation. Given the patient's history of major depressive disorder and a prior suicide attempt, this medication should be avoided as it could potentially exacerbate his mood symptoms. Valproic Acid (option A) and Lacosamide (option B) are not the best choices in this scenario but for different reasons. Thrombocytopenia and hepatic disease are relative contraindications to valproic acid, and first-degree heart block is a contraindication to lacosamide. However, the patient's history doesn't mention these conditions. Carbamazepine (option C) and Oxcarbazepine (option E) are also not the best choices because they can cause hyponatremia. But again, the patient's history doesn't suggest he has this condition. Therefore, given the patient's specific history of major depressive disorder and a prior suicide attempt, Levetiracetam (option D) should be avoided.

42. The correct answer is E. Thiamine.

The patient's presentation of ataxia, ophthalmoparesis, and altered mental status are indicative of Wernicke encephalopathy, a life-threatening condition resulting from thiamine (Vitamin B1) deficiency. This condition is often seen in individuals with alcohol use disorder, especially those who have poor dietary intake. The deficiency in thiamine impairs energy metabolism in the brain and can lead to rapid neurological degeneration if not promptly treated. The treatment of Wernicke's encephalopathy involves immediate repletion of thiamine, often in high doses and via intravenous route. As for the other options, riboflavin deficiency typically causes stomatitis. Pyridoxine deficiency usually results in skin abnormalities, neuropathy, and sometimes somnolence or confusion. Cyanocobalamin deficiency typically leads to anemia and/or neurologic symptoms, including subacute combined degeneration of the spinal cord. Folate deficiency can lead to megaloblastic anemia, but does not present with this patient's symptoms. Therefore, these options are less likely given the patient's presentation.

43. Answer: (A) Delirium tremens

Delirium tremens is a severe form of alcohol withdrawal that can occur within 2 to 3 days of stopping alcohol use in people who have been drinking heavily for a long time. The symptoms of delirium tremens can include hallucinations, confusion, disorientation, agitation, and seizures. Delirium tremens can be fatal if not treated promptly. The patient in this question has a history of alcohol abuse and presents with all of the classic symptoms of delirium tremens. Therefore, the most likely diagnosis is delirium tremens. The other answer choices are less likely diagnoses. Schizoaffective disorder, posttraumatic stress disorder, and depression are all mental health conditions that can cause hallucinations, but they would not be expected to have the vital sign abnormalities that the patient in this question has. Delirium tremens is a medical emergency. Treatment typically involves hospitalization and the use of benzodiazepines to control the symptoms. Most people with delirium tremens make a full recovery, but some may experience long-term cognitive impairment. If you or someone you know is experiencing alcohol withdrawal, it is important to seek medical attention immediately.

44. Answer: (A) Alprazolam

Alprazolam is a short-acting benzodiazepine. Short-acting benzodiazepines are not recommended for the management of delirium tremens because of their short half-life and potential for causing rebound seizures. The other answer choices are all appropriate to consider for the management of delirium tremens. Chlordiazepoxide, diazepam, and lorazepam are all long-acting benzodiazepines that can be used to control the symptoms of delirium tremens. Propofol is a sedative hypnotic that can be used in severe cases of delirium tremens. The treatment of delirium tremens is typically supportive care and benzodiazepines to control the symptoms. Benzodiazepines are used because they can rapidly calm the patient and reduce the risk of seizures. Long-acting benzodiazepines are preferred over short-acting benzodiazepines for the management of delirium tremens because they provide more sustained sedation and reduce the risk of rebound seizures. Propofol is a sedative hypnotic that can be used in severe cases of delirium tremens when benzodiazepines are not effective. Propofol provides rapid sedation and amnesia, but it can also cause respiratory depression. Therefore, propofol should only be used in a setting where close monitoring and airway management is available.

45. Correct Answer:D) Vestibular neuritis.

The patient's presentation is indicative of a peripheral cause of her dizziness, as suggested by a positive head thrust test, no skew, and unilaterally beating nystagmus. With continuous symptoms for hours and no reported association with head movement, benign paroxysmal positional vertigo is unlikely. Labyrinthitis can be ruled out due to the absence of hearing loss. Central nystagmus often presents with direction-changing nystagmus, and there are no other localizing symptoms in this patient that would suggest a posterior circulation stroke. Therefore, the most likely diagnosis is vestibular neuritis.

46. Answer: (A) Benign paroxysmal positional vertigo

The patient's presentation is most suggestive of benign paroxysmal positional vertigo (BPPV). BPPV is a common disorder of the inner ear that causes brief episodes of dizziness when the head is moved in a certain way. The other answer choices are less likely diagnoses. Vestibular neuritis is an inflammation of the vestibular nerve, which is the nerve that carries information from the inner ear to the brain about balance and movement. Vestibular neuritis can cause dizziness, but the episodes typically last for hours or days, rather than seconds or minutes. Migraine can also cause dizziness, but it is usually accompanied by other symptoms, such as headache, nausea, and vomiting. Concussion can also cause dizziness, but it is usually accompanied by other symptoms, such as headache, amnesia, and difficulty concentrating. Vertebrobasilar insufficiency is a condition in which the blood supply to the back of the brain is reduced. Vertebrobasilar insufficiency can cause a variety of symptoms, including dizziness, but it is usually accompanied by other symptoms, such as vision changes, numbness or weakness in the arms or legs, and speech problems. BPPV is a benign condition that usually goes away on its own within a few weeks or months. However, there are simple treatments available that can help to speed up recovery.

47.Answer: (A) Finger-to-nose coordination test

The HINTS test is a bedside test that is used to distinguish between central and peripheral causes of vertigo. The test consists of three parts: the head impulse test, the nystagmus test, and the test of skew. The finger-to-nose coordination test is not a component of the HINTS test. The finger-to-nose coordination test is used to assess cerebellar function. While cerebellar dysfunction can be a feature of posterior circulation stroke, it is not necessary to perform the finger-to-nose coordination test to diagnose a central cause of vertigo. The HINTS test is a very sensitive and specific test for central causes of vertigo. If the HINTS test is abnormal, then the patient should undergo further evaluation, such as MRI of the brain, to rule out a central cause of vertigo. Central causes of vertigo include stroke, hemorrhage, and tumor. Peripheral causes of vertigo include labyrinthitis, vestibular neuritis, and benign paroxysmal positional vertigo (BPPV). Treatment for vertigo depends on the underlying cause. If the vertigo is caused by a central cause, then the patient should be treated for the underlying condition. If the vertigo is caused by a peripheral cause, then the patient may be treated with medications to suppress the nausea and vomiting, and with physical therapy to help improve balance and coordination.

48. Correct Answer: A. Left middle cerebral artery (MCA)

This patient's symptoms of sudden speech loss , right-side paralysis, and leftward gaze deviation are indicative of a stroke affecting the left middle cerebral artery (MCA). The left MCA supplies the area of the brain responsible for language in the majority of people , as well as the left motor strip which controls the right side of the body. In strokes, the eyes typically deviate towards the affected side. The other options are less likely given the patient's specific symptoms and their typical presentations. For instance, a right anterior cerebral artery stroke would likely present with more significant left leg than arm weakness and wouldn't typically impact language. Similarly, a right

MCA stroke would cause left-side weakness and potentially evidence of neglect. A left posterior cerebral artery stroke would primarily cause visual symptoms, like right homonymous hemianopia, and a right posterior inferior cerebellar artery stroke (also known as a lateral medullary syndrome) would typically cause vertigo, ipsilateral (right-sided) hemiataxia, dysarthria, ptosis, and miosis (ie, ipsilateral Horner's syndrome).

49. Answer: D. Administer tissue plasminogen activator immediately

The patient in this scenario is presenting within the 4.5-hour window from symptom onset and does not have any exclusion criteria for tissue plasminogen activator (tPA) administration. tPA is an emergency treatment for ischemic stroke that works by dissolving the clot and improving blood flow to the part of the brain being deprived of blood flow. Choices A and E are incorrect because the patient is presenting within the 4.5-hour tPA window and delaying treatment or referral could lead to worse outcomes. Choice B is incorrect because recent surgery is a relative contraindication for tPA due to the increased risk of bleeding. Choice C is incorrect because recent intracerebral hemorrhage is a contraindication for tPA due to the significantly increased risk of recurrent bleeding.

50. Answer: (C) MRI brain

Non-contrast CT head is not the most appropriate imaging study for this patient because it is not sensitive for detecting acute ischemic stroke within 6 hours of onset. Contrast-enhanced CT head is not the most appropriate imaging study for this patient because he has end-stage renal disease and is therefore at high risk of contrast-induced nephropathy. MRI brain is the most appropriate imaging study for this patient because it is sensitive for detecting acute ischemic stroke within 6 hours of onset and can also be used to determine the extent of the infarct. CT angiography is an important component of the acute stroke assessment, but it is not necessary for this patient because he cannot receive CT contrast. Carotid duplex ultrasound is not the most appropriate imaging study for this patient because it is not sensitive for detecting acute ischemic stroke. Patients with end-stage renal disease and allergy to iodine should receive MRI brain without contrast for the evaluation of acute ischemic stroke. Gadolinium contrast should be avoided in patients with end-stage renal disease due to the risk of nephrogenic systemic fibrosis. If MRI is not available, then CT angiography can be performed with MR angiography time-of-flight protocol. MR angiography time-of-flight protocol does not require IV contrast with gadolinium or a carotid duplex ultrasound. Carotid duplex ultrasound is not as sensitive for detecting acute ischemic stroke as MRI or CT angiography, but it can be used to evaluate for carotid stenosis. Carotid stenosis is a risk factor for ischemic stroke, so carotid duplex ultrasound may be helpful in determining the underlying etiology of the stroke.

51. Answer: (E) Hypertension

Hypertension is the most common cause of intracerebral hemorrhage (ICH). It is responsible for over 60% of all ICH cases. Hypertension causes damage to the blood vessels, making them more likely to rupture. Arteriovenous malformations (AVMs) and cerebral amyloid angiopathy (CAA) are less common causes of ICH. AVMs are congenital abnormalities of the blood vessels in the brain. CAA is a condition that causes amyloid plaques to build up in the walls of the blood vessels in the brain. Intracranial aneurysms are also less common causes of ICH. Intracranial aneurysms are balloon-like outpouchings in the walls of the blood vessels in the brain. Neoplastic lesions are rare causes of ICH. Neoplastic lesions are tumors that can form in the brain. The patient in this question has a history of hypertension and presents with a left-sided hemiplegia and aphasia, which are consistent with a hemorrhage in the right basal ganglia. The MRI brain shows a hemorrhage in the right basal ganglia, which confirms the diagnosis. The other answer choices are less likely causes of ICH in this patient. AVMs, CAA, and intracranial aneurysms typically cause more peripheral lobar hemorrhages. Neoplastic lesions are rare causes of ICH and are not typically associated with hypertension. Patients with ICH should be treated in a hospital setting. Treatment may involve blood pressure control, surgical evacuation of the hemorrhage, and supportive care.

52. Answer: C. Intravenous immunoglobulin (IVIG)

Explanation: The patient's presentation is suggestive of acute inflammatory demyelinating polyneuropathy, also known as Guillain-Barré syndrome. Symptoms typically develop over a few days and peak in severity at 2 to 4 weeks. The condition is characterized by the presence of symmetric proximal and distal limb weakness, areflexia, and distal paresthesias/sensory loss. Lumbar puncture often shows cytoalbuminologic dissociation (elevated protein without CSF pleocytosis). The first-line treatment for Guillain-Barré syndrome is either IVIG or plasmapheresis. While EMG/nerve conduction studies can be helpful, they can be normal early in the disease course and are not required for diagnosis. MRI of the spine may show nerve root enhancement but is not a sensitive sign. Steroids have not been shown to have benefit in acute inflammatory demyelinating polyneuropathy and are not recommended. Even though acute inflammatory demyelinating polyneuropathy is often preceded by an infection, this patient does not have signs of active infection or meningitis/encephalitis requiring antibiotics or antivirals.

53. Correct Answer: A. Nonsteroidal anti-inflammatory drugs (NSAIDs)

This patient's symptoms are indicative of neuropathic pain commonly seen in diabetic neuropathy. First-line treatments for neuropathic pain include gabapentin, pregabalin, tricyclic antidepressants (like amitriptyline), and serotonin and norepinephrine reuptake inhibitors (like duloxetine). Nonsteroidal anti-inflammatory drugs (NSAIDs), option A, are not typically recommended for the treatment of neuropathic pain as they are more useful for nociceptive pain (pain that arises from actual or threatened damage to non-neuronal tissue and is due to the activation of nociceptors). Thus, initiating treatment with NSAIDs would not be the best choice in this patient's case. While the other options listed can be effective for treating neuropathic pain, it is important to consider the patient's overall medical condition and potential side effects before deciding on a treatment plan. For instance, tricyclic antidepressants should be used with caution in patients with cardiovascular disease, while duloxetine should be avoided in patients with severe renal impairment.

54. Answer: (A) 3,4-Diaminopyridine (3,4-DAP)

The patient in this question has a presentation that is consistent with Lambert-Eaton myasthenic syndrome (LEMS). LEMS is a rare autoimmune disorder that affects the neuromuscular junction. LEMS is characterized by proximal muscle weakness, fatigability, and hyporeflexia. The most effective symptomatic treatment for LEMS is 3,4-DAP. 3,4-DAP is a potassium channel blocker that increases the release of acetylcholine from the presynaptic nerve terminal. Edrophonium, pyridostigmine, prednisone, and rituximab are not effective treatments for LEMS. Edrophonium and pyridostigmine are cholinesterase inhibitors that are used to treat myasthenia gravis, but they are not effective in LEMS. Prednisone and rituximab are immunosuppressive medications that are used to treat autoimmune disorders, but they are not effective in LEMS. LEMS is often associated with small cell lung cancer. Therefore, it is important to screen patients with LEMS for small cell lung cancer. Treatment for LEMS typically involves 3,4-DAP and supportive care. With treatment, most patients with LEMS can improve their quality of life. However, there is no cure for LEMS.

55. Answer: (B) Perifascicular atrophy and perivascular inflammation

The patient in this question has a presentation that is consistent with dermatomyositis. Dermatomyositis is an autoimmune inflammatory myopathy that is characterized by proximal muscle weakness, skin rash, and elevated muscle enzymes. The characteristic histopathological findings of dermatomyositis on muscle biopsy are perifascicular atrophy and perivascular inflammation. Perifascicular atrophy refers to the presence of atrophic muscle fibers at the edges of muscle fascicles. Perivascular inflammation refers to the presence of inflammatory cells, such as macrophages, B-cells, and plasma cells, around blood vessels. The other answer choices are not characteristic histopathological findings of dermatomyositis. Eosinophilic myositis, vacuolar myopathy, necrotizing myopathy, and granulomatous myositis are other types of inflammatory myopathies, but they have different histopathological findings. The diagnosis of dermatomyositis is based on a combination of clinical features, laboratory findings, and muscle biopsy results. Treatment for dermatomyositis typically involves corticosteroids and immunosuppressive medications. With treatment, most patients with dermatomyositis can improve their muscle strength and quality of life. However, there is no cure for dermatomyositis.

56. The correct answer is A) Cluster headache.

This patient's history is classic for a cluster headache, characterized by unilateral, severe, periorbital pain, often associated with autonomic symptoms such as lacrimation, conjunctival injection, and rhinorrhea. The attacks often occur in clusters lasting weeks to months, with headache-free periods in between. The other options are less likely given the patient's symptoms and presentation: B) Short-lasting unilateral neuralgiform pain with conjunctival injection and tearing syndrome is characterized by brief and more frequent attacks of pain. C) Trigeminal neuralgia presents as shooting facial pain. D) Tension headaches are typically bilateral and present as a mild-to-moderate pressure-like pain. E) Secondary headache is usually associated with red flag symptoms such as explosive onset, signs of increased intracranial pressure, vision symptoms, abnormal neurologic examination, age >50 years, and immunosuppressed state, none of which are present in this case.

57. Answer: A. Indomethacin

Explanation: The patient's presentation is consistent with hemicrania continua—a chronic headache syndrome that should resolve completely with indomethacin. This treatment response is part of the diagnostic criteria. The indomethacin trial is typically done over several days with incremental dose increases. After a successful trial, the headache resolves and indomethacin is stopped. If the headache does not completely resolve, an alternative diagnosis should be considered. Tricyclic antidepressants and topiramate are treatments for many headache types, but not for hemicrania continua. Verapamil is particularly effective in cluster headache while triptans are used as abortive medications for migraines. However, none of these treatments is as effective for hemicrania continua as indomethacin, making option A the best choice.

58. Answer: (E) Send thrombophilia workup and start therapeutic anticoagulation with heparin.

The patient in this question has a clinical presentation and imaging findings that are consistent with cerebral venous sinus thrombosis (CVST). CVST is a condition in which a blood clot forms in one or more of the veins that drain blood from the brain. The patient's headaches, nausea, vomiting, and papilledema are all symptoms of elevated intracranial pressure. The nonvisualization of the right transverse, sigmoid, and jugular venous system on magnetic resonance venogram is a sign of CVST. The most appropriate next step in the management of this patient is to send thrombophilia workup and start therapeutic anticoagulation with heparin. Thrombophilia workup is performed to identify any underlying conditions that may predispose the patient to blood clots. Heparin is a blood thinner that can help to prevent the blood clot from growing larger and causing further damage to the brain. The other answer choices are not the most appropriate next step in the management of this patient. An EEG is used to diagnose seizures, but there is no evidence that the patient is having seizures. A lumbar puncture is used to diagnose meningitis and encephalitis, but there is no evidence that the patient has either of these conditions. Admitting the patient to the hospital for observation is not the best next step because the patient is not in immediate danger. Starting the patient on anticonvulsant medication is not the best next step because there is no evidence that the patient has seizures.

59. Answer: (B) L5

The patient's symptoms are consistent with an L5 radiculopathy. L5 radiculopathy is caused by compression of the L5 nerve root, which exits the spine at the L4-L5 level. The L5 nerve root innervates the tibialis anterior muscle, which is responsible for dorsiflexion of the foot. Therefore, weakness of the tibialis anterior muscle is a classic sign of L5 radiculopathy. The other answer choices are less likely. L4 radiculopathy would cause weakness of the quadriceps muscle, which is responsible for knee extension. S1 radiculopathy would cause weakness of the gastrocnemius muscle, which is responsible for plantar flexion of the foot. A thoracic spinal cord lesion would cause more widespread sensory and motor deficits. Peroneal neuropathy is another common cause of foot drop, but it is distinguished from L5 radiculopathy by the sparing of foot inversion. L5 radiculopathy is a common cause of foot drop, especially in older adults. It is most often caused by herniation of the L4-L5 disc. Treatment for L5 radiculopathy typically involves rest, physical therapy, and pain medication. If these treatments are not effective, surgery may be considered. Most patients with L5 radiculopathy make a full recovery with treatment. However, some patients may experience long-term numbness and weakness in the affected leg.

60. Answer: A. Administer dexamethasone 10 mg IV, with urgent evaluation for thoracic spine decompression This patient is presenting with rapidly progressing symptoms suggestive of spinal cord compression, likely due to metastatic disease given the presence of an epidural mass lesion. The most appropriate next step in management is to administer dexamethasone to reduce inflammation and edema around the spinal cord, and to urgently evaluate the patient for surgical decompression to relieve pressure on the spinal cord. Options B (Administer a high dose of morphine for pain control), C (Immediate referral to a physical therapist), D (Initiate aggressive chemotherapy regimen), and E (Start radiation therapy) may be a part of the patient's overall treatment plan but are not the immediate priority in this acute setting.

Index

INDEX

Dr Rafael Zioni

INDEX

Made in the USA
Las Vegas, NV
31 January 2024

85132922R10201